James McNair's
favorites

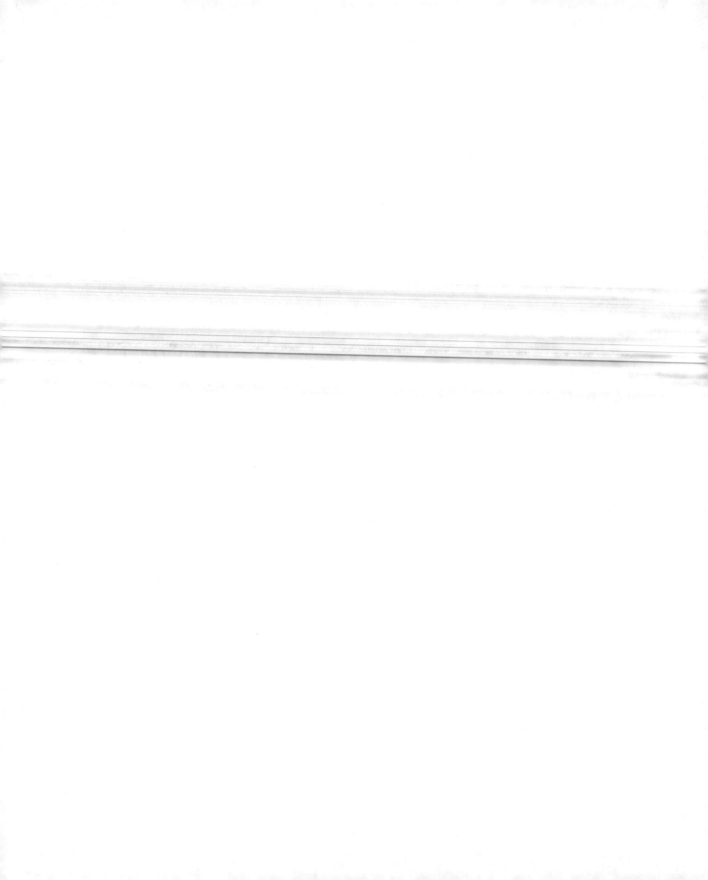

JAMES MCNAIR'S
favorites

CHRONICLE BOOKS

SAN FRANCISCO

Library of Congress Cataloging-in-Publication Data available.

ISBN 0-8118-0115-2

Printed in the United States of America.

Recipes compiled and updated by James McNair and Andrew Moore,
The Rockpile Press, Lake Tahoe and San Francisco.

Photograph styling by James McNair

Designed by Reuter Design, San Francisco

Distributed in Canada by Raincoast Books

8680 Cambie Street

Vancouver, British Columbia V6P 6M9

10 9 8 7 6 5 4 3 2 1

Chronicle Books

85 Second Street

San Francisco, California 94105

www.chroniclebooks.com

*For my devoted partner, Andrew Moore,
without whose valued contributions this book and
my life would not be nearly as good.*

*And in memory of my late partner, Lin Cotton,
without whom my food career and my work for
Chronicle Books would probably never have happened.*

Previous James McNair cookbooks published by Chronicle Books:

Bar & Grill Cookbook (1986)

Chicken (1987)

Cold Pasta (1985)

James McNair's Beans and Grains (1997)

James McNair's Beef Cookbook (1989)

James McNair's Breakfast, Revised Edition (1998)

James McNair's Burgers (1992)

James McNair's Cakes (1999)

James McNair's Cheese Cookbook (1986 and 1989)

James McNair's Cold Cuisine (1988)

James McNair Cooks Italian (1994)

James McNair Cooks Southeast Asian (1996)

James McNair's Corn Cookbook (1990)

James McNair's Custards, Mousses, and Puddings (1992)

James McNair's Fish Cookbook (1991)

James McNair's Grill Cookbook (1990)

James McNair's Pasta Cookbook (1990)

James McNair's Pie Cookbook (1989)

James McNair's Potato Cookbook (1989)

James McNair's Rice Cookbook (1988)

James McNair's Salads (1991)

James McNair's Salmon Cookbook (1987)

James McNair's Soups (1990)

James McNair's Squash Cookbook (1989)

James McNair's Stews and Casseroles (1991)

James McNair's Vegetarian Pizza (1993)

Pizza (1987)

Power Food (1986)

CONTENTS

A CULINARY JOURNEY

I entered the world shortly after a traditional Southern midday Thanksgiving dinner. Perhaps it was the smell of turkey and dressing wafting through the halls of the old Baptist Hospital in Alexandria, Louisiana, that lured me out and sparked my lifelong interest in good food.

When I was two months old, my family settled in Jonesville, Louisiana, where my daddy was to serve as the Baptist minister for forty-five years. Even as a young child I was fascinated by cooking, and one of my favorite playtimes involved fantasy creations with pots and pans in the middle of the kitchen floor. An early clue to my interest in food presentation began with the creation and arrangement of delicacies from the mud along the levee that separated Little River from the parsonage where we lived.

Life in a typical small town in the Deep South of the 1940s and 1950s was filled with food-centered events, and Jonesville had more than its share of good cooks. Each church lady showed off her best efforts at the dinners-on-the-grounds that frequently followed Sunday morning services. I always looked forward to those feasts of fried chicken, dumplings, baked ham, sweet potato casseroles, fresh butter beans, deviled eggs, and shimmering fruit- or vegetable-filled gelatin molds of every shape — the salads of the Southern table. Another long table or two groaned under an array of incredible desserts. My favorite was the lemon icebox pie, a sweet my mother wouldn't make at home because it contained raw eggs.

My childhood and teenage years were punctuated with numerous barbecues, catfish fries, and picnics, either under moss-draped trees along the banks of the countless rivers and lakes that dot Catahoula Parish, or atop Fort Hill, a Civil War battle site in the parish (county) seat of Harrisonburg. My mother and I also decorated and helped with the food for hundreds of weddings and receptions, and we were always in charge of the lavishly decorated annual spring banquet, an event for which I loved planning menus and designing waitress costumes that fit the fantasy themes.

I learned to cook through these hometown experiences by observing and questioning my mother, daddy, grandmothers, and family friends, so that by adolescence I was doing much of the baking and table decorating for our family. Many recipes from those formative years have remained in my repertoire, and my own versions appear in this collection, such as Mawmaw Mackie's custardy banana pudding, Mawmaw Keith's old-fashioned cherry cream pie, Mother's lemon meringue pie and pear relish, Daddy's succulent barbecued chicken, Aunt Doris's white buttermilk biscuits, and the pecan pie and baked corn of my fifth-grade teacher, Eula Cain.

During my teen years I was a devoted fan of *Looking at Cooking*, a television show hosted by Mildred Swift on KNOE-TV in Monroe, Louisiana. The homespun show was a predecessor of the PBS cooking shows, and many years before the advent of California cuisine, Mrs. Swift emphasized gardening to insure having the freshest possible ingredients.

At Louisiana College, a Southern Baptist campus in Pineville, President Guinn dubbed me King McNair because I was a bit of a rebel and definitely more interested in editing three yearbooks, founding and directing a Miss America preliminary beauty pageant, and running other campus events than I was in academia. Fortunately, I still managed to graduate with honors. Even though I was always involved in planning campus party menus, this was an era of my life in which food was limited to survival fare, with a Coke and cupcake serving as a quick breakfast en route to morning classes, bologna-on-white-bread sandwiches substituting for the sometimes undistinguishable dining hall choices, and midnight after-study hunger satisfied by a run to an all-night coffee shop across the Red River in neighboring Alexandria for an order of pecan waffles. I made up for any food deprivation by returning home on weekends, where I worked as organist and youth director in my daddy's church and continued to enjoy those communal dinners, my folks' home cooking, and numerous wonderful Sunday meals in the homes of parishioners who lavishly entertained the preacher's family.

Attempting to follow in my father's footsteps, I secured a master's degree at the New Orleans Baptist Theological Seminary. During those sequestered years, my friend Cary Griffin and I would save up our spending money in order to play hooky from the requisite chapel services occasionally and visit famous New Orleans restaurants. These hallowed institutions added to my knowledge of good cooking and sustained my spirit.

After a stint working as director of public relations for the Louisiana Baptist Convention in Alexandria, I realized that church work was not my calling. So it was back to New Orleans and teaching positions in the public schools. I also further educated myself about both the vibrant country-style Cajun cooking and the elegant Creole fare of that magical food city. During those days, large amounts of garlic, chiles, herbs, and spices became permanent additions to my seasoning palette. My recipes for gumbo, red beans and rice, and grilled trout with toasted pecan butter and Champagne sauce have been included in this volume.

Next stop on my culinary educational tour was New York City, an eye-opening mecca for a young man from rural Louisiana. My first job was as a designer in a flower shop that catered to East Side high society. Whenever we installed floral displays for parties in some of Manhattan's most beautiful homes, I always took note of what was being prepared in the kitchen. Next I helped manage an upscale ultracontemporary Fifth Avenue plant-and-flower store, where I created countless bouquets for the rich and famous, designed tabletop decorations for Tiffany and Company, and constructed weekly horticultural displays for everyone from Bonwit Teller to Revlon.

I was a true flower child back then, and as my hair grew to well below my shoulders, my eyes were opened wide to the infinite variety of international foods. Like that proverbial kid in a candy store, my companion, Lenny Meyer, and I explored the tables of Chinatown, Little Italy, lower East Side Jewish delicatessens, midtown French bastions of haute cuisine, West Side Cuban sidewalk cafes, and tiny cross-cultural ethnic restaurants. Among the recipes I have included from those days is one for Turkish stuffed eggplant as prepared by Hussan, the chef-owner-waiter-dishwasher of the quintessential hole-in-the-wall restaurant.

In those years, I seriously pursued my culinary self-education. Like most home cooks of the era, I watched Julia Child and Graham Kerr introduce America to new ingredients and techniques. And I read Craig Claiborne and James Beard and became more adventuresome and experimental in my cooking. Even though my apartment kitchen had once been a closet and my refrigerator was in the entry hall, I turned out incredible feasts for my friends.

A trip to San Francisco in 1973 to install the decorations for a party to celebrate the tenth anniversary of the local Tiffany store was all it took to convince me to transplant myself to California. My backgrounds in writing and horticulture converged with a position at Ortho Books, where I wrote and edited fourteen books on gardening and cooking. There was no such thing as a food stylist on the West Coast, so I prepared my own food for the cameras, a practice that I've continued throughout my publishing career. As a result of my years with Ortho, I met Marian May, my last editor there, who has remained one of my best friends and greatest influences.

Growing out of my Ortho book on picnics, my late partner, Lin Cotton, and I opened Picnic Productions, a party planning and catering service that specialized in fanciful al fresco events, and Twin Peaks Grocery, one of San Francisco's first gourmet emporiums to offer freshly cooked take-out meals. Our store, incidentally, was named for its location at the base of towering Twin Peaks in the center of San Francisco, not for the trendy television show that came some years later.

Food retailing and catering have to be two of the world's most demanding jobs. Lin and I rarely saw our Mill Valley home in daylight. We left for the produce market before sunrise and returned after dark, following a long day of shopping, cooking, cleaning, displaying, stocking, selling, and a lot of schlepping. We encountered the myriad problems of running a store stocked with fresh cheeses, perishable produce, garden flowers, just-baked pastries, fine wines, the first Starbucks coffee sold outside of Seattle, and a variety of hot and cold dishes cooked daily.

But we also had great fun operating the store. The space was basic black and white to allow us to change the colorful accents at whim. Each month had a different theme with extensive decorations to carry it out. During the holiday season, we installed a grand piano in the tiny space and secured our friends, including society pianist Peter Mintun, to play as people shopped by candlelight and were waited on by our tuxedoed staff. A rear-projection screen continuously showed pictures of our food and catering events.

As part of a concerted effort to get the local press to visit our shop and write about it, we sent a fabulous basket of our products and a special invitation to Jane Benet, then food editor of the *San Francisco Chronicle*. We asked that she call so we could arrange for her a special tour of our unusual store, but there was no response. Early one morning, as Lin and I were frantically unloading the goods from our predawn shopping and getting the daily specials underway, a woman opened the unlocked door, although a sign read Closed. I told her politely that we did not open for another hour, but she pushed right on in and insisted that she just wanted to look around. After we explained that we took great pride in the appearance of our store and did not like people to see it before it was beautifully displayed for the day, she refused to return when we were opened, and we insisted she leave. The woman stormed out in a huff. You can probably guess the rest of the story. The woman was Jane Benet, who announced to her staff that she had been rudely thrown out of the Twin Peaks Grocery and would see to it that the store and its owners were never mentioned in the paper.

Years later, after I'd published several of my single-subject cookbooks, I was greatly amused that Jane Benet, in a review of one of them, dubbed me "the king of single-subject cookbooks," a title often repeated by other food writers from coast to coast.

Perhaps the only thing harder than running a retail gourmet shop or a restaurant is catering. You usually have to haul everything you need to set up a temporary kitchen and dining room to serve a fabulous meal in places never intended for such purposes. Back then I cooked steaks on a hot plate on the floor of a back office, grilled chicken in a downtown alley, offered up a multicourse dinner in an underground railway station, maintained a steady hand while setting up a cold buffet on a rocking yacht on windy San Francisco Bay, served a hot breakfast in the middle of a vineyard, and pulled off an elegant dinner for seven hundred in a downtown shopping mall.

Even with all the hard work, many loyal fans, and great publicity from popular local columnists Herb Caen and Armistead Maupin and the Bay Area's

television stations, Lin and I were forced to close Twin Peaks Grocery after only a year and a half. In retrospect, we had chosen a location that was off the beaten path for successful retailing and had invested too much in redoing the building. As we retreated back to Mill Valley and Lake Tahoe and slowly recovered from the loss of our dream, I eked out a living through a variety of writing projects, including magazine articles, a volume on entertaining for Sunset Books, a weekly column with Lin on landscaping for the *Chronicle*, and the ghostwriting of a cookbook for a famous singer.

Then in 1984, after numerous failed attempts to sell several cookbook ideas to a number of New York publishers, I took my ideas to the fledgling Chronicle Books in San Francisco. Although they had never published a cookbook, I admired their work. Then-publisher Larry Smith quickly snapped up one of my book ideas, *Cold Pasta*, a collection of recipes for room-temperature pastas that I'd prepared for Twin Peaks Grocery. Bill LeBlond was assigned to be my editor, a job he has ably done on the twenty-seven titles that followed *Cold Pasta*. If you think only of Italian-inspired pasta salads, be sure to check my recipes for noodles with poached chicken in peanut sauce and cold spicy noodles coated with sesame dressing.

Being in California has greatly expanded my cooking knowledge. We are lucky to live in a land of great abundance, where there is year-round fresh produce from farmers' markets, daily catches from the Pacific Ocean, fresh noodles from Asian shops, still-warm handmade tortillas from Hispanic markets, fresh and packaged products from every corner of the planet, and, of course, fabulous wines from the nearby vineyards. Each new wave of arrivals has brought a wealth of delicacies that have been adopted as our own and fused to our local ingredients and cooking methods. I've learned to cook the exciting foods of China, Japan, and Southeast Asia, as evidenced by the inclusion of hot-and-sour soup, bagged sushi, Thai curries, and Vietnamese spring rolls in the chapters that follow.

Travels abroad or across North America always introduce me to new dishes. Whether at home in San Francisco or in faraway places, I visit restaurants to glean ideas as other writers might use a library. Research has never been more fun! Later at home I attempt to re-create those remembered tastes or develop a recipe with influences from those dining experiences. In this book are my recollections or interpretations of Korean barbecued beef, Sicilian stuffed rice balls, Moroccan *tagine*, southwestern tamales, and Florentine *panna cotta*.

My California relatives and friends continue to inspire my cooking. My sister, Martha, who insists that my parents and I never gave her a chance to learn to cook, says she learned how from my early books. Now I've learned some good things from her, such as how she seasons black beans. A couple of recipes for grilled fare that originated with my brother-in-law, John Richardson, have been included among my favorites. Auntie Naila Gallagher is not only one of my staunchest fans, but never hesitates to share her pearls of wisdom for ways to improve a recipe in progress. Kristi Spence helped me create a superb salad of eggplant, goat cheese, and pine nuts, and her sister, Gail High, shared her favorite way of cooking chicken that has become a standard in my own kitchen. For all my previous books, I've sent out the first-draft recipes to a group of family and friends across the country, who've graciously tested them in their own kitchens and reported back to me with improvements to my concept or writing.

Likewise, I've been inspired and taught by as well as gleaned ideas from the writings of my peers, including Antonia Allegra, Lee Bailey, Rick Bayless, Rose Beranbaum, Flo Braker, Hugh Carpenter and Teri Sandison, Irena Chalmers, Amy Coleman, Shirley Corriher, Marion Cunningham, Carol Field, Joyce Goldstein, Marcella Hazan, Emily Luchetti, Sheila Lukins and Julee Rosso, Nick Malgieri, Nancie McDermott, Mark Miller, Paulette Mitchell, Martha Stewart, Zanne Stewart, Barbara Tropp, and Anne Willan. Through the International Association of Culinary Professionals (IACP), many of these respected food authorities have not only shared their knowledge but have become friends.

No matter what the source of a recipe — a family heirloom, a recollected restaurant experience, a friend's favorite, an updated classic, a middle-of-the-night inspiration — I acknowledge that nothing in the world of food is totally original. But what I do with the recipe to adapt it to my taste makes it my own.

I invite you now to join me in a culinary journey that includes my favorite dishes from the twenty-eight cookbooks that I've previously published with Chronicle Books. As part of my ongoing education, I was not content merely to reprint the recipes as they first appeared. During the past two years, my partner, Andrew Moore, and I have revisited each recipe and have updated, retested, and/or rewritten it for the modern kitchen. Plus Andrew, who has an excellent palate, has contributed many new ideas to my original work. Whenever appropriate, the amount of fat has been reduced to create a lighter version. But I refuse to sacrifice flavor and instead advocate a well-balanced diet that maintains both a healthy body and spirit.

The growing availability of international products has been taken into account, too, although I have included substitutions for some of the harder-to-find items. If an ingredient is unfamiliar, check for a listing on pages 600-603. Methods and techniques have been updated to reflect the modern kitchen, taking for granted that most of my readers have food processors, electric mixers, and other useful appliances, as well as such helpful items as instant-read thermometers and salad spinners. All of these changes are intended to make cooking easier and more pleasurable for you.

Joseph Conrad once wrote, "The intention of every other piece of prose may be discussed and even mistrusted, but the purpose of a cookery book is one and unmistakable. Its object can conceivably be no other than to increase the happiness of mankind." It is my sincere hope that this collection of recipes will become a trusted friend of your twenty-first-century kitchen and serve as a guide to enriching the pleasures of your table.

Whether you're looking for a nourishing breakfast at the beginning of the day or a tasty prelude to lunch or dinner, here are some delicious ways to get off to a great start.

Breakfast

MANY nutritionists insist breakfast is the most important meal of the day. Most of us use up more energy during the morning hours and therefore need the long-lasting fuel provided by a well-balanced meal. Yet I find breakfast to be much more than just necessary fodder.

Through the years the morning meal has provided me with some of life's most pleasurable moments. Whether it's Champagne and puffed oven-baked pancakes at a table set with crisp linens, beautiful dishes, and fresh flowers for a cheerful celebration with friends, or a solitary cup of coffee and a simple bowl of crisp granola in a peaceful nook, a relaxed breakfast sets the tone for a happy and productive day.

In addition to the offerings that follow, please see Breads, beginning on page 410, for biscuits that are comforting additions to the breakfast table.

BUTTERMILK PANCAKES

Although best when eaten immediately, pancakes may be kept in a warm oven for up to 15 minutes. Serve with warm maple syrup, Ginger Syrup (page 598), or your favorite toppings.

IN a bowl, combine the flour, sugar, salt, baking powder, and baking soda and stir to mix well. Set aside.

IN another bowl, combine the buttermilk, ½ cup milk for thick pancakes or up to 1 cup milk for thinner pancakes, eggs, and melted butter and blend well. Add the flour mixture and stir until the ingredients are just blended.

MEANWHILE, heat a nonstick griddle or large, heavy skillet over medium heat. Using a pastry brush, lightly grease with butter, or coat with spray.

WORKING in batches and using about ¼ cup batter for each pancake, pour the batter onto the hot cooking surface; do not crowd the pancakes. Cook until the tops are bubbly, about 1 minute. Then turn and cook until the bottoms are browned, about 1 minute longer. Serve hot.

Makes 4 to 6 servings.

VARIATIONS

STIR 1 cup chopped banana or other soft fruit or ½ cup chopped toasted nuts (see page 554) into the batter.

SPRINKLE fresh blueberries or raspberries over the top after pouring onto the griddle or skillet.

2 cups all-purpose flour

1 tablespoon sugar

1 teaspoon salt

1 teaspoon baking powder

½ teaspoon baking soda

1½ cups buttermilk, at room temperature

½ to 1 cup milk (not fat free), at room temperature

2 eggs, at room temperature

¼ cup (½ stick) unsalted butter, melted and cooled slightly

Unsalted butter, at room temperature, or cooking spray for greasing

OVEN-PUFFED PANCAKES

FOR EACH SERVING

1 tablespoon unsalted butter

1 egg

¼ cup milk (not fat free)

¼ cup all-purpose flour

⅛ teaspoon salt

Known by the picturesque name Dutch babies, these showy German classics are among my favorite breakfast treats for entertaining. The basic recipe is for individual pancakes. For larger groups, multiply all of the ingredients as you increase the pan size. I often bake showstopping giant versions in a shallow paella pan that holds a dozen times the batter recipe.

Choose an ovenproof skillet, pie pan, or other shallow baking dish that will accommodate the desired number of servings. For a single serving, use a 4-inch diameter container; for a 2-egg individual pancake, use a 6-inch pan; for 4 to 6 eggs, use a 9- to 10-inch pan; for 6 to 8 eggs, use a 12-inch pan; for 10 to 12 eggs, use a 14- to 16-inch pan. As a general rule, larger pans that spread the batter thinner yield a drier and puffier pancake, while a thicker layer of batter in smaller pans produces a more custardy result and may take a bit longer to cook completely.

The classic topping is a generous sprinkling of powdered sugar and a squeeze of lemon or lime. Other possibilities include fresh berries, sliced peaches or other soft fruit, cooked apple or pear, warm maple syrup, jelly, curd (see page 593), or other favorite breakfast toppings. No matter which toppings you choose, present them at the table for adding to taste. Be sure to have the whole breakfast on the table and everyone seated before bringing the showy pancake directly from the oven.

PREHEAT an oven to 475° F.

SELECT a baking pan or dish (see recipe introduction). Add the butter (you'll need enough to coat the bottom generously) and heat in the oven until the butter is melted and the container is hot; watch carefully to avoid burning the butter.

MEANWHILE, calculate the number of servings and multiply the ingredients accordingly. In a blender or a bowl, combine the egg(s), milk, flour, and salt and blend or whisk until smooth. Pour the batter into the heated baking pan or dish and return the pan to the oven. Cook until the pancake is well puffed and golden, about 12 minutes, or longer for larger pancakes or those with a thicker layer of batter.

SERVE at once. When you make larger pancakes, cut them into wedges at the table. For a change of pace, spread large pancakes with selected topping, roll up jelly-roll fashion, and cut crosswise into slices at the table.

LEMON SOUFFLÉ PANCAKES

6 eggs, at room temperature, separated

2 cups small-curd cottage cheese or
   ricotta cheese (not fat free)

¼ cup canola or other high-quality
   vegetable oil

2 tablespoons sugar

½ teaspoon salt

4 teaspoons freshly squeezed lemon
   juice, preferably from Meyer variety

1 teaspoon grated or minced fresh
   lemon zest

4 teaspoons baking powder

1 cup all-purpose flour

Unsalted butter, at room temperature,
   or cooking spray for greasing

*Light as air, these lemony pancakes are a special morning treat. Serve
with your favorite toppings.*

IN a metal bowl, beat the egg whites with an electric mixer at
medium speed until they form peaks that are stiff but not dry
when the beater is raised. Set aside.

IN a food processor or blender, combine the egg yolks, cottage or
ricotta cheese, oil, sugar, salt, lemon juice and zest, baking
powder, and flour. Blend until smooth. Transfer to a bowl and
fold in the beaten egg whites.

MEANWHILE, heat a nonstick griddle or large, heavy skillet over
medium-high heat. Using a pastry brush, lightly grease with
butter, or coat with spray.

WORKING in batches and using about ¼ cup batter for each
pancake, pour the batter onto the hot cooking surface; do not
crowd the pancakes. Cook until the tops are bubbly, about
2 minutes. Then turn and cook until the bottoms are browned,
about 1 minute longer. Serve hot.

Makes 4 to 6 servings.

BLUEBERRY CORN PANCAKES

These are my very favorite pancakes, especially when topped with warm maple syrup. The golden color and crunchy texture of the corn are a good counterpoint to the dark and juicy blueberries. When fresh berries are not available, unsweetened frozen ones work well.

IN a bowl, combine the cornmeal, flour, baking powder, baking soda, and salt and stir to blend well. Set aside.

IN another bowl, combine the buttermilk, syrup or honey, oil, and egg, and stir to blend well. Add the cornmeal mixture and stir until the ingredients are just combined. Set aside for 10 minutes to soften the cornmeal.

HEAT a nonstick griddle or large, heavy skillet over medium-high heat. Using a pastry brush, lightly grease with melted butter, or coat with spray.

WORKING in batches and using about ¼ cup batter for each pancake, pour the batter onto the hot cooking surface; do not crowd the pancakes. Scatter the berries over the batter and cook until the tops of the pancakes are bubbly, about 1 minute. Then turn and cook until the bottoms are browned, about 1 minute longer. Between batches, wipe the pan with paper toweling to remove blueberry stains. Serve hot.

Makes 4 servings.

1½ cups yellow cornmeal

½ cup all-purpose flour

1 teaspoon baking powder

½ teaspoon baking soda

½ teaspoon salt

2 cups buttermilk

2 tablespoons pure maple syrup
  or honey

2 tablespoons canola or other high-
  quality vegetable oil

1 egg

Unsalted butter, at room temperature,
  or cooking spray for greasing

About 1½ cups fresh blueberries

BUTTER-RICH WAFFLES

Unsalted butter, at room temperature, or cooking spray for greasing

2 eggs, at room temperature, separated

1½ cups milk (not fat free), at room temperature

2 teaspoons baking powder

1 cup sifted all-purpose flour

½ cup (1 stick) unsalted butter, melted and cooled slightly

On an occasion when indulging is justified, try these delectable waffles, a special favorite of my late good friend, Martha Jane Cotton. Although I like to cook waffles in a deep-pocketed Belgian waffle iron, any type of iron will do. For a romantic change of pace, try a heart-shaped Scandinavian waffle maker.

Warm pure maple syrup is the perfect topping for waffles.

PREHEAT a waffle iron. Using a pastry brush, generously grease the grids with melted butter, or coat with spray.

IN a metal bowl, beat the egg whites with an electric mixer at medium speed until they form peaks that are stiff but not dry when the beaters are raised. Set aside.

IN another bowl, combine the egg yolks, milk, baking powder, flour, and melted butter and beat until smooth. Fold in the beaten egg whites.

BAKE until crisp in the waffle iron according to the manufacturer's directions. Serve hot.

Makes 4 servings.

SCONES WITH ORANGE BUTTER

Many Americans find these butter-rich British biscuits comforting for breakfast or at a coffee break. Traditionalists serve them with afternoon tea.

TO make the Orange Butter, in a food processor, combine the orange zest, powdered sugar, and butter and blend until well mixed. Transfer to a small bowl, cover, and refrigerate until shortly before serving.

TO make the scones, position racks so that the scones will bake in the middle of an oven and preheat the oven to 350° F. Using a pastry brush, lightly grease a baking sheet with butter or vegetable shortening, or coat with cooking spray or line with kitchen parchment. Set aside.

IN a bowl or food processor, combine the flour, granulated sugar, baking powder, baking soda, and salt. Cut in the cold butter with your fingertips, a pastry blender, or the steel blade until the mixture resembles coarse bread crumbs. If using a food processor, transfer the mixture to a bowl. Add the buttermilk, dried fruits or ginger, and zest and stir just until the mixture sticks together.

TURN out the dough onto a lightly floured surface and knead lightly and quickly, about 30 seconds. Pat the dough into a ball and flatten it to form a disk, then roll out with a lightly floured rolling pin into a round about ½ inch thick. Using a floured knife, cut into 8 wedges. Place on the prepared baking sheet, leaving space between each scone.

BRUSH the tops with melted butter and sprinkle with sugar. Bake until golden brown, 20 to 25 minutes. Serve warm with the Orange Butter.

Makes 8 scones.

VARIATION

Whole-Wheat Scones. Substitute 1 cup whole-wheat pastry flour for 1 cup of the all-purpose flour. Sprinkle with a mixture of ground cinnamon and sugar instead of just sugar.

ORANGE BUTTER

2 tablespoons grated or minced fresh orange zest

3 tablespoons powdered sugar

½ cup (1 stick) unsalted butter, at room temperature

SCONES

Unsalted butter or solid vegetable shortening, at room temperature, or cooking spray for greasing (optional)

2 cups all-purpose flour

3 tablespoons granulated sugar

1 teaspoon baking powder

½ teaspoon baking soda

½ teaspoon salt

½ cup (1 stick) very cold unsalted butter, cut into small pieces

⅔ cup buttermilk

⅓ cup dried cherries, cranberries, currants, or raisins or chopped crystallized ginger

1 tablespoon grated or minced fresh lemon or orange zest

Unsalted butter, melted, for brushing

Granulated sugar for sprinkling

CROISSANTS

3 tablespoons sugar

1 envelope (¼ ounce) quick-rising
active dry yeast

2⅔ cups all-purpose flour

1½ teaspoons salt

1 cup whole milk

1 cup (2 sticks) cold unsalted butter

Unsalted butter or solid vegetable
shortening, at room temperature, or
cooking spray for greasing (optional)

1 egg beaten with 1 tablespoon water
for brushing

Any day that I wish to relive my mornings in Paris, I indulge in a buttery croissant with café au lait. *The technique for making these flaky French rolls is easy, but the chilling between steps makes the preparation a long one. Don't try to reduce the number of foldings, however, or the rolls will not be flaky.*

IN a small bowl, combine ¼ cup warm water (110° to 115° F) and 1 tablespoon of the sugar, sprinkle with the yeast, stir to dissolve, and let stand until soft and foamy, about 5 minutes. (Discard the mixture and start over with a fresh envelope of yeast if bubbles have not formed within 5 minutes.)

IN a bowl, combine the remaining 2 tablespoons sugar, the flour, and salt and stir to blend well. Add the milk and foamy yeast mixture and stir until moistened, scraping down the sides of the bowl. The dough should be rather loose, much like unkneaded biscuit dough. Cover the bowl tightly with plastic wrap, and set aside at room temperature to relax the gluten for about 30 minutes, then refrigerate for at least 5 hours or for up to overnight.

PLACE the cold butter on a generously floured work surface. Using a rolling pin, pound the butter until softened, turning often to coat with the flour from the board, then roll the butter into a flat piece about 5 by 6 inches and set aside. (Refrigerate briefly if the butter begins to get warm; when ready to use it should be about the same temperature as the dough in the following step.)

SCRAPE up all traces of butter from the work surface and sprinkle lightly with flour. Turn out the chilled dough and roll it out into a rectangle about 8 by 12 inches, with the long side facing you. Place the butter with its short side facing you over the right half of the dough. Brush off excess flour from the dough, fold the left side over the buttered half, and press the edges together to seal. Press and roll the folded dough out lengthwise to form a rectangle about 10 by 20 inches. Brushing off excess flour from the dough as you fold, bring the bottom third of the dough up over the middle third, then fold the top third down over it as you would a letter. Place on a baking sheet, cover with plastic wrap, and refrigerate for 45 minutes.

TO "turn" the chilled dough, position it on a lightly floured surface with the long sealed side toward the right and roll it out into a rectangle about 10 by 20 inches. Again brushing off excess flour from the dough, fold it over in thirds as you would a letter. Place on a baking sheet, cover with plastic wrap, and refrigerate until well chilled, about 45 minutes.

REPEAT the turning and chilling step 2 more times. After the final folding, refrigerate the dough for up to overnight.

USING a pastry brush, lightly grease 2 baking sheets with butter or vegetable shortening, or coat with cooking spray or line with kitchen parchment. Set aside.

ON a lightly floured surface, roll out the dough into a 12-by-18-inch rectangle, lifting the dough to relax it and flouring the surface as needed. Using a sharp knife or pastry wheel, cut the dough lengthwise in half. Gently stretch 2 opposite corners of each piece to create diagonal edges, then cut each piece into 8 equal triangles with 4-inch bases. Hold each triangle by the wide end and pull toward the tip to stretch the dough while rolling it up from the wide end. Tuck the tip of the triangle slightly underneath the roll and curve the ends in toward the tip to form a crescent shape. Place about 2 inches apart on the prepared baking sheets. (At this point, the croissants can be covered and refrigerated overnight.) Lightly brush the tops and sides with the egg-and-water mixture, cover loosely with plastic wrap or a cloth kitchen towel, and let rise in a warm place until almost doubled in bulk, 1 to 2 hours.

POSITION racks so that the croissants will bake in the middle of an oven and preheat the oven to 425° F.

GENTLY brush the risen croissants again with the egg-and-water mixture. Bake for 10 minutes, then reduce the heat to 375° F and bake until golden brown, about 7 minutes longer. Transfer to wire racks to cool slightly before serving.

Makes 16 croissants.

STICKY BUNS

SWEET YEAST DOUGH

½ cup sugar

2 envelopes (¼ ounce each) quick-
rising active dry yeast

3 eggs, at room temperature

1½ teaspoons salt

1 cup milk (not fat free), at room
temperature

½ cup (1 stick) unsalted butter,
melted and cooled slightly

5¾ cups all-purpose flour

Unsalted butter, at room temperature,
for greasing

CURRANT-PECAN FILLING

1½ cups firmly packed brown sugar

½ cup (1 stick) unsalted butter, at
room temperature

1½ tablespoons ground cinnamon

½ cup dried currants

¾ cup finely chopped pecans

STICKY PECAN GLAZE

1 cup (2 sticks) unsalted butter, at
room temperature

1¾ cups firmly packed brown sugar

¼ cup light corn syrup

¾ cup small pecan halves or
coarsely chopped pecans

Those gooey glazed sticky buns, the rage at bakeries from coast to coast, are easy to make at home. See the variations for how to make equally delectable cinnamon rolls.

TO make the Sweet Yeast Dough, in a small bowl, combine ¼ cup warm water (110° to 115° F) and 1 tablespoon of the sugar. Sprinkle with the yeast, stir to dissolve, and set aside until soft and foamy, about 5 minutes. (Discard the mixture and start over with fresh envelopes if bubbles have not formed within 5 minutes.)

IN the bowl of a heavy-duty stand mixer fitted with a flat beater, combine the remaining 7 tablespoons sugar, the eggs, salt, milk, butter, and the foamy yeast mixture and mix at the lowest speed until smooth. With the mixer running at low speed, add the flour, ½ cup at a time, until well incorporated, stopping to scrape down the bowl and beater as necessary. Exchange the beater for a dough hook. Knead at medium speed until the dough is smooth, elastic, and no longer sticky, about 3 minutes.

USING a pastry brush, lightly grease a bowl with butter. Gather the dough into a ball, transfer to the prepared bowl, turn the dough to coat all sides with butter, cover the bowl tightly with plastic wrap, and set the dough aside to rise in a warm place until doubled in bulk, about 1 hour.

MEANWHILE, to make the Currant-Pecan Filling, in a bowl, combine all of the filling ingredients, stir to mix well, and set aside.

USING a pastry brush, generously grease the bottoms of two 9-inch round cake pans with butter and set aside.

TO make the Sticky Pecan Glaze, in a bowl, combine the butter, brown sugar, and corn syrup and beat until well mixed. Divide the mixture evenly between the prepared pans, then spread it evenly with a rubber spatula. Sprinkle with the pecans and set aside.

PUNCH down the risen dough and turn it out onto a lightly
   floured surface. Roll out into a 14-by-24-inch rectangle.
   Sprinkle the reserved filling over the dough, gently pressing
   the mixture into the dough with your fingers. Beginning with a
   narrow end, roll up the dough like a jelly roll. Slice crosswise
   into 1-inch-wide pieces to make a total of 14 slices. Arrange
   7 slices on top of the glaze in each pan. Cover with a kitchen
   towel and let stand in a warm place until puffy and almost
   doubled in bulk, about 1 hour.

POSITION racks so that the buns will bake in the middle of an
   oven and preheat the oven to 375° F.

BAKE the buns until golden brown on top, about 20 minutes.
   Remove from the oven, immediately cover each pan with an
   inverted serving platter, quickly invert each pan and platter
   together, and lift off the pans. The glaze will dribble down
   the sides. Pull apart and serve warm.

Makes 14 buns.

VARIATIONS

FOR a heartier bun, substitute 2 cups whole-wheat flour for
   2 cups of the all-purpose flour.

TO make cinnamon rolls, omit the Sticky Pecan Glaze. Bake the
   rolls in buttered pans, then turn out and brush the tops with a
   mixture of ¾ cup powdered sugar, 1 tablespoon warm water,
   and 1 tablespoon freshly squeezed lemon juice. Serve warm.

SUNSHINE GRANOLA

6 cups rolled grains such as barley,
    oats, rye, triticale, or wheat, one
    type or a mixture

1 cup raw sunflower seeds

1 cup chopped raw or blanched
    almonds or other nuts

2 tablespoons grated or minced fresh
    orange zest (optional)

1 can (12 ounces) frozen orange
    juice concentrate, thawed

Most commercial granolas contain added oil or butter and are too sweet. This version lets the taste of the grains shine through. If you prefer a richer blend, mix the grains with about ½ cup high-quality vegetable oil or melted butter before toasting. For a sweeter product, add about ¼ cup honey to the raw mixture. If desired, stir 1 cup raisins, dried cherries or cranberries, chopped dates or other dried fruit, or a combination of dried fruits into the slightly cooled granola.

PREHEAT an oven to 300° F.

IN a large mixing bowl, combine the rolled grain(s), sunflower seeds, nuts, and orange zest (if using) and mix well. Add the orange juice concentrate and mix thoroughly. Transfer the mixture to large, shallow baking pans and spread in a thin layer. Bake, stirring occasionally, until dry and toasted, about 45 minutes.

POUR into a large mixing bowl to cool, stirring occasionally. When completely cooled, store in an airtight container at room temperature for up to a week.

Makes 8 cups for 8 servings.

SOFT-COOKED EGGS

I first came to enjoy soft-cooked eggs in Holland, where they star at almost every breakfast along with sliced cold cuts, assorted cheeses, and breads. For an elegant presentation, top the cracked eggs with dollops of caviar, sour cream, and minced chives, or sauteed crab or tiny shrimp.

Eggs, at room temperature

Salt

Freshly ground black pepper

IN a saucepan, combine the eggs with just enough water to cover, then remove the eggs. Place the pot of water over medium heat and bring just to a simmer. Carefully lower the eggs into the water. Adjust the heat to maintain a simmer and cook, uncovered, until the eggs are done to your taste, 3 to 5 minutes.

DRAIN and transfer the eggs to egg cups. To eat, crack the tops gently with a knife, peel away about ½ inch of the shell, season to taste with salt and pepper, and eat with a spoon.

ALTERNATIVELY, crack and peel the eggs and serve in small bowls.

Each cooked egg makes 1 serving.

HARD-COOKED EGGS

Eggs, at room temperature

Don't call them "boiled" eggs, because boiling turns the insides rubbery and cracks the shells, which then leak and create watery eggs.

IN a saucepan, place the eggs in a single uncrowded layer and add just enough water to cover them. Place over high heat. Just as soon as the water begins to simmer, reduce the heat to maintain a gentle simmer and cook for 15 to 18 minutes, depending on the size of the eggs.

DRAIN the eggs and cover immediately with cold water to halt cooking. Tap each egg all over to crack the shell, then place under running cold water and peel off the shell.

Each cooked egg makes 1 serving.

SCRAMBLED EGGS

Basic to so many breakfasts, scrambled eggs can be wonderful when properly cooked or rubbery when overcooked. Avoid overcooking, as they will continue to cook after removing from the heat.

Eggs, at room temperature

Milk (not fat free) or cream

Salt

Unsalted butter

Freshly ground black pepper

BREAK the eggs into a bowl. For each egg, add 1 teaspoon milk or cream and ⅛ teaspoon salt, or to taste, and beat with a whisk or fork until well blended but not frothy.

IN a skillet, heat about 1 teaspoon butter for each egg over medium-low heat. Pour in the eggs. As soon as they begin to thicken, stir them with a fork, lifting the edges to let uncooked egg pour underneath. Cook the eggs, stirring, just until they are almost set but still creamy. Remove immediately to a warmed serving dish and serve. Pass pepper at the table.

2 scrambled eggs make 1 or 2 servings.

VARIATIONS

COOK onions, shallots, garlic, mushrooms, sweet peppers, ham, or other meat in the butter before adding the eggs. Or add crumbled cooked bacon, grated cheese, toasted sunflower seeds, minced fresh herbs, or slivered truffles when the eggs are almost set. Top plain scrambled eggs with caviar or smoked salmon.

POACHED EGGS

1 tablespoon white wine vinegar

Eggs, at room temperature

Salt

Freshly ground black pepper

Poached eggs are delicious on their own and even better when smothered in Hollandaise sauce as directed in the adjacent recipes.

IN a large skillet or saute pan, pour in water to a depth of about 2½ inches. Add the vinegar and bring to a boil over medium-high heat, then reduce the heat so that the water barely bubbles. Break an egg into a small bowl. Using the tip of a slotted spoon, swirl a section of the water to activate it, then immediately slip the egg into the center of the whirlpool. Repeat with as many eggs as desired without crowding the pan. Reduce the heat to low and let the eggs steep in the hot water until the whites are set, about 3 minutes.

USING a slotted spoon, remove the eggs from the water, drain well, and serve at once. Pass salt and pepper at the table.

Each cooked egg makes 1 serving.

EGGS AND HOLLANDAISE CLASSICS

Prepare Hollandaise Sauce as directed on page 572 and poach eggs as directed in the preceding recipe, then combine them with a variety of other ingredients as suggested here to create some of America's favorite fancy breakfast dishes. Whichever combination you choose, be sure to serve immediately after assembling.

Eggs Benedict. Toast and butter rounds of Holland rusk or English muffin halves. Cover each round with a slice of broiled ham or Canadian bacon. Top with a poached egg, then cover with Hollandaise Sauce.

Eggs Blackstone. Toast and butter English muffin halves. Top each with a slice of broiled tomato, then crumbled crisply fried bacon, and a poached egg. Cover with Hollandaise Sauce and garnish with a bit of crumbled bacon.

Eggs Sardou. Place 1 or 2 cooked large artichoke bottoms on each plate. Top each bottom with a little warm creamed spinach, then a poached egg. Cover with Hollandaise Sauce.

Eggs with Salmon. Fill freshly baked puff pastry shells with slivered smoked salmon, top with a poached egg, and cover with Hollandaise Sauce. Garnish with additional salmon and fresh caviar.

Eggs on Scones. Split warm Scones (page 21), top with slices of fried ham, and then place a poached egg on each. Cover with Hollandaise Sauce made with orange juice and garnish with thin strips of orange zest.

OMELETS

Once you've mastered the technique, omelets are a quick yet elegant breakfast presentation. If there's a crowd, cook at the table over a portable electric burner. Omelets may be served plain, with fillings, or topped with a sauce such as fresh tomato or cheese.

FOR EACH SERVING

3 eggs

Salt

Freshly ground black or white pepper

1 tablespoon Clarified Butter (page 571)

OPTIONAL FILLINGS

Avocado slices

Caviar and sour cream

Cooked and shredded chicken, beef,
  or pork

Cooked lobster, shrimp, or crab

Creamed spinach

Crumbled crisply cooked bacon

Grated or crumbled cheese, one kind
  or a combination

Jams or jellies

Salsa

Sauteed mushrooms

Smoked salmon, sour cream, and
  minced fresh chives

Steamed or sauteed asparagus tips or
  broccoli florets

IN a small bowl, beat the eggs with a whisk or fork until well blended but not frothy. Add salt and pepper to taste.

HEAT an 8-inch nonstick skillet over high heat. Add the clarified butter and heat until very hot but not smoking. Add the eggs and move the pan continuously over the heat to prevent sticking, using a thin spatula to keep eggs away from the sides of the pan. When the bottom sets up, use the spatula to lift up the sides and let any uncooked egg flow underneath. If you wish, just before the top is set, add about 1/3 cup filling down the center of the omelet. Tilting the pan and using the spatula, roll one-third of the omelet over the filling. Hold the pan over a serving plate so the unfolded side begins to slide out. Using the spatula, flip the omelet so the folded side folds over with the center on the top; total cooking time should be less than 1 minute.

ADD a compatible sauce, if you wish, and a garnish appropriate to the filling.

Makes 1 serving.

BACON AND EGGS CASSEROLE

Here's a new twist on traditional American breakfast fare that holds up for easy morning entertaining.

IN a saute pan or skillet, melt 2 tablespoons of the butter over medium-high heat. Add the mushrooms and cook, stirring constantly, for about 2 minutes. Reduce the heat to medium-low and cook, stirring frequently, until tender, about 8 minutes longer, depending on the variety and size. Set aside.

IN a skillet, fry the bacon over medium heat until crisp, then transfer to paper toweling to drain. Discard the bacon fat from the skillet.

IN the skillet, melt 4 tablespoons of the remaining butter over low heat. Add most of the drained bacon (save some for garnishing) and about three-fourths of the mushrooms. Mix well and sprinkle with the flour and salt and black pepper to taste. Gradually stir in the milk and cook, stirring constantly, until the mixture is smooth and thickened, about 20 minutes. Cover and set aside.

PREHEAT an oven to 350° F. Using a pastry brush, generously grease a 9-inch soufflé dish with butter and set aside.

IN another skillet, melt the remaining 2 tablespoons butter over medium-low heat. In a bowl, combine the eggs, cream, and 1 teaspoon salt, or to taste. Pour into the skillet and scramble with a fork just until barely set; do not overcook. Immediately transfer to a bowl.

IN the prepared dish, alternately layer the scrambled eggs and the bacon white sauce, ending with sauce. Top with the remaining mushrooms and reserved bacon. Bake, uncovered, until heated through, 15 to 20 minutes.

GARNISH with chives and serve warm.

Makes 8 servings.

½ cup (1 stick) unsalted butter

8 ounces flavorful fresh mushrooms such as chanterelle, portobello, or shiitake, sliced

8 ounces thick-sliced bacon, preferably pepper-cured, cut into small pieces

½ cup all-purpose flour

Salt

Freshly ground black pepper

1 quart milk (not fat free)

Unsalted butter, at room temperature, for greasing

12 eggs, lightly beaten

¾ cup light cream or half-and-half

Fresh chives for garnish

CORNED BEEF HASH

1 pound boiling potatoes, unpeeled

2 tablespoons canola or other high-quality vegetable oil

¼ cup (½ stick) unsalted butter

1 cup sliced onion

2 red sweet peppers, stems, seeds, and membranes discarded, cut into narrow strips

1 teaspoon minced garlic

3 to 4 cups cooked corned beef brisket, thinly sliced, then cut into narrow strips

1 tablespoon minced fresh thyme, or 1 teaspoon crumbled dried thyme

1 tablespoon Worcestershire sauce, or to taste

Salt

Freshly ground black pepper or ground cayenne

½ cup chopped fresh flat-leaf parsley

4 to 6 poached eggs (page 30)

Fresh parsley or thyme sprigs for garnish

Always start with high-quality cooked corned beef, never canned. I prefer hash without the traditional crust that results from overcooking. If you feel differently, cook on one side until brown and crusty, invert, and cook the other side until crusty. Hash is one dish that I enjoy with tomato catsup.

PLACE the potatoes in a saucepan and add water to cover by about 2 inches, then remove the potatoes. Bring the water to a boil over medium-high heat, return the potatoes, and cook until just tender when pierced with a wooden skewer or small, sharp knife, 15 to 45 minutes, depending on size. Drain well, then return the potatoes to the pan, place over the heat, and shake the pan until excess moisture evaporates and the potatoes are dry to the touch. Set aside to cool. As soon as the potatoes are cool enough to handle, peel them, cut into narrow strips, and set aside.

IN a saute pan or skillet, heat the oil and 2 tablespoons of the butter over medium heat. Add the onion and sweet pepper and cook, stirring frequently, until the vegetables are very soft but not browned, about 10 minutes. Stir in the garlic and cook about 1 minute longer. Add the remaining 2 tablespoons butter, the reserved potatoes, corned beef, thyme, Worcestershire sauce, and salt and pepper or cayenne to taste. Cook until the meat and potatoes are heated through, about 8 minutes. Stir in the chopped parsley.

TO serve, distribute the hash evenly on 4 to 6 warmed plates. Top each serving with a poached egg and garnish with parsley or thyme sprigs.

Makes 4 to 6 servings.

GRILLADES AND GRITS

The Creole kitchen of New Orleans gave America this special dish of braised veal, which is usually accompanied with grits to soak up the rich gravy. Although traditionally served as a breakfast or brunch dish, it is equally satisfying at lunch or dinner. Lard is still used for cooking the veal in many New Orleans kitchens, but oil and butter have been used here.

QUICKLY rinse the veal under cold running water, pat dry with paper toweling, and cut into pieces 2 to 3 inches in diameter. Place each piece between 2 sheets of waxed paper or plastic wrap and pound with a mallet or other flat instrument to a uniform thickness of about ¼ inch. Generously season with salt, pepper, and cayenne. Dip the meat into the flour to coat lightly, shaking off excess flour.

IN a saute pan or skillet, heat 1 tablespoon of the oil and 1 tablespoon of the butter over medium heat. Add as many of the veal pieces as will fit without crowding the pan and brown on both sides. Using a slotted utensil or tongs, transfer the veal to a plate. Brown the remaining veal pieces in the same manner, adding more oil and butter as necessary to prevent sticking.

ADD enough oil and butter to that remaining in the pan to total 2 tablespoons and heat over medium-high heat. Add the onion and cook, stirring frequently, until soft but not browned, about 5 minutes. Stir in the garlic and cook for 1 minute. Add the tomato, stock or broth, and bay leaves, and bring the mixture to a boil. Reduce the heat to achieve a simmer, cover partially, and cook for 20 minutes.

ADD the reserved veal and simmer, partially covered, turning the veal every 10 minutes to coat with the gravy, until the flavors are well blended and the meat is tender when pierced with a sharp knife, about 30 minutes.

MEANWHILE, cook the grits according to the package directions, and keep warm.

TO serve, mound the grits on warmed plates, add the veal grillades, cover both with the pan gravy, and serve immediately.

Makes 6 servings.

6 boneless veal round steaks (5 to 6 ounces *each*), about ½ inch thick, trimmed of excess fat

Salt

Freshly ground black pepper

Ground cayenne

All-purpose flour for dredging

About 2 tablespoons canola or other high-quality vegetable oil

About 2 tablespoons unsalted butter

2½ cups chopped yellow or white onion

1½ tablespoons minced garlic

2 cups peeled, seeded, drained, and chopped ripe or canned tomato

2 cups White Stock (page 578) or canned reduced-sodium chicken broth

2 bay leaves

1½ cups grits

Appetizers

OFTEN my favorite part of a meal is the appetizer, and sometimes I enjoy making a complete meal of several of them.

Here are some of my best dips, spreads, finger foods, and other small plates to begin a meal or to star on their own at a party. You'll find recipes that make great snacks or picnic fare, as well as some that can be expanded into main courses or complete light meals by offering larger portions.

Most can be set on the cocktail or party table for self-service or passed on trays, while others can be plated as first courses at the table.

GRANNY'S ONION DIP

Mary Knecht, grandmother of my late partner, Lin Cotton, used to serve this often at our Lake Tahoe compound, something we current residents still do. Potato chips must have been invented to team up with this dip, although steamed or blanched fresh vegetables are also great dippers.

If you wish to reduce the amount of fat and calories, choose lower fat cream cheese and substitute plain nonfat yogurt for the mayonnaise.

IN a food processor, combine all of the ingredients, including salt to taste, and blend until smooth. Transfer to a bowl and serve at room temperature.

Makes about 2 cups for 12 servings.

12 ounces cream cheese, at room temperature

3 tablespoons Mayonnaise (page 388) or high-quality commercial mayonnaise

2 tablespoons heavy (whipping) cream, light cream, or half-and-half

½ cup chopped yellow or white onion, or to taste

1 teaspoon minced garlic (optional)

1 tablespoon Worcestershire sauce

Salt

SUN-DRIED TOMATO AND GARLIC SPREAD

1 tablespoon chopped garlic or
  2 tablespoons peeled Roasted
  Garlic (page 551)
¼ cup drained sun-dried tomatoes
  packed in olive oil
4 ounces fresh goat cheese, at room
  temperature
4 ounces cream cheese, at room
  temperature
Salt
Oil from sun-dried tomatoes

Quick and easy, this delicious appetizer is always popular with guests. In addition to offering it with baguette slices or crackers, I frequently serve it with tiny Roasted Potatoes with Garlic and Rosemary (page 306).

IN a food processor, combine all of the ingredients, including salt to taste and a little of the oil as needed, and blend until smooth. Transfer to a bowl and serve at room temperature.

Makes about 1½ cups for 8 servings.

CHILI BEAN DIP

Mexicali Beans (page 348)
2 tablespoons tomato paste
1½ teaspoons minced canned
  chipotle chile in *adobo* sauce,
  or to taste
1½ teaspoons *adobo* sauce from
  canned chiles, or to taste
Fresh cilantro (coriander) sprigs
  for garnish

Use this technique with any cooked beans and favorite seasonings to create your own flavorful dips. Serve with corn tortilla chips.

COOK the Mexicali Beans as directed. Measure out 2 cups of the cooked beans and drain well. (Save the remaining beans for another use.)

IN a food processor, combine the beans, tomato paste, chile, and *adobo* sauce and blend until smooth. Transfer to a bowl, garnish with cilantro sprigs, and serve at room temperature.

Makes about 2 cups for 8 servings.

ROASTED GARLIC AND BEAN SPREAD

Use cannellini, flageolet, navy, or other small white beans for this Mediterranean-style spread. Serve with sliced whole-grain French or Italian bread.

After preparing this favorite from my Beans & Grains *book on the PBS television show* Home Cooking with Amy Coleman, *Amy suggested the addition of a splash of balsamic vinegar, an excellent idea that I've continued.*

2 or 3 whole garlic heads

2 cups cooked dried or canned
   small white beans (see page 340)

Extra-virgin olive oil

Balsamic vinegar

Salt

Freshly ground black pepper

ROAST the garlic as directed on page 551. Squeeze the cloves from the skin into a bowl and set aside.

DRAIN the beans and transfer to a food processor. Add the garlic and blend until fairly smooth. Season to taste with oil, vinegar, salt, and pepper. Transfer to a small crock and serve at room temperature.

Makes about 2 cups for 8 servings.

MIDDLE EASTERN GARBANZO SPREAD ~ *Hummus* ~

½ cup sesame seed paste (tahini)

6 tablespoons extra-virgin olive oil

1 tablespoon minced garlic

2 cups cooked dried or canned
garbanzo beans (see page 340)

¼ cup freshly squeezed lemon juice,
or more if needed

Salt

1 tablespoon paprika

Pomegranate seeds for garnish
(optional)

Fresh mint sprigs for garnish

Pureed garbanzo beans (chickpeas) blended with sesame seed paste (tahini) is a quickly prepared and highly nutritious appetizer. Traditionally used as a spread or dip with small wedges of pita bread, the mixture also goes well with crusty French bread, toasted whole-grain bread, or vegetables. Hummus can be thinned with lemon juice and olive oil to taste for a tangy salad dressing or combined with plain yogurt for a sandwich spread.

Tahini is available in Greek and Middle Eastern specialty stores and most gourmet or natural-foods markets, as well as many supermarkets.

IN a food processor, combine the sesame seed paste, 2 tablespoons of the oil, and the garlic and blend well. Drain the beans and reserve the liquid. Transfer the beans and ½ cup of the reserved liquid to the sesame seed mixture. Add the lemon juice and blend to a creamy consistency, adding more of the reserved bean liquid if necessary. Season to taste with salt and more lemon juice if needed. Transfer to a bowl, cover, and set aside at room temperature for about 2 hours or refrigerate overnight; return to room temperature before serving.

IN a small saucepan, combine the remaining ¼ cup oil and the paprika. Place over medium heat and heat, stirring frequently, until the oil turns bright red, about 3 minutes. Strain the oil through a fine-mesh strainer into a small bowl. Set aside.

TO serve, spread the hummus on a serving plate. Using the back of a spoon, form an indentation in the center and fill with the red-tinted oil. Sprinkle with pomegranate seeds (if using) and garnish with mint sprigs.

Makes about 2 cups for 8 servings.

CHUTNEY-GLAZED CHEESE

Everything is done ahead of time for this festive addition to the appetizer table. Serve with English whole-wheat (wheatmeal) biscuits, crackers, or bite-sized muffins.

DAMPEN two 12-inch squares of cheesecloth with water, wring dry, and stack flat, one on top of the other. Smoothly line a 3-cup bowl with the cheesecloth.

IN a food processor, combine the cream cheese, butter, and orange juice and zest and blend until smooth and fluffy. Remove about half of the mixture and reserve. Add the curry powder to the remaining mixture and blend until thoroughly mixed. Spoon about one-third of the reserved cheese mixture into the lined mold, pressing with your fingertips or a spatula to compress the mixture and eliminate air pockets. Add about one-third of the curried cheese mixture, pressing in the same manner. Continue alternately layering the cheese mixtures until both are used up. Bring the excess cheesecloth up over the top to cover the cheese completely and refrigerate until the cheese feels firm when gently pressed, about 1½ hours.

UNFOLD the cheesecloth, invert the mold onto a serving plate, and gently pull off the container and the cheesecloth. If not serving within a couple of hours, wrap tightly with plastic wrap and refrigerate for up to 2 days.

IN a small saucepan, melt the chutney over low heat. While the chutney is melting, gently press the cashews into the surface of the cheese. Remove the chutney from the heat and cool to room temperature, then spoon it over the cheese to cover completely; use a small spatula to spread it evenly onto the sides. Refrigerate the cheese for about 30 minutes to allow the glaze to set.

REMOVE from the refrigerator about 20 minutes before serving. Garnish with orange zest.

Makes 8 to 10 servings.

1 pound cream cheese, at room temperature

½ cup (1 stick) unsalted butter, at room temperature

¼ cup freshly squeezed orange juice

1½ teaspoons grated or minced fresh orange zest

1½ tablespoons Indian-Style Curry Powder (page 556) or high-quality commercial curry powder, or to taste

½ cup finely chopped mango or other chutney (a favorite recipe or high-quality commercial product)

½ cup roasted whole cashews

Shredded fresh orange zest for garnish

SWEET CRUNCHY NUTS

2 cups pecan or walnut halves or
    whole cashews, skinned hazelnuts,
    or other nuts
¼ cup sugar
Canola or other high-quality vegetable
    oil for frying (optional)
Salt

A bowl of these crisp treats set out with cocktails always disappears quickly. Whether left as halves or chopped, they are also delicious sprinkled over a green salad or a hot fudge sundae.

IN a saucepan, bring 3 cups water to a boil over high heat. Add the nuts, return to a boil, and cook for 1 minute. Drain the nuts, rinse under warm running water, and drain again. Transfer the warm nuts to a bowl, pour the sugar over the nuts, and stir until the sugar is dissolved.

TO fry the nuts, in a saucepan, pour in oil to a depth of 1 inch and heat to 360° F. Using a slotted utensil, transfer the nuts to the oil and cook, stirring frequently, until golden, about 3 minutes; watch carefully to prevent burning. Again using a slotted utensil, transfer the nuts to a colander set over a bowl or in the sink to drain. Season to taste with salt and stir frequently until cool to keep the nuts from sticking together.

TO toast the nuts, preheat an oven to 350° F. Transfer the sugared nuts to a shallow baking pan and toast in the oven, stirring frequently, until dry, mahogany colored, and fragrant, 15 to 20 minutes. Transfer the nuts to a bowl, season to taste with salt, and stir frequently until cool. When cool enough to handle, use your hands to break apart any nuts that are stuck together.

Makes 2 cups for 8 servings.

GORGONZOLA WAFERS

These thin savory cookies are excellent paired with full-bodied red wines.

IN a bowl, combine the butter and cheese and beat with an electric mixer until smooth and creamy. Add the flour, pine nuts, and salt and mix well. Divide the dough in half. Using your palms, form the dough into 2 logs, each about 1½ inches in diameter. Wrap in waxed paper or plastic wrap and refrigerate until well chilled and firm, at least 3 hours or for up to 2 days.

PREHEAT an oven to 375° F. Using a pastry brush, lightly grease 2 baking sheets with butter, or coat with spray or line with kitchen parchment.

SLICE the chilled dough into rounds about ⅛ inch thick and place about 2 inches apart on the prepared baking sheets. Bake until golden brown, about 12 minutes. Immediately remove from the baking sheets and transfer to a wire rack to cool completely.

SERVE immediately or store in airtight containers at room temperature for up to 3 days.

Makes about 30 wafers for 10 servings.

½ cup (1 stick) unsalted butter, at room temperature

8 ounces Gorgonzola or other blue cheese, finely crumbled

1 cup all-purpose flour

¾ cup pine nuts

½ teaspoon salt

Unsalted butter, at room temperature, or cooking spray for greasing (optional)

MEXICAN BEAN-FILLED CORN SHELLS ~ *SOPES* ~

Mexicali Beans (page 348) or
    Southwestern Beans (page 351)

SOPES

1 pound prepared Mexican corn
    dough *(masa)*, or 2 cups Mexican
    corn flour *(masa harina)*
¼ cup all-purpose flour
1 teaspoon baking powder
½ teaspoon salt
2 tablespoons high-quality pure lard,
    unsalted butter, or solid vegetable
    shortening
Canola or other high-quality vegetable
    oil for frying

Fresh Tomato Salsa (page 392)
¾ cup crumbled fresh Mexican
    cheese *(queso fresco)* or farmer
    cheese (about 3 ounces)
Fresh cilantro (coriander) sprigs for
    garnish

Throughout Mexico, crispy masa *shells are known as* sopes, *as well as by a variety of other names depending on their shape and origin. Elongated boat shapes are called* chalupas. *The same dough is also used to fashion round* gordas *or* gorditas *or football-shaped* memelos, *small, fat tortillas over which the filling is spooned.*

If you are unfamiliar with Mexican corn dough (masa) *and corn flour* (masa harina), *please read about them on page 602.*

COOK the Mexicali or Southwestern Beans as directed. Measure out 1½ cups of the cooked beans and set aside. (Save the remaining beans for another use.)

TO make the *sopes,* if using *masa,* place it in a mixing bowl. If using corn flour, place in a bowl and gradually stir in about 1⅓ cups warm water, using just enough water to form a dough that holds together. Cover and set aside to cool completely.

TO the *masa* or moistened corn flour, add the all-purpose flour, baking powder, salt, and lard, butter, or shortening. Using your hands, knead the mixture until well blended and light. If the mixture is too dry, add a little warm water. The finished dough should feel soft but not sticky.

MOISTEN your hands with water and form the dough into 12 walnut-sized balls. Place the balls in a bowl and cover tightly with plastic wrap.

PLACE a flat Mexican griddle *(comal),* other griddle, or heavy skillet over medium heat. Moisten your hands with water. Working with 1 dough ball at a time, pat it between the palms of your hands into a flat disk about 3 inches in diameter and ¼ inch thick. Place it on the hot griddle and cook until the bottom is partially set and lightly browned, about 1 minute.

Turn and cook the other side until partially set, about 30 seconds. Remove to a work surface, last cooked side up, and pinch up the edge with your fingertips to form a ¼- to ½-inch lip all around; dip your fingers in cold water if the dough is too hot to handle. Set aside. Cook and shape the remaining dough in the same manner. (At this point the *sopes* can be cooled, tightly covered, and refrigerated for up to 2 days.)

ABOUT 30 minutes before serving, prepare the Fresh Tomato Salsa as directed, begin to reheat the beans over low heat, and fry the *sopes*.

TO fry the *sopes*, in a skillet or saucepan, pour in oil to a depth of ½ inch and heat to 375° F. Preheat an oven to 200° F. Place a wire rack on a baking sheet and position alongside the stove top.

CAREFULLY add a few of the *sopes* to the hot oil; avoid crowding the pan. Fry until golden brown, 30 seconds to 1 minute. Using a slotted utensil, transfer the *sopes* to the wire rack to drain well, then place the rack and baking sheet in the oven to keep warm. Fry the remaining *sopes* in the same manner, allowing the oil to return to 375° F between batches.

JUST before serving, drain the salsa and the reheated beans. Spoon about 2 tablespoons of the beans into each hot shell. Sprinkle each with about 1 tablespoon of the cheese, and top with about 1 tablespoon of the salsa. Place on a serving dish or arrange on individual plates and garnish with cilantro sprigs.

Makes 6 servings.

SUSHI POCKETS
~ *INARI-ZUSHI* OR *AGE-ZUSHI* ~

SOYBEAN CAKE POCKETS

12 large rectangular or 24 small
    square packaged fried soybean
    cakes *(aburage)*; see recipe
    introduction)
1½ cups Vegetable Stock (page 580),
    White Stock (page 578) made with
    chicken, or canned vegetable or
    reduced-sodium chicken broth
    (optional)
1 tablespoon soy sauce
3 tablespoons sugar
½ teaspoon salt (optional)

SUSHI RICE

3 cups medium-grain white rice
¾ cup unseasoned rice vinegar
¾ cup sugar
1 tablespoon salt

Auntie Naila Gallagher, who shared her Hawaiian version of this traditional Japanese sushi, calls this tasty snack "cone sushi," since the soybean pockets serve as cones for the sweet-and-sour rice filling.

Airy fried soybean cakes (aburage), sometimes sold as tofu puffs, can be purchased from Japanese markets. Shop carefully, however, as they are not the same as pieces of dense, heavy fried soybean curd.

Rice for sushi is cooked in less water than normally used for cooking the grain to allow for absorption of the vinegar mixture. If desired, add about 1 cup finely chopped cooked chicken or shrimp to the rice along with the vegetables.

TO prepare the Soybean Cake Pockets, cut each large rectangular cake in half crosswise, or make a slit along one side of each small square cake. Gently pull open the center of each to form a little bag. Transfer to a saucepan, add water to cover, place over medium-high heat, and bring to a boil. Reduce the heat to maintain a simmer and cook for about 15 minutes. Drain. (This procedure removes the excess oily taste from the fried cakes.)

IN a saucepan, combine the stock or broth (if using) or 1½ cups water with the soy sauce, sugar, and salt (if using unsalted stock or water). Bring to a boil over medium-high heat. Add the soybean cake pockets, adjust the heat to achieve a simmer and cook, uncovered, carefully turning the pockets occasionally, until they are soft and the liquid is absorbed, about 1 hour. Remove from the heat and let stand until cool. (At this point, the pockets can be covered and refrigerated for up to 24 hours.)

TO make the Sushi Rice, wash the rice as directed on page 365, then cover with cold water and soak for about 1 hour. Drain and cook the rice in 3 cups cold water as directed on page 365.

JUST before the rice is ready, in a small saucepan, combine the vinegar, sugar, and salt. Place over medium-high heat and cook, stirring constantly, just until the sugar is dissolved, about 2 minutes; do not boil. Let cool briefly.

FLUFF the warm rice with a fork and transfer it to a large mixing bowl. Pouring in a little at a time, add the vinegar mixture to the rice, turning the rice carefully with a rice paddle or spatula to avoid crushing the kernels and to distribute the vinegar mixture evenly. After the vinegar mixture is incorporated, turn the rice continuously with the paddle or spatula while fanning it with a handheld fan or a hair dryer set on cool until the rice is cool, about 5 minutes. Cover with a damp cloth towel and set aside at room temperature to absorb the vinegar mixture, at least 30 minutes or for up to several hours; do not refrigerate.

TO make the Seasoned Vegetables, in a saucepan, combine the sugar, salt, and ¾ cup water and bring to a boil over medium-high heat, stirring to dissolve the sugar and salt. Separately add and cook the carrot, green beans, and mushrooms, cooking each vegetable until tender but not mushy, about 5 minutes for the carrot and beans and about 2 minutes for the mushrooms. As soon as each vegetable is done, remove it with a wire skimmer, or drain it through a strainer, catching the liquid in a bowl and returning it to the saucepan to reheat for the next vegetable. Squeeze the mushrooms to remove excess liquid that can stain the rice. Gently combine the vegetables with the cooled rice.

USING your hands, squeeze each piece of soybean cake to release excess liquid; work carefully to prevent tearing the pockets. Dampen your hands with water and stuff about ⅓ cup of the rice mixture into each pocket.

TO serve, arrange the sushi on a tray, open side up, and garnish with pickled ginger or offer it alongside.

Makes 8 servings.

SEASONED VEGETABLES

3 tablespoons sugar

1½ teaspoons salt

¾ cup finely chopped or diced carrot

¾ cup thinly sliced green beans (cut crosswise)

1½ cups finely chopped fresh shiitake mushroom caps; or ¾ ounce Chinese dried black mushrooms, rinsed thoroughly and soaked in warm water until soft, then stemmed and finely chopped

Pickled ginger slices

FRITTATA WITH SUMMER SQUASH

6 eggs

2 tablespoons light cream or half-and-half

¼ cup freshly grated Parmesan cheese (about 1 ounce), preferably Parmigiano-Reggiano

1 teaspoon salt, or to taste

½ teaspoon freshly ground black pepper, or to taste

1 tablespoon olive oil, preferably extra-virgin

1 tablespoon unsalted butter

½ cup minced onion

1 teaspoon minced garlic

1½ cups sliced, shredded, or chopped summer squash, steamed or sauteed in olive oil until tender

¾ cup chopped summer squash blossoms (optional)

Mixed minced fresh herbs such as basil, chervil, chives, mint, oregano, and flat-leaf parsley

Summer squash blossoms for garnish (optional)

Almost any ingredient can be substituted for the squash in this Italian-style omelet. See the variations for a few suggestions. If adding squash blossoms to the mixture, please read the introduction to Fried Stuffed Squash Blossoms (page 51).

When I make a frittata for a large group, I prepare the baked variation, then cut it into bite-sized pieces and arrange them on a serving tray.

IN a bowl, lightly beat the eggs. Add the cream or half-and-half, cheese, salt, and pepper. Beat until well blended. Set aside.

IN a 10-inch skillet, preferably nonstick, heat the olive oil and butter over medium heat. Add the onion and cook, stirring frequently, until soft but not browned, about 5 minutes. Add the garlic and cook for 1 minute longer.

DISTRIBUTE the squash and the chopped squash blossoms (if using) evenly in the skillet, then pour the egg mixture over the squash. Reduce the heat to low and cook undisturbed until the frittata is set around the edges. Using a spatula, gently lift the edges of the frittata and tilt the skillet to let any uncooked egg run down under the bottom. Continue cooking until the frittata has almost set on top.

INVERT a plate over the top of the skillet, invert the plate and skillet together, and lift off the skillet. Slide the frittata, cooked side up, back into the skillet. Cook until the bottom is set, 1 to 2 minutes. Alternatively, do not turn the frittata. Instead, place the skillet under a preheated broiler until the top of the frittata is set and tinged with brown, about 30 seconds; be sure that you are using a flameproof skillet and be careful not to burn or overcook the frittata.

AGAIN, invert a flat serving plate over the skillet, invert them together, and lift off the skillet. Or, if you have finished the frittata in a broiler, loosen the edges with a spatula and slide the frittata onto the plate.

TO serve, sprinkle with the herb mixture, garnish with the squash blossoms (if using), and cut into wedges.

Makes 4 servings.

VARIATIONS

SUBSTITUTE any favorite vegetable or combination of vegetables for the squash.

COOK about 6 ounces American-style smoked bacon or Italian bacon (*pancetta*) until crisp. Crumble the bacon and sprinkle it over the cooked vegetables before pouring on the egg mixture.

RINSE and pat dry 6 flat anchovy fillets, mince, and add to the egg mixture.

OMIT the vegetables. Distribute a layer of leftover cooked spaghetti or other pasta over the onion and garlic.

OMIT the vegetables. Add 4 more eggs and ¼ cup minced fresh herb(s) of choice to the egg mixture.

FOR a lower-cholesterol frittata, use 9 egg whites instead of 6 whole eggs.

FOR a baked frittata, triple the recipe or any of the variations, pour the mixture into a greased 13-by-9-inch pan and bake in a 350° F oven until puffed and firm to the touch, about 30 minutes. If the top begins to brown too quickly during baking, cover loosely with aluminum foil.

SICILIAN EGGPLANT RELISH
~ *CAPONATA* ~

6 tablespoons olive oil, preferably
    extra-virgin

2 pounds eggplants, peeled, if
    desired, and cut into 1-inch cubes

2 cups chopped yellow onion

1 cup chopped fennel or celery

1 cup chopped red sweet pepper

1 teaspoon minced garlic

2½ cups peeled, seeded, drained,
    and chopped ripe or canned tomato

¼ cup red wine vinegar, or more if
    needed

2 tablespoons sugar, or more if
    needed

½ teaspoon salt, or to taste

¼ teaspoon freshly ground black
    pepper, or to taste

¼ cup drained small capers

¼ cup pitted and quartered green
    olives, preferably Sicilian

¼ cup pine nuts

½ cup chopped fresh basil

This sweet-and-sour concoction may be made in quantity when the garden is at its peak and then preserved in jars for year-round enjoyment as directed for Bread-and-Butter Pickles on page 404. When offering as an appetizer, serve alone, arrange on greens, spread atop grilled or toasted bread, or add to an antipasto platter. It is also a tasty accompaniment to grilled fish, poultry, or meats, and makes an unusual sauce for hot or cold pasta.

IN a saute pan or skillet, heat 4 tablespoons of the oil over medium-high heat. Add the eggplant and cook, stirring frequently, until soft and browned, about 10 minutes. Remove to a bowl and set aside.

ADD the remaining 2 tablespoons oil to the same pan and place over medium-high heat. Add the onion, fennel or celery, and sweet pepper and cook, stirring frequently, until soft, about 5 minutes. Stir in the garlic and cook for about 1 minute longer. Add the browned eggplant, tomato, vinegar, sugar, salt, and pepper. Bring the mixture to a boil, then reduce the heat to achieve a simmer and simmer uncovered, stirring frequently, for about 10 minutes.

STIR in the capers and olives and continue to simmer until the eggplant is tender, about 15 minutes longer. Taste and adjust the vinegar, sugar, and salt to achieve a good balance of sour, sweet, and salty. Stir in the nuts and basil and simmer until heated through, about 5 minutes longer. Remove from the heat and let cool to room temperature before serving, or cool, cover, and refrigerate for up to 2 weeks.

Makes 6 servings.

FRIED STUFFED SQUASH BLOSSOMS

Serve this gardening-season treat as an appetizer or as an accompaniment to grilled or roasted meats or fish.

Look for blossoms at farmers' markets or specialty produce stores. When harvesting from the garden, it is generally better to pick large male blossoms, those without a swollen base at the stem end. Be sure to leave a few males intact to insure continued pollination. Or carefully cut female flowers from the tiny developing squashes.

16 large squash blossoms

¼ cup ricotta cheese (about 2 ounces)

½ teaspoon minced garlic

1 tablespoon pine nuts

2 tablespoons minced fresh basil

Salt

Freshly ground black pepper

⅔ cup sifted all-purpose flour

Canola or other high-quality vegetable oil for frying

Freshly grated Parmesan cheese, preferably Parmigiano-Reggiano

QUICKLY rinse the squash blossoms under cold running water and gently pat dry with paper toweling. Cut off and discard the stems. Set aside.

IN a bowl, combine the ricotta cheese, garlic, pine nuts, basil, and salt and pepper to taste and mix well. Open up the blossoms and spoon about 1½ teaspoons of the mixture into the center of each; avoid overfilling. Twist the top of each blossom together to close. Place on a baking sheet and refrigerate for about 15 minutes.

IN a shallow bowl, combine the flour and 1 cup cold water and beat with a wire whisk until smooth and creamy. Let stand for about 15 minutes.

IN a deep skillet or saucepan, pour in oil to a depth of ¾ inch and heat to 350° F. Preheat an oven to 200° F. Place a wire rack on a baking sheet and position alongside the stove top.

BRIEFLY dip a stuffed blossom into the batter, then carefully slip it into the hot oil. Dip and add a few more blossoms to the oil; avoid crowding the pan. Fry until golden brown on one side, then turn and continue to fry until golden brown on all sides, about 3 minutes total. Using a slotted utensil, transfer the blossoms to the rack to drain well, then place the rack and baking sheet in the oven to keep warm. Fry the remaining blossoms in the same manner, allowing the oil to return to 350° F between batches.

SPRINKLE with salt and cheese to taste, arrange on a serving plate, and serve hot.

Makes 4 to 6 servings.

EASTERN MEDITERRANEAN STUFFED GRAPE LEAVES ~ *DOLMADES* ~

1 cup long-grain white rice

½ cup olive oil, preferably extra-virgin

1 cup finely chopped yellow or white onion

¼ cup finely chopped green onion, including green tops

¼ cup minced fresh flat-leaf parsley (reserve stalks)

2 tablespoons minced fresh mint

2 tablespoons minced fresh dill

½ cup pine nuts

½ teaspoon salt, or to taste

¼ teaspoon freshly ground black pepper, or to taste

1 jar (8 ounces) grape leaves packed in brine

¾ cup freshly squeezed lemon juice

About 1 quart Vegetable Stock (page 580), White Stock (page 578) made with chicken, or canned vegetable or reduced-sodium chicken broth (optional)

Freshly squeezed lemon juice for serving

Grated or minced fresh lemon zest for garnish

The Turkish word dolma *means "something stuffed." Versions of this well-known appetizer are served in Turkey, Greece, and other countries in the region.*

If you have access to fresh young grape leaves, blanch them in boiling water to soften and use as directed for the readily available jarred ones. Tender fresh fig leaves or less-exotic cabbage leaves may be substituted for grape leaves.

Although the dolmades are delicious on their own, you may offer a traditional sauce of plain yogurt with minced garlic and salt to taste.

WASH and drain the rice as directed on page 364.

IN a saute pan or skillet, heat ¼ cup of the oil over medium-high heat. Add the yellow or white onion and cook, stirring frequently, until soft but not browned, about 5 minutes. Add the drained rice and ¼ cup water and cook, stirring frequently, just until the rice has absorbed the liquid. Stir in the green onion, minced herbs, pine nuts, and salt and pepper. Cover and set aside for about 10 minutes.

RINSE the grape leaves under cold running water to remove as much brine as possible, pat dry with paper toweling, and stack on a plate. Place 1 leaf at a time, shiny side down, on a flat work surface. Cut off and discard the tough stem end. Spoon about 1 tablespoon of the rice mixture in the center near the base of the leaf. Fold the stem end over to cover the filling, then fold both sides inward and tightly roll the leaf toward the pointed tip end to form a compact packet. Repeat with the remaining leaves and filling.

LINE the bottom of a large pot with a layer of grape leaves and/or parsley stalks to prevent the dolmades from sticking. Arrange the stuffed leaves, seam side down, on top of the parsley, making as many layers as necessary. Drizzle the remaining ¼ cup oil and the ¾ cup lemon juice over the dolmades. Pour in just enough stock or broth (if using) or water to barely cover the dolmades. Top with a heat-resistant plate and nontoxic weight (such as a bowl filled with pie weights or an aluminum foil-wrapped brick) to keep the dolmades submerged during cooking. Cover the pot, place over medium heat, and bring to a gentle boil, then reduce the heat to achieve a simmer and cook until the grape leaves and rice are tender, 45 minutes to 1 hour. During cooking, add a little more liquid if needed to keep the dolmades moist. Remove from the heat and let cool in the pot.

TO serve, arrange on a serving platter, sprinkle with lemon juice to taste, and garnish with lemon zest.

Makes about 36 dolmades for 6 to 8 servings.

MARINATED ROASTED SWEET PEPPERS

6 orange, red, or yellow sweet
   peppers, or a combination

½ cup extra-virgin olive oil

2 tablespoons freshly squeezed
   lemon juice

1 tablespoon balsamic or red wine
   vinegar

Salt

Freshly ground black pepper

A common element of an antipasto platter, these also make an excellent accompaniment to such second courses as grilled or roasted poultry, fish, or meat. And they're great on sandwiches of salami, grilled eggplant, or Italian cheese.

Minced garlic and chopped fresh basil, oregano, or rosemary may be added along with the marinade.

ROAST the peppers as directed on page 552. If roasted whole, cut the peppers in half lengthwise and remove and discard the stems, seeds, and membranes. Cut lengthwise into narrow strips and set aside.

IN a nonreactive bowl, combine the oil, lemon juice, vinegar, and salt and pepper to taste and mix well. Add the pepper strips and stir to coat evenly with the marinade. Cover and let stand, stirring occasionally, for about 30 minutes, or refrigerate for up to 1 week; return to room temperature before serving.

Makes 6 to 8 servings.

FONTINA AND ROASTED PEPPERS

During my stint as a gourmet grocer, I made huge platters of this savory combination several times a week to satisfy the cravings of addicted customers.

ROAST the peppers as directed on page 552. If roasted whole, cut the peppers in half lengthwise and remove and discard the stems, seeds, and membranes. Cut lengthwise into ½-inch-wide strips and set aside.

IN a nonreactive bowl, combine the oil, vinegar or lemon juice, garlic, basil or oregano, and salt to taste and mix well. Add the pepper strips and stir to coat evenly with the marinade. Cover and let stand, stirring occasionally, for at least 1 hour, or refrigerate for up to 1 week.

CUT the cheese into ½-inch wide strips that are as long as the pepper strips. Remove the pepper strips from the marinade, reserving the marinade. Arrange the pepper strips on individual plates or a serving platter, alternating them with the cheese strips. Drizzle with a bit of the marinade and let stand for about 30 minutes.

TO serve, sprinkle with the capers, then garnish with the herb sprigs (if using).

Makes 6 to 8 servings.

4 red sweet peppers

½ cup extra-virgin olive oil

¼ cup red wine vinegar or freshly squeezed lemon juice

2 to 3 teaspoons minced garlic

1 tablespoon minced fresh basil or oregano, or 1 teaspoon crumbled dried oregano

Salt

8 ounces Italian Fontina cheese, sliced ⅛ inch thick

1 tablespoon drained small capers

Fresh basil or oregano sprigs for garnish (optional)

BAKED NUT-CRUSTED CAMEMBERT

½ cup pecans or other nuts

1 whole round or oval Camembert
    cheese (about 8 ounces)

1 egg

Apple or pear slices

Sliced and lightly toasted rich bread
    such as brioche, panettone, or
    raisin pumpernickel

Any creamy cheese with a thin rind can be served this way.

PREHEAT an oven to 350° F.

TOAST the nuts as directed on page 554. Chop coarsely and place
    in a shallow bowl.

CUT off and discard the top rind of the Camembert. In a shallow
    bowl, beat the egg, add the cheese, and turn to coat on all
    sides with the egg. Transfer the cheese to the bowl with the
    nuts. Turning the cheese, press the nuts onto all sides to cover
    completely. Transfer the cheese to a baking sheet, cut side up,
    cover, and refrigerate for about 1 hour.

PREHEAT an oven to 400° F.

BAKE the cheese until the interior is warm and runny, about
    15 minutes.

TO serve, transfer the warm cheese to a serving plate and
    surround with fruit and bread slices.

Makes 8 servings.

GRILLED CHEESE-STUFFED CHILES

Warm chiles filled with a smooth mixture of three cheeses can open a meal or be served as a side dish with grilled meats or fish. If you prefer a smoother sauce, puree the Guacamole in a blender or food processor.

ROAST the chiles whole as directed on page 552. Leaving the stems intact, carefully slit each chile down one side. Using your fingertips, remove the seeds, being careful not to tear the skins.

IN a bowl, combine the 3 cheeses and mix together with a fork. Carefully stuff each chile with an equal portion of the cheese mixture. Refrigerate to chill the cheese slightly.

PREPARE a grill for moderate direct-heat cooking or preheat a broiler.

PREPARE the Guacamole as directed and set aside.

USING a pastry brush, lightly coat the chiles all over with olive oil. Grill or broil, turning once, until the cheese melts, 6 to 8 minutes.

TO serve, spoon the guacamole onto warmed plates, top with chiles, and garnish with red pepper strips and/or cilantro sprigs. Serve with tortilla chips.

Makes 6 servings.

6 fresh mild to medium-hot chiles such as Anaheim, New Mexico, or *poblano*

¼ cup crumbled fresh goat cheese (about 1 ounce)

¾ cup freshly shredded Jarlsberg cheese (about 2¼ ounces)

½ cup freshly shredded fresh mozzarella cheese (about 3 ounces)

Guacamole (page 395)

Olive oil for brushing

Red sweet pepper strips and/or fresh cilantro (coriander) sprigs for garnish

Corn tortilla chips for serving

STUFFED EGGPLANT, TURKISH STYLE ~ *Imam Bayildi* ~

2 large globe eggplants (about
    1 pound each)

Coarse salt

About ¾ cup olive oil, preferably
    extra-virgin

3 cups finely chopped yellow or white
    onion

3 cups peeled, seeded, drained, and
    chopped ripe or canned tomato

1 tablespoon minced garlic

3 tablespoons minced fresh flat-leaf
    parsley

3 tablespoons freshly squeezed
    lemon juice

½ teaspoon sugar

Freshly ground black pepper

Fresh flat-leaf parsley sprigs for
    garnish

This has been one of my favorite eggplant preparations since first sampling it in New York years ago at a tiny hole-in-the-wall West Side restaurant where Hussan, the owner-chef-waiter, prepared it as I've written. Since then I've found numerous recipes that call for whole or halved eggplants, but I still prefer thick slices for a more elegant presentation.

The Turkish name for this dish roughly translates to "the priest fainted." Legend has it that he swooned from ecstasy upon tasting the dish, although other theories maintain that his sinking spell occurred when he learned how much precious olive oil had been used in the preparation. I've given the traditional cooking method, but if you wish to reduce the amount of oil, omit adding the oil to the pan for softening the eggplant; instead, using a pastry brush, coat the slices lightly with olive oil, place on baking sheets, and bake in a 350° F oven until soft.

DISCARD the stems and blossom ends from the eggplants, then cut away and discard a thin slice of peeling from opposite sides of the eggplant. Cut each unpeeled vegetable lengthwise into 4 or 5 slices about ¾ inch thick. Sprinkle both sides of the slices with salt. Lay the slices on paper toweling, cover with more paper toweling, top with a cutting board and heavy weights (such as aluminum foil-wrapped bricks or canned foods), and let stand for about 30 minutes to draw out excess moisture.

IN a large saute pan or skillet, heat ¼ cup of the oil over medium-high heat. Add the onion and cook, stirring frequently, until soft but not browned, about 5 minutes. Add the tomato, garlic, minced parsley, lemon juice, sugar, and salt and pepper to taste and cook for about 3 minutes longer. Set aside.

PREHEAT an oven to 350° F.

USING paper toweling, blot excess salt from the eggplant slices. To create a pocket in each slice for stuffing, make a deep incision into the pulp at the blossom end, leaving about 1 inch uncut all around the remaining sides.

IN a large saute pan or skillet, heat ¼ cup of the remaining oil over medium-high heat. Add the eggplant slices, about 3 at a time, and cook, turning once or twice, until the flesh begins to soften, about 2 minutes per side. As they are done, remove the eggplant slices to a platter. Soften the remaining eggplant slices in the same manner, adding oil as necessary.

STUFF as much of the onion mixture as possible into each eggplant slit; the tender flesh may tear, but just re-form the slice as well as possible. Place the slices in two 13-by-9-inch pans and spoon any remaining onion mixture over the top. Pour ¼ cup water around the eggplant in each pan, cover the pans tightly with aluminum foil, and bake until the eggplant is very tender when pierced with a small, sharp knife and most of the liquid has been absorbed, about 45 minutes.

TRANSFER the pans to a work surface to cool completely, then cover and refrigerate for at least 2 hours or for up to 2 days; return to room temperature before serving.

TO serve, using a wide spatula, transfer the eggplant slices to serving plates and garnish with the parsley sprigs.

Makes 8 to 10 servings.

GOAT CHEESE, EGGPLANT, AND RED PEPPER TART

3 red sweet peppers

4 to 6 slender Asian eggplants, or
2 small globe eggplants

Extra-virgin olive oil for brushing

1 tablespoon minced garlic

Salt

Freshly ground black pepper

8 ounces puff pastry, thawed in the
refrigerator if frozen

Unsalted butter, melted and cooled
slightly, for brushing

4 cups finely crumbled fresh goat
cheese (about 1 pound)

½ cup shredded fresh basil or
minced fresh flat-leaf parsley

Make your own puff pastry from a reliable recipe, purchase the pastry from a French-style bakery, or check the supermarket freezer for a high-quality product.

ROAST the peppers as directed on page 552. If roasted whole, cut the peppers in half lengthwise and remove and discard the stems, seeds, and membranes. Cut lengthwise into narrow strips and set aside.

PREHEAT an oven to 375° F.

CUT unpeeled eggplants crosswise into ½-inch-thick slices. Using a pastry brush, coat both sides of the eggplant slices lightly with oil and arrange in single layers on baking sheets. Sprinkle with the garlic and salt and pepper to taste. Bake until the eggplant is lightly browned and tender but still intact, about 20 minutes.

INCREASE the oven temperature to 400° F. Lightly brush a clean baking sheet with oil.

ON a lightly floured surface, roll out the puff pastry into a 12-by-16-inch rectangle about ⅛ inch thick. Fold the pastry loosely in half and transfer to the prepared baking sheet, then unfold. Alternatively, cut the rectangle into eight 4-by-6-inch pieces to form individual tarts and transfer each to the baking sheet.

LEAVING a 1-inch border uncovered around the entire perimeter of the pastry, brush the pastry with melted butter and sprinkle evenly with the cheese. Top with the baked eggplant slices and then the roasted pepper strips. (If making individual tarts, distribute cheese, eggplant, and pepper strips equally among the 8 pastry pieces.) Brush uncovered pastry edges with water, fold edges in half to form a rim, and press together to make an attractive ridge around the pastry.

BAKE until the pastry is puffed and golden, 10 to 15 minutes.

TO serve, sprinkle with the basil or parsley, cut the large tart into small squares or rectangles, and transfer to serving plates.

Makes 8 servings.

SEVICHE ~ or Ceviche ~

Lean white fish such as sole, snapper, or flounder are customarily used in this refreshing dish eaten throughout the Caribbean and Latin America. Almost any saltwater fish can be used. If you choose salmon or another anadromous fish, first freeze the fish for 48 hours to kill any potentially harmful parasites that it may have picked up when it entered freshwater. Farm-raised baby salmon may be used without freezing. A mixture of several types of fish with flesh of varying colors makes a striking dish.

QUICKLY rinse the fish under cold running water and pat dry with paper toweling. Cut into bite-sized cubes or strips.

IN a nonreactive container, combine the fish and lime juice and toss well. Cover tightly and refrigerate for at least 5 hours but for no more than 24 hours, stirring several times. (If the fish cannot be served within a short time after 24 hours, drain off the liquid and toss the fish with a little olive oil to prevent it from drying out.)

SHORTLY before serving, add the oil, onion, garlic, ginger, cilantro, and tomato. Season to taste with salt and hot sauce and stir well.

Makes 8 servings.

VARIATION

FOR Polynesian-style cured fish, served throughout the South Pacific, stir about 1 cup Fresh Coconut Milk (page 562) or high-quality commercial coconut milk into the fish along with the oil and other ingredients.

1½ pounds fish fillet (see recipe introduction), skinned

1 cup freshly squeezed lime juice

3 tablespoons light olive oil or high-quality vegetable oil

⅓ cup finely chopped green onion, including green tops

½ teaspoon minced garlic

½ teaspoon minced fresh ginger

⅓ cup finely chopped fresh cilantro (coriander)

½ cup peeled, seeded, drained, and finely chopped ripe tomato

Salt

Hot sauce

SWEDISH CURED SALMON
~ *GRAVLAX* ~

2 pieces center-cut very fresh salmon
    fillets (1½ to 2 pounds each), skin
    intact

12 fresh dill sprigs

⅓ cup coarse salt

⅓ cup sugar

2 tablespoons black or white
    peppercorns, cracked

¼ cup aquavit, vodka, or Cognac

Compound Butter, made with fresh
    dill (page 402), and/or Dilled
    Mustard Sauce (page 387)

Fresh dill sprigs for garnish

Lemon or cucumber slices for garnish

Thin brown bread slices, toasted

Drained small capers

When making gravlax, the Swedes traditionally lay pine or spruce twigs in the bottom of the container before adding the fish. Although picturesque, this touch of nature is not necessary to create this Scandinavian treat, also known as gravad lax.

For a fanciful presentation, cut thinly sliced brown bread into rounds and toast until crisp, then spread with the butter or add a dollop of sauce. Roll each gravlax slice into a rosette shape, place on the bread, and garnish the center of each with a caper.

QUICKLY rinse the salmon under cold running water and pat dry with paper toweling. Set aside.

PLACE 4 of the dill sprigs in a flat glass or ceramic dish large enough to hold the salmon fillets in a single layer.

IN a bowl, combine the salt, sugar, peppercorns, and aquavit, vodka, or Cognac. Rub the fleshy side of 1 salmon fillet with half of the salt mixture and place it, skin side down, on top of the dill in the dish. Top with 4 of the remaining dill sprigs. Rub the other fillet with the remaining salt mixture and place it, skin side up, on top of the first piece of salmon, placing thick width to thin width to create a uniform thickness. Arrange the remaining 4 dill sprigs over the fish. Cover the dish loosely with plastic wrap and evenly place about 5 pounds of weights (such as aluminum foil-wrapped bricks or canned foods) on top to press the fish down. Refrigerate for 2 to 3 days. During refrigeration, remove the weights and plastic cover every 12 hours, separate the fillets, and baste the cut sides with the juices that have accumulated in the dish. Place the fillets together again, turn them over, cover, and reposition the weights.

PREPARE the Compound Butter and/or Dilled Mustard Sauce as directed and set aside.

TO serve the gravlax, discard the dill and use a brush or paper toweling to remove the salt mixture. Place the fillets skin side down on a cutting board and slice the fillets on the diagonal into thin strips, freeing them from the skin. Arrange on a platter and garnish with fresh dill sprigs and lemon or cucumber slices. Offer toasted bread, capers, and the Compound Butter and/or Dilled Mustard Sauce alongside.

Makes about 20 servings.

SMOKED SALMON SPREAD

8 ounces cream cheese, at room
  temperature
3 tablespoons heavy (whipping)
  cream
5 ounces smoked salmon, minced
1 tablespoon minced fresh chives or
  green onion, including green tops
Freshly squeezed lemon juice
Ground cayenne
Freshly ground black pepper

Delicious on bagels, brioche, croissants, or French or pumpernickel bread, as well as a dip for vegetables, this spread is a great way to use the more economical trimmings from smoked salmon.

IN a bowl, combine the cream cheese and cream and beat with a hand mixer until light and fluffy. Stir in the smoked salmon, chives or green onion, and lemon juice, cayenne, and black pepper to taste.

Makes 8 servings.

SALMON CAKES WITH ROASTED RED PEPPER CREAM

SALMON CAKES

3 cups fine fresh bread crumbs, from about 10 ounces good-textured white bread, preferably French

⅓ cup coarsely chopped fresh flat-leaf parsley

¼ cup chopped green onion, including green tops, or shallot

2 eggs

2 tablespoons unsalted butter, melted and cooled slightly

2 tablespoons Mayonnaise (page 388) or high-quality commercial mayonnaise

1 tablespoon Dijon mustard

2 teaspoons freshly squeezed lemon juice

2½ cups flaked cooked fresh salmon

Salt

Freshly ground black pepper

When I was growing up, my only experience with salmon was panfried croquettes made with canned fish, all that was available at that time in rural Louisiana. These little cakes are a fresh update on those memories.

To pass at a party, form the mixture into bite-sized patties, cook as directed, and pass on a tray with toothpicks and the sauce for dipping. Tomato Sauce (page 573) or Rémoulade (page 390) make good alternatives to the luxurious cream sauce.

TO begin the Salmon Cakes, in a food processor, combine 1½ cups of the bread crumbs, the chopped parsley, green onion or shallot, eggs, melted butter, mayonnaise, mustard, and lemon juice. Pulse on and off several times until well mixed. Add the salmon and process briefly to combine; do not overmix. Season to taste with salt and pepper. Transfer to a bowl, cover, and refrigerate for at least 30 minutes or for up to overnight.

TO make the Roasted Red Pepper Cream, roast the peppers as directed on page 552. If roasted whole, cut the peppers in half and remove and discard the stems, seeds, and membranes. Coarsely chop the peppers and transfer to a saucepan. Add the light cream or half-and-half, place over medium heat, and cook, stirring frequently, until the cream is reduced by half, about 8 minutes. Transfer to a food processor or blender and puree until smooth. Return the mixture to the pan, season to taste with salt and chile, and set aside.

USING about ¼ cup of the chilled salmon mixture for each cake, shape the mixture into 12 round or oval patties about ½ inch thick and 3 inches in diameter. Evenly coat the salmon patties on all sides with the remaining 1½ cups bread crumbs, using 2 tablespoons per patty and patting lightly to adhere the crumbs. Let stand for 5 minutes.

PREHEAT an oven to 200° F. Place a wire rack on a baking sheet and position alongside the stove top.

IN a saute pan or skillet, pour in oil to a depth of ¼ inch and heat over medium-high heat. Fry the patties, a few at a time, turning once, until golden and crisp on each side, 1 to 2 minutes per side. Using a slotted spatula, transfer the cakes to the rack to drain well, then place the rack and baking sheet in the oven to keep warm. Fry the remaining patties in the same manner, adding more oil as needed.

TO serve, reheat the Roasted Red Pepper Cream over low heat, then spoon it onto 6 warmed individual plates. Arrange 2 cakes on top of each portion, sprinkle with minced parsley, and serve immediately.

Makes 6 servings.

ROASTED RED PEPPER CREAM

3 red sweet peppers
1½ cups light cream or
   half-and-half
Salt
Ground cayenne or other dried
   hot chile

Canola or other high-quality
   vegetable oil for frying
Minced fresh flat-leaf parsley for
   garnish

GRILLED HERB-MARINATED
SHRIMP

HERB MARINADE

1 cup fruity olive oil, preferably
   extra-virgin

2 tablespoons freshly squeezed lemon
   juice or white wine vinegar

¼ cup mixed minced fresh herbs
   such as oregano, flat-leaf parsley,
   rosemary, and thyme

2 teaspoons minced garlic

Salt

Freshly ground black pepper

Ground cayenne or other dried
   hot chile

2 pounds large shrimp in shells

Vegetable oil for brushing grill rack
   or basket

My brother-in-law, John Richardson, sets out mounds of these delectables as an appetizer. The communal shelling is a guaranteed icebreaker, although the shrimp may also be served on individual plates. For a fancier presentation or for fastidious guests, peel the shrimp before serving them.

TO make the marinade, in a nonreactive bowl, combine all of the marinade ingredients, including salt, pepper, and chile to taste, and mix well.

ADD the shrimp to the marinade and stir to coat evenly. Cover and let stand, stirring occasionally, for about 30 minutes, or refrigerate for up to 3 hours.

PREPARE an open grill for hot direct-heat cooking.

REMOVE the shrimp from the marinade, reserving the marinade, and set aside.

IN a saucepan, bring the marinade to a boil over medium-high heat, then set alongside the grill.

WHEN the fire is ready, lightly brush the grill rack or a grill basket with oil. Place the shrimp on the rack or in the basket and grill, turning several times and brushing with the marinade, until the shells turn bright pink and the meat is just opaque, 4 to 5 minutes in all.

TO serve, transfer to a serving bowl or platter.

Makes 8 servings.

CAJUN CHICKEN BITES WITH APRICOT MUSTARD

A fruity mustard dipping sauce provides a good foil for the hot spices in this easy appetizer. Offer toothpicks or tiny appetizer forks for dipping the chicken pieces.

TO make the Cajun Spice Mix, in a small bowl or plastic bag, combine all of the spice mix ingredients and stir or shake to mix well. Set aside.

TO make the Apricot Mustard, in a small saucepan, combine the preserves and mustard. Place over low heat and stir until the preserves melt and are thoroughly blended with the mustard. Set aside to cool.

QUICKLY rinse the chicken under cold running water and pat dry with paper toweling. Cut into bite-sized pieces, toss in the reserved spice mix to coat well, and let stand for about 20 minutes.

PREHEAT an oven to 200° F. Place a wire rack on a baking sheet and position alongside the stove top.

IN a large saute pan or skillet, combine 2 tablespoons butter and 2 tablespoons oil and heat over medium-high heat. Add as many chicken pieces as will fit without crowding the pan and cook, turning frequently, just until the chicken turns opaque throughout, about 5 minutes; to check for doneness, cut into a piece with a small, sharp knife. Using a slotted utensil, transfer the chicken pieces to the rack to drain well, then place the rack and baking sheet in the oven to keep warm. Cook the remaining chicken in the same manner, adding more butter and oil as needed.

SERVE warm with the Apricot Mustard for dipping.

Makes 8 to 10 servings.

CAJUN SPICE MIX

1 tablespoon garlic powder

2 teaspoons crumbled dried thyme

2 teaspoons ground cayenne or other dried hot chile

2 teaspoons freshly ground black pepper

1 teaspoon freshly ground white pepper

1 teaspoon salt

APRICOT MUSTARD

1½ cups apricot preserves

6 tablespoons Creole or Dijon mustard

5 boned and skinned chicken breast halves

Unsalted butter for frying

Canola or other high-quality vegetable oil for frying

OVEN-BARBECUED CITRUS-FLAVORED CHICKEN DRUMMETTES

2 cups tomato-based barbecue sauce (a favorite recipe or high-quality commercial product)

1 cup firmly packed brown sugar

¾ cup freshly squeezed orange juice

¼ cup freshly squeezed lemon juice

36 to 40 chicken drummettes (about 3 pounds trimmed wings)

3 small oranges, sliced, then slices cut in half

2 or 3 lemons, sliced, then slices cut in half

About 3 tablespoons minced fresh chives or cilantro (coriander)

Always a big hit at parties, this dish reminds me of my late friend Stephen Marcus, who originated the concept.

The drummette is the large joint of the wing that resembles a miniature drumstick. Supermarkets often sell them by the package. Alternatively, buy whole wings, disjoint them, and reserve the tip and middle joints for the stockpot.

IN a saucepan, combine the barbecue sauce, sugar, and fruit juices. Place over medium heat and cook, stirring occasionally, until the sugar melts and the flavors are well blended, about 10 minutes.

PREHEAT an oven to 325° F.

IN a shallow baking dish or pan, arrange the drummettes in rows in a single layer. Alternate the orange and lemon slices between the wings. Pour the barbecue sauce mixture over the top, cover with aluminum foil, and bake for 1 hour.

REMOVE the foil and continue baking until the wings are very tender when pierced with a fork and the sauce is thick, about 45 minutes longer.

TO serve, arrange on a large platter and sprinkle with the minced herb.

Makes 10 to 12 servings.

FRIED CHICKEN WINGS, THAI STYLE ~ *GAI TOTE* ~

Thai cooks are famous for their fried stuffed chicken wings, known to American patrons of Thai restaurants as angel wings. They are wonderful to eat, yet highly labor intensive to make, since the wings must be boned before stuffing. Here is a simplified unstuffed version.

If you wish, substitute 16 chicken wing drummettes (large wing joints) for the whole wings.

Thai Sweet Chile-Garlic Sauce
  (page 400)

8 chicken wings

Salt

Canola or other high-quality
  vegetable oil for frying

Rice flour (not sweet rice flour) for
  dusting

Finely chopped green onion,
  including green tops, for garnish

PREPARE the Thai Sweet Chile-Garlic Sauce as directed and set aside.

QUICKLY rinse the chicken wings under cold running water, then pat dry with paper toweling. Cut each wing at the two joints; reserve the tips for making stock. Lightly sprinkle the 16 wing pieces with salt and set aside.

IN a wok, deep fryer, or saucepan, pour in oil to a depth of 2 inches and heat to 375° F. Preheat an oven to 200° F. Place a wire rack on a baking sheet and position alongside the stove top or fryer.

WHILE the oil is heating, lightly dust the chicken pieces all over with rice flour, shaking off any excess flour.

CAREFULLY add a few chicken pieces to the hot oil; avoid crowding the pan. Fry until crispy and golden brown all over, about 10 minutes. Using tongs or a slotted utensil, transfer the chicken pieces to the rack to drain well, then place the rack and baking sheet in the oven to keep warm. Fry the remaining wings in the same manner, allowing the oil to return to 375° F between batches.

TO serve, arrange the chicken wings on a serving dish, spoon the sauce over them, and sprinkle with green onion.

Makes 4 servings.

VEGETARIAN VARIATION

USE 1 pound firm tofu in place of the chicken. Drain well, cut into bite-sized cubes, lightly dust with rice flour, and fry as directed until golden brown, about 5 minutes.

SLICED ARTICHOKE-FILLED CHICKEN ROLLS

70

Juice of 1 lemon (if using fresh
   artichokes)

4 large, 6 medium-sized, or 12 very
   small fresh artichokes, or 1 package
   (9 ounces) frozen artichoke hearts,
   thawed

1 cup freshly grated Parmesan cheese
   (about 4 ounces), preferably
   Parmigiano-Reggiano

¼ cup Mayonnaise (page 388) or
   high-quality commercial mayonnaise

1 teaspoon minced garlic

3 tablespoons minced fresh basil

6 boned and skinned chicken
   breast halves

Salt

Freshly ground white pepper

6 thin slices prosciutto or other
   flavorful ham

2 tablespoons olive oil

3 tablespoons unsalted butter

Pass these attractive rounds on a platter or arrange three on a plate for a sit-down first course. If desired, serve with Tomato Sauce (page 573).

IF using fresh artichokes, in a large bowl, pour in enough cold water to cover all of the artichokes once they are added. Stir in the lemon juice and set aside. Cut off the stem and top one-third of each artichoke and remove the tough outer leaves. As each artichoke is prepared, drop it into the lemon water to prevent discoloration.

DRAIN the fresh artichokes, place them in a pan, and add water to cover. Place over medium-high heat, bring to a boil, and cook until tender when pierced, 25 to 45 minutes, depending on size. (Alternatively, steam over boiling water until tender.) Drain and let cool. When cool enough to handle, remove the leaves and reserve for another purpose. Cut away and discard the fuzzy chokes.

IN a food processor, combine the artichoke hearts, cheese, mayonnaise, garlic, and basil and puree until fairly smooth. Set aside.

QUICKLY rinse the chicken under cold running water and pat dry with paper toweling. Discard tendons and any connecting tissue or fat from the chicken; separate the little fillet and use it for another purpose or leave it attached and tuck it under the larger muscle. Leave small breasts whole; slice thicker ones in half horizontally. Place each piece between 2 sheets of waxed paper or plastic wrap. Using a mallet or other flat instrument, pound the chicken to a uniform thickness of about ⅛ inch. Lightly sprinkle both sides with salt and pepper.

TOP each pounded chicken piece with a slice of prosciutto cut to fit the shape of the chicken. Spread a thin layer of the artichoke mixture over the prosciutto. Roll up like a jelly-roll and secure lengthwise with a skewer or toothpicks, or tie crosswise in several places with cotton string.

PREHEAT an oven to 350° F.

IN an ovenproof saute pan or skillet, heat the oil and butter over medium heat. Add the chicken rolls and cook, turning frequently, until lightly browned all over, about 5 minutes. Transfer the pan to the oven and bake for 10 minutes. Remove the chicken from the oven and let stand until just cool enough to handle.

TO serve, remove the skewers or string and slice the rolls horizontally on a slight diagonal into ⅓-inch-wide pieces.

Makes 10 to 12 servings.

FRUIT-STUFFED PORK MEDALLIONS

½ cup pecans or walnuts

½ cup pitted prunes

¼ cup golden raisins

¼ cup dried apricots

2 tablespoons coarsely chopped
   fresh ginger

2¼ teaspoons chopped fresh sage, or
   ¾ teaspoon crumbled dried sage

1½ teaspoons fresh thyme, or
   ½ teaspoon crumbled dried thyme

2 tablespoons Dijon mustard

½ cup Cognac

2 whole pork tenderloins (about
   12 ounces *each*)

Salt

Freshly ground black pepper

1 cup White Stock (page 578) or
   canned reduced-sodium chicken
   broth

1 bay leaf, crumbled

Tiny fresh mint leaves or shredded
   large mint leaves for garnish

Here's a particularly tasty version of one of my favorite food combinations, fruit and pork. This preparation can also be served warm from the oven in thick slices as a main dish. It cannot be thinly sliced for finger food, however, until it is well chilled.

TOAST the nuts as directed on page 554 and set aside to cool.

IN a food processor, combine the toasted nuts, prunes, raisins, apricots, ginger, sage, and thyme and chop coarsely. Add the mustard and 2 tablespoons of the Cognac and quickly blend; do not overmix. Set aside.

BUTTERFLY each pork tenderloin by slicing lengthwise down the center, cutting almost but not completely through the meat, and then opening the halves to form a flat piece. Using a meat mallet or other flat instrument, pound the pork to a uniform thickness of about ½ inch. Lightly sprinkle with salt and pepper, then evenly spread half of the nut-fruit mixture over each piece of meat. Working from one long side of each tenderloin, roll the meat up like a jelly-roll. Wrap each roll in several layers of cheesecloth and tie at 1-inch intervals with cotton string.

PREHEAT an oven to 375° F.

IN a dutch oven or other large, ovenproof pot, combine the stock or broth, the remaining 6 tablespoons Cognac, and the bay leaf. Bring to a boil over medium heat, then add the pork rolls. Cover, transfer to the oven, and cook, turning several times, until an instant-read thermometer inserted into the meat registers 140° F, about 30 minutes. (To test thin meat, insert the thermometer well into the meat from the end of the roll.) Remove the meat from the pan and let cool to room temperature.

REMOVE the string and cheesecloth from the cooled pork, then wrap the rolls tightly in plastic wrap or aluminum foil and refrigerate overnight.

TO serve, return the pork rolls almost to room temperature, then carve into ¼- to ½-inch-thick slices. Arrange on a platter and garnish each slice with mint.

Makes 8 to 10 servings.

SATAY

12 ounces boneless lean beef, lamb,
   or pork or boned and skinned
   chicken breast

MARINADE

¼ cup fish sauce, preferably Thai or
   Vietnamese

¼ cup freshly squeezed lime juice

2 tablespoons finely ground unsalted
   dry-roasted peanuts or peanut
   butter

1 tablespoon Thai Red Curry Paste
   (page 557) or canned Thai red
   curry paste

1 tablespoon palm sugar

1 teaspoon minced fresh lemongrass,
   tender bulb portion only

1 teaspoon minced garlic

Peanut sauce (pages 397-398; see
   recipe introduction)

Vegetable oil for brushing grill rack

*Satay, or saté, is a specialty of Indonesia and Malaysia that has spread
throughout tropical Asia and has become a new favorite on our continent.
Pork is taboo among followers of Islam, but it is popular with Southeast
Asians of other beliefs, so I've included it among the meats of choice. This
recipe is merely an example of the countless versions sold by street vendors
or prepared by home cooks from Myanmar to Bali.*

*In addition to the meats and chicken suggested in the recipe,
small meatballs, whole shrimp, chunks of fish, or firm tofu cubes are
excellent prepared this way.*

*Most Americans think of peanut sauce as the perfect partner
to satay. Select the creamy Indonesian Peanut Sauce (page 397) or the
spicier Thai Peanut Sauce (page 398) to accompany the skewered meat. Or
for a change of pace, serve the grilled meat with Thai Sweet Chile-Garlic
Sauce (page 400).*

*Thai Cucumber Relish (page 403) is a traditional accompaniment
to the satay of Thailand.*

QUICKLY rinse the meat or chicken under cold running water
   and pat dry with paper toweling. To facilitate slicing, wrap the
   meat or chicken in freezer wrap or plastic wrap and place in a
   freezer until very cold but not frozen hard, about 2 hours.

TO make the marinade, in a nonreactive bowl, combine all of the
   marinade ingredients, mix well, and set aside.

USING an electric slicer or very sharp knife, slice the meat or
   chicken very thinly, then cut into strips from 3 to 4 inches
   long and about 1 inch wide. Place in the marinade and stir to
   coat evenly, cover, and refrigerate for at least 2 hours or,
   preferably, overnight.

ABOUT 30 minutes before cooking, place 8 to 10 bamboo skewers in a shallow container, cover with water, and set aside to soak. Prepare an open grill for moderate direct-heat cooking.

PREPARE the selected peanut sauce as directed and set aside.

REMOVE the meat or chicken pieces from the marinade, reserving the marinade, and thread onto the skewers, weaving the skewers in and out of the meat and using 2 pieces per skewer. Set aside.

IN a saucepan, bring the marinade to a boil over medium-high heat, then set alongside the grill.

WHEN the fire is ready, lightly brush the grill rack with oil. Place the skewered meat or chicken on the rack and grill, turning frequently and brushing with the marinade, until done, 4 to 5 minutes.

TO serve, arrange the skewers on a serving platter or individual plates with the peanut sauce alongside.

Makes 4 servings.

THAI TOAST ~ *Kanom Pang Na Moo* ~

Thai Peanut Sauce (page 398)

Thai Cucumber Relish (page 403)

5 ounces ground lean pork

2½ tablespoons finely chopped green
   onion, including green tops

1 tablespoon finely chopped fresh
   cilantro (coriander), preferably roots
   or lower stem portions

1 teaspoon minced garlic

2 teaspoons fish sauce, preferably
   Thai or Vietnamese

1 egg, lightly beaten

1 teaspoon freshly ground white
   pepper

¼ teaspoon salt

About 6 slices stale fine-textured
   white bread

Canola or other high-quality vegetable
   oil for frying

Fresh cilantro (coriander) leaves for
   garnish

Thinly slivered sweet red pepper or
   red hot chile for garnish

Among the first words my nephew Devereux spoke were "Thai toast," his favorite dish at Swatdee restaurant in San Francisco, and among his earliest solid foods. All ages delight in this traditional appetizer or snack.

These little tidbits fry best at around 350° F; any hotter will brown them too quickly before the spread is done.

PREPARE the Thai Peanut Sauce and Thai Cucumber Relish as directed. Set each aside.

IN a food processor or mixing bowl, combine the pork, onion, chopped cilantro, garlic, fish sauce, egg, pepper, and salt and process or mix well with your hands until the mixture is thick and sticky. (At this point the mixture can be covered and refrigerated for up to 24 hours before assembling the toasts.)

TRIM the crusts from each slice of bread, then cut each slice into 4 triangles or squares. Spread each piece of bread with an equal portion of the pork mixture, mounding the mixture slightly in the center and tapering toward the edges; be sure to spread the mixture all the way to the edges of the bread.

IN a wok, deep fryer, or saucepan, pour in oil to a depth of 2 inches and heat to 350° F. Preheat an oven to 200° F. Place a wire rack on a baking sheet and position alongside the stove top or fryer.

CAREFULLY add a few pieces of the bread, meat side down, to the hot oil; avoid crowding the pan. Fry until crisp and golden brown, about 1 minute, turning the toasts during the last 10 seconds to brown the bottoms. Using tongs or a slotted utensil, transfer the toasts to the rack, meat side down, to drain well, then turn the toasts meat side up and place the rack and baking sheet in the oven to keep warm. Fry the remaining bread pieces in the same manner, allowing the oil to return to 350° F between batches.

TO serve, garnish each piece of hot toast with a cilantro leaf and a sliver or two of sweet pepper or chile. Place the cucumber relish alongside and offer the peanut sauce at the table.

Makes 4 to 6 servings.

OVEN-ROASTED BURGERS

I've always called these open-faced, oven-roasted tidbits "Knecht Burgers," because they are a specialty of Dorothy Knecht, the vivacious aunt of my late partner, Lin Cotton. In fact, the first time I encountered them was at a Christmas party at Dorothy's, and I couldn't stop eating them. Cooked in a blistering-hot oven, the French bread gets crisp and the juice from the lean beef permeates the bread.

The uncooked burgers can be prepared ahead of time and frozen for quick-and-easy party appetizers or unexpected lunch guests. The burgers may also be served in larger portions as a main course. For smaller groups, spread the meat mixture on small French rolls for individual burgers. In any case, be sure that the meat covers all exposed top surfaces of the bread to prevent the bread from burning around the edges during the high-heat cooking.

Add minced fresh herbs, chopped mushrooms, or other seasonings to the beef for variety. Or replace the mustard spread with catsup or barbecue sauce.

1 sweet French or Italian baguette, about 2½ inches wide, split lengthwise

Unsalted butter, at room temperature, for spreading

1½ pounds ground lean beef

¼ cup finely chopped yellow onion

2 tablespoons Worcestershire sauce, or to taste

Salt

Freshly ground black pepper

Dijon or yellow American mustard for spreading

PREHEAT an oven to 400° F.

SPREAD the bread with a thin coating of the butter. Set aside.

IN a bowl, combine the beef, onion, Worcestershire sauce, and salt and pepper to taste. Spread the mixture over the buttered bread in an even layer about ¼ inch thick. Be sure that the meat covers the edges of the bread; any exposed bread will burn during roasting. Press the meat down around the edges with a fork or your fingers to adhere it to the bread. Spread a layer of mustard to taste over the meat.

PLACE the burgers on ungreased baking sheets and roast until done to preference, 6 to 7 minutes for medium-rare.

TRANSFER the burgers to a cutting surface and cut each piece crosswise into 8 equal sections, or as desired. Serve hot.

Makes 8 servings.

VEAL AND PORK TERRINE

1 pound boned veal, with some fat, cut into 1-inch cubes

1 pound boned pork, with some fat, cut into 1-inch cubes

1 pound thick-sliced bacon, coarsely chopped

1 tablespoon minced garlic

1 tablespoon juniper berries

2 tablespoons minced fresh thyme, or 2 teaspoons crumbled dried thyme

1 tablespoon minced fresh sage, or 1 teaspoon crumbled dried sage

1 tablespoon minced fresh marjoram, or 1 teaspoon crumbled dried marjoram

1 bay leaf, finely crumbled

½ teaspoon freshly grated nutmeg

2 teaspoons salt, or to taste

1 teaspoon freshly ground black pepper, or to taste

½ cup dry white wine

2 eggs, lightly beaten

12 ounces pork fatback, thinly sliced (optional)

Juniper berries for garnish

Bay leaves for garnish

Serve this easy-to-make, country-style pâté right from its baking dish with good crusty bread, your favorite mustard, and gherkins (cornichons), olives, or pickled onions.

IN a large bowl, combine the veal, pork, bacon, garlic, the 1 tablespoon juniper berries, minced or crumbled herbs and bay leaf, nutmeg, salt, and pepper. Stir in the wine, cover tightly with plastic wrap, and refrigerate overnight.

PUT the meat mixture through a food grinder. Alternatively, working in batches, place the mixture in a food processor and coarsely chop; avoid getting the mixture too fine. Transfer to a large bowl, add the eggs, and mix until well blended. (To test the seasonings, in a small skillet over medium-high heat, cook a small nugget of the mixture until browned. Taste and add seasonings to the mixture as needed.)

PREHEAT an oven to 325° F.

LINE a 2-quart earthenware terrine with the sliced fat (if using) to keep the meat moist, fill with the meat mixture, and smooth the top. Arrange juniper berries and bay leaves on the top. Cut a piece of kitchen parchment to fit snugly inside the terrine and cover the top of the meat. Cover with a tight-fitting lid or aluminum foil and place the dish in a large, deep pan. Pour enough hot (not boiling) water into the pan to come halfway up the sides of the terrine. Bake until set and an instant-read thermometer registers 150° to 160° F when inserted into the center of the terrine, about 1½ hours.

TRANSFER the terrine from the water bath to a work surface to cool slightly, then remove the lid and place heavy weights, such as canned foods or aluminum foil–wrapped bricks, on top to compress the meat. Set aside to cool completely, then remove the weights, cover tightly, and refrigerate for at least 3 days or for up to 1 week to allow the flavors to mellow.

TO serve, cut into slices about ¼ inch thick and offer the condiments suggested in the recipe introduction.

Makes 8 to 10 servings.

ITALIAN POACHED VEAL IN TUNA SAUCE *~ Vitello Tonnato ~*

Plan to make this classic Italian pairing the day before serving to allow time for the flavors to blend.

Pork tenderloins, boned and skinned chicken breasts, or skinless fish fillets may be substituted for the veal (do not roll); adjust poaching times to avoid overcooking and remove from the poaching liquid to cool.

TO make the Tuna Sauce, in a food processor or blender, combine the tuna, anchovies, the 3 tablespoons capers, oil, and lemon juice and blend until well mixed. Transfer to a bowl, add the mayonnaise, and fold together until well blended. Season to taste with salt and pepper. Cover and refrigerate for several hours.

TO prepare the veal, rinse it under cold running water and pat dry with paper toweling. Roll it tightly and tie with cotton string at 1-inch intervals. Place it in a pot in which it just barely fits. Add the onion, carrot, celery, parsley, bay leaves, and peppercorns. Add just enough wine or a combination of water and wine to cover. Remove the veal. Bring the liquid to a boil over medium heat, add the veal, and adjust the heat to maintain a low simmer, then cover and poach until the meat tests very tender when pierced with a skewer or fork, about 2 hours. Remove the pot from the heat and let the veal cool in the liquid.

REMOVE the strings from the cooled veal and slice it into ¼-inch-thick slices. Spread a thin layer of the chilled sauce on a platter. Arrange a layer of sliced veal over the sauce, then lightly cover with more sauce. Continue layering until all the veal and sauce are used, ending with a layer of sauce. Cover tightly with plastic wrap and refrigerate at least overnight or for up to 3 days. Remove from the refrigerator a few minutes before serving.

TO serve, sprinkle with the 1 tablespoon capers, minced parsley, and lemon zest. Garnish with lemon slices.

Makes 8 to 10 servings.

TUNA SAUCE

1 can (6 ounces) tuna, preferably packed in olive oil, drained

6 flat anchovy fillets, rinsed and patted dry

3 tablespoons drained small capers

½ cup extra-virgin olive oil

3 tablespoons freshly squeezed lemon juice, or to taste

½ cup Mayonnaise (page 388), preferably made with olive oil, or high-quality commercial mayonnaise

Salt

Freshly ground white pepper

POACHED VEAL

2½ pounds lean boned veal top round

1 onion, sliced

1 carrot, cut into 2-inch pieces

1 celery stalk, cut into 2-inch pieces

3 fresh flat-leaf parsley sprigs

2 bay leaves

1 teaspoon white peppercorns

Dry white wine for poaching

1 tablespoon drained small capers

2 tablespoons minced fresh flat-leaf parsley

1 tablespoon minced fresh lemon zest

Thin lemon slices for garnish

SICILIAN STUFFED RICE BALLS
~ *Arancini* ~

2 cups short-grain white rice, preferably Italian Arborio

½ teaspoon crumbled saffron threads

1 quart White Stock (page 578) or canned reduced-sodium chicken broth

Salt

2 tablespoons olive oil, preferably extra-virgin

½ cup finely chopped yellow or white onion

4 ounces ground lean pork or beef

1½ teaspoons minced fresh rosemary, or ½ teaspoon crumbled dried rosemary

¼ cup Tomato Sauce (page 573) or canned tomato sauce

¼ cup dry white wine

⅓ cup shelled fresh or thawed frozen green (English) peas

Freshly ground black pepper

4 eggs

½ cup freshly grated pecorino cheese (about 2 ounces), preferably pecorino-romano, or Parmesan cheese (about 2 ounces), preferably Parmigiano-Reggiano

2 cups unseasoned very fine dried bread crumbs, preferably from Italian or French bread

Olive oil or high-quality vegetable oil for frying

Called "little oranges" because of their shape and finished color, arancini *make an intriguing appetizer or satisfying snack.*

WASH and drain the rice as directed on page 365.

IN a saucepan, combine the saffron, stock or broth, and drained rice. Place over medium-high heat and bring to a boil. Stir the rice, cover tightly, reduce the heat to very low, and cook until the liquid is absorbed and the rice is tender but still firm to the bite and slightly sticky, about 17 minutes. Remove from the heat, transfer to a bowl, stir in salt to taste, and set aside to cool to room temperature.

IN a sauté pan or skillet, heat the 2 tablespoons olive oil over medium-high heat. Add the onion and cook, stirring frequently, until soft but not browned, about 5 minutes. Add the ground meat and rosemary and cook, stirring frequently and breaking up the meat, until the meat just loses its raw color, about 5 minutes longer. Add the tomato sauce, wine, and peas and cook until the liquid evaporates and the peas are just tender, about 10 minutes longer for fresh peas, or about 5 minutes for thawed. Season to taste with salt and pepper.

IN a mixing bowl, beat 2 of the eggs. Add the cooled rice and grated cheese and mix thoroughly. Moisten your hands with water. Scoop about ¼ cup of the rice mixture into the palm of one hand and press it out to form an even round, then press the center to form an indention. Place about 1 tablespoon of the meat mixture in the indention, then gently close your hand to encase the filling in the rice. Use both hands to roll the stuffed rice into a ball. Continue making balls until both mixtures are used up.

IN a small bowl, beat the remaining 2 eggs. In a shallow bowl, place the bread crumbs and position alongside the bowl containing the beaten eggs. Roll each rice ball in the egg to coat completely, then roll in the bread crumbs to cover well. Set aside until all of the balls are coated.

IN a deep fryer or saucepan, pour in oil to a depth of 3 inches and heat to 360° F. Preheat an oven to 200° F. Place a wire rack on a baking sheet and position alongside the fryer or stove top.

CAREFULLY add a few of the rice balls to the hot oil; avoid crowding the pan. Fry, turning frequently, until golden brown all over, 2 to 3 minutes. Using a slotted utensil, transfer the rice balls to the rack to drain well, then place the rack and baking sheet in the oven to keep warm. Fry the remaining rice balls in the same manner, allowing the oil to return to 360° F between batches.

SERVE warm.

Makes about 12 *arancini* for 6 servings.

ASIAN PANFRIED DUMPLINGS
~ *GYOZA* OR POTSTICKERS ~

10 ounces ground lean pork

1 cup finely chopped yellow or white
onion

1 cup finely chopped napa cabbage

2 tablespoons minced or grated fresh
ginger

1 tablespoon Asian sesame oil

1 tablespoon soy sauce

½ teaspoon salt, or to taste

¼ teaspoon freshly ground black
pepper, or to taste

About 48 fresh round *gyoza* or
potsticker skins or square wonton
wrappers, trimmed into circles
(available in Asian markets and
some supermarkets)

Canola or other high-quality vegetable
oil for frying

About 2 cups White Stock (page 578)
made with chicken or canned
reduced-sodium chicken broth

Chinese chives for garnish (optional)

CONDIMENTS FOR DIPPING

Soy sauce

Unseasoned rice vinegar or Chinese
black vinegar

Asian sesame oil

Asian chile sauce

Known as Japanese gyoza or Chinese potstickers, these tasty morsels are one of my all-time favorite appetizers.

IN a bowl, combine the pork, onion, cabbage, ginger, sesame oil, soy sauce, salt, and pepper and mix well. Set aside.

WORKING with 1 wrapper at a time (keep the rest covered to prevent drying out), place about 2 teaspoons of the pork mixture onto the wrapper and just off center. Form the mixture into a half-circle shape with your fingertips. Moisten the inside edge of the wrapper with water, fold the wrapper over the filling so that the edges meet, and pinch the center of the joined edges to adhere. On the side of the dumpling facing you, and beginning just to one side of the pinched center, fold the top piece of dough to form 3 little pleats with edges that face toward the center; pinch together at the top to seal tightly. Repeat the pleating on the other side of the pinched center, reversing the folds so that the pleat edges face the center. Leave the back side of the dumpling unpleated. Repeat with the remaining wrappers until the filling is used up. (At this point, the dumplings may be covered and refrigerated for up to several hours or frozen for up to 1 month; thaw before cooking.)

IN a large, heavy skillet, pour in just enough oil to cover the bottom of the pan and heat over medium heat. Working in batches if necessary, add the dumplings, smooth side down, so that they touch each other in straight rows or in a circle.

Cook until the bottoms are browned, then pour in enough stock or broth to come halfway up the sides of the dumplings. Reduce the heat so that the liquid simmers, cover the pan, and cook until the liquid is almost absorbed, about 15 minutes. Uncover, increase the heat to medium, and cook until the bottoms of the dumplings are crisp, adding a bit more oil underneath the dumplings, if necessary. Remove from the heat; keep warm if cooking in batches.

TO serve, using a spatula, transfer the hot dumplings to a serving platter and garnish with chives (if using). Offer the condiments at the table; each diner mixes ingredients to taste for dipping the dumplings.

Makes about 48 dumplings for 8 servings.

VIETNAMESE SPRING ROLLS
~ *CHA GIO* ~

Vietnamese Chile Dipping Sauce
(page 396)

CHICKEN AND SHRIMP FILLING

2 ounces very thin, wiry dried rice
noodles

8 ounces shrimp, peeled and
deveined

1 pound finely ground chicken breast

½ cup finely chopped Chinese chives
or green onion, including green
tops

¼ cup finely minced carrot

1 teaspoon salt, or to taste

½ teaspoon freshly ground black
pepper, or to taste

Vegetable oil or cooking spray for
greasing

About 24 Vietnamese round dried
rice paper wrappers *(bahn trang)*,
about 8 inches in diameter

About 24 large, crisp lettuce leaves

1 cup packed fresh cilantro (coriander)
leaves

1 cup packed fresh mint leaves

1 cup packed fresh Asian basil leaves

Canola or other high-quality vegetable
oil for frying

*Pork, beef, or crab are often used in the filling for this popular appetizer
or snack.*

PREPARE the Vietnamese Chile Dipping Sauce as directed and
set aside.

TO make the filling, break the rice noodles into short lengths and
place in a bowl, add hot water to cover, and let stand, stirring
occasionally, until softened but still firm to the bite, about
15 minutes. Drain in a colander set in a sink and rinse thoroughly
under cold running water to remove surface starch. Transfer
to a cutting board, coarsely chop, then transfer to a bowl.

QUICKLY rinse the shrimp under cold running water and pat dry
with paper toweling. Coarsely chop and add to the noodles.
Add the remaining filling ingredients, mix well, and set aside.

USING a pastry brush, lightly grease a baking sheet with oil, or
coat with spray. Set aside.

TO assemble the rolls, place the filling and wrappers on a work
surface and fill a wide, shallow bowl with warm water. Working
with 1 sheet at a time, dip a rice paper round into the warm
water to soften, then lay the wrapper flat on the work surface.
Spoon 2 rounded tablespoons of the filling onto the lower third
of the wrapper and form the filling into a cylinder, leaving
about 1 inch of space along the bottom and sides. Fold the
bottom up around the filling and fold each side over to encase
the filling, then roll to form a cylinder and place seam side
down on the prepared baking sheet. Repeat with the remaining
wrappers until the filling is used up.

ARRANGE the lettuce leaves and herbs on a tray or serving platter and set on the table. Spoon the dipping sauce into small bowls and position at each place.

IN a wok, deep fryer, or saucepan, pour in oil to a depth of 2 inches and heat to 375° F. Preheat an oven to 200° F. Place a wire rack on a baking sheet and position alongside the stove top or fryer.

CAREFULLY add a few of the rolls to the hot oil; avoid crowding the pan. Fry, turning frequently, until golden brown, about 6 minutes. Using tongs or a slotted utensil, transfer the rolls to the rack to drain well, then place the rack and baking sheet in the oven to keep warm. Fry the remaining rolls in the same manner, allowing the oil to return to 375° F between batches.

TO serve, leave whole or diagonally slice each roll into 2 pieces and arrange on a serving platter. To eat, place a few herb leaves on a lettuce leaf, add a spring roll, and wrap firmly in the lettuce. Dip into the sauce and enjoy.

Makes about 24 rolls for 8 servings.

MOVING ON

Within this section is a wide variety of first courses,
most of which can also double as the main course for
a light meal. Choose from soups, starter salads, pastas
and noodles, risotto, polenta, dumplings, and pizza.

Soups

A STEAMING hot bowl of homemade soup is one of
life's greatest comforts. And a bowl of chilled soup
on a hot day is extremely refreshing.

Here are soups for all seasons from all over the
world that range from simple vegetable preparations
to complex meaty meals in a bowl. Many benefit
from being made the day before serving, refrigerated
overnight, and gently reheated before serving.

GAZPACHO

Use yellow tomatoes with their juice and yellow peppers to create a
sunny new look for an old favorite that is usually red. Or choose ripe
green tomato varieties such as Evergreen or Green Zebra and combine
them with green peppers. In any case, be sure the tomatoes are ripe
and flavorful.

IN a bowl, combine the tomatoes, onion, sweet pepper, and
cucumber. Stir in the tomato juice, shallot, garlic, vinegar, and
oil. Working in batches if necessary, transfer the mixture to a
food processor or blender and puree until the mixture is fairly
smooth yet still has some small chunky bits. Transfer to a bowl
and season to taste with salt and pepper. Cover and refrigerate
for at least 4 hours or for up to overnight. Let stand at room
temperature for about 15 minutes before serving.

TO serve, stir the soup, ladle it into chilled bowls or goblets, and
add a sprinkling of each garnish, or pass the garnishes for
adding to taste at the table.

Makes 6 servings.

2½ pounds ripe tomatoes, peeled,
    seeded, and coarsely chopped

1 cup coarsely chopped red onion

1 cup coarsely chopped sweet pepper

1 cup peeled, seeded, and coarsely
    chopped cucumber

¾ cup fresh or canned tomato juice

¼ cup chopped shallot

1½ teaspoons chopped garlic

¼ cup sherry vinegar or red or white
    wine vinegar

3 tablespoons extra-virgin olive oil

Salt

Freshly ground black pepper

GARNISHES

Croutons (page 555), made with
    ¼-inch bread cubes

Peeled, seeded, and chopped tomato

Minced fresh chives

Peeled, seeded, and diced cucumber

Minced fresh basil, dill, oregano, or
    thyme

Pesticide-free edible flowers or petals
    such as calendula, tiny French
    marigold, or nasturtium (optional)

FLORENTINE ONION SOUP
~ *CARABACCIA* ~

¼ cup olive oil, preferably
   extra-virgin

4 pounds yellow onions (see recipe
   introduction), cut in half
   lengthwise, then thinly sliced

2 teaspoons sugar

Salt

1 bottle (750 ml) dry white wine

3 cups Brown Stock (page 576),
   White Stock (page 578), Vegetable
   Stock (page 580), or canned broth

1 cinnamon stick

4 cups torn or cut very stale Italian or
   French bread (about 5 ounces)

Whole fresh chives for garnish
   (optional)

Freshly grated Parmesan cheese,
   preferably Parmigiano-Reggiano,
   for serving

Carabaccia has been served in Florence since the Middle Ages. The name translates to "a combination of simple things," which is exactly what goes into this thick soup. Like many soups, it tastes better when made a day ahead and reheated. Although usually eaten hot, this hearty soup is often presented at room temperature on warm summer days.

For good caramelization, choose onions that are somewhat dry. Freshly picked onions contain so much water that they fall apart by the time they achieve good color.

IN a heavy soup pot, heat the oil over medium heat. Add the onions and toss well to coat with the oil. Cover, reduce the heat to medium-low, and cook, stirring occasionally, until the onions just begin to color, about 30 minutes.

UNCOVER the onions, increase the heat to medium, sprinkle with the sugar and a little salt, and cook, stirring frequently, until the onions are richly browned and caramelized, 20 minutes or longer, depending upon moisture content of onions.

ADD the wine, stock or broth, 1 cup water, and cinnamon stick. Stir well and bring to a boil. Cover tightly, reduce the heat to achieve a simmer, and simmer gently, stirring occasionally, for 1 hour.

ADD the bread to the simmering soup and continue cooking until the bread disintegrates, 30 to 45 minutes longer; stir occasionally to prevent the soup from sticking to the bottom of the pot and add a bit of water if the soup gets too thick.

REMOVE and discard the cinnamon stick. Using a wire whisk, whip the soup until the bread is well incorporated. Taste and add more salt if needed. (At this point, the soup can be cooled completely, then covered and refrigerated for up to 2 days. Slowly reheat before serving.)

TO serve, ladle the hot soup into warmed bowls and garnish with chives (if using). Pass the cheese at the table for sprinkling over the soup.

Makes 6 servings.

OVEN-PUFFED

PANCAKES

(page 16)

———

SCONES WITH

ORANGE BUTTER

(page 21)

ROASTED GARLIC
AND BEAN SPREAD
(page 39)

———————

SUSHI POCKETS
(page 46)

SEVICHE
(page 61)

————

SATAY
(page 74)

VEAL AND PORK
TERRINE
(page 78)

———

TUSCAN
CREAMY SWEET
PEPPER SOUP
(page 97)

THAI COCONUT
CHICKEN SOUP
(page 110)

———

MEDITERRANEAN
FISH SOUP
(page 108)

VIETNAMESE BEEF
SOUP WITH NOODLES

(page 118)

———

CAESAR SALAD

(page 121)

FRUIT, NUTS, AND
GREENS SALAD

(page 122)

————

FENNEL AND
ORANGE SALAD

(page 134)

GREEN PAPAYA
SALAD

(page 128)

———

THAI FIERY GRILLED
SHRIMP SALAD

(page 132)

TUSCAN CREAMY SWEET PEPPER SOUP ~ *Zuppa Crema di Peperoni* ~

*For an attractive presentation, make two batches of this creamy —
yet creamless — soup, one with red peppers and the other with yellow
peppers. Ladle one soup into warmed bowls to fill halfway, then ladle
the second soup into the center of the first soup. Draw a wooden
skewer through the surface to create an interesting pattern.*

ROAST the peppers as directed on page 552. If roasted whole, cut
the peppers in half and remove and discard the stems, seeds,
and membranes. Chop coarsely and set aside.

IN a soup pot or large saucepan, melt the butter over medium-
high heat. Add the onion and cook, stirring frequently, until
soft but not browned, about 5 minutes. Add the potato, 1 quart
stock or broth, and 2 cups water. Increase the heat to high,
bring to a boil, and cook for 15 minutes.

REDUCE the heat to achieve a simmer. Enclose the thyme and bay
leaves in a small square of cheesecloth, tie with cotton string to
form a bag, and add to the simmering soup. Add the chopped
peppers and simmer until the potatoes are falling apart and
creamy, about 45 minutes longer; add more stock, broth, or
water if the soup becomes too thick.

DISCARD the bag of herbs. Working in batches if necessary,
transfer the soup to a food processor or blender and puree
until smooth. Season to taste with salt and pepper. (At this
point, the soup can be cooled completely, then covered and
refrigerated for up to 2 days. Slowly reheat before serving.)

TO serve, pour the soup into a clean pot and heat over low heat.
Ladle the hot soup into warmed bowls, drizzle with olive oil
(if using), and sprinkle with cheese.

Makes 4 servings.

4 large red or yellow sweet peppers

2 tablespoons unsalted butter

1 cup chopped yellow onion

1 large baking potato (about 8 ounces),
    peeled and chopped

About 1 quart Vegetable Stock (page
    580), White Stock (page 578), or
    canned vegetable or reduced-sodium
    chicken broth

2 fresh thyme sprigs

2 bay leaves

Salt

Freshly ground white pepper

Extra-virgin olive oil for serving
    (optional)

Freshly grated Parmesan cheese,
    preferably Parmigiano-Reggiano,
    for serving

CREAMY BEAN SOUP

2 cups dried beans (see recipe
introduction)

2 tablespoons olive oil, preferably
extra-virgin

1 cup chopped yellow onion

1 cup chopped celery

1 tablespoon chopped fresh jalapeño
or other hot chile, or to taste

1 tablespoon minced garlic

1 tablespoon minced fresh oregano,
or 1 teaspoon crumbled dried
oregano

1 tablespoon minced fresh thyme, or
1 teaspoon crumbled dried thyme

2 teaspoons ground cumin

1 teaspoon ground coriander

2 bay leaves

About 3 quarts unsalted Brown Stock
(page 576), unsalted Vegetable
Stock (page 580), unsalted White
Stock (page 578), or canned
reduced-sodium broth (see recipe
introduction)

½ cup tomato puree (optional)

Salt

Freshly ground black pepper

Any dried beans can be used for this soup. Sometimes I like to make two batches from different-colored beans, such as black and white, and ladle them into the bowls simultaneously from opposite sides. Then I swirl a wooden skewer through the soups to create a pattern and often add a drizzle of pureed roasted red pepper or hot sauce for a splash of color.

Because cooking dried beans with salt adds considerably to the cooking time, I recommend using unsalted homemade stock and seasoning with salt after the beans are tender. If you choose to use canned broth, allow for a longer cooking time. Since the acid in tomatoes prevents some bean types from ever getting tender, the tomato puree should not be added until the beans are done.

The use of a pressure cooker can reduce the cooking time by more than half due to the higher temperature that occurs inside the pressurized pot. Follow the manufacturer's directions and cook the soup until the beans are tender before adding the tomato puree and salt, then finish cooking the soup conventionally.

CLEAN and soak the beans as directed on page 342. Drain and set aside.

IN a soup pot or large saucepan, heat the oil over medium-high heat. Add the onion, celery, and chile and cook, stirring frequently, until soft and golden, about 8 minutes. Add the garlic, oregano, thyme, cumin, and coriander and cook for about 1 minute longer. Add the beans, bay leaves, and enough stock or broth to cover the beans by about 3 inches. Bring to a boil and cook for about 10 minutes, then reduce the heat to achieve a simmer, cover partially, and simmer until the beans are very tender, 30 minutes to 2 hours, or even longer, depending on type and size of bean and length of storage. Add more liquid during cooking if necessary to maintain a "soupy" consistency.

STIR the tomato puree (if using) into the beans and season to taste with salt and pepper. Cover and simmer until the flavors are well blended, about 20 minutes.

REMOVE and discard the bay leaves from the soup. Working in batches, if necessary, transfer the beans and their liquid to a food processor or blender and puree until fairly smooth. For a smoother soup, grind or press thick-skinned beans through a food mill or strainer after pureeing to remove the skins. (At this point, the soup can be cooled completely, then covered and refrigerated for up to 2 days. Slowly reheat before serving.)

TO serve, pour into a clean pot and heat over low heat. Ladle the hot soup into warmed bowls.

Makes 6 servings.

NORTH AFRICAN POTATO SOUP

¼ cup canola or other high-quality
   vegetable oil

2 cups coarsely chopped yellow or
   white onion

2 cups chopped red or yellow sweet
   pepper

1 tablespoon ground cumin

2 teaspoons ground coriander

¼ cup coarsely chopped garlic

2 pounds boiling or baking potatoes
   or sweet potatoes (not orange "yam"
   varieties), peeled and cut into
   bite-sized pieces

3 cups peeled, seeded, drained, and
   chopped ripe or canned tomato

1 quart Vegetable Stock (page 580),
   White Stock (page 578) made with
   chicken, or canned vegetable or
   reduced-sodium chicken broth

2 tablespoons freshly squeezed
   lemon juice

1 tablespoon grated or minced fresh
   lemon zest

Salt

Freshly ground black pepper

Ground cayenne or other dried
   hot chile

3 tablespoons chopped fresh mint

Shredded fresh lemon zest for garnish

Fresh mint leaves for garnish

For a smooth version of this exotic porridge, transfer it to a food processor or blender and puree; reheat before serving.

IN a soup pot or large saucepan, heat the oil over medium-high heat. Add the onion and cook, stirring frequently, until soft but not browned, about 5 minutes. Add the sweet pepper, cumin, and coriander and cook, stirring frequently, about 5 minutes longer. Stir in the garlic, reduce the heat to low, and cook, stirring occasionally, until the onion is almost caramelized, about 20 minutes.

ADD the potato slices, tomato, stock or broth, lemon juice, and grated or minced lemon zest. Increase the heat to medium-high and bring to a boil, then cover, reduce the heat to achieve a simmer, and simmer until the potatoes are tender, about 30 minutes. Season to taste with salt, pepper, and chile. (At this point, the soup can be cooled completely, then covered and refrigerated for up to 2 days. Slowly reheat before serving.)

TO serve, stir in the chopped mint and ladle the hot soup into warmed bowls. Sprinkle each serving with shredded lemon zest and garnish with mint leaves.

Makes 4 to 6 servings.

TUSCAN BREAD AND TOMATO SOUP ~ *PAPA AL POMODORO* ~

European peasant soups originated as a bowl of stale bread covered with broth. This traditional recipe from Tuscany is a good example. Be sure to use stale country-style Italian or French bread and very flavorful tomatoes.

IN a soup pot or large saucepan, heat the 3 tablespoons oil over medium-high heat. Add the onion and cook, stirring frequently, until soft but not browned, about 5 minutes. Add the garlic and cook for about 1 minute longer. Add the chopped tomato, reduce the heat to low, and cook, stirring frequently, for about 10 minutes.

COMBINE the reserved tomato liquid with enough water to equal 4 cups and stir into the tomato mixture. Add the stock or broth and salt and pepper to taste. Increase the heat to medium-high and bring to a boil, then reduce the heat to achieve a simmer, stir in the bread, cover, and simmer until the bread falls apart and the soup is well flavored, about 45 minutes. Taste and adjust seasonings if necessary. If a smoother soup is desired, working in batches, transfer the mixture to a food processor or blender and blend well, then return the soup to the pot. (At this point, the soup can be cooled completely, then covered and refrigerated for up to 2 days. Slowly reheat before serving.)

TO serve, stir the shredded basil into the hot soup, then ladle into warmed bowls, drizzle with a little olive oil, and garnish with basil leaves. Pass the cheese at the table for sprinkling over the soup.

Makes 8 servings.

3 tablespoons olive oil, preferably extra-virgin

1 cup finely chopped yellow or white onion

2 tablespoons minced garlic

4 cups peeled, seeded, drained, and chopped ripe or canned tomato (reserve liquid)

1 quart Brown Stock (page 576), Vegetable Stock (page 580), White Stock (page 578), or canned broth

Salt

Freshly ground black pepper

8 cups torn or cut very stale Italian or French bread (about 10 ounces)

½ cup chopped or shredded fresh basil

Extra-virgin olive oil for drizzling

Fresh basil leaves for garnish

Freshly grated Parmesan cheese, preferably Parmigiano-Reggiano, for serving

GINGERED CARROT SOUP

3 tablespoons unsalted butter

1 cup sliced leek, including pale
green portion

1 tablespoon minced fresh ginger

1½ pounds carrots, peeled and cut
into 1-inch lengths

2 cups Vegetable Stock (page 580),
White Stock (page 578), or canned
vegetable or reduced-sodium
chicken broth

Salt

Freshly ground white pepper

2 cups freshly squeezed orange juice

¼ cup chopped fresh mint

Shredded fresh orange zest for
garnish

During my days of running the Twin Peaks Grocery in San Francisco, we simmered countless vats of this soup, which we sold freshly made or frozen. Although I prefer it as a refreshing cold dish on a summer day, it is also good hot, especially with a little light cream stirred in to enrich and smooth the warm soup.

IN a soup pot or large saucepan, melt the butter over medium-high heat. Add the leek and ginger and cook, stirring frequently, until soft but not browned, about 5 minutes. Add the carrots and stir until coated with butter. Stir in the stock or broth and bring to a boil, then reduce the heat to achieve a simmer, cover partially, and simmer until the carrots are very tender, about 30 minutes.

WORKING in batches, if necessary, transfer the soup to a food processor or blender and puree until smooth. Season to taste with salt and pepper. (At this point, the soup can be cooled completely, then covered and refrigerated for up to 2 days.)

TO serve hot, pour the soup into a clean pot, stir in the orange juice, and heat over low heat. Ladle into warmed bowls and sprinkle with the mint and orange zest.

TO serve cold, cool completely, then cover and refrigerate until well chilled, at least 2 hours or for up to 2 days. Stir in the orange juice, ladle into chilled bowls, and sprinkle with the mint and orange zest.

Makes 4 servings.

POTATO AND ONION
FAMILY SOUP

Although many cooks prefer to use only leeks in this French-inspired soup, I've added other members of the onion family for a more complex flavor. Served warm, it's hearty fare. Presented chilled, this creamy potato soup goes by the fancy American moniker vichyssoise. A garnish of pesticide-free edible flowers, such as viola, allium, borage, lavender, or other herb blossoms, adds color to the cold soup.

Purple-fleshed Peruvian potatoes create a pale lilac version; Yukon Gold or other varieties with yellow flesh render a butter-hued soup. For a pale green rendition, add the leek tops and a handful of minced fresh herbs instead of the bouquet garni. Sweet potatoes create an unusual variation; swirl a dollop of crème fraîche (see page 591) or whipped sour cream into the hot soup, or chill and garnish with slivered fresh orange zest and mint leaves.

2 tablespoons unsalted butter

1½ cups chopped white onion

1¼ cups chopped leek, white part only

½ cup chopped shallot

2 tablespoons chopped garlic

1 pound boiling or baking potatoes, peeled and sliced

Several fresh chervil, marjoram, flat-leaf parsley, and/or savory sprigs, tied together with cotton string into a bouquet garni

1 quart Vegetable Stock (page 580), White Stock (page 578), or canned vegetable or reduced-sodium chicken broth

1 cup heavy (whipping) cream, light cream, or half-and-half

Salt

Freshly ground white pepper

Whole or minced fresh chives for garnish

IN a soup pot or large saucepan, melt the butter over medium-high heat. Add the onion, leek, and shallot and cook, stirring frequently, until soft but not browned, about 5 minutes. Stir in the garlic and cook for about 1 minute longer. Add the potato slices, bouquet garni, and stock or broth. Bring to a boil, cover partially, reduce the heat to achieve a simmer, and simmer until the potatoes are very soft, about 30 minutes. Discard the bouquet garni.

WORKING in batches if necessary, transfer the soup to a food processor or blender and puree until very smooth. Stir in the cream or half-and-half and season to taste with salt and white pepper. (At this point, the soup can be cooled completely, then covered and refrigerated for up to 2 days.)

TO serve hot, pour the soup into a clean pot and heat over low heat; do not allow to come to a boil. Ladle the hot soup into warmed bowls and garnish with chives.

TO serve cold, cool completely, cover, and refrigerate until well chilled, at least 2 hours or for up to 2 days. Whisk to recombine, ladle into chilled bowls, and garnish with chives.

Makes 4 to 6 servings.

CORN CHOWDER

About 8 medium-sized ears corn, or
4 cups thawed frozen or drained
canned corn kernels

6 ounces salt pork, trimmed of rind
and cut into small cubes, or 6 thick
slices bacon, cut crosswise into
1-inch lengths

2 tablespoons canola or other high-
quality vegetable oil, if using salt
pork

1½ cups finely chopped leek,
including pale green portion

2 cups finely chopped yellow or white
onion

3 tablespoons all-purpose flour

4 cups Vegetable Stock (page 580),
White Stock (page 578), or canned
vegetable or reduced-sodium
chicken broth

4 cups diced or sliced peeled boiling
potatoes (about 2 pounds)

2 tablespoons minced fresh thyme, or
2 teaspoons crumbled dried thyme

2 bay leaves

1 cup heavy (whipping) cream, light
cream, or half-and-half

Salt

Freshly ground black or white pepper

Ground cayenne or other dried hot
chile or hot sauce

Fresh thyme sprigs for garnish

*Although this all-American favorite is best made with fresh corn, drained
canned or thawed frozen corn kernels make an acceptable chowder.*

IF using fresh corn, cut the kernels from the cobs as directed for
Sauteed Corn on page 358 and measure out 4 cups into a bowl.
If using thawed or canned corn, place in a bowl.

TRANSFER half of the corn to a food processor or blender and
puree until smooth. Return the pureed corn to the bowl with
the remaining corn and set aside.

IF using salt pork, in a saucepan, combine the pork and enough
water to cover and bring to a boil over high heat. Boil for
5 minutes to remove excess salt; drain. In a soup pot or large
saucepan, heat the oil over medium-high heat, add the salt
pork, and cook until browned.

IF using bacon, in a soup pot or large saucepan, cook over
medium-high heat until crisp.

ADD the leek and onion to the salt pork or bacon and cook,
stirring frequently, until soft but not browned, about 5 minutes.
Stir in the flour and cook, stirring constantly, about 2 minutes.
Add the stock or broth, potatoes, minced or crumbled thyme,
and bay leaves. Bring to a boil, then reduce the heat to achieve
a simmer, cover partially, and simmer until the potatoes are
tender, about 30 minutes.

STIR the reserved corn into the soup and simmer for about
3 minutes. Stir in the cream or half-and-half and season to
taste with salt, pepper, and chile or hot sauce. Simmer until
heated through, about 5 minutes longer; do not allow to come
to a boil. (At this point, the soup can be cooled completely,
then covered and refrigerated for up to 2 days. Slowly reheat
before serving.)

TO serve, ladle the hot soup into warmed bowls and garnish
with thyme sprigs.

Makes 6 servings.

SEAFOOD VARIATION

SUBSTITUTE Fish Stock (page 575) or bottled clam juice for the
chicken stock or broth. When adding the cream, stir in about
3 cups of one or a mixture of the following: shucked raw small
oysters, shucked steamed clams or mussels, raw small scallops
or peeled shrimp, cooked crab or lobster meat, chopped
smoked fish, or bite-sized chunks of firm fish fillets such as
halibut, cod, or salmon.

CORN, CHEESE, AND CHILE SOUP

About 6 medium-sized ears corn, or
    3 cups thawed frozen or drained
    canned corn kernels

2 tablespoons unsalted butter

2 tablespoons canola or other high-
    quality vegetable oil

1 cup chopped yellow or white onion

2 teaspoons minced garlic

2 tablespoons all-purpose flour

1 cup finely chopped fresh, thawed
    frozen, or drained canned green
    mild to medium-hot chile such as
    Anaheim, New Mexico, or *poblano*

1 cup peeled, seeded, drained, and
    chopped ripe or canned tomato

3 cups Vegetable Stock (page 580),
    White Stock (page 578), or canned
    vegetable or reduced-sodium
    chicken broth

12 ounces Velveeta or similar
    processed cheese (not fat free),
    freshly shredded

2 cups heavy (whipping) cream, light
    cream, or half-and-half, or 1 can
    (13 ounces) evaporated milk (not
    fat free)

Salt

Ground cayenne or other dried hot
    chile

Red chile or red sweet pepper, cut
    into narrow strips or fanciful
    shapes, for garnish

My sister, Martha, always makes this velvety soup for our outdoor Thanksgiving feasts on the terrace of her Napa Valley home.

*   I don't normally advocate the use of processed cheeses, but these products, natural cheeses that have been melted and blended with emulsifiers, do make an exceptionally smooth soup. If instead you prefer to use natural cheese, choose Cheddar, be sure to melt it slowly, and never allow the soup to approach a boil; also, this soup does not reheat well when made with natural cheese.*

*   For a smoother version of this rich, delicious soup, puree it in a food processor or blender before stirring in the cream and cheese.*

IF using fresh corn, cut the kernels from the cobs as directed for Sauteed Corn on page 358, measure out 3 cups, and set aside. If using thawed or canned corn, reserve for later use.

IN a soup pot or large saucepan, combine the butter and oil and heat over medium-high heat. Add the onion and cook, stirring frequently, until soft but not browned, about 5 minutes. Stir in the garlic and cook for about 1 minute longer. Add the flour and cook, stirring constantly, for 2 minutes longer. Add the corn, green chile, tomato, and stock or broth. Bring to a boil, then reduce the heat to achieve a simmer and simmer, stirring occasionally, for about 15 minutes.

STIR the cheese and cream, half-and-half, or evaporated milk into the soup and simmer, stirring, until the cheese melts, about 5 minutes; do not allow to come to a boil. Season to taste with salt and ground chile. (At this point, the soup can be cooled completely, then covered and refrigerated for up to 2 days. Slowly reheat before serving.)

TO serve, ladle the hot soup into warmed bowls and garnish with red chile or sweet pepper.

Makes 6 to 8 servings.

THAI SPICY SEAFOOD SOUP
~ TOM YAM GOONG ~

Inspiration for this highly fragrant soup came from similar soups that I've enjoyed in Thai restaurants. Cracked crab or lobster, sliced squid, or oysters may be added and cooked in the simmering broth.

PEEL and devein the shrimp, reserving the shells. Quickly rinse the shrimp under cold running water, pat dry with paper toweling, cover, and refrigerate for later use.

IN a soup pot or large saucepan over medium-high heat, combine the oil and shrimp shells and cook, stirring frequently, until the shells turn bright pink. Add the stock, lemongrass, lime zest and leaves, galanga or ginger, and chopped chiles. Bring to a boil, then reduce the heat to achieve a simmer, cover, and simmer for 25 minutes. Pour the broth through a fine-mesh strainer into a clean pot; discard the strained solids.

BRING the strained soup to a boil over medium-high heat. Add the mussels or clams, cover, and cook until the shells open, about 2 minutes. Remove from the heat. Using a slotted utensil, transfer the mussels or clams to a bowl. Break off and discard the top shell from each. Return the mussels or clams on the half shell to the broth and place over medium-high heat. Add the shrimp and cook until the shrimp turn opaque, about 2 minutes. Reduce the heat to achieve a simmer, stir in the lime juice, fish sauce, cilantro, slivered chile, green onion, and salt to taste and simmer for about 1 minute.

TO serve, ladle the hot soup into warmed bowls and garnish with lime slices.

Makes 6 servings.

1 pound medium-sized shrimp in shells

1 tablespoon canola or other high-quality vegetable oil

2 quarts Fish Stock (page 575)

3 fresh lemongrass stalks, coarsely chopped

Shredded zest of 1 lime

6 to 8 fresh or thawed frozen kaffir lime leaves

2 tablespoons sliced fresh galanga or ginger

4 fresh Thai bird or other hot chiles, chopped

24 small to medium-sized mussels or clams in shells, well scrubbed (mussels debearded)

2 tablespoons freshly squeezed lime juice

2 tablespoons fish sauce, preferably Thai or Vietnamese

3 tablespoons chopped fresh cilantro (coriander)

1 tablespoon slivered fresh red Thai bird or other hot chile, or to taste

¼ cup chopped green onion, including green tops

Salt

Thin lime slices for garnish

MEDITERRANEAN FISH SOUP

2 quarts Fish Stock (page 575)

Provençal Red Garlic Sauce (page 391)

8 slices French bread, about ½ inch thick, or 16 slices skinny baguette, about ½ inch thick

Extra-virgin olive oil for brushing

2 pounds white fish fillets (see recipe introduction), skinned

2 tablespoons unsalted butter

2 tablespoons extra-virgin olive oil

2 cups thinly sliced leek, including pale green portion

1 tablespoon minced garlic

⅛ teaspoon crumbled saffron threads

1 cup peeled, seeded, drained, and chopped ripe or canned tomato

Salt

Freshly ground black pepper

Minced fresh flat-leaf parsley for garnish

Here I have combined elements of several classic fish soups served along the shores of the Mediterranean to create my California version. Choose firm-fleshed fish, such as sea bass, halibut, or monkfish, or flaky-fleshed fish, such as orange roughy or red snapper.

Sometimes I offer Aïoli (page 389) for adding extra richness at the table.

PREPARE the Fish Stock and Provençal Red Garlic Sauce as directed, cover, and refrigerate for up to 2 days. Bring the sauce to room temperature before serving.

PREHEAT an oven to 350° F.

LIGHTLY brush the bread slices on both sides with oil. Place on a baking sheet and bake until golden brown and crisp, about 25 minutes.

QUICKLY rinse the fish under cold running water, pat dry with paper toweling, and cut into large bite-sized chunks. Set aside.

IN a soup pot or large saucepan, melt the butter with the 2 table-spoons oil over medium-high heat. Add the leek and cook, stirring frequently, until soft but not browned, about 5 minutes. Add the garlic and saffron and cook for about 1 minute longer. Stir in the tomato, stock, and salt and pepper to taste. Bring to a boil, then reduce the heat to achieve a simmer. Add the fish and cook until the fish is just opaque when cut into at the thickest part with a small, sharp knife, about 10 minutes, or until done to preference.

TO serve, ladle the hot soup into warmed bowls, add 1 or 2 slice(s) of toasted bread and dollops of Provençal Red Garlic Sauce to each bowl, and sprinkle with parsley.

Makes 8 servings.

CAMBODIAN RED CHICKEN
SOUP WITH PINEAPPLE

My initial taste of this exotic concoction was love at first slurp.

IF using Tamarind Liquid, prepare as directed and set aside. If using tamarind paste, reserve for later use.

QUICKLY rinse the chicken under cold running water and pat dry with paper toweling. Cut into bite-sized pieces and set aside.

IN a soup pot or large saucepan, combine the stock or broth and coconut milk and place over medium-high heat. Bring to a boil, then reduce the heat to achieve a simmer. Stir the curry paste into the simmering liquid until well blended. Add the tamarind liquid or paste, pineapple, fish sauce, sugar, and fresh and ground chile. Simmer for about 4 minutes. Add the chicken and simmer just until the chicken turns opaque throughout, about 5 minutes; to check for doneness, cut into a piece with a small, sharp knife. Do not allow the soup to boil or the chicken will be overcooked and tough. Stir in salt to taste.

TO serve, stir the mint into the hot soup and ladle into warmed bowls.

Makes 4 servings.

Tamarind Liquid (page 561), or 2 tablespoons tamarind paste

2 boned and skinned chicken breast
halves

2 cups White Stock (page 578) made
with chicken or canned reduced-
sodium chicken broth

2 cups Fresh Coconut Milk (page 562)
or high-quality commercial coconut
milk

2 tablespoons Thai Red Curry Paste
(page 557) or canned Thai red curry
paste, or to taste

1½ cups coarsely chopped fresh or
drained canned pineapple

1 tablespoon fish sauce, preferably Thai
or Vietnamese

2 teaspoons palm sugar

1 teaspoon minced fresh red Thai bird
or other hot chile, or to taste

1 teaspoon ground cayenne or other
dried hot chile, or to taste

Salt

½ cup small fresh mint leaves or
shredded fresh mint

THAI COCONUT CHICKEN SOUP ~ *Tom Kha Gai* ~

1 tablespoon canola or other high-quality vegetable oil, if using fresh mushrooms

6 ounces fresh meaty mushrooms such as shiitake or portobello, sliced or cut into pieces of equal size, or 1 cup drained canned whole straw mushrooms, or a combination of fresh mushrooms and canned straw mushrooms

4 cups Fresh Coconut Milk (page 562) or high-quality commercial coconut milk

2 cups White Stock (page 578) made with chicken or canned reduced-sodium chicken broth

3 tablespoons minced fresh galanga or ginger

2 tablespoons minced fresh lemongrass, tender bulb portion only

2 teaspoons minced fresh Thai bird or other hot chile, or to taste

1 tablespoon slivered fresh or thawed frozen kaffir lime leaves

$\frac{1}{8}$ teaspoon black or white peppercorns

2 boned and skinned chicken breast halves

3 tablespoons fish sauce, preferably Thai or Vietnamese, or more if needed

1 tablespoon freshly squeezed lime juice, or more if needed

1½ teaspoons palm sugar, or more if needed

2 tablespoons finely chopped green onion, including green tops

This fragrant blend of chicken, coconut milk, and exotic seasonings is my favorite Southeast Asian soup. For my vegetarian friends, I created the variation that follows, which captures much of the essence of the Thai original.

Straw mushrooms, imported canned or dried from China and Southeast Asia, have rounded, elongated heads and a delicate flavor.

IF using fresh mushrooms, place a wok, saute pan, or skillet over high heat. When the pan is hot, add the oil and swirl to coat the pan. When the oil is hot but not yet smoking, add the mushrooms and stir-fry for 1 minute. Reduce the heat to medium and stir-fry until the mushrooms are tender, 3 to 5 minutes longer. Remove from the heat and set aside. If using canned straw mushrooms, set aside.

IN a soup pot or large saucepan, combine the coconut milk, stock or broth, galanga or ginger, lemongrass, chile, lime leaves, and peppercorns. Place over medium-high heat and bring to a boil. Reduce the heat to achieve a simmer and simmer, uncovered, for 10 minutes.

QUICKLY rinse the chicken under cold running water, pat dry with paper toweling, and slice into bite-sized pieces. Add the chicken to the simmering soup and continue to simmer just until the chicken turns opaque throughout, about 5 minutes; to check for doneness, cut into a piece with a small, sharp knife. Do not allow the soup to boil or the chicken will be overcooked and tough.

STIR the reserved mushrooms, fish sauce, lime juice, and sugar into the simmering soup and simmer until heated through, about 3 minutes longer. Remove from the heat, taste, and adjust with fish sauce, sugar, and/or lime juice to achieve a good balance of salty, sweet, and sour.

TO serve, ladle the hot soup into warmed bowls and sprinkle with
the green onion.

Makes 6 servings.

VARIATION

Mushroom Coconut Soup (*Tom Yam Hed Ga-Ti*). Increase
the mushroom quantity to 12 ounces fresh or 2 cups canned.
If using fresh mushrooms, increase the amount of oil to
2 tablespoons. Use Vegetable Stock (page 580) or canned
broth in place of the chicken stock or broth. Omit the chicken
breasts. Simmer the soup for 15 minutes before adding the
mushrooms and remaining ingredients; substitute soy sauce
for the fish sauce, if desired.

INDONESIAN SPICY CHICKEN SOUP ~ *SOTO AYAM* ~

1 chicken (about 4 pounds), cut up

2 quarts White Stock (page 578) made with chicken or canned reduced- sodium chicken broth

1 large yellow onion, quartered

3 fresh lemongrass stalks, coarsely chopped

¼ cup sliced fresh galanga or ginger

2 cinnamon sticks

1 teaspoon cardamom seed (not whole pods)

½ teaspoon black peppercorns

Salt

SEASONING PASTE *(BUMBU)*

1 cup coarsely chopped shallot

1 tablespoon coarsely chopped fresh galanga or ginger

½ teaspoon firm dried shrimp paste (Indonesian *trasi* or Malaysian *blachan*)

2 teaspoons coriander seed

2 teaspoons fennel seed

1½ teaspoons cumin seed

This flavorful meal-in-a-bowl originated in Java but is now served throughout Indonesia, as well as in Malaysia. Rice noodles, prepared as directed in the recipe for Vietnamese Beef Soup with Noodles (page 118), may be substituted for the mung bean noodles.

QUICKLY rinse the chicken under cold running water and pat dry with paper toweling.

IN a soup pot or large saucepan, combine the stock or broth, dark meat chicken pieces (reserve the breast for later use), yellow onion, lemongrass, sliced galanga or ginger, cinnamon, cardamom seed, and peppercorns. Bring to a boil over medium-high heat, then reduce the heat to achieve a simmer, cover, and simmer for 25 minutes.

ADD the chicken breast to the soup and simmer, covered, until the breast just turns opaque, 15 to 20 minutes longer.

REMOVE the chicken pieces from the stock and set aside to cool. Remove the stock from the heat and let cool for a few minutes.

LINE a colander or strainer with several layers of dampened cheesecloth and place in a large bowl set in a larger bowl filled with ice. Pour the stock through the colander or strainer into the bowl, pressing against the onion to release all the liquid; there should be about 2 quarts. Discard the strained solids. Season the stock with salt to taste and stir occasionally until cold.

MEANWHILE, as soon as the chicken is cool enough to handle, pull off and discard the skin and bones. Cut the meat into bite-sized pieces, cover, and refrigerate for later use. Cover the cooled stock and refrigerate until well chilled.

TO make the Seasoning Paste, in a food processor or heavy mortar with a pestle, combine the shallot, chopped galanga or ginger, shrimp paste, and coriander, fennel, and cumin seed. Grind to a thick paste, adding about 1 tablespoon water if needed to facilitate blending.

PLACE a wok, saute pan, or heavy skillet over medium heat. When the pan is hot, add the oil and swirl to coat the pan. When the oil is hot, add the Seasoning Paste and cook, stirring constantly, until the mixture is very fragrant and darker and the oil begins to separate from the paste, about 8 minutes. Remove from the heat and drain off and discard excess oil.

REMOVE any fat that has solidified on the surface of the chilled stock. Transfer the stock to a soup pot or large saucepan, place over medium-high heat, and bring to a boil, then reduce the heat to achieve a simmer. Add a little of the hot stock to the cooked paste and blend well, then stir the mixture into the stock. Stir in 1 tablespoon sugar and the salt, cover, and simmer while you prepare the remaining ingredients. (At this point, the soup can be cooled completely, then covered and refrigerated for up to 2 days. Slowly reheat before proceeding.)

PLACE the noodles in a bowl, cover with hot water, and let stand until softened but still firm to the bite, about 10 minutes, then drain. Using kitchen scissors, cut into short lengths and set aside.

PREPARE and arrange as many of the additions and seasonings as you wish in bowls and/or on a large platter and place on the table, or divide among individual serving trays.

STIR the chicken and noodles into the simmering stock and heat through, about 5 minutes. Taste and add more sugar and salt if needed.

TO serve, ladle the hot soup into warmed bowls. Diners select additions and seasonings to add to their bowls to taste.

Makes 6 servings.

¼ cup canola or other high-quality vegetable oil

1 tablespoon palm sugar, or more if needed

1 teaspoon salt, or to taste

4 ounces mung bean noodles

ADDITIONS AND SEASONINGS

Indonesian red chile sauce *(sambal ulek)* or other Asian chile sauce

Indonesian spiced chile sauce *(sambal bajak)*

Sliced green onion, including green tops

Mung bean sprouts

Chopped fresh celery leaves, preferably Chinese variety (Indonesian *seledri*)

Chopped fresh red or green hot chile

Crumbled potato chips

Diced boiled new potato

Chopped or sliced hard-cooked egg or chopped egg yolk

SICHUAN HOT AND SOUR SOUP
~ *SUAN-LA TANG* ~

8 ounces boneless lean pork

1 teaspoon cornstarch

2 tablespoons soy sauce

1 teaspoon Chinese rice wine
(*Shaoxing*) or dry sherry

1 teaspoon minced fresh ginger

1½ teaspoons Asian sesame oil

20 dried lily buds

¼ cup small cloud ears (dried black
fungus)

6 medium-sized fresh shiitake or
dried Chinese black mushrooms

6 cups White Stock, Asian-Style
Variation (page 579), or canned
reduced-sodium chicken broth

½ cup slivered canned bamboo
shoots

½ pound drained firm tofu, cut into
bite-sized cubes

3 tablespoons cornstarch dissolved
in ¼ cup water

½ cup unseasoned rice vinegar,
or more if needed

2 teaspoons freshly ground Sichuan
or black pepper, or to taste

1 egg, lightly beaten

About 2 tablespoons thinly sliced
green onion, including green tops

Salt

Unseasoned rice vinegar for serving

Asian chile sauce for serving

Don't skimp on the pepper or vinegar, as the soup should be both very hot and very tart. Although the components can be readied earlier, cook the soup shortly before serving.

QUICKLY rinse the pork under cold running water, then pat dry with paper toweling. Slice the pork across the grain into ¼-inch-thick slices. Cut each slice lengthwise into ¼-inch-wide slivers, then cut the slivers crosswise into 1½-inch lengths. Set aside.

IN a bowl, combine the 1 teaspoon cornstarch, soy sauce, wine or sherry, ginger, and ½ teaspoon of the sesame oil and mix well. Add the pork and stir to coat evenly with the marinade. Cover and let stand at room temperature for about 25 minutes.

IN separate bowls, cover the lily buds, cloud ears, and dried mushrooms (if using) with water and soak until softened, about 30 minutes. Drain and rinse well. Cut off and discard the hard stem ends from the lily buds, the stems from the mushrooms, and any hard sections from the cloud ears. Slice the lily buds in half lengthwise and thinly slice the mushrooms and cloud ears. If using fresh mushrooms, discard the stems and thinly slice. Set aside.

IN a soup pot or large saucepan, bring the stock or broth to a simmer over medium-high heat. Add the marinated pork, adjust the heat to achieve a simmer, and simmer, uncovered, for 5 minutes. Skim off any foam that rises to the top.

ADD the lily buds, cloud ears, mushrooms, bamboo shoots, and tofu. Cover and simmer for about 2 minutes longer.

ADD the dissolved cornstarch to the simmering soup and stir until slightly thickened, about 30 seconds. Add ½ cup vinegar and the pepper and simmer for about 30 seconds longer. Remove from the heat and slowly pour in the egg, stirring gently to distribute. Stir in the remaining 1 teaspoon sesame oil and the green onion. Taste and add more vinegar, salt, and pepper if needed.

TO serve, ladle the hot soup into warmed bowls. Offer vinegar and chile sauce for diners to add to taste to their portions.

Makes 6 servings.

APPLEFEST SOUP

This soup was created to take to an Applefest picnic, once a charming annual event at the Strybing Arboretum in Golden Gate Park. Like most soups, it is best made ahead and gently reheated before serving.

Choose flavorful, not-too-tart apple varieties such as Golden Delicious, Gravenstein, or McIntosh.

IN a heavy soup pot or large saucepan, heat the oil over medium heat. Add the onion and toss well to coat with the oil. Cover, reduce the heat to medium-low, and cook, stirring occasionally, until the onion just begins to color, about 30 minutes.

REMOVE the cover, increase the heat to medium, and cook, stirring occasionally, until the onion is almost caramelized, about 25 minutes.

STIR the garlic, apple, juniper berries, cinnamon, cloves, and ham into the onion and cook, stirring frequently, for about 1 minute. Add the ham bone (if using), mustard, stock or broth, and cider. Increase the heat to medium-high and bring to a boil, then reduce the heat to achieve a simmer, cover partially, and simmer until the apples are very tender, about 35 minutes. Season to taste with salt and pepper. (At this point, the soup can be cooled completely, then covered and refrigerated for up to 2 days. Slowly reheat before serving.)

TO serve, ladle the hot soup into warmed bowls and top with dollops of yogurt or crème fraîche.

Makes 6 servings.

3 tablespoons olive oil

2 cups chopped yellow onion

1 teaspoon minced garlic

4 cups peeled, cored, and sliced apple (see recipe introduction)

½ teaspoon juniper berries, crushed

½ teaspoon ground cinnamon

¼ teaspoon ground cloves

2 cups chopped flavorful baked ham (about 8 ounces)

1 ham bone (optional)

1 tablespoon sweet-and-hot mustard

4 cups Brown Stock (page 576), White Stock (page 578), or canned broth

4 cups apple cider

Salt

Freshly ground black pepper

Plain yogurt, Crème Fraîche (page 591), or commercial crème fraîche

LOUISIANA GUMBO

½ cup canola or other high-quality
    vegetable oil

½ cup all-purpose flour

1½ cups chopped yellow onion

1½ cups chopped celery

½ cup chopped green sweet pepper

½ cup chopped fresh flat-leaf
    parsley

1 teaspoon minced garlic

2 tablespoons canola or other high-
    quality vegetable oil, if using okra

8 ounces fresh or thawed frozen okra,
    stemmed and sliced (optional)

7 cups Brown Stock (page 576), White
    Stock (page 578), or canned broth

¼ cup Worcestershire sauce

¼ cup catsup

¼ teaspoon Louisiana hot sauce,
    or to taste

1 cup peeled, seeded, drained, and
    chopped ripe or canned tomato

2 teaspoons salt, or to taste

8 ounces flavorful baked ham, cut
    into small cubes

1 bay leaf

1½ teaspoons minced fresh thyme, or
    ½ teaspoon crumbled dried thyme

1½ teaspoons minced fresh
    rosemary, or ½ teaspoon crumbled
    dried rosemary

¼ teaspoon crushed dried hot chile,
    or to taste

This is one of my all-time favorite gumbo recipes, which was given to me by Ruth Dosher, one of the best cooks in my hometown of Jonesville, Louisiana. Since making the dark roux is time-consuming, I always double the recipe so there will be plenty of gumbo for several days or for a party.

Most Louisiana cooks add either okra or filé (ground dried sassafras leaves) to their gumbo, but never in combination. Filé can be found in gourmet groceries and many supermarkets.

IN a heavy soup pot or large saucepan, heat the ½ cup oil over medium-low heat. Whisk in the flour. Stir frequently for 20 minutes, then stir constantly until the roux is very dark brown, about 25 minutes longer; do not allow to burn.

ADD the onion, celery, sweet pepper, parsley, and garlic and cook, stirring frequently, until the vegetables are very soft, about 45 minutes.

MEANWHILE, if using okra, in a saute pan or skillet, heat the 2 tablespoons oil over medium heat. Add the okra and cook, stirring frequently, until tender, about 15 minutes. Transfer the okra to the roux mixture.

ADD the stock or broth, Worcestershire sauce, catsup, hot sauce, tomato, salt, ham, bay leaf, thyme, rosemary, and chile to the roux mixture. Increase the heat to medium-high and bring to a boil, then reduce the heat to achieve a simmer, cover, and simmer for 3 to 4 hours, stirring occasionally. (At this point, the soup can be cooled completely, then covered and refrigerated for up to 2 days. Slowly reheat before proceeding.)

ABOUT 30 minutes before serving, cook the rice as directed on page 364 and keep warm.

ABOUT 20 minutes before serving, add the chicken, crab, and shrimp to the simmering soup; stir occasionally. About 10 minutes before serving, stir in the oysters and their liquor (if using), the sugar, and lemon juice. Taste and adjust the seasonings. If you have not used okra, remove the pot from the heat and stir in the filé.

TO serve, ladle the hot soup into warmed bowls, add a scoop of rice, and sprinkle with parsley and/or green onion.

Makes 6 servings.

2 cups long-grain white rice

1 cup shredded cooked chicken

1 pound cooked crabmeat

1½ pounds cooked shrimp, peeled and deveined

12 small oysters, freshly shucked, with liquor, or 8 ounces jarred oysters with liquor (optional)

1 tablespoon brown sugar, or to taste

2 tablespoons freshly squeezed lemon juice, or to taste

1½ teaspoons filé, if not using okra

Minced fresh flat-leaf parsley and/or chopped green onion, including green tops, for garnish

VIETNAMESE BEEF SOUP WITH NOODLES ~ *PHO BO* ~

STOCK

6 pounds beef bones with some meat
   attached, such as ribs or shank

1 pound boneless beef chuck, in one
   piece

2 yellow onions, unpeeled, sliced

1 piece fresh ginger, about 3 inches
   long, thinly sliced

1 cinnamon stick

5 whole star anise pods

1 teaspoon black peppercorns

Salt or fish sauce, preferably Thai or
   Vietnamese

10 ounces boneless sirloin or other
   tender beef, trimmed of all excess
   fat and connective tissue

9 ounces dried rice noodles, about
   ⅛ inch wide

10 ounces mung bean sprouts

In Vietnam this hearty soup is a favorite breakfast treat, but it may be enjoyed at any time of the day. Both in Vietnam and in Vietnamese communities in America, entire restaurants are devoted to this singular fare.

Eight-pointed star anise pods hold tiny seeds that impart their distinct flavor to the soup.

TO make the stock, quickly rinse the bones under cold running water. In a large soup pot, combine the bones with water to cover. Place over medium heat, bring to a boil, and cook for 10 minutes. Drain. Add fresh cold water to cover by about 2 inches and return to a boil. Using a slotted utensil or wire skimmer, remove any foamy scum that rises to the surface. Continue cooking until the foaming stops, about 15 minutes.

QUICKLY rinse the chuck under cold running water and add to the stock. Stir in the onion slices, ginger, cinnamon stick, star anise, and peppercorns and reduce the heat so that the mixture barely simmers. Cover and simmer until the chuck is tender but not falling apart, 1½ to 2 hours. Remove the chuck and set aside to cool, then cover and refrigerate for later use. Season the stock lightly with salt or fish sauce and continue to simmer until the stock is well flavored, 6 to 8 hours longer.

WHEN the stock is ready, remove from the heat and let cool for a few minutes. Line a colander or strainer with several layers of dampened cheesecloth and place in a large bowl set in a larger bowl filled with ice. Pour the stock through the colander or strainer into the bowl, pressing against the onions and meat to release all the liquid; there should be about 3 quarts. Discard the strained solids. Season the stock to taste with salt or fish sauce and stir occasionally until cold, then cover and refrigerate until well chilled. When the stock is well chilled, remove any fat that has solidified on the surface. (At this point, the soup can be covered and refrigerated for up to 2 days.)

ABOUT 2 hours before serving, quickly rinse the raw beef under cold running water and pat dry with paper toweling. To facilitate slicing, wrap the beef in freezer wrap or plastic wrap and place in a freezer until very cold but not frozen hard, about 2 hours.

PLACE the noodles in a bowl, add hot water to cover, and let stand, stirring occasionally, until softened but still firm to the bite, about 20 minutes. Drain in a colander set in a sink and rinse thoroughly under cold running water to remove surface starch. Return the noodles to the bowl, cover with cold water to keep them from clumping together, and set aside.

SLICE the cooked chuck and the chilled raw beef across the grain as thinly as possible. Place the chuck, raw beef, and bean sprouts in separate bowls and set aside.

TRANSFER the stock to a soup pot or large saucepan, place over medium-high heat, and bring to a boil, then reduce the heat to low, cover, and keep warm while you prepare the additions and seasonings.

ARRANGE as many of the additions and seasonings as you wish in bowls and/or on a large platter and place on the table, or divide among individual serving trays.

TO serve, drain the noodles and divide them evenly among large warmed bowls. Distribute equal portions of the chuck, raw beef, and bean sprouts over the noodles and ladle the hot stock over the ingredients; it will quickly cook the raw beef slices. Diners select additions and seasonings to add to their bowls to taste.

Makes 6 to 8 servings.

VARIATION

Vietnamese Chicken Soup with Noodles (*Pho Ga*). Substitute 6 pounds bony chicken pieces for the beef bones when making the stock. Poach a whole chicken in place of the chuck, removing it from the stock as soon as it is very tender. Shred the cooled chicken and add the meat when reheating the stock for serving. Omit the raw beef.

ADDITIONS AND SEASONINGS

3 ripe tomatoes, cut in half lengthwise, then sliced

6 green onions, including green tops, thinly sliced

1 red or yellow onion, very thinly sliced, then cut into half rings

3 or 4 fresh Thai bird or other hot chiles, thinly sliced or chopped

1 cup fresh cilantro (coriander) leaves

1 cup fresh mint leaves or sprigs

1 cup fresh Asian basil leaves or sprigs

Fish sauce, preferably Thai or Vietnamese

Vietnamese red chile sauce (*tuong ot*), Vietnamese chile-garlic sauce (*tuong ot toi*), or other Asian chile or chile-garlic sauce

Lime or lemon wedges

Salads

A SALAD can appear at any time during a meal. Here are some that seem appropriate as American-style starters, yet are just as good alongside or after the main course.

Check pages 376–385 for salads that are best as side dishes and pages 283–299 for heartier main-dish salads.

CAESAR SALAD

Since its inception in a Tijuana restaurant, this Mexican classic has never gone completely out of favor. Like chef Caesar, I prefer to serve the lettuce leaves whole, to be picked up with the fingertips for nibbling. Tradition dictates mixing the dressing in a wooden salad bowl and then adding the lettuce, but I like to make the dressing separately in order to have more control over the amount that ends up tossed with the greens.

Eggs may contain dangerous bacteria that are only killed once the egg and yolk are firmly set. If you prefer not to use the traditional coddled eggs, a touch of cream or mayonnaise will add the richness normally provided by the yolks.

WASH the lettuce leaves under cold running water. Place in a salad spinner and spin to remove as much water as possible. Pat dry with paper toweling. Wrap in a cloth kitchen towel or paper toweling and refrigerate for at least 30 minutes to crisp, or place the wrapped leaves in a plastic bag and refrigerate for up to several hours.

PREPARE the Garlic Croutons as directed and set aside.

JUST before serving the salad, prepare the dressing. Bring a small pot of water to a rapid boil over high heat. Place the eggs, one at a time, on a spoon, lower them into the boiling water, and boil for 1 minute. Transfer the eggs to a bowl of cold water to cool. Break the eggs, separating the yolks into a small bowl; discard the whites. Add the anchovies, garlic, mustard, oil, and 1½ tablespoons lemon juice to the yolks and whisk to blend. Whisk in the salt and pepper. Taste and add more lemon juice if needed.

IN a large bowl, combine the whole lettuce leaves, about half of the croutons, and half of the cheese. Add the dressing to taste and toss well.

TO serve, immediately arrange the salad on a serving platter or chilled plates. Sprinkle with the remaining croutons and cheese and serve immediately. Pass a pepper mill at the table.

Makes 4 servings.

---

2 medium-sized heads romaine lettuce, tough outer leaves discarded, separated into about 24 leaves

2 cups Garlic Croutons (page 555)

CAESAR DRESSING

2 eggs

3 flat anchovy fillets, rinsed, patted dry, and minced

1½ teaspoons minced garlic

1 teaspoon Dijon mustard

½ cup extra-virgin olive oil

1½ tablespoons freshly squeezed lemon juice, or more if needed

¼ teaspoon salt, or to taste

½ teaspoon freshly ground black pepper, or to taste

¼ cup freshly grated or shaved Parmesan cheese (about 1 ounce), preferably Parmigiano-Reggiano

Freshly ground black pepper for serving

FRUIT, NUTS, AND GREENS SALAD

About 8 cups small whole or torn
tender young salad greens, one
kind or a combination

Sweet Crunchy Nuts (page 42), or
1 cup pecans, walnuts, or other nuts

Berry Vinaigrette (page 565)

3 medium-sized apples or pears

About 2 tablespoons freshly squeezed
lemon juice

1 cup berries (same kind as used in
vinaigrette)

The pairing of crisp greens with sliced fruit sprinkled with toasted nuts is a new American classic with many variations. I like to serve a combination of watercress, toasted hazelnuts (filberts), apples, and cranberries on a Thanksgiving dinner menu. As an elegant autumn opener or main course, combine julienned apples and shredded Belgian endives, top with smoked or grilled quail, sprinkle with fresh pomegranate seeds and toasted macadamia nuts, and drizzle with Basic Vinaigrette (page 564).

On Christmas Eve, I traditionally choose blueberries or raspberries and sweet crunchy pecans for the salad and top individual servings with shredded smoked chicken, a few thin slivers of red onion, and a little triple-crème blue cheese.

Pears, walnuts, and Belgian endives, a popular restaurant combination, are frequently teamed with chunks of blue cheese and tossed in Walnut Vinaigrette (page 567). For an offbeat trio, mix spinach, sliced bananas, and cashews in Creamy Vinaigrette (page 565) made with canned evaporated milk.

WASH the greens under cold running water. Place in a salad spinner and spin to remove as much water as possible. Pat dry with paper toweling. Wrap in a cloth kitchen towel or paper toweling and refrigerate for at least 30 minutes to crisp, or place the wrapped greens in a plastic bag and refrigerate for up to several hours.

IF using the Sweet Crunchy Nuts, prepare as directed, then coarsely chop and set aside.

IF using plain nuts, toast as directed on page 554. Chop coarsely and set aside.

PREPARE the Berry Vinaigrette as directed and set aside.

JUST before serving, quarter the apples or pears lengthwise and core them. Thinly slice the quarters and transfer to a bowl. Add the lemon juice and stir well to keep the fruit from discoloring.

IN a salad bowl, combine the greens, nuts, apple or pear slices, and berries. Pour the vinaigrette to taste over the salad and toss thoroughly. Serve immediately on chilled plates.

Makes 6 to 8 servings.

ITALIAN BREAD AND TOMATO SALAD ~ *Panzanella* ~

10 ounces stale Italian bread,
   sliced about ¾ inch thick

3 to 4 cups chopped ripe tomato,
   peeled and seeded if desired

1 cup minced red onion

1 teaspoon minced garlic

½ cup extra-virgin olive oil

3 tablespoons red wine vinegar,
   or to taste

Salt

Freshly ground black pepper

1 cup packed fresh basil leaves,
   torn if large

Fresh basil sprigs for garnish

Almost nothing is wasted in the Italian kitchen, and here is a wonderful use of stale bread, usually eaten as an antipasto or as a first course. Be sure to choose hearty, coarse-grained or whole-grain bread, not soft types that will turn mushy and fall apart when soaked. Seeded or herbed bread adds a nice touch.

Some Italian cooks toss in chopped cucumber, sweet peppers, celery, anchovy fillets, hard-cooked eggs, grated Parmesan cheese, or other favorite salad components. The addition of cooked beans, fish, poultry, or meats or of drained canned tuna turns the simple salad into a complete meal. No matter what else you choose to add, flavorful vine-ripened tomatoes are absolutely essential; don't ever use those hard red things that are available all year from most supermarkets!

IN a large bowl, combine the bread with enough cold water to cover. Set aside for about 20 minutes.

DRAIN off the water from the bread. Using your hands, squeeze out as much water as possible from the soaked bread and crumble it into a bowl. Add the tomato, onion, and garlic and toss to mix well. Pour the olive oil over the salad, sprinkle with the vinegar and salt and pepper to taste, and toss thoroughly. (At this point, the salad may be covered and refrigerated for up to 2 hours; return to room temperature before proceeding.)

TO serve, add the basil leaves and toss to mix well. Transfer to a serving bowl or platter and garnish with basil sprigs.

Makes 8 servings.

VARIATIONS

FOR toasted bread salad, cut the bread slices into 1-inch cubes, arrange them in a single layer on a baking sheet, and toast in a 300° F oven, stirring frequently, until golden, about 15 minutes. Remove the bread cubes from the oven and let them cool to room temperature. Do not soak the bread in water. Toss the toasted bread with about 5 cups mixed tender salad greens (washed, dried, and chilled as directed for Fruit, Nuts, and Greens Salad on page 122) and the tomato and other remaining ingredients and serve immediately; do not chill.

FOR *pane a caponata*, combine the toasted bread with the tomatoes and about 2 cups chopped assorted pickled vegetables.

BURMESE GINGER SALAD
~ GHIN THOKE ~

½ cup dried yellow split peas

½ cup dried fava beans

Canola or other high-quality vegetable
oil for frying

½ cup unsalted dry-roasted peanuts

2 tablespoons freshly squeezed lime
juice

1 tablespoon juice from Pickled
Ginger (page 406) or high-quality
commercial pickled ginger

2 teaspoons fish sauce, preferably
Thai or Vietnamese

4 teaspoons minced Pickled Garlic
(page 405), or 2 teaspoons minced
fresh garlic

Salt

1½ cups finely shredded green
cabbage

½ cup finely shredded purple
cabbage

¼ cup minced Pickled Ginger (page
406) or high-quality commercial
pickled ginger

¼ cup minced fresh ginger

¼ cup minced shallot

¼ cup minced red sweet pepper
mixed with 2 teaspoons minced
fresh red or green Thai bird or
other hot chile, or to taste

Lime wedges for serving

I use a combination of fresh and sweet pickled ginger in this "salad" from Myanmar (formerly Burma), where it is traditionally enjoyed as a dessert or snack. Most Westerners, however, will prefer to eat it as an appetizer salad or accompaniment.

If you wish, use 1 cup dried yellow split peas or fava beans instead of the combination given. Packaged fried fava beans and split peas, sold in Asian markets, can be used in place of the home-fried ones. Optional additions include about ¼ cup toasted shredded coconut and/or toasted sesame seed and about the same amount of crisply fried shallot.

PLACE the split peas in a saucepan and the fava beans in a second pan. Add enough water to each pan to cover the legumes by about 1 inch. Place over medium heat and bring to a boil, then reduce the heat to achieve a simmer. Simmer the split peas until barely tender, 10 to 15 minutes, then drain and set aside. Simmer the fava beans until the skins soften enough to be peeled off, about 20 minutes. Using a slotted utensil, remove the beans and reserve the water in the pan. Using your thumbnail, peel off and discard the skins. Return the peeled beans to the water, adjust the heat to achieve a simmer, and simmer, uncovered, until the beans are plumped and barely tender, 15 to 20 minutes longer, then drain and set aside.

IN a wok, deep fryer, or saucepan, pour in oil to a depth of 1 inch and heat to 350° F. Carefully add the split peas to the hot oil and fry until golden brown and crisp, 3 to 4 minutes. Using a slotted utensil, transfer the peas to paper toweling to drain well. Return the oil to 350° F, add the fava beans, and fry until golden brown and crisp, 4 to 5 minutes. Drain on paper toweling. Fry and drain the peanuts in the same way; they should cook in 2 to 3 minutes. Set aside.

IN a bowl, combine the lime juice, ginger juice, fish sauce, garlic, and salt to taste; mix well. Set aside.

A FEW minutes before serving, combine the green and purple cabbages and mound in the center of a serving plate. Arrange the fried peas and beans and peanuts, pickled and fresh ginger, shallot, and sweet pepper-chile mixture in separate mounds around the cabbage. Pour the lime dressing over the top.

AT the table, toss the ingredients together to combine well before serving. Offer lime wedges for squeezing over individual portions.

Makes 8 servings.

GREEN PAPAYA SALAD

2 tablespoons sesame seed

¼ cup freshly squeezed lime juice

3 tablespoons fish sauce, preferably Thai or Vietnamese

2 teaspoons palm sugar

1 tablespoon minced garlic

1 tablespoon minced fresh Thai bird or other hot chile, or to taste

3 cups peeled, seeded, and shredded green (unripe) papaya

½ cup peeled and shredded carrot

½ cup thinly slivered red sweet pepper

¼ cup coarsely chopped fresh mint

¼ cup coarsely chopped fresh cilantro (coriander)

3 tablespoons minced green onion, including green tops

½ cup peeled, seeded, drained, and chopped ripe tomato

1 tablespoon dried shrimp powder or finely ground dried shrimp (ground in a spice grinder, blender, or mortar with a pestle)

2 tablespoons coarsely chopped unsalted dry-roasted peanuts

Fresh mint sprigs for garnish

Throughout tropical Asia, unripe papaya is eaten as a vegetable, and one of the most popular uses is in salads such as Vietnamese goi du du, *Thai* som tum, *or Burmese* thinnbawthee thoke, *all inspirations for my version. Most Americans can locate firm green papayas in Asian and Latin American markets.*

For a heartier dish, toss about 1 cup cooked small shrimp or shredded cooked chicken, beef, or pork into the mixture along with the tomato and other final ingredients.

TOAST the sesame seed as directed on page 553 and set aside.

IN a large bowl, combine the lime juice, fish sauce, and sugar and stir to dissolve the sugar. Stir in the garlic and chile until well mixed. Add the papaya, carrot, sweet pepper, mint, cilantro, and green onion. Using your hands, gently squeeze the mixture to release the flavors and soften the vegetables. Add the tomato, shrimp powder or ground shrimp, peanuts, and toasted sesame seed and toss to mix well.

TO serve, mound the salad on a serving plate or on chilled plates and garnish with mint sprigs

Makes 4 servings.

SESAME EGGPLANT SALAD

This intriguing salad makes a great beginning or addition to an Asian meal.

PLACE a wok, saute pan, or skillet over high heat. When the pan is hot, add the 2 tablespoons canola or other vegetable oil and swirl to coat the pan. When the oil is hot but not yet smoking, add the eggplant and stir-fry for about 1 minute. Add ¼ cup water, or a little more as needed, and continue to stir-fry, moving the pan off and on the heat as necessary to prevent scorching, until the water evaporates and the eggplant is tender when pierced, about 5 minutes. Transfer to a bowl and let cool to room temperature.

TO make the Sesame Dressing, toast the sesame seed as directed on page 553 and pour into a bowl. Add the remaining dressing ingredients and whisk to blend. Pour over the cooled eggplant and toss to coat well.

TO serve, mound the eggplant on a serving plate and sprinkle with the green onion.

Makes 4 to 6 servings.

2 tablespoons canola or other
   high-quality vegetable oil
1½ pounds slender Asian eggplants,
   thinly sliced crosswise into rounds

SESAME DRESSING

2 tablespoons sesame seed
2 tablespoons unseasoned rice
   vinegar
2 tablespoons soy sauce
1 tablespoon Asian sesame oil
1 tablespoon canola or other
   high-quality vegetable oil
1 teaspoon sugar
1 teaspoon minced ginger
½ teaspoon minced garlic
½ teaspoon Asian chile sauce,
   or to taste

3 tablespoons minced or slivered
   green onion, including green tops

MEDITERRANEAN EGGPLANT SALAD

2 heads butter lettuce or other tender
    lettuce, separated into leaves

1 pound globe eggplant

Coarse salt

½ cup pine nuts

Fruity olive oil, preferably extra-virgin,
    for frying, roasting, or grilling

Mustard Vinaigrette (page 566),
    made with Dijon mustard

1 cup crumbled fresh or semidry goat
    cheese (about 4 ounces)

My "sister" and Tahoe neighbor, Kristi Spence, and I created this salad one warm summer night when these ingredients were all we had on hand. It's been a favorite and oft-repeated combination ever since.

WASH the lettuce leaves under cold running water. Place in a salad spinner and spin to remove as much water as possible. Pat dry with paper toweling. Wrap in a cloth kitchen towel or paper toweling and refrigerate for at least 30 minutes to crisp, or place the wrapped leaves in a plastic bag and refrigerate for up to several hours.

PEEL the eggplant and slice crosswise into ¼-inch-thick slices. Sprinkle both sides of each slice with salt. Lay the slices on paper toweling, cover with more paper toweling, top with a cutting board and heavy weights (such as aluminum foil-wrapped bricks or canned foods), and let stand for about 30 minutes to draw out excess moisture.

TOAST the pine nuts as directed on page 553 and set aside.

USING paper toweling, blot excess salt from the eggplant slices.

TO panfry the eggplant, place a wire rack on a baking sheet and position it alongside the stove top. In a saute pan or skillet, pour in oil to cover the bottom of the pan barely. Add the eggplant slices, a few at a time, and cook until tender and lightly browned on both sides, about 10 minutes total; add more oil as needed. Using a slotted utensil, transfer the eggplant to the rack to drain and cool.

TO roast the eggplant, preheat an oven to 400° F. Using a pastry
brush, coat the slices lightly with oil, spread on a baking sheet,
roast in the oven, turning once, until tender, about 15 minutes.
Set aside to cool.

TO grill the eggplant, prepare an open grill for moderate direct-
heat cooking. Using a pastry brush, coat the slices generously
with oil and grill, turning once, until browned and tender,
about
15 minutes. Set aside to cool.

PREPARE the Mustard Vinaigrette as directed and set aside.

TO serve, tear the lettuce leaves into bite-sized pieces and place
in a salad bowl. Cut the cooled eggplant slices into quarters and
add to the lettuce. Add the toasted pine nuts, cheese, and the
vinaigrette to taste, toss well, and serve on chilled plates.

Makes 4 servings.

THAI FIERY GRILLED SHRIMP SALAD ~ *YUM GOONG YAHNG PHET* ~

2 cups mixed young salad greens

1 pound medium-sized or large shrimp in shells

Vegetable oil for brushing grill rack or basket

2 ounces snow peas

1 teaspoon salt

1 teaspoon minced fresh lemongrass, tender bulb portion only

¼ cup chopped fresh cilantro (coriander)

6 tablespoons freshly squeezed lime juice

¼ cup fish sauce, preferably Thai or Vietnamese

2 tablespoons sugar

1 tablespoon Thai Red Curry Paste (page 557) or canned Thai red curry paste

½ cup thinly sliced shallot

2 tablespoons thinly sliced green onion, including green tops

½ cup packed fresh small mint leaves or chopped larger leaves

¼ cup packed fresh Asian basil leaves

Lime slices for garnish

Fresh Asian basil and/or mint sprigs for garnish

Pesticide-free edible flowers such as borage, garlic, or pineapple sage for garnish (optional)

Cool, crisp greens and refreshing mint balance the fiery dressing for the shrimp. I've also enjoyed this salad made with home-smoked shrimp (just follow the manufacturer's directions for your smoker). When you don't wish to fire up a grill or a smoker, the shrimp can be boiled, or they can be stir-fried in a wok with a little vegetable oil.

Avoid using bitter or assertive greens such as endive or radicchio in the salad mix.

WASH the greens under cold running water. Place in a salad spinner and spin to remove as much water as possible. Wrap in a cloth kitchen towel or paper toweling and refrigerate for at least 30 minutes to crisp, or place the wrapped greens in a plastic bag and refrigerate for up to several hours.

PREPARE an open grill for hot direct-heat cooking.

QUICKLY rinse the shrimp under cold running water and pat dry with paper toweling. Set aside.

WHEN the fire is ready, lightly brush the grill rack or a grill basket with oil. Place the shrimp on the rack or in the basket and grill, turning once, until the shells turn bright pink and the meat is just opaque, 4 to 5 minutes in all. Remove from the grill and transfer to a plate to cool.

TRIM the ends and remove any strings from the peas. Bring a small pot of water to a boil over high heat and prepare a bowl of iced water. When the water boils, stir in the salt, drop in the peas, and cook until crisp-tender, 2 to 3 minutes. Quickly drain and transfer to the iced water to halt cooking. Drain again and set aside.

IN a bowl, combine the lemongrass, cilantro, lime juice, fish sauce, sugar, and curry paste. Blend well.

WHEN the shrimp are cool enough to handle, peel and devein. Add them to the fish sauce mixture, along with the shallot, green onion, and snow peas; toss well.

TO serve, line a serving plate with the chilled greens and sprinkle with the mint and basil leaves. Using tongs or a slotted utensil, remove the shrimp and snow peas from the dressing and arrange on the greens. Drizzle the dressing over the greens. Garnish with the lime slices, herb sprigs, and flowers (if using).

Makes 4 servings.

FENNEL AND ORANGE SALAD

3 cups mixed tender bitter greens
   such as radicchio, Belgian endive,
   and frisée

3 oranges

1 fennel bulb

Extra-virgin olive oil

Freshly squeezed lemon juice

Salt

Freshly ground black pepper

The fragrant anise flavor of fennel combines well with bitter greens and sweet oranges in this refreshing salad.

WASH the greens under cold running water. Place in a salad spinner and spin to remove as much water as possible. Pat dry with paper toweling. Wrap in a cloth kitchen towel or paper toweling and refrigerate for at least 30 minutes to crisp, or place the wrapped greens in a plastic bag and refrigerate for up to several hours.

PEEL the oranges, removing all white pith and outer membrane. Slice crosswise and set aside.

TRIM the fennel bulb, thinly slice, and set aside.

JUST before serving, place the crisp greens in a bowl. Drizzle lightly with olive oil and toss to coat. Add lemon juice, salt, and pepper to taste and toss lightly but thoroughly.

TO serve, transfer the greens to a serving platter or distribute among chilled plates. Arrange the fennel and orange slices over the greens. Drizzle the slices with a little olive oil and lemon juice.

Makes 4 servings.

TROPICAL FRUIT SALAD WITH PASSION FRUIT DRESSING

Add or substitute other tropical fruits for those suggested here.

IN a skillet, place the coconut over medium heat and toast, shaking the pan or stirring frequently, until lightly golden and fragrant, about 5 minutes. Pour onto a plate to cool and set aside.

PREPARE the Passion Fruit Dressing as directed and set aside.

IN a large bowl, combine all of the fruits. Add the dressing to taste and toss gently.

TO serve, transfer to a serving platter or arrange on chilled plates, sprinkle with the toasted coconut and macadamia nuts, and garnish with pineapple leaves and flowers (if using).

Makes 6 to 8 servings.

1 cup grated or shredded fresh or packaged sweetened coconut (see page 562)

Passion Fruit Dressing (page 571)

2 mangoes, peeled, pitted, and sliced or cut into bite-sized pieces

2 medium-sized papayas, peeled, seeded, and sliced or cut into bite-sized pieces

1 small pineapple, peeled, cored, and sliced or cut into bite-sized pieces

3 medium-sized bananas, peeled, sliced, and tossed in about 1 tablespoon freshly squeezed lemon juice to prevent discoloring

2 starfruits, sliced

2 or 3 kiwifruits, peeled and sliced

1 cup unsalted roasted macadamia nuts

Leaves from pineapple top for plate garnish (optional)

Pesticide-free, nontoxic tropical flowers such as miniature orchids for garnish (optional)

Noodles, Pasta, Polenta, Risotto & Gnocchi

ASIAN noodles and Italian pasta, as well as other starches traditionally served as first courses, have become indispensable components of the American diet. In Asia, noodles are served as snacks or as one of a galaxy of dishes put out at the same time, while in North America we often enjoy them as a light meal or as a separate course. Many modern Italians and most Americans are happy to serve the traditional first-course pasta or risotto in a larger portion as a satisfying main dish.

BANGKOK FRAGRANT HERB NOODLES ~ *KWAYTIOW PAHT* ~

There's so much flavor packed into this simple dish that meat, although traditional, is unnecessary. If you wish, however, add 1 pound boneless tender pork or beef or boned and skinned chicken, finely chopped, along with the shallot and stir-fry until opaque.

Adjust the amount of chile according to the heat level of the available varieties. Keep in mind, however, that the finished noodles should cause your mouth to smoke.

If you have access to fresh rice noodles, or make your own, cut them from ½ to almost 1 inch wide, typical Thai sizes for stir-frying; they'll require less soaking time than dried noodles and will need to be separated with your fingers while soaking.

IN a bowl, cover the noodles with hot water and let stand, stirring occasionally, until softened but still firm to the bite, 20 to 30 minutes. Drain in a colander set in a sink and rinse thoroughly under cold running water to remove surface starch. Return the noodles to the bowl, cover with cold water to keep them from clumping together, and set aside.

READY the remaining ingredients, except the garnish, and place them alongside the stove top.

PLACE a wok, large saute pan, or large, heavy skillet over medium-high heat. When the pan is hot, add the oil and swirl to coat the pan. When the oil is hot but not yet smoking, add the shallot and stir-fry for about 1 minute. Add the garlic and chile and stir-fry for about 30 seconds longer. Stir in the fish sauce, soy sauce, oyster sauce, sugar, and pepper to taste and cook, stirring frequently, until the mixture thickens, about 5 minutes longer.

DRAIN the noodles, add them to the sauce, and gently stir-fry until tender, 3 to 5 minutes, adding a little more oil if the noodles begin to stick. Add the basil and mint leaves and gently toss the noodles until the leaves wilt, about 1 minute. Remove from the heat.

TO serve, transfer the noodles to a serving platter or warmed plates and garnish with herb sprigs.

Makes 8 first-course or 4 main-course servings.

1 pound dried rice noodles, ⅛ to
   ½ inch wide
¼ cup canola or other high-quality
   vegetable oil, or more if needed
4 cups sliced shallot
3 tablespoons finely chopped garlic
2 tablespoons chopped fresh Thai
   bird or other hot chile, or to taste
¼ cup fish sauce, preferably Thai or
   Vietnamese
¼ cup soy sauce
¼ cup oyster sauce
¼ cup palm sugar
Freshly ground black pepper
2 cups packed fresh Asian basil
   leaves
2 cups packed fresh mint leaves
Fresh Asian basil and/or mint sprigs
   for garnish

THAI NOODLES ~ *PAHT THAI* ~

1 pound dried rice noodles, about ⅛ inch wide

8 ounces boneless lean pork or boned and skinned chicken

8 ounces medium-sized shrimp in shells

¾ cup fish sauce, preferably Thai or Vietnamese

4 teaspoons distilled white vinegar

2 tablespoons palm sugar

4 teaspoons paprika, or ¼ cup catsup or tomato paste

5 tablespoons canola or other high-quality vegetable oil, or more if needed

½ cup sliced shallot

2 tablespoons minced garlic

1 tablespoon minced fresh Thai bird or other hot chile, or to taste

4 eggs, lightly beaten

¼ cup thinly sliced green onion, including green tops

10 ounces mung bean sprouts

½ cup chopped unsalted dry-roasted peanuts

¼ cup chopped fresh cilantro (coriander)

2 tablespoons dried shrimp powder or finely ground dried shrimp (ground in a spice grinder, blender, or mortar with a pestle)

Fresh cilantro (coriander) sprigs for garnish

Lime wedges for serving

If you have access to fresh rice noodles, or make your own, substitute them for the more readily available dried ones; they'll require less soaking time than dried noodles and will need to be separated with your fingers while soaking.

IN a bowl, cover the noodles with hot water and let stand, stirring occasionally, until softened but still firm to the bite, about 20 minutes. Drain in a colander set in a sink and rinse thoroughly under cold running water to remove surface starch. Return the noodles to the bowl, cover with cold water to keep them from clumping together, and set aside.

QUICKLY rinse the pork or chicken under cold running water and pat dry with paper toweling. Cut into very small pieces and place alongside the stove top.

PEEL and devein the shrimp, leaving the tails intact. Quickly rinse under cold running water, pat dry with paper toweling, and place alongside the stove top.

IN a small bowl, combine the fish sauce, vinegar, sugar, and paprika, catsup, or tomato paste and place alongside the stove top.

READY the remaining ingredients, except garnishes, and place them alongside the stove top.

PLACE a wok, large saute pan, or large, heavy skillet over medium-high heat. When the pan is hot, add 2 tablespoons of the oil and swirl to coat the pan. When the oil is hot but not yet smoking, add the shallot and stir-fry for about 1 minute. Add the pork or chicken, garlic, and chile and stir-fry until the meat is opaque throughout, about 1 minute. Transfer to a bowl and set aside.

HEAT 1 tablespoon of the remaining oil in the wok. Add the eggs and cook just until slightly set, then break them up and transfer to the bowl with the pork or chicken. Heat 1 tablespoon of the remaining oil in the wok. Add the shrimp and stir-fry just until they turn pink. Transfer to the bowl with the other stir-fried ingredients.

DRAIN the noodles and place alongside the wok. Heat the remaining 1 tablespoon oil, add the noodles, and gently stir-fry until tender, 3 to 5 minutes, adding a little more oil if the noodles begin to stick. Add the reserved fish sauce mixture and stir-fry to coat the noodles, about 30 seconds. Return the reserved stir-fried ingredients to the pan. Add the green onion, most of the bean sprouts, and ¼ cup of the peanuts and stir-fry until the ingredients are well mixed and the sprouts and onions are crisp-tender, 1 to 2 minutes.

TO serve, transfer the noodles to a serving plate, sprinkle with the chopped cilantro, remaining ¼ cup peanuts, and shrimp powder or ground shrimp. Garnish with the remaining bean sprouts and the cilantro sprigs and place the lime wedges alongside for squeezing over individual portions.

Makes 8 first-course or 4 main-course servings.

FRESH PASTA

About 2 cups all-purpose flour

3 eggs, at room temperature

1 teaspoon olive oil, preferably extra-virgin (optional)

½ teaspoon salt (optional)

All-purpose flour for dusting

All-purpose flour yields the most tender pasta. Semolina flour, sometimes sold as pasta flour, is best left for making commercial dried pasta products.

Italian pasta makers do not traditionally add oil or salt to their dough, but I like the added flavor. Nor do they generally add seasonings or colorings, other than spinach, except in the Piedmont region, where they sometimes add vegetables such as beet or tomato. To achieve these colors and flavors, add about 1 cup vegetable puree along with the eggs. If you wish to be more adventuresome with colors and flavorings, please see James McNair's Pasta Cookbook *for detailed directions.*

TO make pasta dough by hand, shape 2 cups flour into a mound on a smooth work surface. Place your fist in the center of the mound and move it in a circular motion to spread out the flour and form a wide, shallow well in the center. Add the eggs and the oil and salt (if using) to the well. Using a fork or your fingertips, gently break the egg yolks. Using a circular motion of the fork or with your fingertips, draw the flour from the inside wall of the well and gradually incorporate it into the egg mixture. While mixing with one hand, use your free hand to keep the wall of flour intact.

WHEN the eggs are no longer runny, push most of the flour over them, reserving to one side any flour you think will not be necessary. Knead the dough with both hands until it forms a crumbly mass. If the dough feels too sticky, gradually work in more flour. If it is too dry and crumbly, work in a few drops of water at a time until it seems moist enough.

POSITION the dough to one side of the work surface, and scrape off all bits of flour and egg from the work surface with a dough scraper. Wash and dry your hands, then lightly sprinkle them and the work surface with flour. Place the dough in the center of the flour-dusted area and knead by pressing down on it with the heels of your palms. Fold the dough in half over itself, give it a half turn, and repeat this kneading procedure until the dough feels elastic and smooth and doesn't break apart easily when you pull it, 10 to 12 minutes. Knead in additional flour as necessary. Test the dough by inserting your finger into the center. If it comes out dry and clean, the dough has enough flour incorporated; if your finger is moist or has dough attached, more flour is required.

SHAPE the dough into a ball and dust it lightly with flour. Wrap in plastic wrap or cover with an inverted bowl and let stand at room temperature for at least 25 minutes or up to 2 hours to allow it to rest.

TO make pasta dough in a food processor, combine the eggs and the oil and salt (if using) in the bowl and pulse until well mixed. Add 1¾ cups of the flour and run the machine until the dough gathers together into a ball. Add as much remaining flour as necessary to form a dough that doesn't feel too sticky. Transfer to a lightly floured surface and knead by hand as described in the hand method. Form into a ball and let rest as directed.

TO roll out pasta dough by hand, lightly dust a clean, flat work surface with flour. If you wish, divide the dough into sections to make rolling easier; keep extra dough covered while working with one piece at a time. Position the dough in the center of the work surface and flatten it with your hands. Using a very long, cylindrical rolling pin without handles, roll back and forth over the dough, without applying heavy downward pressure, until the dough is about ⅛ inch thick. After each roll, turn the dough a quarter turn to keep it from sticking to the surface. When the dough has been flattened to the correct thickness, begin to curl the dough around the rolling pin. As you pull the dough back and forth with the pin, move your cupped hands along the length of the pin to stretch the dough further in all directions. Work as quickly as possible to keep the dough from drying out, and continue to turn it each time your repeat the rolling and stretching. Dust with flour whenever the dough feels sticky. Roll and stretch until the dough is the desired thickness; avoid rolling too thin or the dough may crack and disintegrate during cooking.

continues ~

TO roll out pasta dough with a hand-cranked pasta machine,
set the machine on its widest opening. Pull off a piece of the
dough about the size of an egg; keep the remaining dough
covered to prevent it from drying out. Feed the piece of dough
through the pasta machine until it is very smooth and elastic,
8 to 10 times. Each time the dough strip comes out, fold it in
half before feeding it into the machine again. If the dough
becomes sticky, dust lightly with flour. Adjust the roller to the
next setting and pass the dough through, this time leaving the
strip unfolded. Roll the dough through the machine 1 or 2
more times at the same opening. Continue feeding the strip of
dough through the rollers, narrowing the opening down one
step every 2 or 3 times to thin out the dough to the desired
degree. Avoid rolling too thinly or the dough may crack and
disintegrate during cooking. Repeat the rolling and thinning
with the remaining dough.

IF the dough will be used for stuffed pasta, cut immediately by
hand as directed in recipes and fill while pliable and still a bit
sticky; it may crack or become too dry to adhere tightly if not
used at once.

IF the dough will be cut into noodles, dust the dough with flour
and let it dry for about 15 minutes for wide noodles or for up
to 25 minutes for thin noodles; turn the dough over several
times during drying. It is ready for cutting when it no longer
sticks to other pieces of dough but is still pliable and soft.

TO cut noodles by hand, position a metal ruler on the flat sheet
of dough and cut the dough into the desired width with a sharp
knife or a plain or fluted rolling pastry wheel; cut to about
⅙ inch wide for tagliarini, ⅛ inch wide for fettuccine, ¼ inch
wide for *tagliatelle*, 1 inch or wider for *pappardelle*. Separate
the noodles and spread them out to dry, preferably on cloth
kitchen towels, for about 15 minutes. Alternatively, roll up the
dough sheet jelly-roll fashion, then flatten the top slightly and
cut with sharp knife across the roll into desired widths. Unroll
and let dry as above.

TO cut noodles with a hand-cranked pasta machine, adjust the blades of the machine to the selected cutting width, then roll each dried strip of pasta through the machine. Hang or spread the noodles out to dry again for about 15 minutes.

Makes about 1 pound for 8 first-course or 4 main-course servings.

MULTICOLORED VARIATION

PREPARE fresh pasta in two or more colors and flavors by adding vegetable purees (see recipe introduction) and/or enough food coloring pastes to achieve desired hues along with the eggs. Using a hand-cranked pasta machine, roll out each pasta into wide strips. Cover the strips of one color and set aside while you cut the other strips into noodles. Do not allow to dry.

USING a pastry brush, coat a strip of wide pasta lightly with water, then overlay it with the colored noodles to form a desired pattern, leaving some space between the noodles for the wide strip to show through. Press the top pasta noodles with your fingertips to seal them to the wide strip. Dust the pasta with flour and roll lightly with a rolling pin to bind the colors together.

SPINACH-STUFFED PASTA PACKAGES WITH CITRUS CREAM

CITRUS CREAM

4 cups heavy (whipping) cream,
light cream, or half-and-half

½ cup freshly squeezed lemon and/or
lime juice

¼ cup grated or minced fresh lemon
and/or lime zest

Salt

Freshly ground white pepper

Roman-Style Spinach (page 315)

All-purpose flour for dusting

Fresh Pasta (page 140), rolled into
sheets, or 1 pound purchased fresh
pasta sheets

1 tablespoon salt

Extra-virgin olive oil or unsalted
butter, melted and cooled slightly,
for brushing

32 whole fresh chives, blanched in
boiling water until tender (optional)

Lemon and lime zest strips for
garnish

Freshly grated Parmesan cheese,
preferably Parmigiano-Reggiano,
for passing

*Here, a Roman-inspired combination of spinach, prosciutto, pine nuts,
and raisins is used as a surprise filling in pasta packets twisted shut at
each end and served atop a luxurious sauce. If you have the time, prepare
sheets of striped pasta as directed in the variation for Fresh Pasta (page
143), using 2 or 3 colors of fresh pasta.*

TO make the Citrus Cream, place the cream or half-and-half in a
saucepan over medium heat and bring to a boil, then stir in
the citrus juice and zest. Cook, whisking almost constantly,
until the mixture is reduced to 2 cups. Season to taste with salt
and pepper. Remove from the heat and immediately place a
piece of plastic wrap directly onto the surface of the sauce to
prevent a skin from forming. Set aside for up to 2 hours.

PREPARE the Roman-Style Spinach as directed and set aside to
cool completely.

LIGHTLY dust a work surface with flour. Cut the pasta into 16
rectangles each about 6 by 4 inches and spread out on the floured
surface. Place about 2 tablespoons of the spinach mixture in the
center of each piece of pasta, then using a pastry brush, coat the
exposed edges of the pasta lightly with water. Beginning with a long
side, roll the pasta up around the filling and twist each end to seal.

IN a large pot, bring 4 quarts water to a rapid boil over high heat, then
stir in the 1 tablespoon salt. Using a slotted utensil, carefully lower
the pasta packages into the water and cook, occasionally stirring
gently, until the pasta is tender but still firm to the bite. Drain and
lightly brush each package with oil or melted butter. Tie the ends
with chives, if desired.

MEANWHILE, reheat the Citrus Cream over low heat, whisking
constantly until smooth.

TO serve, spoon ¼ to ½ cup of the Citrus Cream, depending upon
the number of packages being served, onto each plate. Arrange
2 to 4 packages on each plate. Garnish with citrus zest strips and
serve immediately. Pass the cheese at the table for sprinkling
over individual portions.

Makes 8 first-course or 4 main-course servings.

AVOCADO TOMATO PASTA

This simple dish climaxed one of the most decadent days of my life. On a sultry night in a tropical rainforest garden in Manhattan Beach, California, creative cook Jerry Needle served this pasta after a large group of friends had stomped what seemed like tons of grapes with our bare feet as a prelude to Jerry's wine making. The uncooked sauce that melds with the hot pasta has since become a staple in my summer entertaining.

When vine-ripened tomatoes are not in season, or perfectly ripe avocados are unavailable, please choose another recipe.

IN a large pot, bring 4 quarts water to a rapid boil over high heat, then stir in 1 tablespoon salt. Drop in the pasta and cook, stirring frequently, until tender but still firm to the bite.

MEANWHILE, scoop the avocado pulp into a large bowl. Using a fork, mash the avocado coarsely, leaving a few small chunks. Add the lime or lemon juice, onion, tomato, chopped basil, and salt and pepper to taste and mix gently.

DRAIN the pasta, transfer to the bowl with the avocado mixture, and toss well. Garnish with basil sprigs and serve immediately. Pass the cheese at the table for sprinkling over individual servings.

Makes 8 first-course or 4 main-course servings.

Salt

Fresh Pasta (page 140) or 1 pound purchased fresh pasta, cut into narrow noodles, or 1 pound high-quality dried linguine or other pasta made with hard durum wheat

3 large, ripe avocados

3 tablespoons freshly squeezed lime or lemon juice

¾ cup finely chopped red onion

3 cups peeled, seeded, and chopped ripe tomato

2 cups chopped fresh basil

Freshly ground black pepper

Fresh basil sprigs for garnish

Freshly grated Parmesan cheese, preferably Parmigiano-Reggiano, for passing

FETTUCCINE WITH PEAS
AND PROSCIUTTO CREAM

½ cup (1 stick) unsalted butter

4 ounces thinly sliced prosciutto, slivered

1 cup shelled fresh or thawed frozen green (English) peas

½ cup heavy (whipping) cream, light cream, or half-and-half

1 cup freshly grated Parmesan cheese (about 4 ounces), preferably Parmigiano-Reggiano, plus more for passing

Salt

Freshly ground white pepper

Freshly grated nutmeg

Fresh Pasta (page 140) or 1 pound purchased fresh pasta, cut into ⅛-inch-wide noodles, or 1 pound high-quality dried fettuccine or other pasta made with hard durum wheat

This preparation has long been a favorite, and I frequently make it using the easy directions that follow. When I wish to create a fanciful presentation, I make a 3-inch-wide, tricolor ribbon of carrot, red sweet pepper, and spinach pastas, arranged in alternating stripes as described in the variation for Fresh Pasta (page 143).

IN a saute pan or skillet, melt the butter over medium heat. Add the prosciutto and cook, stirring frequently, until translucent, about 3 minutes. Add the peas and continue cooking until the peas are crisp-tender, about 10 minutes for fresh peas, or about 5 minutes for thawed peas. Stir in the cream or half-and-half, the 1 cup cheese, and salt, pepper, and nutmeg to taste. Reduce the heat to very low and heat through; do not allow to boil. Keep warm.

MEANWHILE, in a large pot, bring 4 quarts water to a rapid boil over high heat, then stir in 1 tablespoon salt. Drop in the pasta and cook, stirring frequently, until tender but still firm to the bite.

DRAIN the pasta, transfer to a heated bowl, add the sauce, and toss well. Serve immediately. Pass additional cheese at the table for sprinkling over individual servings.

Makes 8 first-course or 4 main-course servings.

SPAGHETTI CARBONARA

The origin of this dish has been attributed to various sources. Some food historians insist it was a popular dish of coal miners, while others say it was a favorite of charcoal makers. Its composition can be anything from a very simple one of pasta, bacon, eggs, and cheese to a far richer one. I've tasted numerous versions over the years and prefer this creamy one made without the onions that are sometimes added to the dish.

Although traditionally made with spaghetti, other dried pasta forms offer variety. Some Italian cooks call for smoked American-style bacon, but my preference is strongly in favor of unsmoked, salt-and-spice-cured Italian bacon (pancetta).

Obviously, this pasta is not diet food. Indeed, it has even been referred to as "heart attack on a plate," but we all deserve an occasional indulgence if our health allows.

2 tablespoons olive oil, preferably extra-virgin

2 cups diced *pancetta* (about 10 ounces)

¼ cup (½ stick) unsalted butter

Salt

1 pound high-quality spaghetti or other dried pasta made with hard durum wheat

6 egg yolks, at room temperature

1½ cups freshly grated Parmesan cheese (about 6 ounces), preferably Parmigiano-Reggiano, plus more for passing

¾ cup heavy (whipping) cream

Freshly ground black pepper

¼ cup minced fresh flat-leaf parsley

TO begin the sauce, in a saute pan or skillet, heat the oil over medium heat. Add the pancetta and cook, stirring frequently, until the meat is translucent, about 5 minutes. Reduce the heat to low, add the butter, and stir until the butter melts. Remove from the heat and set aside.

IN a large pot, bring 4 quarts water to a rapid boil over high heat, then stir in 1 tablespoon salt. Drop in the pasta and cook, stirring frequently, until tender but still firm to the bite.

MEANWHILE, in a large bowl, combine the egg yolks, the 1½ cups cheese, cream, and salt and pepper to taste. Stir in the cooled *pancetta* and butter.

DRAIN the pasta, transfer to the bowl with the sauce, and toss well. Sprinkle with the parsley and serve immediately. Pass additional cheese at the table for sprinkling over individual servings.

Makes 8 first-course or 4 main-course servings.

BACON AND TOMATO PASTA

8 ounces sliced smoked bacon, cut
into 1-inch lengths

1 cup finely chopped yellow onion

2 cups peeled, seeded, drained, and
chopped ripe or canned tomato

½ cup packed fresh basil leaves

Salt

1 pound high-quality *penne*, rigatoni,
or other dried pasta made with hard
durum wheat

½ cup heavy (whipping) cream

½ cup chopped fresh basil

Freshly ground black pepper

Fresh basil sprigs for garnish

Freshly grated Parmesan cheese,
preferably Parmigiano-Reggiano,
for passing

Joe Bevacqua, the Emmy-winning set designer of The Young and the
Restless, *shared this recipe that Sophia Loren gave to him when they
worked together on a television special. He claims that it's her favorite
pasta, so my family refers to it as Sophia's pasta.*

*Surprisingly, the sauce is made with American-style smoked
bacon instead of Italian* pancetta *and served over cooked dried pasta.
It's too hearty for delicate fresh noodles.*

IN a saute pan or skillet, cook the bacon over medium-high heat
until all of the fat is rendered and the bacon is done but not
crisp. Add the onion and cook, stirring frequently, until the
onion is soft and lightly golden, about 5 minutes.

IN a food processor or blender, combine the tomato and basil leaves
and puree coarsely. Transfer to the bacon and onion mixture.
Bring the mixture to a boil, then reduce the heat to achieve a
simmer and simmer for about 30 minutes.

IN a large pot, bring 4 quarts water to a rapid boil over high heat,
then stir in 1 tablespoon salt. Drop in the pasta and cook, stirring
frequently, until tender but still firm to the bite.

MEANWHILE, add the cream, chopped basil, and salt and pepper to
taste to the simmering sauce and heat through.

DRAIN the pasta, transfer to a heated bowl, add the sauce, and toss
well. Garnish with basil sprigs and serve immediately. Pass the
cheese at the table for sprinkling over individual servings.

Makes 8 first-course or 4 main-course servings.

ROMAN-STYLE SPAGHETTI WITH GARLIC AND OLIVE OIL
~ *SPAGHETTI AGLIO E OLIO* ~

My variation on this old Roman specialty has long been comfort food to me, so it had to have a place in this book of favorite recipes. It's quick, easy, and very satisfying, making it a great supper after working too long or when there's little time for cooking.

This is one dish in which I take on any number of Italian cooks and authors. Most brown the garlic in the oil, then discard it; I use a more gentle hand in cooking the garlic so that it never browns and adds bitterness, and I leave it in the oil for added flavor. And for some unexplained reason that I fail to comprehend, the Italians serve this dish without any cheese. I much prefer my California version, which is showered with the world's finest cheese.

IN a large pot, bring 4 quarts water to a rapid boil over high heat, then stir in 1 tablespoon salt. Drop in the spaghetti and cook, stirring frequently, until tender but still firm to the bite.

MEANWHILE, in a large saute pan or skillet, combine the oil, garlic, and anchovies (if using) over low heat and cook until the garlic just begins to take on a hint of color; do not brown the garlic. Remove from the heat.

DRAIN the spaghetti, transfer to the pan holding the garlicky olive oil, season to taste with salt and pepper or chile, and toss well. Sprinkle with the parsley, crown lavishly with cheese, and serve immediately.

Makes 8 first-course or 4 main-course servings.

Salt

12 ounces high-quality spaghetti or other dried pasta made with hard durum wheat

½ cup extra-virgin olive oil

1 tablespoon minced garlic, or to taste

3 flat anchovy fillets, rinsed, patted dry, and minced (optional)

Freshly ground black pepper or crushed dried hot chile

2 tablespoons minced fresh flat-leaf parsley

Freshly grated Parmesan cheese, preferably Parmigiano-Reggiano, for serving

PASTA WITH CARAMELIZED ONIONS

½ cup olive oil, preferably
    extra-virgin

5 pounds onions, cut in half, then
    thinly sliced

⅓ cup coarsely chopped garlic

Salt

Freshly ground black pepper

1 cup dry red or white wine

1 tablespoon minced mixed fresh
    aromatic herbs such as bay leaf,
    lavender blossoms, marjoram,
    rosemary, summer savory, and
    thyme; or 1 teaspoon crumbled
    dried *herbes de Provence*, or to
    taste

1 pound high-quality *orecchiette* (little
    ears) or other dried pasta made
    with hard durum wheat

Fresh herb sprigs (same as used in
    sauce) for garnish (optional)

Freshly grated Parmesan cheese,
    preferably Parmigiano-Reggiano,
    for passing

One of my favorite cold-weather pastas, this dish relies on a simple sauce of onions, cooked until caramelized. Choose onions that are somewhat dried for storage; freshly dug bulbs contain so much moisture that they fall apart and do not caramelize easily.

Unfortunately, an editorial error in my pasta cookbook called for too much of the herb mixture. If you tried that recipe and found the herbs overwhelming, please make this corrected version.

TO make the sauce, in a large, heavy pot, heat the oil over medium heat. Add the onions and toss well to coat with the oil. Cover, reduce the heat to medium-low, and cook, stirring occasionally, until the onions just begin to color, about 20 minutes.

UNCOVER, add the garlic, increase the heat to medium, and season to taste with salt and a generous amount of pepper. Cook, stirring frequently, until the onions are caramelized, 20 minutes or longer, depending on the moisture content of the onions.

INCREASE the heat to medium-high, add the wine and minced or crumbled herbs, and cook until the wine evaporates, about 5 minutes.

MEANWHILE, in a large pot, bring 4 quarts water to a rapid boil over high heat, then stir in 1 tablespoon salt. Drop in the pasta and cook, stirring frequently, until tender but still firm to the bite.

DRAIN the pasta, transfer to a heated bowl, add the onion mixture, and toss well. Garnish with herb sprigs (if using) and serve immediately. Pass the cheese at the table for sprinkling over individual servings.

Makes 8 first-course or 4 main-course servings.

VARIATION

FOR a zesty counterpoint, slice 12 ounces hot Italian or other spicy sausage and saute until browned. Using a slotted utensil, transfer to the onions just before adding the wine.

ITALIAN RICE AND PEAS
~ *RISI E BISI* ~

Some Italian cooks prefer this dish quite moist and served in a bowl with a soup spoon. If you wish to follow suit, add a little extra stock or broth. Either way the combination makes a great beginning or a light main course.

WASH and drain the rice as directed on page 365. Set aside.

IN a saucepan, melt the butter over medium-high heat. Add the onion and cook, stirring frequently, until soft but not browned, about 5 minutes. Add the drained rice and stir until all the grains are well coated with butter, about 2 minutes. Add the stock or broth and wine and bring to a boil, then reduce the heat to achieve a simmer, cover, and simmer, stirring occasionally, until the rice is tender but firm to the bite and most of the liquid has been absorbed, about 20 minutes.

MEANWHILE, prepare a bowl of iced water and set aside. In a saucepan, combine the peas with just enough water to cover barely. Place over medium-high heat and cook until crisp-tender, 5 to 10 minutes for fresh peas, or about 5 minutes for frozen peas. Quickly drain and transfer to the iced water to halt cooking.

WHEN the rice is cooked, stir in the peas, prosciutto (if using), cheese, and salt and pepper to taste and heat through.

TO serve, immediately spoon onto warmed plates or into shallow bowls. Pass additional cheese for sprinkling over individual portions.

Makes 8 first-course or 4 main-course servings.

2 cups short-grain white rice,
    preferably Italian Arborio

¼ cup (½ stick) unsalted butter

½ cup minced yellow onion

5 cups Vegetable Stock (page 580),
    White Stock (page 578), or canned
    vegetable or reduced-sodium
    chicken broth

1 cup dry white wine

3 cups shelled fresh or thawed
    frozen green (English) peas

8 ounces thinly sliced prosciutto,
    slivered (optional)

1 cup freshly grated Parmesan
    cheese (about 4 ounces), preferably
    Parmigiano-Reggiano

Salt

Freshly ground black pepper

Freshly grated Parmesan cheese,
    preferably Parmigiano-Reggiano,
    for passing

AFGHANISTAN-STYLE LEEK-STUFFED PASTA WITH YOGURT AND MEAT SAUCES ~ *AUSHAK* ~

SPICED MEAT SAUCE

2 tablespoons unsalted butter

½ cup chopped leek, including pale
    green portion

½ cup finely chopped carrot

12 ounces ground lamb, veal, or beef

1 cup dry white wine

2 cups peeled, seeded, and chopped
    ripe or canned tomato

1 bay leaf

2 teaspoons ground cinnamon

2 teaspoons ground cumin

1 teaspoon ground coriander

Salt

Freshly ground black pepper

LEEK FILLING

3 tablespoons olive oil, preferably
    extra-virgin

1½ cups chopped leek, including
    pale green portion

Salt

Freshly ground black pepper

YOGURT SAUCE

2 cups plain yogurt

1 teaspoon minced garlic

¼ cup minced fresh mint

Salt

Some food historians credit Central and Southwest Asians with being the first cooks to stuff noodle dough. The idea spread to China as wontons and potstickers and to Italy as ravioli and other stuffed pastas. Since Afghanistan lay along the trade routes, the idea was adapted to local flavorings.

TO make the Spiced Meat Sauce, in a heavy saucepan, melt the butter over medium heat. Add the leek and carrot and cook, stirring frequently, until soft but not browned, about 5 minutes. Add the ground meat and cook, stirring frequently and breaking up the meat, just until it loses its color; do not brown. Increase the heat to medium-high, add the wine and cook, stirring frequently, until the wine evaporates. Add the tomato, bay leaf, cinnamon, cumin, coriander, and salt and pepper to taste. Bring almost to a boil, then reduce the heat to achieve a simmer, cover, and simmer, stirring occasionally, until the meat is very tender and flavorful, 3 to 4 hours. (At this point, the meat sauce can be cooled completely, then covered and refrigerated for up to 3 days; reheat before proceeding.)

TO make the Leek Filling, in a saute pan or skillet, heat the oil over medium heat. Add the chopped leek and cook, stirring frequently, until very tender, about 10 minutes. Season to taste with salt and pepper. Remove from the heat and set aside.

TO make the Yogurt Sauce, in a bowl, combine the yogurt, garlic, minced mint, and salt to taste. Cover and set aside.

IF using fresh pasta, lightly flour a work surface. Spread out half of the pasta sheets. Mound 1 teaspoon of the filling at 2-inch intervals along the pasta. Using a pastry brush, coat the exposed dough lightly with water, then cover loosely with the remaining pasta sheets. Press down around the filling to force out air and seal the dough. Using a pastry wheel or sharp knife, cut between the filling mounds to form 2-inch squares; there should be about 48 total. Set aside on cloth kitchen towels.

IF using wonton wrappers, lightly flour a work surface and spread out half of the wrappers. Mound 1 teaspoon of the filling in the center of half of the wrappers. Brush the exposed dough with water, then cover with the remaining wrappers. Press around the filling to seal. Trim edges with a pastry wheel. Set aside on cloth kitchen towels.

IN a large pot, bring 4 quarts water to a rapid boil over high heat, then stir in the 1 tablespoon salt. Drop in the pasta packets and cook, stirring frequently, until tender but still firm to the bite. Drain, transfer to a warmed bowl, add the melted butter, and toss gently but well.

TO serve, spoon ¼ or ½ cup of the Yogurt Sauce, depending on the size of the portions being served, onto each plate. Top with 6 or 12 pasta packets and spoon some of the reserved meat sauce over the top. Garnish with leek greens and mint leaves and serve immediately.

Makes 8 first-course or 4 main-course servings.

Fresh Pasta (page 140), thinly rolled
into sheets; 1 pound purchased
fresh pasta sheets; or about
48 wonton wrappers (available
in most supermarkets)

All-purpose flour for dusting

1 tablespoon salt

3 tablespoons unsalted butter,
melted

Slivered leek greens for garnish

Fresh mint leaves for garnish

POLENTA

2 quarts Brown Stock (page 576),
Vegetable Stock (page 580), White
Stock (page 578), or canned broth
(all optional)

Salt

2 cups cornmeal (see recipe
introduction)

OPTIONAL ADDITIONS

½ cup (1 stick) unsalted butter

⅔ cup freshly grated Parmesan
cheese (about 3 ounces), preferably
Parmigiano-Reggiano

2 cups freshly shredded good-melting
cheese such as Italian Fontina
(about 10 ounces) or crumbled
Gorgonzola or mild, creamy goat
cheese (about 8 ounces)

2 tablespoons minced fresh herb of
choice, or 2 teaspoons crumbled
dried herb of choice

1 cup sauteed finely chopped flavorful
fresh mushrooms such as porcino
or chanterelle

1 cup chopped cooked spinach,
Swiss chard, or other green

¼ cup minced drained sun-dried
tomatoes packed in olive oil

Unsalted butter or extra-virgin olive
oil if frying, grilling, broiling, or
roasting

Polenta is the Italian name for both cornmeal and the cooked mush made from it. Although in the United States we identify Italian cornmeal with the coarse yellow variety sold here as polenta, in Italy the type of cornmeal varies with the region. Finely ground yellow or white cornmeal is favored in the Veneto; a coarser yellow meal is preferred in Piedmont and Lombardy.

The finished dish may be served freshly cooked as a side dish or as a bed for stews and sauces. Frequently it is cooled, then sliced and reheated for serving as a side dish or used as a component in other dishes.

Italian kitchen tradition calls for continuous stirring of barely simmering polenta for about 45 minutes. The revolutionary techniques in this recipe are based on methods used by modern chefs and yield the same creamy results with much less attention.

TO cook polenta on a stove top, select a large metal bowl that will fit over a larger pot to create a double boiler arrangement or use a large double boiler. Fill the bottom pot with water, keeping the level well below the bottom of the insert. Place the pot over high heat and bring the water to a boil, then reduce the heat to maintain a simmer.

MEANWHILE, combine the stock or broth or 2 quarts water with salt to taste in the top portion of the double boiler. Stir the water in one direction to create a whirlpool in the center. While stirring, slowly pour the cornmeal in a thin stream into the center of the swirling water until completely mixed.

COVER the polenta container tightly with a lid or aluminum foil and set it over the simmering water. Cook, uncovering and using a rubber spatula to scrape the bottom and sides of the container several times, until the polenta is thick and smooth, 1½ to 2 hours; adjust the heat to maintain simmering water throughout cooking, adding boiling water if needed to maintain water level.

TO cook polenta in an oven, preheat an oven to 325° F. In a large ovenproof pot or flameproof casserole, combine the stock or broth or 2 quarts water with salt to taste. Place over high heat and bring to a boil.

STIR the water in one direction to create a whirlpool in the center. While stirring, slowly pour the cornmeal in a thin stream into the center of the swirling water until completely mixed. Return the mixture to a boil, cover tightly with a lid or aluminum foil, transfer to the oven, and bake until the polenta is thick and smooth, about 20 minutes.

AFTER cooking the polenta by one of the preceding methods, remove it from the heat or the oven and, if desired, stir in any one or a compatible combination of the suggested additions. If adding butter or cheese, stir until melted.

TO serve warm, pour the mixture onto a platter or other flat surface and smooth the top with a damp wooden spoon. Alternatively, pour the polenta into a bowl that has been dampened with water and let stand a few minutes, then unmold onto a serving plate. Cut the polenta into wedges and serve immediately.

TO reheat later or use in other dishes, after stirring in any selected additions as directed above, pour the hot mixture into a greased 9-by-5-inch loaf pan, 13-by-9-inch baking pan, or 9-inch round cake pan and smooth the top with a damp wooden spoon or spatula. Let cool to room temperature, then cover and refrigerate until firm, at least 2 hours or for up to 3 days. Turn the chilled polenta out onto a cutting surface and slice or cut into fanciful shapes. Use as directed in recipes or fry in butter or olive oil. Alternatively, using a pastry brush, coat the slices generously on both sides with melted butter or olive oil and heat them on a grill rack over a medium-hot fire, under a preheated broiler, or in a 450° F oven until crispy on the outside.

Makes 8 servings.

VARIATION

Soft Polenta (*Polentina*). Increase the amount of stock, broth, or water to 10 cups and cook until the mixture thickens to the texture of cream of wheat, about 1 hour if using the stove top method, or about 15 minutes if using the oven method; add more liquid if necessary to achieve a smooth, soft consistency. Pour or ladle into large, shallow warmed bowls, and top with *mascarpone*, Gorgonzola, or other soft creamy cheese or freshly grated Parmesan cheese, or your favorite pasta sauce or stew.

NORTHERN ITALIAN POLENTA CASSEROLE ~ *POLENTA PASTICCIATA* ~

Polenta (page 154), made with coarse
yellow cornmeal and, preferably,
cooked in chicken or vegetable
stock or broth

Unsalted butter, at room temperature,
or cooking spray for greasing

½ cup pine nuts

1 cup freshly shredded Italian
Fontina cheese (about 5 ounces)

1 cup crumbled creamy sweet
Gorgonzola cheese (about 4 ounces)

½ cup freshly grated Parmesan
cheese (about 2 ounces), preferably
Parmigiano-Reggiano

3 cups Tomato Sauce (page 573) or
high-quality commercial tomato
pasta sauce

Shredded fresh basil or chopped flat-
leaf parsley for sprinkling

Vary this meatless dish by substituting a favorite meat sauce for the cheese filling. Or fill with sauteed mushrooms, a combination of other cheeses, cooked spinach or other vegetables, or other lasagna fillings.

For a larger group, make the polenta with 12 cups liquid and 3 cups cornmeal and divide it among three 13-by-9-inch baking pans; make 1½ times the amount of filling and sauce.

If you wish a richer polenta, add the butter and Parmesan cheese as suggested in the basic polenta recipe.

COOK the polenta as directed.

MEANWHILE, using a pastry brush, generously grease a 9-inch springform pan and two 9-inch round cake pans with butter, or coat with spray. Set aside.

POUR the polenta into the 3 prepared pans, dividing equally. Smooth the tops with a damp wooden spoon or spatula to make each layer as flat as possible. Let cool to room temperature, then cover tightly and refrigerate until firm, at least 2 hours or for up to 3 days.

TOAST the pine nuts as directed on page 553 and set aside.

DISTRIBUTE half of the Fontina and Gorgonzola cheeses in an even layer over the polenta in the springform pan and sprinkle with about one-third of the toasted pine nuts. Turn the polenta out from the cake pans and place 1 round over the cheese-topped layer. Add the remaining Fontina and Gorgonzola and half of the remaining pine nuts. Cover with the final round of polenta. Sprinkle the Parmesan cheese and remaining pine nuts evenly over the top. (At this point the casserole can be covered and refrigerated for up to 12 hours; return to room temperature before proceeding.)

PREHEAT an oven to 350° F. Line a baking sheet with kitchen parchment or aluminum foil. Place the casserole on the prepared baking sheet and bake until the cheeses melt and the casserole is heated through, about 1 hour. Set aside to cool slightly.

JUST before serving, heat the Tomato Sauce or pasta sauce over low heat.

TO serve, ladle ¼ or ½ cup of the warm sauce, depending on the size of the portions being served, onto each individual plate. Remove the springform ring, slice the casserole into wedges, and place on top of the sauce. Sprinkle each serving with basil or parsley.

Makes 12 first-course or 6 main-course servings.

ROASTED POLENTA WITH RED CHILE SAUCE AND CHORIZO-CORN SAUTE

Polenta (page 154)

Unsalted butter, at room temperature, or cooking spray for greasing

3 cups Red Chile Sauce (page 574)

1 cup Crème Fraîche (page 591), commercial crème fraîche, or sour cream

2 tablespoons freshly squeezed lime juice

3 tablespoons finely chopped fresh mint

About 4 medium-sized ears corn, or 2 cups thawed frozen or drained canned corn kernels

2 tablespoons olive oil

¾ pound chorizo (spicy Spanish sausage), casings discarded, crumbled

Unsalted butter, melted and cooled slightly, or olive oil for brushing

Lime zest strips for garnish

Fresh mint sprigs for garnish

Serve this zesty combo as an opener or as a one-dish brunch or supper.

COOK the polenta as directed.

MEANWHILE, using a pastry brush, generously grease a 9-by-5-inch loaf pan with butter, or coat with spray. Set aside.

POUR the polenta into the prepared pan. Let cool to room temperature, then cover tightly and refrigerate until firm, at least 2 hours or for up to 3 days.

PREPARE the Red Chile Sauce as directed and set aside.

IN a bowl, combine the crème fraîche or sour cream, lime juice, and chopped mint and stir to mix thoroughly. Set aside.

IF using fresh corn, cut the kernels from the cobs as directed for Sauteed Corn on page 358, measure out 2 cups, and set aside. If using thawed or canned corn, reserve for later use.

IN a saute pan or skillet, heat the 2 tablespoons oil over medium-low heat. Add the chorizo and cook, stirring occasionally to break up the meat, until done, about 10 minutes. With a slotted spoon, transfer to a small bowl. Discard all but 2 tablespoons fat from the skillet. Add the corn and cook, stirring frequently, until the corn is tender, about 4 minutes for young corn, or 8 minutes for older corn. Stir in the reserved chorizo. Set aside.

PREHEAT an oven to 450° F.

TURN the polenta out onto a cutting surface. Cut into 12 slices about ¾-inch thick, then cut each slice on the diagonal into 2 triangles to make a total of 24 pieces.

LIGHTLY brush the polenta triangles on all sides with melted butter or oil and place on baking sheets. Roast in the oven

until the triangles are crisp and golden on the bottoms, about
10 minutes. Turn and roast until golden on the other sides, 5 to
10 minutes longer.

MEANWHILE, reheat the Red Chile Sauce and the chorizo-corn
mixture separately over low heat.

TO serve, spoon ¼ or ½ cup of the Red Chile Sauce, depending
on the size of the portions being served, onto warmed plates.
Arrange 2 or 4 polenta slices in the center of each pool of sauce
and spoon a portion of the chorizo-corn mixture around the
edge of the plate or over the top of the polenta. Add a dollop of
the reserved minted cream to each serving and garnish with
lime zest strips and mint sprigs.

Makes 12 first-course or 6 main-course servings.

BASIC RISOTTO WITH PARMESAN CHEESE ~ *Risotto al Parmigiano* ~

2 cups short-grain white rice, preferably Italian Arborio, Carnaroli, or Vialone Nano

About 7 cups Brown Stock (page 576), Vegetable Stock (page 580), White Stock (page 578), or canned broth

¼ cup (½ stick) unsalted butter

⅔ cup finely chopped yellow onion

1½ teaspoons minced garlic

½ cup dry white wine

1 cup freshly grated Parmesan cheese (about 4 ounces), preferably Parmigiano-Reggiano

Salt

Freshly ground black pepper

Freshly grated Parmesan cheese, preferably Parmigiano-Reggiano, for sprinkling and passing

Use this basic recipe as a guide for preparing the suggested variations or creating your own recipes with a host of optional additions. Saffron Risotto is a classic accompaniment to Ossobuco (page 262) and roasted chicken or meats. Don't miss the Smoked Chicken Risotto variation, an excellent cold-weather dish. And my partner, Andrew, is crazy about the Winter Squash Risotto.

Most Italian recipe writers urge the use of a lightly flavored broth and abhor the use of canned broth; I enjoy stock with a bit more flavor and do not find canned substitutes objectionable.

Form leftover cold risotto into small cakes, panfry in unsalted butter until golden brown on both sides, and serve as a side dish. Or form the risotto into small balls, poke a small cube of fresh mozzarella into the center of each ball, deep-fry in olive oil or vegetable oil until golden, and serve as an antipasto.

WASH and drain the rice as directed on page 365. Set aside.

IN a saucepan, bring the stock or broth to a simmer over high heat, then reduce the heat to maintain a simmer while cooking the rice.

IN a heavy, deep saute pan or skillet, melt the butter over medium-high heat. Add the onion and cook, stirring frequently, until soft but not browned, about 5 minutes. Add the garlic and drained rice and stir until all the grains are well coated, about 2 minutes. Add the wine and cook, stirring constantly, until the wine has evaporated, about 3 minutes. Add ½ cup of the simmering stock or broth, adjusting the heat under the rice if the liquid is evaporating too quickly. Keep the rice at a simmer and stir almost continuously, scraping the bottom and sides of the pan, until the liquid has been absorbed.

CONTINUE to add the stock or broth ½ cup at a time each time the rice becomes dry, and continue to stir the rice as it cooks. As the risotto approaches completion, add the stock or broth only ¼ cup at a time. You may not need it all before the rice is done, or you may need more liquid, in which case add more stock or broth or hot water. Cook until the rice is tender but firm to the bite, about 25 minutes in all.

WHEN the rice is done, add the cheese and stir for about 2 minutes. Completed risotto should be creamy but not soupy; if it is too dry, add a little more stock, broth, or hot water. Season to taste with salt and pepper.

TO serve, spoon onto warmed plates and sprinkle lightly with cheese. Pass additional cheese at the table for sprinkling over individual servings.

Makes 8 first-course or 4 main-course servings.

VARIATIONS

Basil Risotto (*Risotto al Basilico*). Add a large handful of fresh basil leaves to the stock or broth when heating. Strain out the basil before using the liquid. Just before the risotto is done, chop or shred enough fresh basil to equal 1 cup packed and stir it into the rice along with the cheese.

Lobster Risotto (*Risotto di Aragosta*). Cook 4 live Maine lobsters (about 1 pound each) in boiling water until the shells turn bright red and the meat is opaque, about 12 minutes. Drain well, reserving the cooking liquid, and set aside to cool. Remove the meat from the tails and claws, chop into bite-sized pieces, and refrigerate until needed. (You may wish to save the whole claws and tail fins for garnish.) Rinse out the contents of the bodies and use the shells and the water from cooking the lobsters in place of fish to make Fish Stock (page 575) to use in cooking the risotto. About 5 minutes before the rice is done, stir in the reserved lobster meat and 1 cup cooked fresh or thawed frozen green (English) peas (see page 338). Omit the cheese. Spoon the risotto into bowls and scatter slivered leek and cherry tomatoes over the top.

continues ~

Saffron Risotto (*Risotto alla Milanese*). Add ½ teaspoon crumbled saffron threads to ½ cup of the warm stock or broth and set aside. Add the saffron-infused stock or broth to the rice about halfway through the cooking.

Seafood Risotto (*Risotto ai Frutti di Mare*). Substitute mildly flavored Fish Stock (page 575) or water for the stock or broth. Cut mixed cooked shellfish and/or fish into small pieces to equal 2 cups. About 5 minutes before the rice is done, stir in the shellfish and/or fish and 3 tablespoons freshly squeezed lemon juice, or to taste. Omit the cheese.

Smoked Chicken Risotto (*Risotto di Pollo Affumicato*). Use chicken stock or broth. Add ½ teaspoon crumbled saffron threads to ½ cup of the warm stock or broth and set aside. Add the saffron-infused stock or broth to the rice about halfway through the cooking. Substitute shallot for the onion and add 1⅓ cups chopped flavorful fresh mushrooms such as porcino, chanterelle, or portobello along with the shallot. Add ⅓ cup chopped drained sun-dried tomatoes packed in olive oil along with the garlic and rice. About 5 minutes before you think the rice will be done, stir in 2 cups chopped or shredded smoked chicken.

Vegetable Risotto (*Risotto al Verdura*). Use vegetable stock or broth. Cut vegetables such as broccoli, carrots, or squash into small pieces to equal 3 cups. After cooking the onion and garlic, stir in the vegetables and cook until crisp-tender. Remove about half of the vegetables to a bowl and set aside. Add the drained rice to the pan and proceed as directed in the basic recipe. Stir in the reserved vegetables about 5 minutes before the rice is done. Alternatively, in a separate pot, cook tender vegetables such as asparagus or green (English) peas until crisp-tender, then stir the drained vegetables into the rice about halfway through cooking.

Winter Squash Risotto (*Risotto con la Zucca*). Peel and seed 2 pounds of Butternut or other flavorful winter squash and cut into ½-inch cubes. Increase stock or broth to 8 cups. After cooking the onion and garlic, add the squash and 1 cup of the stock or broth and cook for about 5 minutes, then add the rice and complete the risotto as directed.

ROMAN BAKED SEMOLINA
DUPLINGS ~ *Gnocchi alla Romana* ~

*Unlike most Italian first courses, this dish can be prepared a day or two
ahead and refrigerated, then baked at the last minute. Semolina is
ground from hard durum wheat; look for it in specialty-food stores,
Italian markets, and some supermarkets.*

IN a heavy-bottomed saucepan, combine the milk, salt, pepper,
and nutmeg. Place over medium heat and bring almost to a boil,
then reduce the heat to very low. Gradually pour in the semolina
in a thin, steady stream, stirring constantly. The mixture will
thicken quickly, but continue cooking and stirring, scraping
the bottom of the pan, until the mixture forms a very thick mass
that pulls away from the sides of the pan, about 15 minutes.
Remove from the heat.

QUICKLY stir ¾ cup of the cheese, the egg yolks, sage, and 2 tablespoons of the melted butter into the hot semolina mixture,
mixing well.

USING a pastry brush, lightly grease a large, shallow-rimmed
baking sheet with butter. Using a metal spatula dipped in cold
water from time to time, spread the thick mixture into the
prepared pan, making a layer about ¼ inch thick. Let cool to
room temperature, then cover and refrigerate until the mixture
is cold and firm, about 1 hour.

USING a biscuit cutter or straight-sided glass 1½ to 2 inches in
diameter, cut the semolina sheet into rounds, dipping the cutter
into cold water between cuts. Place the dumplings in a greased
13-by-9-inch pan, or divide among gratin dishes, arranging them
in slightly overlapping rows to form a single layer. Dot with
softened butter and sprinkle with the remaining ¼ cup cheese.
(At this point, the dumplings can be covered and refrigerated
for up to 2 days; return to room temperature before proceeding.)

PREHEAT an oven to 400° F.

BAKE until the dumplings are golden and crusty, about 20 minutes.
Remove from the oven and let stand for about 5 minutes before
serving directly from the pan or dishes.

Makes 8 to 12 servings.

5 cups milk

1½ teaspoons salt, or to taste

½ teaspoon freshly ground black
pepper, or to taste

⅛ teaspoon freshly grated nutmeg,
or to taste

1½ cups coarsely ground semolina
flour

1 cup freshly grated Parmesan
cheese (about 4 ounces), preferably
Parmigiano-Reggiano

3 egg yolks, lightly beaten

3 tablespoons minced fresh sage, or
1 tablespoon crumbled dried sage

¼ cup (½ stick) unsalted butter,
melted

Unsalted butter, at room temperature,
for brushing and dotting

ITALIAN POTATO DUMPLINGS
~ *Gnocchi di Patate* ~

2 pounds baking potatoes

About 1 cup all-purpose flour

Salt

¼ cup (½ stick) unsalted butter, melted

1½ cups freshly grated Parmesan cheese (about 6 ounces), preferably Parmigiano-Reggiano

Minced fresh flat-leaf parsley, sage, or thyme (optional)

Freshly grated Parmesan cheese, preferably Parmigiano-Reggiano, for passing

I'd always used boiling potatoes when making gnocchi until I discovered that baking potatoes yield dumplings that are lighter and a bit drier. Toss the cooked gnocchi with melted butter and cheese as directed in the recipe, or select Tomato Sauce (page 573), Pesto (page 399), or a favorite Italian pasta sauce for mixing with the dumplings.

BAKE the potatoes as directed on page 314.

WHEN the potatoes are cool enough to handle, peel and cut into large chunks. Using a ricer, press the warm potatoes into a large bowl. Stir in 1 cup flour and about 1 teaspoon salt, or to taste. Lightly flour a work surface, then turn out the potato mixture onto it and knead with your fingers until smooth, adding more flour a little at a time until the dough is barely sticky. Form the mixture into a loaf.

CUT off a crosswise piece of the dough about 1½ inches thick. Roll the dough on the work surface with your palms into a rope about ¾ inch thick. Cut into 1-inch lengths. Dust your fingertips with flour and press and roll each piece of the dough against the inside of a flour-dipped fork so that one side has the impression of the tines and the other has a dent in the middle made by your thumb; set aside. Repeat this process with the remaining dough.

MEANWHILE, in a large pot, bring 4 quarts water to a rapid boil over high heat, then stir in 1 tablespoon salt.

DROP about 12 of the dumplings at a time into the boiling water. After they rise to the surface, continue to cook for about 10 to 15 seconds. Using a slotted utensil, quickly transfer the dumplings to a warmed bowl, add a little of the melted butter, and toss to coat. Cover the bowl to keep the contents warm while you cook the remaining dumplings, adding each batch to the bowl with a little melted butter and tossing as they are done.

WHEN all of the gnocchi are done, add the remaining butter and the cheese and toss well.

TO serve, transfer to a serving bowl or spoon onto warmed plates and sprinkle with minced herb. Pass additional cheese at the table for sprinkling over individual servings.

Makes 6 servings.

MILANESE SPINACH DUMPLINGS IN GORGONZOLA SAUCE
~ *GNOCCHI VERDE CON GORGONZOLA* ~

SPINACH DUMPLINGS

8 ounces fresh spinach

¾ cup ricotta cheese (about
   6 ounces), drained

½ cup unseasoned dried bread
   crumbs, preferably from Italian or
   French bread

1 egg, lightly beaten

¼ cup freshly grated Parmesan
   cheese (about 1 ounce), preferably
   Parmigiano-Reggiano

2 tablespoons finely chopped green
   onion, including green tops

¼ teaspoon salt, or to taste

⅛ teaspoon freshly grated nutmeg

All-purpose flour for dusting

GORGONZOLA SAUCE

1 cup heavy (whipping) cream, light
   cream, or half-and-half

1 cup crumbled creamy Gorgonzola
   cheese (about 4 ounces)

Salt

Freshly ground black pepper

1 tablespoon salt for cooking
   dumplings

Freshly grated Parmesan cheese,
   preferably Parmigiano-Reggiano,
   for serving

Serve these cloud-light dumplings with the rich sauce, or place the combination in gratin dishes and bake until the top is crusty. Cooked potato gnocchi (page 164) may be used in place of the spinach dumplings.

TO make the dumplings, wash the spinach carefully to remove any sand or grit and discard any tough stems. Place the damp spinach in a saute pan or heavy skillet and cook over high heat, stirring frequently, until the spinach wilts and turns bright green, about 5 minutes. Drain in a colander set in a sink or large bowl and squeeze out as much liquid as possible. Transfer to a food processor and chop finely. Alternatively, finely chop the spinach with a sharp knife and transfer to a bowl.

ADD the ricotta cheese, bread crumbs, egg, Parmesan cheese, onion, salt, and nutmeg to the spinach and blend thoroughly. Cover tightly and refrigerate for about 2 hours.

MOISTEN your hands. Using about 2 teaspoons to form each dumpling, roll the spinach mixture between your palms to form balls. Roll the balls lightly in flour to dust them on all sides, then arrange them on a tray lined with waxed paper. Cover and refrigerate for about 30 minutes.

TO make the sauce, in a heavy-bottomed saucepan, combine the cream or half-and-half and Gorgonzola. Place over medium heat and bring to a boil, stirring frequently. Reduce the heat to low and stir until slightly thickened, about 5 minutes. Season to taste with salt and pepper, and continue to stir until smooth, about 2 minutes longer. Keep warm.

IN a large pot, bring 4 quarts water to a simmer, then stir in the 1 tablespoon salt. Drop the dumplings, a few at a time, into the simmering water; do not crowd the pan. Regulate the heat so that the water remains at a simmer and cook until the dumplings pop up to the surface, about 2 minutes. Cook for about 2 minutes longer. Using a slotted utensil, remove the dumplings to a tray lined with paper toweling to drain well. Cook the remaining dumplings in the same manner.

TO serve, divide the sauce evenly among warmed plates or shallow bowls. Top with the dumplings and sprinkle with additional cheese.

ALTERNATIVELY, to serve as a gratin, preheat an oven to 350° F. Grease 4 individual flameproof gratin dishes or other shallow baking dishes. Divide about half of the sauce evenly among the dishes. Arrange the dumplings over the sauce, then spoon the remaining sauce over the dumplings. Bake for 10 minutes.

MEANWHILE, preheat a broiler.

REMOVE the gratins from the oven. Sprinkle with the bread crumbs and Parmesan cheese. Place under the preheated broiler until the cheese melts and a light crust forms, 2 to 3 minutes. Serve immediately.

Makes 4 servings.

FOR GRATIN (optional)

3 tablespoons unseasoned fine dried bread crumbs, preferably from Italian or French bread

2 tablespoons freshly grated Parmesan cheese, preferably Parmigiano-Reggiano

Pizza

AFTER publishing two books on pizza baking, it was difficult to condense one of my favorite subjects into a few pages. The detailed basic recipe will teach you everything you need to know about making perfect pizza. A few of my favorite toppings follow.

PIZZA

Read this master recipe through several times before starting to make a pizza to understand the steps necessary for creating all sizes and types. Once you fully grasp the various elements — mixing, kneading, shaping, and baking — of pizza making, the process will become clear and quite easy. With just a little practice, you will be quickly turning out the most scrumptious pizzas you've ever tasted and creating your own countless variations.

My favorite pizzas are the original flat versions, for which I've given directions for shaping and baking following the basic dough recipe. For directions on making stuffed pizzas, calzones, and deep-dish pizzas, please see my books Pizza *and* Vegetarian Pizza.

For well-textured, extra-crisp crusts, choose bread flour or semolina flour. Bread flour, used by most pizzerias, is made from hard northern spring wheat. It has a high gluten content that raises yeast dough to its maximum volume, which results in a dough that can be stretched quite thinly. Semolina flour, the same type used in quality dried pasta, is milled from hard durum wheat. It requires the addition of a little more water to the dough than is necessary with bread flour or all-purpose flour. Dough made of semolina or bread flour takes longer to knead and rise than dough made with all-purpose flour, but the resulting crisp crusts may make the extra effort and time worthwhile.

Although all-purpose flour is a blend of hard and soft wheats, its gluten content is high enough to make excellent crusts. It requires less moisture, kneading, and rising time than bread or semolina flour. If you use all-purpose flour, omit the second rising described in the directions.

Alter the taste and texture of the crust by using one of the flavorful dough variations on page 175; be sure that the crust will complement the toppings. The dough recipe can be doubled if you're entertaining a crowd or just want to prepare extra dough for freezing.

For quick-and-easy pizza crusts, I highly recommend using a heavy-duty stand mixer with a dough hook attachment. In about 10 minutes the dough can be mixed, kneaded, and set aside to rise.

continues ~

BASIC PIZZA DOUGH

1 tablespoon sugar

1 cup warm water (110° to 115° F)

1 envelope (¼ ounce) active dry
yeast or quick-rising yeast

3¼ cups bread, semolina, or
all-purpose flour (see recipe
introduction)

1 teaspoon salt

¼ cup olive oil, preferably
extra-virgin, or canola or other
high-quality vegetable oil (select
an oil that complements
the toppings)

Oil for brushing (same type as used
in dough)

Cornmeal for sprinkling on pizza peel
(if using)

Selected toppings (use your favorite
ingredients or see A Few of My
Favorite Pizzas on pages 176-179)

The single most important piece of pizza baking equipment in my kitchen is the pizza screen, a round of heavy-gauge wire mesh bordered with strong wire tape. Since discovering pizza screens, sold in restaurant-equipment outlets and well-stocked kitchenware stores, I never bother with lining my oven floor with quarry tiles or baking on pizza stones (which are usually too small to be effective). A screen is far easier to use than assembling a pizza on a peel, the paddle-shaped spatula made for transferring pizzas directly onto a preheated stone surface. Screen-baked pizzas have a wonderfully crisp crust, although it may be even slightly crispier if you place the screen directly on preheated tiles or a stone.

If you cannot locate pizza screens and do not wish to bake directly on hot tiles, purchase a flat pizza pan with ventilation holes that allow direct heat to reach the bottom of the crust. Old-fashioned pizza pans without such holes should be avoided, as the crust gets too greasy and/or soggy when trapped inside a pan.

Top the pizza dough with your favorite ingredients, being sure not to overload it with too many conflicting elements or pile it up with too much of a good thing. Or make one of my favorite pizzas as directed on pages 176-179.

IN a small bowl, dissolve the sugar in the warm water. Sprinkle the yeast over the water, stir to dissolve, and let stand until soft and foamy, about 5 minutes. (Discard and start over with fresh yeast if bubbles have not formed within 5 minutes.)

TO mix and knead the dough by hand, in a large mixing bowl, combine 3 cups of the flour with the salt. Make a well in the center of the flour and pour in the yeast mixture and the ¼ cup oil. Using a wooden spoon, vigorously stir the flour into the well, beginning in the center and working toward the sides of the bowl, until the flour is incorporated and the soft dough just begins to hold together.

TURN the dough out onto a lightly floured surface. Dust your hands with flour and knead the dough gently in the following manner: press down on the dough with the heels of your hands and push it away from you, then partially fold it back over itself. Shift it a quarter turn and repeat the procedure. While kneading, very gradually add just enough of the remaining ¼ cup flour until the dough is no longer sticky or tacky; this should take about 5 minutes. As you work, use a dough scraper to pry up any bits of dough that stick to the work surface. Continue kneading until the dough is smooth, elastic, and shiny, 10 to 15 minutes longer. Knead the dough only until it feels smooth and springy; too much kneading overdevelops the gluten in the flour and results in a tough crust.

TO mix and knead the dough with a food processor, in the bowl, combine 3 cups of the flour and the salt and process to mix well, about 5 seconds. Add the yeast mixture and the ¼ cup oil and process continuously until the dough forms a single ball or several masses on top of the blade, about 30 seconds. Pinch off a piece of dough and feel it. If it is sticky, continue processing while gradually adding just enough of the remaining ¼ cup flour for the dough to lose its stickiness. If the dough is dry and crumbly, add warm water, a tablespoon at a time, until the dough is smooth. Turn the dough out onto a lightly floured surface and knead by hand as described in the previous paragraph for about 2 minutes.

TO mix and knead the dough with a heavy-duty stand mixer, in the bowl, combine 3 cups of the flour, the salt, yeast mixture, and ¼ cup oil. Attach the flat beater and mix well at the lowest speed for 1 minute. Replace the flat beater with the dough hook and knead at medium speed until the dough is smooth and elastic, about 5 minutes. Pinch off a piece of dough and feel it. If it is sticky, continue kneading while gradually adding just enough of the remaining ¼ cup flour for the dough to lose its stickiness. If the dough is dry and crumbly, add warm water, a tablespoon at a time, until the dough is smooth and elastic.

AFTER mixing and kneading the dough by one of the preceding methods, using a pastry brush, generously grease a large bowl with oil, shape the dough into a ball, place it in the bowl, and turn to coat all over with oil. Cover the bowl tightly with plastic wrap to prevent moisture loss and set aside in a draft-free warm place for the dough to rise until doubled in bulk, about 45 minutes if using quick-rising yeast or about 1½ hours if using regular yeast.

continues ~

WHILE the dough is rising, prepare an oven for baking as follows.

IF baking directly on a piping-hot baking surface, line an oven with unglazed quarry tiles or position a baking stone: in a gas oven, position the tiles or stone directly on the oven floor; in an electric oven, arrange the tiles or stone on the lowest rack of the oven.

IF baking on a pizza screen or vented flat pan without the use of tiles or a stone, position an oven rack at the highest position.

PREHEAT the prepared oven to 500° F for about 30 minutes before assembling the pizza.

AS soon as the dough has doubled in bulk, use your fist to punch it down to prevent overrising. Squeeze the dough into a ball, pressing out all the air bubbles. If you are using bread flour or semolina flour, turn the dough in an oiled bowl to coat once more, cover the bowl tightly with plastic wrap, and refrigerate it until the dough is puffy, from 35 minutes to 1 hour (omit this step if using all-purpose flour).

IF you cannot bake the pizza dough within 2 hours of its rising, punch the dough down again, turn it in an oiled bowl to coat once more, cover the bowl tightly with plastic wrap, and refrigerate. (The dough can be punched down a total of 4 times and kept refrigerated for up to 36 hours before the yeast is exhausted and the dough unusable.) Let chilled dough come to room temperature before proceeding with shaping.

TO prepare the dough for shaping, pull the top of the dough and tuck all seams under the bottom to create a ball with a smooth top. To make a 15- to 16-inch pizza, keep the dough in a single ball. To make two 12-inch pizzas, divide the dough into 2 equal-sized smooth balls. To make individual 8-inch pizzas, divide the dough into 4 to 6 equal-sized portions. To make appetizer-sized *pizzette*, divide the dough into 18 equal-sized portions.

IF you wish to freeze dough for later use, wrap the pieces tightly in plastic wrap or seal in airtight plastic containers and freeze for up to 4 months. Before using, thaw in the refrigerator for 1 or 2 days or for a few hours at room temperature.

SHAPE the risen dough into crusts by one of the following methods. To achieve a superthin crust, use the stretching method.

TO shape with a rolling pin, place a ball of dough on a lightly floured surface and dust the top of the dough lightly with flour. Using the heels of your hands, press the dough into a circle or other desired shape, then roll it out with a lightly floured rolling pin until it is about ¼ inch thick, keeping the edges a little thicker than the center. While rolling the dough, pick it up and turn it over several times to stretch it. Add a little flour to the surface of the dough whenever needed to keep it from sticking. Rest one hand near the edge of the dough round and use the other hand to push the dough against it to form a slight rim around the dough, working your way completely around the perimeter of the dough.

TO shape by stretching, knead the dough for about 1 minute. Lightly flour the work surface. Shape the dough ball into a flat disk about 1 inch thick and lightly flour both sides. Starting from the center of the dough, press it out quickly with the heels of your hands, working around the dough to create the desired shape, usually a circle, until the dough is about ½ inch thick. Dust with flour whenever needed to prevent sticking. Stop stretching before you reach the outer edge of the dough, which will form the rim of the pizza.

REST one of your hands on the surface of the dough. Lift up a portion of the dough with your other hand and pull it gently away from the center, stretching it as thinly as possible. Continue moving around the dough, stretching it until it reaches the desired shape and size and is between ⅛ and ¼ inch thick. If a hole forms, pinch it closed. (Be very careful when shaping the cornmeal or whole-wheat variations by this method, as those doughs tear easily.) Next, rest one of your hands near the edge of the dough and use your other hand to push the dough against it to form a slight rim, working your way completely around the perimeter of the dough.

ONCE the dough is shaped, sprinkle a pizza peel with cornmeal or lightly brush 1 or more pizza screens or vented pizza pans with oil. Lay the dough on the cornmeal-dusted peel or oiled screen(s). Lightly brush the dough all over with oil. Add toppings, leaving a ½-inch border around the edges, and bake immediately.

continues ~

IF using a pizza peel, before transferring the assembled pizza to the oven, give the peel a quick, short jerk to be sure the bottom of the crust has not stuck to it. Place the peel in the oven, holding the pizza over the stone or tiles, then quickly jerk the peel back 2 or 3 times, hopefully leaving the pizza centered on the cooking surface. (It takes a bit of practice, so don't be discouraged if you lose a few pizzas.) Bake until the crust is puffed and golden, about 10 minutes. Slide the peel underneath the crust and remove the pizza from the oven. Use a metal spatula to lift a portion of the crust, if necessary, in order to slip the peel underneath.

IF using a pizza screen or vented pizza pan, before transferring the assembled pizza or calzone to the oven, give the screen a quick jerk to be sure the dough is not stuck to the wire. Place the screen or pan directly on the hot tiles or pizza stone. If you have not lined the oven with tiles or a stone, place the screen or pan on the top rack of the preheated oven to prevent the direct heat from burning the bottom of the crust. Bake until the crust is puffed and golden, about 10 minutes.

TO bake and serve multiple pizzas, assemble and bake as many pies at one time as the oven will accommodate; several screens are easier to work with when baking several pies at once. Remove each pizza as soon as it is done. If you cannot serve it immediately, do not cover it with aluminum foil to keep it warm; the crust will get soggy. If you wish to serve several pizzas at one time, it is best to bake them up to 1 hour ahead and, just before serving, reheat each one briefly, 2 or 3 minutes, in a preheated 500° F oven.

TO cut a pizza for serving, quickly jerk the pizza off the peel or slide it off the screen or pan onto a metal cutting tray or a flat cutting surface. Lightly brush the edges of the crust with oil. Using a rolling cutting wheel or a serrated bread knife, quickly and firmly cut all the way across the pizza in several places to form wedges. Serve sliced large pizzas directly from the cutting tray or transfer to a platter for passing. Slice small pizzas and serve on individual plates. Serve piping hot.

Makes one 15- to 16-inch round pizza, two 12-inch round pizzas, four to six 8-inch round individual pizzas, or eighteen 3-inch round appetizer-sized *pizzette*; for 8 to 10 appetizer servings or 4 to 6 main-course servings.

PIZZA DOUGH VARIATIONS

TO create crusts with a variety of flavors and textures, make the following changes to the recipe for Basic Pizza Dough. Use an oil that complements the other dough ingredients and pizza toppings.

Cornmeal Dough. Substitute 1 cup yellow cornmeal or polenta (coarse cornmeal) for an equal amount of the flour. Stir the cornmeal, flour, and salt together before adding the yeast mixture.

Cracked Pepper Dough. Add about 3 tablespoons freshly cracked black pepper while kneading the dough.

Curried Dough. Add about 2 tablespoons Indian-Style Curry Powder (page 556) or high-quality commercial curry powder along with the salt. Use canola or other bland vegetable oil.

Herbed Dough. Add about 3 tablespoons minced fresh herbs or 1 tablespoon crumbled dried herbs while kneading the dough.

Seeded Dough. Add about ¼ cup sesame seed, lightly toasted (see page 553), or ¼ cup poppy seed while kneading the dough.

Spicy Dough. Add 2 tablespoons paprika and 1 tablespoon ground cayenne or other dried hot chile along with the salt.

Sweet Dough. Add ¼ cup sugar with the flour and reduce the salt to ½ teaspoon. Use canola or other bland vegetable oil.

Whole-Wheat Dough. Substitute 1 cup whole-wheat flour for an equal amount of the white flour. Stir the flours and the salt together before adding the yeast mixture.

A FEW OF MY FAVORITE PIZZAS

Use the preceding master recipe to make some of my prized combinations.

BARBECUED CHICKEN PIZZA. Combine 5 boned and skinned chicken breast halves with 1 cup of your favorite tomato-based barbecue sauce and marinate for at least 4 hours or up to overnight. Place the chicken and marinade in a baking pan or dish, cover tightly with a lid or aluminum foil, and bake in a preheated 350° F oven until tender and just past the pink stage inside, about 30 minutes. Let the chicken cool, then cut the meat into bite-sized pieces. (Alternatively, grill the chicken over a moderate charcoal fire.) Make the Basic Pizza Dough as directed. Shape the risen dough as desired and brush it all over with oil. Top with a mixture of about 1½ cups freshly shredded Italian Fontina cheese (about 8 ounces) and about 1½ cups freshly shredded smoked Gouda cheese (about 6 ounces). Spoon a thin layer of barbecue sauce over the cheeses. Arrange the chicken and thinly sliced red onion rings over the top and drizzle lightly with oil. Bake as directed. Remove to a cutting surface and lightly brush the edges of the crust with oil. Sprinkle with chopped fresh cilantro (coriander).

CALIFORNIA PIZZA. Roast about 12 garlic cloves as directed on page 551. Make the Basic Pizza Dough with olive oil as directed. Shape the risen dough as desired and brush it all over with olive oil. Top with about 2 cups freshly shredded fresh mozzarella cheese (about 12 ounces) and about 1 cup crumbled fresh or semidry goat cheese (about 4 ounces). Sliver about 12 sun-dried tomatoes packed in olive oil and scatter them over the cheese. Squeeze the roasted garlic from the skin, chop coarsely, and scatter over the pizza. Season to taste with salt and pepper and drizzle lightly with olive oil. Bake as directed. Remove to a cutting surface and lightly brush the edges of the crust with olive oil. Sprinkle with about ¼ cup freshly grated Parmesan cheese (about 1 ounce), preferably Parmigiano-Reggiano.

CARAMELIZED ONION AND SAUSAGE PIZZA. Caramelize 6 cups sliced onion in ½ cup olive oil as directed on page 551. Season to taste with salt and pepper, then stir in 2 tablespoons minced garlic, 12 ounces hot Italian sausage slices, and ½ cup dry white wine and cook until the wine is reduced. Stir in 3 tablespoons chopped fresh flat-leaf parsley. Make the Basic Pizza Dough with olive oil as directed. Shape the risen dough as desired and brush it all over with oil. Distribute a mixture of about 1½ cups freshly shredded Italian Fontina cheese (about 8 ounces), about 1½ cups freshly shredded fresh mozzarella cheese (about 9 ounces), and ¼ cup freshly grated Parmesan cheese (about 1 ounce), preferably Parmigiano-Reggiano, over the dough, then top with the onion and sausage mixture. Bake as directed. Remove to a cutting surface and lightly brush the edges of the crust with olive oil. Sprinkle with more freshly grated Parmesan cheese, minced red sweet pepper, and minced fresh flat-leaf parsley.

FRENCH PIZZA *(PISSALADIÈRE)*. Combine 6 cups sliced yellow or white onion (about 3 pounds) with 2 tablespoons minced garlic, 3 tablespoons fresh thyme leaves or 1 tablespoon crumbled dried thyme, and 1 bay leaf and caramelize as directed on page 551, then season to taste with salt and pepper and discard the bay leaf. Make the Basic Pizza Dough with olive oil as directed. Shape the risen dough as desired and brush it all over with oil. Top with the caramelized onion mixture. Rinse 12 flat anchovy fillets, pat dry with paper toweling, and arrange them over the onion layer. Top with 1 cup pitted Niçoise or other flavorful ripe olives, 1 table-spoon drained capers, and 1½ tablespoons pine nuts and drizzle lightly with olive oil. Bake as directed. Remove to a cutting surface and lightly brush the edges of the crust with olive oil. Sprinkle with minced fresh flat-leaf parsley.

continues ∼

FRESH FIG, BLUE CHEESE, AND HONEY PIZZA DOLCE. Make the Sweet Variation of the Basic Pizza Dough with walnut or almond oil as directed. Shape the dough as desired and brush it all over with oil. Top with about 3 cups crumbled creamy blue cheese such as Gorgonzola or Cambozola (about 12 ounces). Slice about 20 fresh figs in half lengthwise and arrange, cut side up, over the cheese. Drizzle with high-quality honey to taste. Bake as directed. Remove to a cutting surface and lightly brush the edges of the crust with oil. Scatter with about 1 cup Sweet Crunchy Nuts (page 42) or toasted walnuts or almonds (see page 554).

ITALIAN MOZZARELLA AND TOMATO PIZZA (*PIZZA MARGHERITA*). Make the Basic Pizza Dough with olive oil as directed. Shape the risen dough as desired and brush it all over with oil. Sprinkle with about 3 cups freshly shredded fresh mozzarella cheese (about 18 ounces). Scatter 4 cups peeled, seeded, drained, and chopped ripe or canned tomato over the cheese. Sprinkle with 1 tablespoon minced fresh oregano or 1 teaspoon crumbled dried oregano, salt to taste, and ¼ cup freshly grated Parmesan cheese (about 1 ounce), preferably Parmigiano-Reggiano, and drizzle lightly with olive oil. Bake as directed. Remove to a cutting surface, lightly brush the edges of the crust with olive oil, and sprinkle with more freshly grated Parmesan cheese and shredded fresh basil.

TOMATO BASIL PIZZA (*PIZZA CON POMODORO E BASILICO*). Make the Basic Pizza Dough with olive oil as directed. Shape the risen dough as desired and brush it all over with oil. Sprinkle with thinly sliced or minced garlic to taste. Top with 3 pounds sliced vine-ripened plum tomatoes. Sprinkle with salt to taste and drizzle lightly with olive oil. Bake as directed. Remove to a cutting surface, lightly brush the edges of the crust with olive oil, and sprinkle generously with whole basil leaves or shredded or chopped basil or oregano.

OLIVE PASTA PIZZA. Prepare Provençal Olive Paste (page 400). Make the Basic Pizza Dough with olive oil as directed. Shape the risen dough as desired and brush it all over with oil. Spread with the olive paste. Distribute about 3 cups freshly shredded semisoft cheese such as *morbier*, Port-du-Salut, or Taleggio (about 15 ounces) over the olive paste. Top with 2 cups peeled, seeded, drained, and chopped ripe or canned tomato and 1 cup thinly sliced red onion, separated into half rings, and drizzle lightly with olive oil. Bake as directed. Remove to a cutting surface and lightly brush the edges of the crust with oil. Sprinkle with shredded fresh basil and finely chopped fresh red or yellow sweet peppers.

PORK AND PINEAPPLE PIZZA. Make the Basic Pizza Dough with canola or other bland vegetable oil as directed. Shape the risen dough as desired and brush all over with oil. Spoon about ¼ cup tomato paste or sauce over the dough and spread evenly. Top with a mixture of about 1½ cups freshly shredded fresh mozzarella cheese (about 9 ounces) and about 1½ cups freshly shredded Gruyère cheese (about 5 ounces). Top the cheeses with about 8 ounces Canadian bacon or baked ham, thinly sliced and cut into small pieces, and 2 cups chopped fresh pineapple or drained canned crushed pineapple or pineapple chunks. Sprinkle with salt and pepper to taste. Bake as directed. Remove to a cutting surface and lightly brush the edges of the crust with oil. Sprinkle with ¼ cup sliced green onion, including green tops.

SALAD PIZZA. Wash, dry, and chill 4 cups small whole or torn tender young salad greens as directed for Fruit, Nuts, and Greens Salad on page 122. Make the Whole-Wheat or Herbed Variation of the Basic Pizza Dough with olive oil as directed. Shape the risen dough as desired into individual-sized pizzas and brush all over with oil. Sprinkle with minced garlic and freshly grated Parmesan cheese, preferably Parmigiano-Reggiano, to taste. Bake as directed. Meanwhile, prepare Balsamic Vinaigrette (page 565). Just before the pizzas are done, in a bowl, combine the salad greens with ½ small red onion, thinly sliced and separated into half rings, and toss with the vinaigrette to taste. Remove the pizzas to a cutting surface and lightly brush the edges of the crusts with oil. Mound the salad on the pizzas and serve immediately. Instruct diners to fold the pizzas around the salad and eat out of hand like a sandwich.

DEEP-FRIED PIZZA POCKETS
~ *PANZAROTTI* ~

Basic Pizza Dough (page 170)

2 cups freshly shredded fresh
   mozzarella cheese (about 12 ounces)

½ cup freshly grated Parmesan
   cheese (about 2 ounces), preferably
   Parmigiano-Reggiano

¾ cup peeled, seeded, drained, and
   chopped ripe or canned tomatoes

¼ cup chopped fresh basil,
   2 tablespoons chopped fresh
   oregano, or 2 teaspoons crumbled
   dried oregano

Salt

Olive oil for frying

Many years ago in Milan, my late partner, Lin, and I kept encountering people eating handheld fried pies that looked and smelled delicious. After a bit of sleuthing and following our noses, we finally located the hole-in-the-wall shop on a little side street that featured these mouth-watering panzarotti.

One evening on our way to dinner at a fancy Milan restaurant over a decade later, Andrew and I stumbled upon the same little shop with lines of people waiting for the pies to come out of the hot oil. As each one was ready, the southern-Italian proprietor wrapped it in a section of waxed paper for eating out of hand. We decided to share one as an antipasto before continuing on to the restaurant. But we ended up returning to the little shop and dining on several of these scrumptious treats while window shopping on nearby via Montenapoleoni. It turned into one of our most memorable meals in all of Italy.

For variety, add other ingredients such as chopped prosciutto, olives, or sun-dried tomatoes to the filling. Or use any good-melting cheese in place of the mozzarella.

MAKE the Basic Pizza Dough with olive oil as directed.

IN a bowl, combine the cheeses and mix well.

DIVIDE the risen dough into 8 equal portions. Roll out each portion to form a round about 5 inches in diameter. Using half of the cheese mixture, divide it equally among the rounds, covering half of each dough round with the mixture and leaving a ½-inch border around the edges uncovered. Sprinkle the tomato, basil or oregano, and salt to taste evenly over the cheese. Top the tomato with the remaining cheese mixture, again dividing it equally. Using a pastry brush, moisten the exposed edges of the dough with water, fold the uncovered halves over the filling, and press the edges of the dough together to seal well. Using a wooden skewer or fork, punch several holes along the side opposite the sealed side to allow steam to escape during cooking.

IN a deep fryer or dutch oven, pour in olive oil to a depth of 2 inches and heat to 360° F. Place a wire rack on a baking sheet and position alongside the fryer or stove top. Carefully slip a few of the *panzarotti* into the hot oil; avoid crowding the pan. Fry, turning frequently, until golden, about 5 minutes. Using tongs or a slotted utensil, transfer the *panzarotti* to the rack to drain well. Fry the remaining *panzarotti* in the same manner, allowing the oil to return to 360° F between batches.

SERVE piping hot.

Makes 8 servings.

BIG ADVENTURES

Most cooks plan their meals around the main dish. The
recipes in this section offer infinite variety, and many of
the dishes can be served in smaller quantities as starters.
And when the temperature soars, choose one of the cool,
yet satisfying main dishes beginning on page 282.

Hot & Hearty Main Dishes

MANY of us opt for vegetarian fare at least part of the
time, so my selection of main dishes begins with
preparations in which vegetables star. As a bonus,
many of the vegetarian dishes in the Starting Out
and Moving On sections can be served in larger
quantities as satisfying main events.

The recipes that feature fish and shellfish, chicken
and other poultry, and meats call on a wide range of
cooking methods. You'll find both quick and easy
entrées for everyday meals and elaborate preparations
for special occasions. In addition, cooks who entertain
will be delighted to discover a number of dishes that
can be prepared ahead for a more relaxed meal for
guests and hosts alike.

CORNBREAD-CRUSTED
BEAN CHILI

This hearty chili may also be prepared from pinto beans or a combination of beans and topped with any cornbread recipe (see page 423; baking times may vary). For smaller groups, cut the recipe in half and bake it in an 8-inch square baking pan or 2-quart baking dish. The chili also makes a satisfying dish without the cornbread topping.

TO make the Bean Chili, in a small skillet, combine the cumin seed, oregano, and torn chiles. Place over medium heat and toast, shaking the pan or stirring frequently, until fragrant, about 3 minutes; do not allow to burn. Pour onto a plate to cool, then transfer to a spice grinder or heavy mortar with a pestle and grind to a fine powder. Set aside.

IN a large, heavy pot, heat the oil over medium-high heat. Add the onion and cook, stirring frequently, until soft but not browned, about 5 minutes. Add the garlic, cayenne, paprika, and ground chile mixture and cook for about 1 minute longer. Stir in the tomato and *chipotle* chile and bring to a boil, then reduce the heat to achieve a simmer and cook, stirring occasionally, for about 15 minutes.

DRAIN the beans and reserve the liquid. Stir the beans into the simmering mixture. Add enough reserved bean liquid to cover the beans barely, adding water if needed. Add salt to taste and simmer until the mixture is well flavored, about 30 minutes.

REMOVE the chili from the heat and stir in the lime juice or vinegar and cilantro. Taste and adjust seasonings. Set aside.

PREHEAT an oven to 350° F. Using a pastry brush, lightly grease a shallow 3-quart baking dish, a 13-by-9-inch pan, or eight 2-cup baking dishes with oil, or coat with spray. Set aside.

PREPARE the Tex-Mex Cornbread batter as directed.

DRAIN the chili to remove excess liquid, if necessary. Transfer to the prepared baking dish(es). Spread the cornbread batter evenly over the top of the chili, dividing it equally if using individual baking dishes. Bake until golden brown and a wooden skewer inserted into the center of the cornbread layer comes out clean, about 45 minutes.

GARNISH with cilantro sprigs or leaves and serve hot.

Makes 8 servings.

BEAN CHILI

1½ tablespoons cumin seed

1½ tablespoons dried oregano

2 or 3 whole *ancho*, *guajillo*, New Mexico, *pasilla*, or other large dried mild to medium-hot chiles, stems and seeds discarded, torn into small pieces

3 tablespoons olive oil

3 cups chopped onion

2 teaspoons minced garlic

½ teaspoon ground cayenne

1½ tablespoons paprika

4 cups peeled, seeded, drained, and chopped ripe or canned tomato

1 teaspoon chopped canned *chipotle* chile in *adobo* sauce

6 cups cooked dried or canned black (turtle) beans (see page 340)

Salt

1 tablespoon freshly squeezed lime juice or red wine vinegar

¼ cup chopped fresh cilantro (coriander)

Vegetable oil for brushing or cooking spray

Tex-Mex Cornbread batter (page 425)

Fresh cilantro (coriander) sprigs or leaves for garnish

CHILES STUFFED WITH BEANS AND CORN

Mexicali Beans (page 348)
or Southwestern Beans (page 351)

ROASTED TOMATO SALSA

4 pounds ripe tomatoes, cored, cut in
half crosswise, seeded, and drained

4 teaspoons olive oil, preferably
extra-virgin

1½ cups chopped white onion

¼ cup chopped fresh jalapeño or
other hot chile, or to taste

2 teaspoons chopped garlic

Salt

Freshly ground black pepper

8 fresh large mild to medium-hot
chiles such as Anaheim or *poblano*

About 3 medium-sized ears corn

1 cup freshly shredded Monterey Jack
or white Cheddar cheese (about
3 ounces)

¼ cup finely chopped fresh cilantro
(coriander)

Salt

Freshly ground black pepper

Olive oil for brushing

Mexican cultured cream *(crema)*,
Crème Fraîche (page 591), or
commercial crème fraîche, placed
in a squeeze bottle

Fresh epazote, cilantro (coriander), or
flat-leaf parsley sprigs for garnish

Most of us who reside north of the Rio Grande are familiar with battered and fried chiles rellenos. Mexican cooks, however, usually omit the batter and frying when chiles are stuffed with ingredients other than cheese.

COOK the Mexicali or Southwestern beans as directed. Measure out 1½ cups of the cooked beans and set aside. (Save the remaining beans for another use.)

TO make the Roasted Tomato Salsa, preheat an oven to 350° F and line a baking sheet with aluminum foil or kitchen parchment. Place the tomatoes, cut side down, on the prepared baking sheet and roast until the tomatoes are very shriveled and fairly dry but not burned, 1 to 1½ hours. Remove from the oven and let cool briefly, then remove and discard the skins and transfer the pulp to a food processor or blender.

IN a saucepan, heat the oil over medium-high heat. Add the onion and chopped chile and cook, stirring frequently, until the onion is very soft and golden, about 8 minutes. Add the garlic and cook for about 1 minute longer. Transfer to the food processor or blender with the roasted tomato pulp and blend until fairly smooth. Return the mixture to the pan, season to taste with salt and pepper, and set aside.

ROAST the chiles whole as directed on page 552 and set aside.

CUT the corn kernels from the cobs as directed for Sauteed Corn on page 358, measure out 1½ cups, and set aside.

DRAIN the beans and transfer to a bowl. Add the corn, cheese, chopped cilantro, and salt and pepper to taste. Set aside.

LEAVING the stems intact, carefully slit each chile lengthwise down one side. Using your fingertips, remove the seeds and veins, being careful not to tear the chile skin. Sprinkle the insides of the chiles with salt to taste.

PREHEAT an oven to 350° F. Select a baking dish large enough to hold all of the chiles and, using a pastry brush, lightly grease with oil.

STUFF each chile with an equal portion of the bean-corn mixture. Transfer seam side down to the prepared baking dish and lightly brush with oil. Bake until the filling is heated through, about 20 minutes.

TO serve, reheat the Roasted Tomato Salsa and spoon it onto warmed plates. Arrange the chiles on top of each portion, squeeze the cream or crème fraîche over the chiles to create an interesting pattern, and garnish with the herb sprigs.

Makes 4 servings.

CRISPY RICE FLOUR CREPES
~ Cambodian *Nuom am Baing*, Thai *Kanom Bueng Yuan*, or Vietnamese *Bahn Xeo* ~

Thai Chile Dipping Sauce (page 396)
or Vietnamese Chile Dipping Sauce
(page 396)

BATTER

1½ cups Fresh Coconut Milk (page
562) or high-quality commercial
coconut milk

2 eggs

1 cup rice flour (not sweet rice flour)

½ teaspoon sugar

½ teaspoon salt

1 teaspoon ground turmeric

Stir-fried shrimp and pork are traditional fillings for these crunchy crepes, sometimes called crispy omelets, but my vegetable mixture is equally tasty. Vary the filling according to whim.

In Vietnam, the crepes are sometimes served as roll ups. Diners break off pieces of the filled crepe and roll it up in lettuce leaves with fresh herbs and bits of vegetables before dipping it in the sauce and eating it out of hand.

PREPARE the Thai or Vietnamese Chile Dipping Sauce as directed and set aside.

TO make the batter, in a bowl or a blender, combine all of the batter ingredients and whisk or blend until smooth. Refrigerate until cooking time. Stir well to blend just before cooking; if the mixture becomes too thick to pour easily, thin with a little water or coconut milk to the consistency of heavy cream.

TO make the filling, place a wok, large saute pan, or large, heavy skillet over high heat. When the pan is hot, add 2 tablespoons of the oil and swirl to coat the pan. When the oil is hot but not yet smoking, add the shallot and garlic and stir-fry until well coated with the oil, about 1 minute. Add the mushrooms and stir-fry until the mushrooms are tender, about 3 minutes. Transfer to a bowl and set aside. Return the pan to the heat and add the remaining 2 tablespoons oil. When the oil is hot but not yet smoking, add the cabbage and coconut and stir-fry until the cabbage wilts, about 2 minutes. Return the mushroom mixture to the pan. Add the cilantro, fish sauce, and pepper to taste and stir-fry until heated through, about 1 minute. Remove from the heat and stir in the bean sprouts. Set aside.

PREHEAT an oven to 200° F if serving all of the crepes at one time.

TO cook the crepes, in an 8-inch nonstick skillet, pour in 2 table-spoons oil and place over medium-high heat. When the oil is hot but not yet smoking, using a measuring cup, pour in ⅓ cup of the crepe batter and quickly tilt and rotate the pan to spread the batter to form a thin pancake. Cook until brown and crispy on the bottom, 3 to 5 minutes. Using a wide spatula, lift the crepe from the pan and drain off as much oil as possible, then transfer the crepe to a work surface. Spoon about ¾ cup of the filling mixture over one-half of the crepe, then fold the other half of the crepe over the filling. Serve immediately as described below or transfer to a baking sheet and keep warm in the oven. Repeat this process to make and fill 5 more crepes, adding oil to the skillet as needed to equal 2 tablespoons for cooking each crepe.

TO serve, divide the sauce among 6 small bowls and position a bowl at each place. Place the crepes on warmed plates and garnish with cilantro sprigs.

Makes 6 servings.

FILLING

4 tablespoons canola or other
 high-quality vegetable oil

2 cups thinly sliced shallot

2 tablespoons minced garlic

4 cups thinly sliced flavorful fresh
 mushrooms such as chanterelle,
 portobello, porcino, or shiitake

3 cups thinly shredded cabbage,
 preferably napa or other Asian
 variety

½ cup grated or shredded fresh
 coconut (see page 562) or
 unsweetened dried (desiccated)
 coconut

1 cup fresh cilantro (coriander)
 leaves

2 tablespoons fish sauce, preferably
 Thai or Vietnamese

Freshly ground white pepper

4 cups mung bean sprouts

Canola or other high-quality
 vegetable oil for cooking crepes

Fresh cilantro (coriander) sprigs for
 garnish

EGGPLANT PARMIGIANA

2 pounds globe eggplants

Salt

2 cups White Sauce (page 572)

2 cups Tomato Sauce (page 573)

All-purpose flour for dredging

Olive oil for frying, brushing, and
    drizzling

Freshly ground black pepper

1 cup freshly grated Parmesan
    cheese (about 4 ounces), preferably
    Parmigiano-Reggiano

About 30 small whole fresh basil
    leaves, or 3 tablespoons minced
    fresh basil or oregano

Fresh basil or oregano sprigs for
    garnish

*In this lighter version of a venerable favorite, white sauce replaces
mozzarella cheese.*

PEEL the eggplants and slice crosswise into ½-inch-thick slices.
    Sprinkle both sides of each eggplant slice with salt. Lay the
    slices on paper toweling, cover with more paper toweling, top
    with a cutting board and heavy weights (such as aluminum
    foil-wrapped bricks or canned foods), and let stand for about
    30 minutes to draw out excess moisture.

MEANWHILE, prepare the White Sauce and Tomato Sauce as
    directed. Set aside.

USING paper toweling, blot excess salt from the eggplant slices.
    Dredge lightly with flour. In a saute pan or heavy skillet, pour in
    oil to a depth of ¼ inch and heat over medium-high heat. Add as
    many of the eggplant slices as will fit without crowding the pan
    and brown on both sides. Continue to cook, turning several times,
    until tender, about 5 minutes. Using a slotted utensil or tongs,
    transfer the eggplant to paper toweling to drain, then season to
    taste with salt and pepper. Brown the remaining eggplant slices
    in the same manner, adding more oil as necessary.

PREHEAT an oven to 350° F. Using a pastry brush, lightly grease a
    13-by-9-inch pan with oil.

ARRANGE a layer of the eggplant slices in the prepared pan. Spoon
    1 cup of the White Sauce over the eggplant, then top with
    1 cup of the Tomato Sauce. Sprinkle with ½ cup of the cheese.
    Repeat with another layer of eggplant, White Sauce, Tomato
    Sauce, and cheese. Drizzle evenly with olive oil.

BAKE until heated through and the cheese is bubbly, about 20
    minutes. Remove from the oven and let stand to cool for about
    15 minutes.

TO serve, sprinkle with the basil leaves or minced herb and garnish
    with herb sprigs. Cut into pieces and transfer to warmed plates.

Makes 6 servings.

PUEBLO VEGETABLE STEW

If you wish to serve this Native American—inspired stew in squash shells, pierce the shells of whole small squashes such as Golden Nugget variety in several places with the tines of a fork or a small, sharp knife and bake in a 400° F oven until tender when pierced with a wooden skewer. Wearing oven mitts, position the hot baked squashes on a cutting surface and cut off the tops. Using a spoon, scrape out and discard the seeds and stringy portions. Carefully peel off and discard the skin, if desired.

IN a small skillet, combine the cumin seed, torn dried chiles, and oregano. Place over medium heat and toast, shaking the pan or stirring frequently, until fragrant, about 3 minutes; do not allow to burn. Pour onto a plate to cool, then transfer to a spice grinder or heavy mortar with a pestle and grind to a fine powder. Set aside.

IN a saute pan or heavy stew pot such as a dutch oven, heat the oil over medium-high heat. Add the onion and cook, stirring frequently, until soft but not browned, about 5 minutes. Add the minced fresh chile, garlic, cinnamon, and ground chile mixture and cook for 1 minute longer. Add the tomato and 1/2 cup of the stock or broth. Bring to a boil, then reduce the heat to achieve a simmer and simmer for about 5 minutes.

ADD the squash and about 2 cups of the remaining stock or broth and cook until the squash is slightly soft when pierced with a small, sharp knife or wooden skewer, about 10 minutes.

DRAIN the beans and reserve the liquid. Stir the beans and corn into the simmering vegetables and cook until the squash is tender, about 10 minutes, adding more stock, broth, or reserved bean liquid if the stew gets too dry. A few minutes before serving, stir in the chopped herb.

MEANWHILE, toast the pine nuts as directed on page 553 and set aside.

TO serve, ladle the warm stew into warmed shallow bowls, sprinkle with the pine nuts, and garnish with herb sprigs.

Makes 6 servings.

1½ teaspoons cumin seed

1 or 2 whole *ancho, guajillo, pasilla,* or other large dried mild to medium-hot chiles, stems and seeds discarded, torn into small pieces

2 tablespoons minced fresh oregano, or 2 teaspoons crumbled dried oregano

¼ cup canola or other high-quality vegetable oil

1½ cups chopped white or yellow onion

1 tablespoon minced fresh jalapeño or other hot chile

1 teaspoon minced garlic

¼ teaspoon ground cinnamon

2 cups peeled, seeded, drained, and chopped ripe or canned tomato

About 3 cups Vegetable Stock (page 580), White Stock (page 578), or canned vegetable or reduced-sodium chicken broth

About 1¾ pounds winter squash such as Buttercup, Butternut, Golden Nugget, or one of the sweet pumpkin varieties, peeled, seeded, and cut into 1-inch cubes

2 cups cooked dried or canned beans such as Anasazi or pinto (see page 340)

2 cups fresh, thawed frozen, or drained canned corn kernels

½ cup chopped fresh cilantro (coriander) or flat-leaf parsley

½ cup pine nuts

Fresh cilantro (coriander) or parsley sprigs for garnish

VEGETABLE POT PIE WITH SPICY CREAM CHEESE PASTRY

WINTER VEGETABLE RAGOUT

- 6 tablespoons (¾ stick) unsalted butter
- 3 tablespoons canola or other high-quality vegetable oil
- 2 cups chopped leek, including pale green portion
- 1 cup thinly sliced fennel
- 2 teaspoons minced garlic
- 12 ounces carrots, peeled and cut into matchsticks (about 2 cups)
- 12 ounces rutabagas or turnips, peeled and cut into matchsticks (about 2 cups)
- 12 ounces parsnips, peeled and cut into matchsticks (about 2 cups)
- 12 ounces sweet potatoes (preferably not orange "yam" varieties), peeled and cut into matchsticks (about 2 cups)
- ¼ cup chopped fresh flat-leaf parsley, summer savory, or tarragon
- ½ cup dry white wine
- 2 cups Vegetable Stock (page 580), White Stock (page 578), or canned vegetable or reduced-sodium chicken broth
- 2 tablespoons all-purpose flour
- ½ cup half-and-half

If you wish to turn this into a chicken or turkey pot pie, brown bite-sized pieces of boned chicken or turkey in the butter and oil and remove to a bowl before adding the vegetables. Return the fowl to the pot before adding the wine and stock and cook until the meat is tender. The vegetable ragout may also be served on its own without the crust.

TO make the Winter Vegetable Ragout, in a heavy stew pot such as a dutch oven, combine 3 tablespoons of the butter with the oil and place over medium-high heat. When the butter is melted, add the leek and fennel and cook, stirring frequently, until soft but not browned, about 3 minutes. Stir in the garlic, carrots, rutabagas or turnips, parsnips, sweet potatoes, and about half of the herbs and cook for about 3 minutes. Add the wine and stock or broth and bring to a boil. Reduce the heat to achieve a simmer, cover, and simmer until the vegetables are tender, 15 to 20 minutes.

STRAIN the cooking liquid into a bowl and transfer the vegetables to a separate bowl. Melt the remaining 3 tablespoons butter in the stew pot over low heat. Add the flour and cook, whisking frequently, for 3 minutes. Gradually whisk in the cooking liquid and half-and-half. Cook, whisking frequently, until the liquid is thickened to sauce consistency, about 5 minutes.

COMBINE the sauce, vegetables, and the remaining herbs and spoon the mixture into a shallow 2-quart casserole or 6 shallow ramekins or other baking dishes that measure 5 to 6 inches in diameter. Cover and refrigerate until quite cold, for up to 2 days.

TO make the Spicy Cream Cheese Pastry, in a bowl, combine the flour, salt, and ground chile and stir together. Using a pastry blender or two knives, cut in the butter and cream cheese to form a soft dough. Alternatively, combine the dry ingredients in a food processor. Add the butter and cream cheese and process with short pulses until the dough just sticks together. Gather the dough into a ball, wrap in plastic wrap or waxed paper, and chill for at least 30 minutes or up to several hours.

ON a lightly floured board, roll out the dough about ¼ inch thick. Using a ruler as a straight edge and a sharp knife or rolling pastry cutter, cut into long strips about ½ inch wide. Surround the edge of the dish with a strip of dough and pinch the edges to form a decorative pattern. Cut the remaining dough strips to a length that will fit across the top of the casserole. Crisscross the dough strips to form a lattice design over the filling. Using a pastry brush, moisten the ends of each dough strip with beaten egg white and press together with the strip surrounding the dish edges. Pinch off any excess dough and smooth the edges with your fingers. Brush the top of the pastry with the egg-cream mixture. Refrigerate for at least 30 minutes before baking.

ALTERNATIVELY, roll out the dough to fit the top of the baking dish, allowing for an overlap of about 1½ inches. Place the dough over the top of the dish and press with your fingers to secure the edges to the baking dish. Cut slits in the pastry and brush all over with the egg-cream mixture. Refrigerate for at least 30 minutes before baking.

POSITION racks so that the pie will bake in the middle of an oven and preheat the oven to 450° F.

BAKE the pie for 10 minutes, then reduce the heat to 350° F and continue baking until the crust is golden and crisp, 20 to 25 minutes.

TRANSFER to a wire rack to cool for about 15 minutes before serving.

Makes 6 servings.

SPICY CREAM CHEESE PASTRY

- 2 cups all-purpose flour
- ½ teaspoon salt
- 2 teaspoons ground cayenne or other dried hot chile
- 1 cup (2 sticks) very cold unsalted butter, cut into small pieces
- 6 ounces very cold cream cheese (not fat free), cut into small pieces

- 1 egg white, lightly beaten, for moistening
- 1 egg yolk lightly beaten with 1 tablespoon heavy (whipping) cream for brushing

SOUTHWESTERN TAMALE CASSEROLE

Southwestern Beans (page 351)
   made with black beans
¼ cup chopped fresh mint
About 6 medium-sized ears corn,
   or 3 cups thawed frozen or drained
   canned corn kernels
2 cups milk
3 cups Mexican corn flour (*masa
   harina*)
¾ cup high-quality pure lard, solid
   vegetable shortening, or unsalted
   butter, at room temperature
2 teaspoons baking powder
1 teaspoon salt, or to taste
Lard, solid vegetable shortening,
   or unsalted butter, at room
   temperature, for brushing, or
   cooking spray
2 cups crumbled fresh goat cheese
   (about 8 ounces)
2 cups freshly shredded Monterey
   Jack or Cheddar cheese (about
   6 ounces)
Shredded fresh mint for garnish

If you like, substitute crumbled cooked spicy Spanish sausage (chorizo), or Bean Chili (page 183) or Beef Chili (page 279), drained of excess liquid, for the black bean mixture. Please read about masa harina *and the choice of lard on page 602.*

Serve with Fresh Tomato Salsa (page 392), Tomatillo-Chile Salsa (page 393), or other favorite salsa.

COOK the Southwestern Beans as directed. Measure out 4 cups of the cooked beans into a bowl, stir in the chopped mint, and set aside. (Save the remaining beans for another use.)

IF using fresh corn, cut the kernels from the cobs as directed for Sauteed Corn on page 358 and measure out 3 cups.

IN a saucepan, combine the corn and milk. Place over medium heat and bring to a simmer, then adjust the heat to maintain a simmer and cook until the corn is very tender, 10 to 12 minutes. Transfer the mixture to a food processor or blender and puree coarsely. Transfer to a bowl, stir in the corn flour, and mix well. Cover and set aside to cool completely.

IN a bowl, combine the ¾ cup lard, shortening, or butter with the baking powder and salt and beat with an electric mixer at medium speed until light and creamy. Add the corn flour mixture, a little at a time, and mix well after each addition. After all of the corn flour mixture has been incorporated, continue to beat at medium speed for about 1 minute to achieve a light, fluffy dough (it will be sticky). Set aside.

PREHEAT an oven to 350° F. Using a pastry brush, lightly grease a 13-by-9-inch baking pan with lard, vegetable shortening, or butter, or coat with spray.

PRESS half of the corn dough in an even layer into the prepared
pan. Drain the beans of excess liquid if necessary and distribute
evenly over the corn dough. Top with half of each of the cheeses,
then cover with the remaining corn dough, spreading evenly.
Sprinkle with the remaining cheese. Bake until the cheese
melts and the dough is lightly browned and springs back when
lightly pressed with your finger, about 45 minutes. Remove
from the oven and let stand for about 10 minutes.

TO serve, cut into squares, transfer to warmed plates, and sprinkle
with shredded mint.

Makes 8 servings.

NEW ORLEANS BEANS AND RICE

2 cups dried small red beans or small
white beans such as navy

12 ounces flavorful baked ham or
smoked pork, cut into 1-inch
cubes

12 ounces *andouille* or other smoked
hot pork sausage, sliced into
¾-inch lengths

2 cups chopped yellow onion

1 cup chopped celery

1 cup chopped green sweet pepper

1 tablespoon minced garlic

½ cup sliced green onion, including
green tops

¼ cup minced fresh flat-leaf parsley

3 bay leaves

2 tablespoons minced fresh thyme, or
2 teaspoons crumbled dried thyme

1 tablespoon minced fresh oregano,
or 1 teaspoon crumbled dried
oregano

About 2 quarts unsalted Brown Stock
(page 576), Vegetable Stock (page
580), or White Stock (page 578;
all optional)

Salt

Freshly ground black pepper

Ground cayenne

Louisiana hot sauce

2 cups long-grain white rice

Chopped fresh flat-leaf parsley or
green onion, including green tops,
for garnish

Every Monday in New Orleans, as has been the custom for over two centuries, spoonfuls of creamy beans are ladled over mounds of white rice, a carryover from the old washday lunch when beans gently simmered while the laundry slowly dried on clotheslines in the Louisiana humidity. Most people think this classic is only prepared with red beans, but many New Orleans cooks work the same wonders with white beans.

CLEAN and soak the beans as directed on page 342.

IN a large, heavy pot, combine the ham or smoked pork and sausage, place over medium-high heat, and cook until the fat is rendered. Add the onion, celery, and sweet pepper and cook, stirring frequently, until soft and golden, about 8 minutes. Add the garlic and cook for about 1 minute longer.

DRAIN the beans and stir them into the pot. Add the sliced green onion, the minced parsley, bay leaves, thyme, and oregano and enough stock or water to cover by ½ inch. Place over medium-high heat and bring to a boil. Using a wire skimmer or slotted utensil, remove any foam that comes to the surface. Boil for 10 minutes, then reduce the heat to achieve a simmer, cover partially, and simmer, stirring occasionally, until the beans are tender but still hold their shape and have absorbed most of the liquid, about 2 hours. Test frequently toward the end and taste several beans for consistency. Add a little liquid as required if the beans get too dry, but use as little liquid as possible, keeping the beans only slightly submerged. Avoid overcooking at any point to prevent the beans from becoming mushy. Once the beans are tender, season to taste with salt, pepper, cayenne, and hot sauce. (To thicken the bean liquid, if desired, remove and mash about ½ cup of the beans, then stir them back into the pot.)

MEANWHILE, cook the rice as directed on page 364.

TO serve, place a scoop of rice in the center of warmed rimmed plates, ladle the beans all around, and sprinkle with minced parsley or green onion.

Makes 6 servings.

NEUCHÂTEL FONDUE

It's unfortunate that fondue keeps passing in and out of vogue in America. This venerable Swiss dish is always a fun and easy way to entertain and is especially satisfying on a cold winter's night. If you haven't indulged in a fondue supper in a while, dig out those old utensils or adapt what you have on hand and give it another chance.

Originating with the Wavre family of Neuchâtel, Switzerland, this recipe made its way to the Borel-Cotton clan, part of my adopted California family. A crunchy green salad, chilled white wine, and fruit dessert round out the meal.

Kirsch, or kirschwasser, is a clear, colorless brandy distilled from cherries with a distinct bitter almond flavor. Tradition dictates dipping the bread into a glass of kirsch before it goes into the fondue, as well as a kiss from a dining companion each time a piece of bread falls off the dipping fork into the simmering cheese.

IN a large bowl, combine the cheeses and set aside.

CUT the garlic cloves in half and rub the cut surfaces all over the interior of a fondue pot, chafing dish, or other pan that evenly distributes heat. Add the butter and place over medium heat until melted. In a bowl, combine the wine and cornstarch and stir until the cornstarch is dissolved, then add it to the melted butter. When the wine is hot but not boiling, add a handful of the cheese. Using a wooden spoon, stir in one direction until the cheese melts and the mixture is quite smooth. Continue adding cheese, a handful at a time, stirring until it has all been added and melted. Season to taste with salt, pepper, and nutmeg. Stir in the kirsch and heat through.

PLACE the pot of melted cheese over a votive candle or very low flame. Put the bread in a basket or other container alongside. Provide long-handled fondue forks or skewers for each person to spear the bread for dipping. Offer small containers of kirsch for those who wish to dip their bread into the liqueur before dipping it into the fondue.

Makes 8 servings.

8 cups freshly shredded Emmentaler
cheese (about 1½ pounds)

6 cups freshly shredded Gruyère
cheese (about 18 ounces)

3 cups freshly shredded Monterey
Jack cheese (about 9 ounces)

2 garlic cloves

3 tablespoons unsalted butter

2 cups dry white wine

3 tablespoons cornstarch

Salt

Freshly ground black pepper

Freshly grated nutmeg

1 cup kirsch (kirschwasser)

1 to 2 French baguettes, sliced
½ inch thick, then slices cut into
bite-sized pieces

Additional kirsch for dipping
(optional)

SUMMER SQUASH, LEEK, AND GOAT CHEESE TART IN WILD RICE CRUST

WILD RICE CRUST

1 egg

½ cup freshly grated Parmesan cheese (about 2 ounces), preferably Parmigiano-Reggiano

3 tablespoons unsalted butter, melted and cooled slightly

2 tablespoons freshly squeezed lemon juice

2½ cups cooked wild rice (page 364)

Salt

Freshly ground black pepper

CUSTARD FILLING

2 cups finely chopped or coarsely shredded summer squash

Salt

½ cup (1 stick) unsalted butter

2 cups thinly sliced leek, including pale green portion

Freshly ground black pepper

4 eggs

1½ cups heavy (whipping) cream, light cream, or half-and-half

1 teaspoon Dijon mustard

1 cup crumbled fresh goat cheese (about 4 ounces)

1 tablespoon chopped fresh marjoram or savory, or 1 teaspoon crumbled dried marjoram

Crunchy wild rice is a satisfying counterpoint to the creamy French custard filling. Cooked brown or white rice (page 364) can be substituted for the wild rice for a more subtle flavor.

PREHEAT an oven to 350° F.

TO make the Wild Rice Crust, in a bowl, combine the 1 egg, Parmesan cheese, melted butter, and lemon juice and whisk to combine. Stir in the cooked rice and season to taste with salt and pepper. Transfer to a 9-inch pie pan and press with your fingertips to cover the bottom and sides evenly. Bake until set and crisp, about 15 minutes. Remove to a wire rack to cool for about 30 minutes. (At this point, the crust can be covered and refrigerated for up to 12 hours; return to room temperature before filling.)

MEANWHILE, to make the Custard Filling, place the squash in a colander set over a bowl or in a sink. Generously sprinkle with salt, mix with your fingertips to distribute the salt, and let stand for 30 minutes. Rinse and drain well, then gently squeeze to release excess moisture. Set aside.

IN a saute pan or skillet, melt the ½ cup butter over medium-high heat. Add the leek and cook, stirring frequently, until soft, about 5 minutes. Add the squash and salt and pepper to taste and cook for about 5 minutes longer. Remove from the heat and set aside.

IN a bowl, combine the 4 eggs, cream or half-and-half, mustard, goat cheese, marjoram or savory, and salt and pepper to taste and whisk to blend well. Stir in the leek-squash mixture, pour into the rice shell, and bake until the filling is set and the top is golden, 30 to 35 minutes.

TRANSFER to a wire rack to cool for about 15 minutes.

TO serve, cut the tart into wedges and transfer to warmed plates.

Makes 6 servings.

GRILLED SESAME TOFU

Even nonvegetarians won't miss the meat when served this intensely flavored tofu with a crispy crust.

DRAIN the tofu, slice each block horizontally in half, and arrange in a single layer on a baking sheet or tray lined with several thicknesses of paper toweling. Cover with more paper toweling and a second baking sheet or cutting board, top with a heavy weight (such as aluminum foil-wrapped bricks or canned foods), and let stand for 1 to 2 hours to remove excess moisture.

TO make the Sesame Marinade, in a nonreactive bowl, combine all of the marinade ingredients, mix well, and set aside.

CUT each slab of drained tofu into 4 rectangles and arrange them in a shallow nonreactive container. Pour the marinade over the tofu, cover, and refrigerate, turning occasionally, for at least 24 hours or up to 6 days; return to room temperature before cooking.

ABOUT 30 minutes before cooking, place 8 bamboo skewers in a shallow container, cover with water, and set aside to soak. Prepare an open grill for moderate direct-heat cooking.

IN a small skillet, place the sesame seed over medium heat and toast, shaking the pan or stirring frequently, until fragrant, about 5 minutes. Pour onto a plate to cool.

REMOVE the tofu from the marinade, reserving the marinade. If using the green onions, cut each onion into 3 pieces of equal length. Then, working with 1 onion at a time and beginning with the root end, thread the 3 onion pieces lengthwise onto the soaked skewers, alternating them with 2 pieces of the tofu; thread the onion pieces in order to simulate the look of a whole onion. Alternatively, thread the tofu onto the skewers.

WHEN the fire is ready, lightly brush the grill rack with oil. Place the skewered tofu on the rack and cook, turning frequently and brushing with the marinade, until lightly browned on all sides, 12 to 15 minutes.

TO serve, sprinkle the tofu with the toasted sesame seed and arrange on warmed plates.

Makes 4 servings.

2 packages (about 14 ounces each) extra-firm tofu

SESAME MARINADE

½ cup soy sauce

½ cup red wine

½ cup unseasoned rice vinegar

½ cup Asian sesame oil

¼ cup fruity olive oil, preferably extra-virgin

2 tablespoons hot chile oil, or to taste

1 tablespoon minced garlic

Salt

½ cup sesame seed, preferably black variety

8 green onions, including green tops (optional)

Vegetable oil for brushing grill rack

THAI GRILLED FISH WITH RED CURRY
SAUCE ~ *PLAH YAHNG GAENG PEHT* ~

2 pounds fish fillet (see recipe
  introduction), skinned and cut into
  4 equal pieces
Salt
3 tablespoons Thai Red Curry Paste
  (page 557) or canned Thai red
  curry paste, or to taste
1¼ cups chilled Fresh Coconut Milk
  (page 562) or unshaken high-quality
  commercial coconut milk
2 teaspoons fish sauce, preferably
  Thai or Vietnamese, or to taste
2 teaspoons soy sauce, or to taste
1 teaspoon palm sugar, or to taste
Vegetable oil for brushing grill rack
  or basket
Slivered green onion tops for garnish

Although any fish may be grilled, those with soft flesh, such as sole, have a tendency to fall apart when they are turned. For this preparation, I prefer salmon, sea bass, catfish, or swordfish, but choose whatever is freshest at the market.

QUICKLY rinse the fish under cold running water and pat dry with paper toweling. Measure the fish at the thickest point and note the measurement. Season to taste with salt and rub about 1½ tablespoons of the curry paste over the entire surface of the fish. Cover and refrigerate for at least 4 hours or for up to overnight; return the fish to room temperature just before cooking.

PREPARE an open grill for hot direct-heat cooking.

SCOOP ¼ cup coconut cream from the top of the coconut milk and transfer to a small saucepan. Place over medium heat and bring to a boil. Stir in the remaining 1½ tablespoons curry paste and cook, stirring constantly, until very fragrant, about 5 minutes.

STIR the remaining 1 cup coconut milk to achieve a smooth consistency, then slowly stir it into the curry paste mixture. Add the fish sauce, soy sauce, and sugar. Bring to a boil, stirring constantly, then adjust the heat to achieve a simmer and cook, stirring frequently, until thickened to a thin sauce consistency, about 10 minutes. Taste and adjust with fish sauce, soy sauce, and palm sugar to achieve a good balance of salty and sweet. Keep warm.

WHEN the fire is ready, lightly brush the grill rack or a grill basket with oil. Place the fish on the rack or in the basket. Grill, turning once, until the flesh is opaque when cut into at the thickest part with a small, sharp knife, about 10 minutes per inch of thickness, or until done to preference; avoid overcooking. Transfer to a cutting surface and remove any skin.

TO serve, pool the sauce onto a serving dish or divide evenly among 4 warmed plates, top with the fish, and scatter green onion over the top. Serve warm.

Makes 4 servings.

BARBECUED SALMON

In contrast to the usual method of grilling fish directly over a hot fire, Babs Lonon, a great salmon cook, taught me her secret of grilling the prized fish indirectly over a fairly slow mesquite fire in a covered grill. She closes the air vents for a short time during the cooking to impart a hint of smoky flavor. Use the same method to cook salmon steaks or fillets.

PREPARE a covered grill for moderately low indirect-heat cooking. Position a drip pan in the center of the fuel grate.

TO make Babs's Barbecue Sauce, in a saucepan, combine all of the sauce ingredients and place over low heat. Simmer until the butter is melted and the flavors are well blended, about 15 minutes. Remove from the heat and set aside.

QUICKLY rinse the salmon under cold running water and pat dry with paper toweling. If using a salmon section, butterfly it by cutting from the inside of the cavity along both sides of the central bone to release the bone from the flesh; be careful not to cut through the flesh and skin. Discard the bone and spread out the two sides of the fish so it lies flat. To determine the cooking time, measure the roast at its thickest point, or measure the whole fish across the back (hold the ruler perpendicular to the spine) at its widest point. Season to taste with salt and pepper and brush the fish all over with some of the sauce.

WHEN the fire is ready, lightly brush the grill rack with oil. Place the fish, skin side down, on the rack directly over the drip pan. Cook the fish, brushing frequently with the sauce and turning only once, until the flesh is just opaque when cut into at the thickest part with a small, sharp knife, about 10 minutes per inch of thickness. Cover the grill and close the air vents during at least part of the cooking to add smoky flavor.

REMOVE and discard the garlic from any remaining sauce, bring to a boil over medium-high heat, and serve with the fish.

Makes 6 to 10 servings.

BABS'S BARBECUE SAUCE

1 cup (2 sticks) unsalted butter

2 garlic cloves, halved

¼ cup soy sauce

2 tablespoons yellow American mustard

1 tablespoon Worcestershire sauce

2 teaspoons catsup, or to taste

1 salmon section (about 5 pounds), skin intact, or 1 whole 6- to 10-pound salmon, dressed

Salt

Freshly ground black pepper

Vegetable oil for brushing grill rack

CORN-WRAPPED SALMON AND SCALLOPS

4 ears corn, unhusked

1 pound salmon fillet, skinned and cut into 4 equal pieces

1 pound small sea scallops, or 1 pound larger scallops, cut into small pieces

¼ cup freshly squeezed lemon juice

4 green onions, including green tops, thinly sliced

Salt

Freshly ground black pepper

¼ cup (½ stick) unsalted butter

Vegetable oil for brushing grill rack

The summer combination of grilled salmon and garden-fresh corn is an unbeatable one. Here's an unusual presentation of the classic team. Since sea scallops cook in about the same amount of time as salmon, they're perfect additions to the colorful bundles. Although certainly less picturesque, aluminum foil may be used instead of the corn husks.

PREPARE an open grill for hot direct-heat cooking.

REMOVE the husks and silks from the corn, being careful not to tear the husks and keeping them as fully intact as possible. Remove 1 sturdy leaf from each set of husks and cut each of these lengthwise into 2 strips; reserve all of the husks. Cut the corn kernels from the cobs as directed for Sauteed Corn on page 358 and set aside.

QUICKLY rinse the salmon and scallops under cold running water, pat dry with paper toweling, and set aside.

SPREAD out the 4 sets of corn husks on a flat surface, making sure the leaves overlap to prevent leakage during cooking. Spoon one-fourth of the corn kernels into the center of each husk set. Top the corn with a piece of salmon and one-fourth of the scallops. Sprinkle each packet with the lemon juice, green onions, and salt and pepper to taste, and dot with the butter. Bring the husks together to enclose the contents completely and tie each end with a strip of husk.

WHEN the fire is ready, lightly brush the grill rack with oil. Place the packets on the rack and grill, turning once, until the salmon is just opaque when cut into at the thickest part with a small, sharp knife, about 10 minutes. Test by opening a packet.

TRANSFER the packets to warmed plates and serve immediately, allowing diners to open packets at the table.

Makes 4 servings.

ROASTED FISH IN A LEMON-NUT CRUST

Here, a venerable cooking method is updated with the sprightly flavors of lemon, herbs, and chopped nuts. The result is moist fish with a crunchy coating.

Serve with Old-fashioned Tartar Sauce (page 387), a sweet-hot mustard, or fresh salsa (see pages 392-395).

PREHEAT an oven to 350° F.

TOAST the nuts as directed on page 554. Chop finely and set aside.

POSITION racks so that the fish will roast in the upper third of the oven and increase the oven temperature to 550° F.

IN a shallow bowl, combine the chopped nuts, bread crumbs, minced or crumbled thyme, and minced or grated lemon zest. Pour the milk into a second shallow bowl. Set the crumb mixture and milk aside.

QUICKLY rinse the fish under cold running water and pat dry with paper toweling. Season to taste with salt and pepper. Dip each piece of the fish into the milk and then into the crumb mixture to cover completely; with your fingertips, pat the fish all over so that the crumbs are well adhered.

SET a rack in a shallow baking or roasting pan and lightly brush the rack with oil or coat with spray. Arrange the fish without touching on the rack and drizzle the butter or oil over the fish. Roast until golden on the outside and the flesh is just opaque when cut into at the thickest part with a small, sharp knife, about 10 minutes per inch of thickness, or until done to preference.

TO serve, transfer the fish pieces to warmed plates or a platter and garnish with shredded lemon zest (if using) and herb sprigs.

Makes 4 servings.

1 cup pecans, hazelnuts (filberts), or other nuts

½ cup fine unseasoned dried bread crumbs, preferably made from French bread

¼ cup minced fresh thyme, preferably lemon variety, or 2 tablespoons crumbled dried thyme

1 tablespoon minced or grated fresh lemon zest

1 cup milk

2 pounds fish fillet, skinned and cut into 8 equal pieces

Salt

Freshly ground black pepper

Vegetable oil or cooking spray for greasing

½ cup (1 stick) unsalted butter, melted, or fruity olive oil, preferably extra-virgin

Shredded fresh lemon zest for garnish (optional)

Fresh thyme, preferably lemon variety, or other herb sprigs for garnish

PARCHMENT-WRAPPED FISH

Unsalted butter, at room temperature, vegetable oil, or cooking spray for greasing

About 2 medium-sized ears corn, or 1 cup thawed frozen or drained canned corn kernels

2 small carrots, peeled and slivered

2 green onions, including green tops, slivered

½ large red sweet pepper, stem, membranes, and seeds discarded, slivered

1 or 2 fresh serrano or other small hot chiles, stems, membranes, and seeds discarded, slivered

½ cup coarsely chopped fresh cilantro (coriander)

6 firm-fleshed or flaky-fleshed fish steaks, about 8 ounces each and 1 inch thick, or 3 pounds fish fillet, skinned and cut into 6 equal pieces

6 tablespoons tequila

6 tablespoons freshly squeezed lime juice

3 tablespoons unsalted butter, melted

Salt

Ground *ancho*, *pasilla*, or other dried mild to medium-hot chile

6 thin lime slices

Fresh cilantro (coriander) sprigs for garnish

Diners are greeted by aromatic bursts of southwestern flavors when they cut open these puffed packets. The rest of the meal should be completely ready so that the parchment bundles can go directly from the oven to the table.

The only problem with this cooking method is the inability to test the fish to see if it is done; you'll have to rely on measuring the thickness of the fish beforehand and cooking it 10 minutes per inch for completely opaque fish, or a little less if you prefer moister fish. Choose firm-fleshed or flaky-fleshed fish for this method; soft-fleshed fish cooks too quickly.

PREHEAT an oven to 475° F.

CUT kitchen parchment into 6 rectangles measuring 10 by 20 inches each. Using a pastry brush, lightly brush one side of each sheet with butter or oil, or coat with spray. Fold each rectangle in half to form a square with greased sides facing each other. Set aside.

IF using fresh corn, cut the kernels from the cobs as directed for Sauteed Corn on page 358 and measure out 1 cup.

IN a bowl, combine the corn, carrots, onions, sweet pepper, fresh chiles, and chopped cilantro. Open the greased parchment and scatter half of the mixture evenly over one half of each piece of parchment, dividing equally and leaving at least a 2-inch border all around each piece.

QUICKLY rinse the fish under cold running water and pat dry with paper toweling. Place a piece of fish on top of the vegetables on each piece of parchment.

IN a small bowl, stir together the tequila and lime juice. Spoon 2 tablespoons of the mixture over each piece of fish. Drizzle the fish evenly with the melted butter and sprinkle with salt and ground chile to taste. Place a lime slice on each piece of fish and scatter the remaining vegetable mixture evenly over the tops.

FOLD the other halves of the parchment over the fish and seal each
packet securely by making a series of tight overlapping folds
along each side to form a square. Place the packets on a baking
sheet and bake until the packets puff up, about 10 minutes.

TRANSFER the packets to warmed plates, garnish with cilantro
sprigs, and serve immediately, allowing diners to open packets
at the table.

Makes 6 servings.

CHINESE DRAGON FISH

GINGERED CITRUS SAUCE

½ cup sugar

1½ tablespoons cornstarch

¼ cup freshly squeezed lemon or
 lime juice

2 tablespoons unsalted butter

3 tablespoons minced fresh ginger

1 tablespoon grated or minced fresh
 lemon or lime zest

2 tablespoons minced fresh cilantro
 (coriander)

2 pounds firm-fleshed fish fillet, skin
 intact, cut into 4 equal pieces

Canola or other high-quality vegetable
 oil for frying

All-purpose flour for dredging

Lemon slices or Pickled Ginger (page
 406) for garnish

Fresh herb sprigs such as cilantro
 (cilantro), chervil, or flat-leaf
 parsley for garnish

*Choose sea bass, catfish, red snapper, rockfish, or other firm-fleshed or
flaky-fleshed fish for this dish, which is traditionally prepared with a
whole fish. Fish fillets make preparation and serving easier. Although
usually accompanied with a sweet-and-sour sauce, I find this sweet yet
tangy citrus sauce highly complementary.*

TO make the Gingered Citrus Sauce, in a small saucepan, combine
 the sugar, cornstarch, and 1 cup cold water. Place over medium
 heat and cook, whisking constantly, until thickened, 3 to 5
 minutes. Add the lemon or lime juice, butter, ginger, zest, and
 minced cilantro and whisk until the butter is melted. Set aside.

QUICKLY rinse the fish under cold running water and pat dry with
 paper toweling. Lay the fish fillets, skin side down, on a flat
 work surface. Holding a sharp knife at a 45-degree angle, score
 each fillet in a diamond-shaped pattern almost through to
 the skin.

BRING a pot of water to a simmer over medium-high heat. Holding
 a fish fillet at both ends with the flesh side down, dip it briefly
 into the simmering water to shrink the meat slightly. (This
 step will help to accent the pattern when the fillets are cooked.)
 Transfer to paper toweling to drain and repeat with the
 remaining fillets.

IN a deep fryer or saucepan, pour in oil to a depth of 2 inches and
 heat to 375° F. Place a wire rack on a baking sheet and position
 alongside the fryer or stove top. Preheat an oven to 200° F.

DREDGE the fish on all sides with flour, shaking off excess flour.
 Hold a piece of the fish at both ends skin side up and carefully
 and slowly immerse it into the hot oil. Cook until golden on the
 outside and the flesh is opaque when cut into at the thickest
 part with a small, sharp knife, 5 to 8 minutes, depending on size
 of the fillet, or until done to preference. Using a slotted utensil,
 transfer the fish to the rack to drain well, then place the rack
 and baking sheet in the oven to keep warm. Fry the remaining
 fish in the same manner, allowing the oil to return to 375° F
 between batches.

MEANWHILE, slowly reheat the sauce.

TO serve, place a fish fillet on each of 4 warmed plates. Spoon a
little of the sauce over and around the fish and spoon the rest
into small bowls placed on each plate. Garnish the fish with
lemon or ginger slices and herb sprigs.

Makes 4 servings.

LEAF-WRAPPED STUFFED SALMON

Unsalted butter, at room temperature,
vegetable oil, or cooking spray
for greasing

3 heads lettuce, preferably butter
type, or 1 pound fresh young sorrel
leaves

1 cup fresh bread crumbs, preferably
from French bread

1 cup unblanched almonds

1 cup fresh flat-leaf parsley sprigs

1 tablespoon fresh tarragon or thyme
leaves

3 tablespoons grated or minced fresh
lemon zest

¼ cup freshly squeezed lemon juice

½ cup (1 stick) unsalted butter, at
room temperature

Salt

Freshly ground black pepper

Ground cayenne

1 whole 5- to 8-pound salmon,
dressed and boned

Gourmet extraordinaire Stephen Suzman shared this memorable salmon presentation. The stuffing is so good, you may wish to cook an extra batch in a baking dish or in hollowed-out lemons to place on each plate. Serve the salmon with lemon and butter or melted Compound Butter made with ginger (page 402). For individual servings, divide the stuffing and wrapping among six 1-pound farm-raised fish.

PREHEAT an oven to 350° F. Using a pastry brush, lightly grease a baking sheet with butter or vegetable oil or coat with spray. Set aside.

BRING a pot of water to a boil over high heat and prepare a bowl of iced water. Working in batches, dip the lettuce or sorrel leaves in the boiling water just until wilted, immediately dip in the iced water, then transfer to paper toweling to drain. Set aside.

IN a food processor, combine the bread crumbs, almonds, and parsley and process just until coarsely chopped and well mixed. Add the tarragon or thyme, lemon zest and juice, and ½ cup butter and mix thoroughly. Season to taste with salt, pepper, and cayenne.

QUICKLY rinse the salmon under cold running water and pat dry with paper toweling. To determine the cooking time, measure the fish across the back (hold the ruler perpendicular to the spine) at its widest point. Stuff the cavity of the salmon with the bread crumb mixture. Place the fish on the prepared baking sheet. Drain the blanched lettuce or sorrel leaves and wrap the fish in the leaves, overlapping them as you work and covering the fish completely with several layers.

BAKE the salmon until the flesh is barely opaque when cut into at the thickest part with a small, sharp knife, about 10 minutes per inch of thickness.

TO serve, at the table, cut the fish crosswise into 1-inch-thick slices and place on warmed plates.

Makes 6 to 8 servings.

THAI PINEAPPLE SHRIMP CURRY
~ *Gaeng Sapbhalot Goong* ~

Using canned pineapple makes this curry easier to prepare, although you may wish to substitute fresh fruit; you'll need 1 cup chopped fruit and 2 cups cut into bite-sized pieces.

PEEL and devein the shrimp, quickly rinse under cold running water, pat dry with paper toweling, and slice in half lengthwise. Cover and refrigerate until needed.

SCOOP ½ cup coconut cream from the top of the coconut milk and transfer to a wok or heavy saucepan. Place over medium heat and bring to a boil. Stir in the curry paste and cook, stirring constantly, until very fragrant, about 5 minutes.

STIR the remaining 1½ cups coconut milk to achieve a smooth consistency, then slowly stir it into the curry paste mixture. Add the crushed pineapple, fish sauce, and sugar. Bring to a simmer and cook for about 3 minutes.

ADD the shrimp to the simmering curry and cook until the shrimp curl and turn opaque, 1 to 2 minutes. Stir in the pineapple chunks, lime juice, and about 2 tablespoons each of the green onion and shredded mint and heat through.

LADLE into a serving bowl and sprinkle with the lime zest and the remaining green onion and shredded mint. Garnish with whole mint leaves and serve warm.

Makes 4 servings.

10 ounces large shrimp in shells

2 cups chilled Fresh Coconut Milk (page 562) or unshaken high-quality commercial coconut milk

2 tablespoons Thai Yellow Curry Paste (page 559) or canned Thai yellow curry paste, or to taste

1 can (8 ounces) crushed pineapple, drained

3 tablespoons fish sauce, preferably Thai or Vietnamese

1 tablespoon palm sugar

1 can (20 ounces) pineapple chunks, drained

2 tablespoons freshly squeezed lime juice

3 tablespoons finely chopped green onion, including green tops

3 tablespoons shredded fresh mint leaves

Shredded or minced zest of 1 lime

Whole fresh mint leaves for garnish

CURRIED SHELLFISH STEW

2 tablespoons canola or other high-quality vegetable oil

1 cup chopped shallot or red onion

1 cup chopped yellow or red sweet pepper

1 tablespoon Indian-Style Curry Powder (page 556) or high-quality commercial curry powder, or to taste

1 teaspoon minced garlic

2 fresh Scotch bonnet, *habanero*, or other hot chiles, stems, seeds, and membranes discarded, cut length-wise into narrow strips

1 cup Fish Stock (page 575), White Stock (page 578) made with chicken, or canned reduced-sodium chicken broth

1 cup Fresh Coconut Milk (page 562) or high-quality commercial coconut milk

4 tablespoons freshly squeezed lime juice

18 large shrimp in shells

1 pound scallops

12 mussels in shells, well scrubbed and debearded

12 clams in shells, well scrubbed

1 pound cooked lobster meat

3 tablespoons minced fresh cilantro (coriander)

2 tablespoons unsalted butter

Salt

Freshly ground black pepper

Minced fresh lime zest for garnish

Use any combination of fresh shellfish in this tropical island-inspired stew. Serve with white rice, quinoa, or Couscous (pages 364 or 371). A crisp vegetable salad of asparagus or green beans is a good accompaniment.

IN a large, nonreactive pot (avoid cast iron, which will turn coconut milk gray), heat the oil over medium-high heat. Add the shallot or onion, sweet pepper, and curry powder and cook, stirring frequently, until the vegetables are soft, about 5 minutes. Stir in the garlic and chiles and cook for about 1 minute longer.

ADD the stock or broth, coconut milk, and 2 tablespoons of the lime juice. Bring to a boil, then adjust the heat to achieve a simmer, cover partially, and simmer for about 15 minutes.

MEANWHILE, quickly rinse the shrimp and scallops under cold running water and pat dry with paper toweling. Peel and devein the shrimp.

ADD the shrimp, scallops, mussels, and clams to the simmering coconut milk mixture. Cover and cook until the mussels and clams open and the shrimp and scallop meat is opaque, about 5 minutes. Discard any clams or mussels that do not open. Stir in the lobster meat, the remaining 2 tablespoons lime juice, cilantro, butter, and salt and pepper to taste. Reduce the heat to low and cook, uncovered, until the butter melts and the lobster is heated through, about 3 minutes.

TO serve, ladle the hot stew into warmed bowls and sprinkle each portion with lime zest.

Makes 6 servings.

BANGKOK
FRAGRANT HERB
NOODLES

(page 137)

———

SPINACH-STUFFED
PASTA PACKAGES
WITH CITRUS CREAM

(page 144)

LOBSTER RISOTTO

(page 161)

———

COLD SPICY NOODLES
WITH CHICKEN IN
CREAMY SESAME DRESSING

(page 294)

NORTHERN ITALIAN
POLENTA CASSEROLE
(page 156)

———

ROMAN BAKED
SEMOLINA DUMPLINGS
(page 163)

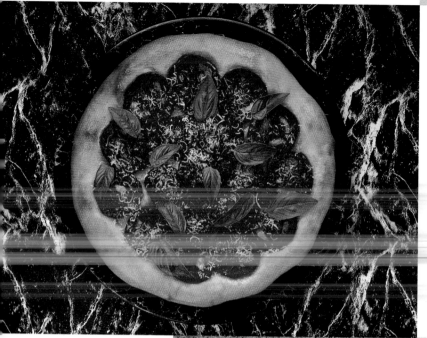

TOMATO BASIL
PIZZA
(page 178)

———

SALAD PIZZA

(page 179)

FRESH FIG, BLUE
CHEESE, AND HONEY
PIZZA DOLCE
(page 178)

———

VEGETABLE
POT PIE
(page 190)

GRILLED
SESAME TOFU
(page 197)

———

PARCHMENT-WRAPPED
FISH
(page 202)

SALMON TERIYAKI

(page 220)

———

ROMAN
CHICKEN CUTLETS
WITH PROSCIUTTO
AND SAGE

(page 221)

INDIAN-STYLE
CHICKEN CURRY
(page 225)

———

THAI CURRY

(page 226)

FISH STEAKS WITH GINGERED MANGO SAUCE

Steaks from large, whole firm-fleshed fish may be cut crosswise from the center of the fish or on the diagonal from one of the fillets. Tuna is a popular choice for grilling on the West Coast; East Coast residents are more likely to opt for swordfish. Bluefish, mahi-mahi, salmon, sea bass, shark, and sturgeon are other good candidates for this preparation.

TO begin the Gingered Mango Sauce, in a saucepan, melt the butter over medium-high heat. Add the shallot or onion and cook, stirring frequently, until soft but not browned, about 5 minutes. Add the ginger and garlic and cook for 1 minute longer. Pour in the wine and cook until the wine is reduced to about ¼ cup. Transfer the mixture to a food processor or blender. Add the mango and stock or broth and puree until smooth. Return the mixture to the saucepan and place over medium-high heat. Add the cream, lime juice, and salt and pepper to taste and cook until the sauce is reduced by half. Set aside. Reserve the chopped mint for later use.

PREPARE an open grill for hot direct-heat cooking.

QUICKLY rinse the fish under cold running water and pat dry with paper toweling.

WHEN the fire is ready, lightly brush the grill rack with oil. Using a pastry brush, coat the fish lightly with oil and sprinkle with salt and pepper. Place the fish on the grill rack directly over the heat for about 1 minute. Reposition the steaks on the same side at a 45-degree angle to the original position to create classic crosshatched grill marks. Cook, turning once, until the flesh is just opaque when cut into with a small, sharp knife, 6 to 8 minutes total.

MEANWHILE, slowly reheat the sauce and stir in the chopped mint.

TO serve, spoon a portion of the sauce onto 4 warmed plates. Top with the steaks and garnish with lime slices and mint sprigs.

Makes 4 servings.

GINGERED MANGO SAUCE

2 tablespoons unsalted butter

6 tablespoons chopped shallot or red onion

2 tablespoons minced fresh ginger

1 teaspoon minced garlic

1 cup dry white wine

2 cups sliced ripe mango

1 cup Fish Stock (page 575), White Stock (page 578) made with chicken, or canned reduced-sodium chicken broth

½ cup heavy (whipping) cream, light cream, or half-and-half

¼ cup freshly squeezed lime juice

Salt

Freshly ground white pepper

¼ cup chopped fresh mint

Four ¾-inch-thick tuna or swordfish steaks (about 8 ounces each)

Vegetable oil for brushing grill rack

Canola or other high-quality vegetable oil for brushing fish

Salt

Freshly ground black pepper

Lime slices for garnish

Fresh mint sprigs for garnish

GRILLED TROUT WITH TOASTED PECAN BUTTER AND CHAMPAGNE CREAM

TOASTED PECAN BUTTER

1½ cups pecans

6 tablespoons (¾ stick) unsalted
butter, at room temperature

2 tablespoons freshly squeezed
lemon juice

2 teaspoons Worcestershire sauce

CHAMPAGNE CREAM

1 bottle (750 ml) brut Champagne or
other dry sparkling wine

¾ cup minced shallot or red onion

2 cups Fish Stock (page 575) or
bottled clam juice

1 quart heavy (whipping) cream

2 tablespoons Worcestershire sauce

½ cup (1 stick) unsalted butter, cut
into 8 equal pieces

⅓ cup minced fresh chervil or other
mild herb

Freshly squeezed lemon juice

Salt

Ground cayenne

6 trout (about ½ pound *each*),
preferably boned

Canola or other high-quality vegetable
oil for brushing fish

Salt

Freshly ground black pepper

Vegetable oil for brushing grill rack or
basket

This recipe, inspired by a similar preparation I've enjoyed at one of my favorite dining spots, Commander's Palace in New Orleans, illustrates the rich excesses of the haute Creole cuisine of that old romantic city. Although the grilled fish is quite tasty with only the pecan butter, a crown of Champagne Cream creates an even more luxurious dish.

TO make the Toasted Pecan Butter, toast the nuts as directed on page 554, then transfer ¾ cup of the nuts to a food processor. Add the butter, lemon juice, and Worcestershire sauce and blend until smooth. Transfer to a bowl and set aside. Chop the remaining ¾ cup pecans for garnishing and set aside.

TO make the Champagne Cream, in a small saucepan, combine the Champagne or other sparkling wine and the shallot or onion. Place over medium-high heat, bring to a boil, and cook until the liquid is reduced to about ¼ cup, about 20 minutes. Add the stock or clam juice and continue cooking until slightly reduced, about 10 minutes. Reduce the heat to medium, add the cream and Worcestershire sauce, and cook, whisking almost constantly, until reduced to about 2 cups, about 20 minutes longer.

REDUCE the heat to low and add the butter, a piece at a time, stirring after each addition with a wooden spoon or wire whisk until the butter melts. When all of the butter has been added, stir in the minced herb and lemon juice, salt, and cayenne to taste. Remove from the heat and immediately place a piece of plastic wrap directly onto the surface of the sauce to prevent a skin from forming. Set aside.

PREPARE an open grill for hot direct-heat cooking.

QUICKLY rinse the trout inside and out under cold running water and pat dry with paper toweling. Using a pastry brush, coat the trout lightly with oil and sprinkle with salt and pepper to taste.

WHEN the fire is ready, lightly brush the grill rack or a grill basket with oil. Place the fish on the rack or in the basket and grill, turning once, until the flesh is just opaque when cut into the thickest part with a small, sharp knife, 6 to 8 minutes total cooking time.

MEANWHILE, slowly reheat the Champagne Cream.

TO serve, using a wide metal spatula, transfer the trout to warmed plates. Top each fish with a dollop of Toasted Pecan Butter and sprinkle with the reserved chopped pecans. Spoon the Champagne Cream around the fish and drizzle a little over the top.

Makes 6 servings.

FISH OR CHICKEN TERIYAKI

TERIYAKI MARINADE

1 cup soy sauce

⅓ cup sweet Japanese cooking wine
   (mirin) or dry sherry

6 tablespoons sugar

1 tablespoon grated or minced fresh
   ginger

2 teaspoons minced garlic

4 fish steaks (about 8 ounces each),
   skinned and central bones removed
   to cut each steak into 2 strips;
   2 pounds fish fillet (skin intact),
   cut into 4 equal portions; or
   8 boned and skinned chicken
   breast halves or thighs

Vegetable oil for brushing grill or
   broiler rack

Sliced green onion, including green
   tops, for garnish

Fresh shiso leaves for garnish
   (optional)

*Use this very flavorful marinade to infuse Japanese seasonings into fish or
chicken. Serve with medium-grain white rice (page 364).*

TO make the Teriyaki Marinade, in a bowl, combine all of the
   marinade ingredients and stir until the sugar dissolves.

QUICKLY rinse the fish or chicken under cold running water and pat
   dry with paper toweling.

PLACE the fish or chicken in a shallow glass or ceramic container
   and pour the marinade over. Cover and refrigerate, turning
   occasionally, for at least 2 hours or for up to 24 hours; return to
   room temperature before cooking.

PREPARE an open grill for hot direct-heat cooking, or preheat a broiler.
   Remove the fish or chicken from the marinade, reserving the
   marinade, and set aside.

POUR ½ cup of the marinade into a saucepan, place over medium-
   high heat and bring to a boil. Remove from the heat and set
   alongside the grill or broiler. Place the remaining marinade in
   another saucepan and reserve for later use.

WHEN the fire or broiler is ready, lightly brush the grill or broiler
   rack with oil. Place the fish or chicken on the rack and grill or
   broil, turning once and brushing with the boiled marinade, until
   the flesh is just opaque, 3 to 5 minutes per side for fish, depending on thickness, or 8 to 12 minutes total for chicken.

MEANWHILE, place the reserved saucepan of marinade over
   medium-high heat, bring to a boil, and cook until reduced
   and thickened, 4 to 5 minutes.

TO serve, arrange the fish or chicken on a platter or warmed plates
   and sprinkle with green onion. Pass the reduced marinade at the
   table as a sauce.

Makes 4 servings.

ROMAN CHICKEN CUTLETS WITH PROSCIUTTO AND SAGE
~ *Saltimbocca di Pollo alla Romana* ~

Many of my friends avoid eating veal, so here's a version of this Roman favorite made with chicken. You may choose to substitute about 1 pound thinly sliced veal. Saltimbocca *translates to "jump in the mouth."*

QUICKLY rinse the chicken under cold running water and pat dry with paper toweling. Discard the tendons and any connective tissue or fat, then separate the little fillet from each piece and save it for another purpose or leave it attached and tuck it under the larger muscle. Place each piece between 2 sheets of plastic wrap and pound with a flat instrument to a uniform thickness of about ¼ inch. Lightly sprinkle both sides of the pieces with salt and pepper.

TRIM the prosciutto slices to fit atop the chicken pieces precisely. Top each chicken piece with a slice of prosciutto and 2 sage leaves, securing each leaf in place with a toothpick.

IN a heavy-bottomed saute pan or skillet (without a nonstick coating), combine 2 tablespoons butter and 2 tablespoons olive oil and heat over medium-high heat. Add as many of the chicken pieces as will fit without crowding the pan. Cook until browned on the bottoms, then turn and cook the other sides until browned and the chicken is opaque throughout, 4 to 5 minutes total; to check for doneness, cut into a piece with a small, sharp knife. Remove the chicken to a warmed platter and cover to keep warm. Cook the remaining chicken in the same manner, adding a little more butter and oil if necessary to prevent sticking.

WHEN all of the chicken is cooked, discard the cooking fat from the pan. Return the pan to medium-high heat. Add the wine and salt and pepper to taste to the pan and scrape the bottom of the pan with a utensil to loosen any browned bits. Cook the wine until reduced to about ½ cup, then add the 2 tablespoons cold butter and stir until melted.

TO serve, discard the toothpicks from the chicken, transfer the pieces to warmed plates, and pour the pan sauce over the chicken.

Makes 4 servings.

4 boned and skinned chicken
   breast halves

Salt

Freshly ground black pepper

4 thin slices prosciutto

8 whole fresh sage leaves

About 2 tablespoons unsalted butter

About 2 tablespoons olive oil

1 cup dry white wine

2 tablespoons very cold unsalted
   butter

PAELLA

24 small clams in shells, well scrubbed

4 cups Fish Stock (page 575) or dry
white wine (optional)

24 mussels in shells, well scrubbed
and debearded

8 to 10 large shrimp in shells

1 pound lean boneless pork

4 boned and skinned chicken thighs

4 boned and skinned chicken
breast halves

1½ pounds squid

Olive oil for sauteing

1 pound spicy Spanish sausage
(chorizo), sliced into ¼-inch-thick
rounds

1½ cups finely chopped yellow onion

6 green onions, including green tops,
sliced

2 red sweet peppers, stems, seeds,
and membranes discarded, cut
lengthwise into narrow strips

2 tablespoons minced garlic

2 cups peeled, seeded, drained, and
chopped ripe or canned tomato

¼ cup minced fresh flat-leaf parsley

3 cups short-grain white rice,
preferably Spanish Valencia

*I felt that my complex version for this famous dish from Valencia was
worth the trouble when the world-renowned Spanish dancers Angela del
Moral and Pascual Olivera proclaimed the recipe to be "perfect!"*

*Vary the shellfish with whatever is fresh and available; chunks
of lobster meat are especially good.*

IN a large pot, combine the clams and 2 cups of the stock or wine
(if using) or 2 cups water. Cover tightly and place over high
heat, shaking the pot or stirring occasionally, just until most of
the shells open, about 5 minutes. Drain and discard any clams
that did not open. Steam the mussels in the same manner.
Cover and refrigerate until needed.

QUICKLY rinse the shrimp, pork, and chicken under cold running
water and pat dry with paper toweling. Peel and devein the
shrimp and set aside. Cut the pork into ½-inch cubes and set
aside. Set the chicken aside.

HOLD the squid under cold running water and pull off the speckled
membranes that cover the sacs, or hoods, then gently pull to
separate the sacs from the tentacles. Pull out and discard the
shells, or swords, and any remaining contents from the sacs.
Rinse the insides of the sacs and set aside. Slice off the tentacle
portions just above the eyes and discard everything except the
tentacles. Squeeze out and discard the hard beak found at the
base of each tentacle. Pat the sacs and tentacles dry with paper
toweling. Slice the sacs crosswise into ½-inch-wide rings,
leave the tentacles whole, and set aside.

IN a paella pan or very large skillet, heat 2 tablespoons of the olive
oil over medium-high heat. Add the shrimp and cook, stirring
frequently, just until bright pink on the outside and the meat
turns opaque, about 3 minutes; remove to a plate, cover, and
refrigerate until needed. Add olive oil, a little at a time, as
needed throughout the rest of the cooking. Add the squid rings
and tentacles to the pan and cook, stirring frequently, just
until opaque, about 2 minutes; remove to a plate, cover, and
refrigerate until needed.

ADD the pork to the pan and cook, turning frequently, until well browned, about 10 minutes; remove to a plate, cover, and refrigerate until needed. Add the chicken pieces to the pan and cook, turning frequently, until golden brown all over, about 10 minutes; remove to a plate, cover, and refrigerate until needed. Add the sausage to the pan and cook, turning frequently, until browned, about 10 minutes; remove to a plate, cover, and refrigerate until needed.

POUR enough oil into the pan drippings to total about ¼ cup. Add the yellow and green onions and sweet peppers and cook, stirring frequently, until very soft and golden, about 8 minutes. Add the garlic, tomato, and parsley and cook until most of the liquid has evaporated, about 10 minutes.

MEANWHILE wash and drain the rice as directed on page 365. In a saucepan, place the chicken stock or broth over medium heat and bring to a simmer; keep warm.

ADD the drained rice to the paella pan and cook, stirring constantly, until all of the grains are well coated with oil, about 3 minutes. Add the reserved squid, pork, chicken, and sausage. Stir in the saffron-infused wine, the warm stock or broth, and salt and pepper to taste. Adjust the heat to maintain a gentle simmer and simmer, stirring occasionally, until the liquid is absorbed, about 20 minutes. About 5 minutes before the rice is done, arrange the reserved shrimp, clams, and mussels on top and heat through.

REMOVE from the heat and let stand for 10 minutes.

GARNISH with asparagus and roasted pepper strips (if using) and serve at the table.

Makes 8 servings.

5 cups White Stock (page 578) made with chicken or canned reduced-sodium chicken broth

1 teaspoon crumbled saffron threads soaked in ½ cup dry white wine

Salt

Freshly ground black pepper

Asparagus tips, cooked until crisp-tender, for garnish (optional)

Roasted red sweet pepper (page 552), cut into strips for garnish (optional)

THAI GRILLED CHICKEN
~ *GAI YAHNG* ~

One chicken (about 4 pounds), cut into serving pieces, or 2 poussins (young chickens) or Cornish hens, split in half

¾ cup Fresh Coconut Milk (page 562) or high-quality commercial coconut milk

2 tablespoons minced garlic

3 tablespoons minced fresh cilantro (coriander), preferably roots or lower stem portions

2 tablespoons fish sauce, preferably Thai or Vietnamese

1 tablespoon soy sauce, preferably dark Chinese style

1 teaspoon ground turmeric

1 teaspoon sugar

½ teaspoon freshly ground white pepper

Thai Sweet Chile-Garlic Sauce (page 400)

Vegetable oil for brushing grill rack

Fresh cilantro (coriander) sprigs for garnish

Succulent grilled chicken, which usually appears as barbecued chicken on menus in American Thai restaurants, is marinated in a spiced coconut mixture before it goes on the grill.

QUICKLY rinse the chicken under cold running water and pat dry with paper toweling.

IN a bowl, combine the coconut milk, garlic, minced cilantro, fish sauce, soy sauce, turmeric, sugar, and pepper; mix well. Add the chicken and turn to coat on all sides. Cover and refrigerate, turning occasionally, for at least 4 hours or, preferably, overnight.

PREPARE the Thai Sweet Chile-Garlic Sauce as directed and set aside.

PREPARE a covered grill for moderate indirect-heat cooking. Position a drip pan in the center of the fuel grate.

REMOVE the chicken from the marinade, reserving the marinade, and set aside.

IN a saucepan, bring the marinade to a boil over medium-high heat, then set alongside the grill.

WHEN the fire is ready, lightly brush the grill rack with oil. Place the chicken on the rack directly over the heat and sear briefly on all sides, then position over the drip pan and cover the grill. Cook, turning and brushing with the marinade every 6 to 7 minutes, until the juices run clear when the chicken is pierced with a fork near the joint, about 30 minutes in all.

IF desired, transfer the chicken to a cutting surface and, using a heavy cleaver, chop into small pieces.

TO serve, distribute the sauce among 4 individual bowls for dipping and position at each place, or transfer to a serving bowl for passing and spooning over the chicken at the table. Arrange the chicken on a serving platter or on warmed plates and garnish with cilantro sprigs.

Makes 4 servings.

INDIAN-STYLE CHICKEN CURRY

Almost everyone enjoys an Indian curry. This version is simple and quickly made yet quite satisfying.

Offer diners plenty of hot cooked rice (page 364), preferably the delicately flavored basmati type, with this pleasantly robust dish.

QUICKLY rinse the chicken under cold running water and pat dry with paper toweling. Cut the breasts lengthwise into finger-wide strips. Sprinkle lightly with salt and pepper. Set aside.

IN a saute pan or heavy stew pot, combine 1 tablespoon oil and 1 tablespoon butter. Place over medium-high heat. When the butter melts, add as many of the chicken strips as will fit without crowding the pan and cook, turning frequently, until opaque all over. Using tongs or a slotted utensil, transfer the chicken to a plate. Cook the remaining chicken in the same manner, adding more oil and butter if necessary to prevent sticking.

ADD 2 tablespoons butter to the pan and melt over medium-low heat. Add the shallot and curry powder and cook, stirring frequently, until the shallot is soft, about 5 minutes. Sprinkle with the flour and cook for about 3 minutes longer.

STIR in the coconut milk and stock or broth and bring to a simmer. Return the chicken to the pan. Reduce the heat to low, cover, and simmer until the sauce thickens to the consistency of heavy (whipping) cream and the chicken is opaque all the way through when tested by cutting with a small, sharp knife at the thickest portion, about 10 minutes. Season to taste with salt and pepper.

TO serve, arrange the condiments in small bowls and place on the table. Ladle the curry into a warmed serving bowl.

Makes 8 servings.

8 boned and skinned chicken
   breast halves

Salt

Freshly ground black pepper

About 1 tablespoon canola or other
   high-quality vegetable oil

About 3 tablespoons unsalted butter

¾ cup chopped shallot

¼ cup Indian-Style Curry Powder
   (page 556) or high-quality
   commercial curry powder,
   or to taste

3 tablespoons all-purpose flour

1½ cups Fresh Coconut Milk (page
   562) or high-quality commercial
   coconut milk

1½ cups White Stock (page 578)
   made with chicken or canned
   reduced-sodium chicken broth

CONDIMENTS

Grated or shredded fresh coconut
   (see page 562) or packaged
   sweetened coconut

Coarsely chopped unsalted
   dry-roasted peanuts or cashews

Minced green onion, including
   green tops

Chutney (a favorite recipe or high-
   quality commercial product)

Dried currants or raisins

THAI CURRY ~ *GAENG* ~

1 pound boned and skinned chicken or boneless tender beef, lamb, or pork; or 2 cups cut-up roasted or barbecued boned duck; or 1 pound skinned fish fillet or peeled shellfish

About 2 medium-sized ears corn, or ¾ cup thawed frozen or drained canned corn kernels

2½ cups chilled Fresh Coconut Milk (page 562) or unshaken high-quality commercial coconut milk

2 tablespoons Thai Red, Green, or Yellow Curry Paste (pages 557, 558, or 559) or canned Thai red, green, or yellow curry paste, or to taste

3 tablespoons fish sauce, preferably Thai or Vietnamese

1 tablespoon palm sugar

¾ cup sliced canned bamboo shoots

1 red sweet pepper, stem, seeds, and membranes discarded, sliced lengthwise into narrow strips

6 whole fresh Thai bird or other tiny hot chiles, or 3 serrano or other small hot chiles, stems, seeds and membranes discarded, sliced lengthwise into quarters

¾ cup fresh Asian basil leaves

6 fresh or thawed frozen kaffir lime leaves (optional)

2 tablespoons freshly squeezed lime juice, or to taste

A big bowl of fragrant Thai curry is guaranteed to thrill chile addicts. This recipe is a guide to the basic method for making curry. It can be greatly varied by using any one of a rainbow of Thai curry pastes, a range of meats or fish, and whatever vegetables are appealing. A particularly delicious version is made with roasted or barbecued duck, available whole from Chinese markets or restaurants or cooked at home.

Contrary to popular opinion, not all curries need to be rich with coconut milk in order to be flavorful. To reduce the amount of calorie-laden coconut milk, blend some coconut milk with flavorful stock or water to equal the amount of liquid called for in the recipe. To prepare a noncoconut curry, fry the curry paste in vegetable oil, then substitute water, a light broth, or a combination of water and stock for the coconut milk.

Serve with plenty of fluffy Thai jasmine rice (page 364).

IF using chicken, quickly rinse under cold running water, pat dry with paper toweling, and cut into bite-sized pieces; set aside. If using meat, quickly rinse under cold running water, pat dry with paper toweling, slice across the grain as thinly as possible, and cut each slice into pieces about 2 inches long by ½ inch wide; set aside. If using cooked duck, set aside. If using fish or shellfish, quickly rinse under cold running water, pat dry with paper toweling, and cut fish or large shellfish into bite-sized pieces; set aside.

IF using fresh corn, cut the kernels from the cobs as directed for Sauteed Corn on page 358, measure out ¾ cup, and set aside. If using frozen or canned corn, reserve for later use.

SCOOP ½ cup coconut cream from the top of the coconut milk and transfer to a wok or heavy saucepan. Place over medium heat and bring to a boil. Stir in the curry paste and cook, stirring constantly, until very fragrant, about 5 minutes. If using chicken or meat, add it to the pan and cook, stirring frequently, until the meat is opaque, about 5 minutes. If using cooked duck, add it to the pan and cook, stirring frequently, for about 1 minute.

STIR the remaining 2 cups coconut milk to achieve a smooth consistency, then slowly stir it into the pan. If using fish or shellfish, add it to the pan. Stir in the fish sauce and sugar. Add the corn, bamboo shoots, sweet pepper, chiles, ½ cup of the basil leaves, and the lime leaves (if using). Bring to a simmer and cook until the chicken or meat is done, 5 to 15 minutes, depending on type; or until the duck is heated through, about 5 minutes; or until the fish or shellfish turns opaque, about 5 minutes. Stir in the lime juice. Taste and add more fish sauce, sugar, and/or lime juice if needed to achieve a good balance of salty, sweet, and sour.

TO serve, ladle into a serving bowl and sprinkle with the remaining ¼ cup basil leaves.

Makes 4 servings.

VEGETARIAN VARIATION

USE 1 pound drained firm tofu, eggplant, or other vegetables, cut into bite-sized cubes, in place of the meat and cook until tender. If using vegetables that cook at different times, start with those that require the longest cooking and add quicker-cooking vegetables near the end. Substitute 1½ tablespoons soy sauce for the fish sauce.

CHILE-MARINATED TURKEY WITH PINEAPPLE SALSA

CHILE MARINADE

1 tablespoon ground *pequín* or other
    dried hot chile

1 tablespoon minced shallot or red
    onion

2 teaspoons minced garlic

¼ cup chopped fresh cilantro
    (coriander)

2 tablespoons chopped fresh oregano,
    or 2 teaspoons crumbled dried
    oregano

1 teaspoon ground cumin

¼ cup freshly squeezed lime or
    lemon juice

¼ cup fruity olive oil, preferably
    extra-virgin

Salt

Freshly ground black pepper

Ground cayenne

3 skinned turkey breast fillets (about
    8 ounces each)

Pineapple Salsa (page 392) or Citrus
    Salsa (page 394)

Vegetable oil for brushing grill rack

Fresh cilantro (coriander) or mint
    sprigs for garnish

Here, in a change of pace from the traditional roasted turkey, a fiery marinade is tempered by a tangy sweet salsa. A boned and skinned half turkey breast may be substituted for the tender fillets; increase the cooking time.

TO make the marinade, in a small nonreactive bowl, combine all of the marinade ingredients, including salt, pepper, and cayenne to taste. Mix well and set aside.

QUICKLY rinse the turkey fillets under cold running water and pat dry with paper toweling. Place in a shallow nonreactive container, pour the marinade over, and turn to coat thoroughly. Cover and refrigerate, turning occasionally, for at least 8 hours or for up to 24 hours. Return to room temperature before cooking.

PREPARE the selected salsa and set aside.

PREPARE an open grill for moderate direct-heat cooking.

WHEN the fire is ready, lightly brush the grill rack with oil. Remove the turkey fillets and brush off excess marinade with your fingertips. Place the turkey on the grill rack and cook for 7 to 8 minutes, then turn and cook until done but still juicy inside, 5 to 7 minutes longer. Remove to a cutting surface, cover loosely with foil, and let stand for about 5 minutes.

TO serve, cut the turkey fillets on the diagonal into slices about ¼ inch thick. Arrange on a serving platter or warmed plates, spoon the salsa alongside, and garnish with herb sprigs.

Makes 6 servings.

CHICKEN OREGANO

Some years ago, for one of the first events staged by our fledgling former San Francisco company, Picnic Productions, three good friends helped my late partner, Lin, and me prepare 800 chicken breasts for this dish in our tiny kitchen. In spite of that large-scale production, the recipe, with some updated flourishes, has remained a reliable old friend. It can be served warm from the oven, but makes such good picnic fare that I usually serve it at room temperature.

PREHEAT an oven to 350° F. Using a pastry brush, lightly grease a wire rack with oil, or coat with spray, and place on a baking sheet.

QUICKLY rinse the chicken under cold running water and pat dry with paper toweling. Remove the fillet from each chicken breast. Cut the remaining portion of each breast into strips about the same size as the fillet. Set aside.

IN a shallow bowl, stir together the eggs and milk.

IN a food processor, combine the bread crumbs, cheese, pine nuts, minced or crumbled oregano, and salt and pepper to taste and blend until fine.

DIP the chicken pieces into the egg mixture, then transfer to a plate and sprinkle generously with the crumb mixture, patting crumbs so that they adhere well to all sides of the chicken. Place on the prepared rack, transfer the rack and baking sheet to the oven, and bake until the meat is just opaque throughout and the coating is golden brown and crisp, about 35 minutes.

TO serve, transfer to a serving platter and garnish with oregano sprigs.

Makes 6 servings.

Vegetable oil or cooking spray for greasing

6 boned and skinned chicken breast halves

2 eggs, lightly beaten

¼ cup milk

2 cups fresh bread crumbs, preferably from French bread

1 cup freshly grated Parmesan cheese (about 4 ounces), preferably Parmigiano-Reggiano

½ cup pine nuts

¼ cup minced fresh oregano, or 1½ tablespoons crumbled dried oregano

Salt

Freshly ground black pepper

Fresh oregano sprigs for garnish

CHICKEN TAMALE CASSEROLE

About 4 medium-sized ears corn, or
    2 cups thawed frozen or drained
    canned corn kernels

¼ cup fruity olive oil, preferably
    extra-virgin

1 cup finely chopped yellow onion

1 tablespoon minced garlic

3 tablespoons ground *ancho*, *pasilla*,
    or other dried mild to medium-hot
    chile, or to taste

4 cups peeled, seeded, drained, and
    chopped ripe or canned tomato

1 tablespoon salt, or to taste

Vegetable oil or cooking spray for
    greasing

3 eggs

1 cup milk (not fat free)

½ cup yellow cornmeal

2 cups coarsely chopped cooked
    chicken

1 cup pitted brine-cured ripe olives
    such as Niçoise

1 cup freshly shredded Monterey Jack
    cheese (about 3 ounces)

1 cup freshly shredded sharp
    Cheddar cheese (about 3 ounces)

Olive oil for drizzling

Minced fresh flat-leaf parsley for
    sprinkling

In my chicken cookbook, I called this preparation a tamale pie, an old California name for the dish in which a thick cornmeal crust is mixed right into the other ingredients. Although I've heard from numerous readers who love the recipe and have family members who make it frequently, one irate East Coast reader was quite upset that she couldn't slice it into wedges for serving like the name, pie, implied. To avoid confusion, and to better describe the dish, it is now called a casserole.

This was a specialty of my late friend M. J. Cotton of Hillsborough, California. She called it President's Pie because it was a particular favorite of Richard Nixon's, whom she frequently entertained. Although I was not a fan of President Nixon's politics, I'd vote for his "pie" any day.

IF using fresh corn, cut the kernels from the cobs as directed for Sauteed Corn on page 358, measure out 2 cups, and set aside. If using thawed or canned corn, reserve for later use.

IN a large saucepan, heat the oil over medium-high heat. Add the onion and cook, stirring frequently, until soft but not browned, about 5 minutes. Add the corn, garlic, and chile and cook for about 1 minute longer. Stir in the tomato and salt, reduce the heat to medium, and cook, stirring frequently, for about 15 minutes.

PREHEAT an oven to 350° F. Using a pastry brush, lightly grease a shallow ovenproof baking dish with oil, or coat with spray. Set aside.

IN a bowl, combine the eggs, milk, and cornmeal and mix until well blended. Add to the tomato mixture and cook, stirring almost constantly to prevent the bottom from scorching, until thickened, about 15 minutes.

STIR the chicken and olives into the cornmeal mixture and pour into the prepared baking dish. Sprinkle with the cheeses, lightly drizzle with oil, and bake until bubbling hot and the cheese is crusty, about 40 minutes.

TO serve, spoon the warm casserole onto warmed plates and sprinkle with parsley.

Makes 6 servings.

CHICKEN BREASTS WITH TOMATILLO-CHILE CREAM

When there's little time to prepare dinner and there's no homemade salsa on hand, I sometimes reach for a high-quality commercial hot green salsa to stir up this quick and satisfying dish. It can also be made with 1 pound boneless pork in lieu of the chicken.

Serve with cooked pasta or rice, or turn the dish into "white tacos," as my sister, Martha, does for her boys, offering them warm tortillas in which to roll up the mixture.

4 boned and skinned chicken
  breast halves

1 tablespoon olive oil

1 tablespoon unsalted butter

1 cup sour cream (not fat free)

¼ cup Tomatillo-Chile Salsa (page
  393) or high-quality commercial
  tomatillo salsa

Freshly grated aged Mexican cheese
  (queso añejo) or Parmesan
  cheese, preferably Parmigiano-
  Reggiano, for sprinkling

Chopped fresh cilantro (coriander)
  for garnish

QUICKLY rinse the chicken under cold running water and pat dry with paper toweling. Remove the fillet from each chicken breast. Cut the remaining portion of each breast vertically into strips about the same width as the fillet. Set aside.

IN a saute pan or skillet, combine the oil and butter and place over medium heat. When the butter is melted, add the chicken strips and cook, turning frequently, until opaque on all sides, about 3 minutes. Stir in the sour cream and salsa, reduce the heat to very low, and cook until the chicken is tender but still moist inside and the sour cream and salsa have blended into a thick sauce, about 10 minutes.

TO serve, arrange the chicken on warmed plates and sprinkle lightly with cheese and cilantro.

Makes 4 servings.

HERB, GARLIC, AND LEMON ROASTED CHICKEN

Vegetable oil or cooking spray for greasing

1 teaspoon salt

½ teaspoon freshly ground black pepper

1 tablespoon minced fresh sage, or 1 teaspoon crumbled dried sage

1 tablespoon minced fresh rosemary, or 1 teaspoon crumbled dried rosemary

1 tablespoon minced fresh thyme, or 1 teaspoon crumbled dried thyme

1 chicken (about 4 pounds) or roasting chicken (about 6 pounds)

1 lemon, pricked all over with a sharp knife

3 garlic cloves, crushed

Soy sauce for rubbing

Unsalted butter, melted and cooled slightly, for brushing

PAN GRAVY (optional)

1 cup White Stock (page 578) made with chicken or reduced-sodium chicken broth

1 tablespoon cold unsalted butter

Fresh sage, rosemary, and/or thyme sprigs for garnish

Perfectly roasted chicken is one of my favorite meals, and I know I am not alone. There are countless ways to season chickens, stuffed or plain, for roasting. The roasted chicken that I like best is fragrant with garlic, lemon, and herbs. I prefer stuffings, or "dressings" as we called them in the South, cooked in a separate pan alongside the bird.

Andrew and I roasted dozens of chickens while retesting the recipe from my chicken book for this collection. We tried a wide range of oven temperatures and rotated the birds in many different ways during roasting. This simple method was our favorite.

A bit of soy sauce rubbed onto the skin helps make the skin brown beautifully while having little influence on the flavor. Truss the chicken cavity closed and tie the legs together with cotton string if you wish. I find that leaving the legs and cavity open helps the bird cook more evenly; just fill the cavity opening with fresh herbs after roasting.

PREHEAT an oven to 375° F. Using a pastry brush, lightly grease a V-rack with oil, or coat with spray. Place the rack in a roasting pan and set aside.

IN a small bowl, combine the salt, pepper, sage, rosemary, and thyme and blend well. Set aside.

QUICKLY rinse the chicken, inside and out, under cold running water, then pat dry with paper toweling. Insert the lemon and garlic into the cavity. Rub the entire outside surface of the chicken with soy sauce, then, using a pastry brush, coat generously with melted butter. Sprinkle with the herb mixture, distributing evenly all over the bird. Place on the prepared rack breast side up and roast until an instant-read thermometer registers 170° to 175° F when inserted into the thickest part of the thigh, 50 to 60 minutes for a 4-pound chicken, or 60 to 70 minutes for a roasting chicken.

TRANSFER the chicken to a platter or a cutting board with a well to rest for 10 to 15 minutes. This helps to distribute the juices throughout the bird.

MEANWHILE, to make Pan Gravy (if desired), pour the drippings from the pan into a fat separator pitcher or small bowl. Pour or spoon off and discard as much fat as possible, then pour the juices back into the pan. Add the chicken stock or broth and any juices that have collected from the resting chicken. Place the pan over medium-high heat and bring the liquid to a boil, using a spoon to scrape up any browned bits from the bottom of the pan. Cook, stirring frequently, until the juices and stock or broth are reduced by half, 4 to 5 minutes. Add the cold butter and stir until melted. Pour the gravy into a bowl for serving.

TO serve, transfer the bird to a serving platter and stuff the cavity opening with fresh herbs. Carve at the table and place on warmed plates. Pass the gravy for drizzling over the chicken.

A 4-pound chicken makes 4 servings, and a roasting chicken makes 6 servings.

BOLOGNESE CHICKEN BREASTS STUFFED WITH HERBS AND CHEESE
~ *PETTI DI POLLO ALLA BOLOGNESE* ~

8 boned and skinned chicken breast halves

Salt

Freshly ground white pepper

½ cup (1 stick) unsalted butter, at room temperature

3 tablespoons minced fresh flat-leaf parsley

2 tablespoons minced fresh oregano, or 2 teaspoons crumbled dried oregano

1½ tablespoons minced fresh marjoram, or 1½ teaspoons crumbled dried marjoram

½ teaspoon freshly grated nutmeg

4 ounces Italian Fontina or Bel Paese cheese

Flour for dredging

2 eggs, lightly beaten

1 cup unseasoned fine dried bread crumbs, preferably from Italian or French bread

Olive oil for brushing and frying

½ cup dry white wine

Fresh flat-leaf parsley, oregano, and/or marjoram sprigs for garnish

The city of Bologna, in Italy's prosperous Emilia-Romagna region, is world famous for its rich and sophisticated cuisine, which includes this preparation for stuffed chicken breasts.

QUICKLY rinse the chicken under cold running water and pat dry with paper toweling. Discard the tendons and any connective tissue or fat, then separate the little fillet and save it for another purpose or leave it attached and tuck it under the larger muscle. Place each piece between 2 sheets of waxed paper or plastic wrap and pound with a mallet or other flat instrument to a uniform thickness of about ¼ inch. Lightly sprinkle both sides of the chicken pieces with salt and pepper and set aside.

IN a bowl, beat the butter with a hand mixer until light and fluffy. Add the minced or crumbled herbs and nutmeg and blend well. Set aside.

CUT the cheese lengthwise into 8 equal-sized pieces, and place 1 piece crosswise on each reserved chicken piece. Equally distribute about half of the reserved herb butter among the chicken pieces, spreading it over the cheese. Roll the breasts tightly around the cheese and secure with toothpicks.

PLACE the flour, eggs, and bread crumbs in 3 separate shallow bowls. Dredge each chicken roll lightly in the flour, dip into the egg mixture, then transfer to a plate and sprinkle generously with the crumbs, patting crumbs so that they adhere well to all sides of the chicken.

PREHEAT an oven to 350° F. Using a pastry brush, lightly grease a shallow baking dish with oil and set aside.

IN a saute pan or heavy skillet, pour in just enough oil to cover the bottom of the pan and place over medium heat. When the oil is hot, add the chicken rolls and cook, turning occasionally, until lightly browned all over, about 5 minutes. Transfer, seam side down, to the baking dish.

IN a small saucepan, melt the remaining herb butter over medium heat, stir in the wine, and pour the mixture over the chicken. Bake, basting occasionally, until the chicken rolls are golden brown and tender, about 15 minutes.

TO serve, arrange the chicken on warmed plates, spoon the pan drippings over the top, and garnish with herb sprigs.

Makes 8 servings.

MOROCCAN PHYLLO-WRAPPED CHICKEN PIE ~ *BISTEEYA* ~

SPICED CHICKEN FILLING

1 chicken (about 4 pounds)
  with giblets

½ cup finely chopped onion

1 teaspoon minced garlic

1 tablespoon ground turmeric

1 teaspoon ground cinnamon

½ teaspoon ground cumin

½ teaspoon ground allspice

¼ teaspoon ground cloves

¼ teaspoon ground coriander

¼ teaspoon ground mace

2 tablespoons minced fresh flat-leaf
  parsley

1½ teaspoons minced fresh thyme,
  or ½ teaspoon crumbled dried
  thyme

1½ cups apple cider

1 cup apricot nectar

½ teaspoon salt, or to taste

½ teaspoon freshly ground black
  pepper, or to taste

EGG FILLING

Stock remaining from cooking chicken

6 eggs, at room temperature

Salt

Freshly ground black pepper

The Moroccans call this heavenly creation "food for the gods." In its nat-ural habitat, the flaky sweet-and-savory pie is most often made with pigeon, although chicken makes a divine version.

As a carryover from my days of running Twin Peaks Grocery, where we made dozens of these pies each week and sold them freshly baked or frozen for home baking, I frequently double or triple this recipe and freeze the extra pie(s) before baking for a future meal.

TO make the Spiced Chicken Filling, quickly rinse the chicken, including all the giblets except the liver, under cold running water and pat dry with paper toweling. Transfer to a stockpot or other large pot. Add the onion, garlic, turmeric, cinnamon, cumin, allspice, cloves, coriander, mace, parsley, thyme, apple cider, apricot nectar, salt, and pepper. If necessary, add a little water to cover the chicken barely. Bring to a boil over high heat and skim off any scum. Reduce the heat to achieve a simmer, cover, and simmer until the chicken is very tender and falls off the bone, about 2 hours. Remove from the heat and set aside to cool in the stock.

WHEN cool enough to handle, remove the chicken from the stock to a work surface and reserve the stock. Discard the skin and bones and cut or shred the meat into small pieces; set aside.

TO make the Egg Filling, strain the reserved stock into a saucepan. Place over high heat and cook until reduced to about 1 cup, then reduce the heat to achieve a simmer.

IN a bowl, combine the eggs with salt and pepper to taste and beat well. Stirring constantly with a whisk or wooden spoon, drizzle the beaten eggs into the simmering stock and cook, stirring frequently, until thick and creamy, about 15 minutes. Remove from the heat. Using a slotted spoon, transfer the eggs to a bowl, leaving behind any stock that has not been incorporated.

TO make the Almond Filling, in a skillet, melt the butter over medium heat. Add the almonds and toast, shaking the pan or stirring frequently, until lightly golden and fragrant, about 5 minutes. Pour into a bowl to cool, then stir in the powdered sugar and cinnamon. Set aside.

TO assemble, unwrap the phyllo and cover with a lightly dampened cloth kitchen towel to prevent drying out. Place 1 sheet of the phyllo on a flat work surface. Using a wide pastry brush, lightly brush the sheet with melted butter to cover completely. Top with a second phyllo sheet placed at a 45-degree angle to the first sheet and brush it lightly with butter. Repeat until 8 sheets in all are used and the sheets form a rough circle of dough.

SCATTER half of the almond filling over the phyllo stack to form an 8-inch circle in the middle of the dough. Cover the nuts with about half of the egg filling, then top with the chicken filling. Cover the chicken with the remaining egg filling, then top with the remaining almond filling. Bring one side of the phyllo up and over to cover as much of the filling as possible, and brush the exposed dough with butter. Bring the remaining phyllo sides up and around the filling, one by one, buttering and overlapping them as you go, until all sides of the phyllo have been folded over the filling to form a compact package.

POSITION racks so that the pie will bake in the middle of an oven and preheat the oven to 375° F. Brush a wire rack with melted butter, position it on a rimmed baking sheet, and set aside.

BRUSH 1 sheet of the remaining phyllo with butter and lay it over the top of the filled pie. Butter and overlap 7 more sheets, positioning them at angles to form a circle of sheets over the filled pie, as done for the base. Butter the underside of a section of the top stack and fold it down under the pie. Continue buttering, overlapping, and folding down to form a smooth, slightly hexagonal shape.

PLACE the pie on the rack, transfer the rack and baking sheet to the oven, and bake until golden brown and crisp, 45 to 55 minutes.

SET aside on the rack to cool for about 10 minutes.

TO serve, generously sprinkle the *bisteeya* with powdered sugar and ground cinnamon, transfer to a serving platter, and place within easy reach of diners. To eat in the Moroccan tradition, break off pieces of the *bisteeya* with three fingers of your right hand and transfer the food directly to your mouth.

Makes 4 servings.

ALMOND FILLING

1 tablespoon unsalted butter
½ cup chopped blanched almonds
1 tablespoon powdered sugar
½ teaspoon ground cinnamon

16 sheets fresh or thawed (in the refrigerator) frozen phyllo dough (about ¾ pound)
About ½ cup (1 stick) unsalted butter, melted and cooled slightly, for brushing
Sifted powdered sugar for garnish
Ground cinnamon for garnish

SWEET-AND-TANGY
CHICKEN THIGHS

6 slices bacon, cut into ½-inch
    pieces

8 boned chicken thighs

All-purpose flour for dredging

⅔ cup honey

6 tablespoons Dijon mustard

2 teaspoons Indian-Style Curry
    Powder (page 556) or high-quality
    commercial curry powder

Salt

Ground cayenne or other dried hot
    chile

Minced fresh chives or flat-leaf
    parsley for garnish

This recipe is a variation on a wonderful chicken dish introduced to me by Gail High, my "sister" and Lake Tahoe neighbor. Gail uses breasts, while I prefer thighs for baking. If you wish to use breasts, reduce the baking time to about 20 minutes.

Of course, the chicken tastes wonderful with its skin intact, but the dish works well with skinned thighs, which your own thighs may appreciate. Also, when I've wanted to trim the fat, I've omitted the bacon altogether, or discarded the saturated drippings and browned the chicken pieces in a little olive oil.

IN a skillet, cook the bacon over medium heat until crisp, 6 to 8 minutes. Using a slotted spoon, transfer to paper toweling to drain; reserve the pan drippings.

PREHEAT an oven to 350° F.

QUICKLY rinse the chicken under cold running water and pat dry with paper toweling. Dredge the chicken with flour, shaking off excess. Place the skillet with the reserved bacon drippings over medium heat, add the chicken, and cook until the pieces are browned on all sides, about 10 minutes. Using tongs, transfer the chicken to an 8-inch square baking dish.

IN a small bowl, combine the honey, mustard, curry powder, and salt and ground chile to taste. Drizzle the mixture over the chicken and bake, uncovered, until tender, about 45 minutes.

TO serve, transfer to a serving platter or warmed plates and sprinkle with the bacon and minced chives or parsley.

Makes 4 to 6 servings.

BARBECUED CHICKEN,
LOUISIANA STYLE

My daddy's slowly cooked barbecued chicken is the best I've ever eaten. When I was growing up, my mother always made a sauce from scratch. Since the advent of good commercial products, Daddy has concocted an easy sauce with complex flavors. For years, friends have begged me for the recipe for this "homemade" sauce and some "gourmets" are surprised when they learn it's based on commercial products.

TO make Daddy's Barbecue Sauce, in a heavy saucepan, melt the butter over medium-high heat. Add the onion and cook, stirring frequently, until soft but not browned, about 5 minutes. Stir in the barbecue sauce, steak sauce, Worcestershire sauce, soy sauce, honey, brown sugar, lemon quarters, and orange juice. Bring to a boil, then reduce the heat to achieve a simmer and simmer until the mixture is thick and the flavors are well blended, about 30 minutes. Remove from the heat, discard the lemons, and set aside.

QUICKLY rinse the chicken under cold running water and pat dry with paper toweling. Transfer to a large pot and add enough cold water to cover barely. Place over medium-high heat and bring just to a simmer, then immediately remove the chicken and drain well.

MEANWHILE, prepare a covered grill for moderate indirect-heat cooking. Position a drip pan in the center of the fuel grate. Soak a handful of hickory or other flavorful wood chips in water. Set the barbecue sauce alongside the grill.

WHEN the fire is ready, lightly brush the grill rack and the chicken with oil. Place the chicken on the rack directly over the heat and sear briefly on all sides, then position over the drip pan and add the soaked chips to the fire to create smoke. Brush the chicken generously with the sauce, cover the grill, and cook, turning and brushing the chicken with the sauce every 10 minutes, until tender, about 1 hour for breast quarters and about 1½ hours for dark meat. If cooking over wood or charcoal, add more fuel and adjust the air vents as needed to maintain an even temperature.

IN a saucepan, bring any unused sauce to a boil, then transfer to a bowl and serve with the chicken.

Makes 8 servings.

DADDY'S BARBECUE SAUCE

½ cup (1 stick) unsalted butter

1 cup finely chopped onion

1 bottle (18 ounces) high-quality hickory-flavored or spicy barbecue sauce

1 bottle (5 ounces) steak sauce

¼ cup Worcestershire sauce

2 tablespoons soy sauce, or to taste

3 tablespoons honey, or to taste

1 tablespoon firmly packed brown sugar, or to taste

2 lemons, quartered

¾ cup freshly squeezed orange juice

2 chickens (about 4 pounds *each*), quartered

Canola or other high-quality vegetable oil for brushing

MINCED CHICKEN WITH LETTUCE LEAVES

2 tablespoons minced fresh ginger

1 tablespoon minced garlic

2 tablespoons oyster sauce

1 tablespoon soy sauce

1 tablespoon dry sherry

½ teaspoon sugar

5 boned and skinned chicken thighs

About 18 small whole or halved
   large lettuce leaves (see recipe
   introduction)

6 Chinese dried black mushrooms or
   medium-sized fresh shiitake mushroom caps

3 tablespoons sesame seed

¼ cup canola or other high-quality
   vegetable oil

¾ cup minced fresh or canned water
   chestnuts

3 tablespoons finely chopped green
   onion, including green tops

1 teaspoon Asian sesame oil

1 teaspoon cornstarch dissolved in
   2 tablespoons water

Salt

Freshly ground white pepper

Red sweet pepper strips for garnish

One of my favorite Chinese dishes is minced squab that's eaten rolled in lettuce leaves. This is my adaption, using the dark meat of chicken to approximate the richness of the pigeon.

Choose crisp romaine or iceberg lettuce to contrast with the cooked chicken, or select softer leaves such as Bibb (also known as limestone, butter, or Boston) or one of the delicate loose-leaf lettuces.

IN a bowl, combine the ginger, garlic, oyster sauce, soy sauce, sherry, and sugar and stir well. Set aside.

QUICKLY rinse the chicken under cold running water and pat dry with paper toweling. Using a very sharp knife, mince the chicken as finely as possible and add to the ginger mixture; mix well. Cover and refrigerate for at least 2 hours or up to overnight; return to room temperature before cooking.

WASH the lettuce leaves under cold running water. Place in a salad spinner and spin to remove as much water as possible. Pat dry with paper toweling. Wrap in a cloth kitchen towel or paper toweling and refrigerate for at least 30 minutes to crisp, or place the wrapped leaves in a plastic bag and refrigerate for up to several hours.

IF using dried mushrooms, cover with warm water and let stand until softened, about 25 minutes. Drain and squeeze out as much liquid as possible. Discard tough stems. Mince the fresh or softened mushrooms and set aside.

TOAST the sesame seed as directed on page 553 and set aside.

ARRANGE the chicken and the remaining ingredients alongside the stove top.

PLACE a wok, large saute pan, or large, heavy skillet over high heat. When the pan is hot, add 2 tablespoons of the oil and swirl to coat the pan. When the oil is hot but not yet smoking, add the chicken mixture and stir-fry, moving the pan off and on the heat as necessary to prevent scorching, until the chicken turns opaque throughout, about 2 minutes. Using a slotted utensil, transfer the chicken to a bowl.

ADD the remaining 2 tablespoons oil to the pan. Add the mushrooms and water chestnuts and stir-fry until the mushrooms are tender, about 2 minutes. Return the chicken to the pan. Add the sesame seed, green onion, sesame oil, and cornstarch mixture and stir-fry until well blended and the sauce is slightly thickened, 1 to 2 minutes. Season to taste with salt and pepper.

TO serve, arrange the chilled lettuce leaves on a platter and place on the table. Transfer the chicken to a serving platter and garnish with the pepper strips.

TO eat, place about 1 tablespoon of the chicken mixture on a lettuce leaf, roll or fold the lettuce, and eat out of hand.

Makes 4 to 6 servings.

GARLIC-GLAZED CHICKEN

6 boned and skinned chicken
  breast halves

¼ cup sesame seed

½ cup coarsely chopped garlic

1½ cups unseasoned rice vinegar

½ cup soy sauce

5 tablespoons honey

2 teaspoons crushed dried hot chile

2 tablespoons canola or other
  high-quality vegetable oil

¼ cup chopped green onion,
  including green tops

Even garlic lovers might be alarmed by the huge quantity of the aromatic bulb in this preparation, but it turns sweet and succulent during the cooking. Great on its own or served over rice or pasta, the chicken also makes a wonderful topping for pizza (page 168).

QUICKLY rinse the chicken under cold running water and pat dry with paper toweling. Cut into bite-sized pieces and set aside.

TOAST the sesame seed as directed on page 553 and set aside.

IN a bowl, combine the garlic, vinegar, soy sauce, honey, and chile and set aside.

PLACE a wok, large saute pan, or large, heavy skillet over high heat. When the pan is hot, add the oil and swirl to coat the pan. When the oil is hot but not yet smoking, add the chicken and stir-fry, moving the pan off and on the heat as necessary to prevent scorching, until the chicken turns opaque throughout, about 3 minutes. Using a slotted utensil, transfer the chicken to a colander set over a bowl to drain well.

POUR the garlic mixture into the pan and cook over medium-high heat, stirring frequently, until the sauce is reduced to the consistency of syrup, about 15 minutes. Return the chicken to the pan and cook, stirring constantly, until the pieces are lightly glazed, about 2 minutes.

TO serve, transfer the chicken to a serving bowl and sprinkle with the green onion and sesame seed.

Makes 6 servings.

PUERTO RICAN RICE AND CHICKEN STEW ~ *Asopao de Pollo* ~

Very similar to the arroz con pollo *that's ubiquitous throughout Spanish-speaking countries, this version of rice and chicken remains soupy, or* asapao, *and is usually eaten with both a fork and a spoon.*

QUICKLY rinse the chicken under cold running water and pat dry with paper toweling.

IN a small bowl, combine the garlic, oregano, cumin, salt, pepper, and cayenne. Rub the spice mixture on the chicken pieces. Place the chicken on a plate, cover, and let stand for about 30 minutes, or refrigerate for up to overnight.

IN a heavy stew pot, heat 2 tablespoons oil over medium-high heat. Add the chicken and cook, stirring occasionally, until opaque and lightly browned all over, about 10 minutes. Transfer to a plate and set aside.

ADD enough oil to that remaining in the pan to total 2 tablespoons. Add the onion and sweet pepper and cook, stirring frequently, until soft but not browned, about 5 minutes. Add the ham and tomato and cook for about 5 minutes longer. Return the chicken to the pot, reduce the heat to achieve a simmer, cover, and simmer until the chicken is tender, about 20 minutes.

USING tongs, remove the chicken to a cutting board and set aside to cool. Increase the heat to medium-high. Add the rice and stir until all the grains are well coated, about 2 minutes. Stir in the stock or broth and bring to a boil. Reduce the heat to low, cover tightly, and simmer until the rice is tender but still soupy, about 15 minutes.

MEANWHILE, if using fresh peas, blanch as directed on page 338.

CUT the cooled chicken into bite-sized pieces and stir it into the cooked rice. Add the peas, cheese, olives, and capers and stir to mix well. Cover and simmer just until the cheese melts and the other additions are heated through, about 5 minutes.

TO serve, ladle the warm stew into warmed shallow bowls and garnish with the pepper strips.

Makes 6 servings.

6 boned chicken thighs or breast halves, skinned if desired

2 teaspoons minced garlic

1 tablespoon minced fresh oregano, or 1 teaspoon crumbled dried oregano

1 teaspoon ground cumin

1 teaspoon salt, or to taste

1 teaspoon freshly ground black pepper, or to taste

½ teaspoon ground cayenne, or to taste

About 3 tablespoons olive oil

1 cup finely chopped onion

1 cup finely chopped green sweet pepper

4 ounces flavorful baked ham, chopped

1 cup peeled, seeded, and chopped ripe or canned tomato

2 cups long-grain white rice

6 cups White Stock (page 578) made with chicken or canned reduced-sodium chicken broth

1 cup shelled fresh or thawed frozen green (English) peas

½ cup freshly grated aged Mexican cheese *(queso añejo)* or dry Monterey Jack or Asiago cheese (about 2 ounces)

¼ cup pitted green olives, sliced

1 tablespoon drained small capers

Roasted Peppers (page 552) made with red sweet peppers, or canned pimiento, cut into strips, for garnish

CHICKEN ENCHILADAS WITH TOMATILLO-CHILE SALSA

Tomatillo-Chile Salsa (page 393)

1 chicken (about 4 pounds), cut up

4 cups freshly shredded Monterey Jack cheese (about 12 ounces)

1 tablespoon minced fresh oregano, or 1 teaspoon crumbled dried oregano

Salt

Freshly ground black pepper

Vegetable oil or cooking spray for greasing

12 corn tortillas

Fresh cilantro (coriander) sprigs for garnish

CONDIMENTS

Avocado slices or Guacamole (page 395)

Chopped ripe tomato

Mexican cultured cream (*crema*) or sour cream

Ripe olives

Thinly sliced radishes

Chopped fresh cilantro (coriander)

Fresh cilantro sprigs for garnish

Once upon a hot summer afternoon, I created this dish at the request of Gail High, my Lake Tahoe neighbor and "sister," and will always remember enjoying it with Gail and her daughter, Tanya, and our good friend, Mary McCoy, under the shelter of a white umbrella. Even without the fresh strawberry margaritas that we enjoyed that steamy August night, it has remained a favorite dish.

PREPARE the Tomatillo-Chile Salsa as directed and set aside.

QUICKLY rinse the chicken pieces under cold running water. Place in a heavy pot and add enough water to cover barely. Place over medium-high heat and bring to a boil. Skim off any scum that rises to the surface. Reduce the heat to achieve a simmer, cover, and simmer until the chicken is very tender, about 2 hours. Remove from the heat and set the pot aside to cool.

WHEN the chicken is cool enough to handle, transfer to a work surface and discard the skin and bones. Shred or chop the chicken into very small pieces. Transfer to a bowl, add 2 cups of the cheese, the oregano, and salt and pepper to taste. Mix well and set aside.

PREHEAT an oven to 350° F. Using a pastry brush, lightly grease a 13-by-9-inch pan with oil, or coat with spray. Set aside.

IN a nonstick skillet over medium heat, heat 1 tortilla for a few seconds on each side just to soften. Alternatively, using tongs, move the tortilla back and forth directly over an open flame until softened. Lay the tortilla on a flat surface, spoon a scant ½ cup of the chicken mixture down the center, spread about 2 teaspoons of the Tomatillo-Chile Salsa over the chicken, roll the tortilla around the filling to form a cylinder, and place, seam side down, in the prepared pan. Soften, fill, and roll the remaining tortillas in the same manner.

SPOON a little of the remaining Tomatillo-Chile Salsa over the tops of the enchiladas, sprinkle with the remaining 2 cups cheese, and bake until heated through and the cheese is bubbly, 15 to 20 minutes.

MEANWHILE, place the condiments in small bowls on the table.

TO serve, spoon some of the remaining Tomatillo-Chile Salsa onto warmed plates, top with 2 enchiladas, and garnish with cilantro sprigs.

Makes 6 servings.

TAMALES

About 3 ounces dried corn husks
(hojas de maiz)
Red Chile Sauce (page 574)

TAMALE DOUGH

1 pound prepared Mexican corn
dough (masa), or 2 cups Mexican
corn flour (masa harina)
½ cup high-quality pure lard, solid
vegetable shortening, or unsalted
butter, at room temperature
2 tablespoons ground ancho, pasilla,
or other dried mild to medium-hot
chile
1 teaspoon baking powder
1 teaspoon salt, or to taste
⅔ cup White Stock (page 578)
made with chicken or canned
reduced-sodium chicken broth

CHICKEN FILLING

1 tablespoon canola or other
high-quality vegetable oil
¾ cup finely chopped onion
1 teaspoon minced garlic
2 cups chopped or shredded cooked
chicken
¼ cup Red Chile Sauce (prepared
previously as directed)
3 tablespoons chopped fresh
cilantro (coriander)
Salt

I've chosen a simple chicken filling to illustrate how to make tamales. Use this basic recipe to create an infinite variety of tamales by trying the filling suggestions that follow on page 248 or by creating your own tamale stuffings from complementary mixtures.

Please read about masa, masa harina, *and the choice of lard on page 602.*

Tamales may be wrapped in banana leaves in place of corn husks for an exotic tropical appearance or in aluminum foil for a less-glamorous presentation.

PLACE the corn husks in a large bowl and cover with warm water. Place a large plate on the husks to keep them submerged and soak to soften, at least 1 hour or for up to overnight.

PREPARE the Red Chile Sauce as directed and set aside.

TO make the Tamale Dough, if using *masa*, reserve for later use. If using corn flour, place in a large bowl and gradually stir in about 1⅓ cups warm water, using just enough water to form a dough that holds together. Cover and set aside to cool completely.

IN a bowl, combine the lard, shortening, or butter with the ground chile, baking powder, and salt and beat with an electric mixer until light and creamy. Add the *masa* or moistened corn flour, a little at a time, and mix well after each addition. With the mixer running, slowly add the stock or broth and mix well, then continue to beat about 1 minute longer to achieve a light, fluffy dough (it will be sticky). Cover and set aside while you prepare the filling or refrigerate for up to 3 days; return to room temperature before using.

TO make the Chicken Filling, in a saute pan or skillet, heat the oil over medium-high heat. Add the onion and cook, stirring frequently, until very soft and golden, about 8 minutes. Add the garlic and cook for about 1 minute longer. Stir in the cooked chicken, the ¼ cup Red Chile Sauce, and cilantro. Remove from the heat, season to taste with salt, and set aside.

TO assemble the tamales, shake the excess water off the soaked
corn husks and pat dry with paper toweling. Lay 1 large husk or
overlap 2 medium-sized husks, smooth side up, on a flat surface.
Moisten your hands with water and scoop up about 3 tablespoons
of the dough. Form a rectangle in the center of the husk with
the dough, leaving about 2 inches uncovered husk at each end
and about 1 inch on either side. Spoon about 2 tablespoons of
the filling down the center of the dough rectangle. Fold the
husk sides up and overlap loosely to allow for expansion during
cooking. Tie each end with narrow strips of torn husk, cotton
string, or nonsoluble ribbon or twine. For a festive presentation,
use scissors to fringe the ends of the wrappers. Repeat with the
remaining husks, dough, and filling to assemble a total of
about 16 tamales.

TO prepare for steaming, place a rack in a large pot with a tight-
fitting lid. Cover the rack with a layer of extra corn husks. Pour
in water to a level just below the rack and place over high heat.
Bring the water to a boil, then adjust the heat to achieve a simmer.

STACK the tamales, seam side down, on the rack in up to 3 layers;
do not crowd. Cover the tamales with 2 or 3 layers of extra
husks. Cover the pot with the lid and steam until the tamale
dough is plump, slightly firm, and easily comes free from the
wrapper, 1 to 1½ hours; unwrap a tamale to test for doneness.
Adjust the heat to maintain simmering water throughout cooking,
adding boiling water as needed to maintain water level.

SHORTLY before serving, slowly reheat the remaining Red Chile
Sauce and transfer to a serving bowl.

TO serve, transfer the hot tamales to warmed plates. Diners open
the wrappers at the table and spoon the sauce over the tamales.

Makes about 16 tamales for 8 servings.

variations follow ~

PREPARE the tamale dough as directed in the preceding recipe, substitute any of the following for the chicken filling, and steam as directed in the recipe.

Black Bean Filling. Cook ¾ cup chopped white or yellow onion in 1 tablespoon canola or other high-quality vegetable oil. Add 1 teaspoon minced garlic and ¼ cup chopped fresh cilantro (coriander). Stir in 2 cups well-drained cooked dried or canned black beans (see page 340) and season to taste with ground dried hot chile, ground cumin, and salt.

Cheese Filling. Use about 4 cups freshly shredded Cheddar or Monterey Jack cheese (about 12 ounces) or 3 cups crumbled blue or goat cheese (about 12 ounces).

Corn Filling. Use 2 cups Sauteed Corn (page 358).

Fish Filling. Using about 1 pound fish, brush ½-inch-thick skinned fillets of salmon, sturgeon, swordfish, or other firm-fleshed fish with melted butter and grill over a hot fire or under a preheated broiler just until well seared on the outside. Cut pieces to fit within the rectangle of tamale dough.

Meat Filling. Substitute cooked sliced or ground beef or pork for the chicken in the filling recipe.

Mushroom Filling. Chop 1 pound fresh mushrooms, preferably flavorful varieties, and saute in 3 tablespoons butter or olive oil until tender. Season to taste with salt, freshly ground black pepper, and minced fresh or crumbled dried sage or thyme.

Shellfish Filling. Grill or saute about 1 pound peeled and deveined shrimp, lobster tail meat, or scallops. Coarsely chop and combine with ¼ cup Tomatillo-Chile Salsa (page 393) or high-quality commercial tomatillo salsa.

Sweet Filling. When preparing the tamale dough, add ½ cup sugar. Use about 2 cups mincemeat, mashed cooked pumpkin or other winter squash, raisins, chopped banana, or other tropical fruits for the filling. Alternatively, add about ¾ cup grated or shredded fresh coconut (see page 562) or packaged sweetened coconut, chopped toasted nuts, chopped dried fruit, or pureed berries to the sweetened dough and omit the filling.

THAI GARLIC PORK
~ *Moo Gratiem* ~

Of all the delectable Thai ways with pork, this simple preparation is my favorite. Serve with plenty of white rice (page 364), preferably jasmine variety, as a foil to the saltiness of the meat.

QUICKLY rinse the pork under running cold water and pat dry with paper toweling. To facilitate slicing, wrap the pork in plastic wrap and place in a freezer until very cold but not frozen hard, about 2 hours.

USING an electric slicer or very sharp knife, slice the pork across the grain as thinly as possible, then cut each slice into pieces about 2 inches long by ½-inch wide. Transfer the pork to a bowl, add the garlic and pepper, and toss to mix well. Cover and refrigerate for at least 1 hour or for up to overnight; return to room temperature before cooking.

IN a small bowl, combine the oyster sauce, fish sauce, and sugar and stir to dissolve the sugar; set aside.

PLACE a wok, large saute pan, or large, heavy skillet over medium-high heat. When the pan is hot, add the oil and swirl to coat the pan. When the oil is hot but not smoking, add the shallot and stir-fry for about 1 minute. Add the pork mixture and stir-fry until the meat is no longer pink, about 2 minutes. Add the oyster sauce mixture and cook until the meat is well coated and the liquid thickens slightly, about 1 minute longer.

TO serve, transfer to a serving bowl or platter and garnish with cilantro sprigs.

Makes 4 servings.

1 pound boneless lean pork

¼ cup minced garlic

2 teaspoons freshly ground white pepper

¼ cup oyster sauce

3 tablespoons fish sauce, preferably Thai or Vietnamese

2 tablespoons palm sugar

2 tablespoons canola or other high-quality vegetable oil

½ cup chopped shallot

Fresh cilantro (coriander) sprigs for garnish

HONEY-GLAZED BARBECUED PORK TENDERLOINS

2 whole pork tenderloins (about 12 ounces *each*), trimmed of excess fat

HERB-AND-GARLIC SPICE MIX

2 tablespoons minced fresh flat-leaf parsley

2 tablespoons minced fresh oregano, or 2 teaspoons crumbled dried oregano

1½ teaspoons minced fresh rosemary, or ½ teaspoon crumbled dried rosemary

1½ teaspoons minced fresh thyme, or ½ teaspoon crumbled dried thyme

1 tablespoon minced garlic

1 tablespoon dried beef bouillon base (optional)

1½ teaspoons salt, or to taste

1½ teaspoons freshly ground black pepper, or to taste

1 teaspoon ground cayenne, or to taste

HONEY-MUSTARD GLAZE

2 tablespoons coarse-grained Dijon mustard

2 tablespoons firmly packed brown sugar

5 tablespoons honey

Vegetable oil for brushing grill rack

Fresh flat-leaf parsley, oregano, and/or rosemary sprigs for garnish

My brother-in-law, John Richardson, is famed among friends for originating this cooking technique. John successfully uses packets of "Italian" salad dressing mix in place of my spice combination. Slow cooking and soaked wood chips thrown on the fire add a special smoky flavor to the meat.

QUICKLY rinse the tenderloins under cold running water and pat dry with paper toweling. Set aside.

TO make the Herb-and-Garlic Spice Mix, in a small bowl, combine all of the spice mix ingredients and blend well. Rub the mixture all over the tenderloins and let stand at room temperature for about 30 minutes.

PREPARE a covered grill for moderately low indirect-heat cooking. Position a drip pan in the center of the fuel grate. Soak a handful of hickory or other flavorful wood chips in water.

TO make the Honey-Mustard Glaze, in a small saucepan, combine all of the glaze ingredients. Place over low heat and simmer until the sugar melts, about 5 minutes.

WHEN the fire is ready, lightly brush the grill rack with oil. Place the tenderloins on the rack directly over the heat and sear briefly on all sides, then position over the drip pan, add the soaked chips to the fire to create smoke, and cover the grill. Cook, turning every 10 to 15 minutes and brushing with the glaze, until an instant-read thermometer inserted into the thickest part of the meat registers 140° F, 45 minutes to 1 hour. If cooking over wood or charcoal, add more fuel and adjust the air vents as needed to maintain an even temperature.

TRANSFER the tenderloins to a cutting surface, cover loosely with foil, and let stand for about 5 minutes.

TO serve, cut crosswise into slices about ¼ inch thick, arrange on a serving platter or warmed plates, and garnish with herb sprigs.

Makes 6 servings.

MAPLE BABY BACK RIBS

Tender meaty pork ribs are always popular. When unavailable, substitute separated meaty, country-style ribs; allow three or four per person. The smoky flavor gained from adding soaked hickory, mesquite, or other flavorful wood chips to the fire is essential for great ribs.

TO make the Maple Marinade, in a nonreactive bowl, combine all of the marinade ingredients and mix well.

QUICKLY rinse the ribs under cold running water and pat dry with paper toweling. Place in a shallow nonreactive container, pour the marinade over, and turn to coat thoroughly. Cover and refrigerate, turning occasionally, for at least 12 hours or up to 2 days; return to room temperature before cooking.

PREHEAT an oven to 300° F.

REMOVE the rib racks from the marinade, reserving the marinade. Arrange the ribs in a baking pan, cover tightly with aluminum foil, and bake for about 50 minutes to tenderize.

PREPARE a covered grill for moderate direct-heat cooking. Soak about 3 cups hickory or other flavorful wood chips in water.

STRAIN the marinade into a saucepan, place over high heat, and cook, stirring frequently, until reduced to about 1½ cups.

WHEN the fire is ready, add the soaked chips to the fire and lightly brush the grill rack with oil. Place the ribs on the rack, cover, and cook, turning and brushing frequently with the reduced marinade, until the meat is tender and well glazed, about 30 minutes.

TRANSFER the ribs to a cutting surface and slice into individual portions.

TO serve, arrange the ribs on a serving platter and garnish with parsley.

Makes 4 servings.

MAPLE MARINADE

1½ cups pure maple syrup

1½ cups apple cider vinegar

1 cup canola or other high-quality vegetable oil

½ cup light molasses

½ cup soy sauce

3 tablespoons sweet-and-hot mustard

2 tablespoons juniper berries, crushed

4 racks (about 1½ pounds *each*) baby back pork ribs, cracked along the backbone

Vegetable oil for brushing grill rack

Fresh flat-leaf parsley sprigs for garnish

NEW MEXICAN GREEN CHILE PORK STEW

Tomatillo-Chile Salsa (page 393)

3 pounds boneless pork, trimmed of
excess fat

1 tablespoon minced fresh oregano,
or 1 teaspoon crumbled dried
oregano

All-purpose flour for dredging

2 tablespoons canola or other
high-quality vegetable oil, or more
if needed

About 1 cup White Stock (page 578)
made with chicken or canned
reduced-sodium chicken broth

Finely diced fresh red and green
sweet peppers and/or hot chiles
for garnish

*In New Mexico, this traditional stew is usually prepared with fiery hot
green chiles. Since not all of us have access to the explosive varieties, I've
used my Tomatillo-Chile Salsa, which calls for a combination of mild
and hot chiles. Feel free to boost the heat with more chile.*

PREPARE the Tomatillo-Chile Salsa as directed and set aside.

QUICKLY rinse the pork under cold running water, pat dry with
paper toweling, and cut into 1-inch cubes. Sprinkle with about
half of the oregano, then dredge in flour to coat lightly all over.
Shake off excess flour.

IN a heavy stew pot, heat 2 tablespoons oil over medium-high heat.
Add as many of the pork cubes as will fit without crowding the
pot and brown on all sides. Using a slotted utensil or tongs,
transfer the browned pork to a plate. Brown the remaining pork
cubes in the same manner, adding more oil as necessary to
prevent sticking.

WHEN all of the meat is browned, return it to the pot. Pour the
Tomatillo-Chile Salsa and 1 cup stock or broth over the pork and
scrape up any browned bits from the bottom of the pot. Bring to
a boil, then reduce the heat to achieve a simmer, cover, and
simmer until the pork is very tender when pierced with a small,
sharp knife or wooden skewer, 45 minutes to 1 hour. Add a bit
of stock or broth if the stew begins to dry out.

TO serve, ladle the stew into warmed shallow bowls and sprinkle
with diced sweet peppers and/or chiles.

Makes 8 servings.

CHILE AND CHORIZO QUICHE

Julia Child has urged us to bring those long-forgotten fluted quiche pans or dishes out of the cupboard once again and rediscover the pleasures of a well-made quiche. I agree with her. Mexican seasonings add zest to this variation on the venerable French custard-and-cheese pie.

PREPARE the pastry as directed, omitting the sugar. After rolling out, press the crust into a 10-inch quiche dish or tart ring. Trim the edges of the pastry even with the rim of the dish or ring. Chill and fully bake as directed. Set aside to cool completely.

TO make the filling, crumble the chorizo into a skillet. Place over medium heat and cook until the chorizo is done. Using a slotted utensil, transfer to paper toweling to drain well. Discard the fat from the skillet.

IN the same skillet, melt the butter over medium-high heat. Add the onion and minced chile and cook, stirring frequently, until soft but not browned, about 5 minutes. Add the garlic and cook for about 1 minute longer. Set aside.

PREHEAT an oven to 375° F.

IN a bowl, combine the eggs, cream or half-and-half, salt, and ground chile to taste and beat until smooth. Stir in the drained chorizo, onion mixture, and cheeses. Pour into the cooled crust and bake until the center is set, about 30 minutes.

REMOVE the pan to a wire rack to cool for about 10 minutes, then remove the ring (if using). Cut the quiche into wedges and transfer to warmed plates.

Makes 6 servings.

½ recipe Basic Pie Crust (page 490), preferably Cornmeal Crust Variation (page 495)

FILLING

4 ounces spicy Spanish sausage (chorizo), casings discarded

1 tablespoon unsalted butter

¼ cup minced onion

¼ cup minced fresh mild to hot chile, or to taste

1 teaspoon minced garlic

3 eggs, at room temperature

2 cups light cream or half-and-half

½ teaspoon salt, or to taste

Ground *ancho* or other dried mild to medium-hot chile, or *pequín* or other dried hot chile

½ cup freshly shredded Monterey Jack cheese (about 1½ ounces)

¼ cup freshly shredded Cheddar cheese (about ¾ ounce)

SPANISH RICE WITH GREEN BEANS AND PEAS

3 tablespoons olive oil

1 large yellow onion, sliced vertically into thin wedges

2 large red sweet peppers, stems, seeds, and membranes discarded, sliced lengthwise into ¼-inch-wide strips

10 ounces spicy Spanish sausage (chorizo), casings discarded, sliced about ½ inch thick

½ cup chopped drained sun-dried tomatoes packed in olive oil

1 tablespoon minced garlic

2 cups short-grain white rice, preferably Spanish Valencia

3 cups Brown Stock (page 576), Vegetable Stock (page 580), White Stock (page 578), or canned broth

1 cup dry white wine

¼ cup minced fresh flat-leaf parsley

1 tablespoon tomato paste

1 teaspoon paprika

½ teaspoon crumbled saffron threads (optional)

Salt

Freshly ground black pepper

1 pound green beans, trimmed and cut into ¾-inch lengths

2 cups tender shelled fresh or thawed frozen green (English) peas

¾ cup sliced pitted green or brine-cured ripe olives

Chopped fresh flat-leaf parsley for garnish

Shredded fresh orange zest for garnish

This combination captures the zesty essence of Spanish Mediterranean cooking.

PREHEAT an oven to 375° F.

IN a saute pan or large, heavy skillet, heat the oil over medium-high heat. Add the onion and sweet peppers and cook, stirring frequently, until soft, about 5 minutes. Add the chorizo, sun-dried tomatoes, and garlic and cook for about 2 minutes longer. Add the rice and cook, stirring frequently, until the grains are well coated, about 5 minutes. Stir in the stock or broth, wine, minced parsley, tomato paste, paprika, saffron (if using), and salt and pepper to taste. Bring to a boil, stirring constantly, then transfer to a large, shallow baking dish, preferably made of earthenware. Cover tightly with a lid or aluminum foil and bake for 20 minutes.

MEANWHILE, blanch the green beans as directed on page 338.

REMOVE the rice from the oven, uncover, and add the beans, peas, and olives, stirring well to distribute the ingredients evenly. Cover tightly, return to the oven, and bake until the liquid is absorbed and the rice is tender, about 10 minutes; if the rice gets too dry before it is done, add a bit more stock, broth, or water.

REMOVE the dish from the oven and let stand for about 10 minutes, then sprinkle with chopped parsley and orange zest. At the table, spoon onto warmed plates.

Makes 8 servings.

ROMAN GRILLED LAMB CHOPS
~ *Costolette d'Agnello a Scottadito* ~

These little chops are traditionally eaten by holding the bone between the fingers.

QUICKLY rinse the lamb chops under cold running water and pat dry with paper toweling. Place in a shallow nonreactive container. Generously drizzle oil and lemon juice over the lamb and sprinkle with the garlic and minced rosemary. Cover and let stand at room temperature for about 1 hour, turning occasionally.

PREPARE an open grill for moderate direct-heat cooking.

REMOVE the lamb and pat dry with paper toweling. Sprinkle with salt and pepper to taste.

WHEN the fire is ready, lightly brush the grill rack with oil. Place the lamb chops on the rack and cook, turning once, until done to preference, about 3 minutes on each side for medium-rare.

TO serve, arrange the lamb on warmed plates, garnish with rosemary sprigs, and place lemon wedges alongside for squeezing over the lamb.

Makes 4 servings.

12 small lamb chops, cut from rack of young spring lamb
Olive oil for drizzling
Freshly squeezed lemon juice for drizzling
2 tablespoons minced garlic
2 tablespoons minced fresh rosemary
Salt
Freshly ground black pepper
Vegetable oil for brushing grill rack
Fresh rosemary sprigs for garnish
Lemon wedges for serving

GRILLED LAMB KABOBS

MARINADE

¾ cup fruity olive oil, preferably
  extra-virgin

1½ tablespoons minced fresh thyme,
  or 1½ teaspoons crumbled dried
  thyme

4 bay leaves, crumbled

3 cups grated onion

1 tablespoon minced garlic

½ cup freshly squeezed lemon juice

Salt

Freshly ground black pepper

Hot sauce

1 leg of lamb (about 5 pounds),
  boned

3 medium-sized leeks, including pale
  green portions, cut into 1-inch
  pieces, or 2 red onions, cut into
  small wedges

1 red sweet pepper, stem, seeds, and
  membranes discarded, cut into
  1-inch squares

1 pound fresh small mushrooms

About 20 cherry tomatoes

Salt

Freshly ground black pepper

Vegetable oil for brushing grill rack

Minced fresh thyme or flat-leaf
  parsley for garnish

*We Americans have adopted classic Middle Eastern kabobs as our own.
Serve with Couscous (page 371) and a cucumber-tomato salad.*

TO make the marinade, in a large nonreactive bowl, combine all of
  the marinade ingredients, including salt, pepper, and hot sauce
  to taste. Mix well and set aside.

QUICKLY rinse the lamb under cold running water, pat dry with
  paper toweling, and cut into 1-inch cubes. Add the lamb to the
  marinade and stir to coat evenly. Cover and refrigerate, stirring
  occasionally, for 4 to 5 hours or for up to overnight; return to
  room temperature before cooking.

PREPARE a covered grill for moderate direct-heat cooking. If using
  bamboo skewers, about 30 minutes before cooking, place them
  in a shallow container, cover with water, and set aside to soak.

REMOVE the lamb from the marinade, reserving the marinade.
  Thread the meat on metal or soaked bamboo skewers. Thread
  each type of vegetable on separate skewers. Sprinkle the meat
  and vegetables with salt and pepper to taste. Set aside.

IN a saucepan, bring the marinade to a boil over medium-high heat,
  then set alongside the grill.

WHEN the fire is ready, lightly brush the grill rack with oil. Place
  the skewers on the rack, cover, and cook, turning frequently and
  basting the meat and vegetables with the marinade, until the
  lamb is done to preference, about 8 minutes for medium-rare.
  Remove each vegetable as it is done, from 5 to 10 minutes.

TO serve, slide the meat and vegetables off the skewers, arrange on
  warmed plates, and sprinkle with minced thyme or parsley.

Makes 8 servings.

MOROCCAN LAMB OR
BEEF STEW ~ *TAGINE* ~

*During the days when my late partner, Lin Cotton, and I ran a catering
company, we once served lamb tagine to 100 costumed guests seated at
low tables on rose petal-sprinkled Persian carpets in a tent draped with
gauze hangings and exotic lamps. A few years later, I served it under a
canopy of redwoods at the famed Bohemian Grove to forty guests on Lin's
fortieth birthday.*

*Unlike most other stews, the meat is not browned when making
a tagine. But like most stews, it tastes best when made the day before. For
each serving, place a scoop of Couscous (page 371) alongside the tagine in
a shallow bowl or deep plate.*

TOAST the coriander and sesame seed separately as directed on
page 553 and set aside to cool. Transfer the coriander seed to a
spice grinder or mortar with a pestle and grind to a fine powder.
Set aside.

QUICKLY rinse the lamb or beef under cold running water, pat
dry with paper toweling, and cut into 1½-inch cubes.

IN a heavy stew pot, combine the lamb or beef with enough stock or
broth (if using) or water to cover barely. Add the ground coriander,
cinnamon, onion, garlic, tomato puree, oil, rosemary, saffron,
and salt and pepper. Place over medium-high heat and bring
to a boil, then reduce the heat to achieve a simmer, cover, and
simmer until the meat is tender, about 2 hours. Add a little
more liquid if the stew becomes too dry. (At this point, the
stew may be cooled completely, then covered and refrigerated
for up to overnight. Slowly reheat before proceeding.)

STIR the prunes into the stew, cover, and simmer until the prunes
are plumped, about 15 minutes. Stir in the honey and simmer,
uncovered, about 10 minutes longer.

TO serve, ladle the warm *tagine* into warmed shallow bowls and
sprinkle with orange flower water and the toasted sesame seed.

Makes 6 servings.

1 teaspoon coriander seed

¼ cup sesame seed

3 pounds boned lamb leg or shoulder
or boneless chuck, trimmed of
excess fat

About 3 cups Brown Stock (page
576), Vegetable Stock (page 580),
or canned vegetable broth (optional)

1 tablespoon ground cinnamon

2 cups finely chopped onion

1 teaspoon minced garlic

¼ cup fresh or canned tomato
puree

3 tablespoons fruity olive oil,
preferably extra-virgin

1 tablespoon minced fresh rosemary,
or 1 teaspoon crumbled dried
rosemary

½ teaspoon crumbled saffron
threads

1 teaspoon salt, or to taste

1 teaspoon freshly ground black
pepper, or to taste

12 ounces pitted prunes

3 tablespoons honey, or to taste

Orange flower water (available where
alcoholic drink mixes are sold)

LAMB STEW WITH CARAMELIZED VEGETABLES

3 pounds boned lamb leg or shoulder, trimmed of excess fat

About ¼ cup fruity olive oil, preferably extra-virgin

2 cups chopped yellow onion

1 tablespoon minced garlic

⅓ cup hearty red wine such as California Zinfandel or Italian Barolo

⅓ cup red wine vinegar

3 cups peeled, seeded, and finely chopped or coarsely pureed fresh or canned tomato

¼ cup chopped fresh chervil or flat-leaf parsley

2 tablespoons minced fresh rosemary or thyme, or 2 teaspoons crumbled dried rosemary or thyme

Salt

Freshly ground black pepper

Caramelized Vegetables (page 323)

Polenta (page 154)

Minced fresh chervil or flat-leaf parsley for sprinkling

Fresh rosemary or thyme sprigs for garnish

This meltingly tender winter stew is also good served over rice or other cooked grains (page 364).

QUICKLY rinse the lamb under cold running water, pat dry with paper toweling, and cut into 1½-inch cubes.

IN a heavy stew pot, heat 2 tablespoons of the oil over medium-high heat. Add as many of the lamb cubes as will fit without crowding the pot and brown on all sides. Using a slotted utensil or tongs, transfer the lamb to a plate. Brown the remaining lamb cubes in the same manner, adding more oil as necessary to prevent sticking.

ADD enough oil to that remaining in the pot to total 2 tablespoons and heat over medium-high heat. Add the onion and cook, stirring frequently, until very soft and golden, about 8 minutes. Add the garlic and cook for 1 minute longer. Add the wine and vinegar and cook for about 2 minutes, scraping the pan bottom to loosen any browned bits.

RETURN the browned lamb to the pot and stir in the tomato, chopped chervil or parsley, minced or crumbled rosemary or thyme, and salt and pepper to taste. Bring to a boil, then reduce the heat to achieve a simmer, cover, and simmer until the meat is very tender when pierced with a small, sharp knife or a wooden skewer, 1½ to 2 hours. Add a little water if the stew dries out before the meat is tender.

ALTERNATIVELY, transfer the covered stew to a preheated 350° F oven and cook, stirring occasionally, until the meat is tender, 1½ to 2 hours; be sure to use an ovenproof pot.

MEANWHILE, prepare the Caramelized Vegetables and Polenta as directed and keep them warm. A few minutes before serving, stir the Caramelized Vegetables into the stew.

TO serve, spoon the warm Polenta into warmed shallow bowls, top with the lamb stew, sprinkle with minced chervil or parsley, and garnish with herb sprigs.

Makes 6 servings.

ITALIAN VEAL STEW
~ *Spezzatino di Vitello* ~

To add a bit of piquancy to this familiar dish, stir in 2 to 3 tablespoons drained small capers or chopped pitted brine-cured olives a few minutes before serving.

QUICKLY rinse the veal under cold running water, pat dry with paper toweling, and cut into 1-inch cubes. Dredge the meat in flour to coat lightly all over. Shake off excess flour.

IN a saute pan or heavy stew pot such as a dutch oven, combine 1 tablespoon oil and 1 tablespoon butter and place over medium-high heat. When the butter melts, add as many of the veal cubes as will fit without crowding the pot and brown well on all sides. Using a slotted utensil or tongs, transfer the veal to a plate. Brown the remaining veal cubes in the same manner, adding more oil and butter as necessary to prevent sticking.

ADD the shallot to the pan and cook, stirring frequently, until soft, about 3 minutes. Add the wine and bring to a boil, scraping the pan to loosen any browned bits. Return the veal to the pan, stir in the sage, salt, and pepper, then reduce the heat to achieve a simmer, cover, and simmer, turning the meat occasionally, until the veal is tender when pierced with a small, sharp knife, about 1 hour.

MEANWHILE, to make the Puff Pastry Cutouts (if using), position racks so that the cutouts will bake in the middle of an oven and preheat the oven to 350° F. Using a pastry brush, lightly grease a baking sheet with melted butter, or coat with spray or line with kitchen parchment. Set aside.

ON a lightly floured work surface, roll out the homemade pastry to a rectangle about 20 by 24 inches or spread out thawed dough sheets. Using a sharp knife or rolling pastry cutter, cut the dough into 18 decorative or geometric shapes. Place the pastry pieces on the prepared baking sheet and brush the tops with melted butter. Bake until the pastry is puffed, crisp, and golden brown, about 15 minutes. Remove from the oven to a wire rack to cool.

TO serve, ladle the warm stew into warmed shallow bowls, top each portion with 3 pastry cutouts (if using), and garnish with herb sprigs.

Makes 6 servings.

3 pounds boneless veal, trimmed of excess fat

All-purpose flour for dredging

About 2 tablespoons olive oil

About 2 tablespoons unsalted butter

3 tablespoons finely chopped shallot

1¼ cups dry white wine

2 tablespoons minced fresh sage, or 2 teaspoons crumbled dried sage

1 teaspoon salt, or to taste

1 teaspoon freshly ground white pepper, or to taste

PUFF PASTRY CUTOUTS (optional)

Unsalted butter, at room temperature, or cooking spray for greasing (optional)

1 pound homemade or frozen puff pastry, thawed in the refrigerator if frozen

Unsalted butter, melted and cooled slightly, for brushing

Fresh marjoram, oregano, or savory sprigs for garnish

FRENCH WHITE VEAL STEW
~ *Blanquette de Veau* ~

3 pounds boneless veal, trimmed of
   excess fat

About ½ cup (1 stick) unsalted
   butter

1 cup finely chopped leek, including
   pale green portion

1 cup finely chopped white or yellow
   onion

1 cup finely chopped celery

1 teaspoon minced garlic

1 bay leaf, crumbled

2 tablespoons minced fresh chervil,
   dill, or flat-leaf parsley

1 teaspoon grated or minced fresh
   lemon zest

About 3 cups White Stock (page 578)
   or canned reduced-sodium chicken
   broth

Salt

Freshly ground white pepper

1 pound pearl onions

8 ounces fresh small white button
   mushrooms

2 tablespoons all-purpose flour

1 cup heavy (whipping) cream

2 cups shelled fresh or thawed frozen
   green (English) peas

8 ounces tender asparagus, trimmed
   and cut on the diagonal into 1-inch
   lengths

¼ cup freshly squeezed lemon juice

Fresh chervil, dill, or flat-leaf parsley
   sprigs for garnish

This delicately seasoned stew, prepared throughout France by chefs and home cooks, celebrates the arrival of spring. Avoid using a cast-iron pot, which can darken the light color of the dish. The beautiful green vegetables in the cream-colored stew made the dish a perfect choice for a St. Patrick's Day birthday feast for my mother during a California visit.

QUICKLY rinse the veal under cold running water, pat dry with paper toweling, and cut into 1-inch cubes.

IN a heavy stew pot, melt 2 tablespoons of the butter over medium heat. Add as many of the veal cubes as will fit without crowding the pot and sear lightly on all sides; do not brown. With a slotted utensil or tongs, transfer the veal to a plate. Sear the remaining veal cubes in the same manner, adding more butter as necessary to prevent sticking.

ADD enough butter to that remaining in the pot to total 3 tablespoons and melt over medium heat. Add the leek, onion, and celery and cook, stirring frequently, until the vegetables are soft but not browned, about 8 minutes. Add the garlic, bay leaf, minced herb, and lemon zest and cook for 1 minute. Return the veal to the pot. Pour in enough stock or broth to cover barely and season to taste with salt and pepper. Bring to a boil, then reduce the heat to achieve a simmer, cover partially, and simmer for 30 minutes.

MEANWHILE, cut a small X in the root end of each pearl onion. Bring a large pot of water to a boil over high heat. Drop the onions into the water. After about 30 seconds, drain the onions. As soon as they are cool enough to handle, pull off the skin and detach the roots; be careful not to remove any of the onion layers.

ADD the pearl onions and mushrooms to the stew and continue simmering, stirring occasionally, until the vegetables and veal are tender, 45 minutes to 1 hour. Add a little more stock or broth if the stew becomes too dry.

STRAIN the liquid from the stew into a vessel with a pouring spout and set the stew aside. In a heavy saucepan, melt 2 tablespoons butter over low heat. Stir in the flour and cook, stirring, for 3 to 4 minutes; do not brown. Gradually whisk in the reserved cooking liquid, then stir in the cream, increase the heat to medium, and cook until reduced to about 3 cups, about 15 minutes.

MEANWHILE, blanch the peas as directed on page 338 and set aside. Blanch the asparagus in the same manner and set aside.

STIR the lemon juice into the reduced cream sauce and season to taste with salt and pepper. Stir in the reserved veal-vegetable mixture, peas, and asparagus. Taste and adjust seasonings. Gently heat the stew to serving temperature, about 3 minutes.

TO serve, ladle the warm stew into warmed shallow bowls and garnish with herb sprigs.

Makes 6 servings.

MILANESE BRAISED VEAL SHANKS
~ OSSOBUCO ~

8 large veal shanks (about 14 ounces
  each)

Salt

Freshly ground black pepper

All-purpose flour for dredging

About 2 tablespoons unsalted butter

About 2 tablespoons fruity olive oil,
  preferably extra-virgin

1 cup finely chopped yellow onion

½ cup finely chopped carrot

½ cup finely chopped celery

2 teaspoons minced garlic

¾ teaspoon minced fresh sage, or
  ¼ teaspoon crumbled dried sage

¾ teaspoon minced fresh rosemary,
  or ¼ teaspoon crumbled dried
  rosemary

1 bay leaf, crumbled

1 cup dry white wine

½ cup fresh or canned tomato puree

2 cups Brown Stock (page 576),
  White Stock (page 578), or canned
  beef or reduced-sodium chicken
  broth

A number of years ago, Luciano Parolari, chef at Lake Como's world-class Villa d'Este Hotel, showed me how to prepare this Lombardian specialty in the hotel kitchen. Saffron-infused risotto alla milanese (page 162) traditionally accompanies the dish.

You'll want to provide small spoons or forks for diners to dig out the marvelously flavored soft marrow from the bone.

QUICKLY rinse the veal shanks under cold running water and pat dry with paper toweling. Lightly salt and pepper the shanks, then dredge in flour to coat lightly all over. Shake off excess flour.

IN a heavy saute pan or stew pot, combine 1 tablespoon butter and 1 tablespoon oil and place over medium-high heat. When the butter is melted, add as many of the veal shanks as will fit without crowding the pan, and brown well on all sides. Using tongs, remove the shanks to a plate. Brown the remaining shanks in the same manner, adding more butter and oil as necessary to prevent sticking.

ADD enough butter and oil to that remaining in the pan to equal 2 tablespoons. Add the onion, carrot, and celery and cook, stirring frequently, until soft but not browned, about 5 minutes. Stir in the garlic, sage, rosemary, and bay leaf and cook for 1 minute longer. Add the wine, bring to a boil, and cook until most of the liquid evaporates, about 5 minutes.

ARRANGE the browned meat in the pan with the vegetables, keeping the shanks upright to prevent the marrow from escaping. Add the tomato puree and stock or broth. Bring to a boil, then reduce the heat to achieve a simmer, cover, and simmer until the meat is very tender and almost falling off the bones, about 2 hours.

REMOVE the pan from the heat and let stand for about 10 minutes before serving.

TO make the *Gremolada*, in a small bowl, combine the parsley, garlic, and lemon zest and mix well. Set aside.

TO serve, transfer the veal shanks to warmed plates and sprinkle with the *Gremolada*.

Makes 8 servings.

GREMOLADA

3 tablespoons minced fresh flat-leaf parsley

1 teaspoon minced garlic

1 tablespoon grated or minced fresh lemon zest

STAR ANISE BEEF

3 pounds round or other boneless lean
    beef, trimmed of excess fat and
    connective tissue

Salt

Freshly ground black pepper

About ¼ cup canola or other high-
    quality vegetable oil

1 cup chopped yellow or white onion

¾ cup sliced green onion, including
    green tops

2 tablespoons minced fresh ginger

1 teaspoon minced garlic

6 tablespoons soy sauce

6 tablespoons Chinese rice wine
    (Shaoxing) or dry sherry

3 tablespoons unseasoned rice vinegar

3 tablespoons firmly packed light
    brown sugar

3 whole star anise pods

8 ounces fresh shiitake mushroom
    caps, sliced

2 tablespoons cornstarch dissolved
    in 6 tablespoons water

Stir-fried slivered snow peas for
    garnish (see page 339)

Sliced kumquats for garnish (optional)

*Eight-pointed star anise pods hold tiny seeds that impart an exotic
flavor. If fresh shiitake mushrooms are unavailable, soak about 8 dried
Chinese black mushrooms in warm water to cover until softened, about
30 minutes; drain, discard tough stems, and slice.*

Serve with fluffy long-grain white rice (page 364).

QUICKLY rinse the beef under cold running water, pat dry with
    paper toweling, and cut into 1-inch cubes. Sprinkle lightly with
    salt and pepper.

IN a heavy stew pot, heat 2 tablespoons of the oil over medium-
    high heat. Add as many of the beef pieces as will fit without
    crowding the pot and brown on all sides. Using a slotted utensil
    or tongs, transfer the beef to a plate. Brown the remaining beef
    cubes in the same manner, adding more oil as necessary to
    prevent sticking.

ADD enough oil to that remaining in the pot to equal 2 tablespoons.
    Add the yellow or white onion and cook, stirring frequently,
    until soft but not browned, about 5 minutes. Add the green
    onion, ginger, and garlic and cook for 1 minute longer. Return
    the beef to the pan. Add the soy sauce, rice wine or sherry,
    vinegar, brown sugar, and star anise. Season generously to
    taste with pepper. Bring to a boil, then reduce the heat to
    achieve a simmer, cover, and simmer until the meat is very
    tender, 2 to 2½ hours. About 30 minutes before the meat is
    done, stir in the mushrooms.

USING a slotted utensil, transfer the beef and mushrooms to a
    bowl. Strain the cooking liquid into a bowl and remove excess
    fat from the top of the liquid. Return the liquid to the pot, stir
    in the cornstarch mixture, place over medium heat, and cook,
    stirring frequently, until thickened to a sauce consistency,
    about 5 minutes. Return the beef and mushrooms to the pot
    and simmer until heated through.

TO serve, ladle the stew into warmed bowls and sprinkle with the
    snow peas and kumquats (if using).

Makes 6 servings.

SOUTH AMERICAN SPICY
BEEF STEW ~ *PICADILLO* ~

In the heyday of Twin Peaks Grocery, I cooked up many gallons of this delicious concoction for ladling into take-out containers. Still one of my favorite stews, it is unique because the meat and flavorful sauce are traditionally cooked separately, then combined for the last few minutes.

QUICKLY rinse the beef under cold running water and pat dry with paper toweling. Cut into 1-inch cubes.

PLACE the beef in a heavy stew pot. Sprinkle with about 2 teaspoons salt and add just enough water to cover. Place over medium-high heat and bring to a boil, then reduce the heat to achieve a simmer, cover, and simmer until the beef is tender, about 1½ hours. Uncover and simmer until most of the liquid has evaporated, about 1 hour longer.

WHILE the meat cooks, in a large saute pan or heavy skillet, heat the oil over medium-high heat. Add the onion and sweet pepper and cook, stirring frequently, until soft but not browned, about 5 minutes. Add the garlic and cook about 1 minute longer. Stir in the tomato, olives, cumin, cloves, and vinegar. Bring to a boil, then reduce the heat to achieve a simmer, cover, and simmer for 15 minutes. Uncover and cook until the sauce is thickened, about 30 minutes longer.

TRANSFER the sauce to the pot with the cooked beef. Stir in the raisins and simmer, stirring frequently, for 10 minutes. Stir in the almonds and heat through.

TO serve, ladle the stew into warmed shallow bowls.

Makes 8 servings.

2 pounds round or other boneless lean beef, trimmed of excess fat and connective tissue

Salt

2 tablespoons olive oil, preferably extra-virgin

1 cup finely chopped white or yellow onion

1 cup finely chopped red sweet pepper

2 teaspoons minced garlic

3 cups peeled, seeded, and chopped ripe or canned tomato

⅓ cup small pimiento-stuffed green olives

½ teaspoon ground cumin

¼ teaspoon ground cloves

1 tablespoon red wine vinegar

¾ cup raisins

½ cup slivered blanched almonds

SOUTH AFRICAN CURRIED BEEF
~ *Bobotie* ~

Unsalted butter, at room temperature, vegetable oil, or cooking spray for greasing

1 thick slice bread

About 1 cup milk (not fat free)

2 tablespoons olive oil

2 cups finely chopped yellow or white onion

1 pound ground lamb

1 pound ground beef

2 teaspoons coriander seed

2 tablespoons apricot jam or fruit chutney (a favorite recipe or high-quality commercial product)

¼ cup freshly squeezed lemon juice

3 heaping tablespoons Indian-Style Curry Powder (page 556) or high-quality commercial curry powder

¼ cup slivered blanched almonds

½ cup golden raisins

½ cup halved or quartered dried apricots

5 eggs

Salt

Freshly ground black pepper

Fresh or dried lemon leaves or bay leaves

San Francisco garden designer Stephen Suzman shared this Cape Malay specialty from his homeland. The casserole is usually served with rice cooked with a pinch of saffron or turmeric and toasted coconut. If desired, scatter chopped toasted nuts over the finished dish and pass fruit chutney at the table.

PREHEAT an oven to 350° F. Using a pastry brush, lightly grease a 13-by-9-inch pan with butter or oil, or coat with spray. Set aside.

PLACE the bread in a small bowl, add milk to cover, and let stand until the bread is soft, about 5 minutes.

IN a saute pan or skillet, heat the oil over medium-high heat. Add the onion and cook, stirring frequently, until soft but not browned, about 5 minutes. Add the lamb and beef and cook, breaking up the meats with a spoon, until the meats are lightly colored but still a little pink, about 8 minutes. Transfer the mixture to a large bowl.

TOAST the coriander seed as directed on page 553. Pour onto a plate to cool, then transfer to a spice grinder or mortar with a pestle and grind to a fine powder. Set aside.

SQUEEZE the milk from the soaked bread, reserving the milk. Tear the bread into small pieces and add it to the meat-onion mixture. Add the ground coriander, jam or chutney, lemon juice, curry powder, almonds, raisins, apricots, and 1 of the eggs to the meat mixture and mix lightly but thoroughly. Season to taste with salt and pepper. Spread the mixture in an even layer in the prepared baking pan. Bake until the meat just begins to brown, about 15 minutes.

REMOVE the casserole from the oven. Distribute several lemon or
bay leaves over the top of the meat and press them down lightly.
Measure the reserved milk and add more, if needed, to equal
1 cup. In a bowl, combine the remaining 4 eggs and the milk
and beat lightly to blend well. Carefully pour the egg mixture
over the meat mixture and leaves. Return the casserole to the
oven and bake until the custard is set, about 30 minutes.

REMOVE the casserole from the oven and let stand for about
15 minutes before cutting into squares. Serve warm or at room
temperature.

Makes 8 servings.

THAI CHILE BEEF WITH FRAGRANT HERBS ~ *NUEA PAD PRIK* ~

1 pound sirloin, flank, or other
   boneless tender lean beef

3 tablespoons fish sauce

3 tablespoons soy sauce

3 tablespoons oyster sauce

3 tablespoons palm sugar

½ teaspoon freshly ground white
   pepper

2 tablespoons canola or other high-
   quality vegetable oil

¾ cup thinly sliced shallot

1½ tablespoons minced garlic

3 tablespoons minced fresh Thai bird
   or other hot chile, or to taste

4 green onions, including green tops,
   cut into 1-inch lengths

1 cup fresh mint leaves

1 cup fresh Asian basil leaves

Fresh mint sprigs for garnish

Fresh Asian basil sprigs for garnish

As with any stir-fried dish, be sure to prepare all the ingredients in advance of cooking and arrange in small bowls alongside the stove top. This preparation is also wonderful made with lamb.

QUICKLY rinse the beef under cold running water and pat dry with paper toweling. To facilitate slicing, wrap the beef in plastic wrap and place in a freezer until very cold but not frozen hard, about 2 hours.

USING an electric slicer or very sharp knife, slice the beef across the grain as thinly as possible, then cut each slice into pieces about 2 inches long by ½ inch wide.

IN a small bowl, combine the fish sauce, soy sauce, oyster sauce, sugar, and pepper and stir to dissolve the sugar; set aside.

PLACE a wok, large saute pan, or large, heavy skillet over high heat. When the pan is hot, add the oil and swirl to coat the pan. When the oil is hot but not smoking, add the shallot and stir-fry for about 1 minute. Add the garlic and chile and stir-fry for about 30 seconds. Add the beef and stir-fry, moving the pan off and on the heat as necessary to prevent scorching, until the meat is barely past the pink stage, about 2 minutes.

ADD the green onions, mint leaves, basil leaves, and the reserved fish sauce mixture; stir-fry until the leaves wilt and the meat is well coated with the sauce, about 2 minutes.

TO serve, transfer to a serving dish and garnish with mint and basil sprigs.

Makes 4 servings.

MALAYSIAN DRY BEEF CURRY IN LIME SAUCE *~ Rendang ~*

Rendang is a style of curry in which the sauce becomes a thick, almost dry coating that adheres to the meat. This version is redolent with the flavor of lime from the use of kaffir lime leaves.

I use tender, lean beef such as sirloin or top round, which renders a succulent stew within a couple of hours. If you prefer to use stewing beef such as chuck or rump roast, increase the final simmering time to about 3 hours, adding a little more coconut milk or water as needed to keep the meat from drying out completely. Lamb makes a tasty substitute for the beef.

TO make the Seasoning Paste, in a food processor, blender, or heavy mortar with a pestle, combine all of the paste ingredients and blend to a thick paste, adding up to 3 tablespoons water if needed to facilitate blending. Set aside.

QUICKLY rinse the beef under cold running water, pat dry with paper toweling, cut into 1-inch cubes, and set aside.

PLACE a wok, large saute pan, or large, heavy skillet over medium heat. When the pan is hot, add the oil and swirl to coat the pan. When the oil is hot, add the seasoning paste and cook, stirring constantly, until the mixture is very fragrant and darker and the oil begins to separate from the paste, about 8 minutes.

ADD the reserved beef, coconut milk, and lime leaves. Adjust the heat so that the mixture barely simmers; do not allow it to boil. Simmer, uncovered and stirring occasionally, for about 45 minutes.

STIR the sugar, lime juice, and salt into the simmering stew. Continue to simmer until the meat is very tender, almost falling apart, and the sauce is thick and adheres to the beef, about 1½ hours longer; add a little hot water if the sauce becomes too thick. Taste and add more sugar, lime juice, and salt if needed to achieve a good balance of sweet, sour, and salty.

TO serve, transfer the warm stew to a serving dish or warmed plates and garnish with lime slices.

Makes 4 servings.

SEASONING PASTE *(REMPAH)*

2 cups coarsely chopped shallot

5 tablespoons coarsely chopped fresh galanga or ginger

3 tablespoons sliced fresh lemongrass, tender bulb portion only

2 tablespoons coarsely chopped garlic

1 tablespoon Indonesian red chile sauce *(sambal ulek)* or other Asian chile sauce

1 tablespoon paprika

1½ pounds boneless beef, trimmed of excess fat and connective tissue (see recipe introduction)

¼ cup canola or other high-quality vegetable oil

1 cup Fresh Coconut Milk (page 562) or high-quality commercial coconut milk

12 fresh or thawed frozen kaffir lime leaves, finely slivered

2 tablespoons palm sugar, or more if needed

2 tablespoons freshly squeezed lime juice, or more if needed

2 teaspoons salt, or to taste

Lime slices for garnish

BETTER BURGERS

1½ pounds beef (see recipe
 introduction)

Worcestershire sauce

Salt

Freshly ground black pepper

Loaf of French bread, cut into
 4 sections each 5 to 6 inches long
 and then split lengthwise, or
 4 Whole-Wheat Buns (page 416) or
 high-quality hamburger buns, split

Vegetable oil for brushing grill rack
 (if grilling)

4 teaspoons unsalted butter

Sliced or crumbled cheese (optional;
 see recipe introduction)

Olive oil or melted unsalted butter for
 brushing on bread or buns

CONDIMENTS

Grilled onion slices or Caramelized
 Onions (page 551)

Mayonnaise or Garlic Mayonnaise
 (page 388) or high-quality
 commercial mayonnaise

Mustard of choice

Ripe tomato slices

Fresh arugula or basil leaves, tender
 lettuce leaves, or other young
 greens

Since 1990, I've judged the annual Build a Better Burger national cookoff, sponsored by Sutter Home Winery in the Napa Valley. Over the years, creative cooks have offered up patties that run the gamut from the expected beef through salmon to black-eyed peas, with winners that feature lamb, pork, and chicken. Coupled with my lifelong love affair with burgers, I've sampled countless variations on the theme. At home, here is how I prefer my burgers.

Most burger cooks agree that chuck or beef with a little fat cooks up particularly juicy and flavorful. Chopped sirloin, round, or other tender lean beef renders a less fatty burger, but it will probably need brushing with a little oil or melted butter during cooking to prevent sticking. Don't forget that great burgers also can be made with ground lamb, pork, and poultry.

I cringe when I read directions, sometimes from otherwise reliable sources, that instruct cooks to press down on the patties while they are cooking. On a grill or under a broiler, that means that all the delicious juices are lost through the grill rack, plus the drips cause flare-ups that will overchar the burgers. On a grill or in a skillet, pressing out the juices compacts the meat and makes it tough and dry. No matter which cooking method you choose, please never press down on a hamburger patty.

Whenever I want a cheeseburger, I look to one of my favorite melting cheeses: Italian Fontina or Gorgonzola, any creamy blue, Swiss Gruyère or Emmentaler, Canadian white Cheddar, and California jalapeño Jack or fresh goat cheese.

QUICKLY rinse the beef under cold running water, pat dry with
 paper toweling, and cut into strips.

USING a food grinder or chef's knife, grind or mince the meat and
 transfer it to a bowl. Sprinkle with 2 tablespoons Worcestershire
 sauce and salt and pepper to taste; be generous with the pepper.
 Handling the beef as little as possible to avoid compacting it,
 mix well. Divide the meat into 4 equal portions and form the
 portions into patties to fit the shape and size of the bread or buns;
 they should be between ¾ and 1 inch thick. Cook immediately,
 or cover and refrigerate for up to 2 hours; return to room
 temperature before cooking.

TO grill the burgers, prepare an open grill for hot direct-heat cooking. When the fire is ready, brush the grill rack with oil. Place the patties on the rack and cook until browned on the bottoms, about 4 minutes. Using a wide spatula, turn the patties. Top each patty with 1 teaspoon butter and sprinkle with Worcestershire sauce to taste. Cook until done to preference, about 4 minutes longer for medium-rare. During the last few minutes of cooking, top each patty with sliced or crumbled cheese (if using). Using a pastry brush, coat the cut sides of the bread or buns lightly with olive oil or butter and place, cut sides down, on the outer edges of the grill to toast lightly.

TO panfry the burgers, place a heavy skillet or griddle over high heat and sprinkle a fine layer of salt over the bottom. When the salt begins to brown and the pan is almost but not quite smoking, add the patties and cook until well browned on the bottoms, about 3 minutes. Using a wide spatula, turn the patties. Top each patty with 1 teaspoon butter and sprinkle with Worcestershire sauce to taste. Reduce the heat to medium-low and cook, turning several times, until done to preference, about 5 minutes longer for medium-rare. During the last few minutes of cooking, top each patty with sliced or crumbled cheese (if using) and lightly toast the buns in a toaster or under a preheated broiler. Using a pastry brush, coat the cut sides of the toasted bread or buns lightly with olive oil or butter.

TRANSFER the patties to the bottom halves of the bread sections or buns. Cover with the bread or bun tops. Offer condiments at the table.

Makes 4 burgers.

KOREAN BARBECUED BEEF

1 pound tenderloin, sirloin, or other tender boneless lean beef, trimmed of excess fat and connective tissue

MARINADE

1 cup soy sauce

½ cup sugar

¼ cup Asian sesame oil

¼ cup finely chopped green onion, including green tops

2 tablespoons minced fresh ginger

2 teaspoons minced garlic

Freshly ground black pepper

About 24 tender lettuce leaves

Condiments (see recipe introduction)

Vegetable oil for brushing grill rack

One of my favorite places to eat in San Francisco is a Korean barbecue house where smoky charcoal grills are brought to the table for cooking paper-thin marinated meats. To save your dining room walls, use your kitchen or outdoor grill or broiler.

This preparation is also delicious with traditional short ribs. Have your butcher slice them through the bone as thinly as possible.

The cooked meat is wrapped in lettuce along with condiments selected from an array of choices: Korean pickled cabbage (kimchee), shredded Japanese white radish (daikon), minced fresh hot chile, raw garlic slices, fresh mung bean sprouts, shredded carrot, sliced green onion, toasted sesame seed, and Asian chile sauce or hot bean paste.

QUICKLY rinse the beef under cold running water and pat dry with paper toweling. To facilitate slicing, wrap the meat in plastic wrap and place in a freezer until very cold but not frozen hard, about 2 hours.

USING a very sharp knife, slice the meat diagonally across the grain as thinly as possible.

TO make the marinade, in a bowl, combine all of the marinade ingredients, including pepper to taste, and mix well. Add the beef slices and stir to coat evenly with the marinade. Cover and refrigerate, stirring occasionally, for at least 4 hours or for up to overnight; return to room temperature before cooking.

WASH the lettuce leaves under cold running water. Place in a salad spinner and spin to remove as much water as possible. Pat dry with paper toweling. Wrap in a cloth kitchen towel or paper toweling and refrigerate for at least 30 minutes to crisp, or place the wrapped leaves in a plastic bag and refrigerate for up to several hours.

PREPARE an open grill for hot direct-heat cooking or preheat
a broiler.

ARRANGE a plate of the chilled lettuce leaves and small bowls of
several selected condiments on the table.

WHEN the fire or broiler is ready, lightly brush the grill or broiler
rack with oil. Remove the beef from the marinade, place on the
rack, and grill or broil, turning once, until done, about 30
seconds. Transfer to a serving platter.

TO eat, place some of the hot meat on a lettuce leaf, top with
selected condiments, wrap the leaf around the meat, and eat
out of hand.

Makes 4 servings.

GRILLED STEAK WITH PEANUT SAUCE

MARINADE

½ cup soy sauce

½ cup freshly squeezed lime juice

2 tablespoons crunchy peanut butter

1 tablespoon palm sugar or brown sugar

1 tablespoon Indian-Style Curry Powder (page 556) or high-quality commercial curry powder

1 teaspoon minced garlic

Crushed dried hot chile

2 pounds flank steak, top round, or other tender boneless lean beef, in a single piece, trimmed of excess fat and connective tissue

Peanut sauce (pages 397-398) of your choice

Vegetable oil for brushing grill or broiler rack

Ever since my partner, Andrew, and I gave his sister, Sara Timpson, a copy of my Beef Cookbook, *this recipe has been a favorite of her family. "Sisi" uses beef from Kealia Ranch, where she works, on the Kona coast of the island of Hawaii. The steak is especially delicious served with fluffy rice (page 364) cooked in coconut milk and sprinkled with toasted shredded coconut.*

TO make the marinade, in a nonreactive bowl, combine all of the marinade ingredients, including chile to taste. Mix well and set aside.

QUICKLY rinse the beef under cold running water and pat dry with paper toweling. Place in a flat, shallow nonreactive dish, pour the marinade over, and turn the meat to coat well on all sides. Cover and refrigerate, turning occasionally, for at least 4 hours or for up to overnight; return to room temperature before cooking.

PREPARE the selected peanut sauce as directed and set aside.

PREPARE an open grill for hot direct-heat cooking or preheat a broiler.

REMOVE the steak from the marinade, reserving the marinade, and set aside.

IN a saucepan, bring the marinade to a boil over medium-high heat, then set alongside the grill.

WHEN the fire or broiler is ready, lightly brush the grill or broiler rack with oil. Place the steak on the rack and grill or broil, turning once and basting occasionally with the marinade, until an instant-read thermometer inserted into the meat registers done to your preference, about 10 minutes per side for medium-rare.

TRANSFER the steak to a cutting surface and let stand for about 5 minutes.

GENTLY reheat the peanut sauce.

TO serve, thinly slice the steak across the grain at a 45-degree angle. Arrange the slices on warmed plates and serve with the warmed peanut sauce.

Makes 6 servings.

BEEF AND WILD MUSHROOM STROGANOFF

A Russian classic is updated with the use of wild mushrooms. Serve over buttered fresh noodles or white rice (page 364).

QUICKLY rinse the beef under cold running water and pat dry with paper toweling. To facilitate slicing, wrap the beef in plastic wrap and place in the freezer until very cold but not frozen hard, about 2 hours.

USING a very sharp knife, slice the beef across the grain into ¼-inch-thick strips, then cut into pieces about 2 inches long. Set aside.

IN a saucepan, bring the stock or broth to a boil over high heat.

MEANWHILE, in a separate saucepan, melt 3 tablespoons of the butter over medium-high heat. Stir in the flour and ½ teaspoon salt and whisk until well blended. Cook, stirring, for about 3 minutes. Add the boiling stock or broth all at once and whisk continuously until the sauce is smooth and thickened to the consistency of cream. Remove from the heat, whisk in the sour cream, and set aside.

IN a saute pan or skillet, melt 3 tablespoons of the remaining butter over medium-high heat. Add the mushrooms and cook, stirring frequently, until tender, 3 to 4 minutes. Season to taste with salt and pepper, transfer to a bowl, and set aside.

IN the same pan, heat the remaining 2 tablespoons butter over medium-high heat. Add the shallot and beef and cook, stirring frequently, until the beef is browned on all sides, 3 to 5 minutes. Stir in the reserved sauce, cooked mushrooms, and the sherry. Season to taste with salt and pepper. Heat until warmed through, 2 to 3 minutes; do not allow to boil or the sauce may curdle.

SPRINKLE each serving with thyme or parsley.

Makes 4 servings.

1½ pounds fillet, sirloin, or other tender boneless lean beef, trimmed of excess fat and connective tissue

1½ cups Brown Stock (page 576) made with beef or canned beef broth

½ cup (1 stick) unsalted butter

1½ tablespoons all-purpose flour

Salt

1 cup sour cream (not nonfat)

1 pound fresh flavorful mushrooms such as chanterelle, morel, porcino, or shiitake, sliced

Freshly ground black pepper

¼ cup minced shallot

3 tablespoons dry sherry, or to taste

Fresh thyme leaves or minced flat-leaf parsley for sprinkling

PANFRIED STEAK

4 tenderloin, sirloin, or other tender
   boneless lean beef steaks, about
   1 inch thick, trimmed of excess fat
   and connective tissue

Freshly ground coarse black pepper

Coarse salt

About 4 tablespoons (½ stick)
   unsalted butter

About ¼ cup Worcestershire sauce

¼ cup minced shallot

¼ cup freshly squeezed lemon juice

1 tablespoon minced fresh flat-leaf
   parsley

*For years, this adaptation of steak au poivre has been my favorite way
of cooking steak. Though any tender beef will work, I most frequently use
fillet because I like the soft texture, and the seasonings impart plenty of
flavor to what can be a rather bland cut. For a chewier steak, choose
rib-eye or New York strip.*

QUICKLY rinse the steaks under cold running water and pat dry
   with paper toweling. Generously sprinkle both sides of the
   steaks with pepper and gently press it into the meat with your
   hands. Loosely cover with plastic wrap and let stand at room
   temperature for about 20 minutes.

IN a saute pan or heavy skillet, sprinkle a fine layer of salt over
   the bottom and place over high heat. When the salt just begins
   to brown and the pan is almost but not quite smoking, add the
   steaks and cook until well browned on the bottoms, about 5
   minutes for medium-rare. Turn the steaks with tongs to prevent
   piercing and releasing juices. Reduce the heat to medium-low.
   Top each steak with about 1 tablespoon butter and sprinkle
   each with about 1 tablespoon Worcestershire sauce, or to taste.
   Add the shallot, distributing it evenly around the steaks, and
   cook until the steaks are done to your preference, about 10
   minutes total for medium-rare. Frequently stir the shallot in
   the pan drippings, adding a bit more butter and Worcestershire
   sauce if needed to prevent the meat from sticking to the pan.

REMOVE the steaks to warmed plates. Add the lemon juice to the
   pan, scraping the sides and bottom to loosen any browned bits
   and cook about 1 minute. Remove from the heat, stir in the
   parsley, and pour over the steaks.

Makes 4 servings.

POT ROAST WITH ROOT VEGETABLES

Enjoy this succulent dish whenever you crave old-fashioned flavors.

PREHEAT an oven to 325° F.

QUICKLY rinse the beef under cold running water and pat dry with paper toweling. If necessary to form a compact mass, tie with cotton string in several places. Set aside.

IN a heavy ovenproof pot, heat the oil over medium-high heat. Add the meat and brown well on all sides. Drain off and discard all but 2 tablespoons of the oil and drippings. Season the meat with salt and pepper to taste. Add all of the Seasoning Mixture ingredients, including enough stock or broth to come halfway up the sides of the roast. Bring to a boil, then cover tightly and transfer to the oven. Cook until the meat is just tender, 1½ to 2 hours, adding a little more stock or broth if necessary to maintain about 2 cups liquid at all times. Remove from the oven and discard the seasoning vegetables.

ARRANGE the root vegetables in the stock remaining around the roast and sprinkle them with salt and pepper. If necessary, add additional stock, broth, or water to come halfway up the depth of the vegetables. Cover tightly, return to the oven, and cook, basting the roast and vegetables occasionally with the liquid, until the vegetables are tender and the meat is very tender but not falling apart, 45 minutes to 1 hour longer.

REMOVE the roast from the pot to a cutting surface and let stand for about 15 minutes. Discard string (if used).

TO serve, carve the roast (don't expect perfect slices) and arrange on a serving platter. Peel the beets and arrange them with the other vegetables around the beef. If the pan drippings seem too thin, whisk in the flour and cook over medium-high heat until the flour loses its raw taste and the gravy is thickened, about 3 minutes. Pour the drippings over the meat and sprinkle with minced herbs.

Makes 6 servings.

3-pound piece eye of round or other
　boneless lean beef cut, trimmed
　of excess fat and connective tissue
2 tablespoons canola or other
　high-quality vegetable oil
Salt
Freshly ground black pepper

SEASONING MIXTURE

2 yellow onions
2 carrots, cut in half
2 celery stalks, cut in half
2 bay leaves
3 fresh flat-leaf parsley sprigs
3 fresh thyme sprigs, or 1 teaspoon
　crumbled dried thyme
About 3 cups Brown Stock (page
　576) made with beef or canned
　beef broth

ROOT VEGETABLES

12 small white onions, peeled
12 small carrots, scraped
12 small parsnips, scraped
12 small new potatoes
12 small turnips or rutabagas, peeled
12 small beets
1 whole garlic head, cloves separated
　and peeled

1 tablespoon all-purpose flour, or
　more if needed (optional)
Minced fresh herbs of choice for
　garnish

SOUTHERN BEEF AND NOODLE CASSEROLE

Salt

6 ounces dried egg noodles or pasta

2 cups White Sauce (page 572)

Unsalted butter, at room temperature,
vegetable oil, or cooking spray for
greasing

2 tablespoons unsalted butter

1 cup finely chopped onion

¾ cup finely chopped sweet pepper

1 tablespoon minced garlic

1½ pounds ground round or other
lean tender beef

8 ounces fresh mushrooms, finely
chopped

3 tablespoons chili powder

Freshly ground black pepper

Ground cayenne or other dried hot
chile

2 cups Tomato Sauce (page 573) or
1 can (15 ounces) tomato sauce

2 cups Creamed Corn (page 358) or
1 can (17 ounces) cream-style corn

1 cup freshly grated Cheddar cheese
(about 3 ounces)

It seems that every family has a version of this casserole, known by various picturesque names such as Italian delight. This one is comfort food from my childhood, a dish that my grandmother Olivia Belle Keith cooked back in Jackson, Mississippi. Years later at my fancy-food take-out store in San Francisco, I made my own version of this old-fashioned casserole in huge quantities, an instant favorite with many customers.

Although Mawmaw Keith always made this dish with flat noodles, fanciful shapes, such as corkscrew pasta, can make it more fun.

IN a large pot, bring 2 quarts water to a boil over high heat, then stir in 1 tablespoon salt. Add the noodles or pasta and cook until tender but still firm to the bite. Drain and rinse in cold water to halt cooking and help keep the noodles or pasta separated. Set aside.

PREPARE the White Sauce as directed and set aside.

PREHEAT an oven to 350° F. Using a pastry brush, lightly grease a 2-quart baking dish with butter or oil, or coat with spray. Set aside.

IN a saute pan or skillet, melt the 2 tablespoons butter over medium-high heat. Add the onion and sweet pepper and cook, stirring frequently, until soft, about 5 minutes. Add the garlic and cook for about 1 minute longer. Stir in the ground beef and mushrooms and cook, stirring to break up the meat, just until the meat loses its raw color, about 5 minutes. Stir in the chili powder. Remove from the heat and season to taste with salt, pepper, and cayenne or other chile.

ARRANGE half of the noodles or pasta in the prepared baking dish, cover with about half of the meat mixture, then half of the tomato sauce, and finally half of the corn. Add the remaining noodles, meat, tomato sauce, and corn in the same order. Cover the top with the reserved white sauce and sprinkle with the cheese. Bake until bubbly, 1 to 1½ hours.

REMOVE from the oven and let stand for about 10 minutes before scooping onto warmed plates.

Makes 6 servings.

BEEF CHILI

Known by the Spanish name chili con carne, *one of America's most popular dishes started out as a campfire stew for hungry Texas cowboys, who laced it with wild chiles to give it plenty of kick. Today there are about as many "authentic" recipes for chili as there are cooks in the Lone Star state, some swearing by cubed beef instead of ground and most arguing against beans that are a preferred addition in other parts of the country.*

This easy yet tasty version comes from my sister, Martha, who serves it with warm tortillas for wrapping the chili to eat out of hand.

QUICKLY rinse the beef under cold running water and pat dry with paper toweling. Using a sharp knife, cut the beef into ½-inch cubes, or chop finely with the knife or in a food processor. Set aside.

IN a heavy stew pot, heat the oil over medium heat. Add the onion and cook until soft but not browned, about 5 minutes. Add the beef and garlic and cook, breaking up the meat with a spoon, until the beef is just past the pink stage. Add the chile, cumin, flour, and salt, pepper, and cayenne to taste. Stir in the tomato sauce, adjust the heat to maintain a simmer, and simmer, uncovered, until thickened and the flavors are well blended, about 1 hour.

DRAIN the beans (if using) and stir them into the chili during the last 20 minutes of cooking. Add a little water to the pot any time during the cooking if the mixture begins to dry out.

TO serve, place the condiments in small bowls on the table. Ladle the chili into warmed bowls and serve hot.

Makes 6 to 8 servings.

3 pounds round or other tender boneless lean beef, trimmed of excess fat and connective tissue

3 tablespoons canola or other high-quality vegetable oil

2 cups finely chopped white or yellow onion

1 tablespoon minced garlic

¾ cup ground dried *ancho, pasilla,* or other mild to medium-hot chile

1 tablespoon ground cumin, or to taste

½ cup all-purpose flour

Salt

Freshly ground black pepper

Ground cayenne

3 cups Tomato Sauce (page 573) or high-quality commercial tomato sauce

4 cups cooked dried or canned black or pinto beans (see page 340; optional)

CONDIMENTS

Freshly shredded cheddar cheese

Sour cream

Finely chopped red onion

Chopped fresh tomato

Fresh cilantro (coriander) leaves

NEW MEXICAN RED BEEF CHILI
~ *Carne en Salsa Roja* ~

3 pounds round or other tender
boneless lean beef, trimmed of
excess fat and connective tissue

12 large *ancho, guajillo,* New
Mexico, *pasilla,* or other dried mild
to medium-hot chiles

1 cup coarsely chopped white or
yellow onion

2 tablespoons coarsely chopped garlic

Salt

Margie Allen, a grand cook who learned to make chili from her late mother, Socoro Sandoval, in Santa Fe, taught me how to make this authentic Southwest dish. I enjoy it spooned over stacked or rolled cheese-filled enchiladas made with blue-cornmeal tortillas. It is also good served in bowls and accompanied with tortillas, chips, or cornbread (page 423) made from the blue cornmeal unique to Southwest pueblos.

PREHEAT an oven to 400° F.

QUICKLY rinse the beef under cold running water and pat dry with paper toweling. Cut into ½-inch cubes and set aside.

DISCARD the stems from the chiles. Slit open and remove the seeds and membranes. Mist the chiles with water and lay them on a baking sheet. Roast in the oven for about 5 minutes.

WORKING in batches if necessary, in a food processor or blender, combine the chiles, onion, garlic, and water to a depth of about 3 inches. Puree until fairly smooth, adding more water if needed to facilitate blending. Transfer to a heavy stew pot.

ADD the reserved beef to the pot. Place over medium-high heat and bring to a boil, then reduce the heat to achieve a simmer, cover, and simmer, stirring occasionally, until the beef is very tender, about 30 minutes. Season to taste with salt.

Makes 6 servings.

BRAISED BEEF BUNDLES

Thin scallops of beef rolled around a stuffing are known as paupiettes
to the French, rollatini *to the Italians,* rouladen *to the Germans, and
sometimes as "birds" or "olives" in the English-speaking world. The
fillings change with the cuisine, but the preparation and the cooking
technique are basically the same.*

QUICKLY rinse the beef under cold running water and pat dry with
paper toweling. To facilitate slicing, wrap in plastic wrap and place
in the freezer until very cold but not frozen hard, about 2 hours.

TO make the stuffing, in a bowl, combine the ham, cheese, walnuts,
drained raisins, mustard, garlic, and salt and pepper to taste and
mix thoroughly. Set aside while you slice the meat.

USING a very sharp knife, thinly slice the meat into 16 pieces. Place
each piece between 2 sheets of waxed paper or plastic wrap and
pound with a mallet or other flat instrument until very thin.
Working with 1 piece of the beef at a time, mound a portion of
the stuffing mixture near one end. Roll the meat from the end
nearest the stuffing, tucking the edges in as you roll to form a
pillow-shaped packet. Tie around the middle and then lengthwise around each roll with cotton string.

IN a pan just large enough to hold all of the meat rolls, heat the oil over
medium-high heat. Add the rolls and brown on all sides, turning
frequently. Blend the stock or broth with the tomato paste and add
to the mixture to a depth of two-thirds up the sides of the beef rolls.
Season to taste with salt and pepper. Bring to a boil, then reduce
the heat to achieve a simmer, cover, and simmer, frequently basting
and turning the rolls, until very tender, 1½ to 2 hours.

REMOVE the beef rolls to a plate. Increase the heat to high and
cook until the sauce is reduced somewhat.

TO serve, cut and remove the strings from the rolls. Arrange on
warmed plates, spoon some of the pan sauce over each bundle,
and sprinkle with parsley.

Makes 8 servings.

2 pounds round, flank, or other tender
boneless lean beef, trimmed of
excess fat and connective tissue

8 ounces thinly sliced flavorful
baked ham, chopped

½ cup freshly grated Parmesan
cheese (about 2 ounces),
preferably Parmigiano-Reggiano

2 tablespoons chopped walnuts

2 tablespoons raisins, soaked in hot
water until plumped, then drained

1 teaspoon Dijon mustard

1 teaspoon minced garlic

Salt

Freshly ground black pepper

2 tablespoons olive oil, preferably
extra-virgin

About 3 cups Brown Stock (page
576) made with beef or canned
beef broth

3 tablespoons tomato paste

Minced fresh flat-leaf parsley for
garnish

WARM weather calls for hearty main-dish salads and other make-ahead fare that is easy on the cook. Although many of these dishes are refrigerated, be sure to return them almost to room temperature before serving. These selections are perfect for transporting in coolers to picnics or potluck get-togethers. Many of the dishes also make great year-round additions to the buffet table.

In addition to the recipes that follow, look through the soups that begin on page 86 for those that can be served chilled as main courses.

TACO SALAD

This Mexicali classic has been lightened for today's preferred dining style, but you may wish to add any favorite taco ingredient, such as seasoned cooked ground beef or shredded chicken, sliced or chopped black olives, and dollops of sour cream or plain yogurt and/or Guacamole (page 395).

∞

COOK the beans as directed. Measure out 4 cups of the cooked beans and set aside to cool. (Save the remaining beans for another use.)

WASH the lettuce leaves under cold running water. Place in a salad spinner and spin to remove as much water as possible. Pat dry with paper toweling. Wrap in a cloth towel or in paper toweling and refrigerate for about 30 minutes to crisp, or place the wrapped leaves in a plastic bag and refrigerate for up to several hours.

TO make the Tomato Dressing, in a small bowl, combine the vinegar, tomato paste, sugar, salt, and pepper to taste and whisk to blend well. Add the oil and whisk until emulsified. Set aside; whisk again just before using if necessary.

TEAR the lettuce leaves into bite-sized pieces to equal about 6 cups.

IN a large bowl, combine the lettuce, tomato, onion, chile, cilantro, cheese, and tortilla chips and toss thoroughly. Drain the beans, add to the salad, and toss thoroughly. Add about half of the reserved dressing and toss to blend well.

TRANSFER the salad to a large serving bowl and serve immediately. Pass the remaining dressing for drizzling over individual servings.

Makes 6 servings.

Mexicali Beans (page 348)

About 2 heads romaine lettuce, tough outer leaves discarded, separated into individual leaves

TOMATO DRESSING

⅓ cup red wine vinegar

3 tablespoons tomato paste

4 teaspoons sugar

1 teaspoon salt, or to taste

Freshly ground black pepper

⅔ cup extra-virgin olive oil

2 cups peeled, seeded, drained and chopped firm, ripe tomato

½ cup chopped red onion

¼ cup chopped fresh jalapeño or other hot chile

½ cup packed fresh cilantro (coriander) leaves

2 cups freshly shredded white Cheddar or Monterey Jack cheese (about 6 ounces)

6 cups lightly crushed white or yellow corn tortilla chips (about 8 ounces)

MARINATED FRIED FISH FILLETS, VENETIAN STYLE ~ *Sfogi in Saor* ~

2 tablespoons olive oil, preferably
    extra-virgin

2 cups chopped yellow onion

1½ cups white wine vinegar

Salt

¼ cup pine nuts

1½ pounds sole or catfish fillets

All-purpose flour for dredging

Canola or other high-quality vegetable
    oil for frying

⅓ cup golden raisins, soaked in hot
    water until plumped, then drained

Freshly ground black pepper

¼ cup minced fresh flat-leaf parsley

On the Feast of the Holy Redeemer, Venetians celebrate with fireworks. This centuries-old dish is commonly a part of the meal served aboard the countless boats that fill the sea and the canals. In Venice it is always made with firm Adriatic sole, but I enjoy it with catfish — my native Louisiana meets my soul country of Italy.

IN a heavy saute pan or skillet, heat the olive oil over medium heat. Add the onion and toss well to coat with the oil. Cover, reduce the heat to medium-low, and cook, stirring occasionally, until the onion just begins to color, about 20 minutes. Uncover, increase the heat to medium, and cook, stirring frequently, until the onion is caramelized, about 20 minutes longer. Increase the heat to high, add the vinegar and salt to taste, and cook until the liquid is almost evaporated, about 5 minutes. Remove from the heat and set aside.

TOAST the pine nuts as directed on page 553 and set aside.

QUICKLY rinse the fish fillets under cold running water and pat dry with paper toweling. Dredge the fillets in flour to coat lightly. Shake off excess flour.

IN a skillet, pour in vegetable oil to a depth of ½ inch and heat over medium-high heat. Place a wire rack on a baking sheet and position alongside the stove top. Carefully add the fish to the hot oil and fry until golden brown on both sides, about 5 minutes. As soon as the pieces are done, remove with a slotted utensil to the rack to drain well. Sprinkle with salt to taste.

PLACE the fish snugly in a dish, overlapping if necessary, then cover with the onion mixture. Sprinkle the pine nuts, raisins, and pepper to taste over the top. Cover tightly with plastic wrap and refrigerate overnight or for up to 2 days. Return to room temperature before serving.

JUST before serving, sprinkle with parsley.

Makes 4 servings.

SALMON SALAD NIÇOISE

This play on a French classic prepared with tuna is perfect for an outdoor hot-weather lunch. Instead of presenting composed salads, each ingredient can be placed in separate bowls for diners to assemble their own salads.

WASH the greens under cold running water. Place in a salad spinner and spin to remove as much water as possible. Pat dry with paper toweling. Wrap in a cloth towel or in paper toweling and refrigerate for about 30 minutes to crisp, or place the wrapped greens in a plastic bag and refrigerate for up to several hours.

PLACE the potatoes in a saucepan and add water to cover by about 2 inches, then remove the potatoes. Bring the water to a boil over medium-high heat, return the potatoes, and cook until just tender when pierced with a wooden skewer or small, sharp knife, about 20 minutes. Drain well, then slice and set aside.

BLANCH the green beans or peas as directed on page 338 and set aside.

PREPARE the Mustard Vinaigrette as directed.

ON individual plates, arrange the salad greens, sliced potatoes, green beans or peas, tomatoes, onion rings, eggs, salmon, and olives. Garnish with anchovies and lemon. Spoon on some of the vinaigrette and serve immediately. Pass the remaining vinaigrette for drizzling over individual servings.

Makes 4 to 6 servings.

About 3 cups young salad greens

6 small thin-skinned potatoes

½ pound tender green beans, tips and strings removed, or edible pod peas

Mustard Vinaigrette (page 566), made with Dijon mustard

4 vine-ripened Italian plum tomatoes, sliced, or 1 cup cherry tomatoes

1 small red sweet onion, thinly sliced and separated into rings

3 hard-cooked chicken eggs (see page 28), peeled and quartered, or 12 hard-cooked quail eggs, peeled

3 cups chopped or flaked cold cooked salmon fillet

½ cup oil-cured ripe olives, preferably Niçoise

Flat anchovy fillets, rinsed and patted dry, for garnish

Lemon wedges for garnish

TRIO OF COLD POACHED FISH WITH WASABI MAYONNAISE

WASABI MAYONNAISE

1 cup Mayonnaise (page 388) or
high-quality commercial mayonnaise

1 tablespoon Japanese horseradish
powder (wasabi), or to taste

3 tablespoons minced fresh herb
such as chervil, chives, or flat-leaf
parsley

COURT BOUILLON

3 cups dry white wine

½ cup freshly squeezed lemon juice
or white wine vinegar

1 cup sliced leek, including green
tops, or chopped yellow onion

1 cup chopped carrot

1 cup chopped celery

4 or 5 fresh flat-leaf parsley sprigs

2 or 3 fresh thyme and/or tarragon
sprigs

1 bay leaf

2 teaspoons salt

1½ teaspoons black peppercorns,
crushed

2 pounds firm-fleshed or flaky-
fleshed fish fillet or steaks (see
recipe introduction)

Fresh herb sprigs such as chervil,
dill, or flat-leaf parsley for garnish

Pesticide-free edible flowers such as
borage for garnish (optional)

Whole fresh chives for garnish

Poached fish makes an elegant and easy dish for entertaining because all of the cooking can be done in advance. I like to combine portions of three types of fish for each serving; in the photo on page 332, I've used tuna, salmon, and sea bass. Ask your fishmonger to recommend three fresh fish species that will render three different colors when cooked.

Before I stopped the questionable practice of eating raw fish, one of the things I most enjoyed about the Japanese preparation of sashimi was the green horseradish condiment, wasabi, which is available at Japanese or Asian markets and some supermarkets. It's also great with cooked fish. Here West and East merge in a mayonnaise flavored with fresh herbs and wasabi.

TO make the Wasabi Mayonnaise, in a small bowl, combine the mayonnaise, wasabi, and minced herb and mix well. Cover and refrigerate until shortly before serving.

TO make the Court Bouillon, in a nonreactive fish poacher or pot large enough to hold the fish with plenty of extra room, combine 2 quarts water and all of the Court Bouillon ingredients and place over medium-high heat. Bring the liquid to a boil, then reduce the heat to achieve a simmer, cover, and simmer until full-flavored, about 30 minutes.

QUICKLY rinse the fish under cold running water and shake off excess water.

IF using fillets, cut each type of fillet into 4 equal pieces.

IF using steaks with a central bone, divide each steak into 2 pieces by cutting along either side of the bone and then dis-carding the bone. Cut away and discard the skin. Form the 2 pieces into 1 disk by interlocking them, wrapping the small end of each half around the large center section of the other half (see the sea bass in the photograph on page 332). Secure with toothpicks, wrap each portion in cheesecloth, and tie with white cotton string to keep the fish intact during cooking. It is not necessary to wrap boneless steak pieces.

PLACE the fish in the simmering liquid; if there's not enough liquid to immerse the fish, add boiling water to cover completely. Adjust the heat to maintain a very gentle simmer and poach the fish until the flesh is opaque when cut into at the thickest part with a small, sharp knife, up to 10 minutes, or until done to preference. Do not let the liquid boil; there should be only a few bubbles breaking on the surface.

WITH a slotted utensil, transfer the fish to paper toweling to drain well. Remove cheesecloth and toothpicks (if using). Remove any protruding pin bones with tweezers or needle-nosed pliers. Cool to room temperature before serving, or cool slightly, cover, and refrigerate for at least 1 hour or up to overnight; return almost to room temperature before serving.

ARRANGE a piece of each type of fish on each plate. Add a dollop of the mayonnaise on the side and garnish the fish with herb sprigs and flowers (if using). Garnish the plates with chives.

Makes 4 servings.

SPICY RICE AND SHRIMP SALAD

288

SESAME-CHILE DRESSING

½ cup unseasoned rice vinegar

½ cup fish sauce, preferably Thai or
Vietnamese

¼ cup freshly squeezed lime juice

¼ cup Asian sesame oil

¼ cup hot chile oil, or to taste

2 cups long-grain white rice,
preferably Thai jasmine

6 green onions, including green tops,
sliced

2 carrots, peeled and diced

1 red sweet pepper, stem, seeds, and
membranes discarded, diced

1 to 2 teaspoons minced fresh Thai
bird or other hot chile, or to taste

½ cup chopped fresh mint

¼ cup chopped fresh cilantro
(coriander)

1 pound medium-sized shrimp,
cooked, peeled, and deveined

⅓ cup chopped unsalted dry-roasted
peanuts

About 2 cups mung bean sprouts
(optional)

Fresh cilantro (coriander) sprigs for
garnish

Lime wedges for garnish

*Fiery hot and refreshingly cool seasonings unique to the cooking of
Southeast Asia give this salad an exotic flair. When available, steamed
fiddlehead fern sprouts make an interesting garnish.*

TO make the Sesame-Chile Dressing, in a small bowl, combine the
vinegar, fish sauce, and lime juice and whisk to blend well. Add
the oils and whisk until emulsified. Set aside; whisk again just
before using if necessary.

COOK the rice as directed on page 364. Fluff with a fork, transfer to
a large bowl, and cool slightly. Gently toss the warm rice with
about one-third of the dressing. Fluff frequently until the rice
cools to room temperature.

ADD the green onions, carrots, sweet pepper, chile, mint, chopped
cilantro, and most of the shrimp, reserving some for garnish.
Toss with the remaining dressing to taste.

TO serve, mound on a serving platter, sprinkle with the peanuts,
surround with the bean sprouts (if using), and garnish with
cilantro sprigs, lime wedges, and the reserved shrimp.

Makes 4 servings.

POACHED CHICKEN BREASTS WITH THAI PEANUT SAUCE AND NOODLES

This elegant yet easy dish was my choice as a main course some years ago at a black-tie bash to celebrate the sale of my first one million cookbooks. It proved to be the perfect selection for one of those rare hot summer evenings in San Francisco, and the fragrance of thousands of gardenias added to the almost-tropical atmosphere.

PREPARE the Thai Peanut Sauce as directed and set aside.

QUICKLY rinse the chicken breasts under cold running water and transfer to a large saucepan. Add just enough cold water to cover the chicken. Place over medium heat and bring to a boil, then immediately reduce the heat so that the water barely ripples. Simmer until the meat is opaque throughout, just beyond the pink stage, about 12 minutes. Using a slotted utensil, remove the chicken to a plate. Let cool to room temperature, then refrigerate until a few minutes before serving.

IN a large pot, bring 4 quarts water to a rapid boil over high heat, then stir in the salt. Drop in the noodles or pasta and cook, stirring frequently, until tender but still firm to the bite. Drain and rinse in cold water, then drain again. Place in a large bowl, toss with the oil, and set aside to cool to room temperature, stirring occasionally to keep the noodles from sticking together.

BLANCH the snow peas as directed on page 338 and set aside.

TOAST the sesame seed as directed on page 553 and set aside.

TO serve, divide the noodles among individual plates. Spoon some of the peanut sauce over the noodles. Slice the poached chicken breasts on the diagonal and reassemble one on top of each pasta serving. Surround the pasta with snow peas to resemble a nest. Sprinkle the chicken and noodles with the green onion, peanuts, and sesame seed. Garnish with cilantro.

Makes 6 servings.

Thai Peanut Sauce (page 398)

6 skinned and boned chicken breast halves

1 tablespoon salt

1 pound fresh or dried thin Chinese wheat noodles *(mein)* or thin pasta such as *spaghettini*

2 tablespoons peanut oil

1 pound snow peas, cut into thin slivers

½ cup thinly sliced green onion, including green tops

½ cup chopped unsalted dry-roasted peanuts

⅓ cup sesame seed

Fresh cilantro (coriander) sprigs for garnish

SOUTHERN FRIED CHICKEN SALAD

About 8 cups dandelion greens or
    mixed salad greens, torn into
    bite-sized pieces

6 boned and skinned chicken breast
    halves

About 1 quart buttermilk

Crispy Bacon Bits (page 553)

Honey-Mustard Dressing (page 570)
    or Mustard Vinaigrette (page 566)

SPICY COATING

1½ cups all-purpose flour

1 tablespoon garlic powder

2 teaspoons freshly ground black
    pepper

2 teaspoons freshly ground white
    pepper

1 teaspoon ground cayenne

1 teaspoon crumbled dried thyme

1 teaspoon salt, or to taste

Peanut or other high-quality vegetable
    oil for frying

About 6 ounces creamy blue cheese,
    broken into chunks

1 cup small whole or sliced pickled
    beets (a favorite recipe or high-
    quality commercial product);
    Bread-and-Butter Pickles (page
    404); or high-quality commercial
    bread-and-butter pickles

It seems that every innovative restaurant chef prepares a fried chicken salad. The counterpoint achieved between warm fried chicken and cool, crisp greens is so good that I had to create my own version of this dish destined to become an American classic.

WASH the greens under cold running water. Place in a salad spinner and spin to remove as much water as possible. Pat dry with paper toweling. Wrap in a cloth kitchen towel or in paper toweling and refrigerate for at least 30 minutes to crisp, or place the wrapped greens in a plastic bag and refrigerate for up to several hours.

QUICKLY rinse the chicken under cold running water and pat dry with paper toweling. Cut the chicken into finger-thick strips or bite-sized chunks. Place in a bowl and add the buttermilk to cover. Cover and refrigerate for at least 2 hours or for up to 12 hours. Return to room temperature before cooking.

PREPARE the Crispy Bacon Bits as directed and set aside.

PREPARE the Honey-Mustard Dressing or Mustard Vinaigrette as directed and set aside; whisk again just before using if necessary.

TO make the Spicy Coating, in a shallow bowl, combine all of the coating ingredients and stir to blend thoroughly. Set aside.

IN a deep fryer or saucepan, pour in oil to a depth of 2 inches and heat to 375° F. Place a wire rack on a baking sheet and position alongside the fryer or stove top. Preheat an oven to 200° F.

DREDGE the chicken pieces in the coating mix, turning to coat all sides. Carefully add a few of the chicken pieces to the hot oil; avoid crowding the pan. Fry, turning occasionally, until crisp and brown, about 8 minutes. Using tongs or a slotted utensil, transfer the chicken to the rack to drain well, then place the rack and baking sheet in the oven to keep warm. Fry the remaining chicken in the same manner, allowing the oil to return to 375° F between batches.

JUST before serving, toss the greens in about half of the dressing or vinaigrette. Arrange the greens on individual plates and top with the fried chicken, cheese, and beets or pickles. Sprinkle with the bacon bits and serve immediately. Pass the remaining dressing or vinaigrette for drizzling over individual servings.

Makes 4 servings.

SMOKED TURKEY AND WILD RICE SALAD

Smoked turkey is readily available in delicatessens and specialty-food markets. Alternatively, smoke your own turkey, following the directions supplied with your smoker.

Prepare the salad and refrigerate at least several hours before serving, or preferably overnight, to allow the flavors to meld. Return the salad to room temperature before serving.

PREPARE the Sweet Crunchy Nuts as directed and set aside.

PREPARE the Papaya-Seed Dressing as directed and set aside; whisk again just before using if necessary.

COOK the wild rice in the stock or broth as directed on page 364. Transfer to a large bowl and let cool to room temperature, stirring occasionally.

ADD the turkey, green and red onions, sweet pepper, parsley, and salt and pepper to taste. Add about three-fourths of the dressing and toss thoroughly. Add more dressing, if needed. Spoon the turkey mixture into papaya halves or serve papaya slices alongside (if using). Sprinkle with the nuts just before serving.

Makes 4 servings.

Sweet Crunchy Nuts (page 42)
 made with walnut or pecan halves
Papaya-Seed Dressing (page 570)
2 cups wild rice
1 quart White Stock (page 578)
 made with turkey or chicken or
 canned reduced-sodium chicken
 broth
3 cups cubed smoked turkey breast
3 green onions, including green
 tops, thinly sliced
½ cup minced red onion
1 cup minced red sweet pepper
½ cup minced fresh flat-leaf parsley
Salt
Freshly ground black pepper
Ripe papaya halves or slices (optional)

JAPANESE-STYLE RICE AND CHICKEN SALAD

1 pound fresh tender spinach leaves

Creamy Japanese-Style Dressing
(page 569)

2 cups long-grain white rice

3 cups White Stock (page 578) made
with chicken or canned reduced-
sodium chicken broth (optional)

4 boned and skinned chicken breast
halves

1 tablespoon sesame seed, preferably
black variety

1 cup diced carrot, steamed or boiled
until crisp-tender, then rinsed in
cold water to halt cooking and
drained

8 ounces whole *enokitake* (slender
Japanese white mushrooms), stem
ends trimmed, or oyster mushrooms
or common white mushrooms,
tough stems discarded, sliced and
steamed until just tender if desired

6 green onions, including green tops,
thinly sliced on the diagonal

Slivered red sweet pepper for garnish

This room-temperature salad combines the flavors of classic mizutaki, *a dish of simmered chicken and vegetables, with a creamy sauce. Although the Japanese prefer slightly sticky medium-grain rice as their daily grain, fluffier long-grain rice works better for this salad.*

WASH the spinach carefully in cold water to remove any sand or grit and discard any tough stems. Place in a salad spinner and spin to remove as much water as possible. Pat dry with paper toweling. Wrap in a cloth kitchen towel or in paper toweling and refrigerate for about 30 minutes to crisp, or place the wrapped greens in a plastic bag and refrigerate for up to several hours.

PREPARE the Creamy Japanese-Style Dressing as directed.

COOK the rice in the stock or broth (if using) or water as directed on page 364. Fluff with a fork and transfer to a large bowl. Add about one-third of the dressing and gently toss. Fluff frequently until the rice cools to room temperature.

MEANWHILE, quickly rinse the chicken breasts under cold running water and transfer to a large saucepan. Add just enough cold water to cover the chicken. Place over medium heat and bring to a boil, then immediately reduce the heat so that the water barely ripples. Simmer until the meat is opaque throughout, just beyond the pink stage, about 12 minutes. Using a slotted utensil, remove the chicken to a plate. Set aside to cool to room temperature, then cut into bite-sized pieces.

TOAST the sesame seed as directed on page 553 and set aside.

ADD the chicken, carrot, mushrooms, and green onions to the cooled rice and toss well. Add the remaining dressing to taste and toss to coat well. Arrange the spinach on a large platter or on individual plates. Top with the rice mixture, sprinkle with the toasted sesame seed, and garnish with sweet pepper.

Makes 4 servings.

SMOKED CHICKEN SALAD WITH BERRY VINAIGRETTE

Smoked chicken can be purchased at gourmet food markets.

PREPARE the Sweet Crunchy Nuts as directed and set aside.

WASH the greens under cold running water. Place in a salad spinner and spin to remove as much water as possible. Pat dry with paper toweling. Wrap in a cloth kitchen towel or in paper toweling and refrigerate for about 30 minutes to crisp, or place the wrapped greens in a plastic bag and refrigerate for up to several hours.

PREPARE the Berry Vinaigrette as directed and set aside; whisk again just before using if necessary.

IN a skillet, cook the bacon over medium-low heat until crisp, 5 to 8 minutes. Using a slotted utensil, transfer to paper toweling to drain.

TO serve, toss the chilled greens with about half of the Berry Vinaigrette, then arrange on individual plates. Top with the chicken, apple slices, and onion rings. Sprinkle with the nuts, berries, and bacon and serve immediately. Pass the remaining vinaigrette for drizzling over individual servings.

Makes 4 servings.

VARIATIONS

TO serve as a warm salad, do not toss the greens in the dressing. Cook the bacon just before serving, then add the chicken to the bacon drippings and heat through. Remove the chicken to the top of the arranged greens, then discard most of the bacon drippings, add the dressing to the pan to heat, and drizzle the warm dressing over the salad.

Sweet Crunchy Nuts (page 42)

About 8 cups mixed young lettuces, spinach, and other garden greens

Berry Vinaigrette (page 565)

8 bacon slices, cut into ½-inch lengths

4 cups shredded smoked chicken

2 crisp apples, peeled, cored, and thinly sliced

½ red onion, thinly sliced and separated into rings

2 cups blueberries or raspberries

COLD SPICY NOODLES WITH CHICKEN IN CREAMY SESAME DRESSING

CREAMY SESAME DRESSING

2 cups Mayonnaise (page 388) or
  high-quality commercial mayonnaise

¼ cup Asian sesame oil

¼ cup soy sauce

1 tablespoon Chinese hot or Dijon
  mustard

1 tablespoon Asian chile sauce or
  chile oil, or to taste

1 tablespoon salt

1 pound fresh or dried thin Chinese
  wheat noodles *(mein)* or thin pasta
  such as *spaghettini*

½ cup soy sauce

2 tablespoons peanut oil

4 boned and skinned chicken breast
  halves

1 cup finely chopped carrot

1 cup finely chopped red sweet pepper

½ cup thinly sliced green onion,
  including green tops

1 cup finely chopped canned sliced
  bamboo shoots

1 cup sliced canned miniature corn
  on the cob

½ cup chopped fresh cilantro
  (coriander)

8 ounces snow peas, cut into
  thin slivers

2 tablespoons sesame seed

Fresh cilantro sprigs for garnish

I concocted this dish for friends Kristi and Bob Spence at Lake Tahoe and published it in my first single-subject cookbook, Cold Pasta. *Since then, it has probably become my best-known recipe, a favorite of caterers and other good cooks from coast to coast.*

The flavor of the dish improves from several hours chilling, but wait until the last minute to add the crunchy snow peas. Please be very generous with the chile sauce or oil; cold noodles can take a lot of heat.

TO make the Creamy Sesame Dressing, in a bowl, combine all of the dressing ingredients and whisk to blend well. Cover and refrigerate until needed; whisk again just before using if necessary.

IN a large pot, bring 4 quarts water to a rapid boil over high heat, then stir in the salt. Drop in the noodles or pasta and cook, stirring frequently, until tender but still very firm to the bite. Drain and rinse in cold water, then drain again. Place in a large bowl and toss with the soy sauce and peanut oil. Set aside to cool to room temperature, stirring occasionally to keep the noodles from sticking together.

MEANWHILE, quickly rinse the chicken breasts under cold running water and transfer to a large saucepan. Add just enough cold water to cover the chicken. Place over medium heat and bring to a boil, then immediately reduce the heat so that the water barely ripples. Simmer until the meat is opaque throughout, just beyond the pink stage, about 12 minutes. Using a slotted utensil, remove the chicken to a plate. Let cool to room temperature.

CUT the chicken into bite-sized pieces and add to the cooled noodles. Add the carrot, sweet pepper, green onion, bamboo shoots, corn, and chopped cilantro and mix gently yet thoroughly. Add the reserved dressing and blend well. Cover and refrigerate for several hours for the flavors to blend or for up to overnight.

ABOUT 30 minutes before serving, remove the noodle mixture from the refrigerator.

BLANCH the snow peas as directed on page 338 and set aside.

TOAST the sesame seed as directed on page 553 and set aside.

TO serve, toss the noodles with the snow peas, adding a little extra soy sauce and peanut oil or mayonnaise if the noodles seem dry. Mound on a platter or transfer to a serving bowl. Garnish with cilantro sprigs and sprinkle with the toasted sesame seed.

Makes 8 servings.

COCONUT-POACHED CHICKEN IN PEANUT AND CHUTNEY CRUST WITH CURRIED YOGURT SAUCE

6 boned and skinned chicken
    breast halves
About 2 cups Fresh Coconut Milk
    (page 562) or high-quality
    commercial coconut milk

CURRIED YOGURT SAUCE

2 teaspoons minced fresh ginger
1 teaspoon minced garlic
¼ cup dried currants or raisins
1 cup plain yogurt
2 tablespoons freshly squeezed lemon
    or lime juice
2 teaspoons ground coriander
1½ teaspoons ground cumin
2 teaspoons ground turmeric
Salt
Ground cayenne

¾ cup mango chutney (a favorite
    recipe or high-quality commercial
    product)
¾ cup Mayonnaise (page 388) or
    high-quality commercial mayonnaise
    or plain yogurt, or a combination
2½ cups finely chopped unsalted
    dry-roasted peanuts
Sliced mango, papaya, or other
    tropical fruit for garnish

In this twist on Indian curry, the usual condiments appear both in the nutty coating and in the slightly sweet, curry-scented sauce. Everything can be done ahead of time for easy summertime entertaining.

QUICKLY rinse the chicken breasts under cold running water and transfer to a large nonreactive saucepan. Add just enough coconut milk to cover the chicken. Place over medium heat and bring to a boil, then immediately reduce the heat so that the coconut milk barely ripples. Simmer until the meat is opaque throughout, just beyond the pink stage, about 12 minutes. Using a slotted utensil, remove the chicken to a plate; reserve the coconut milk. Let the chicken cool to room temperature, then cover and chill for up to several hours.

TO make the Curried Yogurt Sauce, combine the reserved coconut milk, ginger, and garlic over medium-high heat and cook until reduced to about 1 cup. Remove from the heat, stir in the raisins, and set aside to cool.

IN a food processor or blender, combine the cooled coconut milk mixture, yogurt, lemon juice, coriander, cumin, turmeric, and salt and cayenne to taste and blend well. Cover and refrigerate until just before serving.

IN a food processor, combine the chutney and mayonnaise and/or yogurt and blend until smooth. Cover and refrigerate until needed.

UP to 2 hours before serving, dip the chicken breasts into the chutney mixture to cover well, then roll in the chopped peanuts, patting to cover the chicken completely. Place on a wire rack or plate, cover loosely, and chill. Remove from the refrigerator about 15 minutes before serving.

TO serve, spoon some of the Curried Yogurt Sauce onto each plate, top with a piece of chicken, and garnish with fruit slices. Alternatively, spoon all of the sauce onto a platter and arrange the chicken and fruit over the sauce.

Makes 6 servings.

MUFFULETTA PASTA SALAD

OLIVE SALAD

1½ cups chopped pimento-stuffed
green olives (reserve juice)

1 cup chopped pitted brine-cured
ripe olives such as Kalamata or
Niçoise (reserve juice)

⅔ cup extra-virgin olive oil

¼ cup juice from olives

½ cup chopped Roasted Sweet
Peppers (page 552) made with red
sweet peppers or canned pimiento

1 cup drained pickled mixed Italian
vegetables (giardiniera)

1 teaspoon minced garlic

3 flat anchovy fillets, rinsed, patted
dry, and minced

2 tablespoons drained small capers

¾ cup minced fresh flat-leaf parsley

1 tablespoon minced fresh oregano,
or 1 teaspoon crumbled dried
oregano

Crushed dried hot chile

1 tablespoon salt

1 pound dried pasta such as *penne* or
fusilli (corkscrews)

4 ounces thinly sliced mortadella, cut
into narrow strips

4 ounces thinly sliced Italian salami,
cut into narrow strips

2 ounces thinly sliced prosciutto, cut
into narrow strips

4 ounces provolone or Monterey Jack
cheese, cut into small cubes

Whole green and ripe olives for
garnish

During my years in New Orleans I occasionally picked up a giant muffuletta for enjoying in Jackson Square or along the Mississippi riverbank. The city's famous sandwich features a filling of olive salad and Italian cold cuts, which also seems a natural for dressing cold pasta.

TO make the Olive Salad, in a bowl, combine all of the Olive Salad ingredients, including crushed chile to taste, and mix well. Cover and let stand at room temperature for several hours, or cover and refrigerate overnight; return to room temperature before using.

IN a large pot, bring 4 quarts water to a rapid boil over high heat, then stir in the salt. Drop in the pasta and cook, stirring frequently, until tender but still very firm to the bite. Drain and rinse under cold running water. Transfer to a large bowl, add the Olive Salad, and toss to coat thoroughly. Set aside to cool to room temperature, stirring occasionally to keep the noodles from sticking together.

JUST before serving, stir in the meats and cheese and garnish with a few whole olives.

Makes 6 to 8 servings.

THAI BEEF SALAD ~ *YUM NUEA* ~

In Thailand this dish is usually served as a snack. Try it as a light lunch or supper or as part of a festive buffet.

WASH the greens under cold running water. Place in a salad spinner and spin to remove as much water as possible. Pat dry with paper toweling. Wrap in a cloth kitchen towel or in paper toweling and refrigerate for about 30 minutes to crisp, or place the wrapped greens in a plastic bag and refrigerate for up to several hours.

TRIM the beef of excess fat and connective tissue, then quickly rinse under cold running water and pat dry with paper toweling. Grill, broil, or roast the beef until medium-rare. Cool, then slice into pieces about 2 inches long by ½ inch wide. Set aside.

TO make the Lemongrass Dressing, in a bowl, combine all of the dressing ingredients and whisk to blend well.

ADD the reserved beef to the dressing and toss to coat thoroughly.

TO serve, arrange the chilled greens on a platter or individual plates. Spoon on the beef, including the dressing, and top with the onion rings and tomato slices. Garnish with bean sprouts, cilantro sprigs, and lime slices.

Makes 4 servings.

4 cups tender lettuce or other salad greens, torn into bite-sized pieces

2 pounds boneless beef tenderloin or other tender cut

LEMONGRASS DRESSING

½ cup freshly squeezed lime juice

¼ cup fish sauce, preferably Thai or Vietnamese

2 tablespoons sugar

2 tablespoons minced fresh red Thai bird or other hot chile

1 tablespoon minced garlic

¼ cup chopped fresh cilantro (coriander)

¼ cup chopped fresh mint

2 teaspoons minced fresh lemongrass, tender bulb portion only

½ red onion, thinly sliced and separated into rings

1 large ripe yellow or red tomato, sliced

Mung bean sprouts for garnish

Fresh cilantro (coriander) sprigs for garnish

Lime slices for garnish

ALONG THE WAY

Some of the most interesting components of any meal are the side dishes that complement or contrast with the main dish.

Accompaniments

VEGETABLES, including the perennial favorite, potatoes, are essential to a balanced diet. Dried beans and grains in combination offer excellent protein, thereby becoming wonderful and flavorful alternatives to meats. Separately, beans and grains, including corn, which is the only grain eaten fresh, can add infinite variety to side dishes.

Most salads made of cabbage, potatoes, and grains are generally better as an accompaniment than served on their own as a separate course.

Choose side dishes that will add contrasting color, texture, and flavor to the meal.

SICHUAN EGGPLANT

Chinese eggplant in spicy garlic sauce is one of my favorite vegetable dishes.

DISCARD blossom ends from the eggplants and cut crosswise into slices about ½ inch thick, then cut slices into half circles and set aside.

IN a small bowl, combine the soy sauce, sugar, vinegar, cornstarch, and chile with ½ cup water and stir to mix well; set aside.

PLACE a wok, large saute pan, or large, heavy skillet over high heat. When the pan is hot, add the oil and swirl to coat the pan. When the oil is hot but not yet smoking, add the eggplant and garlic, quickly toss to coat with oil, and stir-fry, moving the pan off and on the heat as necessary to prevent scorching, until the eggplant is very tender but not falling apart, about 5 minutes. Stir the reserved soy sauce mixture to recombine, then stir it into the eggplant. Add the sliced green onion and stir until the sauce thickens, about 30 seconds.

TRANSFER to a serving platter or bowl, sprinkle with garlic chives or green onion tops, and serve warm.

Makes 6 servings.

2 pounds slender Asian eggplants

½ cup soy sauce

3 tablespoons sugar

2 tablespoons unseasoned rice vinegar

2 tablespoons cornstarch

2 teaspoons crushed dried hot chile or Asian chile sauce, or to taste

¼ cup canola or other high-quality vegetable oil

¼ cup chopped garlic

½ cup sliced green onion, including green tops

Snipped fresh garlic chives or slivered green onion tops for garnish

SOUTHERN STEWED OKRA

¼ cup (½ stick) unsalted butter

2 cups chopped yellow onion

1½ cups chopped red or green sweet
pepper

2 pounds fresh small okra, stemmed
and sliced crosswise about ½ inch
thick

4 cups peeled, seeded, and chopped
ripe or canned tomato

2 teaspoons red wine vinegar or
balsamic vinegar

2 tablespoons minced fresh thyme,
or 2 teaspoons crumbled dried
thyme

1 teaspoon chili powder

½ teaspoon sugar

Salt

Freshly ground black pepper

Ground cayenne

*Every summer I crave the stewed okra from my Louisiana childhood and
enjoy it as a side dish, pasta sauce, and even pizza topping.*

IN a saute pan or heavy skillet, melt the butter over medium-high
heat. Add the onion and sweet pepper and cook, stirring
frequently, until the vegetables are soft but not browned, about
5 minutes. Reduce the heat to medium, add the okra, and cook,
stirring frequently, until tender, about 15 minutes.

ADD the tomato, vinegar, thyme, chili powder, and sugar to the okra.
Season to taste with salt, pepper, and cayenne. Cover, reduce the
heat to low, and cook, stirring occasionally, until the liquid
evaporates and the mixture is fairly thick, about 30 minutes.

TRANSFER to a serving bowl and serve warm or at room temperature.

Makes 6 servings.

MILANESE SWEET-AND-SOUR ONIONS ~ *CIPOLLE IN AGRODOLCE* ~

Serve these little golden beauties alongside poultry or meats, or add them to a plate of mixed antipasti.

3 pounds pearl onions

3 tablespoons unsalted butter

1 cup golden raisins

¼ cup white wine vinegar

2 teaspoons sugar

Salt

Freshly ground black pepper

TO peel the onions, cut a small *X* in the root end of each onion. Bring a large pot of water to a boil over high heat. Drop the onions into the water. After about 30 seconds, drain the onions. As soon as they are cool enough to handle, pull off the skin and detach the roots; be careful not to remove any of the onion layers.

IN a heavy-bottomed saute pan or skillet in which the onions will fit in a single layer, melt the butter over medium heat. Add the onions and stir until they are well coated with the butter. Add water to a depth of 1 inch. Cook, turning the onions occasionally, until they begin to soften, about 10 minutes.

ADD the raisins, vinegar, sugar, and salt and pepper to taste and stir well. Reduce the heat to achieve a simmer and simmer, stirring occasionally, until the onions are tender when pierced with a wooden skewer, 45 minutes to 1 hour, depending on the size of the onions. If the pan becomes dry during cooking, add a tablespoon or so of water as needed.

INCREASE the heat to medium-high and cook the onions, turning once or twice, until most of the liquid evaporates and the onions are glazed and golden, about 5 minutes. Adjust the seasonings.

TRANSFER to a warmed serving dish and serve hot.

Makes 6 servings.

MASHED POTATOES

2 pounds potatoes (see recipe
   introduction for type)
¾ cup (1½ sticks) unsalted butter,
   melted
About ½ cup heavy (whipping)
   cream, heated
Salt
Freshly ground black or white pepper

While the homey mashed potato has skyrocketed to gourmet status, some food writers have waxed nostalgically about the characteristic lumps. To my way of thinking, those who equate mashed potatoes with lumps were living with lazy cooks who didn't take the time or use the right technique to remove the lumps.

Take your choice as to the type of potato to use: boiling or waxy potatoes whip up smooth and creamy, while baking potatoes produce a fluffy dish. Don't forget varieties with yellow, red, and purple flesh for mashing, as well as sweet potatoes.

No matter which potatoes you cook, a ricer is the tool of choice for mashing them and a worthwhile investment if you enjoy this dish. Avoid using potato mashers or food mills, which break up too many starch-filled cells and cause stickiness. And never subject potatoes to electric mixers or food processors, both of which will whip them into glue.

My mashed potato recipe is no low-fat dish, even though I use little butter in comparison to some recipes of French chefs. It's also possible to get by with less butter than I suggest; adjust the recipe to fit your dietary restrictions. Polyunsaturated margarine, if you can accept the flavor, certainly cuts the amount of saturated fat, although not the calories. The liquid reserved from boiling the potatoes, flavorful stock or broth, half-and-half, low-fat buttermilk, or even low-fat milk can be used instead of the cream for a less-rich dish.

IF desired, peel the potatoes, cut into pieces of uniform size about ¾ inch thick, and rinse under cold running water to remove surface starch.

PLACE the whole or cut potatoes in a saucepan and add water to cover by about 2 inches, then remove the potatoes. Bring the water to a boil over medium-high heat, return the potatoes, and cook until just tender when pierced with a wooden skewer or small, sharp knife, 15 to 45 minutes for whole potatoes, depending on size, or 15 to 20 minutes for pieces; avoid overcooking. Drain well, then return the potatoes to the pan, place over the heat, and shake the pan until excess moisture evaporates and the potatoes are dry to the touch. As soon as whole potatoes are cool enough to handle, peel and cut into chunks.

PRESS the hot potatoes through a ricer into a large bowl. Stir in the melted butter, ½ cup heated cream, and salt and pepper to taste. Using a wooden spoon or whisk, whip the potatoes until light and fluffy, adding additional warm cream if required to form desired consistency; avoid making the potatoes too thin.

TRANSFER to a warmed serving bowl and serve immediately or keep warm in a partially covered container set over warm (not simmering) water for up to 30 minutes.

Makes about 4 cups for 4 to 6 servings.

VARIATIONS

Combo Mashed Potatoes. Combine the riced potatoes with an equal portion of pureed beet, carrot, cauliflower, celeriac (celery root), green bean, lima bean, parsnip, rutabaga, mushroom, or turnip before adding the butter and cream.

Garlic Mashed Potatoes. Separate a head of garlic, peel all of the cloves, and add to the potatoes for cooking. Put the garlic through the ricer along with the potatoes. Alternatively, chop the garlic and saute it in a little butter until tender but not browned, then heat with the cream and add to the potatoes. Or roast 2 whole garlic heads as directed on page 551, then squeeze out the pulp and add it to the potatoes after ricing.

Mashed Potatoes Gratin. Mound the whipped potatoes in a gratin dish or other ovenproof (or flameproof if broiling) serving dish and generously sprinkle the top with freshly grated Parmesan cheese, crumbled Gorgonzola or other blue cheese, shredded Gruyère, or other good-melting cheese. Place in a preheated 400° F oven or under a preheated broiler until the cheese melts and is golden.

Italian-Style Mashed Potatoes. Omit the butter and stir in about ½ cup extra-virgin olive oil, or to taste.

ROASTED POTATOES WITH GARLIC AND ROSEMARY

2 pounds small new potatoes

2 tablespoons coarsely chopped garlic

1 tablespoon coarsely chopped fresh
rosemary, or 1 teaspoon
crumbled dried rosemary

½ cup fruity olive oil, preferably
extra-virgin

Coarse salt

Freshly ground black pepper

This is how I most frequently cook potatoes. They go perfectly with roasted lamb or chicken, grilled or smoked fish or meats, or melted cheese.

For a simple yet sublime starter, offer a bowl of sour cream, plain yogurt, Mayonnaise (page 388), or Sun-Dried Tomato and Garlic Spread (page 38) for dipping.

For fancier appetizers suitable for passing, cut a thin layer from the top of each potato and, using a melon-ball scoop, hollow out an indentation. Fill the hollow with a tasty stuffing — dabs of sour cream with smoked salmon or caviar, soft cheese blended with minced sun-dried tomato, or other favorites. Or stuff with a piece of raclette cheese and a slice of gherkin (cornichon) and heat in the oven until the cheese melts. Garnish each potato with a tiny sprig of fresh herb.

When purchasing the potatoes, consider purple or yellow varieties in addition to regular white ones. When small new potatoes aren't available, larger potatoes can be quartered, sliced, or cut into 1-inch cubes.

PREHEAT an oven to 375° F.

WASH the potatoes under cold running water, scrubbing well to remove all traces of soil. Pat dry with paper toweling.

IN a roasting pan or other large baking pan, place the potatoes in a single layer. Add the garlic, rosemary, oil, and generous sprinklings of salt and pepper. Stir the potatoes in the seasoning to coat all over. Roast, stirring every 10 minutes, until the potatoes are tender when pierced with a wooden skewer, 35 to 45 minutes.

TRANSFER to a warmed serving bowl and serve immediately.

Makes 6 to 8 servings.

SWISS STRAW MAT POTATOES
~ *Rösti* ~

Switzerland's famous panfried potato cakes combine a crunchy crust with a meltingly tender interior. Butter, clarified to prevent burning, is the traditional cooking fat, but cholesterol watchers may choose to substitute canola or other polyunsaturated oil.

Sometimes a sprinkling of grated Emmentaler, Gruyère, or other Swiss cheese is scattered over the top of the potatoes after they are flipped. By the time the bottom is crusty, the cheese will have melted.

2 pounds baking potatoes

Salt

Freshly ground black pepper

½ cup Clarified Butter (page 571)

Minced fresh flat-leaf parsley for sprinkling

PEEL the potatoes and shred them about ⅛ inch thick. Do not rinse; just pat off the excess natural moisture with paper toweling. Season to taste with salt and pepper.

IN a 10-inch skillet, heat ¼ cup of the butter over medium heat. Add the dried potatoes and cook until the bottom is golden brown and crusty, about 5 minutes; shake the pan occasionally to prevent the potatoes from sticking. Reduce the heat to low and cook about 5 minutes longer to cook the interior partially.

INVERT a plate over the top of the skillet, invert the skillet and plate together, and lift off the skillet so that the potatoes are on the plate. Increase the heat to medium and heat the remaining ¼ cup butter in the skillet. Slide the potato cake, cooked side up, back into the skillet and cook, shaking the pan frequently to prevent sticking, until the bottom is crusty, about 5 minutes, then reduce the heat to low and cook until the interior is tender, about 5 minutes longer.

SLIDE the cake onto a serving plate, sprinkle with the parsley, and serve immediately.

Makes 4 servings.

POTATOES ANNA ~ *POMMES ANNA* ~

2½ pounds baking potatoes

Salt

Freshly ground black pepper

¾ cup Clarified Butter (page 571),
   remelted

Special large copper pans are traditionally used by restaurants to cook this grand dish created in honor of a fashionable French woman named Anna Deslions. Various-sized skillets, shallow round baking dishes, or glass pie plates will work in the home kitchen; just distribute the mixture evenly among the smaller pans. Attractive individual servings can be arranged in tart pans with removable bottoms, baked until the top is golden, then transferred, top side up, with a spatula onto plates.

The potatoes may also be served directly from the baking container when a more casual presentation is appropriate.

PEEL the potatoes and trim each lengthwise into an even cylinder. Using a mandoline or other slicing device, cut crosswise into slices about ¹⁄₁₆ inch thick. If desired, trim each slice with a small round biscuit cutter to create a uniform circle. Rinse the slices under cold running water and pat dry with paper toweling. Season the slices with salt and pepper to taste.

PREHEAT an oven to 450° F.

BRUSH about 2 tablespoons of the butter in 2 medium-sized ovenproof skillets or other shallow, round baking dishes (see recipe introduction). In each container, arrange a layer of potatoes in a spiral design, overlapping each slice. Drizzle a bit more of the butter over the layer. Repeat this step two more times, making 3 layers of potatoes in all.

BAKE until the potatoes are tender when pierced with a wooden skewer or small, sharp knife and the bottoms are golden brown, about 45 minutes. Several times during cooking, press the top of the potatoes with a spatula to create compressed cakes of even thickness.

USING a spatula, carefully loosen the sides and bottom of the potato "cakes" from the skillets or baking dishes. Pour off and discard excess butter. Invert a warm serving plate over the top of a skillet or baking dish, invert the plate and skillet or dish together, and lift off the skillet or baking dish. Repeat with the remaining potato skillet or dish. Serve immediately.

Makes 6 servings.

FRENCH FRIED POTATOES
~ *Pommes de Terre Frites* ~

Deep-fried potatoes are crispier when fried twice, in the French manner, although very thin cuts can be cooked successfully at higher heat in only one frying. Potatoes can be cut into a wide variety of shapes for deep frying. A few suggestions follow the recipe.

    An electric deep fryer with a built-in thermostat makes potato frying a breeze, but a deep pot, a long-handled wire basket, and a deep-fat thermometer work just fine.

    Don't forget that sweet potatoes, especially orange "yam" varieties, make unusually scrumptious fries, too. Thin cuts work best.

Baking potatoes (allow 1 medium-sized per person)
Peanut or other high-quality vegetable oil for frying

PEEL the potatoes. Using a mandoline or other slicing device, cut into desired shape (see suggestions on pages 310-311). Be sure that all pieces are about the same size. Rinse in cold water and pat completely dry with paper toweling. Or spin in a salad spinner, then finish drying with paper toweling.

MEANWHILE, in a deep fryer or saucepan, pour in oil to a depth of 2 inches and heat to 325° F.

WORKING in batches if necessary, transfer the dried potatoes to a fry basket and slowly immerse the basket into the hot oil, or carefully drop the dried potatoes by handfuls into the hot oil; avoid crowding the pan. Fry until the potatoes are cooked and soft but not beginning to turn golden, about 3 minutes for thin cuts to about 5 minutes for thick cuts. Using the basket, tongs, or a slotted utensil, transfer the potatoes to paper toweling to drain for at least 5 minutes or for up to several hours.

SHORTLY before serving, heat the oil to 375° F. Return the potatoes to the hot oil and fry until crisp and golden, about 3 minutes for straw cuts to about 5 minutes for thick cuts. Drain briefly on dry paper toweling and pat with additional paper toweling to remove surface grease. (If cooking a lot of potatoes, transfer each batch to a dish and keep warm in a preheated 200° F oven until all are cooked.) Serve hot.

Each medium-sized potato makes 1 serving.

variations follow ~

SUGGESTED CUTS FOR FRENCH FRIED POTATOES

Balls. Form spheres with a melon-ball scoop.

Baskets or nests. Cut as for straw potatoes (following) or as for thin chips. Dip a set of overlapping wire baskets with a long handle (sold in cookware stores) into the hot oil, then remove and arrange the straws or rounds inside the larger basket. Cover with the smaller basket and lower into the hot oil, holding by the handle to keep the baskets together. Fry until the potatoes are completely done and crisp. Carefully remove each potato basket to paper toweling to drain. Keep warm until all the potatoes are fried. Fill at the last minute with sauteed or stir-fried vegetables, purees, or stews or other saucy dishes.

Chips (or British crisps). Slice crosswise into desired thickness, from paper-thin to about ⅛ inch.

Crinkles. Slice on a special ripple-bladed cutter into French fry-sized pieces.

Cubes. Trim into perfect cubes of desired size.

French fries (French *pommes frites* or British chips). Slice lengthwise into sticks about 3 inches long and from ¼ to ½ inch thick.

Scallops (French *collerettes*). Slice crosswise about ⅛ inch thick, then cut with a scalloped cookie cutter; remove center with a small round or scalloped cutter.

Shavings (French *chatouillard* or *copeaux*). Use a rotating vegetable peeler and cut in a continuous spiral to create thin ribbons about ½ inch wide and as long as possible.

Shoestring (French *cordon de soulier*) or Straw (French *paille*). Cut lengthwise into julienne about as thick as matchsticks; leave shoestrings as long as possible, and cut straws into 3-inch lengths.

Puffed (French *soufflé*). Use large baking potatoes that have been stored for 2 to 3 months, or until skin cannot be penetrated with a fingernail. Slice lengthwise ⅛ inch thick. Trim the edges of each slice to form a wide football shape, making all pieces the same size. Slices must be absolutely dry before the first cooking. Stir the potatoes with a wooden spoon or shake the basket during both the first and second fryings to agitate the oil. Depending upon the potato, most slices will puff up and inflate during the second frying; since all will not puff perfectly, start with about twice as many as you plan to serve. Unpuffed slices are just as tasty but lack the drama.

Waffles (French *gaufrettes*). Use a mandoline or other slicing device with a serrated blade to cut thinly crosswise, then rotate a quarter turn before the next cut. Leave round or trim into squares.

POTATOES GRATIN

2 pounds potatoes (see recipe
    introduction)

5 tablespoons unsalted butter

Salt

Freshly ground white pepper

Freshly grated nutmeg

¼ cup minced fresh chives or green
    onion, including green tops

1 tablespoon minced garlic, or to
    taste

1 cup light cream or half-and-half

¾ cup heavy (whipping) cream

Minced chives for garnish

I'll never forget the magical Lake Tahoe night I first tested this dish for my Potato Cookbook. *I took it piping hot down to my neighbor Kristi Spence, and the two of us sat on her deck overhanging the water and watched a lunar eclipse while polishing off the entire gratin with a green salad and some fabulous wine.*

Whether you call it by its fancy French name — gratin de pommes à la crème — or dub it plain old scalloped potatoes, there is no more succulent treatment of potatoes than slices slowly cooked in cream until meltingly tender.

Choose boiling potatoes if you wish the slices to retain their shape during cooking. If you prefer potato layers that almost melt together instead of remaining distinct, use baking potatoes and do not rinse them after slicing; just pat off the excess natural moisture with paper toweling and the starch will help the layers stick together.

Don't forget sweet potatoes and their orange "yam" varieties for a gratin of a different hue and flavor.

PEEL the potatoes. Trim sides to form even cylinders or rectangles, if desired. Using a mandoline or other slicing device, slice the potatoes as thinly as possible. Quickly rinse the slices under cold running water and pat dry with paper toweling.

PREHEAT an oven to 300° F. Select a gratin or other ovenproof serving dish 10 to 12 inches in diameter.

MELT 3 tablespoons of the butter and pour into the baking dish. Using about one-third of the potato slices, arrange a single layer in the bottom of the dish. Sprinkle with salt, pepper, and nutmeg to taste, 2 tablespoons of the minced chives or green onion, and half of the garlic. Add a second layer of potato slices, using about half of what remains, and sprinkle with the seasonings, the remaining 2 tablespoons chives or green onion, and the remaining garlic. Top with a final layer of potato slices; the dish should be no more than three-quarters full. Pour the light and heavy creams over the top to cover the potatoes barely. Cut the remaining 2 tablespoons butter into small pieces and dot the top. Sprinkle with salt and pepper to taste.

BAKE until the potatoes are tender, most of the liquid has been
absorbed, and the top is lightly browned, 1½ to 2 hours. If the
top is not brown, increase the temperature to 375° F during the
last 10 minutes of cooking.

SERVE immediately or keep warm in a 200° F oven for up to 1 hour.
Sprinkle with chives just before serving.

Makes 4 servings.

VARIATIONS

FOR a lighter version, substitute milk, stock, or canned broth for
the creams.

SPRINKLE the top with freshly shredded Gruyère, Cheddar, or
other good-melting cheese before baking.

LAYER sauteed onion between the layers of potatoes in place of
the chives or green onion.

BAKED POTATOES

Large baking potatoes (allow 1 per
person)
Unsalted butter at room temperature
Salt
Freshly ground black pepper

OPTIONAL TOPPINGS

Sour cream, Crème Fraîche (page
591), commercial crème fraîche, or
plain yogurt
Compound Butter (page 402)
Minced fresh chives or green onion
Minced fresh herbs such as basil,
marjoram, oregano, savory, or thyme
Chopped fresh chiles or drained
canned *chipotle* chiles in *adobo*
sauce
Freshly shredded Cheddar, Italian
Fontina, Monterey Jack, or other
good-melting cheese
Freshly grated Parmesan cheese,
preferably Parmigiano-Reggiano
Crumbled goat cheese or blue cheese
Crumbled crisply fried bacon
Chopped drained sun-dried tomatoes
packed in olive oil
Sauteed chopped onion and garlic
Pesto (page 399)
Chopped olives or *Tapénade* (page
400)
Minced fresh or preserved truffles
Caviar

*A perfectly baked potato is a hallmark of good cooking. Choose potatoes
with unblemished skin and with flesh that is white and dry. Once baked,
the nutrient-laden edible skin should be crisp and the interior soft and
dry. Rubbing them with butter or oil before they go in the oven results in
soft skin. And please forget foil wrapping, too; it produces insipid
steamed potatoes with limp skin. Although time-savers, microwaves turn
out a baked potato with unappealing texture and soft skin.*

*Potatoes adapt to a range of oven temperatures and cooking
times, so they can be baked in the oven when it is already in use for other
dishes. At 350° F, they will cook in about 1 hour and 20 minutes; at 450° F,
the potatoes should be done in about 45 minutes.*

*Offer potatoes with one or more of the suggested toppings,
if desired.*

PREHEAT an oven to 375° F.

WASH the potatoes under cold running water, scrubbing well to
remove all traces of soil. Pat dry with paper toweling. Using a
fork, prick each potato in several places. Place directly on an
oven rack and bake until the flesh gives and feels soft when
squeezed through a cloth kitchen towel between your thumb
and fingers, about 1 hour.

PLACE one or more of the suggested toppings in small bowls
(if using).

SPLIT the potatoes and press all around with your fingertips to
loosen the pulp. Add a dollop of butter and serve piping hot.
Diners season the potatoes to taste with salt, pepper, and
toppings (if using).

Each potato makes 1 serving.

ROMAN-STYLE SPINACH
~ *Spinaci alla Romana* ~

Ever since my first visit to Italy, I've made the traditional Roman spinach dish exotically accented with pine nuts and raisins.

WASH the spinach carefully to remove any sand or grit and discard any tough stems. Transfer the damp spinach to a saute pan or heavy skillet and place over medium heat. Cook, stirring frequently, just until the spinach is wilted and bright green, 3 to 5 minutes. Drain in a colander and squeeze out as much liquid as possible. Set aside.

IN a saute pan or skillet, combine the butter and olive oil and place over medium heat. When the butter melts, add the garlic, drained raisins, and pine nuts and cook, stirring frequently, until the pine nuts begin to color, 2 to 3 minutes. Add the drained spinach and salt and pepper to taste and stir until the spinach is well coated and heated through, about 2 minutes longer.

TRANSFER to a serving bowl and serve warm.

Makes 6 servings.

4 pounds young, tender spinach

2 tablespoons unsalted butter

2 tablespoons extra-virgin olive oil

2 tablespoons minced garlic

6 tablespoons golden raisins, soaked in warm water until plumped, then drained

6 tablespoons pine nuts

Salt

Freshly ground black pepper

SPICY SQUASH CAKES

Fresh Tomato Salsa (page 392)

4 cups finely chopped or grated
summer squash (about 1⅓ pounds)

Salt

About 2 medium-sized ears corn, or
1 cup thawed frozen or drained
canned corn kernels

¼ cup finely chopped green onion,
including green tops

1 tablespoon minced fresh hot chile,
or to taste

4 eggs, lightly beaten

½ cup freshly grated Parmesan
cheese (about 2 ounces), preferably
Parmigiano-Reggiano

1 cup freshly shredded sharp
Cheddar cheese (about 3 ounces)

½ cup all-purpose flour

3 tablespoons unsalted butter, melted
and cooled slightly

Freshly ground black pepper

Ground cayenne or other dried hot
chile

Canola or other high-quality vegetable
oil for frying

Mexican cultured cream *(crema),* sour
cream, Crème Fraîche (page 591),
or commercial crème fraîche

Fresh cilantro (coriander) sprigs for
garnish

Control the fieriness of the chiles by adjusting the amount and type used. To pass the cakes as appetizers, cook the squash mixture by teaspoonfuls, arrange on a tray, and top each tiny cake with small dollops of salsa and sour cream.

PREPARE the Fresh Tomato Salsa as directed and set aside.

PLACE the squash in a colander set over a bowl or in a sink, sprinkle with salt, toss to distribute the salt, and let stand for about 30 minutes to draw out excess moisture.

IF using fresh corn, cut the kernels from the cobs as directed for Sauteed Corn on page 358, measure out 1 cup, and set aside. If using thawed or canned corn, reserve for later use.

PREHEAT an oven to 200° F. Line a plate or baking sheet with paper toweling and position alongside the stove top.

GENTLY squeeze the squash to release as much moisture as possible and transfer to a large bowl. Add the corn, green onion, fresh chile, eggs, cheeses, flour, and melted butter and mix well. Season to taste with salt, pepper, and ground chile.

IN a large saute pan or skillet, heat 2 tablespoons oil over medium-high heat. Spoon about 2 tablespoons of the squash mixture per cake into the hot oil and flatten to create uniform thickness; do not crowd the pan. Cook until golden brown on the bottoms, then turn and cook the other sides until golden brown, about 3 minutes total per cake. Transfer to the prepared plate or baking sheet to drain well, then transfer the plate or sheet to the oven to keep warm. Cook the remaining cakes in the same manner, adding more oil as necessary.

TO serve, arrange the cakes on warmed plates with some of the salsa and a dollop of cream or crème fraîche. Garnish with cilantro sprigs.

Makes 6 servings.

FRIED SUMMER SQUASH
AND LEMON SLICES

Malt vinegar and crushed hot chile add a tangy edge to crisply fried squash pieces. In place of the beer batter, dip the squash pieces in flour, then beaten egg, and finally fine dried bread crumbs, or in a mixture of equal parts cornmeal and flour.

IN a bowl, combine the flour, 1 teaspoon salt, egg yolks, beer, and butter and beat until smooth. Let stand at room temperature for about 1 hour.

CUT the squash into sticks about the size of french-fried potatoes or into disks about ½ inch in diameter. Alternatively, use a melon-ball scoop to form rounds from larger squash. Place the squash pieces in a colander set over a bowl or in a sink, sprinkle with salt, toss to distribute the salt, and let stand for about 30 minutes to draw out excess moisture. Pat dry with paper toweling.

IN a deep fryer or saucepan, pour in oil to a depth of 2 inches and heat to 360° F. Preheat an oven to 200° F. Place a wire rack on a baking sheet and position alongside the fryer or stove top.

DIP a few of the squash pieces and lemon slices into the batter and carefully add to the hot oil; avoid crowding the pan. Fry, turning frequently with a slotted spoon or tongs, until they are golden brown and crusty, 3 to 5 minutes total. Using a slotted utensil, remove to the rack to drain well, then blot dry with paper toweling to remove as much oil as possible and place the rack and baking sheet in the oven to keep warm. Fry the remaining squash and lemon slices in the same manner, allowing the oil to return to 360° F between batches.

TO serve, transfer the squash and lemon slices to a serving platter and sprinkle to taste with salt, vinegar, and chile.

Makes 4 servings.

1 cup all-purpose flour

Salt

2 egg yolks, beaten

¾ cup beer

3 tablespoons unsalted butter, melted and cooled slightly

1 pound summer squash

Canola or other high-quality vegetable oil for frying

2 lemons, thinly sliced and seeded

Malt vinegar

Crushed dried hot chile

ROASTED WINTER SQUASH

Winter squash (see recipe
  introduction)

Unsalted butter, melted, for brushing

Brown sugar, pure maple syrup, or
  honey (optional)

Spices such as freshly grated nutmeg
  or ground allspice, cardamom,
  cinnamon, cloves, or ginger, one
  kind or a pleasing combination
  (optional)

Salt

Freshly ground black pepper

"If it were not for pumpkins, we'd be undone soon," penned an American colonist in a 1693 diary, indicating the vital importance of these native squashes to the earliest settlers. Fortunately for modern cooks, we're no longer limited to pumpkins, but have access to the fruits of numerous hard-shelled squash cultivars that are products of modern plant hybridization.

Some of my favorite winter squash do not store or ship as well as Acorn, Butternut, Banana, and other supermarket mainstays. Buttercup, Delicata, and Sweet Dumpling are definitely worth growing in your garden or searching out in farmers' markets and specialty-produce stores.

*Also known by its Japanese name kabocha or its Cantonese name nam gwa, the "Japanese pumpkin" is actually a Western hemisphere native (*Curcurbita moschata*) that made its way to Malaysia, then to China, and finally to Japan, where it was improved over the last few centuries before returning to its American homeland. Several varieties are sold here in Asian markets and better produce shops. The flesh is deeply colored and intensely flavored.*

CUT squash in half or into large pieces. With a metal spoon, scoop out the seeds and all interior stringy portions. If you plan to serve squash halves, cut off a small slice from the bottom of each so they will stand upright. If the squash will be pureed after baking, you may wish to peel it with a vegetable peeler or small, sharp paring knife, then cut into smaller pieces for quicker baking.

PREHEAT an oven to 400° F. Using a pastry brush, coat the surface of the squash flesh lightly with melted butter. Place, cut side up, in a shallow baking pan and roast until almost tender, about 30 minutes.

IF serving squash in its shell, brush with more melted butter, sprinkle with brown sugar or drizzle with maple syrup or honey to taste (if using), dust with spices (if using), and sprinkle with salt and pepper to taste. Continue roasting, brushing occasionally with more melted butter, until tender when pierced with a fork or wooden skewer, 15 to 30 minutes longer. Transfer warm squash directly to serving plates or arrange on a serving platter.

IF pureeing cooked squash, continue roasting until tender when pierced with a fork or wooden skewer, 15 to 30 minutes longer. Remove from the oven and set aside to cool. When cool enough to handle, scrape the flesh from the shell with a spoon into a food processor or blender, or transfer peeled cooked squash pieces to a food processor or blender. Puree until smooth. Use the puree as directed in recipes, or season to taste with melted butter, sweetener (if using), spices (if using), and salt and pepper. Reheat in a saucepan over medium-low heat or in a microwave oven before serving as a side dish.

1 pound cleaned raw squash makes 4 servings and yields about 2 cups puree.

BAKED SWEET POTATOES

Sweet potatoes, 12 ounces to 1 pound each (allow 1 per person)

Unsalted butter, at room temperature or melted, for serving

Vegetable authority Elizabeth Schneider and commercial growers advocate the one-word sweetpotato over the more common two-word sweet potato for the tropical American member of the morning glory family, to distinguish it from nonrelated potatoes, which belong to the nightshade family. Whether you choose the new moniker or stick with tradition, sweet potatoes are too often overlooked.

In some households, sweet potatoes are offered only at Thanksgiving. In my home, this nutritious tuber is an occasional satisfying light meal on its own and appears frequently as a creamy side dish year-round. I enjoy baked sweet potatoes, usually the sweeter, moister orange varieties labeled "yams," with a little butter and a dusting of powdered sugar or some warm pure maple syrup.

PREHEAT an oven to 400° F.

WASH the sweet potatoes under cold running water, scrubbing well to remove all traces of soil. Pat dry with paper toweling. Using a fork, prick each sweet potato in several places. Place directly on an oven rack and cook until the flesh gives and feels soft when squeezed through a cloth kitchen towel between your thumb and fingers, 35 to 55 minutes.

TO serve, split the sweet potatoes, add a dollop or drizzle of butter, and serve piping hot.

Each sweet potato makes 1 serving.

SWEET POTATO KISSES

Whether you offer these delicate morsels as a brunch dish, an unusual accompaniment to afternoon tea, alongside roast pork or duck, or as an airy dessert, be sure to pipe and brown them only minutes before serving.

BAKE the sweet potatoes as directed in the preceding recipe.

AS soon as the sweet potatoes are cool enough to handle, peel them and press through a ricer into a bowl. Add the eggs, sugar, salt to taste, and orange juice or liqueur and zest. Whisk until smooth and fluffy.

PREHEAT a broiler. Using a pastry brush, lightly grease a baking sheet with butter or oil, or coat with spray. Set aside.

TRANSFER the sweet potato mixture to a pastry bag fitted with a large fluted tip. Pipe onto the orange slices. Arrange on the prepared baking sheet and drizzle the tops with melted butter. Place under the broiler until lightly browned, 1 to 2 minutes.

TRANSFER to a warmed serving plate and dust with powdered sugar. Garnish with blossoms (if using) and serve immediately.

Makes 6 servings.

3 pounds orange "yam" variety sweet potatoes

4 eggs

¼ cup sugar, or to taste

Salt

2 tablespoons freshly squeezed orange juice or orange-flavored liqueur

1 tablespoon grated or minced fresh orange zest

Unsalted butter, at room temperature, vegetable oil, or cooking spray for greasing

2 or 3 medium-sized oranges, sliced about ⅛ inch thick

About ¼ cup (½ stick) unsalted butter, melted

Powdered sugar for dusting

Pesticide-free edible flowers such as scented geranium or borage for garnish (optional)

SWEET POTATOES WITH PECAN STREUSEL

3 pounds orange "yam" variety sweet potatoes

Unsalted butter, at room temperature, vegetable oil, or cooking spray for greasing

2 eggs, lightly beaten

¼ cup (½ stick) unsalted butter, melted and cooled slightly

½ cup whole milk or light cream

¼ cup (½ stick) unsalted butter, at room temperature

¼ cup all-purpose flour

⅔ cup firmly packed light brown sugar

1 cup chopped pecans

Fresh mint leaves for garnish (optional)

Back in Lake Providence, Louisiana, Juanita Cheek introduced me to this Southern casserole, and it has remained a favorite way of preparing sweet potatoes. I occasionally pour the mixture into a partially baked pastry crust and bake it as a pie (see page 490).

BAKE the sweet potatoes as directed on page 320. Alternatively, in a saucepan, combine the sweet potatoes and cold water to cover. Bring to a boil over medium-high heat and cook until tender, 35 to 45 minutes. Drain.

PREHEAT an oven to 350° F. Using a pastry brush, lightly grease a 2-quart baking dish with butter or oil, or coat with spray. Set aside.

AS soon as the sweet potatoes are cool enough to handle, peel, cut into chunks, and press through a ricer into a bowl; do not use a food processor as it will make them too smooth. Add the eggs, melted butter, and milk or cream and beat until well blended. Pour into the prepared baking dish.

IN a bowl, combine the room-temperature butter, flour, brown sugar, and pecans and mix well with your fingertips. Sprinkle the mixture evenly over the top of the sweet potatoes. Bake until the topping is bubbly, about 1 hour.

GARNISH with mint (if using) and serve warm or at room temperature.

Makes 6 to 8 servings.

ROASTED VEGETABLES

Roasted vegetables appear frequently on my dining table, usually as a side dish, but sometimes they become the main event, or are served over polenta or tossed with pasta. The slightly sweet caramelized variation is a flavorful addition to meat stews or is quite good as a side dish on its own.

When combining vegetables, add them to the pan in the order required for cooking until tender. If using beets, roast unpeeled separately from other vegetables to prevent bleeding; peel before serving.

2 pounds vegetables such as beets, carrots, leeks, onions, parsnips, potatoes, squash, sweet peppers, rutabagas, and turnips, one type or a combination

Fruity olive oil, preferably extra-virgin

Salt

Freshly ground black pepper

PREHEAT an oven to 400° F.

TRIM or cut all of the vegetables roughly the same size, 1 to 2 inches in diameter and length. Baby vegetables can be left whole or cut in half.

IN a large roasting pan or other large baking pan or pans, spread the vegetables in a single layer; do not crowd the vegetables. Drizzle with olive oil, sprinkle generously to taste with salt and pepper, and stir to coat well. Roast, stirring every 10 minutes, until the vegetables are browned and tender when pierced with a wooden skewer, 30 to 45 minutes.

TRANSFER to a warm serving bowl and serve hot, or cool to room temperature for use in salads.

Makes 6 servings.

VARIATION

Caramelized Vegetables. Combine ¼ cup (½ stick) unsalted butter and 2 tablespoons light brown sugar in the baking pan or pans and heat in the oven until the butter and sugar melt. Add the vegetables and salt and pepper; omit the olive oil. Roast as directed.

GRILLED VEGETABLES

Selected vegetables (pages 325-327)

Vegetable oil for brushing grill rack

Fruity olive oil or other oil or oil-based
    marinade (see recipe introduction)
    for brushing vegetables

Salt

Freshly ground black pepper

Vegetables take on a special flavor when grilled. They're a grand accompaniment to a meal or can be the main course. To serve grilled vegetables as a main dish, plan on about 8 ounces of raw vegetables per person. Add some slices of grilled Polenta (page 154) to round out the plate.

Since vegetables contain little or no fat, brush them with oil or an oil-based marinade to keep them moist and prevent them from sticking to the grill. Bland vegetable oils such as canola, peanut, or safflower will accomplish these tasks, but a variety of other oils, including a fruity olive oil or a nut oil, will double as flavor enhancers. For a distinctive change of pace, marinate in or brush with hot chile oil or mahogany-hued Asian sesame oil.

If you need to reduce fats in your diet, wrap unoiled vegetables in banana, cabbage, grape, lettuce, or spinach leaves; the wrappers will char without flaming and add a slightly smoky taste to the vegetables.

Grilled vegetables are delicious on their own, but you may wish to serve them with Garlic Mayonnaise or one of the other mayonnaise variations (page 388), Tomato Sauce (page 573), Pesto (page 399), or another favorite sauce.

PREPARE the selected vegetables as directed in the following listings. Note that some vegetables should be precooked before adding to the grill.

PREPARE an open grill for moderate to low indirect-heat cooking. Position a drip pan in the center of the fuel grate.

WHEN the fire is ready, lightly brush the grill rack with vegetable oil. Brush the vegetables with oil or marinade and season to taste with salt and pepper. Place the vegetables on the rack directly over the heat and sear briefly on all sides, then position over the drip pan and cook, turning frequently and brushing with oil or marinade, until lightly browned and tender when pierced with a wooden skewer; see vegetable listings for approximate cooking times.

SERVE warm or at room temperature.

FRESH VEGETABLES FOR GRILLING

NO precooking is required for these vegetables. Simply trim as
suggested and marinate or brush with selected oil (except
corn in husks). Grill as described in the basic recipe for
Grilled Vegetables.

Belgian Endives. Cut into halves or quarters. Grill for about
5 minutes.

Chiles. Cut lengthwise, remove and discard stems, seeds, and
membranes, and cut into wide strips if desired. Grill for 8 to
10 minutes.

Corn. Choose ears with ends intact. Pull the husks back but
leave attached at the base; remove silks. Rub the kernels with
softened unsalted butter, if desired, and reposition the husks.
Tie the narrow end of each ear together with a strip of torn
husk or cotton string. Place in a large bowl, add water to cover,
and soak for about 20 minutes. Remove the ears from the water
and pat dry with paper toweling. Grill for about 20 minutes. Or
to grill shucked and silked corn, brush the ears with melted
butter instead of oil. Grill for about 15 minutes.

Eggplants. Leave very small eggplants whole. Cut off the stems of
larger eggplants and slice lengthwise in half or into wedges, or
cut crosswise into thick slices. Leave stems on slender Asian
varieties and slice 3 or 4 times lengthwise almost to the stem,
then fan out the slices on the grill rack. Grill for about 15 minutes.

Fennel. Cut bulbs into wedges or thick slices. Grill for about
15 minutes.

Garlic. Peel off most of the outer layers of skin from whole heads.
Grill for about 20 minutes.

Green Onions. Slice off root ends and trim off some of the green
tops. Grill for 7 to 10 minutes.

Leeks. Slice off root ends and trim away some of the green tops,
then cut lengthwise in half. Or leave whole, but split lengthwise
to within a couple inches of the root end. Rinse well between
layers in both cases. Grill for 5 to 10 minutes.

continues ~

Mushrooms. Cut off tough portion of stem ends. Leave whole or cut very large ones into pieces; skewer if desired. Grill for about 5 minutes.

Onions. Cut unpeeled onions into halves or quarters and grill for 15 to 20 minutes. Or thickly slice peeled onions and grill for about 5 minutes.

Peppers, Sweet. Same as for chiles.

Potatoes and Sweet Potatoes. To grill whole, prick unpeeled tubers in several places with a fork and grill for 25 to 30 minutes for small potatoes or 1 hour or more for large ones. Or cut small potatoes or sweet potatoes in half and larger ones into wedges or 1/2-inch-thick slices and grill for about 30 minutes. If you wish to shorten grilling time, boil potatoes or sweet potatoes until almost tender, then pat dry; grill for 15 to 20 minutes.

Radicchio. Same as for Belgian endives.

Romaine Lettuce. Same as for Belgian endives.

Shallots. Peel and grill for 3 to 4 minutes.

Summer Squashes. Leave small squashes whole. Cut larger ones lengthwise into halves or quarters, or cut on the diagonal into 1/2-inch-thick slices. Grill for 5 to 10 minutes.

Tomatoes. Grill cherry or small tomatoes whole. Cut larger ones into halves or thick slices. Grill 8 to 15 minutes.

PRECOOKED VEGETABLES FOR GRILLING

THE following vegetables should be at least partially cooked before grilling. After precooking, pat them dry with paper toweling before marinating or brushing with selected oil. Grill as described in the basic recipe for Grilled Vegetables.

Artichokes. Trim and boil or steam artichokes until tender as directed for Sliced Artichoke-Filled Chicken Rolls on page 70. Cut lengthwise into halves or quarters and scoop out and discard the fuzzy chokes. Grill for 5 to 10 minutes.

Asparagus. Discard tough ends and peel lower portion of stems. Blanch, steam, or microwave stalks until almost tender. Grill for about 3 minutes.

Beets. Steam, boil, or microwave unpeeled beets until just tender. Cool and peel. Leave small beets whole or cut in half; slice larger ones. Grill for 5 to 10 minutes.

Broccoli. Trim into spears. Blanch, steam, or microwave until crisp-tender. Grill for about 5 minutes.

Carrots. Steam, boil, or microwave until just tender. Leave small ones whole; thickly slice large ones on the diagonal or cut into quarters. Grill for about 10 minutes.

Cauliflower. Slice into wedges. Blanch or steam until crisp-tender. Grill for about 8 minutes.

Parsnips. Same as carrots (see previous listing).

Rutabagas. Peel and slice about ½ inch thick. Blanch or steam until just tender. Grill for about 10 minutes.

Turnips. Same as rutabagas (see previous listing).

Winter Squashes. Peel and cut into ½-inch-thick slices. Blanch or steam until barely tender. Grill for 10 to 15 minutes.

VEGETABLE CUSTARDS

Unsalted butter, at room temperature,
  for greasing
About 1 pound fresh vegetables,
  trimmed, steamed or boiled until
  tender, and drained well
1 cup milk (not fat free)
1 cup heavy (whipping) cream
4 eggs
¼ cup all-purpose flour
¼ cup freshly grated Parmesan
  cheese (about 1 ounce), preferably
  Parmigiano-Reggiano
Salt
Freshly ground black or white pepper
Freshly grated nutmeg
Fresh herb sprigs such as basil,
  mint, sage, or thyme for garnish
  (optional)
Pesticide-free edible flowers such as
  chive, lavender, or nasturtium for
  garnish (optional)

These soufflé-like custards can be made for special occasions with whatever fresh vegetables are available from the garden or market. In the photograph on page 333, clockwise from the top right, are custards made from green pattypan squash, carrot, cauliflower, broccoli, red sweet pepper, and yellow crookneck squash.

PREHEAT an oven to 375° F. Using a pastry brush, generously grease eight 6-ounce custard cups with butter and set aside.

WORKING in batches if necessary, place the cooked vegetables in a food processor and process until smooth. You should have about 2 cups. Transfer the vegetable puree to a bowl. Add the milk, cream, eggs, flour, cheese, and salt, pepper, and nutmeg to taste. Stir to blend well. Distribute the vegetable mixture evenly among the prepared custard cups.

PLACE the cups on a rack (or racks) set in a large, deep baking pan (or pans), transfer to the oven, and pour enough hot (not boiling) water into the baking pan(s) to reach halfway up the sides of the custard containers. Place a sheet of aluminum foil over the pan to cover the tops of the custards loosely. Bake until a knife inserted into the center of the custards comes out barely clean, about 30 minutes.

REMOVE the custard cups from the water bath to a wire rack to cool for about 15 minutes.

TO serve, run a thin, flexible knife blade around the inside edges of each cup. Invert a serving plate over a cup, invert the plate and cup together, and carefully lift off the cup. Repeat with the remaining custards. Garnish each serving with herbs and/or flowers (if using). Serve immediately or at room temperature.

Makes 8 servings.

HERB, GARLIC, AND
LEMON ROASTED
CHICKEN (page 232)
and ROASTED
VEGETABLES
(page 323)

———

FRENCH WHITE
VEAL STEW
(page 260)

ROMAN GRILLED
LAMB CHOPS
(page 255)

———

THAI CHILE
BEEF WITH
FRAGRANT HERBS
(page 268)

MALAYSIAN DRY
BEEF CURRY
(page 269)

———

BETTER BURGERS (page 270)
on WHOLE-WHEAT BUNS
(page 416)
and FRENCH
FRIED POTATOES
(page 309)

TRIO OF COLD
POACHED FISH

(page 286)

———

SOUTHERN FRIED
CHICKEN SALAD

(page 290)

MILANESE
SWEET-AND-SOUR
ONIONS
(page 303)

———

VEGETABLE
CUSTARDS
(page 328)

RICE (page 364)
and STICKY RICE
(page 368)

———

SPANISH RICE
WITH GREEN BEANS
AND PEAS
(page 254)

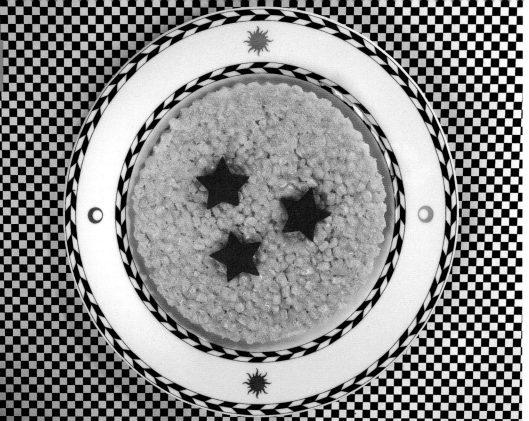

BAKED CORN

(page 360)

———

FRESH TOMATO SALSA,
TOMATILLO-CHILE SALSA,
PINEAPPLE SALSA

(pages 392-393)

ITALIAN POTATO
AND GREEN BEAN
SALAD

(page 379)

———

COUSCOUS AND
GARBANZO SALAD

(page 381)

RATATOUILLE

When cooked separately, then tossed together for a final blending, each vegetable in this Provençal favorite retains its characteristic flavor. For a change, the vegetables can be roasted (see page 323) instead of sauteed. Ratatouille is excellent with roasted or grilled chicken or lamb.

ROAST the peppers as directed on page 552. If roasted whole, cut the peppers in half lengthwise and remove and discard the stems, seeds, and membranes. Slice lengthwise into narrow strips and set aside.

IN a saute pan or heavy stew pot such as a dutch oven, heat ¼ cup of the oil over medium-high heat. Add the onion and cook, stirring frequently, until very soft and golden, about 8 minutes. Add the garlic and reserved pepper strips and cook for 1 minute longer. Transfer the vegetables to a colander set over a bowl; discard the oil that collects in the bowl.

HEAT ¼ cup of the remaining oil in the same pan. Add the eggplant and cook, stirring frequently, until lightly browned, about 8 minutes. Add to the colander with the onion mixture.

HEAT ¼ cup of the remaining oil in the same pan. Add the zucchini and cook, stirring frequently, until lightly browned, about 8 minutes. Add to the other vegetables in the colander.

HEAT the remaining 2 tablespoons oil in the same pan. Add the tomato, minced or crumbled herbs, and sugar and bring to a boil. Stir in the browned vegetables and season to taste with salt and pepper. Return the mixture to a boil, then reduce the heat to achieve a simmer, cover, and simmer, stirring occasionally, until all the vegetables are very tender but still hold their shapes, about 30 minutes.

SERVE warm or at room temperature. Just before serving, stir in the chopped basil.

Makes 8 servings.

3 red or yellow sweet peppers

¾ cup plus 2 tablespoons fruity olive oil, preferably extra-virgin

2 cups sliced yellow onion

2 tablespoons coarsely chopped garlic

1 pound globe eggplant, peeled and cut into ¾-inch cubes

2 pounds zucchini, sliced about ¼ inch thick

6 cups peeled, seeded, drained, and chopped ripe or canned tomato

1 tablespoon minced mixed fresh aromatic herbs such as lavender blossoms, marjoram, rosemary, summer savory, and thyme and fresh or dried bay leaf; or 1 teaspoon crumbled dried *herbes de Provence*

1 teaspoon sugar, or to taste

Salt

Freshly ground black pepper

⅓ cup chopped fresh basil

COOKED FRESH BEANS OR PEAS

Fresh shell beans, unshelled green
soybeans, shelled green (English)
peas, green beans, or edible pod
peas (snow peas or Sugar Snaps)

Sliced bacon, pork sausage, ham, or
blanched salt pork (optional)

Unsalted butter for seasoning or
sauteing (optional)

Salt

Freshly ground black pepper

Olive oil or high-quality vegetable oil
for sauteing or stir-frying (optional)

If you have access to fresh shell beans, enjoy them when available or freeze a quantity of them. To freeze, blanch the shelled beans for 2 to 3 minutes in boiling water, then drain, pack in freezer bags, and freeze for up to 9 months.

Unlike other shell beans, fresh soybeans that are mature yet still green can be cooked in their fuzzy pods. The cooked whole pods are sometimes referred to as "popper beans," because the beans are popped out of their shells at the table.

Today, some types of edible pod peas and green beans are available year-round, although they will have optimum flavor when picked locally in season. Farmers' markets are an excellent source of fresh legumes.

Fresh beans or peas may be cooked by the following methods. Cooking time will vary with age and size.

TO cook shell beans (except fava beans), bring a pot of water to a boil over high heat, add the shelled beans and about 1 ounce bacon, sausage, ham, or salt pork (if using) per cup of beans, cover partially, and reduce the heat to maintain a simmer. Cook, stirring occasionally, until the beans are tender, 25 to 45 minutes, depending on type and size. Season to taste with salt and pepper.

TO cook shelled fava beans, bring a pot of water to a boil over high heat, add the shelled beans, and boil for about 3 minutes. Drain the beans, then peel off and discard the thin layer of skin from each bean. If tender, transfer to a saucepan, stir in a little butter to taste (if desired), season to taste with salt and pepper, and reheat over medium heat. Tough peeled favas should be simmered until tender as directed for shell beans, then seasoned to taste.

TO cook unshelled soybeans, bring a pot of water to a boil over high heat, stir in about 1 tablespoon salt, add the whole pods, and cook until tender, 10 to 15 minutes. Drain and serve in the pods for diners to shell at the table.

TO blanch young green beans, edible pod peas, or shelled green (English) peas for use in recipes, trim the ends and remove any strings from the beans or pea pods. Bring a pot of water to a boil over high heat and ready a bowl of iced water. When the water boils, stir in about 1 tablespoon salt, drop in the beans or peas, and cook until crisp-tender, 2 to 3 minutes. Quickly drain and transfer to the iced water to halt cooking. Drain well and use as directed.

TO cook green beans, edible pod peas, or shelled green peas, trim the ends and remove any strings from the beans or pea pods. Bring a pot of water to a boil over high heat. When the water boils, stir in about 1 tablespoon salt, add the beans or peas, and cook until tender, 5 to 10 minutes. Drain, stir in a little butter to taste (if desired), and season to taste with salt and pepper. Mature green beans can also be cooked with bacon, sausage, ham, or salt pork as directed for shell beans.

TO steam green beans or edible pod peas, trim the ends and remove any strings. Place a rack in a pot with a tight-fitting lid that will be large enough to hold the beans or peas and pour in water to a level just below the rack. Place the pot over high heat and bring the water to a boil, then adjust the heat to achieve a simmer. Place the beans or peas on the rack, cover the pot with the lid, and steam until crisp-tender, 5 to 15 minutes; adjust the heat to maintain simmering water throughout cooking. Transfer to a bowl, stir in a little butter to taste (if desired), and season to taste with salt and pepper.

TO saute green beans or edible pod peas, trim the ends and remove any strings. Cut green beans into 1½-inch lengths; leave pea pods whole or cut as desired. Place 1 tablespoon unsalted butter or olive oil for every 2 cups beans in a saute pan or large, heavy skillet and heat over medium-high heat. Add the beans or peas and cook, stirring frequently, until crisp-tender, 3 to 8 minutes. Season to taste with salt and pepper.

TO stir-fry green beans or edible pod peas, trim and cut as for sauteing. Place a wok, large saute pan, or large, heavy skillet over high heat. When the pan is hot, add about 1 tablespoon high-quality vegetable oil for every 2 cups beans and swirl to coat the pan. When the oil is hot but not yet smoking, add the beans or pea pods and stir-fry until coated with the oil, about 1 minute. Add about 2 tablespoons water, cover, and cook, stirring occasionally, until crisp-tender, 2 to 5 minutes. Season to taste with salt and pepper.

Each cup beans makes 1 or 2 servings.

COOKED DRIED BEANS

This basic recipe works for cooking any type of dried bean or other legume. Except for salt and pepper added at the end, I've omitted seasonings, resulting in a pot of beans that can be used in a variety of dishes. For more flavorful beans to be served on their own, select one of the well-seasoned variations on pages 346-352.

Soaking beans prior to cooking softens them, shortens their cooking time, and makes them more digestible. Although beans can be cooked without soaking, they will take considerably longer to become tender. Lentils, split peas, black (turtle) beans, and some new hybrid beans do not require soaking, however; check packages or ask sellers if in doubt.

Actual soaking time varies with variety; large types such as fava and lima beans need longer soaking periods than smaller beans. Generally, the longer beans are soaked, the shorter the cooking time and the more tender the result.

An exception to the general rules of soaking and cooking is the Italian lupine bean (lupini). It contains a bitter alkaloid that must be leached out by soaking the beans in a saltwater brine for about a week with daily rinsing and fresh brine. Follow supplier's directions for these beans.

Although cooking beans in their soaking water conserves nutrients, disposing of the soaking water, rinsing the beans, and cooking them in fresh liquid helps reduce the amount of insoluble sugars that cause gas. If you choose to soak black (turtle) beans, however, you may want to cook them in the soaking liquid in order to retain more of their rich color pigments.

To preserve both color pigments and nutrients, avoid cooking legumes in too much liquid. Start by immersing soaked beans in liquid to cover by no more than ½ inch, or unsoaked beans by no more than 2 inches, adding more liquid as needed to keep them barely covered.

Legumes absorb the flavors around them during cooking. Onions, garlic, celery, carrots, meat, and fresh and dried herbs may be added to the beans at the beginning. Acidic ingredients, such as tomatoes or tomato products, citrus juice, vinegar, or wine, interfere with the legumes' ability to bind with water, however, and will toughen bean skins and lengthen the cooking time. With some beans, acidic products prevent them from ever getting tender no matter how long they are cooked! Wait until the beans are done before adding these flavorings.

Cooking dried legumes with salt adds considerably to the cooking time, therefore I call for seasoning with salt after the legumes are tender. If you wish to cook legumes in a liquid more flavorful than water, use unsalted stock, or use canned reduced-sodium broth and allow for extra cooking time.

Adding a bit of unsalted butter or vegetable oil to the bean pot helps prevent liquid from overflowing the rim during the boiling period. Some cooks advocate rubbing a little vegetable oil around the top edge of the cooking pot to accomplish this purpose.

Crunchy undercooked beans are not only unappealing to chew, but also can be difficult to digest due to the presence of toxic lectin, which can cause stomachaches, diarrhea, or nausea. On the other hand, overcooked beans turn mushy. The trick is to cook beans until they are just tender and creamy yet still hold their shape; once they begin to split, they turn unpleasantly soft.

Cooking time varies with type of legume, length of storage, altitude, duration of soaking, and the hardness of the water. The older the bean, the longer it takes to cook. Since there are no labels to indicate age, estimating cooking time is a matter of guesswork. Always begin to taste before you think the beans will be done.

Pressure cookers reduce the cooking time by more than half due to the higher temperature that occurs inside the pressurized pot. They make it impossible to gauge when the beans are tender and to adjust the seasonings during cooking, however. To prevent overcooking, follow the manufacturer's directions, but shorten the time by a few minutes. If the beans are not yet done, finish cooking them conventionally.

Since cooking beans is time-consuming, you may wish to cook more dried beans than needed for a specific recipe and store the leftovers for another purpose. Cooked beans can be covered and refrigerated for up to 3 days, or they can be frozen for several months and then thawed before reheating. Liquid drained off of cooked beans makes a delicious addition to soups or stews.

continues ~

Dried beans, peas, or lentils

Unsalted Brown Stock (page 576),
unsalted Vegetable Stock (page
580), or unsalted White Stock
(page 578; all optional)

1 tablespoon unsalted butter or
vegetable oil (optional)

Salt (optional)

Freshly ground black pepper
(optional)

SPREAD the beans, peas, or lentils out on a tray or other flat
surface and carefully pick over by hand to remove any foreign
bits or imperfect legumes. Place the legumes in a colander or
strainer and rinse well under cold running water to remove the
dust accumulated during drying and storing.

IF using split peas, lentils, black (turtle) beans, and some new
varieties of beans that do not require soaking (check packages
or ask sellers if in doubt), you may skip the next three paragraphs
and proceed with cooking. If using other legumes, soak by one
of the following methods.

Quick Hot-Soak Method. In a heavy-bottomed pot, pour in
enough water to cover the legumes by about 3 inches once
they are added. Bring to a boil over high heat. Add the rinsed
legumes, return the water to a boil, and boil for 3 to 5 minutes.
Remove from the heat, cover, and let stand for 1 hour or longer;
extra soaking time will result in shorter cooking time. If soaking
longer than 2 hours, refrigerate after cooling to room temperature
to prevent fermentation.

Long Cold-Soak Method. Place the legumes in a large bowl and
add cold water to cover by about 3 inches. Let stand for several
hours or, preferably, overnight. When soaking during hot
weather, refrigerate to prevent fermentation.

DRAIN the soaked legumes in a colander or strainer, reserving the
liquid for cooking if desired (see recipe introduction). Rinse
the beans under cold running water and drain again.

TRANSFER the drained legumes to a large, heavy pot. If the
legumes were soaked, add enough stock (if using), water, or
reserved soaking liquid to cover by about ½ inch and stir well.
If the legumes were not soaked, add enough liquid to cover by
about 2 inches and stir well. Avoid filling the pot more than
three-quarters full. Add butter or oil, if desired, to reduce the
amount of foaming and help prevent the liquid from boiling
over. Place over medium-high heat and bring to a boil. Using a
wire skimmer or slotted utensil, remove any foam that comes
to the surface.

IF cooking lentils or split peas, immediately reduce the heat to achieve a simmer and cover partially.

IF cooking beans, boil for 10 minutes, then reduce the heat to achieve a simmer and cover partially.

SIMMER, stirring occasionally, until the lentils, peas, or beans are tender but still hold their shape and have absorbed most of the water, about 20 minutes for lentils or split peas, or 20 minutes to 2 hours for most beans and whole peas. Large bean varieties, those stored for long periods, or beans cooked in salted stock or broth may take even longer. Test frequently for doneness and taste several beans for consistency. Add a little liquid as required if the legumes get too dry, but use as little liquid as possible, keeping the beans only slightly submerged. Avoid overcooking at any point to prevent the beans from becoming mushy.

IF serving the legumes on their own, season to taste with salt and pepper after they are tender. (To thicken the bean liquid, if desired, remove and mash about 1/2 cup of the beans, then stir them back into the pot.)

IF using the beans in the following variations or in recipes, season as directed.

Each cup dried legumes yields 2 to 3 cups cooked, depending on variety, for at least 3 servings.

Eliminating the Gas

Human digestion systems are incapable of breaking down the various complex sugars, including raffinose, stachyose, and verbascose, collectively known as alpha-galactrosides, found in beans. Bacteria living in the lower intestines, however, do break them down, resulting in the production of large amounts of several gases, including carbon dioxide, hydrogen, and methane.

Not all legumes are made the same. Greater amounts of the indigestible sugars are found in beans that are native to the Western Hemisphere — kidney, lima, navy, and pinto beans — than are present in the Asian natives — lentils, split peas, and *azuki* and mung beans. And today plant hybridizers are developing bean varieties genetically altered to lower the amount of indigestible sugars.

It seems that almost everyone has a solution to the problem of gases that result from eating beans. For example, Mexican cooks throw a pungent herb, epazote, into the beans as they simmer. Many food writers suggest changing the soaking water several times, then cooking in fresh water. According to the United States Department of Agriculture, however, this latter process does not aid digestibility but merely helps shorten cooking time.

Some food scientists now advocate dropping dried beans into rapidly boiling water and boiling for a few minutes, a procedure that tricks the seeds into beginning the process of growing into a new plant. The hot water softens the plant cell walls that protect the sugars, allowing them to leach into the water. The beans should then be removed from the heat, covered, and soaked for an hour or more. When the soaking water is discarded, about 85 percent of the insoluble sugars are drained off. Of course, some nutrients, as well as color pigment, will also go down the drain, but if you are bothered by intestinal gases from eating beans, it will be worth the slight sacrifice.

Another option is to use Beano, a liquid food additive that contains an enzyme that breaks down the sugars before the intestinal bacteria have a chance to go to work. Many insist that it greatly reduces or eliminates gas problems.

Perhaps the easiest solution is simply to eat more beans. It is believed by some that when one eats beans on a regular basis, the problem of gas lessens over time.

A World of Well-Seasoned Beans

Following are a few of my favorite American regional and international bean dishes. Use the preceding basic recipe as a guide and serve them with the suggested grain (cooked as directed on pages 364-371), or use them as directed in other recipes in this book.

Although I've chosen to stick with the traditional additions of meat for flavoring, any recipe that uses meat can be turned into a vegetarian dish by omitting it, cooking the onions or other vegetables in a little olive oil or vegetable oil, and using unsalted vegetable stock (for optimum flavor) or water.

Each recipe can be transformed into a flavorful soup by increasing the amount of liquid to cover the beans to about 3 inches and adding enough liquid during cooking to maintain a "soupy" consistency. For a creamy soup, simmer until the beans begin to fall apart, then puree in a food processor or blender and, if desired, press through a food mill or fine-mesh strainer to remove the bean skins.

345

BRAZILIAN-STYLE BEANS

2 cups dried black (turtle) beans

8 ounces bacon, chopped

1 cup finely chopped yellow onion

1 teaspoon minced garlic

1 teaspoon ground cumin

2 bay leaves

1 tablespoon brown sugar

½ cup fresh or canned tomato puree

Salt

Freshly ground black pepper

3 tablespoons chopped fresh cilantro
(coriander)

2 tablespoons freshly squeezed lime
juice, or to taste

Serve with long-grain white rice (page 364).

PICK over and rinse the beans as directed on page 342 and set aside.

IN a large, heavy pot, cook the bacon over medium-high heat until the
fat is rendered. Add the onion and cook, stirring frequently, until
soft but not browned, about 5 minutes. Add the beans, garlic, cumin,
bay leaves, brown sugar, and enough water to cover by about 2 inches.
Cook as directed on pages 342–343 until the beans are tender.

ADD the tomato puree and salt and pepper to taste and simmer
until the flavors are well blended, about 20 minutes. Just before
serving, stir in the cilantro and lime juice.

Makes 6 servings.

FRENCH-STYLE BEANS

2 cups dried white beans, preferably
flageolets

2 tablespoons fat from duck or
goose confit

2 cups finely chopped leek, including
pale green portion

1 tablespoon minced garlic

1 to 2 quarts unsalted Vegetable
Stock (page 580) or White Stock
(page 578; both optional)

2 cups peeled, seeded, drained, and
chopped ripe or canned tomato

½ cup minced fresh flat-leaf parsley

6 ounces duck or goose confit, chopped

Salt

Freshly ground black pepper

Serve with Couscous (page 371) or pearled barley (page 364).

CLEAN and soak the beans as directed on page 342.

DRAIN the beans and transfer to a large, heavy pot. Stir in the
confit fat, leek, garlic, and enough stock (if using) or water to
cover by ½ inch. Cooked as directed on pages 342–343 until
the beans are tender.

ADD the tomato, parsley, chopped confit, and salt and pepper
to taste and simmer until the flavors are well blended, about
20 minutes.

Makes 6 servings.

INDIAN LENTILS ~ *DAL* ~

In some versions of dal, the lentils are pureed after cooking, but in this recipe they remain whole. Alternative traditional legumes include split mung beans (moong dal) and yellow split peas (chana dal). Serve with basmati rice (page 364).

PICK over and rinse the lentils as directed on page 342 and set aside.

IN a heavy pot, heat the clarified butter or oil over medium-high heat. Add the shallot or onion, ginger, and chile and cook, stirring frequently, until very soft and golden, about 8 minutes. Add the garlic, ground spices, and nutmeg and cook for about 1 minute longer. Add the lentils and 2 quarts hot water. (For a drier result, add only enough water to cover the lentils by ½ inch.) Bring to a boil, then adjust the heat to maintain a simmer, cover, and cook, stirring occasionally, until the lentils are just tender, about 10 minutes.

ADD the tomato and salt to taste and continue to cook, uncovered, until the lentils are very soft, about 10 minutes longer.

JUST before serving, stir in the lime juice, chopped cilantro, and more salt if needed.

Makes 8 servings.

2 cups red lentils *(masoor dal)*

2 tablespoons Clarified Butter (page 571) or canola or other high-quality vegetable oil

2 cups finely chopped shallot or red onion

¼ cup finely chopped fresh ginger

1 tablespoon minced fresh hot chile, or to taste

2 teaspoons minced garlic

2 teaspoons ground coriander

1 teaspoon ground turmeric

1 teaspoon ground cumin

1 teaspoon ground cayenne, or to taste

1 teaspoon freshly ground black pepper, or to taste

½ teaspoon ground cardamom

½ teaspoon ground cinnamon

¼ teaspoon ground cloves

¼ teaspoon freshly grated nutmeg

2 cups peeled, seeded, drained, and chopped ripe or canned tomato

Salt

2 tablespoons freshly squeezed lime juice, or to taste

½ cup chopped fresh cilantro (coriander)

MEXICALI BEANS

2 cups dried black (turtle), pink,
pinto, kidney, or similar beans

1 tablespoon cumin seed

1 tablespoon dried oregano

1 or 2 whole *ancho*, *guajillo*, New
Mexico, *pasilla*, or other large dried
mild to hot chile(s), stem(s) and
seeds discarded, torn into small
pieces

2 tablespoons olive oil

2 cups chopped yellow onion

2 teaspoons minced garlic

Salt

Freshly ground black pepper

Serve with long-grain white rice (page 364) or Corn Tortillas (page 428).

COOK the beans until tender as directed on pages 342–343; do
not season.

MEANWHILE, in a small skillet, combine the cumin seed, oregano,
and torn chile(s). Place over medium heat and toast, shaking the
pan or stirring frequently, until fragrant, about 3 minutes; do
not allow to burn. Pour onto a plate to cool, then transfer to a
spice grinder or heavy mortar with a pestle and grind to a fine
powder. Set aside.

IN a saute pan or heavy skillet, heat the oil over medium-high heat.
Add the onion and cook, stirring frequently, until very soft and
golden, about 8 minutes. Add the garlic and cook for about
1 minute longer.

STIR the onion mixture and the reserved spice mixture into the
cooked beans and season to taste with salt and pepper. Simmer
until the flavors are well blended, about 20 minutes.

Makes 6 servings.

NORTH AFRICAN–STYLE BEANS

Serve with Couscous (page 371) or wheat berries (page 364).

CLEAN and soak the beans as directed on page 342.

IN a large, heavy pot, heat the oil over medium-high heat. Add the onion and carrot and cook, stirring frequently, until the vegetables are soft but not browned, about 5 minutes. Add the garlic, cinnamon, cloves, and saffron and cook for about 1 minute longer.

DRAIN the beans and stir them into the pot. Add the cilantro and parsley sprigs and enough stock (if using) or water to cover by ½ inch. Cook as directed on pages 342–343 until the beans are tender.

STIR in the tomato and salt and pepper to taste and simmer until the flavors are well blended, about 20 minutes.

Makes 6 servings.

2 cups dried Egyptian fava *(ful medames)* or garbanzo beans (chickpeas)

3 tablespoons olive oil

3 cups chopped yellow onion

1 cup chopped carrot

1 teaspoon minced garlic

1 cinnamon stick

3 whole cloves

½ teaspoon crumbled saffron threads

6 fresh cilantro (coriander) sprigs

6 fresh flat-leaf parsley sprigs

About 2 quarts unsalted Vegetable Stock (page 580) or White Stock (page 578) made with chicken (optional)

1 cup peeled, seeded, drained, and chopped ripe or canned tomato

Salt

Freshly ground black pepper

SOUTHERN BEANS

2 cups dried lima beans or
    black-eyed peas

3 tablespoons bacon drippings or
    canola or other high-quality
    vegetable oil

3 cups sliced yellow onion

1 pound smoked ham, cubed

1 bay leaf

1 to 2 quarts unsalted Brown Stock
    (page 576) or White Stock (page
    578) made with chicken (optional)

Salt

Freshly ground black pepper

Serve with cornbread (page 423).

CLEAN and soak the beans as directed on page 342.

IN a large, heavy pot, heat the bacon drippings or oil over medium-high heat. Add the onion and cook, stirring frequently, until soft but not browned, about 5 minutes.

DRAIN the beans and stir them into the pot. Add the ham, bay leaf, and enough stock (if using) or water to cover by ½ inch. Cook as directed on pages 342–343 until the beans are tender. Season to taste with salt and pepper.

Makes 6 servings.

SPANISH-STYLE BEANS

2 cups dried lima beans

3 tablespoons fruity olive oil,
    preferably extra-virgin

4 cups sliced yellow onion

1 cup chopped leek, including pale
    green portion

1 cup chopped carrot

3 tablespoons minced garlic

1 pound spicy Spanish sausage
    (chorizo), casings discarded, sliced

2 bay leaves

1 tablespoon paprika

1 to 2 quarts unsalted Brown Stock
    (page 576) or White Stock (page
    578; both optional)

Salt

Freshly ground black pepper

Serve with short-grain white rice, preferably Spanish Valencia (page 364).

CLEAN and soak the beans as directed on page 342.

IN a large, heavy pot, heat the oil over low heat. Add the onion, leek, carrot, and garlic and cook, stirring frequently, until the vegetables are almost caramelized, about 45 minutes.

DRAIN the beans and stir them into the pot. Add the sausage, bay leaves, paprika, and enough stock (if using) or water to cover by ½ inch. Cook as directed on pages 342–343 until the beans are tender. Season to taste with salt and pepper.

Makes 6 servings.

SOUTHWESTERN BEANS

Serve with hominy (page 364), Corn Tortillas (page 428), or commercial tortillas.

PICK over and rinse the beans as directed on page 342.

IN a large, heavy pot, cook the bacon over medium-high heat until the fat is rendered. Add the onion, celery, carrot, fresh chile, and bay leaf and cook, stirring frequently, until the vegetables are very soft and golden, about 8 minutes. Add the garlic, chili powder, cumin, and cayenne and pepper to taste and cook for about 2 minutes. Stir in the beans and enough stock (if using) or water to cover by about 2 inches. Cook as directed on pages 342–343 until the beans are tender. Season to taste with salt.

Makes 6 servings.

2 cups dried black (turtle) beans

4 ounces bacon, chopped

1 cup chopped yellow onion

1 cup chopped celery

½ cup chopped carrot

1 tablespoon chopped fresh jalapeño
  or other hot chile

1 bay leaf

4 teaspoons minced garlic

1 tablespoon chili powder

2 teaspoons ground cumin

Ground cayenne

Freshly ground black pepper

About 2 quarts unsalted Vegetable
  Stock (page 580) or White Stock
  (page 578) made with chicken
  (optional)

Salt

TUSCAN BEANS

2 cups dried white beans, preferably
cannellini

1 cup fresh sage leaves, tough stems
discarded

1 teaspoon minced garlic (optional)

2 tablespoons extra-virgin olive oil

Salt

Freshly ground black pepper

Extra-virgin olive oil for serving

The Tuscans have many uses for beans. They are served as an antipasto on their own or combined with canned tuna, as a side dish, or as an addition to soups and stews. The variation with tomatoes, which translates as "beans cooked like birds," is my favorite way to serve them.

CLEAN and soak the beans as directed on page 342.

DRAIN the beans and transfer them to a large, heavy pot. Add the sage, garlic (if using), oil, and enough water to cover by about ½ inch; stir well. Cook as directed on pages 342–343 until the beans are tender. Season to taste with salt and pepper.

JUST before serving, drain off excess water. Pass olive oil at the table for drizzling over the beans.

Makes 6 servings.

VARIATION

Tuscan Beans and Tomato (*Fagioli all'uccelletto*). Cook and drain the beans as directed. In a saute pan or skillet, heat ½ cup extra-virgin olive oil over medium-high heat. Add 4 ounces Italian bacon (*pancetta*), chopped, and cook, stirring frequently, until the bacon is lightly browned, about 4 minutes. Add 2 teaspoons minced garlic and cook for about 1 minute longer. Stir in 2 cups peeled, seeded, drained, and chopped ripe or canned tomato and cook for about 3 minutes. Add to the cooked beans and season to taste with salt and pepper. Place over medium-low heat and cook, stirring occasionally, until the liquid has thickened, about 20 minutes. If the mixture becomes too dry, stir in a little water.

HOPPIN' JOHN

The origin of the odd name of this Southern classic, often served as a traditional New Year's good luck dish, is gone with the wind.

IF using dried peas, clean and soak as directed on page 342, drain, and set aside. If using fresh or frozen peas, reserve for later use.

IF using sliced bacon, cut crosswise into pieces about ½ inch wide. If using slab bacon, cut into ¼-inch dice. Transfer to a large, heavy pot and cook over medium heat, stirring frequently, until browned and crisp, 6 to 7 minutes. Using a slotted utensil, transfer the bacon to paper toweling to drain.

DISCARD all but 3 tablespoons of the bacon fat and place the pot over medium-high heat. Add the onion, celery, and sweet pepper and cook, stirring frequently, until the vegetables are soft but not browned, about 5 minutes. Stir in the peas, garlic, thyme, bay leaf, and just enough water to cover barely. Bring to a boil, then reduce the heat to achieve a simmer, cover partially, and simmer, stirring occasionally, until the peas are tender but still hold their shape, 15 to 25 minutes.

MEANWHILE, cook the rice in the stock or broth as directed on page 364.

STIR the tomato into the peas and simmer, uncovered, about 5 minutes. Stir in the cooked rice, season to taste with salt and generous amounts of ground pepper and hot sauce, and heat through, about 2 minutes. Stir in most of the green onion and chopped parsley.

TO serve, transfer to a serving dish, sprinkle with the reserved bacon and the remaining green onion and chopped parsley, and garnish with parsley sprigs.

Makes 8 servings.

VEGETARIAN VARIATION

OMIT the bacon. Substitute 3 tablespoons high-quality vegetable oil for the bacon renderings. Cook the rice in vegetable stock or water.

1½ cups dried black-eyed peas, or 3 cups shelled fresh or thawed frozen black-eyed peas

4 ounces sliced bacon or slab bacon trimmed of rind

1½ cups chopped yellow onion

1 cup chopped celery

1 cup chopped red or green sweet pepper

1 tablespoon minced garlic

1 tablespoon minced fresh thyme, or 1 teaspoon crumbled dried thyme

1 bay leaf

1 cup long-grain white rice

1½ cups Vegetable Stock (page 580), White Stock (page 578) made with chicken, or canned reduced-sodium chicken or vegetable broth

2 cups peeled, seeded, drained, and chopped ripe or canned tomato

Salt

Freshly ground black pepper

Louisiana hot sauce

¾ cup chopped green onion, including green tops

½ cup chopped fresh flat-leaf parsley

Fresh flat-leaf parsley sprigs for garnish

AMERICAN BAKED BEANS

Vegetable oil or cooking spray for
 greasing

8 ounces salt pork, trimmed of rind
 and cut into small cubes

8 cups cooked dried or canned beans
 (see page 340)

3 cups chopped yellow onion

½ cup light molasses

½ cup firmly packed brown sugar

½ cup catsup

2 tablespoons dry mustard or
 prepared Dijon mustard

1 tablespoon salt, or to taste

1 teaspoon freshly ground black
 pepper, or to taste

354

No all-American celebration would be complete without a side dish of baked beans. This generic recipe illustrates the method for baking, while the variations add typical regional flourishes. For vegetarian beans, substitute 2 tablespoons canola or other high-quality vegetable oil for the seasoning meat.

Choose one type of bean, a packaged mixture of bean varieties that have been selected because they share similar cooking times, or a combination of separately cooked beans.

PREHEAT an oven to 275° F. Using a pastry brush, lightly grease a bean pot or 3-quart baking dish with oil, or coat with spray. Set aside.

IN a saucepan, combine the salt pork and enough water to cover and bring to a boil over high heat. Boil for 5 minutes to remove excess salt; drain and set aside.

DRAIN the beans, reserving the liquid, and transfer to a bowl. Measure the liquid, adding water if necessary to equal 3 cups and stir into the beans. Add the pork, onion, molasses, brown sugar, catsup, mustard, salt, and pepper and mix well. Transfer the mixture to the prepared pot or dish, cover tightly with a lid or aluminum foil, and bake, stirring occasionally, until very tender and well flavored, about 5 hours. If the beans get dry before they are ready, add a little more of the bean liquid or water. If the beans are "soupy," uncover during the final hour or so of cooking to allow some of the liquid to evaporate.

Makes 8 servings.

VARIATIONS

Baked Beans and Rice. Bake the beans according to the basic recipe or any of the following variations. Meanwhile, cook 2 cups brown rice or a mixture of wild and brown rices such as Lundberg Wild Blend as directed on page 364. Combine the cooked rice and the baked beans, transfer to a greased 13-by-9-inch pan, and bake in a 350° F oven until well flavored and bubbly, about 45 minutes. Just before serving, shower the top with minced fresh chives or green onion tops to garnish.

Barbecued Baked Beans. Omit the catsup. Add 1 cup tomato-based barbecue sauce (a favorite recipe or high-quality commercial product).

Boston Baked Beans. Use small white beans, such as navy or Great Northern. Omit the catsup.

Hawaiian Baked Beans. Use navy beans. Omit the salt pork, molasses, catsup, mustard, and salt. Increase the brown sugar to 1 cup. Add 2 cups cubed Spam (about 12 ounces), 2 cups drained canned pineapple chunks (reserve juice and use as part of the liquid stirred into the beans), 1 cup soy sauce, 1/4 cup finely chopped fresh ginger, and 4 teaspoons minced garlic.

New England Baked Beans. Use yellow-eyed beans or small white beans, such as navy or Great Northern. Omit the brown sugar and molasses. Add 1 cup packed maple sugar or pure maple syrup.

Southern Baked Beans. Use kidney, lima, or navy beans. Use the salt pork or 8 ounces chopped bacon or baked ham. Increase the catsup to 1 cup and add 2 tablespoons Worcestershire sauce.

Western Baked Beans. Use black, red kidney, pinto, or similar beans. Add 1/4 cup chopped fresh jalapeño or other hot chile, or to taste, and 2 tablespoons Worcestershire sauce.

CORN ON THE COB

Ears of corn

Unsalted butter, at room temperature
or melted

Salt

Freshly ground black pepper

OPTIONAL SEASONINGS

Ground dried hot chile

Ground cumin

Crushed Sichuan peppercorns

Minced fresh sage or other herb

Freshly squeezed lime or lemon juice

Here are several ways to cook and season corn ears. At the height of the summer, however, butter, salt, and other seasonings are really unnecessary.

TO shuck corn, pull the husks down from the narrow end, then snap them off along the stem. Twist the silks at the top and pull off as many as possible, then complete removal with a dry vegetable brush or a plastic cornsilk brush. Cook corn as soon as possible after husking.

TO boil corn, fill a large pot with enough water to cover the corn once it is added; do not add salt, as it will toughen the corn. Bring the water to a boil over high heat. Add the shucked corn, cover, remove the pot from the heat, and let stand until the corn is tender, about 2 minutes for young, tender corn or about 5 minutes for older corn. Drain well.

TO grill corn, choose ears with ends intact. Pull the husks back but leave attached at the base; remove silks. Rub the kernels with softened unsalted butter, if desired, and reposition the husks. Tie the narrow end of each ear together with a strip of torn husk or cotton string. Place in a large bowl, add water to cover, and soak for about 20 minutes. Remove the ears from the water and pat dry with paper toweling. Grill, turning several times, for about 20 minutes. Or to grill shucked corn, brush the ears with melted butter and grill, turning occasionally, for about 15 minutes.

TO microwave corn, place unshucked ears in a single layer on a platter or directly on a carousel. Cook at full power until tender, about 7 minutes for 1 ear or about 12 minutes for 2 ears when cooking in a small microwave oven, or about 1 minute for 1 ear and for up to 14 minutes for 6 ears when cooking in a regular-sized microwave oven. Using oven mitts or a cloth kitchen towel to prevent burning hands, remove ears from the oven and pull off the husks and silks. Or, to serve ears in husks, pull the husks back without breaking, pull off silks, and reform the husks around the ears.

TO roast corn, prepare ears as for grilled corn (see previous page). Preheat an oven to 375° F. In a roasting pan, arrange the corn in a single layer and roast until done, 15 to 20 minutes. Or, to roast shucked and silked corn, arrange the ears in a roasting pan, brush with melted butter, and roast, turning several times, in a preheated 350° F oven until done, about 15 minutes.

TO steam corn, place a rack in a large pot with a tight-fitting lid and pour in water to a level just below the rack. Place the pot over high heat and bring the water to a boil, then adjust the heat to achieve a simmer. Place shucked corn on the rack, cover the pot with the lid, and steam until the corn is done, about 4 minutes for young, tender corn or for up to 8 minutes for older ears.

SERVE cooked corn immediately. Offer butter, salt, pepper, and/or other seasonings at the table.

Each ear of corn makes 1 serving.

SAUTEED OR CREAMED
FRESH CORN

Ears of corn

Unsalted butter

Salt

Freshly ground black pepper

**Heavy (whipping) cream, light cream,
or half-and-half, if making creamed
corn**

For the field-fresh flavor of corn on the cob without the mess at the table, saute cut corn to serve as a side dish or to use in recipes calling for cooked corn. To cut calories, cook the corn in a little chicken or vegetable stock or broth instead of the butter.

For creamed corn that's far superior to the canned product, add cream to sauteed corn and cook until the mixture is thickened and creamy. For less caloric creamed corn, dissolve 4 teaspoons cornstarch in 1 cup low-fat milk or low-fat canned evaporated milk and use in place of the cream. Serve creamed corn as an accompaniment or use in recipes calling for creamed corn.

TO shuck corn, pull the husks down from the narrow end, then snap them off along the stem. Twist the silks at the top and pull off as many as possible, then complete removal with a dry vegetable brush or a plastic cornsilk brush. Cook corn as soon as possible after husking.

IF making Sauteed Corn, rest the base of an ear of shucked corn on a large, deep plate or inside a large bowl. With a sharp knife, cut down the length of the cob from the tip to the base. Leave behind a bit of the pulp to avoid mixing tough cob fibers into the corn. Turn the knife blade over and scrape the cob with the blunt edge to remove pulp and milky juices. Each medium-sized cob should yield about 1/2 cup kernels.

IF making Creamed Corn, rest the base of an ear of shucked corn on a large, deep plate or inside a large bowl. Run the blade of a sharp knife down the center of each row of kernels the full length of the ear. Turn the knife blade over and with the blunt edge scrape the corn into the plate or bowl. Several passes over the cob may be necessary to release all the juices. Each medium-sized cob should yield about 1/3 cup scraped kernels.

FOR Sauteed Corn, in a saute pan or skillet, for each cup of kernels, melt 1 tablespoon butter over medium heat. Add the corn and cook, stirring frequently, until tender, about 4 minutes for young corn or for up to 8 minutes for older corn. Season to taste with salt and pepper. Transfer to a serving bowl and serve immediately, or use in recipes calling for cooked corn kernels.

FOR Creamed Corn, cook the corn until tender as directed in the previous paragraph and season to taste with salt and pepper. For each cup of scraped kernels, stir about ¼ cup cream or half-and-half into the cooked and seasoned corn and continue to cook, stirring frequently, until slightly thickened, about 10 minutes longer. Transfer to a serving bowl and serve immediately, or use in recipes calling for creamed corn.

Each cup cooked corn makes 1 or 2 servings.

BAKED CORN

Unsalted butter, at room temperature,
    for greasing

About 12 medium-sized ears corn

6 eggs, at room temperature, well
    beaten

1 teaspoon salt

½ cup (1 stick) unsalted butter,
    melted and cooled slightly

Red sweet pepper, stem, seeds, and
    membranes discarded, cut into
    decorative shapes for garnish
    (optional)

This simple preparation has been among my regular summer recipes ever since my fifth grade teacher, Eula Cain, shared it with me many years ago.

PREHEAT an oven to 350° F. Using a pastry brush, lightly grease a 13-by-9-inch pan, two 8-inch tart pans with removable bottoms, or eight 3-inch tart pans with removable bottoms with butter. Set aside.

CUT the kernels from the corn cobs as directed for Sauteed Corn on page 358. Measure out 6 cups and transfer to a bowl. Add the eggs, salt, and melted butter and mix well. Pour into the prepared pan(s) and bake until the center is just set when touched, 30 to 40 minutes.

TRANSFER to a work surface to cool for a few minutes before serving.

SERVE directly from the large pan. If using tart rings, lift up the bottoms and remove the rings, then, using a spatula, carefully slide the corn off the bottoms directly onto serving plates or individual plates. Garnish with sweet pepper (if using).

Makes 8 servings.

CORN AND WILD RICE SAUTE

The idea for this flavorful concoction came from Christy Hill, one of my favorite restaurants on the north shore of Lake Tahoe. The mixture also makes a great stuffing for fowl.

CUT the kernels from the corn cobs as directed for Sauteed Corn on page 358, measure out 3 cups, and set aside.

IN a saute pan or skillet, combine the butter and oil and place over medium-high heat. When the butter is melted, add the garlic and cook for about 30 seconds. Stir in the corn, cooked wild rice, and tomatoes and cook, stirring frequently, until the corn is tender, about 4 minutes for young corn or for up to 8 minutes for older corn.

REMOVE from the heat, stir in the basil, season to taste with salt and pepper, and serve immediately.

Makes 6 servings.

About 6 medium-sized ears corn,
   preferably a sweet white variety
2 tablespoons unsalted butter
2 tablespoons extra-virgin olive oil
1 tablespoon minced garlic
2 cups cooked wild rice (page 364)
3 tablespoons minced drained
   sun-dried tomatoes packed in
   olive oil
1/3 cup chopped fresh basil
Salt
Freshly ground black pepper

361

SMOTHERED CAJUN CORN

About 12 medium-sized ears corn

6 tablespoons (¾ stick) unsalted
  butter

1 cup finely chopped yellow onion

2 tablespoons sugar

½ teaspoon salt, or to taste

Freshly ground black pepper

Ground cayenne

1½ cups peeled, seeded, drained, and
  chopped ripe or canned tomato

1½ cups Vegetable Stock (page 580),
  White Stock (page 578), or canned
  vegetable or reduced-sodium
  chicken broth

½ cup heavy (whipping) cream or
  canned evaporated milk

*It certainly isn't traditional, but this venerable Cajun side dish also
makes an excellent pasta sauce or pizza topping.*

CUT the kernels from the corn cobs as directed for Sauteed Corn
  on page 358, measure out 6 cups, and set aside.

IN a saute pan or heavy skillet, melt 2 tablespoons of the butter over
  medium-high heat. Add the onion and cook, stirring frequently,
  until soft but not browned, about 5 minutes. Stir in the reserved
  corn, sugar, salt, and pepper and cayenne to taste and cook,
  stirring frequently, until the corn begins to stick to the pan,
  about 10 minutes. Stir in the tomato and cook until the liquid
  evaporates, about 5 minutes longer. Add the stock or broth and
  bring to a boil, then adjust the heat to achieve a simmer and
  cook, stirring frequently, until most of the liquid is absorbed,
  about 15 minutes longer.

STIR the remaining 4 tablespoons butter and the cream or evaporated
  milk into the corn. Cook, stirring frequently, until most of the
  liquid is absorbed, about 5 minutes.

Makes 6 servings.

UPSIDE-DOWN CORN CAKE

On balmy summer nights at Lake Tahoe, my Southern roots are satisfied with a simple supper featuring this classic dish accompanied with a plate of sliced ripe tomatoes from the farmers' market and some green beans or fried okra.

Although I often prepare this down-home dish without the hot chile, it does contribute a bit of zing to the crisp-edged corn cake that forms in the smoking-hot skillet. Choose an iron or other heavy pan; nonstick coatings won't produce the essential crisp crust.

The cake is delicious plain or with Fresh Tomato Salsa (page 392) or a dollop of Crème Fraîche (page 591) or commercial crème fraîche.

¼ cup canola or other high-quality vegetable oil

About 8 medium-sized ears corn

1 tablespoon minced fresh hot chile or drained canned *chipotle* chile in *adobo* sauce, or to taste

⅓ cup all-purpose flour

Salt

Freshly ground black pepper

∽

PREHEAT an oven to 425° F.

IN a medium-sized cast-iron or other heavy ovenproof skillet, pour in the oil and place in the oven until sizzling hot but not yet smoking, about 25 minutes.

MEANWHILE, cut the kernels from the corn cobs as directed for Sauteed Corn on page 358, measure out 4 cups, and transfer to a bowl.

ADD the chile, flour, and salt and pepper to taste to the corn and mix well. Transfer the mixture to the hot oiled skillet, quickly smoothing the top to form an even layer; do not stir. Gently press the corn mixture down to compact it. Bake until the corn mixture forms a bottom crust, about 30 minutes.

USING a spatula, loosen the edges of the corn cake from the skillet. Invert a serving plate over the skillet and then invert the skillet and plate together, so the corn cake is on the plate. Lift off the skillet and serve the corn cake piping hot. Cut into wedges at the table.

Makes 6 servings.

COOKED WHOLE GRAINS

Whole Grains (see recipe introduction)

Brown Stock (page 576), Vegetable Stock (page 580), White Stock (page 578), or canned broth (see recipe introduction for type and use and see chart on page 366 for amount; all optional)

Salt (optional; see recipe introduction)

Unsalted butter or canola or other high-quality vegetable oil (optional)

This basic recipe can be used for all whole grains except sticky or glutinous rice (see page 368). Many grains also come in cracked, ground (grits), or flaked form and are usually cooked as a breakfast cereal; follow package directions for cooking these forms.

Rinsing the grains before cooking is advised for washing off the dust that collects from harvesting, drying, and storing, especially imported or bulk grains. Rinsing domestic enriched rice will also wash away the extra vitamins that have been added in a coating, but I often choose to rinse to achieve a fluffier cooked grain. Be certain to wash quinoa very thoroughly to remove the coating of saponin, a natural insect repellant secreted by the plant.

Dried grains can be cooked without soaking, although soaking whole hominy, oats, triticale, and wheat will decrease their cooking times by as much as one-half. Rice may also be soaked for more even cooking.

The exact amount of liquid and cooking time may vary with the size of grain variety, length of storage, altitude, and personal preference. Initially, use the measurements given, then adjust the amount of liquid and/or cooking time if necessary for future pots of the same grain.

When cooking amaranth, hominy, rye, triticale, or wheat, add salt after the grain is cooked, as salt prevents the absorption of liquid and causes these grains to toughen before they are tender. For added flavor, however, these grains can be cooked in unsalted stock (see pages 576–580) instead of water. Other grains can be cooked in salted water, canned reduced-sodium broth, or salted stock.

Grains cooked in water can be eaten immediately with milk or yogurt, sweeteners, or fruits as a breakfast cereal or snack. Cooked whole grains may be served as a side dish, plain or with a savory sauce. Or use them in stuffings, pilafs, puddings, casseroles, and other dishes. Cooked whole amaranth and teff form a sticky mass similar to cooked cornmeal or polenta and are not suitable for use in recipes that call for drier, separated grains, such as salads; use them as cereals or as you would polenta in any favorite recipe.

Cooked grains can be successfully refrigerated in covered containers for up to 1 week; reheat briefly in a microwave oven or with a little liquid in a saucepan over low heat.

SPREAD the grains out on a tray or other flat surface and carefully pick over by hand to remove any foreign bits or imperfect grains. To rinse the grains (see recipe introduction regarding enriched rice), place in a bowl, add cold water to cover, and stir vigorously with your fingertips to wash, then drain off the water through a fine-mesh strainer. Repeat if necessary until the water is clear.

SOAK hominy, oats, triticale, wheat, or rice if desired (see recipe introduction). To soak, place the washed grains in a bowl, add cold water to cover, and set aside to soak, about 1 hour for rice, or overnight for other grains. Drain just before cooking. If desired, reserve the soaking water to use as part of the cooking liquid.

IN a heavy saucepan, combine the grain with the stock or broth (if using) or water and add salt to taste (if using). Place over medium-high heat and bring to a boil. Stir the grain, cover tightly, reduce the heat to very low, and cook until the liquid is absorbed and the grains are tender (some grains will remain a bit chewy when fully cooked); see the chart on page 366 for approximate cooking times. If grains that require a long cooking time become too dry toward the end of cooking, add a little water.

IF cooking amaranth or teff, remove from the heat, stir well, and serve or use immediately, or pour into a dish to cool completely and use as you would polenta. If cooking other grains, remove from the heat, remove the lid, cover the pot with paper toweling, replace the lid, and let rest for the time indicated.

ALTERNATIVELY, for fluffier, separated grains, bring the liquid to a boil. Meanwhile, in a heavy saucepan, heat 2 teaspoons butter or oil per cup of grain over medium heat, add the grain, and cook, stirring continuously, until the grain is fragrant and well coated with the butter or oil, about 2 minutes. Stir in the boiling liquid and salt to taste (if using), cover tightly, reduce the heat to very low, and proceed with cooking as directed previously.

DRAIN off any liquid that remains in the pan after the grains are tender and rested. Season to taste with salt if desired. Using a fork, lift the grain from the bottom to fluff without breaking the tender grains. Serve or use as directed in recipes.

Each cup cooked whole grain makes 1 serving.

COOKING WHOLE GRAINS BY THE ABSORPTION METHOD

GRAIN *Per 1 cup*	LIQUID *Water, stock, or broth*	COOK TIME *Approximate, after adjusting boil to simmer*	REST TIME *Off the heat*	YIELD *Approximate*
AMARANTH	3 cups (unsalted)	25 minutes	None	2½ cups
BARLEY:				
HULLED	3 cups	1 hour	10 minutes	3½ cups
PEARLED	3 cups	30 minutes	10 minutes	3½ cups
BUCKWHEAT	2 cups	15 minutes	5 minutes	3 cups
HOMINY	4 cups (unsalted)	3 hours	10 minutes	3 cups
JOB'S TEARS	3 cups	40 minutes	10 minutes	2½ cups
MILLET	2 cups	15 minutes	10 minutes	4 cups
OATS	3 cups	1 hour	10 minutes	2½ cups
QUINOA	2 cups	12 to 15 minutes	5 minutes	3½ cups
RICE:				
WHITE	1½ cups*	17 minutes	10 minutes	3 cups
BROWN	2 cups	45 minutes	10 minutes	3 to 4 cups
RYE	3 cups (unsalted)	1 hour	10 minutes	3 cups
TEFF	3 cups	20 minutes	None	3 cups
TRITICALE	3 cups (unsalted)	1½ hours	5 minutes	3 cups
WHEAT:	3½ cups (unsalted)	1½ hours	10 minutes	3 cups
SPELT	4 cups (unsalted)	2 hours	10 minutes	3 cups
WILD RICE	4 cups	45 minutes	5 minutes	4 cups

If cooking more than 2 cups white rice, add only 1 cup liquid for each additional cup of grain.

Using a Rice Cooker

If you cook rice frequently and have room for another kitchen appliance, you might invest in an electric rice cooker, which consistently produces perfect rice. It also does a fine job with buckwheat, millet, and quinoa. Use the amount of liquid specified in the accompanying chart and allow the recommended resting time after the cooker shuts itself off.

STICKY RICE

White, brown, or black glutinous rice

Also called glutinous, sweet, or waxy rice, sticky rice is the daily grain of preference in Laos and northeast Thailand. Elsewhere in Southeast Asia and southern China it is generally used to make sweets or snacks, savory stuffings, and ceremonial foods. The use of the word sticky *refers to the fact that the kernels of these rice varieties cling together naturally during cooking. They are stronger in flavor than other varieties as well. Although called* sweet, *the rice is not distinctively sweeter than common indica rice; the name comes from its use in making sweet dishes.*

Plan ahead when cooking sticky rice, as the grains must be soaked prior to cooking. Cooking time will vary according to the length of soaking.

WASH and drain the rice as directed on page 365. Place in a bowl, add enough fresh water to cover completely, and let soak for at least 4 hours or, preferably, overnight.

TO prepare for steaming, position a rack in a wok or pot with a tight-fitting lid that will be large enough to hold a steamer basket or colander. Pour in water to a level just below the steaming rack. Place the wok or pot over high heat and bring the water to a boil, then adjust the heat to achieve a simmer.

IF using a steamer basket or colander with holes that are large enough to allow the rice to fall through, line the steamer basket or colander with several layers of moistened cheesecloth or a piece of banana leaf. Drain the rice and spread it evenly in the prepared container. Transfer to the steamer rack over the simmering water, making sure that the rice does not come in direct contact with the water. Cover the wok or pot with the lid and steam until the rice is tender, 25 to 35 minutes for white rice or about 1 hour for brown or black rice. Adjust the heat to maintain simmering water throughout cooking, adding boiling water if needed to maintain water level. For softer rice, sprinkle about ¼ cup water over the top of the rice 2 or 3 times during steaming.

Each cup uncooked rice yields about 2 cups cooked for 2 servings.

VARIATIONS

Coconut Sticky Rice. Soak 2 cups rice as directed in the recipe. Drain and transfer to a pot. Stir in 3 cups Fresh Coconut Milk (page 562) or high-quality commercial coconut milk and 1 cup water. Place over high heat and bring to a boil, then reduce the heat to very low, cover tightly, and cook until the rice is tender and the liquid has evaporated, about 15 minutes for white rice or 35 to 45 minutes for brown or black rice. Remove from the heat and let stand, covered, for 15 minutes before serving.

Sweet Sticky Rice. Cook as directed in the recipe, then finish as directed for Thai Sticky Rice with Mangoes on page 435.

BULGUR

Bulgur

Boiling Brown Stock (page 576),
Vegetable Stock (page 580), White
Stock (page 578), canned broth,
or water

Bulgur, a popular food of the Middle East and eastern Europe, is actually whole wheat that has been hulled, cleaned, steamed, and dried. It requires no cooking, but needs only to be reconstituted in hot liquid before using in recipes.

WASH and drain the bulgur as directed on page 365 and place in a bowl.

ADD 3 cups boiling liquid per 1 cup bulgur used, stir well, and let stand until the grains are tender yet firm to the bite, about 15 minutes for fine granules, about 30 minutes for medium granules, about 1 hour for coarse granules, or about 1½ hours for whole grains.

LINE a colander or strainer with dampened cheesecloth. Drain the bulgur through the cheesecloth, then gather the cheesecloth into a bag and gently squeeze out excess liquid. Transfer the bulgur to a bowl and, using a fork, lift the bulgur from the bottom to fluff without breaking the tender grains. Serve as a side dish or use as directed in recipes.

**Each cup uncooked bulgur yields about 3 cups cooked for
3 servings.**

COUSCOUS

Made from hard durum wheat, or semolina, this "pasta" from North Africa resembles tiny round grains and is used like a grain.

Traditionally, couscous is alternately steamed and dried several times until very airy in a special two-tiered pot (couscousière) over a simmering stew or salted water. Most of the couscous available in North America is the parboiled quick-cooking variety and merely needs to be soaked in boiling liquid until softened. Although it lacks the airy texture and flavor of authentic couscous, it makes a perfectly reasonable substitute. It tastes best when reconstituted in stock or broth.

The following method differs slightly from package directions.

FOR each 1 cup couscous used, in a saucepan, combine 1½ cups stock or broth (if using) or water and 1 tablespoon butter. Place over medium-high heat and bring to a boil. Add the couscous and salt and pepper to taste and quickly stir to mix well. Tightly cover and let stand until the liquid is absorbed, about 10 minutes.

USING a fork, lift the couscous from the bottom to fluff without breaking the tender granules. Serve or use as directed in recipes.

Each cup uncooked couscous yields about 3 cups cooked for 3 servings.

Quick-cooking couscous

Brown Stock (page 576), Vegetable Stock (page 580), White Stock (page 578), or canned broth (all optional)

Unsalted butter

Salt

Freshly ground black pepper

PERSIAN DILLED RICE WITH LIMA BEANS ~ *POLO* ~

2 cups long-grain white rice,
preferably basmati

Salt

1½ cups shelled fresh small lima
beans, or 1 package (10 ounces)
thawed frozen lima beans

1 cup (2 sticks) unsalted butter,
melted

¼ cup chopped fresh dill, or
2 tablespoons crumbled dried dill

Minced fresh dill for garnish

Fresh dill sprigs for garnish

The Iranians are true rice connoisseurs, devoting much time and attention to its preparation, and this butter-rich presentation is a delicious example of their centuries-old tradition of teaming rice with beans. During cooking, a highly prized, crisp crust, known as dig, *forms on the bottom of the pot.*

For variety, stir cooked chicken, beef, or lamb into the rice before steaming.

WASH and drain the rice as directed on page 365.

IN a large bowl, combine the rice with enough cold water to cover by 1 inch. Stir in 1 tablespoon salt, cover loosely, and let stand overnight.

ON the day of serving, bring a pot of water to a boil over high heat and ready a bowl of iced water. When the water boils, add the lima beans, cover partially, and reduce the heat to maintain a simmer. Cook, stirring occasionally, until the beans are tender, about 25 minutes. Quickly drain and transfer the beans to the iced water to halt cooking, then drain again and set aside.

TRANSFER the rice and soaking water to a large pot. Add 3 quarts cold water and place over high heat. Bring to a boil and cook for 1 minute. Drain immediately through a fine-mesh strainer.

IN a large, heavy pot, pour in just enough of the butter to cover the bottom of the pot. Spread about 1 cup of the rice in the pot.

IN a bowl, combine the remaining rice, the drained beans, chopped or crumbled dill, and salt to taste and mix well. Spoon the mixture on top of the layer of rice in the pot and shape into a cone. Make a slight indention in the top of the rice and bean mixture and pour the remaining butter over. Cover the pot with a cloth kitchen towel to catch and hold the steam as it rises, then cover with a lid and fold the corners of the towel up on top of the lid. Place the pot over medium-low heat for 15 minutes, then reduce the heat to very low and cook until the rice is tender, about 35 minutes. Remove from the heat and set aside for about 5 minutes to cool.

TO serve, spoon the warm rice and beans onto a serving platter, then scrape out pieces of the golden, crisp crust from the bottom of the pot and arrange it over the rice and beans. Sprinkle with minced dill and garnish with dill sprigs.

Makes 8 servings.

CHINESE FRIED RICE

3 cups cooked long-grain white rice
    (page 364)

¼ cup sesame seed

About 3 tablespoons canola or other
    high-quality vegetable oil

3 eggs, beaten

½ cup diagonally cut snow peas

1 cup diced Chinese barbecued pork
    (char siu), baked ham, or cooked
    chicken

1 tablespoon soy sauce, or to taste

1 teaspoon oyster sauce, or to taste

2 tablespoons thinly sliced green
    onion, including green tops

Start with leftover rice or cook and cool a fresh pot, then use this basic recipe as a guide to vary the finished dish by substituting ingredients and seasonings according to whim or what's on hand.

USING your fingers, break up the clumps of cold rice into separate grains and set aside.

TOAST the sesame seed as directed on page 553 and set aside.

PLACE a wok, large saute pan, or large, heavy skillet over high heat. When the pan is hot, add 1 tablespoon of the oil and swirl to coat the pan. When the oil is hot but not yet smoking, add the beaten eggs. They will immediately set up on the bottom. Slide the solid part to one side to allow the uncooked portion to spread onto the pan and cook. When all the egg has set but is still moist, quickly transfer it to a small bowl and break it up with a fork or slice into thin strips and set aside.

RETURN the pan to the heat, pour in another tablespoon of oil, and swirl to coat the pan. When the oil is hot but not yet smoking, add the snow peas and stir-fry, moving the pan off and on the heat as necessary to prevent scorching, until the snow peas are crisp-tender, about 2 minutes. Add the reserved rice, the meat, soy sauce, and oyster sauce and stir-fry until all the rice grains are coated, 2 to 3 minutes longer. Add the green onion and reserved cooked egg and stir-fry just long enough to heat through. Immediately turn out onto a serving platter, sprinkle with the toasted sesame seed, and serve hot.

Makes 4 servings.

WILD RICE CUSTARDS

Delicious with rich meaty stews, game dishes, or roasted meats.

COOK the wild rice as directed on page 364. Transfer the cooked rice to a bowl and set aside.

IN a saute pan or skillet, melt the butter over medium heat. Add the onion and mushrooms and cook, stirring frequently, until soft, about 8 minutes. Add to the rice, stir in the parsley and cheese, and set aside.

PREHEAT an oven to 350° F. Using a pastry brush, generously grease six 6-ounce custard cups with butter or shortening. Dust generously with flour, shaking the cups to coat all over, then invert and tap out excess flour. Set aside.

IN a small saucepan, combine the cream or half-and-half with the grated or minced orange zest and place over low heat until warm.

IN a bowl, lightly beat together the egg yolks and eggs. Pour the warm cream through a fine-mesh strainer into the eggs and whisk together; discard the zest. Season to taste with salt and pepper. Equally distribute the rice mixture among the prepared cups, loosely filling each cup about three-fourths full. Then evenly divide the cream mixture among the cups.

PLACE the cups on a rack set in a large, deep baking pan, transfer to the oven, and pour enough hot (not boiling) water into the baking pan to reach about halfway up the sides of the cups. Place a sheet of aluminum foil over the pan to cover the tops of the custards loosely. Bake until a knife inserted into the center of the custards comes out clean, about 45 minutes.

REMOVE the custard cups from the water bath to a wire rack to cool for a few minutes.

TO serve, run a thin, flexible knife blade around the inside edges of a cup. Invert a serving plate over the cup, invert the plate and cup together, and carefully lift off the cup. Repeat with the remaining custards. Garnish each custard with slivered orange zest and serve immediately.

Makes 6 servings.

1 cup wild rice

1 tablespoon unsalted butter

¾ cup finely chopped yellow onion

3 ounces flavorful fresh mushrooms such as chanterelle, morel, or portobello, sliced

2 tablespoons minced fresh flat-leaf parsley

¼ cup freshly grated Parmesan cheese (about 1 ounce), preferably Parmigiano-Reggiano

Unsalted butter or solid vegetable shortening, at room temperature, for greasing

All-purpose flour for dusting

2¼ cups heavy (whipping) cream, light cream, or half-and-half

1 tablespoon grated or minced fresh orange zest

4 egg yolks

2 eggs

About 1 teaspoon salt

About ½ teaspoon freshly ground white pepper

Thinly slivered fresh orange zest for garnish

PEANUTTY COLESLAW

1 head cabbage (about 1½ pounds)

1 cup Mayonnaise (page 388) or high-quality commercial mayonnaise

⅓ cup Asian sesame oil

⅓ cup smooth peanut butter, at room temperature

3 tablespoons unseasoned rice vinegar or white wine vinegar

2 tablespoons freshly squeezed lemon juice

1 tablespoon soy sauce

Salt

Freshly ground black pepper

Hot chile oil

1 tablespoon unsalted butter

1 cup unsalted dry-roasted peanuts

Outstanding with barbecued or grilled meats, especially baby back ribs, this slaw tastes best when prepared a few hours before serving. If made ahead and refrigerated, however, be sure to bring it back to room temperature before serving.

Any variety of green cabbage may be used alone or combined with different types for diversity in color and flavor. I like to serve the slaw nestled inside a collar made from the leaves of savoy cabbage or colorful edible kale.

DISCARD any wilted outer leaves of the cabbage. Rinse the head under cold running water. Using a food processor or a sharp knife, shred the cabbage and place in a large bowl.

IN a food processor or blender, combine the mayonnaise, sesame oil, peanut butter, vinegar, lemon juice, and soy sauce and blend well. Season to taste with salt, pepper, and chile oil. Pour the mixture over the cabbage and toss thoroughly. Cover and let stand at room temperature for about 2 hours, or cover tightly, refrigerate for up to 24 hours, and return the coleslaw to room temperature before serving.

IN a skillet, melt the butter over low heat. Add the peanuts and cook, stirring frequently, until the peanuts are golden brown and fragrant, about 3 minutes; watch carefully to prevent burning. Transfer to paper toweling to drain and cool.

JUST before serving, stir in most of the peanuts, saving a few to sprinkle over the top.

Makes 8 servings.

NEW-POTATO SALAD IN
RED ONION DRESSING

This simple potato salad is exceptionally good with summer barbecue.
It is also delicious tossed with Mustard Vinaigrette (page 566) instead
of the mayonnaise dressing.

PLACE the potatoes in a saucepan and add water to cover by about
2 inches, then remove the potatoes. Bring the water to a boil
over medium-high heat, return the potatoes, and cook until
just tender when pierced with a wooden skewer or small, sharp
knife, 10 to 20 minutes, depending on the size of the potatoes;
avoid overcooking. Drain well, then return the potatoes to the
pan, place over the heat, and shake the pan until excess moisture
evaporates and the potatoes are dry to the touch.

LEAVE potatoes whole or cut into halves, quarters, or slices.
Transfer to a bowl and season to taste with salt and pepper.
Let cool slightly before dressing.

IN a bowl, combine the mayonnaise, sour cream or yogurt, onion,
and minced dill or parsley and blend well. Pour over the warm
potatoes and toss gently to mix thoroughly. Set aside to cool to
room temperature for about 30 minutes before serving, or cover
tightly, refrigerate for several hours, and return almost to room
temperature before serving.

TO serve, transfer to a serving bowl and garnish with herb sprigs.

Makes 6 servings.

2 pounds small new potatoes

Salt

Freshly ground black pepper

¾ cup Mayonnaise (page 388) or
high-quality commercial
mayonnaise

¾ cup sour cream or plain yogurt

½ cup finely chopped red onion

½ cup minced fresh dill or flat-leaf
parsley

Fresh dill or flat-leaf parsley sprigs
for garnish

ALL-AMERICAN POTATO SALAD

2 pounds boiling potatoes

1 cup Mayonnaise (page 388) or high-quality commercial mayonnaise

1 tablespoon Dijon mustard

2 tablespoons freshly squeezed lemon juice or white wine vinegar, or to taste

3 Hard-Cooked Eggs (page 28), chopped

½ cup minced white or yellow onion

½ cup finely chopped Bread-and-Butter Pickles (page 404) or high-quality commercial bread-and-butter pickles, or ½ cup sweet pickle relish

Salt

Freshly ground black pepper

Crispy Bacon Bits (page 553; optional)

It's hard to beat this simple classic. Vary it according to individual tastes and what is on hand — chopped or minced olives, celery, sweet pepper, green onion, or fresh herbs.

PLACE the potatoes in a saucepan and add water to cover by about 2 inches, then remove the potatoes. Bring the water to a boil over medium-high heat, return the potatoes, and cook until just tender when pierced with a wooden skewer or small, sharp knife, 15 to 45 minutes, depending on size. Drain well, then return the potatoes to the pan, place over the heat, and shake the pan until excess moisture evaporates and the potatoes are dry to the touch.

AS soon as the potatoes are cool enough to handle, peel them, cut into small cubes or thin slices of uniform size, and place in a large bowl.

IN a bowl, combine the mayonnaise, mustard, and lemon juice or vinegar and whisk to blend well. Gently toss enough of the dressing into the warm potatoes to coat completely. Stir in the eggs, onion, pickles or relish, and more dressing if needed. Season to taste with salt and pepper and set aside to cool to room temperature for about 30 minutes, or cover tightly, refrigerate for up to several hours, and return almost to room temperature before serving.

TO serve, transfer to a serving bowl or plate and sprinkle with the bacon (if using).

Makes 6 servings.

ITALIAN POTATO AND GREEN BEAN SALAD ~ *INSALATA DI PATATA E FAGIOLINO* ~

It is best to make this salad just before it is served, allowing only enough time for the vegetables to cool to room temperature and then stand for several minutes. If made too far in advance, the beans will turn dark and the potatoes will become mushy. Serve it alongside or following a second course of meat, poultry, or fish. It also makes a good antipasto.

BLANCH the beans as directed on page 338. Place in a bowl and set aside.

PLACE the potatoes in a saucepan and add water to cover by 2 inches, then remove the potatoes. Bring the water to a boil over medium-high heat, return the potatoes, and cook until just tender when pierced with a wooden skewer or small, sharp knife, 20 to 25 minutes; avoid overcooking. Drain well, then return the potatoes to the pan, place over the heat, and shake the pan until excess moisture evaporates and the potatoes are dry to the touch. Remove the potatoes and set aside to cool slightly.

WHEN the potatoes are cool enough to handle, peel them and cut crosswise into ¼-inch-thick slices. Arrange the slices in a circle around the edge of a serving plate, slightly overlapping them. Sprinkle with vinegar, salt, and pepper to taste and let stand for about 5 minutes.

ADD the onion to the beans and toss to mix. Sprinkle with vinegar, salt, and pepper to taste and toss well, then drizzle with enough olive oil to coat the beans lightly and toss again. Mound the beans in the center of the potato platter. Sprinkle the minced herb(s) and the garlic (if using) over the potatoes and beans. Drizzle the potatoes generously with olive oil and let stand for about 10 minutes before serving.

Makes 4 servings.

8 ounces young green beans

1 pound medium-sized boiling potatoes

Red wine vinegar for sprinkling

Salt

Freshly ground black pepper

¼ cup slivered red onion

Extra-virgin olive oil for drizzling

1 to 2 tablespoon(s) minced fresh basil, chives, oregano, or flat-leaf parsley, one type or a combination

½ teaspoon minced garlic (optional)

GREEN RICE SALAD

1 cup long-grain brown rice

1 cup long-grain white rice

Balsamic Vinaigrette (page 565)

3 tablespoons pine nuts

½ cup finely chopped green onion,
including green tops

1 to 1½ cups minced mixed fresh
herbs such as basil, cilantro
(coriander), mint, flat-leaf parsley,
tarragon, and watercress

½ cup freshly shredded white
Cheddar cheese (about 1½ ounces)

1 cup cooked fresh green (English)
peas (page 338) or thawed frozen
petite green peas

Shredded romaine lettuce

Sprigs of same fresh herbs as above
for garnish

Pesticide-free edible flowers such as
tiny marigold, nasturtium, or wild
mustard (optional)

*Lots of fresh herbs are the secret to this glorious salad that was first
served to me by the late garden master Stephen Marcus. Select herbs in
whatever combination you find appealing.*

IN separate pots, cook the brown and white rices as directed on
page 364.

MEANWHILE, prepare the Balsamic Vinaigrette as directed and set
aside. Toast the pine nuts as directed on page 553 and set aside.

IN a large bowl, combine the cooked brown and white rice, fluff
with a fork, and cool slightly. Add about half of the vinaigrette
and fluff frequently until the rice cools completely.

WHEN the rice is cooled, add the green onion, minced herbs,
cheese, peas, and the remaining vinaigrette. Toss well and let
stand for about 30 minutes for the flavors to blend.

TO serve, arrange a bed of shredded lettuce on a serving platter,
then mound the rice salad on top. Sprinkle with the toasted
pine nuts and garnish with herb sprigs and flowers (if using).

Makes 6 to 8 servings.

COUSCOUS AND GARBANZO SALAD

Although Moroccan cooks would never turn their beloved couscous into a salad, the results of this preparation capture the essence of North African flavors.

For a heartier nonvegetarian salad that can be served as a main dish, poach 6 boned and skinned chicken breast halves in barely simmering chicken stock or canned reduced-sodium broth until just opaque throughout, about 12 minutes. Cool and shred the chicken, then stir it into the salad.

TO make the dressing, in a small bowl, combine all of the dressing ingredients and whisk to blend well. Set aside.

PREPARE the couscous as directed on page 371 and set aside to cool.

DRAIN the beans and transfer to a large bowl. Add the couscous, currants, sweet pepper, onion, mint, and parsley and mix well. Add the dressing and toss to distribute. Cover and let stand at room temperature for about 1 hour, or cover tightly, refrigerate for up to overnight, and return to room temperature before serving.

TOAST the pine nuts as directed on page 553 and set aside.

MOUND the salad on a serving dish or individual plates, sprinkle with the pine nuts, and garnish with tomato wedges.

Makes 12 servings.

DRESSING

½ cup extra-virgin olive oil

½ cup freshly squeezed lemon juice

1 teaspoon minced garlic

½ teaspoon ground cumin

Hot sauce, preferably North African *harissa*, to taste

Salt to taste

Freshly ground black pepper to taste

2 cups quick-cooking couscous

3 cups cooked dried or canned garbanzo beans (see page 340)

⅔ cup dried currants, soaked in hot water until plumped, then drained

⅔ cup finely chopped red sweet pepper

½ cup sliced green onion, including green tops

½ cup chopped fresh mint

½ cup chopped fresh flat-leaf parsley

½ cup pine nuts

Ripe tomato slices cut into small wedge-shaped pieces for garnish

MIXED GRAIN AND HERB TABBOULEH

¼ cup bulgur

½ cup brown rice

½ cup millet

¾ cup minced fresh flat-leaf parsley

¾ cup minced mixed fresh herbs
such as basil, mint, oregano, and
summer savory

½ cup minced green onion, including
green tops

1 cup peeled, seeded, drained, and
chopped ripe tomato

¼ cup freshly squeezed lemon juice,
or more if needed

¼ cup fruity olive oil, preferably
extra-virgin

Salt

Freshly ground black pepper

Pomegranate seeds for garnish
(optional)

*Middle Eastern tabbouleh is usually made with bulgur and fresh
parsley. Here is a change-of-pace version made with several grains
and a bouquet of fresh herbs. For a quick-and-easy variation, increase
the bulgur to 1 cup and omit the rice and millet. In any case, be sure
to use only fresh herbs, never dried.*

PREPARE the bulgur as directed on page 370.

COOK the brown rice and millet separately as directed on page
364, using the alternative method for fluffier, separated
grains. Let each cool to room temperature.

IN a large bowl, combine the drained bulgur, cooled rice and millet,
herbs, onion, tomato, lemon juice, and oil. Season to taste with
salt and pepper and mix well.

TO serve, transfer to a serving bowl or platter and sprinkle with
pomegranate seeds (if using).

Makes 6 servings.

BUCKWHEAT NOODLES WITH ASPARAGUS IN SESAME DRESSING

Japanese buckwheat noodles team up with fresh young asparagus in a simple traditional salad dressing made with dashi, a fish-and-kelp-based stock available in instant form in Japanese markets.

TOAST the sesame seed as directed on page 553 and set aside.

IN a large pot, bring 4 quarts water to a rapid boil over high heat. Drop in the noodles and cook, stirring frequently, until tender but still very firm to the bite. Drain well, then transfer to a large bowl.

IN a blender or food processor combine about half of the toasted sesame seed, the soy sauce, stock or broth, and sugar. Blend well, pour over the warm noodles, and set aside to cool to room temperature, occasionally stirring the noodles to coat thoroughly.

DISCARD the tough ends from the asparagus, then cut the spears on the diagonal into pieces about 1 inch long.

IN a saucepan, pour in water to a depth of 2 inches, place over medium-high heat, and bring to a boil. Ready a bowl of iced water. When the water boils, add the asparagus and cook just until crisp-tender, 2 to 3 minutes. Plunge immediately into the iced water to halt cooking, then drain well.

ADD the cooled asparagus and the green onions to the noodles and toss well. Mound on a serving platter or transfer to a serving bowl. Sprinkle with the remaining sesame seed and garnish with *shiso* leaves (if using). Serve at room temperature.

Makes 10 to 12 servings.

3 tablespoons sesame seed

1 pound dried Japanese buckwheat noodles *(soba)*

1 cup soy sauce

¼ cup reconstituted dashi stock (see package directions), White Stock (page 578) made with chicken, or canned reduced-sodium chicken broth

1 tablespoon sugar

1 pound asparagus

6 green onions, including green tops, cut on the diagonal into ½-inch lengths

Fresh *shiso* (minty Japanese herb) leaves for garnish (optional)

SAFFRON PASTINA WITH CURRANTS, PINE NUTS, AND MINT

SAFFRON DRESSING

½ teaspoon crumbled saffron threads

½ cup extra-virgin olive oil

1 teaspoon minced garlic

3 tablespoons freshly squeezed lemon juice

¼ teaspoon ground cumin

2 teaspoons ground turmeric

1 teaspoon sugar

Salt

Freshly ground black pepper

1 tablespoon salt

1 pound tiny pasta (*pastina*)

⅔ cup pine nuts

½ cup dried currants, soaked in hot water until plumped, then drained

¼ cup chopped fresh mint

¼ cup chopped fresh flat-leaf parsley

3 tablespoons chopped fresh coriander (cilantro)

Orange flower water (available where bar mixes are sold)

Fresh mint sprigs or leaves for garnish

Pomegranate seeds for garnish (optional)

Tiny pastina, *most often used in soups, approximates North African couscous in this cold side dish.*

TO make the Saffron Dressing, in a small bowl, combine the saffron and oil and let stand for about 15 minutes to soften the saffron. Add the garlic, lemon juice, cumin, turmeric, sugar, and salt and pepper to taste. Mix well and set aside.

IN a large pot, bring 4 quarts water to a rapid boil over high heat, then stir in the 1 tablespoon salt. Drop in the *pastina* and cook, stirring frequently, until tender but still very firm to the bite. Drain well, then transfer to a large bowl. Add the dressing, stir to mix well, and set aside to cool to room temperature, occasionally stirring the *pastina* to coat thoroughly.

TOAST the pine nuts as directed on page 553.

ADD the pine nuts, drained currants, and chopped mint, parsley, and cilantro to the *pastina* and stir to mix well.

TO serve, transfer to a serving bowl or platter, sprinkle lightly with orange flower water, and garnish with mint and pomegranate seeds (if using). Serve at room temperature.

Makes 10 to 12 servings.

SPICY BLACK BEAN AND CORN SALAD

Southwestern flavors meld in this robust composition, which I sometimes top with strips of grilled fish fillet or chicken breast or slices of grilled or roasted pork tenderloin. For extra crunch, scatter crushed tortilla chips over the top.

To prepare this salad ahead of time, combine the beans, corn, onions, chopped cilantro, and dressing, then cover and refrigerate for up to overnight; bring to room temperature before adding the tomatoes, garnishing, and serving.

COOK the Mexicali or Southwestern Beans as directed and set aside to cool.

PREPARE the Smoked Chile Vinaigrette as directed and set aside.

IF using fresh corn, cut the kernels from the cobs as directed for Sauteed Corn on page 358, measure out 3 cups, and set aside. If using thawed or canned corn, reserve for later use.

MEASURE out 4 cups of the cooked beans, drain well, and transfer to a large bowl. (Save the remaining beans for another use.) Add the corn, red onion, green onion, chopped cilantro, and the vinaigrette and toss well. Add the tomato and toss gently. Season to taste with salt.

TO serve, transfer to a serving bowl, stick tortilla chips around the edges, and garnish with cilantro sprigs. Serve at room temperature.

Makes 8 servings.

Mexicali Beans (page 348) or
  Southwestern Beans (page 351)
  made with black (turtle) beans
Smoked Chile Vinaigrette (page 567)
About 6 medium-sized ears corn,
  or 3 cups thawed frozen or
  drained canned corn kernels
½ cup minced red onion
½ cup minced green onion,
  including green tops
½ cup chopped fresh cilantro
  (coriander)
2 cups peeled, seeded, drained, and
  chopped ripe tomato or halved
  cherry tomatoes
Salt
Tortilla chips for garnish
Fresh cilantro (coriander) sprigs for
  garnish

Condiments

HERE are sauces from around the world that add zest to a variety of dishes. Choose French-style mayonnaise and flavored butter variations, Mexican-inspired salsas, Mediterranean *tapénade* and pesto, and Southeast Asian dipping sauces to complement a wide variety of foods.

Pickles and relishes made from various fruits and vegetables add crunch and a touch of piquancy to mealtimes with their balanced blends of sweet, sour, and salty.

OLD-FASHIONED TARTAR SAUCE

Some people rate this standby as indispensible with fish. Freshly made, it beats any bottled version that I've tried.

IN a small bowl, combine all of the ingredients and mix well. Cover and refrigerate for at least 1 hour or for up to 2 days. Return almost to room temperature before serving; whisk to blend if the sauce separates.

Makes about 1½ cups for 6 servings.

1 cup Mayonnaise (page 388) or high-quality commercial mayonnaise

½ cup minced dill pickle

2 tablespoons minced green onion, including green tops

2 tablespoons minced fresh flat-leaf parsley

2 teaspoons drained small capers, minced

1 tablespoon freshly squeezed lemon juice

1 teaspoon Worcestershire sauce

½ teaspoon salt, or to taste

¼ teaspoon freshly ground black pepper, or to taste

⅛ teaspoon ground cayenne, or to taste

DILLED MUSTARD SAUCE

Although this sauce is typically served with Scandinavian gravlax (page 62), it also complements baked ham, smoked turkey, and grilled fish or sausages and makes a unique sandwich spread.

IN a food processor or blender, combine the prepared mustard, brown sugar, vinegar or lemon juice, and dry mustard and blend well. With the machine running, very slowly drizzle in the oil and blend until thickened and emulsified. Stir in the minced dill and season to taste with salt and pepper. (At this point, the sauce can be covered and refrigerated for up to several hours; return to room temperature before using.)

Makes about 1½ cups for 12 servings.

½ cup prepared Dijon mustard

⅓ cup firmly packed light brown sugar

¼ cup white wine vinegar or freshly squeezed lemon juice

2 teaspoons dry mustard

⅔ cup canola or other high-quality vegetable oil

2 tablespoons minced fresh dill

Salt

Freshly ground black pepper

MAYONNAISE

1 whole egg, at room temperature

1 egg yolk, at room temperature

1 tablespoon freshly squeezed lemon
   juice, or more if needed

1 teaspoon Dijon mustard

Salt

Freshly ground white pepper

1 cup canola or other high-quality
   vegetable oil

I tend to agree with whoever first described mayonnaise as "fat at its finest." And since food processors or blenders allow us to make foolproof mayonnaise in a flash, there's no reason not to have homemade on hand. For variety, try some of the variations that follow.

IN a food processor or blender, combine the egg, egg yolk, 1 tablespoon lemon juice, mustard, ½ teaspoon salt, and ¼ teaspoon pepper and blend for a few seconds. With the machine running, gradually add the oil in a slow, steady trickle and blend until the mixture is thick and creamy. Turn the machine off.

WITH a rubber or plastic spatula, scrape down any oil from the sides of the container and blend into the mayonnaise. Taste and add more lemon juice, salt, and pepper if needed. Use immediately or transfer to a covered container and refrigerate for up to 2 days.

Makes about 1¼ cups.

MAYONNAISE VARIATIONS

Garlic Mayonnaise. Add 1 tablespoon coarsely chopped garlic or several cloves of Roasted Garlic (page 551) when blending the eggs.

Herbed Mayonnaise. Stir ½ to 1 cup minced fresh herbs into the completed mayonnaise. Use only one herb or a complementary combination. Basil, dill, and tarragon impart their unique flavors and should be used alone or in combination with milder herbs such as chervil or flat-leaf parsley.

Italian *Maionese*. Use another egg yolk in place of the whole egg. Omit the mustard and substitute extra-virgin olive oil for the vegetable oil.

Provençal *Aïoli*. Omit the mustard. Add 2 tablespoons coarsely chopped garlic when blending the eggs. Use black pepper instead of the white.

Red-Hot Chile Mayonnaise. Add ½ cup chopped roasted red sweet pepper (see page 552) and 1 teaspoon minced canned *chipotle* chile in *adobo* sauce, or to taste, when blending the eggs.

Sesame Mayonnaise. Add 2 tablespoons soy sauce when blending the eggs. Substitute 3 tablespoons Asian sesame oil for 3 tablespoons of the vegetable oil and season to taste with hot chile oil.

Spicy Mayonnaise. Add 1 teaspoon chopped canned *chipotle* chile in *adobo* sauce, or to taste, when blending the eggs.

Tangy Mayonnaise. Combine equal parts finished mayonnaise and sour cream.

Tomato Mayonnaise. Coarsely chop about 6 drained sun-dried tomatoes packed in olive oil, then add when blending the eggs.

Truffled Mayonnaise. Stir as much minced black or white truffle, preferably fresh, into the finished mayonnaise as your taste and budget allow.

RÉMOULADE

⅓ cup Mayonnaise (page 388) or
high-quality commercial
mayonnaise

¼ cup Creole or Dijon mustard

¼ cup canola or other high-quality
vegetable oil

1 tablespoon freshly squeezed lemon
juice or apple cider vinegar

1 tablespoon prepared horseradish

2 tablespoons minced fresh flat-leaf
parsley

1½ teaspoons minced fresh tarragon

1½ teaspoons minced gherkin
(cornichon)

1½ teaspoons drained small capers,
chopped

½ teaspoon minced garlic

2 flat anchovy fillets, rinsed, patted
dry, and minced

1 tablespoon paprika

Salt

Freshly ground black pepper

Louisiana hot sauce

*This wonderful French sauce, adapted by the Creoles of New Orleans, is
traditionally served with cold fish, shellfish, or meats.*

IN a small bowl, combine the mayonnaise, mustard, oil, lemon juice
or vinegar, and horseradish and blend well. Stir in the parsley,
tarragon, gherkin, capers, garlic, anchovy, and paprika. Season
to taste with salt, pepper, and hot sauce. Cover and refrigerate
for at least 2 hours before serving or for up to 4 days.

Makes about 1¼ cups for 4 servings.

PROVENÇAL RED GARLIC SAUCE ~ *ROUILLE* ~

I enjoy the color and sweetness that the roasted peppers add to my version of this sauce that is stirred into bouillabaisse or other fish soups. It also makes a tasty condiment for grilled foods. If making to serve with a fish soup, use some of the liquid from the soup in place of the stock or broth.

ROAST the peppers as directed on page 552.

IF roasted whole, cut the peppers in half lengthwise and remove and discard the stems, seeds, and membranes. Coarsely chop the peppers and transfer to a food processor, blender, or mortar. Add the bread crumbs, stock or broth, garlic, and oil and blend or grind with a pestle to a thick paste. If the sauce is too thick, add a little more stock or broth or oil. Season to taste with salt and pepper and a generous amount of cayenne; the finished sauce should be fiery.

Makes about 2 cups for 8 servings.

2 red sweet peppers

¾ cup fine fresh bread crumbs, made from French bread with crust removed

About ¼ cup Fish Stock (page 575) or liquid from fish soup, or 2 tablespoons canned reduced-sodium chicken broth diluted with 2 tablespoons water

2 teaspoons chopped garlic

2 tablespoons fruity olive oil, preferably extra-virgin

Salt

Freshly ground black pepper

Ground cayenne

FRESH TOMATO SALSA

2 cups peeled, seeded, and chopped
ripe tomato, or 2 cups halved or
quartered cherry tomatoes

¼ cup finely chopped red, white,
or yellow onion, or ½ cup
chopped green onion

1 teaspoon minced garlic

2 tablespoons minced fresh hot
chile, or to taste

¼ cup minced fresh cilantro
(coriander)

2 teaspoons freshly squeezed lime
juice

Salt

*Start with flavorful garden ripe tomatoes and vary the other components
to suit your taste.*

IN a bowl, combine all of the ingredients, including salt to taste. Set
aside for about 15 minutes for flavors to blend.

JUST before serving, drain the salsa and transfer to a serving bowl.

Makes about 2 cups for 6 servings.

PINEAPPLE SALSA

1 small- to medium-sized pineapple,
peeled and cored

¾ cup minced red onion

¼ cup finely chopped fresh cilantro
(coriander) and/or mint

1 tablespoon unseasoned rice vinegar
or white wine vinegar

½ teaspoon ground cayenne, or to
taste

Salt

*This spicy, sweet combination is excellent with grilled fish, chicken,
or pork.*

COARSELY chop the pineapple and transfer to a colander set over
a bowl or in a sink to drain for about 5 minutes.

IN a bowl, combine the drained pineapple, onion, cilantro and/or
mint, vinegar, cayenne, and salt to taste. Stir to combine,
cover, and chill for about 1 hour for the flavors to blend.

JUST before serving, drain the salsa and place in a serving bowl.

Makes about 4 cups for 8 servings.

TOMATILLO-CHILE SALSA

In addition to using this salsa for Chicken Enchiladas (page 244) and Chicken Breasts with Tomatillo-Chile Cream (page 231), spoon it over fried or poached eggs or use as a sauce for grilled chicken or fish. And see the variation for a great dip for tortilla chips.

IF using fresh tomatillos, bring a saucepan of water to a boil over medium-high heat. Drop the unhusked tomatillos into the boiling water and blanch for about 2 minutes. Drain. Remove and discard the husks and stems, rinse under cold running water, and drain again. If using canned tomatillos, drain, rinse, and drain again. Set aside.

IN a skillet, heat the oil over medium-high heat. Add the onion and cook, stirring frequently, until soft but not browned, about 5 minutes.

IN a food processor or blender, combine the onion, drained tomatillos, chiles, garlic, oregano, lime juice, sugar, and stock or broth. Blend until fairly smooth, then season to taste with salt.

TRANSFER the salsa to a saucepan. Place over medium-high heat and bring to a boil, then reduce the heat to maintain a simmer, cover, and simmer until the sauce is slightly thickened and the flavors are well blended, about 15 minutes. Pour into a bowl to cool completely.

STIR the cilantro into the cooled salsa and use immediately, or cover and refrigerate for up to 3 days.

Makes about 3 cups for 12 servings.

VARIATION

FOR a chunky dip for corn tortilla chips, omit the stock or broth and quickly blend in the food processor or blender only long enough to yield a coarse puree. Simmer for only 5 minutes.

1½ pounds fresh tomatillos, or 2 cans (13 ounces each) tomatillos

1 tablespoon canola or other high-quality vegetable oil

1 cup chopped white or yellow onion

1 cup coarsely chopped fresh green Anaheim, New Mexico, or other mild to medium-hot chiles, or 1 can (7 ounces) chopped mild green chiles, drained

2 tablespoons chopped green serrano or other hot green chile

1 tablespoon minced garlic

2 tablespoons minced fresh oregano, or 2 teaspoons crumbled dried oregano, preferably from Mexico

2 tablespoons freshly squeezed lime juice

2 teaspoons sugar, or to taste

½ cup White Stock (page 578) made with chicken, Vegetable Stock (page 580), or canned vegetable or reduced-sodium chicken broth

Salt

½ cup finely chopped fresh cilantro (coriander)

CITRUS SALSA

1 large grapefruit, preferably sweet
  pink variety

2 large oranges or tangerines

½ cup minced fresh mint

3 tablespoons minced fresh chives

2 tablespoons freshly squeezed lemon
  or lime juice

1 teaspoon sugar

Hot sauce

Salt

A tangy and sweet foil to spicy grilled dishes.

CUT away the peel and all of the white membrane from the grapefruit
and oranges or tangerines. Cut between the connecting membranes
to remove the sections of the fruits. Coarsely chop the pulp and
place in a colander set over a bowl or in a sink to drain for about
5 minutes.

IN a bowl, combine the drained fruits, mint, chives, lemon or lime
juice, sugar, and hot sauce and salt to taste. Stir to combine,
cover, and chill for about 1 hour for the flavors to blend.

JUST before serving, drain the salsa and place in a serving bowl.

Makes about 3 cups for 6 servings.

TROPICAL SALSA

1 cup finely cubed ripe mango

1 cup finely cubed ripe pineapple

½ cup minced green onion, including
  green tops

2 tablespoons minced fresh hot chile

½ cup minced fresh cilantro (coriander)

1 tablespoon freshly squeezed lime
  juice or unseasoned rice vinegar

Salt

*I originally created this salsa to serve with spicy Jamaican jerk grills, but it
goes well with many other dishes, too.*

IN a bowl, combine all of the ingredients, including salt to taste.
Stir to combine, cover, and chill for about 1 hour for the flavors
to blend.

JUST before serving, drain the salsa and place in a serving bowl.

Makes about 2 cups for 4 servings.

CILANTRO SALSA

Try this zesty blend as a sandwich spread or spoon it onto baked potatoes or grilled meats.

IN a food processor, combine all of the ingredients, including salt to taste. Blend until fairly smooth. Transfer to a serving bowl and serve immediately, or cover and refrigerate for up to several hours.

Makes about ¾ cup for 6 servings.

1½ tablespoons coarsely chopped garlic

1¼ cups coarsely chopped fresh cilantro (coriander)

¼ cup minced fresh jalapeño or other hot chile

1 tablespoon olive oil, preferably extra-virgin

1 tablespoon freshly squeezed lime or lemon juice

1 teaspoon ground cumin

Salt

GUACAMOLE

I'm partial to the creamy Hass avocados from California for guacamole and enjoy it as a dip with lime-flavored tortilla chips. It is also an excellent condiment for grilled fare and burgers.

SCOOP the avocado pulp into a bowl. Using a fork, mash the avocado coarsely, leaving a few small chunky pieces. Stir in the tomato, onion, and lime juice. Season to taste with salt, pepper, and ground chile. Set aside for about 15 minutes for the flavors to mellow or for up to 1 hour; do not refrigerate.

Makes about 3 cups for 6 servings.

3 large ripe avocados

¼ cup peeled, seeded, drained, and chopped ripe tomato

2 tablespoons finely chopped red onion

2 tablespoons freshly squeezed lime juice, or to taste

Salt

Freshly ground black pepper

Ground cayenne or other dried hot chile

THAI CHILE DIPPING SAUCE
~ *Nam Prik* ~

¼ cup minced or sliced fresh Thai
bird or other hot chile

2 teaspoons minced garlic (optional)

¼ cup freshly squeezed lime juice or
distilled white vinegar

3 tablespoons fish sauce, preferably
Thai or Vietnamese

Nearly all Thai cooks make a version of this sauce, which appears at almost every meal and is used along with crushed dried red chiles and chopped peanuts for seasoning dishes.

IN a bowl, combine all of the ingredients and mix well.

USE immediately, or cover tightly and refrigerate for up to
2 months.

Makes about ¾ cup for 6 servings.

VIETNAMESE CHILE DIPPING
SAUCE ~ *Nuoc Cham* ~

3 tablespoons coarsely chopped garlic

3 tablespoons coarsely chopped fresh
red hot chile, or to taste

¾ cup fish sauce, preferably Thai or
Vietnamese

4½ tablespoons sugar, or to taste

6 tablespoons distilled white vinegar

6 tablespoons freshly squeezed lime
juice

3 tablespoons finely chopped unsalted
dry-roasted peanuts (optional)

3 tablespoons finely shredded or
grated carrot (optional)

Numerous variations exist on this ubiquitous condiment that is used in Vietnam, much as salt and pepper are an indispensible part of the American table. To save time, substitute 2 tablespoons chile-garlic sauce (Vietnamese tuong ot tuoi) for the fresh garlic and chile.

IN a food processor or blender, combine ½ cup water with the
garlic, chile, fish sauce, sugar, vinegar, and lime juice and
blend well.

USE immediately, or cover tightly and refrigerate for up to 2 months.
Just before serving, stir in the peanuts and carrot (if using).

Makes about 2 cups for 8 servings.

INDONESIAN PEANUT SAUCE
~ *SAUS KACHANG TANAH* ~

Smooth and creamy, this sauce makes a great foil for Satay *(page 74) and other spicy fare.*

IF using peanuts, in a blender or food processor, combine the peanuts and 2 tablespoons of the oil and blend until a fairly smooth butter forms; set aside. If using prepared peanut butter, reserve.

IN a small saucepan, heat 1 tablespoon oil over medium heat. Add the garlic and ginger and cook, stirring constantly, until the garlic just begins to change color; do not brown. Stir in the peanut butter, coconut milk, stock or broth, soy sauce, sugar, and salt and cayenne to taste. Bring to a boil, then adjust the heat to maintain a simmer and cook, stirring frequently, until the sauce is smooth and thickened, about 5 minutes. Remove from the heat and stir in the lime juice. Pour into a bowl.

SERVE warm or at room temperature, or cover tightly and refrigerate for up to 5 days. If the sauce becomes too thick during storage, thin with coconut milk or slowly reheat just before serving to achieve a consistency for dipping.

Makes about 2 cups for 8 servings.

⅔ cup unsalted dry-roasted peanuts, or ⅔ cup smooth peanut butter

1 or 3 tablespoons peanut or other high-quality vegetable oil

2 teaspoons minced garlic

1 teaspoon grated or minced fresh ginger

1¾ cups Fresh Coconut Milk (page 562) or high-quality commercial coconut milk

¼ cup White Stock (page 578) made with chicken or canned reduced-sodium chicken broth

3 tablespoons soy sauce

2 tablespoons palm sugar

Salt

Ground cayenne

¼ cup freshly squeezed lime juice

THAI PEANUT SAUCE
~ NAM JIM ~

¼ cup Tamarind Liquid (page 561),
or 1 tablespoon tamarind paste

1 cup unsalted dry-roasted peanuts,
or 1 cup smooth peanut butter

2 tablespoons peanut oil or other
high-quality vegetable oil, if using
peanuts

1 cup coconut cream scooped from
the top of chilled Fresh Coconut
Milk (page 562) or unshaken high-
quality commercial coconut milk

¼ cup Thai Red Curry Paste (page
557) or canned Thai red curry
paste, or to taste

1 cup White Stock (page 578) made
with chicken or canned reduced-
sodium chicken broth

6 tablespoons palm sugar

2 tablespoons fish sauce, preferably
Thai or Vietnamese

Salt

The Thais prefer a peanut sauce with a balance of sweet, sour, spicy, and salty tastes. Serve with Satay (page 74) or as a dip for Asian shrimp chips, fried banana or vegetable chips, and raw or steamed vegetables.

IF using tamarind liquid, prepare as directed and set aside. If using tamarind paste, reserve for later use.

IF using peanuts, in a blender or food processor, combine the peanuts and the oil and blend until a fairly smooth butter forms; set aside. If using prepared peanut butter, reserve.

IN a small saucepan, place the coconut cream over medium heat and bring to a boil. Stir in the curry paste and cook, stirring constantly, until quite fragrant, about 5 minutes. Stir in the peanut butter, stock or broth, and sugar. Reduce the heat to maintain a simmer and cook, stirring frequently, until the sauce is smooth and thickened, about 5 minutes. Remove from the heat and stir in the tamarind liquid or paste, fish sauce, and salt to taste. Pour into a bowl.

SERVE warm or at room temperature, or cover tightly and refrigerate for up to 5 days. If the sauce becomes too thick during storage, thin with coconut milk or slowly reheat just before serving to achieve a consistency for dipping.

Makes about 2 cups for 8 servings.

PESTO

In Liguria, the birthplace of this heaven-sent mixture, pecorino fiore sardo *is the cheese of choice. Since only harsher-tasting* pecorino romano *is generally available here, I prefer the sauce made with milder and nuttier Parmigiano-Reggiano. For variety I sometimes make the sauce with almonds, walnuts, or even pecans, and the touch of vinegar in this version is also nontraditional. Some Genoese recipes also call for about 3 table-spoons softened unsalted butter to be stirred in with the cheese.*

Use pesto to crown pasta, pizza, or grilled bread; stir it into soups or risotto; serve it alongside grilled fish; or spread it on sandwiches. The sauce should never be cooked or heated, but tossed with cooked pasta, spooned onto baked pizza, or added to other dishes at the time of serving.

IN a food processor, combine the basil, pine nuts, garlic, and vinegar (if using) and chop finely. With the machine running, slowly add the oil, continuing to blend until well mixed. Transfer to a bowl, stir in the cheese, and season to taste with salt. Alternatively (and traditionally), grind the basil, pine nuts, and garlic in a mortar with a pestle before working in the remaining ingredients.

USE immediately, or transfer to a container, cover with a thin film of olive oil to keep the sauce from darkening, and refrigerate for up to 3 days. To freeze for up to 6 months, omit the cheese during preparation and add it after thawing.

Makes about ¾ cup for 6 servings.

2 cups firmly packed fresh basil leaves

¼ cup pine nuts

1 teaspoon minced garlic

1 teaspoon red wine vinegar or balsamic vinegar (optional)

½ cup extra-virgin olive oil

¾ cup freshly grated Parmesan cheese (about 3 ounces), preferably Parmigiano-Reggiano, or a mixture of ½ cup Parmesan and ¼ cup pecorino romano cheeses

Salt

PROVENÇAL OLIVE PASTE
~ *TAPÉNADE* ~

1 cup pitted brine-cured ripe olives,
  such as Niçoise

½ cup firmly packed fresh basil
  leaves

3 tablespoons drained small capers

2 tablespoons coarsely chopped garlic

3 flat anchovy fillets, rinsed and
  patted dry (optional)

2 teaspoons grated or minced fresh
  lemon zest

¼ cup extra-virgin olive oil

About 2 tablespoons freshly squeezed
  lemon juice

Salt

Freshly ground black pepper

Tapénade, *found throughout Provence, is an intensely flavored puree of olives that makes a delicious spread for crusty French bread or sandwiches and a great topping for pizza. Use only tree-ripened dark olives that have been cured in brine, not the common California black olives, which are green olives that have been cured with lye to darken them.*

For a vegetarian version, omit the anchovies.

IN a food processor, combine the olives, basil, capers, garlic, anchovy fillets (if using), lemon zest, and olive oil. Puree until fairly smooth. Season to taste with lemon juice, salt, and pepper and blend well.

Makes about 1 cup for 8 servings.

THAI SWEET CHILE-GARLIC
SAUCE ~ *NAHN JEEM GRATIEM* ~

2 cups distilled white vinegar

1 cup sugar

1 tablespoon salt

1 tablespoon Asian chile-garlic sauce,
  or 2 teaspoons minced fresh red
  hot chile and 1 teaspoon minced
  garlic

This sauce is a traditional accompaniment to Thai-style barbecued chicken. It also pairs well with spring rolls and any fried or grilled food.

IN a small saucepan, combine the vinegar, sugar, and salt. Place over medium-high heat and bring to a boil, stirring to dissolve the sugar and salt. Cook until the mixture is syrupy, 15 to 20 minutes. Remove from the heat, stir in the chile-garlic sauce or chile and garlic, and set aside to cool to room temperature (the sauce will thicken further as it cools).

USE immediately, or cover tightly and refrigerate indefinitely.

Makes about 1 cup for 6 to 8 servings.

FRENCH WHITE BUTTER SAUCE ~ *Beurre Blanc* ~

An absolute classic with grilled, broiled, or roasted fish or meats.

IN a nonreactive saucepan, combine the shallot, wine, and vinegar. Place over medium-high heat and cook until the shallot is tender but not browned and the liquid is almost evaporated, about 6 minutes; avoid scorching the shallot.

REMOVE the pan from the heat and add 1 piece of the butter, stirring or whisking until the butter is melted. Place the pan over low heat and add the remaining butter, 1 piece at a time, stirring each time until the butter is melted before adding the next piece. When all of the butter has been added, season to taste with salt and pepper; strain out the shallot if desired. Serve immediately or place in a double boiler over barely simmering water for up to 30 minutes.

Makes about ½ cup for 4 servings.

VARIATION

Red Butter Sauce (*Beurre Rouge*). Substitute red wine and red wine vinegar for the white wine and white wine vinegar.

2 tablespoons minced shallot

2 tablespoons dry white wine

2 tablespoons white wine vinegar

½ cup (1 stick) cold unsalted butter, cut into 8 equal pieces

Salt

Freshly ground black or white pepper

COMPOUND BUTTER

1 cup (2 sticks) unsalted butter, at
    room temperature

ADDITIONS

¼ cup minced fresh herb such as
    basil, chives, cilantro (coriander),
    dill, or tarragon

4 teaspoons minced fresh ginger or
    garlic

2 teaspoons prepared mustard or
    horseradish

4 teaspoons drained small capers,
    finely chopped

2 flat anchovy fillets, rinsed, patted
    dry, and minced

2 teaspoons minced drained canned
    chipotle chile in *adobo* sauce

¼ cup freshly squeezed lemon or
    lime juice

4 teaspoons grated or minced fresh
    lemon or lime zest

Salt
Freshly ground black or white pepper
Ground cayenne or other dried
    hot chile

Butter enhanced with fresh herbs or other ingredients makes a simple and delicious sauce for most grilled foods, especially fish. Choose one or a pleasing combination of the suggested additions.

For a whimsical touch, slice the cold butter, trim it with tiny aspic cutters, and place the cutouts on the food just before serving.

IN a bowl, using an electric mixer, or in a food processor, beat the butter until light and fluffy. Add 1 or a pleasing combination of the suggested additions and season to taste with salt and pepper and/or chile; blend well. Transfer to a bowl or form into a cylinder. Cover or wrap with plastic wrap and refrigerate for at least 1 hour or for up to 5 days.

TO serve cold or almost at room temperature, spoon into dollops, scrape into curls, roll into balls, or cut into pats or shapes.

TO serve as a hot sauce, melt the butter in a small saucepan and pour directly over the fare, into a bowl for passing, or into very small individual bowls for dipping.

Makes about 1 cup for 8 servings.

THAI CUCUMBER RELISH
~ *Yam Taeng Kwa* ~

A cooling contrast to the spicy dishes of Thailand, this condiment is traditionally served with fried foods. Although the sweet-sour dressing can be made well in advance, toss it with the cucumber only a short time before serving to keep the vegetable crisp and fresh tasting.

I prefer using seedless cucumbers, also known as English or hothouse varieties, because they do not require peeling or seeding. You may substitute regular cucumbers or Asian varieties, which should be peeled, halved, and seeded before slicing.

¼ cup distilled white vinegar

¼ cup sugar

¼ teaspoon salt

1 cup thinly sliced seedless cucumber

¼ cup thinly sliced red onion half rings

1 teaspoon minced fresh red Thai bird or other hot chile

1 tablespoon finely chopped unsalted dry-roasted peanuts

Fresh cilantro (coriander) leaves for garnish

IN a small saucepan, combine ¼ cup water with the vinegar, sugar, and salt. Place over medium heat and bring to a boil, stirring until the sugar and salt dissolve. Remove from the heat and let cool to room temperature.

A few minutes before serving, add the cucumber, onion, and chile to the cooled vinegar mixture and toss well. Divide among 4 small dishes. Sprinkle each serving with some of the peanuts, garnish with cilantro leaves, and serve immediately.

Makes 4 servings.

BREAD-AND-BUTTER PICKLES

2 quarts distilled white vinegar

4 cups sugar

6 tablespoons salt

4 teaspoons celery seed

4 teaspoons dill seed

1 tablespoon ground turmeric

2 teaspoons dry mustard

4 quarts thinly sliced pickling
cucumber or zucchini (about
5 pounds)

1 quart thinly sliced white onion
(3 or 4 large onions)

Whether made from cucumbers or summer squash, these spicy, sweet pickles are great on burgers, in salads, or as a condiment with many dishes.

IN a saucepan, combine the vinegar, sugar, salt, celery seed, dill seed, turmeric, and mustard. Bring to a boil over medium-high heat, stirring to dissolve the sugar and salt.

MIX the cucumber or zucchini and onion slices in a ceramic bowl, pour the hot vinegar mixture over the top, and let stand at room temperature for 1 hour.

TRANSFER the vegetable mixture to a large pot over medium-high heat. Bring to a boil and cook for 3 minutes.

REMOVE from the heat and set aside to cool to room temperature, then cover tightly and refrigerate for at least 2 weeks before using or for up to 6 months.

ALTERNATIVELY, to preserve for longer storage, pack the hot pickles into sterilized canning jars and pour the vinegar solution over to cover, leaving about ¾-inch headspace between the liquid and the jar rim. Seal and process in a boiling-water bath, following the canning-jar manufacturer's instructions. Check the jars and store those with proper seals in a cool, dark place for up to 1 year. Any jar that does not have a proper seal should be refrigerated as directed in the recipe.

Makes 6 to 7 pints.

PICKLED GARLIC

This sweet-and-sour garlic is a sensational addition to any salad and makes an unusual condiment for everything from burgers to grilled fish.

Although commercially pickled garlic bulbs are available in Asian markets, like most good things to eat, those made at home taste best. Whenever possible, choose freshly dug small bulbs for pickling. If only larger garlic bulbs are available, separate the heads into individual cloves for pickling.

10 young whole garlic heads, or
  5 mature whole garlic heads
1½ cups distilled white vinegar
1½ cups sugar
4½ teaspoons salt

IF using freshly dug young garlic, wash the heads under cold running water to remove all traces of soil. Without cutting into the cloves, cut off and discard the stems and roots. If using mature garlic, separate the heads into unpeeled cloves. Place the garlic in a large pot, add water to cover by 1 inch, then remove the garlic.

PLACE the pot of water over high heat and bring to a boil. Add the garlic, reduce the heat to achieve a simmer, and simmer for 10 minutes. Drain the garlic in a colander, pat dry with paper toweling, then place in a sterilized glass jar or jars.

IN a saucepan, combine the vinegar, sugar, and salt. Place over medium-high heat and bring to a boil, stirring to dissolve the sugar and salt. Remove from the heat and pour over the garlic to cover completely. Set aside to cool to room temperature.

COVER the cooled garlic tightly and refrigerate for at least 2 weeks before using or for up to 6 months. (To preserve for longer storage, make in large quantity, immediately seal the jars after adding the hot vinegar solution, and process as directed for Bread-and-Butter Pickles in the preceding recipe.)

TO use, remove the garlic from the pickling solution and peel just before serving or using as directed in recipes.

Makes about 1 quart.

PICKLED GINGER

2 pounds fresh ginger, preferably
immature

About 1 quart boiling water

2 cups distilled white vinegar

1 cup sugar

1 tablespoon salt

Pickled ginger is a well-known ingredient and condiment in the cooking of Japan and China, and its popularity has spread throughout tropical Asia. It makes a wonderful addition to salads and provides a soothing contrast when served as a condiment with fiery dishes.

Imported in early summer, immature ginger, which has soft, fiberless flesh and a translucent cream-colored skin, is ideal for pickling. Mature brown-skinned ginger will also work; be certain that the tuber has not dried out and is unblemished.

PEEL the ginger. Using a mandoline, slicer, or sharp knife, cut the ginger across the grain into paper-thin slices. Place the slices in a bowl, add boiling water to cover, and let stand for about 2 minutes, then drain in a colander. Transfer the drained ginger to a sterilized glass jar or jars.

IN a saucepan, combine the vinegar, sugar, and salt. Place over medium-high heat and bring to a boil, stirring to dissolve the sugar and salt. Remove from the heat and pour over the ginger to cover completely. Set aside to cool to room temperature.

COVER the cooled ginger tightly and refrigerate for at least 2 weeks before using or for up to 6 months. (To preserve for longer storage, make in larger quantity, immediately seal the jars after adding the hot vinegar solution, and process as directed for Bread-and-Butter Pickles on page 404.)

Makes about 1 quart.

OLD-FASHIONED CORN RELISH

Serve this tangy concoction with grilled or roasted meats or on burgers or other sandwiches.

CUT the kernels from the corn cobs as directed for Sauteed Corn on page 358 and measure out 5 cups.

IN a large pot, heat the oil over medium-high heat. Add the corn and cook, stirring frequently, for 2 minutes. Add the onion, sweet pepper, chile, currants, vinegar, sugar, celery and mustard seeds, cloves, hot sauce, salt, and 2 cups water. Bring to a boil, then adjust the heat to maintain a simmer and simmer, uncovered, for 35 minutes. Taste and adjust the seasonings. Remove from the heat and set aside to cool to room temperature.

COVER the cooled relish tightly and refrigerate for at least 2 weeks before using or for up to 6 months. (To preserve for longer storage, pack the hot relish into sterilized canning jars, seal, and process as directed for Bread-and-Butter Pickles on page 404.)

Makes 4 pints.

About 10 medium-sized ears corn

2 tablespoons canola or other high-quality vegetable oil

1 cup chopped white or yellow onion

1 cup diced red sweet pepper

2 tablespoons minced fresh hot chile

⅔ cup dried currants

2 cups apple cider vinegar or distilled white vinegar

1 cup sugar

1 teaspoon celery seed

1 teaspoon mustard seed

3 whole cloves

½ teaspoon Louisiana hot sauce, or to taste

1 teaspoon salt, or to taste

MOTHER'S PEAR RELISH

4 pounds firm ripe pears, peeled
  and cored

2½ pounds yellow onions

3 or 4 green sweet peppers, stems,
  seeds, and membranes discarded

2 red sweet peppers, stems, seeds,
  and membranes discarded

3 fresh jalapeño or other hot chiles,
  stems, seeds, and
  membranes discarded, or to taste

2 cups sugar

3 tablespoons dry mustard

2½ tablespoons salt

1 tablespoon ground turmeric

3 cups apple cider vinegar

My mother makes this relish in great quantity each year. We've long enjoyed it on burgers made of ground venison from my daddy's hunting successes.

USING a food grinder fitted with a medium disk, grind the pears into a bowl. Using the same disk, grind the onions, sweet peppers, and chiles and add to the pears. Set aside.

IN a large pot, combine the sugar, mustard, salt, and turmeric. Stir in the vinegar, place over high heat, and stir until the sugar dissolves, about 4 minutes.

ADD the ground pear mixture to the vinegar mixture. Bring to a boil, then reduce the heat to achieve a simmer and simmer, uncovered, until the onion is tender but still crisp and most of the liquid evaporates, 30 to 45 minutes.

REMOVE from the heat and set aside to cool to room temperature, then cover tightly and refrigerate for at least 2 weeks before using or for up to 6 months. (To preserve for longer storage, pack the hot relish into sterilized canning jars, seal, and process as directed for Bread-and-Butter Pickles on page 404.)

Makes 6 pints.

TOMATO CHUTNEY

Serve as an accompaniment to meats or add a little to a vinaigrette for tossed greens.

IN a saucepan, combine the onion, vinegar, sugar, allspice, cinnamon, and salt to taste. Enclose the cloves and peppercorns in a small square of cheesecloth, tie with cotton string to form a bag, and add to the mixture. Place over medium-high heat and bring to a boil, then reduce the heat to achieve a simmer, cover, and simmer until the onion is tender, about 20 minutes.

STIR in the tomatoes and continue to simmer, uncovered, until most of the liquid evaporates, about 20 minutes. Remove and discard the cheesecloth bag and season to taste with salt. Remove from the heat and set aside to cool to room temperature.

COVER the cooled chutney tightly and refrigerate for at least 2 weeks before using or for up to 6 months. (To preserve for longer storage, pack the hot chutney into sterilized canning jars, seal, and process as directed for Bread-and-Butter Pickles on page 404.)

Makes about 1 pint.

1½ cups chopped onion

¾ cup apple cider vinegar

½ cup firmly packed light brown sugar

½ teaspoon ground allspice

¼ teaspoon ground cinnamon

About ½ teaspoon salt

4 whole cloves

4 black peppercorns

2 pounds ripe tomatoes, peeled, seeded, and chopped

Breads

WHETHER you choose steamed brown bread from New England or warm tortillas from Mexico, fresh bread makes any meal seem special. Biscuits are at home on both breakfast and supper tables, while rolls and popovers are grand additions to dinner menus. And burgers taste terrific on homemade buns or squares of Italian focaccia.

My Southern heritage makes me love cornbread in any guise, and be sure to try the dressing made from the spicy variation.

BUTTERMILK BISCUITS

For decades, my aunt Doris Keith of Jackson, Mississippi, made a pan of wonderful hot biscuits almost every morning for breakfast and often again for supper. Her recipe is simple; the perfection she exhibits probably comes from the daily practice. While my aunt recommends self-rising flour (which already contains baking powder and salt), I've adapted her recipe to all-purpose flour.

As a youngster, I always asked for "white" biscuits, which meant cooked only until the tops were barely beginning to brown. I still like them this way. If you prefer a browner top, brush the biscuits with melted butter before baking. If you enjoy the sides crusty, arrange the biscuits about 1 inch apart in the baking pan; for soft sides, arrange them touching.

Offer butter and good jelly, jam, honey, or syrup with the biscuits.

Unsalted butter or solid vegetable
    shortening, at room temperature,
    or cooking spray for greasing
    (optional)
2 cups all-purpose flour
2 teaspoons baking powder
½ teaspoon baking soda
½ teaspoon salt
½ cup solid vegetable shortening
¾ cup buttermilk

POSITION racks so that the biscuits will bake in the middle of an oven and preheat the oven to 400° F. Using a pastry brush, lightly grease a baking sheet or pan with butter or shortening, or coat with spray or line with kitchen parchment. Set aside.

IN a bowl or food processor, combine the flour, baking powder, baking soda, and salt. Cut in the shortening with your fingertips, a pastry blender, or the steel blade until the mixture resembles coarse bread crumbs. If using a food processor, transfer the mixture to a bowl. Add the buttermilk and stir just until the mixture sticks together.

TURN the dough out onto a lightly floured surface and knead lightly and quickly, about 30 seconds. Using a lightly floured rolling pin, roll out about ½ inch thick. Using a floured 2½-inch round biscuit cutter, cut out circles. Place on the prepared sheet (see recipe introduction).

BAKE until lightly browned, 10 to 12 minutes. Serve piping hot.

Makes about 12 biscuits.

GOLDEN YEAST ROLLS

2 tablespoons sugar

1 envelope (¼ ounce) active dry
  yeast or quick-rising yeast

1 cup warm milk (110° to 115° F)

3 tablespoons unsalted butter,
  melted and cooled slightly

1 teaspoon salt

About 4 cups sifted all-purpose flour

1 cup pureed Roasted Winter Squash
  (page 318)

Unsalted butter, melted, for
  brushing

Solid vegetable shortening, at room
  temperature, or cooking spray for
  greasing (optional)

Sesame seed or poppy seed for
  sprinkling (optional)

*Instead of fashioning the dough into predictable rounds, treat it in one
of the following ways: cut the dough into strips about 9 inches long by
2 inches wide and loosely tie each into a knot; cut these same long strips
in half lengthwise and braid them together; roll the dough into small
balls and place 3 together in each well of a muffin tin to bake into
cloverleaf shapes; or cut the dough into wedge shapes, roll up from the
broad end, and turn corners to form crescents.*

IN a small bowl, dissolve the sugar in ¼ cup warm water (110° to
115° F). Sprinkle the yeast over the water, stir to dissolve, and
let stand until soft and foamy, about 5 minutes. (Discard the
mixture and start over with a fresh package of yeast if bubbles
have not formed within 5 minutes.)

IN a bowl, combine the foamy yeast, warm milk, the 3 tablespoons
melted butter, and salt and beat to blend thoroughly. Mix in 1 cup
of the flour and the squash puree, then mix in only as much of
the remaining flour as needed to form a soft dough that can be
easily handled. Turn out onto a lightly floured surface and knead
until the dough is no longer sticky, about 5 minutes, adding
more flour, a little at a time, if necessary.

USING a pastry brush, generously brush a large bowl with melted
butter, form the dough into a ball, place it in the bowl, and turn
to coat all over with butter. Cover the bowl tightly with plastic
wrap to prevent moisture loss and set aside in a warm, draft-
free place for the dough to rise until doubled in bulk, about 45
minutes if using quick-rising yeast, or about 1½ hours if using
regular yeast.

USING a pastry brush, lightly grease a baking sheet with butter or
shortening, or coat with spray or line with kitchen parchment.
Set aside.

PUNCH the dough down and turn it out onto a lightly floured surface. Roll the dough into a disk about ½ inch thick. Using a 3- to 4-inch round biscuit or cookie cutter, cut into circles, or cut and shape as described in the recipe introduction. Place rolls about ½ inch apart on the prepared baking sheet. Cover loosely with plastic wrap or a cloth kitchen towel and let rise in a warm place until almost doubled in bulk, about 30 minutes.

POSITION racks so that the rolls will bake in the middle of an oven and preheat the oven to 400° F.

BRUSH the tops of the rolls with melted butter and sprinkle with seed (if using). Bake until lightly golden, about 20 minutes. Transfer to a wire rack to cool briefly. Serve hot.

Makes 6 servings.

YEAST BISCUITS

1 package (¼ ounce) quick-rising
    active dry yeast
5 cups all-purpose flour
5 teaspoons baking powder
½ teaspoon baking soda
3 tablespoons sugar
1 teaspoon salt
1 cup canola or other high-quality
    vegetable oil
2 cups buttermilk
Unsalted butter or solid vegetable
    shortening, at room temperature,
    or cooking spray for greasing
    (optional)

*These airy biscuits, good for any meal of the day, were popular in my
hometown. The dough keeps in the refrigerator for several days. Cut off
and roll out only what you need for a meal.*

Serve piping hot with plenty of butter and good jelly or jam.

IN a small bowl, sprinkle the yeast over 5 tablespoons warm water
    (110° to 115° F), stir to dissolve, and let stand until soft and
    foamy, about 5 minutes. (Discard the mixture and start over
    with a fresh package of yeast if bubbles have not formed within
    5 minutes.)

IN a bowl or food processor, combine the flour, baking powder,
    baking soda, sugar, and salt. Cut the oil into the mixture with a
    pastry blender or the steel blade until the mixture resembles
    coarse bread crumbs. If using a food processor, transfer the
    mixture to a bowl. Pour in the buttermilk and softened yeast.
    Stir the mixture quickly to combine the liquid with the dry
    ingredients. Cover and refrigerate for at least 1 hour or,
    preferably, overnight.

USING a pastry brush, lightly grease 2 baking sheets with butter or
    shortening, or coat with spray or line with kitchen parchment.
    Set aside.

FORM the chilled dough into a ball and turn out onto a generously
    floured surface. Knead lightly and quickly, about 1 minute. Using
    a lightly floured rolling pin, roll out about ½ inch thick. Using
    a floured 2½-inch round biscuit cutter, cut out circles. Place
    barely touching on the prepared sheets. Cover loosely with plastic
    wrap or a kitchen towel and let rise in a warm place just until
    puffy, 20 to 30 minutes.

POSITION racks so that the biscuits will bake in the middle of an
    oven and preheat the oven to 400° F.

BAKE until lightly browned, 10 to 15 minutes. Serve piping hot.

Makes about 48 biscuits.

POPOVERS

For maximum puffiness, avoid opening the oven door until the popovers are almost done. Serve piping hot with plenty of butter and jam or honey.

PREHEAT an oven to 425° F. Using a pastry brush, generously grease eight 6-ounce ovenproof custard cups with butter or shortening, or coat with spray. Set aside.

IN a blender or a bowl, combine the melted butter, eggs, milk, flour, sugar, and salt and blend or whisk until smooth. Divide the batter evenly among the prepared custard cups.

PLACE the cups on a baking sheet, leaving space around each cup for hot air to circulate. Transfer to the oven and bake until well puffed and firm to the touch, about 25 minutes, then reduce the heat to 350° F and bake until browned, about 15 minutes longer.

TRANSFER to a work surface, run a dull knife blade around the inside of each cup to loosen, remove the popovers, and serve immediately.

Makes 8 popovers.

Unsalted butter or solid vegetable shortening, at room temperature, or cooking spray for greasing

3 tablespoons unsalted butter, melted and cooled slightly

4 eggs, at room temperature

1⅓ cups milk (not fat free)

1⅓ cups all-purpose flour

1 tablespoon sugar

½ teaspoon salt

WHOLE-WHEAT BUNS

1 tablespoon sugar

1 envelope (¼ ounce) active dry
    yeast or quick-rising yeast

2 cups whole-wheat flour

About 1½ cups all-purpose flour

1½ teaspoons salt

1 egg, at room temperature, lightly
    beaten

1 cup milk (not fat free), at room
    temperature

5 tablespoons unsalted butter,
    at room temperature, cut into
    small pieces

Unsalted butter or solid vegetable
    shortening, at room temperature,
    for greasing

1 egg, lightly beaten, for brushing

OPTIONAL TOPPINGS

Coarse salt

Freshly cracked black pepper

Caraway seed

Poppy seed

Sesame seed

As with most breads, these buns are best eaten the day they are baked. If you don't plan to use them all, some of the dough can be frozen. After the second rising, the dough can be divided into individual portions, wrapped tightly in plastic freezer wrap, and frozen for up to 2 months. Defrost, allow to rise, and bake as directed.

IN a small bowl, dissolve the sugar in ⅓ cup warm water (110° to 115° F). Sprinkle the yeast over the water, stir to dissolve, and let stand until soft and foamy, about 5 minutes. (Discard the mixture and start over with a fresh package of yeast if bubbles have not formed within 5 minutes.)

TO mix and knead the dough by hand, combine the whole-wheat flour and 1 cup of the all-purpose flour and the salt in a large mixing bowl and stir well. Make a well in the center of the flour and pour in the yeast mixture, egg, and milk. Vigorously stir the flour into the liquid to form a soft dough. Turn the dough out onto a lightly floured surface and knead for about 10 minutes, gradually adding the 5 tablespoons butter a little at a time, then gradually adding just enough of the remaining ½ cup all-purpose flour for the dough to lose its stickiness. Continue kneading just until the dough is soft, smooth, and elastic, 5 to 10 minutes longer; too much kneading overdevelops the gluten in the flour and results in a tough bread. If the dough is dry and crumbly, add warm water, a tablespoon at a time, during kneading.

TO mix and knead the dough with a heavy-duty stand mixer, in the bowl, combine the whole-wheat flour and 1 cup of the all-purpose flour, the salt, yeast mixture, egg, and milk. Attach the flat beater and mix well at the lowest speed for 1 minute. Replace the flat beater with the dough hook and knead at medium speed for 2 minutes. Add the 5 tablespoons butter a little at a time while continuing to knead until the dough is soft, smooth, and elastic, about 3 minutes longer. Pinch off a piece of dough and feel it. If it is sticky, continue kneading while gradually adding just enough of the remaining ½ cup all-purpose flour for the dough to lose its stickiness. If the dough is dry and crumbly, add warm water, a tablespoon at a time, and knead until the dough is smooth and elastic.

AFTER mixing the dough by one of the preceding methods, using a pastry brush, generously grease a large bowl with butter or shortening, shape the dough into a ball, place it in the bowl, and turn to coat all over with butter or shortening. Cover the bowl tightly with plastic wrap to prevent moisture loss and set aside in a warm, draft-free place for the dough to rise until doubled in bulk, about 45 minutes if using quick-rising yeast, or 1½ to 2 hours if using regular yeast.

PUNCH down the dough, form the dough into a smooth ball again, return it to the bowl, cover, and let rise again in a warm place until doubled in bulk, about half as long as the first rising.

USING a pastry brush, lightly grease a baking sheet with butter or shortening, or line with kitchen parchment. Set aside.

TURN out the dough onto a lightly floured surface, keeping the smooth top upright. Using a flour-dusted rolling pin or floured hands, begin at one side and work to the other to press out the air. Divide the dough into 6 equal portions. Using your hands, shape each piece of dough into a smooth round ball, then gently flatten each ball out with your hand or a rolling pin to form a disk about the diameter you want the cooked bun to be; they rise up, not out. Avoid tearing the smooth top of the buns when flattening them. Place the buns on the prepared baking sheet, cover loosely with plastic wrap or a cloth kitchen towel, and let rise in a warm place until doubled in bulk, about 30 minutes.

POSITION oven racks so that the buns will bake in the middle of an oven and preheat the oven to 400° F.

BRUSH the tops of the buns with the beaten egg. Sprinkle the buns with one or a combination of the toppings. Bake until the buns are golden brown all over, about 15 minutes. Transfer the baking sheet to a wire rack and let cool for about 10 minutes, then remove the buns from the pan to a wire rack and let cool completely.

Makes 6 buns.

DILLED POTATO BREAD

½ pound boiling or baking potatoes

1 tablespoon sugar

1 envelope (¼ ounce) active dry
yeast or quick-rising yeast

1 cup buttermilk

2 tablespoons unsalted butter, melted
and cooled slightly, or canola or
other high-quality vegetable oil

1 tablespoon salt

¼ cup finely chopped fresh dill

About 8 cups all-purpose flour

Unsalted butter or solid vegetable
shortening, at room temperature,
for greasing

Pastry flour for dusting

*It is always difficult to wait for this fragrant bread to cool before cutting
a slice.*

BOIL the potatoes as directed on page 304. Drain the potatoes and
reserve the cooking liquid, if desired.

IN a small bowl, dissolve the sugar in 1½ cups warm water or
liquid from cooking potatoes (110° to 115° F). Sprinkle the
yeast over the water, stir to dissolve, and let stand until soft
and foamy, about 5 minutes. (Discard the mixture and start
over with a fresh package of yeast if bubbles have not formed
within 5 minutes.)

PRESS the potatoes through a ricer into a large bowl.

TO mix and knead the dough by hand, add the foamy yeast,
buttermilk, melted butter or oil, salt, and dill to the potatoes
and stir to combine thoroughly. Add 7 cups of the all-purpose
flour and mix well. Turn the dough out onto a lightly floured
surface and knead for about 5 minutes, gradually adding just
enough of the remaining 1 cup all-purpose flour for the dough
to lose its stickiness. Set aside for 10 minutes to relax the
gluten, then continue kneading just until the dough is smooth,
elastic, and shiny, about 10 minutes longer; too much kneading
overdevelops the gluten in the flour and results in a tough
bread. If the dough is dry and crumbly, add warm water, a
tablespoon at a time, during kneading.

TO mix and knead the dough with a heavy-duty stand mixer, in
the bowl, combine the potatoes, the foamy yeast, buttermilk,
melted butter or oil, salt, dill, and 7 cups of the flour. Attach
the flat beater and mix well at the lowest speed for 1 minute.
Replace the flat beater with the dough hook and knead at
medium speed until the dough is quite elastic, supple, and
smooth, about 5 minutes. Pinch off a piece of dough and feel it.

If it is sticky, continue kneading while gradually adding just enough of the remaining 1 cup flour for the dough to lose its stickiness. If the dough is dry and crumbly, add warm water, a tablespoon at a time, and knead until the dough is smooth and elastic.

AFTER mixing the dough by one of the preceding methods, using a pastry brush, generously grease a bowl with butter or vegetable shortening. Shape the dough into a ball, place it in the bowl, and turn to coat all over with butter or shortening. Cover the bowl tightly with plastic wrap to prevent moisture loss and set aside in a warm, draft-free place for the dough to rise until doubled in bulk, about 45 minutes if using quick-rising yeast, or about 1½ hours if using regular yeast.

USING a pastry brush, generously grease the bottom and sides of a shallow, round baking pan about 12 inches in diameter or two 9-by-5-inch loaf pans with butter or shortening. Set aside.

PUNCH down the dough, turn it out onto a lightly floured surface, and knead for about 5 minutes. If using a round baking pan, form the dough into a large round loaf and place in the prepared pan. If using loaf pans, divide the dough in half, form each portion into a loaf, and place in the prepared loaf pans. Cover loosely with plastic wrap or a cloth kitchen towel and let rise in a warm place until almost doubled in bulk, about 30 minutes.

POSITION racks so that the bread will bake in the middle of an oven and preheat the oven to 350° F.

USING a sharp knife or kitchen scissors, slash the top of the loaf (or loaves) with crosses, diamonds, or parallel incisions. Lightly mist the top(s) with warm water and dust with pastry flour. Bake until nicely browned, about 1 hour or more for the large loaf, or 45 to 50 minutes for the smaller loaves. Turn out onto wire racks to cool for about 15 minutes.

Makes one 12-inch round loaf or two 9-by-5-inch loaves for 12 servings.

FOCACCIA

1 tablespoon sugar

1 envelope (¼ ounce) active dry
   yeast or quick-rising yeast

3¼ cups all-purpose flour

2 teaspoons salt

¼ cup extra-virgin olive oil

Extra-virgin olive oil for brushing

Coarse salt

*One gorgeous late-summer Sunday afternoon in the Napa Valley,
Andrew and I found ourselves happily seated around the family table of
Arnie and Alma Tudal, who make excellent Cabernet Sauvignon. We
couldn't stop eating the warm figassa (a dialect term for focaccia)
baked by Grandma May Ceruti, Alma's ninety-something mother. Most
of us split the flat bread in half and stuffed it with flavorful antipasto
ingredients, including vine-ripened tomatoes, marinated red sweet
peppers, red onion, and salami, for eating out of hand.*

*This crusty Italian flatbread can be varied by sprinkling the
top with Caramelized Onions (page 551) or minced fresh herbs before
baking. Or work about 2 tablespoons fresh or 2 teaspoons dried herbs into
the dough during kneading. Other optional toppings include fresh grapes,
chopped dried fruits or sun-dried tomatoes, or a coating of thick
tomato sauce.*

*My recipe calls for baking the dough in a pan so that the bread
can be cut into squares, rectangles, or strips. If you prefer the traditional
Italian round, form the dough into a disk about ¾-inch thick and bake
on a greased baking sheet.*

IN a small bowl, dissolve the sugar in 1 cup warm water (110° to
   115° F). Sprinkle the yeast over the water, stir to dissolve, and
   let stand until soft and foamy, about 5 minutes. (Discard the
   mixture and start over with a fresh package of yeast if bubbles
   have not formed within 5 minutes.)

TO mix and knead the dough by hand, in a large bowl, combine
   3 cups of the flour with the salt. Make a well in the center of the
   flour and pour in the ¼ cup oil and the yeast mixture. Using a
   wooden spoon, vigorously stir the flour into the well, beginning
   in the center and working toward the sides of the bowl, until
   the flour is incorporated and the soft dough just begins to hold
   together. Turn the dough out onto a lightly floured surface and
   knead for about 5 minutes, gradually adding just enough of the
   remaining ¼ cup flour for the dough to lose its stickiness.
   Continue kneading just until the dough is smooth, elastic, and
   shiny, 10 to 15 minutes longer; too much kneading overdevelops

the gluten in the flour and results in a tough bread. If the dough is dry and crumbly, add warm water, a tablespoon at a time, during kneading.

TO mix and knead the dough with a heavy-duty stand mixer, in the bowl, combine 3 cups of the flour, the salt, the ¼ cup oil, and the yeast mixture. Attach the flat beater and mix well at the lowest speed for about 1 minute. Replace the flat beater with the dough hook and knead at medium speed until the dough is smooth and elastic, about 5 minutes. Pinch off a piece of dough and feel it. If it is sticky, continue kneading while gradually adding just enough of the remaining ¼ cup flour for the dough to lose its stickiness. If the dough is dry and crumbly, add warm water, a tablespoon at a time, until the dough is smooth and elastic.

AFTER mixing and kneading the dough by one of the preceding methods, generously brush a large bowl with oil. Shape the dough into a ball, place it in the bowl, and turn to coat all over with oil. Cover the bowl tightly with plastic wrap to prevent moisture loss and set aside in a warm, draft-free place for the dough to rise until tripled in bulk, about 1½ hours if using quick-rising yeast, or about 3 hours if using regular yeast.

POSITION racks so that the focaccia will bake in the middle of an oven and preheat the oven to 375° F. Using a pastry brush, generously grease the bottom and sides of a 13-by-9-inch pan with oil.

PUNCH down the dough and place it in the center of the prepared pan. Using your fingertips, spread the dough to fit the bottom of the pan evenly; it may be springy and a bit difficult to spread. Using a finger, poke deep holes in the top of the dough to create a dimpled effect. Generously brush the dough all over with oil and sprinkle with coarse salt. Bake until golden brown, 30 to 35 minutes.

REMOVE to a wire rack and let cool in the pan for about 5 minutes. Turn out onto the rack to cool for about 10 minutes longer. Cut into squares or rectangles and serve warm.

Makes 6 servings.

STEAMED BROWN BREAD

Unsalted butter or solid vegetable
    shortening, at room temperature,
    or cooking spray for greasing

½ cup whole-wheat flour

½ cup medium rye flour

1 teaspoon baking soda

½ teaspoon salt

½ cup yellow or white cornmeal,
    preferably stone-ground

1 cup buttermilk, at room
    temperature

⅓ cup light molasses

1 tablespoon unsalted butter, melted
    and cooled slightly

½ cup raisins, soaked in dark rum or
    hot water until plumped, then
    drained

Although home cooks have long relied on coffee cans as handy containers for cooking this classic accompaniment to Boston Baked Beans (page 355), reports indicate that cans may release harmful toxins when heated. Safe options include pudding molds, heatproof bowls, or tempered glass can-shaped containers available from baking-supply catalogs and some cookware stores. You can also use a 2-quart container and double the bread recipe and cooking time.

SELECT a 1-quart heatproof container (see recipe introduction) and a pot with a tight-fitting cover large enough to hold the bread container. Place a flat steaming rack in the bottom of the pot. Place the container on the rack and add enough water to the pot to reach about halfway up the sides of the bread container, then remove the container. Using a pastry brush, generously grease the inside of the container with butter or shortening, or coat with spray. Set aside. Place the pot over high heat and bring the water to a boil, then cover and adjust the heat to achieve a simmer.

PLACE the flours, baking soda, and salt together in a strainer or sifter and sift into a bowl. Stir in the cornmeal. Add the buttermilk, molasses, butter, and raisins and stir to blend well. Spoon the mixture into the buttered container, filling no more than two-thirds full. If using a pudding mold with a lid, cover with the lid; if using a mold, bowl, or other container without a lid, cover tightly with aluminum foil. Place the container on the rack inside the pot of simmering water, cover the pot, and simmer until a wooden skewer inserted in the center of the bread comes out clean, about 1½ hours; adjust the heat to maintain simmering water throughout cooking, adding boiling water if needed to maintain water level.

REMOVE the container from the simmering water to a wire rack, remove the lid or foil, and let stand for about 5 minutes. Invert a lightly greased wire rack over the container, invert the rack and container together, and carefully lift off the container. Set aside to cool for a few minutes longer. Using a serrated bread knife, slice the warm bread and serve immediately.

Makes 8 servings.

CORNBREAD

Some residents of each side of the Mason-Dixon Line enjoy bread made from yellow cornmeal and others prefer using white or blue; preference is equally divided on whether to add sweetener.

If you enjoy a fine-textured cornbread, choose American fine or regular grind cornmeal. For a coarser-grained bread, use polenta or other coarsely ground meal. If you prefer a dark, crusty exterior, grease an iron pan and preheat it in the oven while you prepare the batter, then pour the batter into the smoking-hot pan.

I've never found a cornbread that I like better than this standard recipe. For the sake of variety, try some of the suggestions on pages 424-425.

POSITION racks so that the cornbread will bake in the middle of an oven and preheat the oven to 400° F. Using a pastry brush, generously grease an 8-inch square baking pan or 9-inch round cake pan with butter or shortening, or coat with spray. Set aside.

IN a bowl, combine the cornmeal, flour, sugar (if using), baking powder, and salt and mix well.

IN another bowl, combine the eggs, melted butter or oil, and milk and beat well. Pour the wet ingredients into the dry ingredients and stir just until the mixture is blended. Pour into the prepared pan. Bake until golden brown and a wooden skewer inserted into the center of the cornbread comes out clean, 20 to 25 minutes.

SERVE immediately from the pan or turn out onto a wire rack to cool briefly.

Makes 6 to 8 servings.

variations follow ~

Unsalted butter or solid vegetable shortening, at room temperature, or cooking spray for greasing (optional)

1 cup cornmeal, preferably stone-ground

1 cup all-purpose flour

¼ cup sugar (optional)

2 teaspoons baking powder

1 teaspoon salt, or to taste

2 eggs, at room temperature

¼ cup (½ stick) unsalted butter, melted and cooled slightly, or canola or other high-quality vegetable oil

1 cup milk (not fat free), at room temperature

CORNBREAD VARIATIONS

Bacon or Crackling Cornbread. Stir ½ cup crumbled, crisply fried bacon or pork or duck cracklings into the finished batter.

Buttermilk Cornbread. Substitute 1 cup buttermilk for the regular milk.

Cheese Cornbread. Stir 1 cup freshly shredded Cheddar or Monterey Jack cheese (about 3 ounces), crumbled fresh goat or blue cheese (about 4 ounces), or other good-melting cheese into the finished batter.

Chile Cornbread. Stir 2 tablespoons or more ground *pasilla, pequín,* or other dried mild to hot chile into the dry ingredients.

Cornbread Fritters. Prepare the basic batter or one of the variations, then thin the batter with about ½ cup milk to the consistency of pancake batter. Drop by spoonfuls onto a preheated, lightly greased griddle or skillet. Cook until bubbly on the tops, 3 to 4 minutes, then turn with a spatula and cook the other sides until golden. Drain briefly on paper toweling.

Cornbread Sticks. Generously grease cornstick molds and preheat in a 450° F oven until smoking hot. Fill each indention about three-fourths full with basic batter or any one of the variations and return the pan to the hot oven. Bake until set and golden, about 10 minutes.

Corn Muffins. Pour the basic batter or any of the variations into greased muffin tins, filling each about three-fourths full. Bake as directed, but reduce the baking time according to mixture and size of pans.

Custard Cornbread. For cornbread with a center of creamy custard, place 2 tablespoons unsalted butter in the baking pan and heat in a 350° F oven until the butter melts. Combine the dry ingredients as directed, but reduce the baking powder to 1 teaspoon and add ½ teaspoon baking soda. When mixing the wet ingredients, increase the milk to 2 cups, use melted butter instead of oil, and add 1½ tablespoons distilled white vinegar. Pour the batter into the preheated pan, then pour 1 cup heavy (whipping) cream over the top; do not stir. Bake until lightly browned, about 1 hour.

Double-Corn Cornbread. Stir ¾ cup fresh, thawed frozen, or drained canned corn kernels into the finished batter.

Flourless Cornbread. For a thin, crunchy cornbread, omit the flour, sugar, and baking powder. Increase the cornmeal to 2 cups and add 1 teaspoon baking soda to the dry ingredients. Substitute 2 cups buttermilk for the 1 cup regular milk.

Herbed Cornbread. Stir 2 tablespoons minced fresh or 2 teaspoons crumbled dried herbs such as dill, rosemary, sage, or thyme into the finished batter.

Hush Puppies. Increase the cornmeal to 2 cups, reduce the flour to ½ cup, and add 1 teaspoon baking soda to the dry ingredients. Substitute 2 cups buttermilk for the 1 cup regular milk and omit the butter or oil. After combining the wet and dry ingredients, stir in 5 tablespoons grated white onion or minced green onion, and, if desired, 2 or 3 tablespoons minced fresh or canned green hot chile. Pour peanut or other high-quality vegetable oil into a deep fryer or saucepan to a depth of 2 inches and preheat to 375° F. Carefully drop the batter, a scant tablespoon at a time, into the hot oil; avoid crowding the pan. Fry, turning frequently, until crisp and golden, about 5 minutes. Using a slotted utensil, transfer to paper toweling to drain briefly before serving.

Nutty Cornbread. Stir ¾ cup chopped toasted pecans or other nuts (see page 554) or ½ cup crunchy peanut or other nut butter into the finished batter.

Seeded Cornbread. Stir ½ cup toasted sesame seed or sunflower seed (see page 553) or 3 tablespoons caraway seed into the finished batter.

Tex-Mex Cornbread. Preheat an oven to 350° F. Reduce the amount of sugar to 2 tablespoons. When mixing the wet ingredients, add ½ cup sour cream or plain yogurt (not fat free); 2 cups fresh, thawed frozen, or drained canned corn kernels; 2 cups freshly shredded Cheddar cheese (about 6 ounces); ½ cup grated yellow onion; and ¼ cup minced fresh or canned jalapeño or other hot chile. Increase baking time to about 45 minutes.

DOUBLE-CORN SPOON BREAD

Unsalted butter or solid vegetable
   shortening, at room temperature,
   or cooking spray for greasing

About 2 medium-sized ears corn,
   or ¾ cup thawed frozen or
   drained canned corn kernels (see
   recipe introduction)

¾ cup cornmeal, preferably stone-
   ground (see recipe introduction)

2 cups freshly shredded sharp
   Cheddar cheese (about 6 ounces)
   or other good-melting cheese

¼ cup (½ stick) unsalted butter, at
   room temperature

½ teaspoon salt, or to taste

Freshly ground black pepper

1 cup buttermilk, at room
   temperature

4 eggs, at room temperature,
   separated

An Early American favorite, soft cornbread served with a big spoon is a hearty dish for breakfast, lunch, or supper. Use yellow kernels and cornmeal with yellow-tinted Cheddar for a golden version, or combine white corn, cornmeal, and natural cream-colored cheese for a white spoon bread.

PREHEAT an oven to 350° F. Using a pastry brush, generously grease a 2-quart soufflé dish or ovenproof casserole with butter or shortening or coat with spray. Set aside.

IF using fresh corn, cut the kernels from the cobs as directed for Sauteed Corn on page 358, measure out ¾ cup, and set aside. If using thawed or canned corn, reserve for later use.

IN a saucepan, combine the cornmeal and 1¾ cups water and stir well. Place over low heat and cook, stirring frequently and scraping the bottom of the pan, until the cornmeal is smooth and thick, about 10 minutes.

REMOVE the cornmeal from the heat, add the cheese, butter, salt, and pepper to taste, and stir until the cheese melts. Gradually pour in the buttermilk, stirring constantly. In a small bowl, lightly beat the egg yolks. Stir them into the cornmeal mixture along with the corn kernels.

IN a separate bowl, beat the egg whites with an electric mixer at medium speed until they form peaks that are stiff but not dry when the beater is raised. Stir about 2 tablespoons of the egg whites into the cornmeal mixture to lighten it, then gently fold in the remaining whites.

POUR the batter into the prepared dish and bake until firm and golden brown, about 50 minutes. Serve piping hot.

Makes 6 servings.

SMOKY CORNBREAD DRESSING

My brother-in-law, John Richardson, created this unique dressing by adapting a Craig Claiborne recipe. John prepares the dressing, which has become a family Thanksgiving tradition, while a turkey is on the outdoor smoker; a couple of hours before the turkey is ready, he transfers the bird to the top of the dressing, wraps the pan tightly in foil, and completes the cooking of the turkey in a conventional oven. The smoked fowl imparts a marvelous flavor to the dressing. Heating commercially prepared smoked fowl on the dressing accomplishes a similar effect.

The dressing can also be used to stuff a turkey or other fowl. Although it will lack the smoky flavor, the mixture is excellent simply baked in a pan on its own and served alongside roasted or grilled fare.

PREPARE the cornbread as directed. Cool completely, then finely crumble into a large bowl.

PREHEAT an oven to 325° F.

SCATTER the bread cubes on a baking sheet and bake until dry and crisp, about 10 minutes. Toss with the crumbled cornbread.

IN a saute pan or skillet, melt the butter over medium-high heat. Add the onion, sweet pepper, and celery and cook, stirring frequently, until the vegetables are soft but not browned, about 5 minutes. Stir in the sage and garlic and cook for about 1 minute longer. Add the livers and stir just until they lose their raw color. Transfer the mixture to the cornbread mixture. Add the grated eggs, raw eggs, and just enough stock or broth to moisten the mixture.

SPREAD the cornbread mixture in a medium-sized roasting pan and pat down slightly. Add smoked fowl as described in the recipe introduction. Cover tightly with aluminum foil and bake until set, about 2 hours. Serve from the baking dish, or spoon onto a platter and garnish with herb sprigs.

Makes 8 to 10 servings.

Tex-Mex Cornbread (page 425)

5 slices white or whole-wheat bread, cut into small cubes

¼ cup (½ stick) unsalted butter

2½ cups finely chopped yellow onion

1½ cups finely chopped red or green sweet pepper

1½ cups finely chopped celery

2 tablespoons minced fresh sage, or 2 teaspoons crumbled dried sage

2 teaspoons minced garlic

6 chicken livers, finely chopped

2 Hard-Cooked Eggs (page 28), grated

3 eggs, lightly beaten

About ½ cup White Stock (page 578) made with chicken or canned reduced-sodium chicken broth

Smoked fowl (see recipe introduction)

Fresh herb sprigs such as flat-leaf parsley, sage, rosemary, and thyme for garnish

CORN TORTILLAS

2 cups Mexican corn flour *(masa harina)*, or 1 pound prepared Mexican corn dough *(masa)*

Freshly made corn tortillas are easy to prepare and complement Mexican and southwestern dishes. If you don't live near a Latin American market that sells ready-to-use masa dough, use readily available Mexican corn flour (masa harina).

IF using corn flour, place it in a bowl and gradually stir in about 1⅓ cups warm water, using just enough water to form a dough that holds together. Cover and set aside for about 30 minutes.

DIVIDE the moistened corn flour or *masa* into 12 equal-sized pieces and roll each piece between your palms to form a smooth ball. As each ball is formed, transfer it to a bowl and cover the bowl with a damp cloth or moist paper toweling until all of the balls are formed.

FOR thin tortillas, place a ball of dough between 2 sheets of waxed paper or plastic wrap. Flatten the dough with your hand, then roll out with a rolling pin, turning the waxed paper or plastic wrap over several times and rolling in all directions to form a round about 9 inches in diameter. Peel off the waxed paper. If desired, trim the dough into a perfect round with a small, sharp knife, using a saucer as a guide.

ALTERNATIVELY, put each dough ball between two sheets of waxed paper or plastic wrap and place it in a tortilla press, positioning the ball slightly toward the back of the center of the press. Close the press tightly, then open the press, remove the tortilla, and peel away the waxed paper or plastic wrap.

FOR thicker tortillas, pat the dough between your palms to form a flat disk.

TO cook tortillas, place a flat Mexican griddle *(comal)*, other griddle, or heavy skillet over medium-high heat. Add a tortilla and cook until the bottom is lightly speckled with brown, about 30 seconds. Flip over with a wide spatula and cook until the other side is done, about 1 minute longer. Wrap in aluminum foil to keep warm while cooking the remaining tortillas, then serve immediately. Or, for later use, transfer to a work surface to cool completely, then wrap tightly and refrigerate for up to 1 week.

TO reheat, wrap tortillas tightly in aluminum foil and place in a preheated 350° F oven for about 15 minutes. Alternatively, using tongs, hold each tortilla over an open flame or place on a hot griddle or grill until soft and warm. Or enclose tortillas in plastic wrap and place in a microwave oven set at high for about 6 seconds per tortilla; do not overheat or the tortillas will be tough.

Makes 12 tortillas.

SWEET ENDINGS

Although most of us enjoy ending our meals with a little something sweet, I've often thought that the person who first philosophized that "life is too short, so eat dessert first" may have been right.

Desserts

HERE is a wide variety of desserts from which to choose, from simple fruits to elaborate layer cakes, with puddings, ice creams, pies, and other delectables in between.

I'm guilty as charged by one book reviewer of having "an all-American sweet tooth." If you enjoy things less sweet, the sugar in many recipes can be reduced a bit without adversely altering the end results.

VENETIAN GLAZED ORANGES
~ *ARANCE GLASSATE ALLA VENEZIANA* ~

This simple recipe turns fresh oranges into something special.

USING a vegetable peeler, remove enough of the zest (the colored part of the peel with none of the bitter white pith) from the oranges in long, narrow strips to measure ½ cup and set aside. Cut away the peel and all of the white membrane from the oranges, keeping them as round as possible and set aside.

IN a saucepan or other nonreactive pot large enough to hold all of the oranges, combine 1 cup water with the sugar, orange and lemon juices, and the orange zest strips. Place over medium-high heat and bring to a gentle boil, then adjust the heat to maintain the gentle boil and cook until the mixture is thickened to a thin syrup consistency, 5 to 8 minutes.

ADD the oranges to the syrup and continue cooking, turning the oranges frequently to coat evenly with the syrup, for 5 minutes. Remove from the heat and stir in the liqueur (if using). Set aside to cool.

COVER and refrigerate the oranges for at least 2 hours or for up to overnight, turning them occasionally in the syrup.

RETURN almost to room temperature before serving. Spoon into a serving dish or individual dishes and garnish with mint sprigs (if using).

Makes 8 servings.

8 navel oranges or blood oranges

2 cups sugar

1 cup freshly squeezed orange juice

¼ cup freshly squeezed lemon juice

About ¼ cup Italian maraschino
   liqueur (optional)

Fresh mint sprigs for garnish
   (optional)

ITALIAN BAKED STUFFED PEACHES
~ *Pesche Ripiene al Forno* ~

⅓ cup blanched almonds

Unsalted butter, at room temperature,
for greasing

6 large ripe but firm freestone peaches

½ cup finely crushed Italian almond
macaroons (amaretti)

¼ cup unsweetened cocoa (optional)

¼ cup sugar, if using cocoa

1 tablespoon grated or minced fresh
lemon zest

Amaretto liqueur, as needed

About 1 tablespoon unsalted butter,
cut into 12 equal bits

1 to 2 tablespoons sugar for
sprinkling

12 small fresh mint leaves for garnish

Mascarpone cheese (optional)

*I discovered these peaches on my first Italian sojourn and have served
them frequently during peach season ever since. You'll need about
20 small amaretti for the stuffing.*

TOAST the almonds as directed on page 554. Chop finely and set
aside.

PREHEAT an oven to 400° F. Using a pastry brush, lightly grease a
shallow baking dish with butter and set aside.

IN a large saucepan, add enough water to cover the peaches amply
when added later. Place over high heat and bring to a gentle
boil.

DROP the peaches into the boiling water for about 1 minute.
Transfer to a colander to drain. As soon as the peaches are cool
enough to handle, pull off the skins, then split in half vertically
and remove the stones. Using a small, sharp knife and a spoon,
carve out the peaches, removing enough of the pulp to leave a
shell about ½ inch thick. Reserve the scooped-out pulp and set
the peach halves aside.

IN a bowl, combine the reserved peach pulp with the chopped
almonds, crushed macaroons, cocoa (if using), the ¼ cup sugar
(if using cocoa), and lemon zest. Add just enough of the liqueur
to form a thick paste.

DIVIDE the stuffing mixture evenly among the peach halves. Place
the peaches in the prepared baking dish, dot each with a bit of
the butter, and lightly sprinkle with sugar. Bake until the
peaches are tender but still hold their shape, about 15 minutes.

GARNISH each peach half with a mint leaf. Serve warm or at room
temperature with dollops of *mascarpone*, if desired.

Makes 6 servings.

THAI TAPIOCA PUDDING WITH FRUIT ~ *SAKOO PAIK* ~

Southeast Asia produces most of the world's supply of tapioca, also known as sago, the latter of which is the source for the Thai name for this lightly sweetened dessert. This pudding, with its clean, pure flavor and almost-pourable, milky texture, is a refreshing change from the egg-rich tapioca pudding familiar to Westerners.

Imported tapioca comes in a mixture of tinted hues, as well as basic white, and a range of sizes, from tiny beads to large pearls. Actual cooking time varies with the size of the tapioca pearls.

Any fresh or canned tropical fruit may be added to the pudding. Cut the fruit into bite-sized pieces before stirring into the tapioca.

½ cup small tapioca pearls

½ cup sugar

Pinch of salt

½ cup coconut cream scooped from the top of chilled Fresh Coconut Milk (page 562) or unshaken high-quality commercial coconut milk

1 cup cut-up assorted fresh or canned fruits such as young coconut, jackfruit, longan, lychee, mango, mangosteen, palm seed, papaya, and rambutan

Fresh mint sprigs for garnish (optional)

Pesticide-free nontoxic small orchids for garnish (optional)

PLACE the tapioca in a fine-mesh strainer and quickly rinse under cold running water. Drain well, then transfer to a saucepan. Add 1½ cups water, the sugar, and salt and stir well. Place over medium-high heat and bring to a boil, stirring constantly. Reduce the heat so that the tapioca barely simmers and cook, stirring occasionally, until the tapioca turns translucent and is tender when tasted, about 15 minutes. Remove from the heat.

STIR the coconut cream into the warm pudding and set aside to cool to room temperature, or cover tightly and refrigerate until chilled.

TO serve, stir the fruits into the pudding, then spoon into 4 individual dishes and garnish with mint and/or flowers (if using).

Makes 4 servings.

SOUTHEAST ASIAN FRIED BANANAS
~ Thai *Gluay Tord* or Indonesian and Malaysian *Pisang Goreng* ~

½ cup all-purpose flour

½ cup rice flour (not sweet rice flour)

1 tablespoon sugar

1 teaspoon baking powder

¼ teaspoon salt

2 eggs

⅔ cup Fresh Coconut Milk (page 562) or high-quality commercial coconut milk

Canola oil or other high-quality vegetable oil for frying

6 large ripe but firm bananas, or 12 finger-sized bananas

Choose bananas that have just turned yellow all over; overripe ones will fall apart during frying. If desired, roll the batter-coated bananas in shredded coconut and/or sesame seed before frying, or sprinkle the fried bananas with toasted shredded coconut and/or sesame seed after frying. Dusting the fried fruit and plate with a mixture of ground cardamom and powdered sugar adds a flavorful and festive touch.

For a special treat, serve with Thai Frozen Coconut Cream (page 464) or a favorite vanilla, coconut, or ginger ice cream, or top with dollops of coconut cream sweetened to taste with palm sugar.

IN a bowl, combine the flours, sugar, baking powder, and salt and mix well. In a separate bowl, lightly beat the eggs, add ⅓ cup water and the coconut milk, and stir until well blended. Stir into the flour mixture and beat until smooth. Cover and refrigerate for about 2 hours.

IN a wok, deep fryer, or saucepan, pour in oil to a depth of 2 inches and heat to 375° F. Place a wire rack on a baking sheet and position alongside the stove top or fryer.

WHILE the oil is heating, peel the bananas. Slice each large banana crosswise into 3 pieces of equal length; leave small bananas whole.

DIP banana pieces or whole small bananas in the batter to coat completely and carefully lower into the hot oil; avoid crowding the pan. Fry, turning several times, until golden brown all over, about 3 minutes. Using a slotted utensil, transfer the bananas to the wire rack to drain briefly. Fry the remaining bananas in the same manner, allowing the oil to return to 375°F between batches.

ARRANGE on a platter or individual plates and serve warm.

Makes 6 servings.

VARIATION

Fried Pineapple (Thai *sapbhalot tord* or Indonesian and Malaysian *nanas goreng*). For the bananas, substitute 6 round pineapple slices, each about ½ inch thick and cut into 3 wedges; pat dry with paper toweling before dipping in the batter.

THAI STICKY RICE WITH MANGOES ~ *MAMUANG KAO NIEO* ~

Street vendors in Thailand sell sticky rice steeped in coconut milk as a special treat during mango season. Try it with summer peaches or nectarines.

2 cups white sticky rice

1¾ cups Fresh Coconut Milk (page 562) or high-quality commercial coconut milk

½ cup palm sugar

½ teaspoon salt

4 or 5 ripe mangoes

Coconut cream scooped from the top of chilled Fresh Coconut Milk or unshaken commercial coconut milk for serving (optional)

COOK the rice as directed on page 368, then transfer it to a bowl.

IN a saucepan, combine the coconut milk, sugar, and salt. Place over medium-high heat and stir until the sugar is dissolved, about 3 minutes. Pour the mixture over the warm rice, stir to combine, and let stand, uncovered, for at least 30 minutes or for up to 2 hours; do not refrigerate.

TO serve, peel the mangoes and cut each half from their large stones. Slice each half into 4 long pieces. Arrange pieces on individual plates, add a scoop of the rice, and top with a spoonful of coconut cream (if using).

Makes 6 servings.

WINE-POACHED PEARS FILLED WITH MASCARPONE IN CARAMEL SAUCE

FILLING

½ cup *mascarpone* cheese (about
   4 ounces)

¼ cup powdered sugar, or to taste

POACHED PEARS

Juice of 2 lemons

6 large ripe but firm pears,
   preferably Bosc

1 cup granulated sugar

1 bottle (750 ml) fruity red or white
   wine or port

Zest of 1 lemon, cut into thin strips

1 vanilla bean, split (optional)

1 cinnamon stick

Caramel Sauce (page 584)

Mascarpone cheese, whisked until
   smooth, for serving (optional)

Fresh mint leaves for garnish

Cornmeal Biscotti (page 438), Italian
   almond macaroons (amaretti), or
   other crisp cookies for serving

When I first created this recipe, mascarpone, *the luxurious Italian triple-cream cheese, was difficult to locate outside of its homeland. Now many local cheese shops and supermarkets carry it.*

The poaching liquid may be saved for another batch of pears or for sipping after dinner.

TO make the filling, in a small bowl, combine the cheese and powdered sugar and whisk until smooth. Cover and refrigerate until needed.

TO make the Poached Pears, in a large bowl, pour in enough cold water to cover all of the pears once they are added. Stir in the lemon juice and set aside. Working with 1 pear at a time, peel as smoothly as possible, leaving the stem intact. Cut a slice off the bottom of the pear so that it will stand upright. Core the pear from the bottom, place it in the lemon water to prevent discoloration, and prepare the remaining pears. Set aside.

SELECT a saucepan just large enough to hold all of the pears standing upright. Combine the granulated sugar, wine, lemon zest, vanilla bean (if using), and cinnamon stick in the saucepan. Bring the mixture to a boil over high heat, stirring to dissolve the sugar.

REMOVE the pears from the lemon water and fill each pear cavity with crumpled aluminum foil. Stand the pears upright in the boiling poaching liquid, adding enough water to cover them. Adjust the heat to maintain a simmer, cover, and poach the pears until they are tender but still hold their shape, about 20 minutes.

WITH a slotted utensil, carefully remove the pears to a shallow bowl. Increase the heat to medium-high and cook the poaching liquid until reduced to about 1½ cups. Pour over the pears and set aside to cool to room temperature. (At this point, the pears can be covered and refrigerated in the poaching liquid for up to 2 days.)

REMOVE the crumbled foil from the pear cavities. Using a spoon or a pastry bag fitted with a medium-sized plain tip, fill the pears with the reserved *mascarpone* filling. Stand the filled pears upright on a tray or platter, cover, and refrigerate until a few minutes before serving time.

PREPARE the Caramel Sauce as directed and keep warm.

TO serve, place each pear on an individual dessert plate. Add a dollop of whisked *mascarpone* (if using) alongside. Slowly spoon the warm sauce over the top of the pears, letting it run down and pool on the plates. Garnish each pear with a mint leaf alongside the stem and serve immediately with the cookies.

Makes 6 servings.

CORNMEAL BISCOTTI

Unsalted butter or solid vegetable
    shortening, at room temperature,
    or cooking spray for greasing
    (optional)
1⅓ cups all-purpose flour
1 cup yellow cornmeal
1 cup sugar
1½ teaspoons baking powder
¼ teaspoon salt
3 eggs, beaten
1 teaspoon pure almond extract
⅔ cup finely chopped blanched
    almonds or other nuts
1 egg yolk mixed with 1 tablespoon
    milk for brushing

*These Italian-style cookies are great on their own or for dunking in coffee,
hot chocolate, or fruity wine. For larger biscotti, form the dough into only
2 loaves.*

POSITION racks so that the biscotti will bake in the middle of an
    oven and preheat the oven to 400° F. Using a pastry brush, lightly
    grease a baking sheet with butter or shortening, or coat with
    spray or line with kitchen parchment. Set aside.

IN a bowl, combine the flour, cornmeal, sugar, baking powder, salt,
    eggs, and almond extract. Beat with an electric mixer at medium
    speed until the dough is well mixed. Stir in the nuts.

GENEROUSLY dust a work surface and your hands with flour.
    Divide the dough into 4 equal portions. Working with 1 piece
    of dough at a time, knead briefly and roll it into a rope about
    9 inches long and about 2½ inches in diameter; as you roll,
    incorporate flour as needed to keep the dough from sticking to
    the surface and scrape the surface as needed to keep it clean and
    smooth. Place the finished ropes several inches apart on the
    prepared baking sheet. Flatten tops slightly with fingers so that
    the sides of each rope are a little flatter than the center. Brush
    the exposed surface of each piece of dough evenly with the egg
    yolk mixture.

BAKE the loaves until golden, about 20 minutes. Remove the baking
    sheet from the oven and set aside to cool for about 5 minutes.

TRANSFER each cookie loaf to a cutting board and cut crosswise
    into slices about 1 inch thick. Arrange the slices on an ungreased
    baking sheet and return to the oven until dry, about 5 minutes
    longer. Transfer to a wire rack to cool completely.

STORE the cooled cookies in airtight containers.

Makes about 3 dozen biscotti.

MEXICAN PUMPKIN TURNOVERS
~ *Empanadas con Calabaza* ~

Pastry half-moons encased with spicy sweet pumpkin puree are a favorite snack or dessert in Mexico, especially during the Christmas season. Of course, you can use any cooked winter squash in place of pumpkin.

TO make the pastry, place the flour, sugar, baking powder, and ½ teaspoon salt together in a strainer or sifter and sift into a bowl or a food processor. Add the lard or shortening and cut in with a pastry blender or the steel blade just until the mixture resembles coarse bread crumbs. Sprinkle the iced water, a tablespoon at a time, over the dough and mix just until the dough begins to hold together in a shaggy mass. Form into a ball with your hands, wrap in waxed paper or plastic wrap, and refrigerate for 30 minutes.

TO make the filling, in a heavy saucepan, combine the pumpkin puree, brown sugar, aniseed, nutmeg, and ¼ teaspoon salt. Place over medium-high heat and bring to a boil, then adjust the heat to maintain a simmer and simmer, uncovered, for 10 minutes. Remove from the heat and set aside to cool to room temperature before using.

POSITION racks so that the turnovers will bake in the middle of an oven and preheat the oven to 400° F. Using a pastry brush, lightly grease a baking sheet with lard or shortening, or coat with spray or line with kitchen parchment. Set aside.

TURN out the chilled dough onto a lightly floured surface and roll it out into a round about ⅛ inch thick. For *empanadas*, cut the dough into 4- to 5-inch rounds; for *empanaditas*, cut into 3-inch rounds. Spoon a heaping tablespoon of the filling on one-half of each large circle, or a heaping teaspoon on each small circle. Moisten the edges of the circle with water and fold the uncovered side of the circle over the filled side to form a half-moon. Press the edges together with the tines of a fork. Place the pastries on the prepared baking sheet, brush the tops with the egg yolk mixture, and bake until golden brown, about 20 minutes.

REMOVE the turnovers to a wire rack to cool briefly. Sprinkle with the sugar-cinnamon mixture while still hot. Serve warm or at room temperature.

Makes about 12 *empanadas* or 36 *empanaditas*.

PASTRY

2 cups all-purpose flour

2 tablespoons sugar

2 teaspoons baking powder

½ teaspoon salt

⅔ cup high-quality pure lard or solid vegetable shortening, chilled

About ¼ cup iced water

FILLING

1 cup pureed Roasted Winter Squash (page 318) made with pumpkin or canned pumpkin (not pumpkin pie filling)

¼ cup firmly packed brown sugar

2 teaspoons aniseed

½ teaspoon freshly grated nutmeg

¼ teaspoon salt

Lard or solid vegetable shortening, at room temperature, or cooking spray for greasing (optional)

1 egg yolk mixed with 1 tablespoon milk for brushing

2 tablespoons sugar mixed with 2 teaspoons ground cinnamon for sprinkling

CARAMEL-GLAZED CUSTARD
~ FRENCH *CRÈME CARAMEL*, ITALIAN *CREMA CARAMELLA*, OR SPANISH *FLAN* ~

1¾ cups sugar

5 egg yolks

3 eggs

2 cans (12 ounces *each*) evaporated milk (not fat free)

2 teaspoons pure vanilla extract

Pesticide-free edible flowers such as violets for garnish (optional)

By any name, this silky concoction is one of my favorite desserts, especially for capping off a spicy meal.

This Santa Fe version calls for canned milk, which was used in most early New Mexican cooking due to the scarcity of fresh milk. The canned product adds an extra caramel accent, but feel free to substitute the same amount of fresh milk (not fat free), half-and-half, cream, or a combination. For a tangy flavor, substitute fresh or canned evaporated goat's milk.

The process of caramelizing sugar must have your total attention. To prevent the melting sugar from crystallizing, do not stir it once it is dissolved until it is completely melted.

POSITION racks so that the custards will bake in the middle of an oven and preheat the oven to 350° F. Select a 9-by-2-inch round cake pan or eight 6-ounce ovenproof custard cups and set aside. Position a large bowl of iced water alongside the stove top.

IN a heavy saucepan, preferably made of stainless steel or copper, combine 1 cup of the sugar and ¼ cup water and stir well. Place over medium heat, cover, and heat for about 4 minutes. Remove the cover and continue to cook without disturbing the mixture until it begins to color, then continue cooking, slowly swirling the pan occasionally to spread the color evenly, until the syrup turns a rich amber; this will take about 8 minutes after removing the cover from the pan. During cooking, if sugar crystals begin to form around the sides of the pan just above the bubbling syrup, brush them away with a pastry brush moistened with water. As soon as the syrup reaches the desired color, briefly place the pan in the iced water to halt cooking.

CAREFULLY pour the hot caramel syrup into the reserved pan or cups, distributing equally if using cups, and immediately swirl each container to coat the bottom and about one-third of the way up the sides. (If the caramel sets up too quickly in the saucepan, reheat until pourable, avoiding cooking further.) Set the container(s) aside to cool; the syrup will harden very quickly.

IN a large bowl, combine the egg yolks and eggs and beat lightly with a fork; avoid overbeating at any point to prevent too many air bubbles from forming. Slowly stir in the milk, then the remaining ¾ cup sugar and vanilla. Slowly pour the mixture through a fine-mesh strainer into the syrup-lined pan or strain into a pitcher and pour into the prepared cups, distributing evenly.

PLACE the pan or cups on a rack set in a large, deep baking pan, transfer to the oven, and pour enough hot (not boiling) water into the large pan to reach about halfway up the sides of the custard container(s). Place a sheet of aluminum foil over the pan to cover the tops of the custard(s) loosely.

BAKE until the custard(s) are set but still wobble like gelatin when the containers are shaken very gently, 1 hour to 1½ hours for the large custard or about 20 to 30 minutes for the cups. (At high altitudes, the custards may take longer to set.) Regulate the oven temperature during baking to maintain water at the almost-simmering stage; do not allow to boil.

TRANSFER the custard container(s) from the water bath to a wire rack.

TO serve warm, set aside to cool for about 15 minutes. Run a thin, flexible knife blade around the inside edges of a container. Invert a serving plate over the container, invert the plate and container together, and carefully lift off the container; caramel syrup will run down the sides and onto the serving plate to surround the custard. Repeat with any remaining custards. Cut the large custard into wedges and spoon some of the syrup over each portion.

TO serve cold, set aside to cool to room temperature, then cover tightly and refrigerate until well chilled, at least 3 hours or for up to overnight. Just before serving, dip the bottom of the container(s) in a bowl of hot water for about 30 seconds, then loosen the custard(s) and unmold as directed in the previous paragraph. Garnish with flowers (if using).

Makes 8 servings.

CRÈME BRÛLÉE

4 cups heavy (whipping) cream

10 egg yolks

¾ cup sugar, or to taste

Pinch of salt

1 teaspoon pure vanilla extract

Sugar for sprinkling

One of my tests of a good restaurant kitchen lies in the success of its crème brûlée. This popular dessert is now commonly known by its French name, which certainly sounds more delicious than the original English moniker of burnt cream. The name comes from the fact that the creamy custard is topped with sugar that is melted and caramelized, not really burned. This custard itself is actually just a less sweet variation of a pot de crème. For a new twist, try one of the flavor variations on pages 444-445.

Tradition dictates that crème brûlée be baked in deep custard cups. Today many chefs pour the mixture into wide, shallow gratin dishes that allow for a larger expanse of the crisp sugar glaze. Restaurants typically use a heated baker's iron or a salamander to melt the sugar; most home cooks rely on a hot broiler to do the job. A small blowtorch from the hardware store does a terrific job and makes it easy to control the melting; it is well worth the small investment if you enjoy this dessert.

POSITION racks so that the custards will bake in the middle of an oven and preheat the oven to 300° F. Select eight 6-ounce ovenproof custard cups or shallow gratin dishes and set aside.

IN a heavy saucepan, place the cream over medium heat and bring almost to the boiling point, then remove from the heat.

MEANWHILE in a bowl, break the egg yolks with a fork and lightly beat in the ¾ cup sugar and the salt; avoid overbeating at any point to prevent too many air bubbles from forming. Gradually stir in the hot cream until the sugar is dissolved and the mixture is smooth. Stir in the vanilla. Pour the mixture through a fine-mesh strainer into a glass measuring cup or a pitcher, and then carefully pour into the custard cups or dishes, distributing equally.

PLACE the cups or dishes on a rack (or racks) set in a large, deep baking pan (or pans), transfer to the oven, and pour enough hot (not boiling) water into the baking pan(s) to reach about halfway up the sides of the custard containers. Place a sheet of aluminum foil over the pan to cover the tops of the custards loosely.

BAKE until the custards are set but still wobble like gelatin when the containers are shaken very gently, about 30 minutes for gratin dishes or about 1½ hours for cups. (At high altitudes, the custards may take longer to set.) Begin checking early and frequently to avoid overcooking. Cooking time will vary according to the material and thickness of the containers and depth of the custards.

TRANSFER the custard containers from the water bath to a wire rack to cool completely, then cover tightly and refrigerate until well chilled, at least 6 hours or for up to 2 days.

SHORTLY before serving, remove the custards from the refrigerator and gently blot the surfaces with paper toweling to remove any moisture. Sprinkle the tops of the custards with a thin, even layer of sugar.

USING a small propane blowtorch held at an angle so that the flame barely touches the surface of the sugar, melt and caramelize the sugar by moving the flame back and forth over the surface.

IF not using a blowtorch, position a broiler rack so that the tops of the custards will be about 4 inches from the heat source and preheat the broiler to very hot. Arrange the custard dishes on a cloth kitchen towel in a shallow pan. Surround the custard containers with ice. Place under the broiler until the sugar melts and the tops are bubbly, about 1 minute; watch carefully to avoid scorching.

LET stand for a few minutes to harden the crust. If kept for more than 1 hour, the crisp tops will melt.

Makes 8 servings.

variations follow ~

CRÈME BRÛLÉE OR POT DE CRÈME VARIATIONS

Banana Custard. Reduce the cream to 3 cups total. Stir 1 cup banana puree, 2 tablespoons light rum, and ½ teaspoon ground cardamom into the completed custard mix. When serving *pot de crème*, garnish with sliced banana just before serving.

***Cajeta* Custard.** Reduce the cream to 2 cups total. After heating the cream, stir in 2 cups heated Mexican Caramelized Goat's Milk Sauce (page 586).

Caramel Custard. Heat the cream as directed and set aside. Beat the egg yolks as directed, omitting the sugar, and set aside. In a heavy saucepan, preferably made of stainless steel or unlined copper, combine the sugar with 1 tablespoon water and stir well. Place over medium heat and cook without disturbing the mixture until it begins to color, then continue cooking, slowly swirling the pan occasionally to spread the color evenly, until the syrup turns a rich amber. During cooking, if sugar crystals begin to form around the sides of the pan just above the bubbling syrup, brush them away with a pastry brush moistened with water. Immediately remove the syrup from the heat and slowly stir it into the hot cream until smooth. Strain the cream mixture into the beaten egg yolks. For added luxury to *pot de crème*, spoon a little warm Caramel Sauce (page 584) over each custard just before serving.

Carrot Custard. Reduce the cream to 3 cups total. Substitute firmly packed light brown sugar or maple syrup for the sugar. After heating the cream and straining it into the egg mixture, stir in 1 cup pureed cooked carrot and 1 teaspoon ground cinnamon or ginger.

Chocolate Custard. Stir ½ cup unsweetened cocoa, preferably Dutch-processed, or to taste, into the sugar before adding it to the eggs. Or chop 6 to 8 ounces finest-quality sweetened chocolate (milk, semisweet, or bittersweet) and stir the chocolate into the warming cream until melted. Remove from the heat and steep for about 15 minutes before straining.

Chocolate-Studded Custard. Sprinkle 2 teaspoons chopped finest-quality semisweet or bittersweet chocolate in the bottom of each custard dish before adding the custard mixture.

Citrus Custard. Add the chopped or grated zest of 2 or 3 lemons, limes, oranges, or tangerines to the cream before heating. Remove from the heat and steep for about 15 minutes before straining. When serving *pot de crème*, spoon a little warm Lemon Sauce (page 589) over each custard just before serving, if desired.

Coconut Custard. Substitute Fresh Coconut Milk (page 562) or high-quality commercial coconut milk for all of the cream. When serving *pot de crème*, sprinkle each custard with a little toasted shredded coconut just before serving, if desired.

Coffee Custard. Stir 2 tablespoons instant espresso into the heated cream.

Fruited Custard. Divide about 2 cups chopped or cubed banana, mango, papaya, nectarine, or peach or whole blueberries or raspberries among the bottoms of the custard cups before pouring in the custard mixture.

Ginger Custard. Add 2 to 3 tablespoons chopped fresh ginger to the cream before heating. Remove from the heat and steep for about 15 minutes before straining.

Lavender Custard. Add ½ cup fresh lavender blossoms to the cream before heating. Remove from the heat and steep for about 15 minutes before straining.

Maple Custard. Substitute pure maple syrup for the sugar in the egg mixture. When serving *pot de crème*, pour a little warm maple syrup over each custard just before serving, if desired.

Mint or Geranium Custard. Add ½ cup coarsely chopped fresh mint or scented geranium leaves to the cream before heating. Remove from the heat and steep for about 15 minutes before straining.

Pumpkin or Winter Squash Custard. Reduce the cream to 3 cups. Substitute firmly packed light brown sugar for the granulated sugar. After adding the strained cream to the egg mixture, stir in 1 cup pureed Roasted Winter Squash (page 318) or canned pumpkin (not pumpkin pie filling), ¼ teaspoon *each* ground cinnamon and freshly grated nutmeg, and ⅛ teaspoon *each* ground allspice and cloves.

Spirited Custard. Add about ¼ cup sherry, brandy, Marsala, port, or other fortified wine or spirit to the strained warm custard mixture.

POT DE CRÈME

4 cups heavy (whipping) cream

1 vanilla bean, split lengthwise
   (optional)

10 egg yolks

1 cup sugar

Pinch of salt

2 teaspoons pure vanilla extract
   (if not using a vanilla bean)

This smooth and elegant custard, commonly known by its French name, is traditionally cooked and served in small pots with covers, although any small baking dishes work well. It is extremely important, however, not to overcook the custard.

To vary the flavor, use any of the variations on pages 444-445.

POSITION racks so that the custards will bake in the middle of an oven and preheat the oven to 300° F. Select eight 6-ounce ovenproof *pot de crème* pots or custard cups.

IN a heavy saucepan, combine the cream and vanilla bean. Place over medium heat and bring almost to the boiling point, then remove from the heat. If using a vanilla bean, using the tip of a small, sharp knife, scrape the seeds into the cream and stir to combine; discard the bean.

IN a bowl, break the egg yolks with a fork and lightly beat in the sugar and salt; avoid overbeating at any point to prevent too many air bubbles from forming. Gradually stir in the hot cream until the sugar is dissolved and the mixture is smooth. If not using a vanilla bean, stir in the vanilla extract. Pour the mixture through a fine-mesh strainer into a pitcher, and then carefully pour the custard mixture into the pots or custard cups, distributing equally.

PLACE the custard containers on a rack set in a large, deep baking pan, transfer to the oven, and pour enough hot (not boiling) water into the pan to reach about halfway up the sides of the custard containers. Cover the pots with their lids or place a sheet of aluminum foil over the pan to cover the tops of the custards loosely.

BAKE until the custards are set but still wobble like gelatin when the containers are shaken very gently, about 30 minutes. Begin checking early and frequently to avoid overcooking.

TRANSFER the custard containers from the water bath to a wire rack, remove the lids or foil, and set aside to cool to room temperature. Cover tightly and refrigerate for several hours; return almost to room temperature before serving.

Makes 8 servings.

BANANA PUDDING

My grandmother Izetta McNair made the best version of this American classic that I've ever tasted. Unfortunately no one in my family wrote down just how she concocted her divine creation, which she always did without looking at a recipe, of course. My aunt Pauline Wiggington and I have each come close to duplicating Mawmaw Mackie's pudding, but nothing quite lives up to the taste stored in my memory. Perhaps it was the farm-fresh ingredients. Or perhaps it wasn't really any better, but rather just idealized in my childhood memories. Or maybe we were just hungrier back then.

3 eggs yolks (reserve whites for topping)

1 cup sugar

1½ tablespoons cornstarch

Pinch of salt

3 cups whole milk or half-and-half

¼ cup (½ stick) unsalted butter, at room temperature

1½ teaspoons pure vanilla extract

About 30 vanilla wafers

6 ripe bananas

Meringue Topping (page 592)

IN a heavy saucepan, combine the egg yolks, sugar, cornstarch, and salt. Whisk or stir in the milk or half-and-half, a little at a time, until the mixture is smooth. Place over medium heat and cook, stirring and scraping the bottom of the pan constantly to prevent scorching, until the mixture thickens, 8 to 10 minutes. Reduce the heat to very low and cook, stirring constantly, for about 3 minutes longer. Remove from the heat, add the butter and vanilla, and stir until the butter melts.

LINE a 2-quart baking dish or casserole with half of the vanilla wafers. Peel the bananas and slice crosswise about ¼ inch thick. Arrange half of the banana slices over the wafers. Cover with about half of the warm custard. Top with the remaining vanilla wafers in a single layer, then the remaining banana slices. Cover with the remaining custard.

PREHEAT an oven to 325° F.

PREPARE the Meringue Topping as directed. Cover the pudding with meringue and bake as directed on page 592.

REMOVE the pudding to a wire rack to cool. Serve at room temperature. Do not refrigerate.

Makes 6 servings.

FLOATING ISLANDS

8 egg whites, at room temperature

¼ teaspoon cream of tartar

Pinch of salt

1 cup sugar

3 cups whole milk

1 teaspoon pure vanilla extract

Crème Anglaise (page 582)

This classic meringue dessert, called oeufs à la neige, île flottante, *or* snow eggs, *lends itself to infinite variations. The egg yolks that remain once you have assembled the egg whites for the meringues can be used for making the Crème Anglaise.*

IN the bowl of a stand mixer fitted with a wire whip, or in a metal bowl with a hand mixer, combine the egg whites, cream of tartar, and salt and beat at medium speed until soft peaks form when the beater is slowly raised. With the mixer running, gradually add the sugar, about 1 tablespoon at a time, and continue to beat until the whites form peaks that are stiff and shiny but still moist when the beater is raised. Set aside.

IN a large skillet, bring the milk to a gentle boil over medium heat. Stir in the vanilla.

USING an ice cream scoop or large spoon rinsed in cold water, scoop up about one-sixth of the egg white mixture and drop it into the gently boiling milk. Repeat with the remaining egg white mixture, dipping the scoop or spoon in cold water each time and forming 6 equal scoops in all. Poach the meringues, turning gently with a spoon several times, until set, 2 to 3 minutes; do not overcook. Using a slotted utensil, carefully remove the meringues to a cloth kitchen towel to drain well. (Strain the poaching milk into a bowl and reserve for making the Crème Anglaise, if desired.) Transfer the drained meringues to a platter or tray, cover loosely, and refrigerate until cold, about 2 hours.

PREPARE the Crème Anglaise as directed. Set aside until serving time. It may be served warm, at room temperature, or chilled.

TO serve, ladle some of the Crème Anglaise onto individual deep plates or shallow bowls and top with a meringue. Alternatively, pour the sauce into a large serving dish and arrange the meringues over the top. Spoon a meringue and a portion of the sauce into individual serving dishes at the table.

Makes 6 servings.

VARIATIONS

Caramel Floating Islands. Prepare the meringue islands and Crème Anglaise as directed and refrigerate. Prepare caramel syrup as directed for Caramel-Glazed Custard on page 440. Using a fork, drizzle the hot caramel syrup from the tines over the meringues. Serve the islands with the sauce as directed and garnish with fresh or crystallized violets.

Chocolate Floating Islands. Prepare the meringue islands and Chocolate Crème Anglaise (page 582) as directed and refrigerate. Serve the islands with the sauce as directed and sprinkle each island with shavings of the same type of chocolate used in the sauce.

Coffee Floating Islands. Prepare the meringue islands and Coffee Crème Anglaise (page 583) as directed and refrigerate. Serve the islands with the sauce as directed and sprinkle each island with a bit of freshly ground coffee.

Golden Treasure Snow Eggs. Prepare the meringue islands and Orange Crème Anglaise (page 583) as directed and refrigerate. Serve the islands with the sauce as directed and sprinkle each island with grated fresh orange zest.

Tropical Floating Islands. Prepare the meringue islands and Coconut Crème Anglaise (page 583) as directed and refrigerate. In a food processor or blender, puree the pulp of 2 medium-sized mangoes with sugar and freshly squeezed lime juice to taste; cover and refrigerate until serving time. Puree 2 cups raspberries or hulled strawberries with ¼ cup fresh passion fruit juice or passion fruit liqueur and sugar and lemon juice to taste; cover and refrigerate until serving time. Serve the islands with the sauce as directed. Spoon small pools of the mango sauce and passion fruit sauce onto the custard, then draw a wooden skewer through the sauces to create a pattern. Sprinkle each island with lightly toasted shredded coconut.

PANNA COTTA

1 envelope (2½ teaspoons)
   unflavored gelatin

¼ cup whole milk

3 cups heavy (whipping) cream

½ cup sugar

Unsalted butter, at room temperature,
   for greasing

Fresh Berry Sauce (page 589)

Berries for garnish

Some recipes that I've encountered for panna cotta, *or the "cooked cream" of Tuscany and Piedmont, call for heating half of the cream, then cooling it before whipping the remaining cream and folding the two together with softened gelatin and sometimes beaten egg white. To my taste, this creates a texture more akin to a Bavarian cream than to the silky quivering versions of* panna cotta *I've enjoyed in Italy. This one is reminiscent of the version served at Osteria del Cinghiale Bianco in Florence.*

IN a small bowl, combine the gelatin and milk. Stir well and set aside to soften for about 5 minutes.

IN a saucepan, combine the cream and sugar, place over medium heat, and stir frequently until the mixture comes to a boil. Stir in the gelatin mixture and continue to stir until the mixture is smooth and the gelatin is completely dissolved, about 1 minute. Pour into a large glass measuring cup or bowl. Immediately place a piece of plastic wrap directly onto the surface of the cream to prevent a skin from forming. Set aside to cool to room temperature.

USING a pastry brush, lightly grease six 6-ounce custard cups or timbale molds with butter. Pour or spoon the cooled cream mixture into the prepared containers, distributing evenly. Cover tightly with plastic wrap and refrigerate until set, at least 3 hours or for up to 12 hours.

PREPARE the Fresh Berry Sauce as directed.

TO serve, dip the bottom of a container into a bowl of hot water for about 30 seconds, then run a thin, flexible knife blade around the inside edges of the container. Invert a serving plate over a container, invert the plate and container together, and carefully lift off the container. Repeat with the remaining containers. Spoon the sauce over the tops and garnish with berries.

Makes 6 servings.

VARIATIONS

Caramel-Glazed Cooked Cream *(Panna Cotta con Caramello)*.
Prepare caramel syrup and line custard cups as directed for
Caramel-Glazed Custard on page 440. Let cool completely
before spooning in the cream mixture. Omit the sauce and
berry garnish.

Coffee Cooked Cream *(Panna Cotta di Caffè)*. Add 2 tablespoons
instant espresso, or to taste, to the cream while heating. Serve
with Chocolate Sauce (page 587) instead of the berry sauce and
berry garnish.

Vanilla-Citrus Cooked Cream *(Panna Cotta di Vaniglia e
Citrone)*. Add 1 vanilla bean, split lengthwise, and the zest
from 1 lemon or orange to the cream before heating it. Once
the cream comes to a boil, remove the vanilla bean and citrus
zest before stirring in the gelatin mixture. Scrape the seeds
from the vanilla bean into the cream.

ENGLISH TRIFLE

STIRRED CUSTARD

2¾ cups whole milk

1 cup heavy (whipping) cream,
    light cream, or half-and-half

1 vanilla bean, split lengthwise
    (optional)

¾ cup sugar, or more to taste

¼ cup cornstarch

Pinch of salt

4 egg yolks, at room temperature

2 tablespoons cold unsalted butter

2 teaspoons pure vanilla extract (if
    not using a vanilla bean)

3 cups whole blueberries or
    raspberries or sliced strawberries,
    or a mixture

Sugar

Lemon Curd (page 593) or high-
    quality commercial lemon curd

Pound Cake (page 518) or high-quality
    commercial pound cake

Dry sherry for sprinkling

Whipped Cream (page 590) for topping

Berries (same as used in trifle) for
    garnish

Fresh mint leaves for garnish

To show off the multicolored layers of a trifle, choose a straight-sided glass bowl or individual straight-sided glasses. Use my basic recipe as a guide to layer any cake, jam or berry sauce, fresh fruit, and custard. For a lighter-textured trifle, make 2 Hot-Milk Sponge Cakes as directed in the recipe for Passion Fruit Cake on page 546 and use in place of the pound cake.

When making the stirred custard, remember that you must cook it over low heat to insure success. Although I prefer to cook the custard over direct heat and stir constantly to prevent scorching, feel free to place the mixture in the top pan of a double boiler and cook it over simmering water; it may take a bit longer to thicken.

TO make the Stirred Custard, in a heavy saucepan, combine 2 cups of the milk, the cream or half-and-half, and vanilla bean (if using). Place over medium heat and bring almost to the boiling point, then remove from the heat. If using a vanilla bean, using the tip of a small, sharp knife, scrape the seeds into the milk and stir to combine; discard the bean.

IN another heavy saucepan, stir together the sugar, cornstarch, and salt. Stir in the remaining ¾ cup milk and mix well. Add the egg yolks and whisk to blend. Pour the hot milk through a fine-mesh strainer into a pitcher, then slowly whisk it into the sugar mixture. Place over very low heat and cook, whisking constantly, until thickened, 10 to 12 minutes. Cover and cook for about 8 minutes longer, whisking several times. Then, while still over the heat, whisk or beat with a hand mixer at medium speed until very smooth, about 2 minutes.

REMOVE from the heat. Add the butter and stir until the butter melts, then stir in the vanilla extract (if not using a vanilla bean). Transfer to a bowl and immediately place a piece of plastic wrap directly onto the surface of the custard to prevent a skin from forming. Set aside to cool to room temperature and use immediately, or refrigerate the cooled pudding for up to 24 hours.

IN a bowl, lightly sweeten the berries with sugar to taste.

TO assemble the trifle, spoon a thin layer of lemon curd in the bottom of a 2½-quart bowl or 6 to 8 individual containers (see recipe introduction). Top with a layer of custard ¼ to ½ inch thick. Slice the cake ¼ to ½ inch thick. Cut the slices to fit inside the serving dish(es) and arrange over the custard in a single layer; if necessary, use trimmings to fill any holes in the cake layer. Sprinkle the cake layer with sherry to moisten. Spoon on enough lemon curd to cover the cake with a thin layer, spoon on a layer of the chopped berries, top the fruit with another layer of the custard, then add another cake layer and sprinkle with sherry. Continue to layer in this manner until all of the ingredients are used up, ending with the custard.

COVER and refrigerate for at least 5 hours or for up to overnight.

JUST before serving, cover the top of the trifle with Whipped Cream, crown it with a few dollops of lemon curd, and swirl to create a pattern. Garnish with berries and mint leaves.

IF prepared in a large container, spoon up the dessert at the table.

Makes 6 to 8 servings.

TIRAMISÙ

5 egg yolks

½ cup powdered sugar

Pinch of salt

1 pound *mascarpone* cheese

About 2 cups cold espresso or other
strong, dark brewed coffee

About 30 ladyfingers

6 ounces finest-quality milk or
semisweet chocolate, grated or
shaved with a vegetable peeler

For a more delicate version of this Italian "pick me up," use slices of sponge cake (see Hot-Milk Sponge Cake in the recipe for Passion Fruit Cake on page 546) in place of the traditional ladyfingers. Mascarpone, a rich Italian cream cheese, may be found in cheese stores and many supermarkets. For a fluffier version, beat 4 egg whites until stiff peaks form and fold them into the mascarpone *mixture.*

If desired, add hazelnut-, coffee-, or orange-flavored liqueur or dry Marsala to taste to the coffee before dipping the ladyfingers.

IN a bowl, combine the egg yolks, sugar, and salt. Whisk or beat with an electric mixer until thick and pale yellow, about 5 minutes. Add the *mascarpone* and beat until the mixture is smooth and thick. Set aside.

POUR the coffee into a shallow bowl. Dip some of the ladyfingers in the coffee and use them to line the bottom and sides of 6 large coffee cups or a 2½-quart straight-sided bowl. Spoon in about half of the *mascarpone* mixture, distributing equally if using cups, and sprinkle with about half of the chocolate. Dip the remaining ladyfingers in the coffee and arrange them in a single layer atop the *mascarpone.* Top with the remaining *mascarpone* mixture and sprinkle the remaining chocolate over the top.

COVER and refrigerate for at least 4 hours or for up to overnight. If made in a single bowl, spoon into individual dishes when serving.

Makes 6 servings.

WHIPPED WINE CUSTARD
~ French *Sabayon* or Italian *Zabaglione* ~

Italians make their frothy zabaglione *with Marsala. French cooks are
more likely to prepare* sabayon *with dry sherry, Madeira, vermouth, or
with sparkling or dessert wines. For a different flavor, combine the wine
with a spirit such as bourbon, rum, or Calvados or other brandy, or add
a favorite liqueur. Citrus juice and zest, vanilla, or ground ginger or other
spices may be added along with the wine.*

*Although the custard may be eaten on its own, it is frequently
served with fresh berries or sliced fruits. Or offer crisp cookies for dipping
into the custard.*

6 egg yolks

⅓ cup sugar, or to taste

Pinch of salt

½ cup Marsala wine or other
wine or spirit (see recipe
introduction)

IN a round-bottomed copper *zabaglione* pan or the top pan of a
double boiler, combine the egg yolks, sugar, and salt. Using a
wire whisk or hand mixer, beat until the mixture is pale and
creamy, about 3 minutes. Slowly whisk in the wine.

SET over simmering (not boiling) water. Continue to beat
constantly until the custard is thick, foamy, and doubled in
volume, 5 to 8 minutes.

SPOON into stemmed glasses and serve warm.

Makes 4 servings.

VARIATIONS

FOR a lighter custard, in a metal bowl beat 6 egg whites with a hand
mixer at medium speed until stiff peaks form when the beater is
raised. Fold them into the warm custard just before serving.

FOR a cold stabilized custard that holds its shape, remove the warm
custard from the heat and place the pan in a bowl of iced water to
cool rapidly. Beat 2 cups heavy (whipping) cream as directed on
page 590 just until it holds its shape. Using a rubber spatula,
fold the whipped cream into the custard. Cover and chill or
freeze. If frozen, remove from the freezer a few minutes before
serving.

ITALIAN CUSTARD ICE CREAM
~ *Gelato di Crema* ~

2 cups whole milk

2 cups heavy (whipping) cream

Zest of 1 lemon

7 egg yolks

1 cup sugar

¼ teaspoon salt

Some of my fondest gastronomic memories of visits to Italy are centered around this creamy concoction. On a hot September afternoon in the late 1970s, while waiting to meet up with dear friends from California who had been traveling separately from us, Lin and I sampled several flavors from Gelateria Vivoli, a Florence institution near Santa Croce. After Marian and Louis arrived, we all indulged in several other scoops of gelato, including one containing grains of rice. It took a lot of sightseeing to walk off our frozen feast.

On a recent trip I was pleased to discover that Vivoli's gelato still tastes as great as I remember. During our daily pilgrimages to the venerable institution, Andrew and I sampled many flavors, although crema, the plain custard version, remains my favorite.

Here is a basic custard recipe and a few flavor variations to get you started. If you have a large ice cream maker, you can double the recipe. Many Italian cookbooks do not call for cream in their gelato recipes, but it adds the smoothness and richness of products made in Italy.

PLACE a bowl in a larger bowl of iced water and set aside.

IN a heavy saucepan, combine the milk, cream, and lemon zest. Place over medium heat and bring the mixture almost to the boiling point, then remove from the heat.

IN a bowl, combine the egg yolks, sugar, and salt and, using a whisk or an electric mixer, beat until the mixture is pale yellow, about 3 minutes. Slowly stir in the hot milk mixture until smooth. Transfer to the top pan of a double boiler set over barely simmering water. Cook, stirring constantly, until the custard mixture thickens enough to coat the back of a spoon thickly. This will take 15 to 20 minutes; do not allow to boil. Pour through a fine-mesh strainer into the bowl set in iced water. Place a piece of plastic wrap directly onto the surface of the custard to prevent a skin from forming, and let cool for about 15 minutes. Remove the plastic wrap, cover tightly and refrigerate until well chilled, at least 3 hours or, preferably, overnight.

POUR the chilled custard mixture into an ice cream maker and
freeze according to the manufacturer's instructions. Serve when
the gelato holds together but is still soft. Or pack into a container
with a tight-fitting lid and place in a freezer for several hours
or for up to several days. Transfer the freezer container to the
refrigerator about 30 minutes before you plan to serve the ice
cream to allow it to reach the proper consistency. If the gelato
gets icy from long storage in a freezer, whip it with a whisk just
before serving.

Makes about 1 quart for 4 servings.

VARIATIONS

Caramel Ice Cream *(Gelato di Caramello).* Prepare caramel
syrup as directed for Caramel-Glazed Custard (page 440) and
remove from the heat. While whisking or stirring, slowly add
1 cup of the cold cream; don't worry if the caramel syrup begins
to harden. Place over low heat, stirring constantly, until smooth.
Heat the milk with the remaining 1 cup cream as directed in
the basic recipe. Combine the eggs with only ¼ cup sugar and
complete the custard. Stir the warm custard into the caramel
mixture, then strain into the cold bowl. Stir 2 teaspoons pure
vanilla extract into the cooled custard before refrigerating.

Chocolate Ice Cream *(Gelato di Cioccolato).* Reduce the sugar
to ½ cup and omit the lemon zest. Melt 6 to 8 ounces finest-
quality semisweet or bittersweet chocolate as directed on page
595 and stir into the warm custard. Stir 1 teaspoon pure
vanilla extract into the cooled custard before refrigerating.
Alternatively, use the recommended amount of sugar and sift
¼ cup unsweetened cocoa, or more to taste, into the milk
mixture and beat until smooth before heating. Stir in
1 teaspoon pure vanilla extract into the cooled custard before
refrigerating.

continues ~

Chocolate-Hazelnut Ice Cream *(Gelato di Gianduia)*. Omit the lemon zest. Finely chop or grind 2 cups hazelnuts and add to the milk mixture before heating. Remove from the heat and set aside for 30 minutes, then pour through a strainer lined with dampened cheesecloth, pressing against the nuts to release as much liquid as possible. Pour the milk mixture into a saucepan and reheat. Prepare the custard as directed, then melt 4 ounces finest-quality semisweet chocolate as directed on page 595 and stir it into the warm custard. Stir 1 teaspoon pure vanilla extract into the cooled custard before refrigerating.

Coffee Ice Cream *(Gelato di Caffè)*. Omit the lemon zest. Dissolve 3 tablespoons instant espresso, or to taste, in the warm milk mixture.

Lemon Ice Cream *(Gelato di Limone)*. Add the zest of 2 more lemons and ½ cup freshly squeezed lemon juice to the milk and cream before heating.

Nut Ice Cream *(Gelato di Noce)*. Toast 2 cups almonds, hazelnuts (filberts), peanuts, pecans, pine nuts, or other nuts as directed on pages 553 or 554. Transfer the warm nuts to a food processor and grind as finely as possible. Stir into the milk mixture before heating. Remove from the heat and let stand for 30 minutes, then pour through a strainer lined with dampened cheesecloth, pressing against the nuts to release as much liquid as possible. Pour the milk mixture into a saucepan and reheat. (If you enjoy textured ice cream, do not strain.) Continue as directed, adding 1 teaspoon pure vanilla extract or almond or other nut extract to the cooled custard before refrigerating.

Peach Ice Cream *(Gelato di Pesca)*. In a food processor, puree enough peeled and pitted peaches to equal 2 cups puree. Stir the puree and 2 teaspoons pure vanilla extract into the cooled custard before refrigerating.

Rhubarb Ice Cream *(Gelato di Rabarbaro)*. In a heavy-bottomed saucepan, combine 2 quarts chopped rhubarb, ⅔ cup sugar, and ½ cup water. Place over medium heat and cook, stirring occasionally, until the rhubarb is very tender. Transfer to a food processor and puree. Stir in 2 tablespoons freshly squeezed lemon juice and set aside while you prepare the custard as directed. Stir the puree into the warm custard. Stir 1 teaspoon pure vanilla extract into the cooled custard before refrigerating.

Strawberry or Raspberry Ice Cream *(Gelato di Fragola or Gelato di Lampone)*. In a food processor, puree enough berries to equal 3 cups puree. Stir in 2 tablespoons freshly squeezed lemon juice and sweeten to taste with sugar (½ to ¾ cup); the puree should taste slightly too sweet in order to account for reduced sweetness that results from the freezing process. Stir the puree and 1 teaspoon pure vanilla extract into the cooled custard before refrigerating.

Vanilla Ice Cream *(Gelato di Vaniglia)*. Omit the lemon zest. Split 1 vanilla bean lengthwise and add to the milk and cream before heating. Using the tip of a small, sharp knife, scrape the seeds into the heated cream; discard the bean. Set the mixture aside to steep for about 30 minutes, then reheat and continue to prepare the custard as directed. Stir 1 tablespoon pure vanilla extract into the cooled custard before refrigerating.

White Chocolate Ice Cream *(Gelato di Cioccolato Bianco)*. Omit the lemon zest. Melt 1 pound finest-quality white chocolate containing cocoa butter as directed on page 595 and stir into the warm custard. Stir 1 teaspoon pure vanilla extract into the cooled custard before refrigerating.

COFFEE AND VANILLA ICE CREAM DOME WITH BITTERSWEET CHOCOLATE SAUCE

PEANUT BUTTER FILLING

½ cup light corn syrup

⅓ cup crunchy peanut butter,
  at room temperature

1 tablespoon unsalted butter

1 egg, at room temperature

½ teaspoon pure vanilla extract

1 pint Coffee Ice Cream (page 458)
  or high-quality commercial coffee
  gelato or rich ice cream

CHOCOLATE CRUST

1 cup chocolate wafer crumbs (from
  about 24 medium-sized wafers)

¼ cup firmly packed light brown
  sugar

½ teaspoon ground cinnamon

6 tablespoons unsalted butter,
  melted

Either make your own smooth Italian ice creams (see page 456) or purchase a high-quality brand that's rich in butterfat. If you prefer a sweeter sauce, use part or all semisweet chocolate instead of bittersweet.

TO make the Peanut Butter Filling, in a saucepan, combine the corn syrup and 2 tablespoons water, place over medium-high heat, and bring to a boil. Reduce the heat to medium and cook for 5 minutes. Using a whisk, beat in the peanut butter until fairly smooth, then stir in the butter until melted and remove from the heat.

IN a small bowl, lightly beat the egg. Slowly stir about 2 tablespoons of the peanut butter mixture into the beaten egg, then add the egg mixture to the saucepan. Place over low heat and cook, stirring constantly, until the egg is cooked, about 2 minutes. Remove from the heat and set aside to cool to room temperature, then stir in the vanilla, cover, and refrigerate until spreadable, about 30 minutes.

SOFTEN the coffee ice cream until it reaches a spreadable consistency. Spread in an even layer up to the rim of a 5-cup rounded mold or bowl, leaving a cavity inside. Cover tightly with plastic wrap and freeze until the ice cream is firm.

REMOVE the mold from the freezer and spread the Peanut Butter Filling evenly over the coffee ice cream layer. Cover tightly with plastic wrap and freeze until firm.

TO make the Chocolate Crust, combine the chocolate wafer crumbs, brown sugar, and cinnamon in a mixing bowl. Add the melted butter and blend well with a fork. Set aside.

SOFTEN the vanilla ice cream until it reaches a spreadable consistency. Remove the mold from the freezer and spread the vanilla ice cream evenly over the peanut butter layer. Cover with the cookie mixture in an even layer, wrap tightly in aluminum foil, and freeze until firm or for up to overnight. Remove from the freezer about 15 minutes before serving.

PREPARE the Chocolate Sauce as directed and keep warm.

TO unmold the dome, dip the mold or bowl briefly in a bowl of hot water. Invert a serving plate over the mold, invert the plate and mold together, and carefully lift off the mold. Garnish with the coffee beans (if using) and serve immediately. Slice in wedges at the table and serve each slice with the sauce.

Makes 6 to 8 servings.

1 pint Vanilla Ice Cream (page 459) or high-quality commercial vanilla gelato or rich ice cream

Chocolate Sauce (page 587) made with bittersweet chocolate

Chocolate-covered coffee beans for garnish (optional)

ITALIAN FRUIT ICE
~ GRANITA DI FRUTTA ~

Simple Sugar Syrup (page 599)

2 cups pureed berries, apricot,
    kiwifruit, mango, melon, nectarine,
    papaya, peach, pear, persimmon,
    or pineapple; or 2 cups of a favorite
    fruit juice

2 tablespoons freshly squeezed
    lemon, lime, or orange juice
    (if using fruit puree)

Fresh mint sprigs for garnish

Berries or ripe fruit slices for garnish

Italian fruit ices can be made from a variety of perfectly ripe seasonal soft fruits and berries. Usually fruit ices are made from only one kind of fruit; if you like, use a pleasing combination.

I like to keep a bottle of sugar syrup in the refrigerator to use whenever the inspiration strikes to make an ice. The type of fruit and degree of ripeness determines the amount of syrup needed; keep in mind when tasting the mixture that freezing diminishes sweetness, so add more syrup than you may think necessary when the mixture is at room temperature.

The coffee variation is a refreshing way to perk up a hot afternoon or end a warm-weather meal.

PREPARE the Simple Sugar Syrup as directed and refrigerate until well chilled.

PLACE a 13-by-9-by-2-inch metal pan in a freezer to chill thoroughly.

PUT the fruit puree or juice in a bowl. If using puree, add the lemon, lime, or orange juice. Stir in 1½ cups of the chilled Simple Sugar Syrup, or to taste; amount will vary according to sweetness of the fruit.

POUR the mixture into the chilled metal pan, cover tightly with aluminum foil or plastic wrap, and place in the freezer until ice crystals form around the edges of the pan, about 30 minutes.

REMOVE the pan from the freezer. Using a metal fork, stir the ice crystals toward the center of the mixture. Cover and return to the freezer. Repeat this stirring process every 30 minutes until the ice is completely frozen, about 2½ hours.

JUST before serving, break up the ice with a fork and spoon it into glasses. Garnish with mint and a few of the same berries or fruit slices used in the ice.

ALTERNATIVELY, combine the ingredients and refrigerate until well chilled, then pour the mixture into an ice cream maker and freeze according to the manufacturer's instructions.

Makes about 1 quart, enough for 4 servings.

VARIATIONS

Coffee Ice *(Granita di Caffè)*. Combine 2½ cups chilled brewed espresso or other chilled brewed dark-roast coffee and ½ cup Simple Sugar Syrup, or to taste. For *caffè latte* ice, add heavy (whipping) cream to taste. Freeze as directed. Garnish servings with dollops of whipped cream, if desired.

Grapefruit-Campari Ice *(Granita di Pompelmo e Campari)*. Combine 2 cups freshly squeezed grapefruit juice, 1 teaspoon grated or minced fresh grapefruit zest, ¾ cup Campari, and 1 cup Simple Sugar Syrup, or to taste. Freeze as directed.

Lemon Ice *(Granita di Limone)*. Combine 1 cup cold water, ¾ cup freshly squeezed lemon juice, 2 teaspoons minced or grated fresh lemon zest, and 1¼ cup Simple Sugar Syrup, or to taste. Freeze as directed. Garnish servings with lemon slices and lemon leaves or blossoms (if available).

THAI FROZEN COCONUT CREAM
~ *IDEM GA-TI* ~

1½ cups Simple Sugar Syrup
(page 599), or to taste
4 cups Fresh Coconut Milk
(page 562) or high-quality
commercial coconut milk

When I retested this recipe in preparation for this book, using frozen "Hawaiian-style" coconut milk packed in the Philippines, my friend Michele Sordi pronounced it the best dessert she'd ever had. Coming from such a world-class gourmet, it was a high compliment for this softly frozen sweet, a cross between sorbet and ice cream. Don't expect a firm American-style ice cream; the results are more akin to an Italian gelato. The cold cream is a wonderful counterpoint to warm Southeast Asian Fried Bananas (page 434).

PREPARE the Simple Sugar Syrup as directed and set aside to cool.

IN a bowl, combine the coconut milk and syrup and blend well. Cover tightly and refrigerate until well chilled, at least 3 hours or, preferably, overnight.

JUST before freezing, whisk or stir the chilled coconut mixture as smoothly as possible. Pour into an ice cream maker and freeze according to the manufacturer's instructions until the mixture is frozen yet still soft.

SERVE immediately, or pack into a container with a tight-fitting lid and place in a freezer for several hours; transfer to a refrigerator about 20 minutes before serving to allow it to reach the proper consistency.

Makes 4 servings.

VENETIAN GLAZED
ORANGES
(page 431)

———

WINE-POACHED PEARS
FILLED WITH MASCARPONE
IN CARAMEL SAUCE
(page 436)
and CORNMEAL BISCOTTI
(page 438)

CARAMEL-GLAZED
CUSTARD
(page 440)

———

CHOCOLATE
MOUSSE
(page 474)

WHITE CHOCOLATE
MOUSSE
(page 473)

———

CITRUS ORCHARD
MOUSSE
(page 476)

PANNA COTTA

(page 450)

———

ITALIAN

FRUIT ICE

(page 462)

MEXICAN
RICE PUDDING
(page 488)

————

SUMMER BERRY
AND POLENTA PUDDING
(page 514)

469

KEY LIME PIE

(page 502)

———

LEMONY BERRY PIE

(page 499)

AUTUMN
SQUASH PIE

(page 509)

———

FRESH GINGER CAKE

WITH CREAMY

MACADAMIA

NUT FROSTING

(page 530)

NUT CAKE

(page 544)

———

DEVIL'S FOOD CAKE

WITH GANACHE

(page 535)

WHITE CHOCOLATE MOUSSE

At the Twin Peaks Grocery in San Francisco, we turned out gallons of this scrumptious froth to satisfy the demands of numerous customers. Be sure to use white chocolate that contains cocoa butter, not the white coating chocolate made with vegetable oils.

I like to serve this mousse in Chocolate Containers (page 594) or Crisp Cookie Cups (page 597) set on a pool of Fresh Berry Sauce (page 589) made from a blend of strawberries and raspberries.

2 cups heavy (whipping) cream, preferably not ultrapasteurized, well chilled

2 cups sugar

½ cup egg whites (from about 4 eggs), at room temperature

Pinch of cream of tartar

1 pound finest-quality white chocolate containing cocoa butter, finely chopped

PLACE a metal bowl and a wire whisk or the beaters of a hand mixer in a freezer until well chilled.

IN the chilled bowl, beat the cream with the chilled whisk or hand mixer just until it forms soft peaks when the beater is raised; do not overbeat. Cover and refrigerate.

IN a saucepan, combine the sugar and ½ cup water. Place over high heat and cook, without stirring, until the mixture registers between 244° and 248° F (firm-ball stage) on a candy thermometer. Remove from the heat.

MEANWHILE, in a metal bowl with clean beaters, beat the egg whites with an electric mixer at low speed until frothy bubbles cover the surface. Add the cream of tartar, increase the mixer speed to medium, and beat until very soft peaks form when the beater is slowly raised. With the mixer running, gradually drizzle in the hot syrup and beat until the whites form peaks that are stiff but still moist when the beater is raised. Add the white chocolate and beat until the chocolate melts and is well blended into the egg white mixture, about 1 minute. Transfer to a bowl and set aside to cool to room temperature.

FOLD the whipped cream into the egg white mixture, incorporating well. Cover and refrigerate until set, at least 3 hours or for up to overnight.

Makes 8 servings.

CHOCOLATE MOUSSE

CLASSIC CHOCOLATE MOUSSE

8 ounces finest-quality semisweet or bittersweet (not unsweetened) chocolate, finely chopped

6 tablespoons (¾ stick) unsalted butter

3 eggs, at room temperature, separated

2 egg yolks, at room temperature

2 teaspoons pure vanilla extract

1 cup heavy (whipping) cream, preferably not ultrapasteurized, well chilled

Pinch of cream of tartar

3 tablespoons sugar

Here are two versions of this beloved dessert. Since classic mousse uses uncooked egg yolks, some people are afraid to enjoy this venerable favorite due to fear of contracting salmonellosis. If you feel that way due to outbreaks of the disease in your area, try the very simple yet rich-tasting version made without eggs.

For a whimsical presentation, prepare both Chocolate Mousse and White Chocolate Mousse (page 473) and layer them in tall glasses, similar to a parfait, or swirl them together in a bowl to create a marbleized effect.

TO make Classic Chocolate Mousse, place a metal bowl and a wire whisk or the beaters of a hand mixer in a freezer until well chilled.

IN a skillet or shallow saucepan, pour in water to a depth of 1 inch, place over medium heat, bring just to a simmer, and adjust the heat to maintain barely simmering water. Combine the chocolate and butter in a heatproof bowl, set the bowl in the simmering water, and stir the mixture constantly just until melted and smooth; do not allow to burn. Alternatively, combine the chocolate and butter in a microwave-safe measuring cup or bowl and microwave at 50 percent power, stirring every 15 seconds, just until melted and smooth; do not allow to burn. Set the mixture aside to cool for a few minutes, then transfer to a bowl and whisk in the 5 egg yolks, one at a time, until smooth. Stir in the vanilla, cover, and refrigerate.

IN the chilled bowl, beat the cream with the chilled whisk or hand mixer just until it forms soft peaks when the beater is raised; do not overbeat. Cover and refrigerate.

IN a metal bowl with clean beaters, beat the egg whites with an electric mixer at low speed until frothy bubbles cover the surface. Add the cream of tartar, increase the speed to medium, and beat until very soft peaks form when the beater is slowly raised. With the mixer running, gradually add the sugar, about 1 tablespoon at a time, and beat until the whites form peaks that are stiff and shiny but still moist when the beater is raised. Stir about one-fourth of the whites into the chocolate mixture to lighten it, then fold in the remaining whites and the whipped cream, incorporating well. Spoon into a serving bowl or divide evenly among individual bowls or glasses. Cover tightly and chill for about 2 hours.

TO make the **Eggless Chocolate Mousse**, position a large bowl of iced water near the stove top. In a saucepan, combine the chocolate and cream. Place over medium-low heat until the chocolate begins to melt and the cream is almost simmering. Whisk or stir until the chocolate and cream are smooth. Stir in the vanilla and powdered sugar. Remove from the heat and place the pan in the bowl of iced water. Whisk until the mixture is creamy smooth and softly holds its shape. Spoon into a serving bowl or divide evenly among individual bowls or glasses. Cover tightly and chill for about 2 hours.

JUST before serving, prepare the Whipped Cream (if using) and spoon dollops onto each serving.

Makes 6 servings.

VARIATION

Mocha Mousse. Add 1 tablespoon instant espresso dissolved in 1 tablespoon hot water to the warm chocolate mixture.

EGGLESS CHOCOLATE MOUSSE

8 ounces finest-quality semisweet or bittersweet (not unsweetened) chocolate, finely chopped

2 cups heavy (whipping) cream, preferably not ultrapasteurized, well chilled

2 teaspoons pure vanilla extract

½ cup powdered sugar, or to taste

Whipped Cream (page 590) for topping (optional)

CITRUS ORCHARD MOUSSE

3 eggs, separated

2 egg yolks

½ to 1 cup sugar

¾ cup freshly squeezed citrus juice

1 tablespoon grated or minced fresh
  citrus zest (optional)

1 cup heavy (whipping) cream,
  preferably not ultrapasteurized,
  well chilled

Pinch of cream of tartar

Pinch of salt

Thinly sliced citrus slices for garnish

Fresh mint sprigs for garnish

Any citrus juice and zest or a combination of different citrus may be used in this airy dessert.

PLACE a metal bowl and a wire whisk or the beaters of a hand mixer in a freezer until well chilled.

IN the top pan of a double boiler, beat the 5 egg yolks with a whisk or hand mixer until very thick and pale yellow, about 5 minutes. Gradually beat in 1 cup sugar if using lime or lemon juice, or ½ cup sugar if using orange or tangerine juice; adjust amount of sugar to taste and tartness of the fruit. Stir in the citrus juice and zest (if using). Set over simmering (not boiling) water and cook, whisking or beating continuously, until the mixture is slightly thicker than heavy cream, about 5 minutes. It should coat the back of a spoon and your finger should leave a trail when you run it across the spoon; do not overcook or the mixture will curdle. Transfer to a bowl and set aside to cool to room temperature.

IN the chilled bowl, beat the cream with the chilled whisk or hand mixer just until it forms soft peaks when the beater is raised; do not overbeat. Cover and refrigerate.

IN a metal bowl with clean beaters, beat the egg whites with an electric mixer at low speed until frothy bubbles cover the surface. Add the cream of tartar and salt, increase the speed to medium, and beat until the whites form peaks that are stiff and shiny but still moist when the beater is raised. Stir about one-fourth of the beaten egg whites into the citrus mixture to lighten it. Fold in the remaining egg whites and the whipped cream, incorporating well. Spoon into a serving bowl or distribute equally among individual serving dishes or glasses, cover tightly, and chill until the mousse is set, at least 3 hours or for up to overnight.

GARNISH each serving with citrus slices and mint.

Makes 6 servings.

RHUBARB MOUSSE

Once upon a time I enjoyed a lovely visit with Sir Cecil Beaton, noted photographer and designer, at his fairy-tale-setting English country home. The mousse made of fresh rhubarb from his extensive garden was the highlight of lunch. It was an experience right out of his design for My Fair Lady.

The mousse mixture also makes a great pie filling for the Cookie Crumb Crust (page 498) made with sugar cookies.

IN a saucepan, combine the rhubarb and ½ cup water. Place over medium heat and bring to a boil, then cover and cook, stirring occasionally, until the rhubarb is very tender, about 5 minutes. Strain and reserve the liquid.

TRANSFER the rhubarb pulp to a food processor or blender. Add ½ cup of the sugar, the lemon juice, and gelatin and puree until smooth. Bring the reserved liquid to a boil, add ⅓ cup of it to the rhubarb mixture, and blend well. Set aside to cool.

PLACE a metal bowl and a wire whisk or the beaters of a hand mixer in the freezer until well chilled. Position a bowl of iced water alongside the stove top.

IN the top pan of a double boiler, combine the egg yolks and the remaining ¾ cup sugar and blend well. Set over simmering (not boiling) water and cook, stirring or whisking constantly, until the mixture is smooth and thick and just hot to the touch. Set in the bowl of iced water and whisk the mixture until cool, then stir in the rhubarb mixture and let stand in the iced water, stirring frequently, until the mixture reaches the consistency of lightly whipped cream.

IN the chilled bowl, beat the cream with the chilled whisk or hand mixer just until it forms soft peaks when the beater is raised; do not overbeat. Fold it into the rhubarb mixture and spoon into a serving bowl or individual bowls or goblets. Cover and refrigerate until set, 2 to 3 hours.

GARNISH each serving with violets (if using).

Makes 6 servings.

6 cups chopped tender young rhubarb

1¼ cups sugar

2 tablespoons freshly squeezed lemon juice

1 envelope (2½ teaspoons) unflavored gelatin

3 egg yolks

1 cup heavy (whipping) cream, preferably not ultrapasteurized, well chilled

Pesticide-free edible violets for garnish (optional)

LEMON SPONGE PUDDING CAKE

Unsalted butter, at room temperature,
    for greasing

1 cup sugar

¼ cup (½ stick) unsalted butter, at
    room temperature

2 teaspoons finely grated or minced
    fresh lemon zest

3 eggs, at room temperature,
    separated and yolks lightly beaten

¼ cup all-purpose flour

Pinch of salt

1¼ cups milk (not fat free)

½ cup freshly squeezed lemon juice

Seasonal berries (optional)

Here's an old-time pudding cake that separates during baking into spongy cake crowning a creamy sauce. Some people like to serve this chilled, but I only enjoy it warm from the oven.

POSITION racks so that the pudding cake will bake in the middle of an oven and preheat the oven to 350° F. Using a pastry brush, generously grease an 8-inch square pan or a 1½-quart baking dish with butter and set aside.

IN a bowl, combine the sugar, ¼ cup butter, and lemon zest and beat with an electric mixer at medium speed until creamy, about 3 minutes. With the mixer still running, slowly drizzle in the egg yolks and beat well. Stir in the flour, salt, milk, and lemon juice. Set aside.

IN a metal bowl with clean beaters, beat the egg whites at medium speed until they form peaks that are stiff but still moist when the beater is raised. Stir about one-fourth of the whites into the batter to lighten it. Using a rubber spatula, fold in the remaining whites. Pour the mixture into the prepared baking container.

PLACE the pudding container on a rack set in a large, deep baking pan, transfer to the oven, and pour enough hot (not boiling) water into the large pan to reach about halfway up the sides of the pudding container. Bake until the top pudding layer is set and lightly browned, about 45 minutes. Regulate the oven temperature during baking to maintain water at the almost-simmering stage; do not allow to boil.

REMOVE the pudding container from the water bath to a wire rack to cool slightly, then serve warm with berries (if using).

Makes 6 servings.

CREOLE BREAD PUDDING

Years ago when I lived in the French Quarter, I frequently enjoyed this treat at the Coffee Pot, where Pearl made it every day. Before leaving New Orleans, I talked her out of the recipe, which has been a standby in my kitchen ever since.

Later at the Twin Peaks Grocery in San Francisco, one of our employees, Julian Turk, made the recipe so often that we nicknamed him "Pearl."

For variety, try one of the versions on the next two pages.

SLICE enough bread into ½-inch-thick slices to fill an 8-inch square pan in 2 layers, then transfer the bread to a large bowl. Using a pastry brush, lightly grease the pan with butter or shortening, or coat with spray. Set aside.

IN a bowl, combine the eggs, sugar, milk, cream, melted butter, vanilla and almond extracts, currants or raisins, and nutmeg; whisk to blend well. Pour the mixture over the bread slices and set aside, turning the bread as necessary, until the bread is soft and saturated with the mixture, about 30 minutes.

ARRANGE the bread slices in 2 layers in the prepared pan. Pour any unabsorbed egg mixture over the top of the bread, cover, and refrigerate for at least 3 hours or for up to overnight.

PREHEAT an oven to 350° F.

BAKE until the pudding is set and the top is lightly browned, about 45 minutes. During baking, occasionally push the bread down into the sauce with a spatula.

MEANWHILE, prepare the selected sauce and keep warm or reheat just before serving.

TO serve, spoon the warm pudding into shallow bowls and ladle some of the sauce over the top.

Makes 6 servings.

variations follow ~

Stale French bread

Unsalted butter or solid vegetable shortening, at room temperature, or cooking spray for greasing

2 eggs, at room temperature

¾ cup sugar

3 cups milk (not fat free), at room temperature

1 cup heavy (whipping) cream, at room temperature

½ cup (1 stick) unsalted butter, melted and cooled slightly

2 teaspoons pure vanilla extract

1 teaspoon almond extract

½ cup dried currants or raisins

1 teaspoon freshly grated nutmeg, or to taste

Lemon Sauce (page 589) or Warm Liquor Sauce (page 587) made with Southern Comfort or bourbon

Banana Bread Pudding. Use banana bread in place of the French bread; slice and lightly toast in an oven to dry. Substitute chopped crystallized ginger for the currants or raisins. Serve with Crème Anglaise (page 582) or Whipped Cream (page 590).

Bread Loaf Pudding. Substitute a 9-by-5-inch loaf pan for the square pan. Use thinly sliced stale high-quality white bread in place of the French bread. Cut off and discard the crusts and trim the slices so that they will stand upright in the loaf pan. Omit the currants or raisins. Dip the bread slices into the egg mixture, then pack the slices rather tightly in the pan to resemble a loaf of bread. Pour any remaining egg mixture over the bread, cover tightly, and refrigerate overnight. Bake as directed and set aside to cool to room temperature, then cover and refrigerate overnight. To serve, run a thin, flexible knife blade around the inside edges of the pan. Invert a serving plate over the pan, invert the plate and pan together, and carefully lift off the pan. Slice the pudding crosswise. Ladle Crème Anglaise (page 582) onto individual plates, then top with slices of the pudding.

Chocolate Bread Pudding. Use chocolate pound cake in place of the French bread; slice and lightly toast in an oven to dry. Omit the currants or raisins. Add 1 cup chopped toasted pecans (see page 554) to the egg mixture, if desired. Serve with warm Caramel Sauce (page 584), Chocolate Sauce (page 587), or Crème Anglaise (page 582).

Chocolate-Caramel Bread Pudding. This variation was inspired by a dessert that I devoured at Mark Miller's Coyote Cafe in Santa Fe. Use chocolate pound cake in place of the French bread; slice and lightly toast in an oven to dry. Reduce the sugar to ⅓ cup and substitute 1 cup Mexican Caramelized Goat's Milk Sauce (page 586) for the cream. Substitute toasted pine nuts (see page 553) for the currants or raisins. Serve with both Chocolate Sauce (page 587) and Mexican Caramelized Goat's Milk Sauce (page 586).

Croissant Bread Pudding. Use stale Croissants (page 22), sliced horizontally, in place of the French bread. Substitute chopped Candied Orange Zest (page 596) for the currants or raisins. For a chocolate version, add about 1 cup coarsely chopped finest-quality semisweet or milk chocolate to the egg mixture.

Date-Nut Bread Pudding. Substitute chopped pitted dates for the currants or raisins and add 1 cup chopped toasted pecans or other nuts (see page 554) to the egg mixture. Serve with Lemon Sauce (page 589).

Gingerbread Pudding. Use Gingerbread (page 515) in place of the French bread; slice and lightly toast in an oven to dry. Serve warm with Old-fashioned Dessert Sauce (page 588) or Lemon Sauce (page 589).

Pumpkin Bread Pudding. Use pumpkin bread in place of the French bread; slice and lightly toast in an oven to dry. Sweeten the custard with pure maple syrup or light brown sugar instead of the sugar. Use chopped dried dates in place of the currants or raisins. When the pudding comes out of the oven, pour warm Caramel Sauce (page 584) over the top and set aside to cool slightly before serving.

BAKED PERSIMMON PUDDING

Unsalted butter or solid vegetable
shortening, at room temperature,
or cooking spray for greasing

2 cups all-purpose flour

1 teaspoon baking powder

1 teaspoon baking soda

½ teaspoon salt

1½ teaspoons ground cinnamon

1 teaspoon ground ginger

3 eggs, at room temperature

1½ cups granulated or firmly packed
light brown sugar

½ cup (1 stick) unsalted butter,
melted and cooled slightly

1 tablespoon pure vanilla extract,
or 2 tablespoons rum

2 cups light cream or half-and-half,
at room temperature

2 cups pureed persimmon (from very
ripe Hachiya persimmons)

1 cup raisins

1 cup chopped pecans or other nuts

I like to offer both Crème Anglaise (page 582) and Caramel Sauce (page 584) for pouring over scoops of this traditional dessert. Diners may choose either or use both in combination. For an elegant presentation, ladle one of the sauces onto each large plate and top with a scoop of the pudding, then dribble small pools of the other sauce on top of the first sauce and pull a wooden skewer through the sauces to create a pattern. Good topping alternatives include Whipped Cream (page 590) or rich vanilla ice cream.

POSITION racks so that the pudding will bake in the middle of an oven and preheat the oven to 350° F. Using a pastry brush, lightly grease a 13-by-9-inch pan with butter or shortening, or coat with spray. Set aside.

IN a bowl, combine the flour, baking powder, baking soda, salt, cinnamon, and ginger. Whisk to mix well and set aside.

IN a bowl, combine the eggs and sugar and beat with an electric mixer until well blended. Stir in the melted butter and vanilla or rum. Fold in the dry ingredients just until incorporated. Slowly stir in the half-and-half and persimmon puree, then mix in the raisins and pecans. Pour into the prepared pan.

PLACE the pan on a rack set in a larger, deep baking pan, transfer to the oven, and pour enough hot (not boiling) water into the larger pan to reach about halfway up the sides of the pudding pan. Bake until a wooden skewer inserted into the center of the pudding comes out almost clean, about 1 hour. Regulate the oven temperature during baking to maintain water at the almost-simmering stage; do not allow to boil.

REMOVE the pudding pan from the water bath to a wire rack to cool slightly, then serve as suggested in the recipe introduction.

Makes 12 servings.

INDIAN PUDDING

Introduced by native Americans to the English who settled along the northeastern seaboard, this traditional sweet is fabulous teamed with a sauce from the Southwest, Mexican Caramelized Goat's Milk Sauce (page 586). The pudding is also delicious served with a scoop of vanilla ice cream or softly Whipped Cream (page 590).

Unsalted butter or solid vegetable
   shortening, at room temperature,
   or cooking spray for greasing
½ cup cornmeal
4 cups cold milk (not fat free)
1 cup firmly packed dark brown
   sugar
½ cup light molasses
6 tablespoons (¾ stick) unsalted
   butter, melted and cooled slightly
1 tablespoon ground ginger
1 teaspoon freshly grated nutmeg
1½ teaspoons salt
1 cup light cream or half-and-half

POSITION racks so that the pudding will bake in the middle of an oven and preheat the oven to 350° F. Using a pastry brush, generously grease a 2-quart baking dish with butter or shortening, or coat with spray. Set aside.

IN a heavy saucepan, combine the cornmeal and milk and stir well. Place over medium-high heat and bring to a simmer, stirring occasionally. Adjust the heat to maintain a simmer and cook, stirring frequently and scraping the bottom of the pan to prevent scorching, until thick and smooth, about 10 minutes. Remove from the heat and stir in the brown sugar, molasses, melted butter, ginger, nutmeg, and salt. Pour into the prepared baking dish.

PLACE the baking dish on a rack set in a large, deep baking pan, transfer to the oven, and pour enough hot (not boiling) water into the large pan to reach about halfway up the sides of the pudding dish. Bake until bubbly, about 30 minutes.

IN a saucepan, place the cream or half-and-half over medium heat and bring almost to a boil, then pour it over the top of the pudding. Continue baking until set to the touch, about 2 hours longer. Regulate the oven temperature during baking to maintain water at the almost simmering stage; do not allow to boil.

REMOVE the pudding dish from the water bath to a wire rack to cool slightly, then serve as suggested in the recipe introduction.

Makes 6 servings.

STEAMED GINGER PUDDING

Unsalted butter or solid vegetable
shortening, at room temperature,
or cooking spray for greasing

Granulated sugar for dusting

½ cup (1 stick) unsalted butter, at
room temperature

1½ cups firmly packed light brown
sugar

4 eggs, at room temperature, lightly
beaten

1⅓ cups fine fresh white or whole-
wheat bread crumbs

1½ cups all-purpose flour

1 teaspoon baking powder

1 teaspoon salt

2 tablespoons grated or minced fresh
ginger

2 teaspoons ground ginger

½ teaspoon freshly grated nutmeg

½ teaspoon ground cinnamon

2 tablespoons grated or minced fresh
orange zest

1 teaspoon grated or minced fresh
lemon zest

2 teaspoons pure vanilla extract, or
¼ cup brandy or ginger-flavored
liqueur

1½ cups golden raisins

½ cup finely chopped crystallized
ginger or drained preserved ginger
in syrup

*Ginger in three forms adds a special flavor to this English-style pudding,
which is best served warm with Orange Crème Anglaise (page 583), softly
Whipped Cream (page 590), or Crème Fraîche (page 591).*

SELECT a 2-quart pudding mold or heatproof bowl and a pot with
a tight-fitting cover large enough to hold the container. Place a
flat steaming rack in the bottom of the pot. Place the pudding
mold or bowl on the rack and add enough water to the pot to reach
about halfway up the sides of the mold or bowl, then remove the
mold or bowl. Place the pot over high heat and bring the water
to a boil, then cover and adjust the heat to achieve a simmer.

USING a pastry brush, generously grease the mold or bowl with
butter or shortening, or coat with spray. Dust generously with
granulated sugar, shake the mold to coat all over, invert, and
tap out excess sugar. Set aside.

IN a bowl, combine the ½ cup butter and brown sugar and beat
with an electric mixer at medium speed until light and fluffy.
With the mixer still running, slowly drizzle in the eggs and beat
well. Add the bread crumbs, flour, baking powder, salt, fresh
and ground ginger, nutmeg, cinnamon, the 2 tablespoons
orange zest and 1 teaspoon lemon zest, and vanilla, brandy, or
liqueur; mix well. Fold in the raisins and chopped crystallized
or preserved ginger.

SCRAPE the mixture into the prepared mold. If using a pudding
mold with a lid, cover with the lid; if using a bowl or mold
without a lid, cover tightly with aluminum foil. Place the mold
on the rack inside the pot of simmering water, cover the pot,
and simmer until a wooden skewer inserted into the center of
the pudding comes out almost clean, about 1½ hours; adjust
the heat to maintain simmering water throughout cooking,
adding boiling water if needed to maintain water level.

REMOVE the mold from the simmering water to a wire rack to
cool for about 10 minutes, then uncover the mold. Invert a
serving plate over the mold, invert the plate and mold together,
and carefully lift off the mold.

TO serve, lightly dust the warm pudding with powdered sugar,
sprinkle with citrus zest, and garnish with ginger strips. Cut
into wedges at the table.

Makes 8 servings.

Powdered sugar for dusting

Minced fresh orange and lemon
zest for garnish

Crystallized ginger or drained
preserved ginger in syrup, cut
into narrow strips, for garnish

STEAMED WINTER SQUASH PUDDING

Unsalted butter or solid vegetable
　　shortening, at room temperature,
　　or cooking spray for greasing
Granulated sugar for dusting
2 cups pureed Roasted Winter
　　Squash (page 318) or canned
　　pumpkin (not pumpkin pie filling)
1½ cups all-purpose flour
1 cup light cream or half-and-half,
　　at room temperature
1 cup firmly packed light brown sugar
½ cup (1 stick) unsalted butter,
　　melted and cooled slightly
2 eggs, at room temperature, lightly
　　beaten
1 teaspoon pure vanilla extract
1 teaspoon ground cinnamon
1 teaspoon ground cardamom
¾ teaspoon freshly grated nutmeg
1 teaspoon baking soda
½ teaspoon salt

Buttercup, Butternut, or Sweet Dumpling squash makes an exceptionally flavorful pudding, as do any of the sweet pumpkins such as Small Sugar. For a festive touch, garnish the pudding with Candied Orange Zest (page 596) and crystallized violets.

Serve with Orange Crème Anglaise (page 583) or Old-fashioned Dessert Sauce (page 588).

SELECT a 2-quart pudding mold or heatproof bowl and a pot with a tight-fitting cover large enough to hold the container. Place a flat steaming rack in the bottom of the pot. Place the pudding mold or bowl on the rack and add enough water to the pot to reach about halfway up the sides of the mold or bowl, then remove the mold or bowl. Place the pot over high heat and bring the water to a boil, then cover and adjust the heat to achieve a simmer.

USING a pastry brush, generously grease the mold or bowl with butter or shortening, or coat with spray. Dust generously with granulated sugar, shake the mold to coat all over, invert, and tap out excess sugar. Set aside.

IN a bowl, combine the squash puree, flour, cream or half-and-half, brown sugar, melted butter, eggs, vanilla, cinnamon, cardamom, nutmeg, baking soda, and salt and stir just enough to mix thoroughly.

SCRAPE the mixture into the prepared mold. If using a pudding
mold with a lid, cover with the lid; if using a bowl or mold
without a lid, cover tightly with aluminum foil. Place the mold
on the rack inside the pot of simmering water, cover the pot,
and simmer until a wooden skewer inserted into the center of
the pudding comes out almost clean, 2 to 2½ hours; adjust the
heat to maintain simmering water throughout cooking, adding
boiling water if needed to maintain water level.

REMOVE the mold from the simmering water to a wire rack to
cool for about 10 minutes, then uncover the mold. Invert a
serving plate over the mold, invert the plate and mold together,
and carefully lift off the mold.

SERVE as suggested in the recipe introduction and cut into
wedges at the table.

Makes 8 servings.

MEXICAN RICE PUDDING
~ *Arroz con Leche* ~

1½ cups short-grain white rice

2 cinnamon sticks

Zest of 1 lime, removed in 1 piece

¼ teaspoon salt

1 quart milk (not fat free)

2 cups canned evaporated milk
(not fat free)

1¼ cups sugar

½ cup raisins

4 egg yolks, at room temperature,
lightly beaten

1 teaspoon pure vanilla extract

2 tablespoons unsalted butter,
cut into small pieces

Ground cinnamon for sprinkling

The essences of cinnamon and lime are captured in this rendition of Mexican rice pudding, a dessert that's almost as popular as the country's famous flan. It has become my favorite rice dessert.

Best eaten warm, this delectable pudding should still be a bit soft or soupy when served. It is also good at room temperature, and any leftovers can be mixed with milk and reheated for breakfast.

WASH and drain the rice as directed on page 365.

IN a saucepan, combine the cinnamon sticks and lime zest with 3 cups water. Place over medium-high heat and bring to a boil, then add the drained rice and the salt and stir once. Reduce the heat to achieve a simmer, cover, and simmer until the rice is tender and all of the liquid is absorbed, about 17 minutes.

ADD the milk, evaporated milk, sugar, and raisins to the rice and stir well. Increase the heat to medium and cook, stirring and scraping the bottom of the pan frequently to prevent sticking or scorching, just until the mixture begins to thicken, about 20 minutes. Remove from the heat and discard the lime zest.

IN a small bowl, lightly beat the egg yolks. Stir about 3 tablespoons of the hot pudding mixture into the beaten egg yolks, then stir the egg mixture and the vanilla into the pudding.

PREHEAT a broiler.

SCRAPE the pudding into a shallow flameproof serving dish, dot with the butter, and sprinkle with cinnamon to taste. Place the pudding under the broiler just until the top begins to brown lightly, about 3 minutes. Serve immediately or at room temperature.

Makes 8 servings.

MAPLE POPCORN

Mary McCoy, also known as Maple Mary, loves maple syrup almost as much as she does corn. She introduced me to this Vermont tradition that combines two of her favorite foods. Although the recipe should serve six, I must admit that the first time I made it was during a terrific electrical storm over Lake Tahoe, and I devoured the entire batch in one afternoon while watching nature's spectacular light show.

1 cup unpopped popcorn kernels

¾ cup (1½ sticks) unsalted butter

1½ cups pure maple syrup

½ cup light corn syrup

1 teaspoon salt

¼ teaspoon cream of tartar

½ teaspoon baking soda

POP the popcorn according to your favorite method and place in a large bowl. Set aside.

PREHEAT an oven to 200° F.

IN a large saucepan, melt the butter over medium-high heat. Add the maple and corn syrups, salt, and cream of tartar and mix well. Cook, without stirring, until the mixture registers between 234° and 240° F (soft-ball stage) on a candy thermometer. Remove from the heat and quickly stir in the baking soda. Pour the syrup over the popcorn and stir to coat thoroughly.

DISTRIBUTE the popcorn equally between two 13-by-9-inch pans. Bake, stirring several times, until dry and crispy, about 1 hour.

REMOVE the pans to a work surface to cool completely before serving. To store, place in a tightly covered container.

Makes 6 servings.

VARIATION

ADD about 1 cup roasted peanuts or coarsely chopped toasted pecans or other nuts (see page 554) to the popped corn before stirring in the hot syrup.

BASIC PIE CRUST

PASTRY

3 cups bleached all-purpose flour

1 teaspoon salt

2 teaspoons sugar

1 cup (2 sticks) very cold or frozen
  unsalted butter, high-quality pure
  lard, or solid vegetable shortening,
  alone or in combination, cut into
  small pieces (see recipe introduction)

½ cup or more iced water

1 egg white, lightly beaten, for
  brushing

1 egg yolk lightly beaten with
  1 tablespoon heavy (whipping)
  cream for brushing top crust
  (optional)

Sugar for sprinkling (optional)

This recipe yields enough flaky pastry for two single-crust pies or a double-crust pie with enough left over for cutout garnishes. If you're making only one pie without a top crust, either cut the recipe in half, or make the full recipe and freeze half as directed for future use.

Crusts made with all butter are the most flavorful and the easiest to blend and handle. Although a butter crust is not quite as tender as a crust made with lard or vegetable shortening, the special flavor makes it my standard choice. Pure rendered lard assures the tenderest and flakiest crust with a flavor that is especially compatible with apples, dried fruits, or savory fillings. Solid vegetable shortening has as many calories as butter, but is low in cholesterol and produces a very fragile crust. The resulting bland taste is often preferred when filling a pie with ultrarich concoctions. Butter can be combined in equal portions with lard or shortening for crusts that will provide some of the flavor of butter and some of the tenderness that the other fats offer.

When I want to make fanciful decorations that require more handling of the dough than a simple bottom crust, I make the Sweet Crust variation; the egg yolks make it easy to work with and give the sturdy pastry a rich golden color.

TO mix the pastry by hand, in a bowl, combine the flour, salt, and sugar and mix well. Using a pastry blender, 2 dinner knives, or your fingertips, cut the butter or other fat into the dry ingredients as quickly as possible just until the mixture resembles very coarse bread crumbs. Sprinkle ½ cup iced water over the mixture and combine with a fork or your fingertips just until the mixture begins to hold together in a shaggy mass. The dough should be crumbly but not dry; if it seems too crumbly, add more iced water, 1 tablespoon at a time.

TO mix the pastry in a food processor, in the bowl, combine the flour, salt, and sugar and process for 1 or 2 seconds to mix. Add the butter or other fat and cut into the dry ingredients by turning the processor on and off with quick pulses just until the mixture resembles very coarse bread crumbs. Sprinkle ½ cup iced water over the mixture and turn the motor on and off with quick pulses just until the mixture begins to hold together in a shaggy mass. The dough should be crumbly but not dry; if it seems too crumbly, add more iced water, 1 tablespoon at a time. Alternatively, to prevent overmixing, after cutting in the fat, transfer the mixture to a bowl, then sprinkle with the water and use a rubber spatula to fold the mixture until it just comes together as directed.

AFTER mixing by one of the preceding methods, turn half of the mixture onto a piece of waxed paper or plastic wrap. Bring the paper or plastic up around the mixture and knead lightly through the paper or plastic, gather into a ball, and press into a thick, flat disk about 5 inches in diameter. Bring the paper or plastic around to enclose the dough. Repeat with the other half of the mixture. Refrigerate for at least 2 hours or for up to 2 days to "relax" the dough for a more tender crust. (At this point the dough can be placed in a plastic freezer bag and frozen for up to 3 months.)

TO roll out the dough, remove 1 piece of the chilled pastry from the refrigerator and place it in the middle of a piece of lightly floured waxed paper or plastic wrap about 12 inches square. Cover the pastry with a second piece of lightly floured waxed paper or plastic. Allow to soften until the dough feels pliable when squeezed between your fingers, 10 to 20 minutes, depending on the length of refrigeration. Using a rolling pin, roll the dough from the center away from you toward the edges, reducing the pressure as you near the edges, then reposition the pin in the center and roll downward toward you. Lift the dough and rotate it about one-eighth turn, then continue rolling and turning in the same manner until you form a round about ⅛ inch thick. Use an empty pie pan as a guide; the piece of dough should be about 2 inches larger all around than the top of the pan. Lift up and reposition the top piece of waxed paper or plastic whenever it wrinkles.

continues ~

ALTERNATIVELY, place the dough on a lightly floured surface. Sprinkle the top with a little flour and dust a rolling pin with flour. Roll as directed in the previous paragraph. Add a bit more flour as necessary to prevent sticking.

IF the dough breaks during rolling, brush the tear with a dab of cold water and cover the tear with a piece of rolled dough cut from the edge of the circle. Avoid rerolling, as it toughens the dough.

TO line a pie pan, discard the top layer of waxed paper or plastic wrap. Invert the dough into the pan and peel away the waxed paper. Or, if rolled directly on a floured surface, fold the crust into quarters, then place the point in the center of the pan and unfold the dough. Beginning at the center of the pan and working toward the edges, press the dough lightly into the pan with your fingertips. When you near the bottom edge of the pan, lift up the edge of the dough with one hand and use the other hand to press the pastry into the corners gently without stretching it.

TO finish off a single-crust pie shell or the bottom crust of a double-crust pie shell, cut the edge of the pastry with a small sharp knife or kitchen scissors so that it hangs evenly about ¾ inch past the outer edge of the pan. Fold the dough down over itself toward the inside of the pan. Smooth the perimeter with your fingertips to form a thick raised rim. If making a single-crust pie, form attractive edges (see page 497 for suggestions). Refrigerate for about 40 minutes (to "relax" the gluten to minimize shrinkage), then transfer to the freezer for about 20 minutes (to maximize flakiness) before baking. (At this point, crusts in pans can be sealed in plastic freezer bags and frozen for up to several weeks; do not thaw before baking.)

FOR a partially or fully baked pie shell, position racks so that the pie shell will bake in the middle of an oven and preheat the oven to 400° F.

CUT a sheet of kitchen parchment about 2 inches larger than the diameter of the pie. Press it into the pastry shell and fill it with ceramic pie weights, dried beans, or rice. Bake until the crust edges begin to brown very lightly and the crust feels completely set to the touch when the parchment is carefully pulled away, about 20 minutes; if the weights and parchment are removed before the dough is completely set, the sides may shrink.

REMOVE from the oven and carefully lift the parchment and the weights from the crust, then return the shell to the oven.

FOR a partially baked shell that will be filled and baked further, bake until the crust is lightly browned, about 5 minutes longer. Check the crust several times during baking and, if the crust puffs up, prick it with a fork in the areas that puff; do not prick all the way through the dough if using a runny filling.

FOR a fully baked, or "blind baked," pie shell that is to be filled with a ready-to-eat filling, bake until golden brown, about 10 minutes longer. Check the crust several times during baking and, if the crust puffs up, prick it with a fork in the areas that puff; do not prick all the way through the dough if using a runny filling. Cover the rim of the crust with a ring of aluminum foil or a pie crust shield if it begins to get too brown before the rest of the crust is done.

AFTER baking the pie shell, remove the crust to a wire rack to cool for about 3 minutes, then, using a pastry brush, lightly coat the bottom and sides of the warm crust with beaten egg white; do not coat the rim of the crust. Set aside to cool completely before filling; cooling prevents soggy crusts. For the crispiest crust, fill as close to the time the pie will be eaten as possible.

TO cover a double-crust pie completely, fill the partially baked shell as directed in individual recipes. Roll out the second piece of dough into a rough round a little thinner than the bottom crust. Using an empty pie pan as a guide, cut the dough into a round slightly larger than the top of the pie. Brush the rim of the filled pie with lightly beaten egg white. Cover the pie with the top crust and trim it even with the bottom crust. Press the edges together to seal.

USING a sharp knife, cut several slits or designs into the top crust to serve as air vents. If desired, cut out decorations such as leaves, flowers, stars, or other fanciful or geometric shapes with a knife or cookie cutters, then brush the bottom of each with a little cold water and stick onto the top crust in an attractive pattern.

continues ~

TO cover a pie partially, which is especially appropriate when the filling is colorful or particularly attractive, as with a berry pie, fill the partially baked shell as directed in individual recipes. Roll out the second piece of dough into a rough round a little thinner than the bottom crust. For a lattice, striped, or spiral design, use a plain or fluted rolling pastry cutter or sharp knife with a ruler as a guide to cut the dough circle into long narrow strips. Arrange on the top of the pie in the desired pattern. Trim any edges of the strips that overlap the edges of the pie to meet the rim of the pie, lift the strips, brush the undersides with beaten egg white, and press onto the rim of the bottom crust to seal.

THE pie may also be covered with free-form or cookie-cutter cutouts. Arrange them slightly overlapping to cover most of the pie, leaving spaces for air vents in between, or scatter them over the top in any design you wish.

FOR a richer baked color, brush the exposed crust with the beaten egg yolk–cream mixture. For a crackle glaze, sprinkle with granulated sugar or a flavored sugar such as vanilla sugar.

Makes pastry for one 9-inch double-crust pie, or two 9-inch single-crust pies.

VARIATIONS

Almond or Vanilla Crust. For a delicately almond-flavored crust to use with egg custard or nut pies, add ½ teaspoon almond extract along with the iced water. For a flavorful crust that goes well with berry or other fruit pies, add 1 teaspoon pure vanilla extract along with the iced water, or substitute vanilla sugar for the regular sugar.

Brown Sugar Crust. Substitute brown sugar for the granulated sugar and add ½ teaspoon ground cinnamon with the salt.

Cheddar Crust. For an occasional change of pace with apple or pear pie, reduce the butter or other fat to ½ cup and stir in 1 cup finely shredded Cheddar cheese after cutting in the fat.

Chocolate Crust. Whenever a chocolate crust seems compatible with the filling, substitute ¼ cup unsweetened cocoa for ¼ cup of the flour.

Cornmeal Crust. For a bright yellow crust with a bit of crunch and flavor that goes well with pumpkin, nut, or other autumn pies, substitute 1 cup finely ground yellow cornmeal for 1 cup of the flour; a bit more iced water may be required.

Cream Cheese Crust. For a delicate texture and slightly tart flavor, cut 6 ounces very cold cream cheese into the flour before adding the butter. Reduce the iced water to about 3 tablespoons.

Spice Crust. For a spicy crust that goes well with fruit pies, add about ½ teaspoon freshly grated nutmeg or ground cinnamon, cloves, or ginger to the flour-and-salt mixture.

Sweet Crust. For a sweeter fully baked shell to fill with a stirred custard, cream, or mousse filling, reduce the salt to ½ teaspoon, increase the sugar to 3 tablespoons, and beat 2 cold egg yolks with the iced water.

Whole-Wheat Crust. For a crunchy crust that is compatible with heavy fillings such as pumpkin or mincemeat, substitute half whole-wheat pastry flour for the regular flour and add 1 teaspoon baking powder with the salt.

Tips for Perfect Pastry

All fat and liquid ingredients must be very cold; if using a food processor for mixing, freeze the fats before using.

When combining butter and solid shortening or any two types of fat together in a crust, it is best to soften the fats, blend them, and chill before using. Alternatively, first cut in the butter, followed by the softer lard or solid shortening.

Mix the ingredients as quickly as possible. Flaky pastry results from pockets of shortening left to melt in between flour paste layers; overmixing results in a tough crust.

Don't shorten or skip the chilling times of the pastry at any point. Chill before rolling out to allow the flour to absorb all liquid and relax the gluten. Before baking, refrigerate the crust in the pan to again relax the gluten and prevent shrinking, and then chill it in the freezer to help improve the flakiness.

When touching dough, be sure your hands are cold; an occasional rinse in cold water keeps them the correct temperature.

When rolling out and assembling crusts, handle the pastry as quickly and as little as possible. If the butter or other fat gets too soft, it will be absorbed by the flour, resulting in a crust that is heavy and tough.

Decorative Edges for Pies

In addition to the standard practice of pressing the tines of a fork into smoothed pastry all the way around the perimeter to create a fluted edge, use these suggestions to get your own creativity flowing.

APPLIQUÉ. Roll out an extra sheet of pastry and cut it out with tiny aspic cutters or cut out leaves or other shapes with a small, sharp knife. Brush the rim of the crust with cold water and apply the cutouts, slightly overlapping. Gently press to adhere the cutouts to the rim.

BRAID. Cut long strips of extra dough about $1/4$ inch wide and braid 2 or 3 strips together to interlock. Brush the rim of the crust with cold water and apply the braid. Gently press to adhere the braid to the rim.

CHECKERBOARD. Use a sharp knife to cut across the rim at $1/2$-inch intervals. Alternately fold every other piece in toward the center.

FEATHER. Use a sharp pair of kitchen scissors to snip slanted incisions every $1/4$ inch around the perimeter of the pastry.

FLUTE. Position one of your index fingers on the outside of the pastry rim, pointing diagonally inward. Use the index finger and thumb of your other hand to push the pastry against the finger to form wide flutes.

POINT. Position one of your index fingers on the inside of the pastry rim, pointing out. With the index finger and thumb of your other hand, crimp the pastry into pronounced points that go outward.

SCALLOP. Place one of your index fingers on the edge of the rim, pointing in. Use the index finger and the thumb of your other hand to move the dough inward to form scallops around the perimeter.

SPOON SCALLOP. Press the rounded tip of a spoon into the rim to form a scallop pattern. If desired, move the spoon down and repeat with smaller scallops nearer the outer rim.

COOKIE CRUMB CRUST

Unsalted butter, at room temperature,
for greasing

2 cups fine cookie crumbs, from
graham crackers, vanilla wafers,
gingersnaps, amaretti or other dry
macaroons, chocolate wafers,
biscotti, or other crisp cookies (as
suggested in recipes)

6 tablespoons (¾ stick) unsalted
butter, melted and cooled slightly

¼ cup sugar or firmly packed light
brown sugar (if using graham
crackers or other lightly sweetened
cookies)

½ teaspoon ground cinnamon, ginger,
or nutmeg (optional)

A food processor or blender makes fast work of turning cookies into fine crumbs. As a general rule, 8 ounces of cookies yields 2 cups crumbs. Adjust the amount of sugar and spice to suit the cookie type. Substitute finely ground nuts for a portion of the crumbs, if desired.

Use for Key Lime Pie (page 502), Peanut Satin Pie (page 511), or fill with any of the mousses on pages 473-477.

PREHEAT an oven to 325° F.

USING a pastry brush, grease a 9-inch pie pan with butter and set aside.

IN a bowl, combine the crumbs, melted butter, sugar (if using), and spice (if using) and stir to blend thoroughly. Spread in the prepared pan and press with your fingertips to pack the mixture evenly on the bottom and up the sides of the pan. Do not overlap the rim of the pan.

BAKE until fragrant, about 15 minutes.

REMOVE to a wire rack to cool completely before filling.

Makes one 9-inch pie crust.

LEMONY BERRY PIE

This recipe using blueberries adapts to huckleberries, gooseberries, raspberries, blackberries, or other berries as well as grapes and pitted sweet or sour cherries. Vary the amount of sugar and lemon according to the tartness of the fruit.

For years I used flour to thicken fruit pies but have come to favor the use of cornstarch, potato starch, or quick-cooking tapioca (such as Minute brand), which yield a filling that is less starchy and more clear. If you prefer a berry pie with more juice, reduce the amount of thickener or omit it completely.

Serve with Crème Anglaise (page 582), softly Whipped Cream (page 590), or vanilla ice cream.

PREPARE the pastry as directed, roll out half of it, and line a 9-inch pie pan. Partially bake, coat, and set aside to cool completely as directed.

POSITION racks so that the pie will bake in the middle of an oven and preheat the oven to 425° F.

IN a bowl, toss the blueberries with the 1 cup sugar, cornstarch or other thickener, nutmeg, cinnamon, and lemon zest and juice. Pour into the cooled pie shell and dot with the butter.

AS directed on page 494 to cover a pie partially, roll out the remaining pastry, cut into strips or cutouts, and arrange over the filling. Brush the pastry with the egg-cream mixture and sprinkle with sugar. Cover the rim of the crust with a ring of aluminum foil or a pie crust shield to prevent overbrowning during baking. Bake for 10 minutes, then reduce the oven temperature to 350° F and bake until the crust is golden brown and the juices are bubbly, about 45 minutes longer.

REMOVE the pie to a wire rack to cool. Serve warm or at room temperature.

Makes 8 servings.

Basic Pie Crust (page 490)

6 cups blueberries

1 cup sugar, or to taste

¼ cup cornstarch, potato starch, or quick-cooking tapioca

½ teaspoon freshly grated nutmeg

¼ teaspoon ground cinnamon

2 tablespoons grated or minced fresh lemon zest

2 tablespoons freshly squeezed lemon juice

2 tablespoons unsalted butter, cut into small pieces

1 egg lightly beaten with 2 table-spoons heavy (whipping) cream for brushing

Sugar for sprinkling

SUMMER PEACH PIE

Basic Pie Crust (page 490)

6 cups peeled, pitted, and sliced ripe
freestone peaches (about 3 pounds)

¾ cup sugar, preferably vanilla sugar
(see recipe introduction), or to taste

3 tablespoons cornstarch, potato
starch, or quick-cooking tapioca

1 teaspoon pure vanilla extract, if not
using vanilla sugar

½ teaspoon ground ginger

2 tablespoons unsalted butter, cut
into small pieces

1 egg lightly beaten with 2 tablespoons heavy (whipping) cream for
brushing

Sugar, preferably vanilla sugar, for
sprinkling

*When available, try Babcock, Strawberry Nectar, or other white peaches,
or make the pie with nectarines or apricots. I love to use vanilla sugar
with peaches. You can make your own by scraping the seeds from a split
vanilla bean into a canister containing about 2 cups sugar and then
burying the pod halves in the canister. The sugar will be well flavored in
about 1 week.*

*Serve with Crème Anglaise (page 582), softly Whipped Cream
(page 590), or ginger or vanilla ice cream.*

PREPARE the pastry as directed, roll out half of it, and line a
9-inch pie pan. Partially bake, coat, and set aside to cool
completely as directed.

POSITION racks so that the pie will bake in the middle of an oven
and preheat the oven to 425° F.

IN a bowl, combine the peaches, the ¾ cup sugar, cornstarch or
other thickener, vanilla (if using), and ginger and toss to coat the
peaches well. Pour into the cooled pie shell and dot with the butter.

AS directed on page 493 to cover a double-crust pie completely, roll
out the remaining pastry, cover the pie, and cut air vents in the
top crust. Brush the pastry with the egg-cream mixture and
sprinkle with sugar. Cover the rim of the crust with a ring of
aluminum foil or a pie crust shield to prevent overbrowning
during baking. Bake for 10 minutes, then reduce the oven
temperature to 350° F and bake until the crust is golden brown
and the juices are bubbly, about 45 minutes longer.

REMOVE the pie to a wire rack to cool. Serve warm or at room
temperature.

Makes 8 servings.

CHERRY CREAM PIE

This old recipe is one of the best from my grandmother Olivia Belle Keith's Mississippi kitchen and was the all-time favorite dessert of my late friend Gregg King, to whom my Pie Cookbook was dedicated. I wish that I could bake him one right now and watch those big, dark eyes light up as they always did when I brought out this pie.

Mawmaw always used canned cherry pie filling, as I've done here, but purists may choose to simmer 2 cups stemmed and pitted fresh, frozen, or canned sweet Bing or Queen Anne cherries with ½ cup cold water, 2 tablespoons cornstarch, and ¼ to ½ cup sugar until the cherries are tender. While light cream or half-and-half could be used in the custard, evaporated milk adds the old-fashioned slightly caramelized flavor that my grandmother favored.

The pie can be finished with Meringue Topping (page 592) instead of whipped cream. Add the hot filling to the cooled crust, top immediately with the meringue, and brown as directed.

½ recipe Basic Pie Crust (page 490)

3 egg yolks, lightly beaten

1 cup sugar

¼ cup cornstarch

⅛ teaspoon salt

2 cups canned evaporated milk (not fat free)

2 tablespoons unsalted butter

1 teaspoon pure vanilla extract

1 can (1 pound) cherry pie filling

Whipped Cream (page 590)

PREPARE the pastry as directed, roll it out, and line a 9-inch pie pan. Fully bake, coat, and set aside to cool completely as directed.

IN a heavy saucepan, combine the egg yolks, sugar, cornstarch, and salt and mix thoroughly. Slowly whisk in the milk. Place over medium heat and cook, stirring almost constantly, until the mixture thickens, 8 to 10 minutes. Reduce the heat to very low and cook until quite thick, 3 to 4 minutes longer. Remove from the heat, add the butter, and stir until the butter melts. Stir in the vanilla and cherry pie filling. Transfer to a bowl, place a piece of plastic wrap directly onto the surface of the custard to prevent a skin from forming, and let cool for about 15 minutes.

POUR the cooled filling into the cooled pie crust.

WHIP the cream as directed. Spoon it over the top of the pie, or transfer to a pastry bag and pipe over the top in a fanciful pattern. Serve immediately or refrigerate for up to 1 hour.

Makes 8 servings.

KEY LIME PIE

Cookie Crumb Crust (page 498)
  made with graham crackers

6 egg yolks, at room temperature
  (reserve whites if making Meringue
  Topping)

2 tablespoons grated or minced fresh
  lime zest

1½ cans (14 ounces *each*) sweetened
  condensed milk (not evaporated
  milk)

¾ cup freshly squeezed lime juice,
  or more if needed

Meringue Topping (page 592) or
  Whipped Cream (page 590)

Freshly shredded lime zest for
  garnish (optional)

My last conversation with noted food authority Maggie Waldron was at a play-reading party hosted by Antonia Allegra at her "treehouse" in the Napa Valley. My contribution to the potluck supper was this pie. After taking a bite, Maggie asked me where I got the Key limes, which are rarely available in California. I confessed that I had used regular limes, to which she retorted in a rather startled manner, "Then how can you call it Key lime pie?"

This south Florida classic originated with the extremely tart, yet slightly sweet juice of the small, round yellowish Mexican Caribbean limes that grow in the area. To my taste, more readily available and less bitter Persian (also known as Tahitian) limes create an even more delicious filling, but take your choice. Please never use bottled lime juice! No matter which limes you choose or what you call it, this is one of America's greatest original desserts.

Substitute lemon juice to make another old favorite, lemon icebox pie.

Traditional recipes are split on the use of a standard pie crust versus a graham cracker crust; my vote swings toward the latter. If you prefer a pastry crust, prepare ½ recipe Basic Pie Crust (page 490) and fully bake as directed.

I enjoy a thicker layer of filling than many traditional recipes offer for a 9-inch pie. My formula is based on 1½ cans sweetened condensed milk; use the leftover ½ can for another purpose. Depending on the thickness of your crust and height of the pie pan, you may have a little bit of extra filling, but better too much of a good thing than not enough!

You also have a choice of topping the pie with meringue or whipped cream; each has their devotees in Floridian kitchens. Although refrigerating may cause some shrinkage and weeping in the meringue, chilling does improve the flavor of the filling and the topping holds up surprisingly well if completely cooled before refrigerating.

POSITION racks so that the pie will bake in the middle of an oven and preheat the oven to 325° F.

PREPARE the Cookie Crumb Crust with graham crackers and omit the spices. Bake as directed and remove to a wire rack to cool completely.

IN a bowl, combine the egg yolks and grated or minced lime zest and beat with a hand mixer at high speed until the mixture is pale and creamy, about 5 minutes. Add the condensed milk and ¾ cup lime juice and stir until smooth. Taste and add more lime juice if required to create a tart flavor. Pour the mixture into the cooled crust to fill completely; you may have a little extra filling. Bake for 5 minutes if topping with meringue, or for 15 minutes if topping with whipped cream.

IF using Meringue Topping, while the pie is baking, prepare the meringue as directed. As soon as the pie is ready, remove it to a work surface. Spread the meringue over the pie and bake as directed on page 592. Remove the pie to a wire rack to cool completely. Cover loosely without touching the meringue and refrigerate until well chilled, about 4 hours.

IF topping with Whipped Cream, remove the pie to a wire rack and let cool completely, then cover tightly and refrigerate until well chilled, about 4 hours or for up to 24 hours. Prepare the Whipped Cream as directed and spoon it over the top of the pie, or transfer to a pastry bag and pipe over the top in a fanciful pattern. Sprinkle with shredded lime zest (if using) and serve immediately, or cover and refrigerate for up to 1 hour.

Makes 8 servings.

LEMON MERINGUE PIE

½ recipe Basic Pie Crust (page 490)

6 tablespoons cornstarch

1½ cups sugar

¼ teaspoon salt

4 egg yolks (reserve whites for topping)

½ cup freshly squeezed lemon juice

2 teaspoons grated or minced fresh lemon zest

3 tablespoons unsalted butter, at room temperature

Meringue Topping (page 592)

I've always been disappointed in gluelike commercial renditions of this American treasure. Likewise, the "perfected" fillings in recent food magazines seem too curdlike for my taste. Here is my mother's version, which we always ate while still a little warm.

PREPARE the pastry as directed, roll it out, and line a 9-inch pie pan. Fully bake, coat, and set aside to cool completely as directed.

IN a heavy saucepan, combine the cornstarch, sugar, and salt and whisk to blend well. Gradually whisk in 2 cups cold water. Place over medium heat and cook, whisking constantly to prevent lumps, just until the mixture thickens and begins to turn translucent, 3 to 5 minutes. Whisk in the egg yolks, 2 at a time, then the lemon juice and zest and butter. Continue whisking just until the butter melts and the mixture returns to a simmer. Remove from the heat and place a piece of plastic wrap directly onto the surface of the filling to prevent a skin from forming.

PREHEAT an oven to 325° F.

PREPARE the Meringue Topping as directed.

AS soon as the topping is ready, place the filling over low heat and whisk just until hot. Pour the filling into the cooled pie crust. Cover the filling with meringue and bake as directed on page 592.

REMOVE the pie to a wire rack to cool. Serve at room temperature; do not refrigerate.

Makes 8 servings.

SOUTHERN CHESS PIE

This old treasure arrived in the Southern colonies from England. Some folks say the name came from the melodic drawl that turned the common name for this plain buttery pie, "just pie," into "jess pie." In fact, cheese was an old cooking term for curdling milk or thickening egg mixtures with heat, so the name is more likely a shortening of cheese.

PREPARE the pastry as directed, roll it out, and line a 9-inch pie pan. Partially bake, coat, and set aside to cool completely as directed.

POSITION racks so that the pie will bake in the middle of an oven and preheat the oven to 325° F.

IN a large bowl, combine the egg yolks, egg, sugar, cornmeal, salt, and butter and beat well. Blend in the cream or milk, then stir in the lemon juice and vanilla. Pour into the cooled pie shell. Cover the rim of the crust with a ring of aluminum foil or a pie crust shield to prevent overbrowning during baking. Bake until a knife inserted 1 inch from the center of the pie comes out clean, about 40 minutes.

REMOVE the pie to a wire rack to cool. Serve warm or at room temperature.

Makes 8 servings.

½ recipe Basic Pie Crust (page 490)

3 egg yolks, at room temperature

1 egg, at room temperature

1 cup sugar

2 tablespoons yellow cornmeal

⅛ teaspoon salt

½ cup (1 stick) unsalted butter, melted and cooled slightly

½ cup heavy (whipping) cream, light cream, half-and-half, or canned evaporated milk (not fat free), at room temperature

1 tablespoon freshly squeezed lemon juice

2 teaspoons pure vanilla extract

SOUTHERN PECAN PIE

½ recipe Basic Pie Crust (page 490)

2 cups pecan halves

3 eggs, at room temperature, lightly
   beaten

⅔ cup sugar

1 tablespoon all-purpose flour

¼ teaspoon salt

1 cup light corn syrup

4 tablespoons (½ stick) unsalted
   butter, melted and cooled slightly

1 teaspoon pure vanilla extract

This version of a perennial favorite was taught to me years ago by my fifth grade teacher, Eula Cain, and makes regular appearances at my fall and winter celebrations. In recent years, I've found that the flavor is even better when the pecans are toasted before adding them to the filling.

The dense pie is best with a dollop of softly Whipped Cream (page 590) flavored to taste with bourbon or pure vanilla extract.

PREPARE the pastry as directed, roll it out, and line a 9-inch pie pan. Partially bake, coat, and set aside to cool completely as directed.

POSITION racks so that the pie will bake in the middle of an oven and preheat the oven to 350° F.

TOAST the pecans as directed on page 554. Measure out 1 cup of the most attractive pecan halves and set aside. Chop the remaining pecans and set aside.

INCREASE the oven temperature to 375° F.

IN a bowl, combine the eggs, sugar, flour, salt, corn syrup, butter, and vanilla and beat until well blended. Stir in the chopped pecans and pour into the cooled pie shell. Arrange the pecan halves on top of the mixture. Cover the rim of the crust with a ring of aluminum foil or a pie crust shield to prevent overbrowning during baking. Bake until the edges of the pie feel set when touched but the center still wobbles slightly, about 50 minutes. The filling should remain just a bit gooey but not syrupy, and a knife inserted into the center of the pie should still have tracings of filling when removed.

REMOVE the pie to a wire rack to cool. Serve warm or at room temperature.

Makes 8 servings.

VARIATION

SUBSTITUTE walnuts, macadamia nuts, cashews, peanuts, or an array of mixed nuts for the pecans.

SWEET POTATO PIE

Matilda Adams, in my hometown of Jonesville, Louisiana, made the best version of this true Southern pie that I've ever tasted.

PREPARE the pastry as directed, roll it out, and line a 9-inch pie pan. Partially bake, coat, and set aside to cool completely as directed.

PLACE the sweet potatoes in a large saucepan and add enough cold water to cover. Bring to a boil over medium-high heat and cook until almost tender, 35 to 40 minutes, then drain. Alternatively, bake as directed on page 320.

POSITION racks so that the pie will bake in the middle of an oven and preheat the oven to 375° F.

WHEN the sweet potatoes are cool enough to handle, peel them and cut into chunks. Press through a ricer into a bowl. Add the sugar, salt, baking soda, cinnamon, nutmeg, and cloves and stir to mix well. Add the eggs, butter, half-and-half or milk, and vanilla and beat until smooth. Pour the mixture into the cooled pie shell. Cover the rim of the crust with a ring of aluminum foil or a pie crust shield to prevent overbrowning during baking. Bake until the top of the pie feels just firm to the touch and just begins to brown, about 40 minutes.

REMOVE the pie to a wire rack to cool. Serve slightly warm or at room temperature.

Makes 8 servings.

½ recipe Basic Pie Crust (page 490), preferably made with lard

1¼ pounds orange "yam" variety sweet potatoes

1 cup sugar

½ teaspoon salt

¼ teaspoon baking soda

½ teaspoon ground cinnamon

¼ teaspoon freshly grated nutmeg

¼ teaspoon ground cloves

2 eggs, at room temperature

¼ cup (½ stick) unsalted butter, melted and cooled slightly

½ cup half-and-half or whole milk, at room temperature

1 teaspoon pure vanilla extract

CRANBERRY ORANGE PIE

Basic Pie Crust (page 490)

12 ounces (about 3½ cups)
cranberries

1 cup sugar

1 tablespoon cornstarch, potato
starch, or quick-cooking tapioca

¼ teaspoon salt

3 tablespoons freshly squeezed
orange juice

2 tablespoons grated or minced fresh
orange zest

2 tablespoons unsalted butter, melted
and cooled slightly

1 egg lightly beaten with 2 tablespoons heavy (whipping) cream for
brushing

Sugar for sprinkling

After a rich Thanksgiving feast, this slightly tart pie, a variation on an old Cape Cod recipe, is welcome and offers a different way of adding the traditional berries to the menu. The pie is so good that you may wish to freeze several bags of berries during the brief season to enjoy it at other times of the year.

Serve with Crème Anglaise (page 582), softly Whipped Cream (page 590), or vanilla ice cream.

PREPARE the pastry as directed, roll out half of it, and line a 9-inch pie pan. Partially bake, coat, and set aside to cool completely as directed.

POSITION racks so that the pie will bake in the middle of an oven and preheat the oven to 425° F.

IN a bowl, combine the cranberries, the 1 cup sugar, cornstarch or other thickener, salt, orange juice and zest, and butter and toss to blend well. Pour into the cooled pie shell.

AS directed on page 494 to cover a pie partially, roll out the remaining pastry, cut into strips, and arrange in a lattice design over the filling. Brush the pastry with the egg-cream mixture and sprinkle with sugar. Cover the rim of the crust with a ring of aluminum foil or a pie crust shield to prevent overbrowning during baking. Bake for 10 minutes, then reduce the oven temperature to 350° F and bake until the crust is golden brown and the juices are bubbly, about 45 minutes longer.

REMOVE the pie to a wire rack to cool. Serve warm or at room temperature.

Makes 8 servings.

AUTUMN SQUASH PIE

*In the autumn, when winter squash make their annual appearance,
I like to use Butternut, Buttercup, or other flavorful varieties, as well as
any of the sweet pumpkins such as New England Pie, to make the filling
for this pie. These squash taste superior to their field pumpkin relatives,
which are best reserved for decorative carving. Avoid watery Acorn
squash for pies.*

PREPARE the pastry as directed, roll out half of it, and line a
9-inch pie pan. Partially bake, coat, and set aside to cool
completely as directed.

USING a pastry brush, lightly grease a baking sheet with butter
or shortening, or coat with cooking spray, or line with kitchen
parchment. Roll out the remaining pastry and cut out leaf shapes
with a sharp knife or cookie cutter. Using a small, sharp knife,
draw veins on each leaf. Arrange the leaves on the prepared baking
sheet, cover with plastic wrap, and refrigerate for later use.

POSITION racks so that the pie will bake in the middle of an oven
and preheat the oven to 375° F.

IN a bowl, combine the pureed squash, cream, eggs, maple syrup
or sugar, cinnamon, ginger, vanilla, and salt and beat well. Pour
the mixture into the cooled pie shell. Cover the rim of the crust
with a ring of aluminum foil or a pie crust shield to prevent
overbrowning during baking. Bake until a knife inserted into
the center of the pie comes out clean, about 1 hour.

REMOVE the pie to a wire rack to cool.

MEANWHILE, brush the pastry leaves with the egg yolk–cream
mixture and sprinkle with the cinnamon sugar. Bake until
golden, about 15 minutes. Remove to a wire rack to cool.

SHORTLY before serving, arrange the pastry leaves on top of the
pie and serve at room temperature.

Makes 8 servings.

Basic Pie Crust (page 490),
    preferably Brown Sugar Variation
    (page 494)
Unsalted butter or solid vegetable
    shortening, at room temperature,
    or cooking spray for greasing
    (optional)
1½ cups pureed Roasted Winter
    Squash (page 318) or canned
    pumpkin (not pumpkin pie filling)
1 cup heavy (whipping) cream, light
    cream, or half-and-half
4 eggs, lightly beaten
1 cup pure maple syrup or firmly
    packed brown or maple sugar
1 teaspoon ground cinnamon
1 teaspoon ground ginger
1 teaspoon pure vanilla extract
½ teaspoon salt
1 egg yolk lightly beaten with
    1 tablespoon heavy (whipping)
    cream for brushing
1 tablespoon sugar mixed with
    1 teaspoon ground cinnamon
    for sprinkling

DECADENT FUDGE PIE

½ recipe Basic Pie Crust (page 490)

3 ounces unsweetened chocolate, chopped

¾ cup (1½ sticks) unsalted butter, at room temperature

3 eggs, at room temperature

1¾ cups sugar

6 tablespoons all-purpose flour

¼ teaspoon salt

1 tablespoon pure vanilla extract

Although this rich creation is delicious on its own, it is even better with Crème Anglaise (page 582).

PREPARE the pastry as directed, roll it out, and line a 9-inch pie pan. Partially bake, coat, and set aside to cool completely as directed.

IN a skillet or shallow saucepan, pour in water to a depth of 1 inch, place over medium heat, bring just to a simmer, and adjust the heat to maintain barely simmering water. Combine the chocolate and butter in a heatproof bowl, set the bowl in the simmering water, and stir the mixture constantly just until melted and smooth; do not allow to burn. Alternatively, combine the chocolate and butter in a microwave-safe measuring cup or bowl and microwave at 50 percent power, stirring every 15 seconds, just until melted and smooth; do not allow to burn. Set the chocolate aside to cool for a few minutes.

POSITION racks so that the pie will bake in the middle of an oven and preheat the oven to 350° F.

IN a bowl, lightly beat the eggs. Add the sugar, flour, and salt and beat well. Add the cooled chocolate mixture and vanilla and stir until smooth. Pour into the cooled pie shell. Bake until a knife inserted into the center of the pie remains a bit gooey, 30 to 35 minutes.

REMOVE the pie to a wire rack to cool. Serve warm or at room temperature.

Makes 8 servings.

VARIATION

TOAST ½ cup pecans or other nuts as directed on page 554, then finely chop and stir into the filling mixture before pouring into the crust.

PEANUT SATIN PIE

The name for this decadent concoction comes from the ultrasmooth texture.

MAKE the crust as directed and set aside to cool completely.

IN a bowl, combine the cream cheese, peanut butter, butter, and egg yolks and beat with an electric mixer at medium speed until creamy. With the mixer still running, drizzle in the condensed milk and beat until very smooth. Stir in the vanilla. Pour into the pie shell, cover loosely, and refrigerate until the filling is firm and well chilled, at least 3 hours or for up to overnight.

ABOUT 20 minutes before serving, remove the pie from the refrigerator and sprinkle with peanuts. Prepare the Chocolate Sauce as directed and keep warm.

SERVE wedges of the pie with the warm sauce.

Makes 8 servings.

Cookie Crumb Crust (page 498) preferably made with gingersnaps

8 ounces cream cheese (not fat free), at room temperature

¾ cup smooth peanut butter, at room temperature

6 tablespoons (¾ stick) unsalted butter, at room temperature

2 egg yolks, at room temperature

1 can (14 ounces) sweetened condensed milk (not evaporated milk)

1 teaspoon pure vanilla extract

Chopped unsalted dry-roasted peanuts for garnish

Chocolate Sauce (page 587) made with bittersweet chocolate

CAPPUCCINO CHEESECAKE

CRUST

Solid vegetable shortening, at room
   temperature, for greasing

1¼ cups graham cracker crumbs
   (from about 12 graham crackers)

⅓ cup firmly packed brown sugar

1 teaspoon ground cinnamon

¼ cup (½ stick) unsalted butter,
   melted and cooled slightly

FILLING

1½ pounds cream cheese (not fat
   free), at room temperature

1 cup sugar

4 eggs, at room temperature, lightly
   beaten

½ cup instant espresso, or to taste

½ cup coffee-flavored liqueur

1 teaspoon pure vanilla extract

Whipped Cream (page 590)

Sweet ground chocolate (see recipe
   introduction) or grated finest-quality
   semisweet chocolate

This variation of my favorite cheesecake is rich with its layer of strong coffee flavor and a creamy topping. Sprinkle with sweet ground chocolate, a favorite topping for cappuccino in coffee houses. Look for it sold in boxes similar to those used for cocoa.

POSITION racks so that the cheesecake will bake in the middle of an oven and preheat the oven to 350° F.

TO make the crust, using a pastry brush, generously grease the bottom and sides of a 9-inch springform pan with shortening. Set aside.

IN a bowl, combine the graham cracker crumbs, brown sugar, and cinnamon. Add the melted butter and blend well with a fork. Using your fingertips, press the mixture into the bottom and halfway up the sides of the prepared pan. Bake until set, about 10 minutes. Transfer to a work surface. When cool enough to handle, wrap aluminum foil around the bottom and about halfway up the sides of the pan.

REDUCE the oven temperature to 325° F.

TO make the filling, in a bowl, beat the cream cheese with an electric mixer at low speed until soft and creamy, about 45 seconds. With the mixer still running, slowly add the sugar, then stop the mixer and scrape the mixture that clings to the sides of the bowl into the center. Continue beating until light and creamy, about 1 minute. Slowly pour in the eggs and beat just until smooth; avoid overbeating, which will incorporate too much air that may result in a cracked top. Stir in the espresso, liqueur, and vanilla and blend well.

POUR the mixture into the crust. Place the foil-wrapped pan in a large baking pan, transfer to the oven, and pour enough hot (not boiling) water into the large pan to reach about ½ inch up the sides of the cheesecake pan. Bake until the cheesecake is barely set except for the center, which should still wobble when moved, about 45 minutes; do not overbake.

REMOVE the cheesecake pan from the water bath to a wire rack. Remove the foil wrapping and immediately run the blade of a metal frosting spatula or dull knife around the inside edges of the pan to loosen the cheesecake. Set aside to cool to room temperature.

COVER the cooled cheesecake and refrigerate until firm and chilled, at least 5 hours or for up to 24 hours.

ABOUT 25 minutes before serving, carefully unclasp and remove the ring and transfer the cheesecake to a serving plate.

TO serve, prepare the Whipped Cream as directed, spread it over the top of the cheesecake, and sprinkle with ground or grated chocolate.

Makes 12 servings.

SUMMER BERRY AND POLENTA PUDDING

Polenta Cake (page 516)

5 cups seasonal berries, such as
blackberries, boysenberries,
currants, gooseberries, raspberries,
or hulled strawberries, one kind or
a combination

About ¾ cup sugar

Whole berries for garnish

Fresh mint leaves for garnish

Whipped Cream (page 590) flavored
with pure almond extract

An English tradition made with white bread becomes more flavorful when crunchy Italian pound cake is used instead. When I'm feeling particularly indulgent, I love to serve this with a scoop of White Chocolate Mousse (page 473) instead of the cream.

It may not take all of the cake to fill the selected pan. Leftover slices are great on their own or lightly toasted and spread with one of the curds on page 593.

BAKE the Polenta Cake in two 8½-by-4½-by-2½-inch loaf pans as directed and cool completely; do not dust with powdered sugar.

PLACE the 5 cups berries in a bowl, sprinkle with ¾ cup sugar, cover, and let stand at room temperature, stirring occasionally, until very juicy. Pour the berries and resulting juice into a saucepan and place over low heat, stirring gently, until heated through, about 3 minutes. Remove from the heat and sweeten to taste with sugar.

TO assemble, cut the cakes into thin slices. Cut these into wedges and other shapes necessary to line the bottom and sides of a deep, round 5-cup charlotte mold or other straight-sided container, leaving no spaces between the slices. Spoon about half of the berries and some of the juice into the center, then cover with a layer of the cake pieces. Add the remaining berries and cover with another layer of the cake slices. Pour the remaining juice over the top. Cover the pudding with plastic wrap, then with a saucer that fits just inside the mold. Place a heavy weight such as an aluminum foil–wrapped brick or canned food on top of the saucer and refrigerate overnight or for up to 2 days.

SHORTLY before serving, run the blade of a metal frosting spatula or dull knife around the insides of the mold to loosen the pudding. Invert a serving plate over the mold, invert the plate and mold together, and lift off the mold. Garnish the top of the pudding and the plate with berries and mint and refrigerate while you prepare the Whipped Cream as directed.

TO serve, cut into wedges at the table and top with the cream.

Makes 8 servings.

GINGERBREAD

Serve with Old-fashioned Dessert Sauce (page 588), Crème Anglaise (page 582), or your favorite gingerbread accompaniment. The cake can also be baked in a greased and floured 10-inch Bundt or other fluted tube pan for about 1 hour; loosen and invert as directed for Sour Cream Coffee Cake on page 520. For a smaller cake, cut the recipe in half and bake in an 8-inch square pan for about 35 minutes.

POSITION racks so that the cake will bake in the middle of an oven and preheat the oven to 350° F.

USING a pastry brush, generously grease the bottom and sides of a 13-by-9-inch pan with shortening. Set aside.

PLACE the flour, baking powder, baking soda, salt, ginger, cinnamon, pepper, allspice, cloves, and nutmeg together in a strainer or sifter and sift into a bowl. Whisk to mix well and set aside.

IN a bowl, combine the sugar, molasses, butter, milk, and eggs and beat with an electric mixer at medium speed until smooth, about 1 minute. Using the mixer on low speed or a rubber spatula, fold in the flour mixture just until incorporated.

SCRAPE the batter into the prepared pan and smooth the surface with a rubber spatula. Bake until the cake springs back when lightly touched in the center with your fingertip and a wooden skewer inserted into the center of the cake comes out clean, about 45 minutes.

REMOVE the pan to a wire rack to cool for about 15 minutes. Cut into squares and serve warm directly from the pan.

Makes 12 servings.

Solid vegetable shortening, at room temperature, for greasing

3 cups all-purpose flour

2 teaspoons baking powder

¼ teaspoon baking soda

1 teaspoon salt

1 tablespoon ground ginger

2 teaspoons ground cinnamon

1½ teaspoons finely ground black or white pepper

1 teaspoon ground allspice

1 teaspoon ground cloves

1 teaspoon freshly grated nutmeg

2 cups sugar

½ cup dark molasses

1 cup (2 sticks) unsalted butter, melted and cooled slightly

1 cup whole milk, at room temperature

2 eggs, at room temperature

POLENTA CAKE

Solid vegetable shortening, at room
temperature, for greasing

All-purpose flour for dusting (optional)

1 cup all-purpose flour

1 cup yellow cornmeal (see recipe
introduction)

2 teaspoons baking powder

½ teaspoon salt

1 cup (2 sticks) unsalted butter, at
room temperature

1½ cups granulated sugar

6 egg yolks, at room temperature,
lightly beaten

4 eggs, at room temperature, lightly
beaten

1 teaspoon pure vanilla extract

1 teaspoon pure almond extract

Powdered sugar for dusting

Called amor di polenta *in Italian, literally "love of cornmeal," this slightly crunchy cake is traditionally baked in a loaf pan with a rounded, ridged bottom, sold as a deerback pan or saddle of venison mold. Lacking such pans, use 8½-by-4½-by-2½-inch loaf pans.*

For years I used powdered sugar in the batter, as is the custom of many Italian bakers. Granulated sugar, however, yields a more delicate crumb and allows for a higher rise. Regular cornmeal with a fine grind gives a finer texture to the cake, but you may choose coarse grind for a crunchier bite.

Italians often serve a pitcher of heavy (whipping) cream for pouring over the cake. It is also wonderful with fresh berries or perfectly plain.

POSITION racks so that the cake will bake in the middle of an oven and preheat the oven to 350° F.

USING a pastry brush, generously grease two 12-by-4½-by-1¾-inch deerback pans or two 8½-by-4½-by-2½-inch loaf pans with shortening; be sure to coat every nook and cranny. If using deerback pans, dust generously with flour, shake the pans to coat all over, invert, and tap out excess flour. If using loaf pans, line the bottoms with kitchen parchment, then lightly brush the parchment with shortening. Set aside.

PLACE the 1 cup flour, cornmeal, baking powder, and salt together in a strainer or sifter and sift into a bowl. Repeat the process two more times. Whisk to mix well and set aside.

IN the bowl of a stand mixer fitted with a flat beater, or in a bowl with a hand mixer, beat the butter at medium speed until soft and creamy, about 45 seconds. With the mixer still running, slowly add the granulated sugar, then stop the mixer and scrape the mixture that clings to the sides of the bowl into the center. Continue beating at medium speed until very light and fluffy, about 5 minutes. Slowly drizzle in the egg yolks and eggs and beat well; stop at least once to scrape the sides of the bowl. Add the vanilla and almond extracts and blend well.

USING the mixer on low speed or a rubber spatula, fold in about one-third of the flour mixture, scraping the sides of the bowl and folding just until the flour mixture is incorporated. In the same manner, fold in half of the remaining flour mixture, and finally the remaining flour mixture.

SCRAPE the batter into the prepared pans, dividing equally, and smooth the surfaces with a rubber spatula. Bake until each cake springs back when lightly touched in the center with your fingertip and a wooden skewer inserted into the center of each cake comes out clean, 25 to 35 minutes.

REMOVE the pans to a wire rack to cool for 5 to 10 minutes. Run the blade of a metal frosting spatula or dull knife around the insides of each pan to loosen the top edges of the cakes. Invert a lightly greased wire rack over a cake, invert the rack and pan together, and lift off the pan. Repeat with the second cake. If baked in loaf pans, peel off the parchment, place another lightly greased rack over a cake, and invert to turn upright; repeat with the second cake. Let the cakes cool completely, then cover tightly and store at room temperature for up to 2 days.

JUST before serving, lightly dust the top of the cake with powdered sugar.

Makes 16 servings.

VARIATION

ADD 8 ounces packaged almond paste along with the butter. Increase the baking time to about 35 minutes; if the tops begin to brown too quickly during baking, cover loosely with aluminum foil.

POUND CAKE

Solid vegetable shortening, at room
temperature, for greasing

1¾ cups all-purpose flour

½ teaspoon salt

1 cup (2 sticks) unsalted butter, at
room temperature

1½ cups sugar

4 eggs, at room temperature, lightly
beaten

3 egg yolks, at room temperature,
lightly beaten

2 teaspoons pure vanilla extract

*Early recipes for this classic literally called for a pound each of flour,
butter, sugar, and eggs. This contemporary version weighs in a bit lighter
but is equally delicious. For a large pound cake, double the recipe and
bake in a 10-inch angel food or other straight tube pan for about
1½ hours.*

POSITION racks so that the cake will bake in the middle of an
oven and preheat the oven to 325° F.

USING a pastry brush, generously grease the bottom and sides of
a 9-by-5-inch loaf pan with shortening. Line the bottom with
kitchen parchment, then lightly brush the parchment with
shortening. Set aside.

PLACE the flour and salt together in a strainer or sifter and sift
into a bowl. Whisk to mix well and set aside.

IN the bowl of a stand mixer fitted with a flat beater, or in a bowl
with a hand mixer, beat the butter at medium speed until soft
and creamy, about 45 seconds. With the mixer still running,
slowly add the sugar, then stop the mixer and scrape the mixture
that clings to the sides of the bowl into the center. Continue
beating at medium speed until very light and fluffy, about
5 minutes. Slowly drizzle in the eggs and egg yolks and beat
well; stop at least once to scrape the sides of the bowl. Add
the vanilla and blend well.

USING the mixer on low speed or a rubber spatula, fold in about
one-third of the flour mixture, scraping the sides of the bowl
and folding just until the flour mixture is incorporated. In the
same manner, fold in half of the remaining flour mixture, and
finally the remaining flour mixture.

SCRAPE the batter into the prepared pan and smooth the surface
with a rubber spatula. Bake until the cake springs back when
lightly touched in the center with your fingertip and a wooden
skewer inserted into the center of the cake comes out clean,
1 hour to 1¼ hours.

REMOVE the pan to a wire rack to cool for 5 to 10 minutes. Run the blade of a metal frosting spatula or dull knife around the insides of the pan to loosen the cake. Invert a lightly greased wire rack over the cake, invert the rack and pan together, and lift off the pan. Peel off the parchment. Place another lightly greased rack over the cake and invert to turn upright. Let cool completely, then cover tightly and store at room temperature for up to 2 days.

Makes 10 servings.

SOUR CREAM COFFEE CAKE WITH PECAN AND CINNAMON FILLING

Solid vegetable shortening, at room
    temperature, for greasing

All-purpose flour for dusting

1½ cups pecans

¾ cup firmly packed light brown
    sugar

1 tablespoon ground cinnamon

3 cups all-purpose flour

1 tablespoon baking powder

1 teaspoon baking soda

½ teaspoon salt

1 cup (2 sticks) unsalted butter, at
    room temperature

1½ cups sugar

1 tablespoon grated or minced fresh
    lemon zest

3 eggs, at room temperature, lightly
    beaten

1 teaspoon pure vanilla extract

1½ cups sour cream (not fat free),
    at room temperature

Powdered sugar for dusting

*Covered after cooling and stored at room temperature, this easy cake keeps
well for about 2 days.*

POSITION racks so that the cake will bake in the middle of an
    oven and preheat the oven to 350° F.

USING a pastry brush, generously grease the bottom and sides of
    a 10-inch Bundt or other fluted tube pan with shortening; be
    sure to coat every nook and cranny. Dust generously with flour,
    shake the pan to coat all over, invert, and tap out excess flour.
    Set aside.

TOAST the pecans as directed on page 554. Finely chop, transfer
    to a bowl, add the brown sugar and cinnamon, and stir to mix
    well. Set aside.

PLACE the 3 cups flour, baking powder, baking soda, and salt
    together in a strainer or sifter and sift into a bowl. Repeat the
    process two more times. Whisk to mix well and set aside.

IN the bowl of a stand mixer fitted with a flat beater, or in a bowl
    with a hand mixer, beat the butter at medium speed until soft
    and creamy, about 45 seconds. With the mixer still running,
    slowly add the sugar, then stop the mixer and scrape the mixture
    that clings to the sides of the bowl into the center. Add the
    lemon zest and continue beating at medium speed until the
    mixture is very light and fluffy, about 5 minutes. Slowly drizzle
    in the eggs and beat well; stop at least once to scrape the sides
    of the bowl. Add the vanilla and blend well.

USING the mixer on low speed or a rubber spatula, fold in about
    one-third of the flour mixture, then half of the sour cream,
    scraping the sides of the bowl and folding just until incorporated.
    In the same manner, fold in half of the remaining flour
    mixture, then the remaining sour cream, and finally the
    remaining flour mixture.

SCRAPE about half of the batter into the prepared pan. Sprinkle the pecan mixture evenly down the center of the batter, preventing the mixture from touching the sides of the pan. Cover with the remaining batter. Bake until the cake springs back when lightly touched in the thickest part with your fingertip and a wooden skewer inserted into the thickest part of the cake comes out clean, 45 to 55 minutes.

REMOVE the pan to a wire rack to cool for 5 to 10 minutes. Run the blade of a metal frosting spatula or dull knife around the insides of the pan to loosen the top edges of the cake. Invert a lightly greased wire rack over the cake, invert the rack and pan together, and lift off the pan. Let the cake cool completely, then transfer to a serving plate and dust with powdered sugar.

Makes 12 servings.

UPSIDE-DOWN BERRY CAKE

522

Solid vegetable shortening, at room
temperature, for greasing

¾ cup (1½ sticks) unsalted butter, at
room temperature

¾ cup firmly packed light brown
sugar

2½ cups blueberries, blackberries, or
cranberries

1½ cups all-purpose flour

1½ teaspoons baking powder

½ teaspoon salt

¾ cup granulated sugar

1 tablespoon grated or minced fresh
lemon zest, or 2 tablespoons grated
or minced fresh orange zest

2 eggs, at room temperature, lightly
beaten

¼ cup freshly squeezed lemon juice,
or ½ cup freshly squeezed orange
juice

1 teaspoon pure vanilla extract

⅓ cup whole milk, at room
temperature

*The elegant look of this cake belies the quick and easy technique. If you use
blueberries or blackberries, add lemon juice and zest to the batter; when you
choose cranberries, use the orange juice and zest.*

*Serve plain or with Crème Anglaise (page 582), Whipped Cream
(page 590), plain yogurt, or a pitcher of heavy (whipping) cream for pouring
over the cake.*

POSITION racks so that the cake will bake in the middle of an
oven and preheat the oven to 350° F.

USING a pastry brush, generously grease the bottom and sides of
a 9-inch round cake pan with shortening.

IN a saucepan, combine 2 tablespoons of the butter and the brown
sugar. Place over medium heat and cook, stirring occasionally,
until the butter melts and the mixture is slightly caramelized,
about 3 minutes. Pour into the prepared pan and quickly swirl
to coat the bottom of the pan evenly. Spread the berries evenly
over the mixture and set aside.

PLACE the flour, baking powder, and salt together in a strainer or
sifter and sift into a bowl. Repeat the process two more times.
Whisk to mix well and set aside.

IN the bowl of a stand mixer fitted with a flat beater, or in a bowl
with a hand mixer, beat the remaining butter at medium speed
until soft and creamy, about 45 seconds. With the mixer still
running, slowly add the granulated sugar, then stop the mixer
and scrape the mixture that clings to the sides of the bowl into
the center. Add the lemon or orange zest and continue beating
at medium speed until the mixture is very light and fluffy,
about 5 minutes. Slowly drizzle in the eggs and beat well; stop
at least once to scrape the sides of the bowl. Add the lemon or
orange juice and vanilla and blend well.

USING the mixer on low speed or a rubber spatula, fold in about one-third of the flour mixture, then half of the milk, scraping the sides of the bowl and folding just until the ingredients are incorporated. In the same manner, fold in half of the remaining flour mixture, then the remaining milk, and finally the remaining flour mixture.

SCRAPE the batter over the berries in the pan and smooth the surface with a rubber spatula. Bake until the cake springs back when lightly touched in the center with your fingertip and a wooden skewer inserted into the center of the cake comes out clean, 50 to 55 minutes.

REMOVE the pan to a work surface. Run the blade of a metal frosting spatula or dull knife around the insides of the pan to loosen the cake. Invert a serving plate over the cake, invert the pan and plate together, and lift off the pan. If any fruit sticks to the pan, remove it with a spatula and reposition it on the cake. Set aside to cool slightly before serving warm or at room temperature.

Makes 8 servings.

VARIATION

SUBSTITUTE sliced banana, mango, papaya, pineapple, or other fruit for the berries. Omit the fruit zest and juice. Increase the milk to ½ cup.

FLORENTINE DOME CAKE
~ *Zuccotto* ~

Pound Cake (page 518)

1 cup hazelnuts (filberts)

About ½ cup Frangelico liqueur

8 ounces finest-quality semisweet
  chocolate, chopped

2 cups heavy (whipping) cream,
  preferably not ultrapasteurized,
  well chilled

¼ cup powdered sugar

During a research visit to Florence some years ago, I sought out the few places that still offered this historic dessert of the Renaissance city. Food scholars cannot agree as to whether the heavenly confection is named for the dome of the city's cathedral, for the dome-shaped hats worn by cardinals, or for the less holy but equally lofty pumpkin.

Most recipes call for maraschino liqueur or a mixture of spirits, as well as at least two kinds of nuts. I prefer the simplicity and consistency of hazelnut-flavored Frangelico liqueur and chopped hazelnuts, especially with the intense chocolate of the inner layer. The cake can be moistened with Simple Sugar Syrup (page 599) instead of liqueur. For a more delicate result, make 2 Hot-Milk Sponge Cakes as directed in the recipe for Passion Fruit Cake on page 546 and use in place of the pound cake.

PREPARE the Pound Cake as directed and set aside.

PLACE a metal bowl and a wire whisk or the beaters of a hand
  mixer in a freezer until well chilled.

SELECT a 1½ -quart bowl with the roundest bottom possible. Line
  the bowl with a layer of dampened cheesecloth. Set aside.

PREHEAT an oven to 350° F.

TOAST the hazelnuts as directed on page 554. Finely chop and
  set aside.

CUT the cake into slices about ⅜ inch thick, then cut each slice on
  the diagonal into 2 pieces to form triangles. Spiraling out from
  the center of the bottom of the cheesecloth-lined bowl, line
  the bowl with the cake pieces. Reserve the remaining cake pieces.
  Using a pastry brush, moisten the cake in the bowl with the
  Frangelico. Set aside.

MELT 6 ounces of the chocolate as directed on page 595 and set
  aside to cool.

IN the chilled bowl, combine the cream and sugar and beat with the chilled whisk or hand mixer until fairly stiff. Fold the chopped hazelnuts and the remaining 2 ounces chocolate into the cream. Spoon half of the mixture over the cake in the bowl, leaving an indention in the center.

STIR the melted chocolate into the remaining whipped cream mixture and spoon the mixture into the center of the cake.

WORKING with one at a time, brush each remaining cake triangle with the Frangelico and place it atop the cake filling to cover completely. Cut away any exposed cake lining the bowl evenly with the new top cake layer. Cut small pieces of cake to fill any holes in the top layer. Cover with plastic wrap and refrigerate at least overnight or for up to 2 days.

TO serve, invert a serving plate over the bowl, invert the plate and bowl together, and lift off the bowl. Peel off the cheesecloth. Cut into wedges at the table.

Makes 8 servings.

SIENESE SPICE CAKE ~ *Panforte* ~

Candied Orange Zest (page 596)

1 cup blanched almonds

1 cup hazelnuts (filberts)

Solid vegetable shortening, at room
temperature, for greasing

1 cup chopped high-quality glazed
apricots, citron, or other fruit

4 teaspoons grated or minced fresh
lemon zest

1 teaspoon ground cinnamon

½ teaspoon freshly grated nutmeg

½ teaspoon ground aniseed

½ teaspoon ground coriander

¼ teaspoon ground cloves

¼ teaspoon finely ground white
pepper

1 cup all-purpose flour

½ cup honey

¾ cup granulated sugar

2 tablespoons unsalted butter, melted
and cooled slightly

Powdered sugar for dusting

Countless shop windows along the narrow winding streets of Siena display this local specialty. The Crusaders dubbed the dense cake panforte, or "strong bread," because it could be taken on long journeys without spoiling. Thickly laced with nuts and glazed fruit, the confection was nearly heavy enough to double as a weapon.

Instead of using the bland-tasting candied fruits found in most supermarkets, look for high-quality imports from Italy in gourmet shops, especially in the fall; honey-glazed apricots from Australia are also wonderful. When stored in an airtight container, panforte, which is almost like a candy, will last for up to a month.

PREPARE the Candied Orange Zest at least several hours or up to a few days before making the cake. Set aside.

TOAST the almonds and hazelnuts separately as directed on page 554. Coarsely chop the nuts and transfer to a large bowl. Set aside.

POSITION racks so that the cake will bake in the middle of an oven and preheat the oven to 325° F.

USING a pastry brush, lightly grease the bottom and sides of a 9-inch springform pan with shortening. Line the bottom with a kitchen parchment round and the sides with a kitchen parchment strip, then lightly brush the parchment with shortening. Set aside.

CHOP the Candied Orange Zest and add to the nuts. Add the glazed apricots or other fruit, lemon zest, cinnamon, nutmeg, aniseed, coriander, cloves, white pepper, and flour and mix thoroughly; set aside.

IN a heavy saucepan, combine the honey and granulated sugar and place over medium heat. Cook, stirring frequently, until the mixture registers between 234° and 240° F (soft-ball stage) on a candy thermometer. Pour the syrup over the nut-and-fruit mixture, add the melted butter, and stir the sticky dough until all the ingredients are thoroughly incorporated. Turn the mixture out into the prepared pan. Moisten your fingers lightly with water and press out the dough to the edges of the pan to form an even layer.

BAKE until the top of the cake is golden brown, 35 to 40 minutes; the gooey cake will not appear done but will set as it cools.

REMOVE the pan to a wire rack to cool for about 15 minutes. Unclasp and remove the ring and peel off the parchment sides. Invert a lightly greased wire rack over the cake, invert the rack and pan together, and lift off the pan bottom. Invert the cake back onto the first rack, parchment side down, to cool completely, at least 1 hour. After the cake is cooled, invert a plate over the cake, invert the rack and plate together, and peel off and discard the parchment.

TO serve, dust the top of the cake with powdered sugar. Cut into small wedges.

Makes 12 servings.

VARIATIONS

Chocolate Spice Cake *(Panforte di Cioccolata).* Add 3 tablespoons unsweetened cocoa along with the flour. Invert the cooled cake onto a wire rack. Combine 6 ounces finest-quality semisweet or bittersweet chocolate and 2 tablespoons unsalted butter and melt as directed for Chocolate Mousse (page 474); whisk until smooth and spread over the top of the cake. When the glaze has set completely, lightly dust with unsweetened cocoa or sweet ground chocolate (see page 512), if desired.

Peppered Spice Cake *(Panpepato).* Add 3 tablespoons unsweetened cocoa along with the flour and increase the white pepper to 1¼ teaspoons. Dust the finished cake with a mixture of equal parts powdered sugar and ground cinnamon or glaze with chocolate as suggested in the preceding chocolate variation.

GINGERED CARROT CAKE WITH
ORANGE CREAM CHEESE FROSTING

GINGERED CARROT CAKE

6 cups finely chopped or shredded
carrots (about 2 pounds)

2¾ cups sugar

Solid vegetable shortening, at room
temperature, for greasing

2½ cups all-purpose flour

2 teaspoons baking powder

½ teaspoon baking soda

¾ teaspoon salt

¾ cup (1½ sticks) unsalted butter,
melted and cooled slightly

4 eggs, at room temperature, lightly
beaten

½ cup finely chopped drained
preserved ginger in syrup (see
recipe introduction)

¼ cup finely chopped dried apricots

1 tablespoon grated or minced fresh
ginger

*Many carrot cake recipes end up tasting like spice cakes with only a hint of
carrot flavor. My version lets the carrots shine through, complemented by
the addition of ginger and apricot and a zesty orange frosting. Sugaring
and draining the carrots means a large amount can be used in the batter,
which results in a more intense carrot color and flavor in the finished cake.*

*Look for moist preserved ginger packed in syrup, sometimes
labeled "stem ginger," in Asian markets and specialty-food stores.
Readily available crystallized ginger can be substituted, if necessary, but
it lacks the moistness of the syrup-soaked product.*

TO make the Gingered Carrot Cake, place the carrots in a colander
set over a bowl. Sprinkle with ¾ cup of the sugar and set aside
to drain, stirring occasionally, for about 25 minutes.

POSITION racks so that the cake will bake in the middle of an
oven and preheat the oven to 350° F.

USING a pastry brush, generously grease the bottom and sides of
two 9-inch round cake pans with shortening. Line the bottoms
with rounds of kitchen parchment, then lightly brush the
parchment with shortening. Set aside.

PLACE the flour, baking powder, baking soda, and salt together in
a strainer or sifter and sift into a bowl. Repeat the process two
more times. Whisk to mix well and set aside.

IN the bowl of a stand mixer fitted with a flat beater, or in a bowl
with a hand mixer, beat the melted butter and the remaining
2 cups sugar until well blended. Slowly drizzle in the eggs and
beat well; stop at least once to scrape the mixture that clings to
the sides of the bowl into the center.

GENTLY squeeze the carrots to release as much moisture as possible
and add to the butter mixture; discard the liquid drained from
the carrots. Add the preserved ginger, apricots, and fresh
ginger and mix at low speed until well blended.

USING the mixer on low speed or a rubber spatula, fold in the
flour mixture just until incorporated.

DIVIDE the batter evenly between the prepared pans and smooth the surfaces with a rubber spatula. Bake until each cake layer springs back when lightly touched in the center with your fingertip and a wooden skewer inserted into the center of each layer comes out clean, about 40 minutes.

REMOVE the pans to a wire rack to cool for 5 to 10 minutes. Run the blade of a metal frosting spatula or dull knife around the insides of each pan to loosen the cake layers. Invert a lightly greased wire rack over a layer, invert the rack and pan together, and lift off the pan. Peel off the parchment. Place another lightly greased rack over the layer and invert to turn upright. Repeat with the second cake layer. Set aside to cool completely.

TO make the Orange Cream Cheese Frosting, in a bowl, combine the butter and orange zest and beat with an electric mixer at medium speed until soft and fluffy. Add the cream cheese, sour cream or yogurt, vanilla and orange extracts, and salt and beat at low speed just until the mixture is smooth and creamy, about 1 minute; avoid overbeating, which makes the cream cheese too thin and runny. Using a rubber spatula, clean the beaters and scrape the sides of the bowl whenever necessary during beating. Add 1 cup of the powdered sugar and beat at low speed just until incorporated. Add the remaining 2 cups powdered sugar and beat just until smooth and spreadable; add a little cream or milk if the mixture is too thick.

TO assemble, place a cooled cake layer on a serving plate and insert pieces of waxed paper under the edges to prevent frosting from going onto the plate. Spoon about 1 cup of the frosting onto the layer and spread evenly over the top with a long metal frosting spatula. Add the second cake layer and evenly spread the remaining frosting over the top and sides of the cake. Using the spatula or a cake decorating comb, texture the frosting as desired. Carefully remove the pieces of waxed paper. Refrigerate the cake, uncovered, until the frosting is set, at least 1 hour. Cover with a cake dome and refrigerate for up to 2 days.

ABOUT 1 hour before serving, remove the cake from the refrigerator and let come to room temperature.

Makes 12 servings.

ORANGE CREAM CHEESE FROSTING

¾ cup (1½ sticks) unsalted butter, at room temperature

2 tablespoons finely grated or minced fresh orange zest

1 pound cream cheese (not fat free), chilled

¼ cup sour cream or plain yogurt

1 teaspoon pure vanilla extract

½ teaspoon pure orange extract

Pinch of salt

3 cups powdered sugar, sifted

Light cream, half-and-half, or milk (not fat free), if needed

FRESH GINGER CAKE WITH CREAMY MACADAMIA NUT FROSTING

FRESH GINGER CAKE

Solid vegetable shortening, at room
  temperature, for greasing

3 cups all-purpose flour

1 tablespoon baking powder

1 teaspoon salt

1 cup (2 sticks) unsalted butter, at
  room temperature

2 cups sugar

2 tablespoons grated or minced fresh
  lime zest

4 eggs, at room temperature, lightly
  beaten

1 cup finely grated fresh ginger

1 cup whole milk, at room
  temperature

*If you're as addicted to ginger as I am, you'll love this cake! For easier
grating and less ginger fibers, freeze peeled tubers until firm and grate
them directly from the freezer; set aside to come to room temperature
before adding to the batter.*

TO make the Fresh Ginger Cake, position racks so that the cake will
  bake in the middle of an oven and preheat the oven to 350° F.

USING a pastry brush, generously grease the bottom and sides of
  two 9-inch round cake pans with shortening. Line the bottoms
  with rounds of kitchen parchment, then lightly brush the parchment
  with shortening. Set aside.

PLACE the flour, baking powder, and salt together in a strainer or
  sifter and sift into a bowl. Repeat the process two more times.
  Whisk to mix well and set aside.

IN the bowl of a stand mixer fitted with a flat beater, or in a bowl
  with a hand mixer, beat the butter at medium speed until soft
  and creamy, about 45 seconds. With the mixer still running,
  slowly add the sugar, then stop the mixer and scrape the mixture
  that clings to the sides of the bowl into the center. Add the lime
  zest and continue beating at medium speed until the mixture is
  very light and fluffy, about 5 minutes. Slowly drizzle in the eggs
  and beat well; stop at least once to scrape the sides of the bowl.
  Add the ginger and blend well.

USING the mixer on low speed or a rubber spatula, fold in about
  one-third of the flour mixture, then half of the milk, scraping
  the sides of the bowl and folding just until the ingredients are
  incorporated. In the same manner, fold in half of the remaining
  flour mixture, then the remaining milk, and finally the remaining
  flour mixture.

DIVIDE the batter evenly between the prepared pans and smooth
  the surfaces with a rubber spatula. Bake until each cake layer
  springs back when lightly touched in the center with your fingertip
  and a wooden skewer inserted into the center of each layer
  comes out clean, about 35 minutes.

REMOVE the pans to a wire rack to cool for 5 to 10 minutes. Run the blade of a metal frosting spatula or dull knife around the insides of each pan to loosen the cake layers. Invert a lightly greased wire rack over a layer, invert the rack and pan together, and lift off the pan. Peel off the parchment. Place another lightly greased rack over the layer and invert to turn upright. Repeat with the second cake layer. Set aside to cool completely.

TO make the Creamy Macadamia Nut Frosting, toast the nuts as directed on page 554. Finely chop and set aside.

IN a bowl, beat the butter with an electric mixer at medium speed until soft and fluffy. Add the cream cheese, vanilla, and salt and beat at low speed just until the mixture is smooth and creamy, about 1 minute; avoid overbeating, which makes the cream cheese too thin and runny. Using a rubber spatula, clean the beaters and scrape the sides of the bowl whenever necessary during beating. Add 1 cup of the powdered sugar and beat at low speed just until incorporated. Add the remaining 2 cups powdered sugar and beat just until smooth and spreadable; add a little cream or milk if the mixture is too thick. Stir in the macadamia nuts until well blended.

TO assemble, place a cooled cake layer on a serving plate and insert pieces of waxed paper under the edges to prevent frosting from going onto the plate. Spoon about 1 cup of the frosting onto the layer and spread evenly over the top with a long metal frosting spatula. Add the second cake layer and evenly spread the remaining frosting over the top and sides of the cake. Using the spatula or a cake decorating comb, texture the frosting as desired. Carefully remove the pieces of waxed paper. Refrigerate, uncovered, until the frosting is set, at least 1 hour. Cover with a cake dome and keep refrigerated for up to 2 days.

ABOUT 1 hour before serving, remove the cake from the refrigerator and let come to room temperature.

Makes 12 servings.

CREAMY MACADAMIA NUT FROSTING

1 cup raw macadamia nuts

¾ cup (1½ sticks) unsalted butter, at room temperature

1 pound cream cheese (not fat free), chilled

2 teaspoons pure vanilla extract

Pinch of salt

3 cups powdered sugar, sifted

Light cream, half-and-half, or milk (not fat free), if needed

HAWAIIAN COCONUT CAKE

WHITE CAKE

Solid vegetable shortening, at room
    temperature, for greasing

¾ cup egg whites (from about
    6 eggs), at room temperature

1 cup whole milk, at room
    temperature

2 teaspoons pure vanilla extract

2½ cups cake flour

2½ teaspoons baking powder

¾ teaspoon salt

1¾ cups sugar

¾ cup (1½ sticks) unsalted butter,
    at room temperature

HAUPIA FILLING

¾ cup sugar

½ cup cornstarch

3 cups Fresh Coconut Milk (page 562)
    or high-quality commercial coconut
    milk (see recipe introduction)

In Hawaii, a luau often ends with haupia, *a gelatinous dessert made with coconut milk. This cake has the clean, fresh taste of pure coconut, especially when the filling is made with homemade or thawed frozen high-quality coconut milk (sometimes available labeled "Hawaiian style" in Asian markets) and the cake is finished with fresh rather than packaged coconut.*

TO make the White Cake, position racks so that the cake layers will bake in the middle of an oven and preheat the oven to 350° F.

USING a pastry brush, generously grease the bottom and sides of two 9-inch round cake pans with shortening. Line the bottoms with rounds of kitchen parchment, then lightly brush the parchment with shortening. Set aside.

IN a bowl or glass measuring cup, combine the egg whites, milk, and vanilla and whisk to blend well. Set aside.

PLACE the flour, baking powder, and salt together in a strainer or sifter and sift into a bowl. Add the sugar and mix with an electric mixer at low speed until well blended, about 30 seconds. Add the butter and beat at medium speed until the mixture resembles coarse bread crumbs, about 45 seconds.

ADD about 1¼ cups of the egg white mixture and beat at medium speed if using a stand mixer or high speed if using a hand mixer for 1½ minutes, then stop the mixer and scrape the mixture that clings to the sides of the bowl into the center. Add the remaining egg white mixture and beat at the same speed for 30 seconds, then stop and scrape down the sides of the bowl and beat again until creamy smooth, about 30 seconds.

DIVIDE the batter evenly between the prepared pans and smooth the surfaces with a rubber spatula. Bake until each cake layer springs back when lightly touched in the center with your fingertip and a wooden skewer inserted into the center of each layer comes out clean, about 25 minutes.

REMOVE the pans to a wire rack to cool for 5 to 10 minutes. Run the blade of a metal frosting spatula or dull knife around the insides of each pan to loosen the cake layers. Invert a lightly greased wire rack over a layer, invert the rack and pan together, and lift off the pan. Peel off the parchment. Place another lightly greased rack over the layer and invert to turn upright. Repeat with the second cake layer. Set aside to cool completely.

TO make the *Haupia* Filling, in a heavy saucepan, combine the sugar and cornstarch. Gradually whisk in 1½ cups water until the mixture is smooth, then stir in the coconut milk. Place over medium heat and cook, stirring almost constantly, until thickened, about 10 minutes. Remove from the heat and set aside to cool for about 10 minutes.

USING a small, sharp knife, carefully trim off all of the browned crust from the top, bottom, and sides of the cake layers to create completely white layers. Using a long serrated knife, slice each layer horizontally in half to create 4 layers total.

TO assemble, place a cooled cake layer on a serving plate and insert pieces of waxed paper under the edges to prevent frosting from going onto the plate. Spoon about one-fourth of the *Haupia* Filling onto the layer and spread evenly over the top with a long metal frosting spatula. Place another layer on top, spread filling, and continue to add remaining layers and filling in the same manner, ending with filling on top of the cake. Set aside at room temperature for the filling to set while preparing the frosting.

TO make the Whipped Cream Frosting, place a metal bowl and a wire whisk or the beaters of a hand mixer in a freezer until well chilled.

IN a small saucepan, combine the powdered sugar and cornstarch and whisk to mix well. Slowly whisk in ½ cup of the cream until smooth. Place over medium heat and stir constantly to prevent scorching on the bottom until the mixture just begins to thicken and comes almost to a boil. Transfer to a bowl and set aside, stirring occasionally, to cool to room temperature.

continues ~

WHIPPED CREAM FROSTING

¼ cup powdered sugar

2½ teaspoons cornstarch

2 cups heavy (whipping) cream, preferably not ultrapasteurized, well chilled

1 teaspoon pure vanilla extract

2 cups grated or shredded fresh coconut (see page 562) or packaged sweetened coconut

Pesticide-free nontoxic small orchids for garnish (optional)

IN the chilled bowl, combine the remaining 1½ cups cream and the
vanilla and beat with the chilled whisk or hand mixer just until
the cream begins to hold its shape. While still beating, add the
powdered sugar mixture a little at a time and beat just until the
mixture forms stiff peaks when the beater is raised and is
spreadable; be careful not to overbeat.

USING a long metal frosting spatula, cover the sides and a 1-inch
border around the outside perimeter of the top of the cake with
the frosting, leaving the *haupia* on the top exposed. Generously
sprinkle the frosted area with the grated or shredded coconut.
Carefully remove the pieces of waxed paper. Cover with a cake
dome and refrigerate for up to 6 hours.

ABOUT 30 minutes before serving, remove the cake from the
refrigerator and surround with orchids (if using).

Makes 12 servings.

DEVIL'S FOOD CAKE
WITH GANACHE

I enjoy finishing this great American standard with rich ganache. When I'm feeling extravagant, I make a double batch of ganache, then slice each cake layer horizontally in half to create 4 layers total and lavishly spread the ganache.

For the ganache, be sure to choose excellent chocolate that tastes great on its own such as Callebaut, Guitard, Lindt, Scharffen Berger, or Vahlrona.

TO make the Devil's Food Cake, position racks so that the cake will bake in the middle of an oven and preheat the oven to 350° F.

USING a pastry brush, generously grease the bottom and sides of two 9-inch round cake pans with shortening. Line the bottoms with rounds of kitchen parchment, then lightly brush the parchment with shortening. Set aside.

PLACE the cocoa in a heatproof bowl or glass measuring cup, slowly add the boiling water or hot coffee, and stir until smooth. Stir in the milk and set aside to cool to room temperature.

PLACE the flour, baking soda, and salt together in a strainer or sifter and sift into a bowl. Repeat the process two more times. Whisk to mix well and set aside.

IN the bowl of a stand mixer fitted with a flat beater, or in a bowl with a hand mixer, beat the butter at medium speed until soft and creamy, about 45 seconds. With the mixer still running, slowly add the sugar, then stop the mixer and scrape the mixture that clings to the sides of the bowl into the center. Continue beating at medium speed until the mixture is very light and fluffy, about 5 minutes. Slowly drizzle in the eggs and beat well; stop at least once to scrape the sides of the bowl. Add the vanilla and blend well.

continues ~

DEVIL'S FOOD CAKE

Solid vegetable shortening, at room temperature, for greasing

¾ cup unsweetened natural cocoa (not Dutch-processed)

1½ cups boiling water or hot strong brewed coffee

¾ cup whole milk

3 cups all-purpose flour

1 teaspoon baking soda

¾ teaspoon salt

¾ cup (1½ sticks) unsalted butter, at room temperature

2¼ cups sugar

3 eggs, at room temperature, lightly beaten

1½ teaspoons pure vanilla extract

GANACHE

1½ pounds finest-quality bittersweet
   (not unsweetened) or semisweet
   chocolate, finely chopped

6 tablespoons unsalted butter,
   at room temperature, cut into
   small pieces

1½ cups heavy (whipping) cream

3 tablespoons light corn syrup

1 tablespoon pure vanilla extract,
   brandy, or fruit-flavored liqueur

Seedless raspberry jam (a favorite
   recipe or high-quality commercial
   product) for spreading (optional)

USING the mixer on low speed or a rubber spatula, fold in about one-third of the reserved flour mixture, then half of the cocoa mixture, scraping the sides of the bowl and folding just until the ingredients are incorporated. In the same manner, fold in half of the remaining flour mixture, then the remaining cocoa mixture, and finally the remaining flour mixture.

DIVIDE the batter evenly between the prepared pans and smooth the tops with a rubber spatula. Bake until each cake layer springs back when lightly touched in the center with your fingertip and a wooden skewer inserted into the center of each layer comes out clean, about 35 minutes.

REMOVE the pans to a wire rack to cool for 5 to 10 minutes. Run the blade of a metal frosting spatula or dull knife around the insides of each pan to loosen the cake layers. Invert a lightly greased wire rack over a layer, invert the rack and pan together, and lift off the pan. Peel off the parchment. Place another lightly greased rack over the layer and invert to turn upright. Repeat with the second cake layer. Set aside to cool completely.

TO make the Ganache, place the chocolate and butter in a bowl or in a food processor. Set aside.

IN a saucepan, combine the cream and corn syrup. Place over medium heat and bring just to a boil. Pour over the chocolate and butter and stir or process until the chocolate is melted and the mixture is smooth. If using a food processor, transfer the mixture to a bowl. Stir in the vanilla, brandy, or liqueur.

COVER and refrigerate until cool and set to the touch, about 2 hours, or refrigerate for up to overnight.

RETURN the ganache to room temperature. Beat briefly with a hand mixer to smooth and lighten to a spreadable consistency; avoid overbeating.

TO assemble, place one of the cooled cake layers on a serving plate and insert pieces of waxed paper under the edges to prevent frosting from going onto the plate. Spread a thin layer of jam (if using) over the layer, then spoon about 1 cup of the ganache onto the layer and spread evenly over the top with a long metal frosting spatula. Add the second cake layer and spread the remaining ganache over the top and sides. If the ganache becomes too stiff during spreading, dip the spatula into hot water and wipe dry. Using the spatula or a cake decorating comb, texture the frosting as desired. Carefully remove the pieces of waxed paper. Refrigerate the cake, uncovered, until the frosting is set, about 1 hour. Cover with a cake dome and refrigerate for up to 2 days.

AT least 1 hour before serving, remove the cake from the refrigerator and let come to room temperature.

Makes 12 servings.

HEIRLOOM APPLE CAKE

HEIRLOOM APPLE CAKE

Solid vegetable shortening, at room
    temperature, for greasing

All-purpose flour for dusting

1 cup pecans or walnuts

2½ cups all-purpose flour

2½ teaspoons baking powder

1 teaspoon salt

2 cups sugar

1½ cups canola or other high-quality
    flavorless vegetable oil

2 eggs, at room temperature

2 teaspoons pure vanilla extract

3 cups peeled, cored, and finely
    chopped flavorful baking apples
    (see recipe introduction)

1 cup raisins

Although this moist cake is wonderful served warm from the oven with vanilla ice cream or whipped cream, it is even more delectable when crowned with caramel glaze to resemble a big caramel apple. If you choose to make the glaze, don't let anything distract you during the process.

Choose good baking apples, preferably from your backyard, a roadside orchard stand, or a farmers' market. Look for Baldwin, Cortland, Golden Delicious, Gravenstein, Ida Red, Northern Spy, or local heirloom varieties with plenty of flavor and juicy texture. Tart apples such as Granny Smith are best left for pies or crisps.

TO make the Heirloom Apple Cake, position racks so that the cake will bake in the middle of an oven and preheat the oven to 350° F.

USING a pastry brush, generously grease the bottom and sides of a 10-inch Bundt or other fluted tube pan with shortening; be sure to coat every nook and cranny. Dust generously with flour, shake the pan to coat all over, invert, and tap out excess flour. Set aside.

TOAST the nuts as directed on page 554. Chop and set aside.

PLACE the flour, baking powder, and salt together in a strainer or sifter and sift into a bowl. Whisk to mix well and set aside.

IN the bowl of a stand mixer fitted with a flat beater, or in a bowl with a hand mixer, combine the sugar, oil, eggs, and vanilla and beat at medium speed until smooth, about 1 minute.

USING the mixer on low speed, fold in the flour mixture just until incorporated, then fold in the apples, raisins, and nuts until well blended.

SCRAPE the stiff batter into the prepared pan and smooth the surface with a rubber spatula. Bake until the cake springs back when lightly touched in the thickest part with your fingertip and a wooden skewer inserted into the thickest part of the cake comes out clean, 1 hour to 1¼ hours.

REMOVE the pan to a wire rack to cool for about 15 minutes. Run the blade of a metal frosting spatula or dull knife around the insides of the pan to loosen the top edges of the cake. Invert a lightly greased wire rack over the cake, invert the rack and pan together, and lift off the pan.

TO make the Old-fashioned Caramel Glaze (if using), prepare a large bowl of iced water and position it alongside the stove top.

IN a heavy saucepan, preferably made of stainless steel or unlined copper, combine ½ cup of the sugar and 1 tablespoon water and stir well. Place over medium heat and cook without disturbing the syrup until it begins to color, then continue cooking, slowly swirling the pan occasionally to spread the color evenly, until the syrup turns a rich amber. During cooking, if sugar crystals begin to form around the sides of the pan just above the bubbling syrup, brush them away with a pastry brush moistened with water. As soon as the syrup reaches the desired color, briefly place the pan in the iced water to halt the cooking. Remove the pan and set aside.

IN a large heavy saucepan, combine the remaining 2 cups sugar, the egg, and milk and whisk until well blended. Add the butter, place over low heat, and stir until the butter melts, then increase the heat to medium and bring the mixture to a boil, whisking almost constantly.

SHORTLY before the milk mixture reaches a boil, place the pan containing the caramel syrup over medium heat and remelt the syrup to a pourable stage. Slowly whisk it into the hot milk mixture and cook, whisking or stirring constantly and scraping the bottom and sides of the pan to prevent scorching, until the mixture registers between 234° and 240° F (soft-ball stage) on a candy thermometer and is thick and a rich caramel color, 5 to 10 minutes. Remove from the heat and set aside to cool for 2 to 3 minutes.

ADD the vanilla to the caramel mixture and beat with a hand mixer at high speed or whisk just until smooth but still pourable, about 30 seconds. Quickly pour it over the cake to coat completely. If it becomes too hard to pour and run smoothly, place over medium heat and stir just until pourable.

FOR optimal flavor, cover the cake with a cake dome and store at room temperature for 1 to 2 days before serving.

Makes 12 servings.

OLD-FASHIONED CARAMEL GLAZE
(optional)

2½ cups sugar

1 egg

¾ cup whole milk

½ cup (1 stick) unsalted butter

1 teaspoon pure vanilla extract

MOCHA TORTE

Solid vegetable shortening, at room
   temperature, for greasing

6 ounces unsweetened chocolate,
   chopped

¾ cup (1½ sticks) unsalted butter

4 eggs

2¾ cups granulated sugar

¼ teaspoon salt

3 tablespoons instant espresso

2 teaspoons pure vanilla extract

¾ teaspoon pure almond extract

1¼ cups all-purpose flour

1 cup finely ground pecans or
   walnuts

Fresh Berry Sauce (page 589) made
   with raspberries (optional)

Unsweetened Whipped Cream (page
   590) or Crème Fraîche (page 591)
   or commercial crème fraîche
   (optional)

Powdered sugar for dusting

Raspberries for garnish (optional)

*Because several versions of a similar recipe for gooey rich brownies exist,
I haven't been able to trace the origins of the baking technique that I've
adapted for this super-rich gooey torte. Whoever discovered the technique
of chilling batter that is not fully cooked to turn it into a dense sensation
deserves much praise.*

POSITION racks so that the torte will bake in the middle of an
   oven and preheat the oven to 425° F.

USING a pastry brush, generously grease the bottom and sides of a
   9-inch springform pan with shortening. Set aside.

IN a skillet or shallow saucepan, pour in water to a depth of 1 inch,
   place over medium heat, bring just to a simmer, and adjust the
   heat to maintain barely simmering water. Combine the chocolate
   and butter in a heatproof bowl, set the bowl in the simmering
   water, and stir the mixture constantly just until melted and
   smooth; do not allow to burn. Set aside to cool. Alternatively,
   combine the chocolate and butter in a microwave-safe measuring
   cup or bowl and microwave at 50 percent power, stirring every
   15 seconds, just until melted and smooth; do not allow to burn.

IN a bowl, combine the eggs, granulated sugar, salt, espresso, and
   vanilla and almond extracts. Beat with an electric mixer at high
   speed until the mixture is very light and creamy, about 10 minutes.
   Reduce the speed to low and drizzle in the melted chocolate just
   until well blended.

USING the mixer on low speed or a rubber spatula, fold in the flour
   and nuts just until the ingredients are incorporated.

SPOON the batter into the prepared pan and bake for 35 minutes; the
   top should be crusty and the center still runny; do not overbake.

REMOVE the pan to a wire rack to cool to room temperature, then
   cover the pan tightly and refrigerate overnight.

PREPARE the Fresh Berry Sauce (if using) and Whipped Cream or Crème Fraîche (if using) as directed and set each aside.

TO serve, run the blade of a metal frosting spatula or dull knife around the insides of the pan to loosen the torte. Unclasp and remove the pan ring. Run the blade between the torte and the pan bottom to loosen the torte, then slide the torte onto a serving plate. Dust the top with powdered sugar, and garnish with raspberries (if using). Cut into wedges and serve with the berry sauce (if using) and dollops of whipped cream or crème fraîche (if using).

Makes 12 servings.

MOLTEN CHOCOLATE BABYCAKES

Crème Anglaise (page 582)

Solid vegetable shortening, at room
  temperature, for greasing

12 ounces finest-quality bittersweet
  (not unsweetened) or semisweet
  chocolate, finely chopped

3 tablespoons unsalted butter, at
  room temperature

⅔ cup granulated sugar

⅛ teaspoon salt

4 eggs, at room temperature, lightly
  beaten

½ cup cake flour

1 teaspoon pure vanilla extract

Gold leaf for garnish (see recipe
  introduction; optional)

Powdered sugar for dusting, if not
  using gold leaf

Mango and raspberry purees for
  swirling (optional)

To insure that the fudgy centers of these individual cakes are runny, time their preparation so they can be served hot from the oven. Or bake them up to a day ahead, cool, cover, and store at room temperature; reheat uncovered in a 350° F oven for about 10 minutes or in a microwave oven at full power for about 25 seconds, being careful not to cook the cakes further when reheating.

Tissue-thin sheets of gold leaf make a luxurious garnish and reinforce the suggestion of flowing molten lava from the little mounds of cake. The inert metal is edible and may be purchased at art-supply stores and some cake decorating supply stores.

Instead of the suggested custard sauce, consider serving the cakes with Fresh Berry Sauce (page 589), Caramel Sauce (page 584), Chocolate Sauce (page 587) made with white chocolate, or Whipped Cream (page 590).

PREPARE the Crème Anglaise and refrigerate as directed until
  serving.

POSITION racks so that the cakes will bake in the middle of an
  oven and preheat the oven to 400° F.

USING a pastry brush, generously grease the bottom and sides of
  six 6-ounce custard cups or soufflé dishes with shortening.
  Line the bottoms of the containers with rounds of kitchen
  parchment, then lightly brush the parchment with shortening.
  Set aside.

MELT the chocolate as directed on page 595 and set aside to
  cool slightly.

IN a bowl or food processor, combine the butter, granulated sugar,
  salt, and eggs and beat with an electric mixer at medium speed
  or process until well blended. Add the flour and blend well. Add
  the vanilla and cooled chocolate and blend until smooth.

DIVIDE the batter evenly among the prepared baking dishes and smooth the surfaces with a small rubber spatula. Place on a baking sheet, transfer to the oven, and bake until the tops are well puffed, about 17 minutes.

REMOVE the baking dishes to a wire rack to cool for about 5 minutes. Run the blade of a small metal frosting spatula or dull knife around the insides of each baking dish to loosen the cakes. Invert an individual serving plate over a cake, invert the plate and baking dish together, and lift off the baking dish. Peel off the parchment. Repeat with the remaining cakes.

TOP each cake with a sheet of gold leaf (if using) or lightly sift a little powdered sugar over the tops of the cakes. Spoon a portion of the Crème Anglaise around each cake, then add dollops of mango and raspberry purees (if using) and swirl with a wooden skewer.

Makes 6 servings.

NUT CAKE

Solid vegetable shortening, at room
temperature, for greasing

1½ cups blanched almonds, pecans,
or other nuts

1½ cups granulated sugar

¾ cup all-purpose flour

1 teaspoon baking powder

½ teaspoon salt

½ cup (1 stick) unsalted butter, at
room temperature

1 tablespoon grated or minced fresh
orange zest (optional)

5 eggs, at room temperature, lightly
beaten

½ cup light cream or half-and-half,
at room temperature

2 teaspoons pure vanilla extract

1 teaspoon pure almond extract

Powdered sugar for dusting

*Having grown up in a Louisiana town surrounded by acres of pecan trees,
I favor these wonderful nuts for this recipe that dates back to the Old South.
It is also fabulous and a beautiful golden yellow when made with blanched
almonds. Feel free to use your favorite nut or a mixture.*

*The cake is delicious plain warm from the oven or simply adorned
with dollops of Whipped Cream (page 590) and/or Chocolate Sauce (page
587) or Caramel Sauce (page 584).*

POSITION racks so that the cake will bake in the middle of an
oven and preheat the oven to 350° F.

USING a pastry brush, generously grease the bottom and sides of
a 9-inch springform pan with shortening. Line the bottom
with a round of kitchen parchment, then lightly grease the
parchment with shortening. Set aside.

IN a food processor, combine the nuts and ¾ cup of the granulated
sugar and pulverize to form a fine meal. Set aside.

PLACE the flour, baking powder, and salt together in a strainer or
sifter and sift into a bowl. Add the ground nut mixture, whisk
to mix well, and set aside.

IN the bowl of a stand mixer fitted with a flat beater, or in a bowl
with a hand mixer, beat the butter at medium speed until soft
and creamy, about 45 seconds. With the mixer still running,
slowly add the remaining ¾ cup granulated sugar and the
orange zest (if using), then stop the mixer and scrape the
mixture that clings to the sides of the bowl into the center.
Continue beating at medium speed until the mixture is very
light and fluffy, about 5 minutes. Slowly drizzle in the eggs
and beat well; stop at least once to scrape the sides of the
bowl. Add the cream or half-and-half and vanilla and almond
extracts and blend well.

USING the mixer on low speed or a rubber spatula, fold in the nut mixture.

USING a rubber spatula, scrape the batter into the prepared pan. Bake until the cake springs back when lightly touched in the center with your fingertip and a wooden skewer inserted into the center of the cake comes out clean, about 40 minutes.

REMOVE the pan to a wire rack to cool for 5 to 10 minutes. Run the blade of a metal frosting spatula or dull knife around the insides of the pan to loosen the cake. Unclasp and remove the pan ring. Invert a lightly greased wire rack over the cake, invert the rack and pan bottom together, and lift off the pan bottom. Peel off the parchment. Invert a serving plate over the cake and invert the rack and plate together to turn the cake upright. Dust the top with powdered sugar. If desired, cover the cake with a stencil before dusting with powdered sugar, then carefully remove the stencil.

Makes 8 servings.

PASSION FRUIT CAKE

Double recipe Passion Fruit Curd
　(page 593)
Simple Sugar Syrup (page 599) or
　passion fruit liqueur

HOT-MILK SPONGE CAKE

Solid vegetable shortening, at room
　temperature, for greasing
½ cup plus 2 tablespoons cake flour
1 teaspoon baking powder
¼ teaspoon salt
¼ cup whole milk
2 tablespoons unsalted butter
3 eggs
3 egg yolks
¾ cup sugar
1 teaspoon pure vanilla extract

The seductive perfumed fragrance and flavor of passion fruit makes eating it one of life's greatest pleasures. One bite of this heady concoction transports me to an island paradise. When I can't find a plentiful supply of wrinkled fresh passion fruits in the produce market, I purchase packages of the frozen pulp from Latin American markets in San Francisco or use frozen concentrate from Hawaii, where the fruits are known by their ancient Hawaiian name, lilikoi.

You will need two Hot-Milk Sponge Cakes to complete this recipe; due to the delicate structure of the batter, I do not recommend doubling the recipe, but advocate mixing and baking the cakes separately. If you wish to work ahead, the cooled cakes can be tightly wrapped in plastic wrap and refrigerated for up to 2 days before assembling the cake.

PREPARE the Passion Fruit Curd and Simple Sugar Syrup (if using) as directed and set aside or refrigerate for up to 2 days before using. If using passion fruit liqueur, reserve for later use.

TO make the Hot-Milk Sponge Cake, position racks so that the cake will bake in the middle of an oven and preheat the oven to 350° F.

USING a pastry brush, generously grease the bottom of a 9-inch springform pan; do not grease the sides. Line the bottom with a round of kitchen parchment, then lightly grease the parchment with shortening. Set aside.

PLACE the flour, baking powder, and salt together in a strainer or sifter and sift into a bowl. Repeat the process two more times. Whisk to mix well and set aside.

IN a small saucepan, combine the milk and butter. Place over medium heat until the butter is melted. Reduce the heat to keep the mixture warm but not simmering.

IN the metal bowl of a stand mixer or a metal bowl, lightly whisk together the eggs, egg yolks, and sugar. Set the bowl over a pan of simmering water, being sure that the bottom of the bowl doesn't touch the water, and whisk gently just until the mixture is lukewarm to the touch. Remove from the heat. Using the wire whip of a stand mixer or hand mixer, beat the egg mixture at high speed

until light, fluffy, at least tripled in bulk, and a wide ribbon forms
when some of the mixture is lifted and dropped back over the
remainder, about 5 minutes if using a stand mixer, or about
10 minutes if using a hand mixer. Add the vanilla and blend well.

SIFT about one-third of the flour mixture over the egg mixture.
Using a large balloon whisk or rubber spatula, quickly and gently
fold the mixture just until the ingredients are incorporated. In the
same way, quickly and gently fold in the remaining flour mixture
in 2 equal batches; the flour mixture must be well incorporated,
but avoid overmixing and deflating the batter too much. Add
the hot milk mixture and fold just until well incorporated.

SCRAPE the batter into the prepared pan and smooth the surface
with a rubber spatula. Bake until the cake springs back when
lightly touched in the center with your fingertip and a wooden
skewer inserted into the center of the cake comes out clean,
about 25 minutes; to prevent falling, do not open the oven door
until near the end of the minimum baking time.

REMOVE the pan to a wire rack to cool completely.

REPEAT the process to make a second cake.

RUN the blade of a metal frosting spatula or dull knife around the
insides of each pan to loosen the cakes. Unclasp and remove the
pan rings. Invert a lightly greased wire rack over a cake, invert
the rack and pan bottom together, and lift off the pan bottom.
Peel off the parchment. Place another lightly greased rack over
the cake and invert to turn upright. Repeat with the second cake.

USING a small, sharp knife and your fingertips, scrape and pull
off the crust from the top and bottom of both cakes in order for
the syrup or liqueur to penetrate. Using a long serrated knife,
slice each cake horizontally in half to create 4 layers total.
Transfer a layer to a sheet of plastic wrap. Using a small bulb
baster or a spoon, evenly drizzle enough syrup or liqueur onto
the layer to moisten it. Cover with a second sheet of plastic
wrap and carefully invert the layer. Pull off the top sheet of
plastic wrap and moisten the layer with soaking liquid in the
same manner. Repeat the process with the remaining layers.

continues ~

1 envelope (2½ teaspoons)
   unflavored gelatin
2 cups heavy (whipping) cream,
   preferably not ultrapasteurized,
   well chilled
About 2 tablespoons sifted powdered
   sugar
Pesticide-free nontoxic passionflowers
   or small orchids for garnish
   (optional)

548

TO assemble, place 1 cake layer on a serving plate and insert pieces of waxed paper under the edges to prevent frosting from going onto the plate. Spoon about ¾ cup of the Passion Fruit Curd onto the layer and spread evenly over the top with a long metal frosting spatula. Place another layer on top, spread curd, and continue to add the remaining layers and curd in the same manner; do not spread curd on the top layer. (Reserve the remaining curd for the frosting and decorating.) Refrigerate for up to 1 hour.

TO make the frosting, place a metal bowl and a wire whisk or the beaters of a hand mixer in a freezer until well chilled.

IN a small heatproof bowl, place ½ cup of the remaining curd, sprinkle with the gelatin, and set aside to soften for about 5 minutes.

IN a skillet, pour in water to a depth of 1 inch, place over medium heat, bring just to a simmer, and adjust the heat to maintain barely simmering water. Place the bowl of gelatin mixture in the simmering water and stir the mixture constantly until the gelatin is dissolved. Remove from the water, add another ½ cup of the curd, stir to blend well, and set aside to cool slightly.

POUR the cream into the chilled bowl. Beat with the chilled whisk or hand mixer just until the cream begins to thicken. Add the curd mixture and 2 tablespoons powdered sugar and beat just until stiff peaks form when the beater is raised. Taste and blend in more sugar if desired.

USING a long metal frosting spatula, cover the top and sides of the cake with the frosting. Spoon about ¼ cup curd onto the center of the cake and pull a small frosting spatula through it to create a simple pattern on top of the cake. Cover with a cake dome and refrigerate for up to 6 hours.

ABOUT 30 minutes before serving, remove the cake from the refrigerator and surround with passionflowers or orchids (if using).

Makes 12 servings.

High-Altitude Baking

The reduced air pressure at altitudes over 3,000 feet creates numerous complications for cooks. Liquids boil at a lower temperature, which means they evaporate more quickly and foods that are cooked in liquid, including pasta, beans, and stocks, take longer to cook than at lower elevations. This accelerated evaporation can also result in cakes and other baked goods that are dry or have weakened structure. Leavenings cause more expansion, which can lead to collapsed baked goods before starch cells have a chance to set. Sugar becomes more concentrated, and too much sugar may prevent baked goods, especially cakes, from setting.

Unfortunately, there are no definite rules to insure baking success at every altitude, but the following general guidelines, based on recommendations of the USDA and food scientists, should prove helpful. Always make notes in recipe margins and keep experimenting until you reach the right formula for your locale. You may experience a few flops, but once you get it right, you can modify recipes for a lifetime of great cakes and other baked goods.

At any elevation over 3,000 feet above sea level, increase the oven temperature by 25 degrees for faster setting and better texture. When baking pound cakes that use no or very little chemical leavening, reduce each $\frac{1}{2}$ cup (1 stick) butter by 1 to 2 table-

spoons to strengthen the structure of the cake. When baking angel food and other sponge-type recipes that call for beaten egg whites instead of chemical leaveners, beat the whites only until they form soft peaks, not the usual stiff peaks, and either reduce the amount of sugar as suggested below or add a bit of extra flour.

At 3,000 to 5,000 feet above sea level, reduce each teaspoon of baking powder or baking soda by $\frac{1}{8}$ teaspoon, reduce each cup of sugar by 1 tablespoon, and increase each cup of liquid by 2 tablespoons.

At 5,000 to 7,000 feet above sea level, reduce each teaspoon of baking powder or baking soda by $\frac{1}{8}$ to $\frac{1}{4}$ teaspoon, reduce each cup of sugar by 2 tablespoons, and increase each cup of liquid by 2 to 3 tablespoons.

At 7,000 to 10,000 feet above sea level, reduce each teaspoon of baking powder or baking soda by $\frac{1}{4}$ to $\frac{1}{2}$ teaspoon, reduce each cup of sugar by 2 to 3 tablespoons, and increase each cup of liquid by 3 to 4 tablespoons.

At over 10,000 feet above sea level, increase each cup of flour by 1 to 2 tablespoons, reduce each teaspoon of baking powder or baking soda by $\frac{1}{4}$ to $\frac{1}{2}$ teaspoon, reduce each cup of sugar by 2 to 3 tablespoons, add 1 extra egg, and increase each cup of liquid by 3 to 4 tablespoons.

BACK TO BASICS

Following are some recipes that are basic to the modern kitchen and are used as components of other dishes.

Check the ingredients section (pages 600–603) to read about items that may be new to you.

Recipes

ROASTED GARLIC

There's no better spread for good crusty bread than the sweet caramelized garlic that results from roasting.

Whole garlic heads
Olive oil
Salt

PREHEAT an oven to 350° F.

CUT off and discard the top one-fourth of each garlic head to expose individual cloves. Peel away most of the outer papery skin, leaving the heads intact. Place in a baking dish, generously drizzle or rub the cut surfaces with olive oil, and sprinkle with salt to taste. Cover with aluminum foil and bake for 45 minutes, then uncover and roast until soft, about 15 minutes longer.

SQUEEZE the tender cloves from their papery sheaths into a bowl. Spread onto bread or use as directed in recipes.

CARAMELIZED ONION

For good caramelization, choose onions that are somewhat dry. Freshly picked onions contain so much water that they fall apart by the time they achieve good color.

Olive oil or high-quality vegetable oil
Sliced white or yellow onion

IN a heavy saucepan or other pot, heat 1 tablespoon oil for each cup of sliced onion over medium heat. Add the onion and toss well to coat with the oil. Cover, reduce the heat to medium-low, and cook, stirring occasionally, until the onion just begins to color, about 20 minutes.

UNCOVER, increase the heat to medium, and cook, stirring frequently, until the onion is caramelized, 20 minutes or longer, depending on the moisture content of the onion. Use as directed in recipes, or cool to room temperature, then cover and refrigerate for up to 1 week; reheat before using.

Each 1 cup sliced onion makes about ¼ cup caramelized onion.

ROASTED CHILES OR
SWEET PEPPERS

Fresh mild to hot chiles or sweet peppers

You'll find hundreds of uses for mild to hot chiles and sweet peppers that have been roasted to bring out their optimal flavor.

PLACE whole chiles or sweet peppers on a grill rack over a charcoal fire, directly over a gas flame, or under a preheated broiler. Roast, turning several times, until the skin is charred on all sides; the timing will depend on the intensity and proximity of the heat. Transfer to a paper or plastic bag, close the bag loosely, and let stand for about 10 minutes.

ALTERNATIVELY, if the chiles or sweet peppers will not be used whole for stuffing, you may choose to roast them in sections for easier cleaning. Cut off and discard the stem ends and discard the seeds and membranes. Following the natural contours of the chiles or peppers, cut horizontally into wide strips that are as flat as possible. Place the strips, skin side up, on a baking sheet and roast under a preheated broiler until the skin is charred all over. Transfer to a paper or plastic bag, close the bag loosely, and let stand for about 10 minutes.

AFTER roasting by either of the preceding methods, using your fingertips or a small, sharp knife, rub or scrape away the charred skin from the chiles or sweet peppers; do not rinse. Use as directed in recipes.

CRISPY BACON BITS

Freshly cooked bits of crisp bacon are much more flavorful than their commercial counterparts. Prepare only as much as you need for serving, as bacon loses its crispness quickly.

8 ounces bacon

CUT sliced bacon crosswise into pieces about ½ inch wide. If using slab bacon, cut into ¼-inch cubes.

HEAT a heavy skillet over medium heat. Add the bacon and cook, stirring frequently, until browned and crisp, 6 to 7 minutes. Using a slotted utensil, transfer the bacon to paper toweling to drain.

Makes about 1 cup.

PAN-TOASTED SEEDS OR NUTS

Toasted seeds or nuts add nutritious crunch and flavor when sprinkled over or tossed into salads, pastas, and other foods.

Sesame seeds, shelled pumpkin or sunflower seeds, almonds, cashews, pine nuts, or peanuts

IN a small skillet, place the seeds or nuts over medium heat and toast, shaking the pan or stirring frequently, until lightly golden and fragrant, about 5 minutes. Pour onto a plate to cool.

USE as directed in recipes.

OVEN-TOASTED NUTS

Shelled cashews, hazelnuts (filberts), macadamia nuts, pecans, walnuts, or other nuts

Toasting greatly enhances the rich flavor of nuts. Be sure that the nuts are fresh, and toast only as many as you need, as they turn rancid quickly.

PREHEAT an oven to 350° F.

SPREAD the nuts in a single layer in an ovenproof skillet or baking pan. Toast in the oven, stirring occasionally, until lightly browned and fragrant, 10 to 15 minutes. Except when toasting hazelnuts, transfer the toasted nuts to a plate to cool.

IF toasting hazelnuts, immediately pour the toasted nuts onto one-half of a cloth kitchen towel spread on a work surface. Fold the other half of the towel over the nuts and vigorously rub the warm nuts with the towel to remove as much of the loose skins as possible (it is not necessary to remove all of the skins).

USE as directed in recipes.

CROUTONS

For a change from the ubiquitous cube-shaped crouton, cut skinny baguettes into thin slices.

½ cup (1 stick) unsalted butter

About ½ cup fruity olive oil, preferably extra-virgin

4 cups cubed stale bread (¾-inch cubes), preferably French

IN a large saute pan or skillet, melt the butter with the oil over medium-low heat. Add the bread and toss until the bread pieces are well coated.

REDUCE the heat to low (or transfer to a baking sheet and place in a preheated 350° F oven) and cook (or bake), stirring or turning frequently, until the bread is golden on all sides, about 20 minutes.

TRANSFER the bread to paper toweling to drain and cool slightly. Use immediately, or cool completely, then store in an airtight container for up to 1 day.

Makes 4 cups.

VARIATIONS

Garlic Croutons. Add 2 tablespoons minced garlic, or to taste, along with the bread cubes.

Herbed Croutons. Add 3 tablespoons minced fresh herbs of choice, or more to taste, or 1 tablespoon crumbled dried herbs of choice along with the bread.

INDIAN-STYLE CURRY POWDER

1½ teaspoons coriander seed

1½ teaspoons black cardamom seed
(not whole pods)

1 teaspoon cumin seed

1½ teaspoons black peppercorns

1½ teaspoons crushed dried hot chile

1 teaspoon whole cloves

1 tablespoon ground tumeric

1 dried bay leaf, crumbled

1 teaspoon freshly grated nutmeg

In Indian kitchens, each dish has its own blend of spices that vary from cook to cook. In Western kitchens, we are more familiar with a simpler blend originally created to appeal to British tastes.

No matter what the combination, freshly combined curry seasonings are usually superior in flavor to long-stored commercial mixes. Adjust the amount of pepper and chiles to create a mild to fiery mixture according to preference; for mild curry powder, use half the amount of peppercorns and crushed chile.

IN a small skillet, combine the coriander, cardamom, and cumin seeds with the peppercorns, chile, and cloves. Place over medium heat and toast, shaking the pan or stirring frequently, until fragrant, about 3 minutes; do not allow to burn. Pour onto a plate to cool.

IN a spice grinder or mortar with a pestle, combine the toasted spices and all the remaining ingredients and grind to a fine powder. Use immediately, or cover tightly and store at room temperature for up to several weeks.

Makes about ⅓ cup.

THAI RED CURRY PASTE
~ *Krueng Gaeng Peht* ~

This essential ingredient of many Thai dishes gets its fire and color from dried red chiles. It is generally paired with beef, pork, and fish, but can be used with any meat, fish, or poultry.

Although toasted whole spice seeds yield more flavor, ground spices may be substituted for the whole. Even when mixing curry pastes in a food processor, the ingredients should be coarsely chopped for measuring and easier blending.

All curry pastes keep well for several weeks in a refrigerator. They should be stored in glass containers; plastic storage containers become too permeated with the intense fragrance to reuse for other purposes.

½ cup dried red Thai bird or other small red hot chiles

¼ teaspoon black peppercorns

1 tablespoon coriander seed

1 teaspoon cumin seed

3 tablespoons chopped fresh lemongrass, tender bulb portion only

3 tablespoons coarsely chopped garlic

¼ cup coarsely chopped shallot

1 tablespoon coarsely chopped fresh galanga or ginger

1 tablespoon coarsely chopped fresh cilantro, preferably from root or lower stem portions

2 teaspoons grated or minced fresh lime zest

1 teaspoon Thai moist shrimp paste (ga-pi)

1 teaspoon salt

DISCARD the stems from the chiles and shake out and discard the seeds if desired. Place in a small bowl, add warm water to cover, and let stand until softened, about 20 minutes.

IN a small skillet, combine the peppercorns and the coriander and cumin seeds. Place over medium heat and toast, shaking the pan or stirring frequently, until fragrant, about 3 minutes; do not allow to burn. Pour onto a plate to cool, then transfer to a spice grinder or mortar with a pestle and grind to a fine powder. Set aside.

DRAIN the chiles, reserving the soaking water, and transfer to a food processor, blender, or mortar with a pestle. Add the lemongrass, garlic, shallot, galanga or ginger, cilantro, and lime zest and chop or pound until well mixed. Add the shrimp paste, salt, and the ground toasted spices. Blend to a thick paste, adding up to 3 tablespoons of the chile soaking water if needed to facilitate blending.

USE immediately, or transfer to a small glass jar, cover tightly, and refrigerate for up to 4 weeks.

Makes about ⅔ cup.

THAI GREEN CURRY PASTE
~ *Krueng Gaeng Kiow Wahn* ~

1 teaspoon black or white
  peppercorns

4 whole cloves

2 teaspoons coriander seed

1 teaspoon cumin seed

1 teaspoon fennel seed

3 tablespoons chopped fresh lemongrass, tender bulb portion only

3 tablespoons coarsely chopped fresh
  galanga or ginger

3 tablespoons chopped fresh green
  Thai bird or other green hot chile

3 tablespoons coarsely chopped
  shallot

2 tablespoons coarsely chopped garlic

2 teaspoons grated or minced fresh
  lime zest

1 teaspoon Thai moist shrimp paste
  (ga-pi)

1 teaspoon salt

½ cup chopped fresh cilantro
  (coriander), including roots, stems,
  and leaves

Canola or other high-quality vegetable
  oil for storing

Green curries are favored by Thai cooks for chicken, fish, and vegetables, as well as for special religious feasts.

Please read the introduction to Thai Red Curry Paste (page 557) for general information on making and storing Thai curry pastes. A thin layer of oil over the top of the paste helps preserve the bright green color of the chiles and cilantro.

IN a small skillet, combine the peppercorns, cloves, and the coriander, cumin, and fennel seeds. Place over medium heat and toast, shaking the pan or stirring frequently, until fragrant, about 3 minutes; do not allow to burn. Pour onto a plate to cool, then transfer to a spice grinder or a mortar with a pestle and grind to a fine powder. Set aside.

IN a food processor, blender, or mortar with a pestle, combine the lemongrass, galanga or ginger, chile, shallot, garlic, and lime zest and chop or pound until well mixed. Add the shrimp paste, salt, cilantro, and the ground toasted spices. Blend to a thick paste, adding up to 3 tablespoons water if needed to facilitate blending.

USE immediately, or transfer to a small glass jar, top with a thin layer of oil to prevent air from darkening the paste, cover tightly, and refrigerate for up to 4 weeks.

Makes about 1 cup.

THAI YELLOW CURRY PASTE
~ *KRUENG GAENG KAH-REE* ~

Milder than Thai green or red curry pastes, this version is more closely akin to the familiar Indian-style golden curry powders. Thai cooks typically combine it with chicken, fish, and shellfish.

Please read the introduction to Thai Red Curry Paste (page 557) for general information on making and storing Thai curry pastes.

DISCARD the stems from the chiles and shake out the seeds if desired. Place in a small bowl, add warm water to cover, and let stand until softened, about 20 minutes.

IN a small skillet, combine the coriander and cumin seeds. Place over medium heat and toast, shaking the pan or stirring frequently, until fragrant, about 3 minutes; do not allow to burn. Pour onto a plate to cool, then transfer to a spice grinder or a mortar with a pestle and grind to a fine powder. Set aside.

DRAIN the chiles, reserving the soaking water, and transfer to a food processor, blender, or mortar with a pestle. Add the lemongrass, galanga or ginger, shallot, and garlic and chop or pound until well mixed. Add the shrimp paste, salt, turmeric, and the ground toasted spices. Blend to a thick paste, adding up to 3 tablespoons of the chile soaking water if needed to facilitate blending.

USE immediately, or transfer to a small glass jar, cover tightly, and refrigerate for up to 4 weeks.

Makes about 1 cup.

3 tablespoons dried red Thai bird or other small red hot chiles

2 tablespoons coriander seed

2 tablespoons cumin seed

3 tablespoons chopped fresh lemongrass, tender bulb portion only

3 tablespoons coarsely chopped fresh galanga or ginger

¼ cup coarsely chopped shallot

3 tablespoons coarsely chopped garlic

1 teaspoon Thai moist shrimp paste (ga-pi)

2 teaspoons salt

2 teaspoons ground turmeric

THAI MUSSAMUN CURRY PASTE
~ *Krueng Gaeng Mussamun* ~

2 tablespoons dried red Thai bird or other small red hot chiles

1½ tablespoons cumin seed

½ teaspoon coriander seed

½ teaspoon cardamom seed

½ teaspoon black or white peppercorns

½ teaspoon whole cloves

2 tablespoons chopped fresh lemongrass, tender bulb portion only

1 tablespoon coarsely chopped fresh galanga or ginger

⅓ cup coarsely chopped shallot

¼ cup coarsely chopped garlic

1½ teaspoons Thai moist shrimp paste *(ga-pi)*

1 teaspoon salt

1 teaspoon freshly grated nutmeg

½ teaspoon ground cinnamon

Indian immigrants introduced their spices to Thailand, where they were incorporated into various recipes, including this paste, which is customarily teamed with beef and potatoes.

Please read the introduction to Thai Red Curry Paste (page 557) for general information on making and storing Thai curry pastes.

DISCARD the stems from the chiles and shake out and discard the seeds if desired. Place in a small bowl, add warm water to cover, and let stand until softened, about 20 minutes.

IN a small skillet, combine the cumin, coriander, and cardamom seeds with the peppercorns and cloves. Place over medium heat and toast, shaking the pan or stirring frequently, until fragrant, about 3 minutes; do not allow to burn. Pour onto a plate to cool, then transfer to a spice grinder or a mortar with a pestle and grind to a fine powder. Set aside.

DRAIN the chiles, reserving the soaking water, and transfer to a food processor, blender, or mortar with a pestle. Add the lemongrass, galanga or ginger, shallot, and garlic and chop or pound until well mixed. Add the shrimp paste, salt, nutmeg, cinnamon, and the ground toasted spices. Blend to a thick paste, adding up to 3 tablespoons of the chile soaking water if needed to facilitate blending.

USE immediately, or transfer to a small glass jar, cover tightly, and refrigerate for up to 4 weeks.

Makes about ¾ cup.

TAMARIND LIQUID

This sweet-sour liquid is an essential ingredient in many Southeast Asian, Caribbean, and Mexican dishes. As it doesn't keep well, prepare only as much as you will use in a day or two.

Tamarind may be purchased in Asian or Latin American markets as packaged blocks of pulp or as whole pods. It also comes in paste form, which can be used without diluting; substitute 1 tablespoon paste for each ¼ cup reconstituted liquid. Bottled liquid concentrate is also available but lacks the flavor of the other forms.

1 ounce preserved tamarind pulp (a piece about 2 inches by 1 inch by ½ inch), or 6 ripe tamarind pods

IF using tamarind pulp, cut the pulp into ½-inch pieces. If using pods, crack them open and remove the pulp.

PLACE the pulp in a small bowl and add ½ cup hot water. Let stand until the pulp is soft, 20 to 30 minutes, occasionally using your fingers to break up and dissolve the pulp. Pour through a fine-mesh strainer into a small bowl, pressing against the pulp with the back of a spoon to release as much liquid as possible. Scrape the pulp that clings to the bottom of the strainer into the bowl with the liquid; discard the fibrous pulp and seeds that remain in the strainer.

USE immediately, or cover tightly and refrigerate for up to 24 hours.

Makes about ½ cup.

FRESH COCONUT MILK

1 mature coconut with juice inside,
    or 4 cups shredded or flaked
    unsweetened dried (desiccated)
    coconut or thawed frozen grated
    coconut
2 cups boiling water

Traditionally, coconut milk is made by steeping grated coconut in hot water. A richer coconut milk can be achieved by using hot milk in place of the water. Shake coconuts and choose one in which you can hear the juice inside.

IF using a whole coconut, preheat an oven to 400° F.

IF using dried or frozen coconut, skip the next three paragraphs.

USING an ice pick or a nail, pierce holes in the three indented "eyes" on the top of the coconut, invert, and drain out the clear juice into a container. Taste the juice to be sure it is sweet; if rancid, discard and start with a fresh coconut. If the juice is good, drink it as a cook's treat or include it as part of the boiling water used to make the coconut milk.

PLACE the coconut in the oven for 15 minutes, which usually cracks the shell and will cause the pulp to pull away from the shell for easier removal. Transfer to a countertop. If the shell did not crack from the heat, hold the coconut with one of your hands and hit it with a hammer or the blunt edge of a heavy cleaver until the shell cracks. Using an oyster knife or other similar instrument, pry the shell open. With the oyster knife or a dull table knife, pry out sections of the white pulp from the shell.

USING a small, sharp knife or a vegetable peeler, remove the brown skin from the white pulp. Rinse the pulp under running cold water to remove any brown fiber that has clung from the shell. Using a hand grater or food processor, finely grate or chop the coconut; there should be about 4 cups.

PLACE the coconut in a bowl, add the boiling water, stir to mix well, and let steep for 30 minutes. Working in batches, if necessary, transfer the coconut and liquid to a blender or food processor and blend until the mixture is as smooth as possible.

LINE a strainer with several layers of dampened cheesecloth and set over a clean bowl. Pour the coconut mixture through the strainer, pressing against the coconut pulp with the back of a spoon, then wrap the cheesecloth around the pulp and squeeze to extract as much liquid as possible.

USE immediately, or cover tightly and refrigerate for up to 2 days; the milk must be chilled in order for the coconut cream to rise to the top.

WHEN a recipe calls for coconut cream, scoop off and use the thick layer that rises to the top of the chilled liquid.

WHEN coconut milk is called for, stir together the thick cream and the thinner liquid until smooth before using.

Makes about 2 cups.

BASIC VINAIGRETTE

⅓ cup vinegar or freshly squeezed
    lemon or lime juice, or a
    combination of vinegar and
    citrus juice

1 teaspoon sugar, or to taste

½ teaspoon salt, or to taste

½ teaspoon freshly ground black
    pepper, or to taste

⅔ cup extra-virgin olive oil

The proportions of vinegar and oil in classic "French dressing" are a matter of personal taste. Most recipes call for one part acid to three parts oil. I prefer one part acid to two parts oil; weight watchers and those who enjoy a tart dressing may choose to use equal parts. Since acidity varies with the vinegar or citrus juice used, adjust the recipe to suit your taste and the intensity of the ingredients.

Consider the wide range of potential acids, used alone or in combination: freshly squeezed lemon or lime juice, red or white wine vinegar, cider vinegar, balsamic vinegar, Champagne vinegar, sherry vinegar, fruit-infused vinegars, or plain or seasoned rice vinegars.

Likewise, there are numerous oils from which to choose. If you like a light-tasting dressing, choose a high-quality vegetable oil such as canola or safflower. For a richer flavor, choose a light to fruity olive oil. This is no time to skimp on quality, since the olive oil remains uncooked, so choose a virgin or cold-pressed oil for optimal flavor. Sometimes it is desirable to blend oils for a more complex flavor. For example, a little Asian sesame oil adds a rich flavor to plain vegetable oil.

When making vinaigrettes, I generally avoid vinegars and oils that are preflavored with garlic, herbs, or other seasonings, preferring to add my own flavorings. Fresh herbs, vegetables, spices, and mustards offer countless possibilities. Members of the onion family — garlic, onions, shallots, green onions, and leeks — enhance almost any dressing. Sweet peppers and fiery chiles add both color and zest. And don't forget the other "zest": grated or minced fresh lemon, lime, orange, tangerine, or grapefruit zest (be sure to use only the colored portion, never the bitter white pith).

Here is a basic combination to get you started. A number of variations follow. Should you end up with a dressing that tastes too strong, dilute it with a little water to taste.

For a warm vinaigrette to serve over wilted greens or meat salads, combine the oil and all other ingredients, except the vinegar or citrus juice. Place over medium heat or microwave until the mixture is hot, 1 to 2 minutes. Remove from the heat and set aside to cool for about 30 seconds, then slowly whisk in or stir in the vinegar or citrus juice. Serve immediately.

IN a bowl or a jar with a cover, combine the vinegar or juice, sugar, salt, and pepper. Whisk well or cover and shake to blend well. Add the oil and whisk or shake until emulsified. Alternatively, mix the ingredients in a blender. Use immediately or let stand at room temperature for up to overnight.

Makes about 1 cup.

VARIATIONS

Asian-Style Vinaigrette. Use unseasoned rice vinegar. Add ¼ cup soy sauce, 1 tablespoon minced fresh ginger, and 1 teaspoon minced garlic. Use equal parts Asian sesame oil, high-quality vegetable oil, and hot chile oil.

Balsamic Vinaigrette. Use balsamic vinegar. Add ½ teaspoon minced garlic and 1 tablespoon Dijon mustard.

Berry Vinaigrette. Use blueberry-, raspberry-, or strawberry-flavored vinegar. Add a little ground cinnamon to taste and about ¼ cup crushed berries (same as the flavor of the vinegar). Use equal parts olive oil and high-quality vegetable oil. Blend in a food processor or a blender.

Cheese Vinaigrette. Stir in about 3 tablespoons crumbled blue or fresh goat cheese or freshly grated Parmesan cheese, preferably Parmigiano-Reggiano.

Citrus Vinaigrette. Use freshly squeezed lemon, lime, grapefruit, orange, or tangerine juice. Add about 1 tablespoon grated or minced fresh citrus zest from the same fruit. Use olive oil or high-quality vegetable oil.

Creamy Vinaigrette. Use apple cider vinegar. Add ½ teaspoon dry mustard and ¼ cup heavy (whipping) cream or canned evaporated milk. Use high-quality vegetable oil.

continues ~

Curried Vinaigrette. Use freshly squeezed lemon juice. Add 1 teaspoon grated fresh ginger, 1 teaspoon minced garlic, 1 teaspoon Indian-Style Curry Powder (page 556) or high-quality commercial curry powder, and ½ teaspoon dry mustard. Use high-quality vegetable oil.

Garlic Vinaigrette. Add 1 teaspoon minced garlic or 1 tablespoon mashed Roasted Garlic (page 551). Alternatively, add 2 crushed garlic cloves and let stand for about 15 minutes; remove the cloves before using.

Hazelnut (Filbert) Vinaigrette. Use white wine vinegar or sherry vinegar. Add 1 teaspoon Dijon mustard. Use equal parts hazelnut oil and light olive oil. Stir in 2 tablespoons finely chopped toasted hazelnuts (see page 554) if desired.

Herb Vinaigrette. Use balsamic vinegar, wine vinegar, or freshly squeezed lemon juice. Add 1 teaspoon minced garlic and about ¼ cup minced fresh basil, chives, cilantro (coriander), dill, mint, or tarragon, or use a pleasing combination of herbs. When fresh herbs are unavailable, add 1 tablespoon crumbled dried herbs, or to taste.

Horseradish Vinaigrette. Use red or white wine vinegar. Add 1 tablespoon horseradish, preferably freshly grated, or to taste.

Hot Chile Vinaigrette. Use red wine vinegar or freshly squeezed lime juice. Add 1 tablespoon minced fresh jalapeño or other hot chile, or to taste, and 3 tablespoons minced fresh cilantro (coriander). Use light olive oil or high-quality vegetable oil.

Mustard Vinaigrette. Use balsamic vinegar, wine vinegar, or freshly squeezed lemon juice. Add 1 tablespoon Dijon or other favorite mustard and 1 teaspoon minced garlic.

Orange Vinaigrette. Use equal parts sherry and balsamic vinegars. Add 1 tablespoon orange-flavored liqueur, 2 tablespoons freshly squeezed orange juice, and 1 tablespoon minced fresh thyme or 1 teaspoon crumbled dried thyme. Use light olive oil or high-quality vegetable oil.

Seeded Vinaigrette. Use apple cider vinegar or freshly squeezed citrus juice. Add 3 tablespoons sesame seed or poppy seed, 1½ teaspoons minced yellow onion, ¼ teaspoon Worcestershire sauce, and ¼ teaspoon paprika. Use almond oil or high-quality vegetable oil. If serving over fruit, increase the sugar to ¼ cup and omit the onion and Worcestershire sauce.

Smoked Chile Vinaigrette. Use red wine vinegar, apple cider vinegar, or freshly squeezed lime juice. Add 1 canned *chipotle* chile in *adobo* sauce, minced, and about 1 teaspoon of the sauce from the canned chiles; adjust amount of chile and sauce to taste.

Sun-Dried Tomato Vinaigrette. Use balsamic vinegar. Add 1 tablespoon minced shallot, 1 teaspoon minced garlic, 8 drained sun-dried tomatoes packed in olive oil, and 8 to 10 fresh basil leaves. Combine a little of the oil from the tomatoes with the olive oil. Blend in a food processor or blender.

Walnut Vinaigrette. Use sherry vinegar or red wine vinegar. Add about 2 tablespoons finely chopped toasted walnuts (see page 554) and 2 tablespoons minced shallot or fresh chives. Use 2 parts walnut oil to 1 part high-quality vegetable oil.

WARM PANCETTA DRESSING

¼ cup extra-virgin olive oil

5 ounces Italian bacon *(pancetta)*, coarsely chopped

2 tablespoons pine nuts

¼ cup balsamic vinegar or red wine vinegar

3 tablespoons minced fresh basil

1 tablespoon minced fresh pesticide-free lavender flowers, or 1 teaspoon crumbled dried lavender flowers (optional)

Salt

Freshly ground black pepper

I enjoy this scrumptious combination over mixed greens, including some bitter ones, and fresh figs, strawberries, or sliced pears.

IN a saute pan or skillet, heat the oil over medium-high heat. Add the *pancetta* and cook, stirring frequently, until browned and crisp, 6 to 7 minutes. Stir in the pine nuts and heat through. Remove from the heat and stir in the vinegar, basil, and lavender (if using). Season to taste with salt and a generous amount of pepper.

USE immediately, or cool to room temperature, cover, and refrigerate for up to 1 day; reheat before using.

Makes about ¾ cup.

CREAMY CHEESE DRESSING

3 ounces fresh goat cheese, or 4 ounces creamy blue cheese

1 cup heavy (whipping) cream

3 tablespoons minced fresh chives

1½ teaspoons Dijon mustard

½ teaspoon salt, or to taste

¼ teaspoon freshly ground white pepper, or to taste

I prefer to crumble cheese over the top of a salad and then toss the whole salad in vinaigrette. But if you enjoy rich, creamy cheese dressings, be sure to try this one.

IN a small bowl, food processor, or blender, combine the cheese, cream, chives, mustard, salt, and pepper. Whisk or blend until smooth. Cover and refrigerate for at least 6 hours or for up to 1 week to develop the flavors. Return to room temperature and whisk to smooth just before serving.

Makes about 1¼ cups.

BUTTERMILK DRESSING

Americans are enamored with the tangy flavor of old-fashioned "ranch" dressing, which tastes much better when made from scratch. Use with mixed vegetables or potato salad.

IN a small bowl, a jar with a cover, or a blender, combine all of the ingredients. Whisk, shake, or blend until smooth. Cover and refrigerate for at least 1 hour or for up to 4 days. Return almost to room temperature before using.

Makes about 1 cup.

½ cup Mayonnaise (page 388) or high-quality commercial mayonnaise

½ cup buttermilk

1 tablespoon minced fresh chives or green onion, including green tops

½ teaspoon minced garlic

2 teaspoons minced fresh flat-leaf parsley

¼ teaspoon salt, or to taste

¼ teaspoon freshly ground black pepper, or to taste

⅛ teaspoon ground dried hot chile or hot sauce, or to taste

CREAMY JAPANESE-STYLE DRESSING

Although not authentically Japanese, this dressing is similar to a sauce served with mizutaki, *a simple dish of simmered chicken and vegetables, in a venerable San Francisco Japanese restaurant. It makes an interesting dressing for crisp greens, cold noodles or rice, lightly cooked vegetables, or poached chicken.*

IN a bowl, a food processor, or a blender, whisk or blend all of the ingredients. Cover and refrigerate for at least 1 hour or for up to 1 week. Return almost to room temperature before using.

Makes about 2½ cups.

1¼ cups Mayonnaise (page 388) or high-quality commercial mayonnaise

¾ cup sour cream

⅓ cup White Stock (page 578) made with chicken or canned reduced-sodium chicken broth

2 tablespoons soy sauce

2 tablespoons sake

1 teaspoon minced garlic

1¾ teaspoons sugar, or to taste

1 tablespoon freshly ground black pepper, or to taste

PAPAYA-SEED DRESSING

1/3 cup white wine vinegar

1 tablespoon grated yellow onion

2 teaspoons Dijon mustard

2 tablespoons sugar, or to taste

2 teaspoons hot sauce, or to taste

1/2 teaspoon salt, or to taste

2/3 cup canola or other high-quality
vegetable oil

2 tablespoons papaya seeds

Papaya seeds add a peppery crunch to this dressing, which is not only good over fruit, but also with cold chicken or other meats.

IN a food processor or blender, combine the vinegar, onion, mustard, sugar, hot sauce, and salt and mix well. With the machine running, slowly drizzle in the oil, blending until the mixture emulsifies. Add the papaya seeds and blend just until the seeds are coarsely chopped. Use immediately, or cover and refrigerate for up to 1 week. Return to room temperature before using.

Makes about 1 cup.

HONEY-MUSTARD DRESSING

2/3 cup sugar

1/3 cup honey

1/3 cup apple cider vinegar

1 teaspoon dry mustard

1 teaspoon paprika

1 teaspoon celery seed

1/4 teaspoon salt, or to taste

1 teaspoon grated white or yellow onion

1 cup canola or other high-quality
vegetable oil

In addition to taming the spicy chicken in Southern Fried Chicken Salad (page 290), this blend is excellent over fresh fruit or a mixture of fruit and greens.

IN a small bowl, a food processor, or a blender, combine the sugar, honey, vinegar, mustard, paprika, celery seed, salt, and onion and whisk or blend well. If using a bowl, slowly beat in the oil until the mixture emulsifies. If using a blender or a food processor, with the machine running, slowly drizzle in the oil, blending until the mixture emulsifies. Use immediately, or cover and refrigerate for up to 1 week. Return to room temperature and stir to blend before using.

Makes about 2 cups.

PASSION FRUIT DRESSING

This sweet-and-tangy mixture is delicious over salads of mixed tropical fruits. If you can find fresh passion fruits, select about 8 soft, shriveled ones. Cut off the stem ends, scoop the pulp into a fine-mesh strainer set over a nonreactive bowl, and press against the pulp with the back of a spoon to extract the juice; discard the seeds.

½ cup fresh or thawed frozen passion fruit juice

3 tablespoons freshly squeezed orange juice

1 tablespoon freshly squeezed lemon or lime juice

1½ tablespoons sugar, or to taste

5 tablespoons canola or other high-quality vegetable oil

IN a bowl, combine all of the ingredients and mix well. Use immediately, or cover and refrigerate for up to 1 day. Return to room temperature before using.

Makes about 1 cup.

CLARIFIED BUTTER

As butter slowly melts, its water evaporates and the milk solids are separated from the clear pure butterfat, or clarified butter. Without the milk solids that turn rancid quickly and burn at high temperature, clarified butter can be stored longer and used for high-heat cooking without burning.

Unsalted butter

IN a small saucepan, melt the butter over very low heat. Remove from the heat and let cool for a few minutes until the milk solids settle to the bottom of the pan. Pour through a fine-mesh strainer into a container, leaving behind the milk solids in the bottom of the pan. (For flavorful browned clarified butter, cook until the milk solids drop to the bottom of the pan and begin to brown, then strain immediately.)

Use immediately or cover and refrigerate for up to several months.

Each 1 cup (2 sticks) butter makes about ¾ cup clarified butter.

HOLLANDAISE SAUCE

4 egg yolks

3 tablespoons freshly squeezed
lemon juice

1 cup (2 sticks) cold unsalted butter,
cut into 8 equal pieces

Ground cayenne

A brunch classic with poached eggs, this velvety rich sauce is also delicious with asparagus and other green vegetables. For a change of pace, it can be made with orange juice in place of the lemon juice.

IN the top pan of a double boiler, combine the egg yolks, lemon juice, and 2 pieces of the butter. Set over simmering (not boiling) water and whisk until the butter melts. Add the remaining pieces of butter, one at a time, whisking until each melts before adding the next piece. When all the butter has been added, stir in a pinch of cayenne. Keep warm over warm water until ready to serve. If the sauce gets too thick or begins to curdle before serving, briskly whisk in a small amount of boiling water until smooth.

Makes about 2 cups for 8 servings.

WHITE SAUCE

5 tablespoons unsalted butter

5 tablespoons all-purpose flour

3 cups milk (not fat free)

Salt

Freshly ground white pepper

Freshly grated nutmeg (optional)

Whether you call it French béchamel, Italian besciamella, or plain old American white sauce, this smooth concoction is a basic component of many lasagna and cannelloni preparations. It also makes a rich-tasting pasta sauce containing less fat than cream-based toppings.

IN a heavy saucepan, melt the butter over low heat. Add the flour and whisk briskly to blend until smooth; do not brown. Add the milk all at once and whisk until very smooth. Season to taste with salt, pepper, and nutmeg (if using). Simmer, stirring frequently, until thickened to the consistency of heavy cream, about 10 minutes.

USE immediately, or cover and set aside for up to 2 hours and gently reheat before using.

Makes about 3 cups.

TOMATO SAUCE

During tomato season, make several batches of this sauce and freeze for winter use. Whenever flavorful summer tomatoes are unavailable, canned tomatoes make a much better sauce than hothouse supermarket varieties. If you like, add minced fresh or crumbled dried herbs or minced fresh or crushed dried hot chile to taste.

This sauce can be tossed with pasta, stirred into risotto, added to soups, or served over meat, poultry, or fish.

IN a saucepan, heat the oil or butter over medium-high heat. Add the onion, carrot, and celery or fennel and cook, stirring frequently, until soft and lightly golden, about 5 minutes. Add the garlic and cook for 1 minute longer. Stir in the tomato, sugar, and salt to taste. Reduce the heat to achieve a simmer and simmer, uncovered, until thick, about 30 minutes. Use immediately, or cover and refrigerate for up to 5 days. Reheat before using.

FOR a smoother sauce, transfer to a food processor or blender and puree. Pour into a clean saucepan and reheat before using

Makes about 4 cups.

½ cup olive oil, preferably extra-virgin, or ½ cup (1 stick) unsalted butter

1 cup finely chopped yellow onion

1 cup finely chopped carrot

1 cup finely chopped celery or fennel

2 teaspoons minced garlic, or to taste

4 cups peeled, seeded, drained, and chopped ripe or canned tomato

1 teaspoon sugar, or to taste

Salt

RED CHILE SAUCE

12 dried whole *ancho*, *guajillo*, New
 Mexico, *pasilla*, or other large dried
 mild to hot chiles, one kind or an
 assortment

2 tablespoons olive oil

1 cup coarsely chopped white or
 yellow onion

2 teaspoons minced garlic

1 tablespoon minced fresh oregano,
 or 1 teaspoon crumbled dried
 oregano

2 cups Brown Stock (page 576),
 White Stock (page 578), or canned
 beef or reduced-sodium chicken
 broth

½ cup peeled, seeded, drained, and
 chopped ripe or canned tomato

Salt

*My version of this southwestern staple has a hint of tomato to cool the
sometimes fiery chiles. It is excellent with tamales, tostadas, enchiladas,
and other southwestern and Mexican dishes, yet also makes a good
sauce for pasta, polenta, or grilled fare.*

*Dried chiles are available in Latin American groceries, ethnic
sections of supermarkets, or natural-foods stores. An assortment of
chiles creates a more complex flavor.*

PREHEAT an oven to 400° F.

RINSE the chiles well under cold running water to remove dust.
 Shake off excess water and lay the chiles on a baking sheet. Roast
 in the oven until lightly toasted, about 4 minutes; do not burn.
 Cool slightly, then discard the stems. Split the chiles open and
 discard the seeds and membranes. Set aside.

IN a saucepan, heat the oil over medium-high heat. Add the onion
 and cook, stirring frequently, until soft, about 5 minutes. Add
 the garlic and oregano and cook for about 1 minute longer. Add
 the reserved chiles and the stock or broth and bring to a boil,
 then reduce the heat to achieve a simmer, cover, and simmer
 until the chiles are very tender, about 30 minutes.

TRANSFER the chile mixture to a food processor or blender, add
 the tomato, and blend until smooth.

POUR the mixture through a fine-mesh strainer into a clean
 saucepan. Season to taste with salt. Place over medium heat and
 cook until slightly thickened, about 5 minutes. Use immediately,
 or cover and refrigerate for up to 5 days; reheat just before serving.

Makes about 2 cups.

FISH STOCK

Unlike other stocks, fish stock is best when simmered for only a short time; longer cooking turns the stock bitter. Avoid oily fish such as salmon or mackerel. Toss in shells from lobster or other shellfish, if available.

WASH the fish bones and parts under cold running water. Crack the fish heads and set all of the fish parts aside.

IN a stockpot, melt the butter over medium-high heat. Add the onion, leek, and celery and cook, stirring frequently, until the vegetables are soft but not browned, about 5 minutes.

ADD the fish parts, 4 cups water, and the remaining ingredients except salt (if using). Bring to a boil, then reduce the heat to maintain a simmer and simmer, without stirring (which could make the stock cloudy), until the stock is delicately flavored, about 30 minutes. Using a slotted or wire utensil, skim the surface to remove any foamy scum during the early stages of cooking. Season to taste with salt. Remove from the heat and set aside to cool for a few minutes.

LINE a colander or strainer with several layers of dampened cheesecloth and place over a large bowl or pot. Pour the stock through the colander or strainer into the bowl or pot, pressing gently against the vegetables and fish with the back of a spoon to release liquid (do not press if you desire clearer stock); discard the strained solids.

USE immediately, or set the bowl or pot of strained stock in a large bowl of iced water and stir the stock occasionally until cold, then cover tightly and refrigerate for up to 4 days or freeze for up to 6 months; reheat to boiling before using.

Makes about 2 quarts.

3 pounds heads, bones, and trimmings from white-fleshed fish

¼ cup (½ stick) unsalted butter

2 cups finely chopped yellow or white onion

2 cups thinly sliced leek, including green tops

2 cups finely chopped celery, including leaves

4 or 5 fresh flat-leaf parsley sprigs

Freshly shredded zest from 1 lemon

½ teaspoon white peppercorns

4 cups dry white wine

About 1 tablespoon salt

BROWN STOCK

4 to 5 pounds beef, veal, or game
bones such as shin, shank, short
rib, neck, knuckle, or oxtail, with
some meat attached, cut crosswise
into small pieces; or 4 to 5 pounds
chicken or turkey parts, with some
meat attached, including necks,
backs, wings, gizzards, and hearts
(do not use livers)

3 large carrots, unpeeled, cut into
3-inch lengths

2 large parsnips, unpeeled, cut into
3-inch pieces

2 large turnips, unpeeled, cut into
large wedges or chunks (optional)

2 large yellow onions, unpeeled,
thickly sliced

3 celery stalks, including leaves, cut
into 3-inch lengths

1 whole large leek, split lengthwise
and cut into 3-inch lengths

4 or 5 fresh flat-leaf parsley sprigs

4 or 5 fresh thyme sprigs, or 1 tablespoon dried thyme

2 bay leaves

1 teaspoon black peppercorns

Salt (optional)

*Whether you choose chicken, beef, veal, or game for making them, brown
stocks achieve their darker color and extra flavor from roasting the
bones, meat, and vegetables before adding liquid. For a richer stock, use
meatier bones or add some extra chunks of meat. You may wish to save
bones, meat trimmings, and carcasses from roasted chickens and turkeys
in your freezer and make stock when you have enough accumulated.*

*Pressure cookers can reduce the cooking time by more than half
due to the higher temperature that occurs inside the pressurized pot. If
you choose to use this device, follow the manufacturer's directions for
cooking the stock after the initial roasting step. You will probably need to
cut the recipe in half to fit into your pressure cooker.*

PREHEAT an oven to 450° F.

QUICKLY rinse the bones and meat under cold running water, pat
dry with paper toweling, and cut off and discard excess fat.

IN a large roasting pan or pans, place the bones and meat in a
shallow, even layer. Roast in the oven, turning frequently, for
30 minutes. Add the carrots, parsnips, turnips (if using),
onions, celery, and leek and continue roasting, turning frequently,
until the bones, meat, and vegetables are well browned, about
30 minutes longer.

TRANSFER the browned bones, meat, and vegetables to a stockpot.
Pour just enough water into each roasting pan to cover the
bottom(s), place over medium-high heat, and bring the water
to a boil, using a spoon to scrape up any browned bits. Transfer
the liquid to the stockpot and add the parsley, thyme, bay
leaves, peppercorns, and just enough water to cover the contents of the stockpot. Place over medium-high heat and bring
to a boil. Reduce the heat to maintain a simmer, cover partially,
and simmer, without stirring (which could make the stock
cloudy), until the stock is richly flavored, 5 to 8 hours. Using a
slotted or wire utensil, skim the surface to remove any foamy

scum during the early stages of cooking. During the last hour, cook uncovered and season to taste with salt (if using); do not salt if the stock will be used for cooking dried beans or certain grains (see pages 340 and 364). Remove from the heat and set aside to cool for a few minutes.

LINE a colander or strainer with several layers of dampened cheesecloth and place over a large bowl or pot set in a bowl of iced water. Pour the slightly cooled stock through the colander or strainer into the bowl or pot, pressing gently against the vegetables and meat with the back of a spoon to release liquid (do not press if you desire clearer stock); discard the strained solids. Stir the stock occasionally until cold, then cover tightly and refrigerate until well chilled, preferably overnight.

WHEN the stock is well chilled, remove any fat that has solidified on the surface. Reheat the stock to boiling and use immediately. Or cover and refrigerate for up to 4 days or freeze for up to 6 months; reheat to boiling before using.

Makes about 3 quarts.

WHITE STOCK

4 to 5 pounds chicken or turkey
parts, with some meat attached,
including necks, backs, wings,
gizzards, and hearts (do not use
livers); or 4 to 5 pounds veal
bones, with some meat attached,
cut crosswise into small pieces

4 large carrots, unpeeled, cut into
3-inch lengths

2 celery stalks, including leaves,
cut into 3-inch lengths

2 large white or yellow onions,
unpeeled, cut into thick slices

2 whole large leeks, split lengthwise
and cut into 3-inch lengths

4 garlic cloves, unpeeled, smashed

4 or 5 fresh flat-leaf parsley sprigs

2 or 3 fresh thyme sprigs, or
1 tablespoon dried thyme

2 bay leaves

1 teaspoon black or white
peppercorns

Salt (optional)

*Lightly colored stock made from chicken is the most commonly used base
for soups and stews and is also wonderful added to many other dishes.*

*Please read about the use of pressure cookers to reduce cooking
time in the introduction to Brown Stock (page 576).*

QUICKLY rinse the bones and parts under cold running water. Cut
off and discard excess fat. Whack the poultry into small pieces
with a heavy cleaver. Transfer to a stockpot. Add enough cold
water to cover. Place over medium-high heat and bring to a
boil, then reduce the heat to maintain a simmer and simmer
for about 6 minutes. Drain and discard the liquid. Rinse the
bones and meat under cold running water and drain again.

RINSE the stockpot and add the drained bones and meat and the
remaining ingredients except salt (if using). Add just enough
water to cover the contents of the stockpot. Place over medium-
high heat and bring to a boil. Reduce the heat to maintain a
simmer, cover partially, and simmer, without stirring (which
could make the stock cloudy), until the stock is richly flavored,
5 to 8 hours. Using a slotted or wire utensil, skim the surface to
remove any foamy scum during the early stages of cooking.
During the last hour, cook uncovered and season to taste with
salt (if using); do not salt if the stock will be used for cooking
dried beans or certain grains (see pages 340 and 364). Remove
from the heat and set aside to cool for a few minutes.

LINE a colander or strainer with several layers of dampened
cheesecloth and place over a large bowl or pot set in a bowl of
iced water. Pour the slightly cooled stock through the colander
or strainer into the bowl or pot, pressing gently against the
vegetables and meat with the back of a spoon to release liquid
(do not press if you desire clearer stock); discard the strained
solids. Stir the stock occasionally until cold, then cover tightly
and refrigerate until well chilled, preferably overnight.

WHEN the stock is well chilled, remove any fat that has solidified on the surface. Reheat the stock to boiling and use immediately. Or cover and refrigerate for up to 4 days or freeze for up to 6 months; reheat to boiling before using.

Makes about 3 quarts.

VARIATIONS

Asian-Style Stock. Omit the carrots, celery, leeks, and herbs. Add 8 thin slices unpeeled fresh ginger and 4 green onions, including green tops, cut into 3-inch lengths. Substitute Sichuan peppercorns for the black or white ones.

Italian Broth *(Brodo)*. Simmer only about 3 hours for a lighter stock.

VEGETABLE STOCK

4 large yellow or white onions,
  unpeeled, thickly sliced

2 whole large leeks, split lengthwise
  and cut into 3-inch lengths

2 or 3 garlic cloves, unpeeled,
  smashed

6 large carrots, unpeeled, cut into
  3-inch lengths

6 celery stalks, including leaves, cut
  into 3-inch lengths

2 ripe tomatoes, coarsely chopped

½ head cabbage, coarsely chopped

2 bay leaves

About 6 fresh herb sprigs

1 teaspoon black peppercorns

About 1 tablespoon salt (optional)

Add ingredients according to seasonal availability, taste, and how you plan to use the stock. It is generally best not to use strongly flavored vegetables such as asparagus or broccoli or intensely colored vegetables such as beets. Although they add good flavor, potatoes will render stock cloudy. Choose herbs that will blend well with the dish in which the stock will be used.

Please read about the use of pressure cookers to reduce the cooking time in the introduction to Brown Stock (page 576).

IN a large stockpot, combine all of the ingredients, except salt (if using). Add 4 quarts water. Place over medium-high heat and bring to a boil. Reduce the heat to maintain a simmer, cover partially, and simmer, without stirring (which could make the stock cloudy), until the stock is richly flavored, 5 to 8 hours. Using a slotted or wire utensil, skim the surface to remove any foamy scum during the early stages of cooking. During the last hour, cook uncovered and season to taste with salt (if using); do not salt if the stock will be used for cooking dried beans or certain grains (see pages 340 and 364). Remove from the heat and set aside to cool for a few minutes.

LINE a colander or strainer with several layers of dampened cheesecloth and place over a large bowl or pot. Pour the stock through the colander or strainer into the bowl or pot, pressing gently against the vegetables with the back of a spoon to release liquid (do not press if you desire clearer stock); discard the strained solids.

USE immediately, or set the bowl or pot of stock in a large bowl of iced water and stir the stock occasionally until cold, then cover tightly and refrigerate for up to 4 days or freeze for up to 6 months; reheat to boiling before using.

Makes about 3 quarts.

CLARIFIED STOCK

If you desire a clear stock, every trace of fat must be removed. Clarified stock, also known as consommé or bouillon, makes an elegant beginning soup on its own or with the addition of a few slivered vegetables that have been blanched or steamed.

2 quarts Brown Stock (page 576),
   Vegetable Stock (page 580), or
   White Stock (page 578)
About 8 eggs

PREPARE the stock, chill, and discard all of the surface fat as directed.

SEPARATE enough eggs to equal 1 cup egg whites; crush and reserve the shells. (Save the yolks for another use.)

IN a large pot, whisk the egg whites until frothy. Add the crushed shells and the chilled stock. Place over medium-low heat and whisk constantly to keep the egg whites from solidifying until the mixture comes to a boil. Adjust the heat to achieve a simmer and simmer, stirring frequently, until the egg whites have absorbed all of the fat and tiny particles from the stock, about 40 minutes.

LINE a colander or strainer with several layers of dampened cheesecloth and place over a large bowl or pot. Pour the stock through the colander or strainer into the bowl or pot.

FOR an exceptionally clear stock, repeat the entire procedure.

USE immediately, or set the bowl or pot of stock in a large bowl of iced water and stir the stock occasionally until cold, then cover tightly and refrigerate for up to 4 days or freeze for up to 6 months; reheat to boiling before using.

Makes about 2 quarts.

CRÈME ANGLAISE

2 cups whole milk, light cream, or
   half-and-half

1 vanilla bean, split lengthwise
   (optional)

5 egg yolks, at room temperature

½ cup sugar

Pinch of salt

2 teaspoons pure vanilla extract
   (if not using a vanilla bean)

*If you can resist just sitting down and eating this creamy custard sauce
with a spoon, use it as a sauce for thick, rich puddings such as bread or
persimmon pudding, or serve with Floating Islands (page 448), chocolate
cake, gingerbread, fruit pies, and other favorite desserts.*

IN a heavy saucepan, combine the milk, cream, or half-and-half
   and vanilla bean (if using). Place over medium heat and bring
   almost to the boiling point, then remove from the heat. If using
   a vanilla bean, using the tip of a small, sharp knife, scrape the
   seeds from the bean into the sauce and stir to combine; discard
   the bean.

IN another heavy saucepan, combine the egg yolks, sugar, and
   salt and whisk until creamy. Gradually whisk in the hot milk or
   half-and-half. Place over low heat and cook, stirring constantly,
   just until the mixture is thick enough to coat the back of a spoon
   (your finger should leave a trail when you run it across the
   spoon), about 5 minutes. To prevent the eggs from overcooking
   or curdling, do not allow the mixture to approach a boil.

POUR the mixture through a fine-mesh strainer into a bowl. If
   not using a vanilla bean, stir the vanilla extract into the sauce.

SERVE warm, or set aside to cool to room temperature, stirring
   frequently to prevent a skin from forming on the surface, then
   cover tightly and refrigerate until well chilled, at least 4 hours
   or for up to 3 days.

Makes about 2 cups for 8 servings.

VARIATIONS

Chocolate Crème Anglaise. Use the vanilla extract instead of the
   vanilla bean. Grate or finely chop 2 ounces finest-quality
   bittersweet (not unsweetened), semisweet, milk, or white
   chocolate containing cocoa butter, add to the warm finished
   sauce, and stir until the chocolate is melted and well blended.

Coconut Crème Anglaise. Substitute Fresh Coconut Milk (page 562) or high-quality commercial coconut milk for the milk or half-and-half.

Coffee Crème Anglaise. Stir 2 tablespoons instant espresso, or to taste, into the hot milk or half-and-half.

Lemon Crème Anglaise. Add 2 tablespoons grated or minced fresh lemon zest to the milk or half-and-half along with only ½ of the vanilla bean (if using) before heating; if using vanilla extract, use only 1 teaspoon.

Nut Crème Anglaise. In a saucepan, melt 2 tablespoons unsalted butter over medium-low heat. Add 1 cup chopped almonds, cashews, pistachios, or other nuts and cook, stirring frequently, until the nuts are lightly browned and fragrant, about 5 minutes. Stir in 1 cup whole milk or half-and-half, reduce the heat to achieve a simmer, and simmer for about 30 minutes. Pour the milk or half-and-half through a strainer into a measuring cup, pressing against the nuts with the back of a spoon to release as much liquid as possible; discard the nuts. Add enough whole milk or half-and-half to equal 2 cups and prepare the sauce as directed.

Orange Crème Anglaise. Reduce the amount of milk or half-and-half to 1½ cups and add 2 tablespoons grated or minced fresh orange zest along with only ½ of the vanilla bean (if using) before heating; if using vanilla extract, use only 1 teaspoon. When adding the half-and-half to the egg mixture, stir in ½ cup freshly squeezed orange juice.

Spirited Crème Anglaise. Stir 1 tablespoon of a favorite liqueur into the finished sauce.

CARAMEL SAUCE

2 cups sugar

1 cup heavy (whipping) cream

½ cup (1 stick) unsalted butter

This divine sauce goes well with desserts from chocolate cake to Baked Persimmon Pudding (page 482) and is heavenly over vanilla or coffee ice cream.

Always devote your total attention to the process of caramelizing sugar. To prevent the melting sugar from crystallizing, do not stir it once the sugar is dissolved until it is completely melted.

POSITION a large bowl of iced water alongside the stove top.

IN a heavy saucepan, preferably made of stainless steel or unlined copper, combine the sugar and ⅓ cup water and stir well. Place over medium heat, cover, and heat for about 4 minutes.

REMOVE the cover and continue to cook without disturbing the mixture until it begins to color, then continue cooking, slowly swirling the pan occasionally to spread the color evenly, until the mixture turns a rich amber; this will take about 8 minutes after removing the cover from the pan. During cooking, if sugar crystals begin to form around the sides of the pan just above the bubbling syrup, brush them away with a pastry brush moistened with water. As soon as the syrup reaches the desired color, briefly place the pan in the iced water to halt cooking, then set aside.

IN a heavy saucepan, place the cream over medium heat and bring almost to a boil. Stirring constantly, slowly add the hot cream to the syrup. Place over medium heat and stir constantly until the mixture is smooth. Remove from the heat, add the butter, and stir until the butter is melted.

SERVE immediately, or set aside to cool to room temperature, then cover tightly and refrigerate for up to 2 weeks. Slowly reheat, stirring frequently, over low heat or in a microwave oven.

Makes about 2 cups for 8 servings.

VARIATIONS

Caramel Syrup. Substitute 1 cup warm water for the cream. Omit the butter. Use for soaking cakes or as directed in recipes.

Chocolate Caramel Sauce. Finely chop 8 ounces bittersweet (not unsweetened) or semisweet chocolate, add it to the warm finished sauce, and stir until the chocolate is melted.

Coffee Caramel Sauce. Substitute 1 cup brewed espresso or other strong coffee for the cream, or stir 1 tablespoon instant espresso into the warm cream.

Nutty Caramel Sauce. Toast 1 cup pecans or other nuts as directed on page 554, then chop and stir into the finished sauce.

Thin Caramel Sauce. Prepare the sauce with water as in the Caramel Syrup variation, then add the butter.

MEXICAN CARAMELIZED
GOAT'S MILK SAUCE ~ *Cajeta* ~

1 can (12½ ounces) evaporated
goat's milk

1 can (14 ounces) sweetened
condensed milk (not evaporated
milk)

3 tablespoons unsalted butter

Here's a quick and easy version of a normally more time-consuming sweet that is a favorite throughout Mexico and the Southwest. It can be enjoyed as a thin pudding on its own, as a flavoring for other desserts (see Crème Brûlée Variations, page 444), or as a sauce for Indian Pudding (page 483).

One of my favorite sundaes smothers rich vanilla ice cream with cajeta *and a sprinkling of toasted pine nuts (see page 553).*

IN a large, deep saucepan, combine the milks and butter. Place over medium-high heat and bring to a boil. Cook, stirring almost continuously, for 8 minutes. Reduce the heat to low and cook, stirring constantly, until the sauce thickens and is a medium tan, 3 to 5 minutes longer.

SERVE warm or cool to room temperature, cover, and refrigerate for up to 2 weeks. Reheat in a microwave oven, stirring several times, or in a saucepan over low heat, stirring almost continuously, until smooth and warm; stir in a little milk or cream if the mixture gets too thick.

Makes about 1½ cups for 6 servings.

CHOCOLATE SAUCE

Start with the finest chocolate you can buy for this all-purpose sauce for desserts and ice cream. Instead of the vanilla, flavor the sauce with a liqueur such as amaretto, Frangelico, Grand Marnier, or Kahlúa.

10 ounces finest-quality semisweet (not unsweetened) or bittersweet chocolate, finely chopped
3 tablespoons unsalted butter
1¼ cups heavy (whipping) cream
1½ teaspoons pure vanilla extract

IN a heavy saucepan, combine the chocolate, butter, and cream. Place over low heat and cook, stirring frequently, until the chocolate melts and the mixture is smooth. Remove from the heat and stir in the vanilla extract.

SERVE warm, or set aside to cool to room temperature, then cover and refrigerate for up to 1 week. Slowly reheat, stirring frequently, over low heat or in a microwave oven.

Makes about 2 cups for 8 servings.

WARM LIQUOR SAUCE

I make this sauce with Southern Comfort liqueur to serve over Creole Bread Pudding (page 479). It's also excellent with other gooey puddings.

1 cup sugar
¼ cup (½ stick) unsalted butter
3 tablespoons light cream or half-and-half
1 egg, lightly beaten
About ¼ cup bourbon, brandy, dark rum, or Southern Comfort

IN a heavy saucepan, combine the sugar, butter, and light cream or half-and-half.

PLACE over low heat and cook, stirring frequently, until the sugar is completely dissolved. Remove from the heat and stir in the egg until well blended. Cool for about 5 minutes, then stir in the chosen liquor.

SERVE warm.

Makes about 1½ cups for 6 servings.

OLD-FASHIONED DESSERT SAUCE

2 cups sugar

2 tablespoons cornstarch

2 cups milk (not fat free)

½ cup (1 stick) unsalted butter

2 teaspoons pure vanilla extract

My favorite way to enjoy gingerbread is how my mother always serves it: warm from the oven napped with this sauce. The simple preparation is also good with steamed puddings and unfrosted chocolate and spice cakes.

IN a small saucepan, combine the sugar and cornstarch and whisk to blend well. Slowly whisk in the milk. Place over medium heat and bring to a boil, whisking almost constantly. Continue cooking and whisking until the sauce is thickened to the consistency of cream, 3 to 5 minutes. Remove from the heat, add the butter, and stir until the butter melts, then stir in the vanilla.

SERVE warm, or set aside to cool to room temperature, then cover and refrigerate for up to 1 week. Slowly reheat, stirring frequently, over low heat or in a microwave oven.

Makes about 2 cups for 8 servings.

LEMON SAUCE

This is a great topping for Creole Bread Pudding (page 479), but it's also good with other dense puddings and cakes. It may be made ahead, refrigerated, and gently reheated before serving.

IN a saucepan, combine the sugar, salt, and cornstarch. Slowly whisk in 1 cup water, blending well. Place over low heat and cook, stirring constantly, until the sauce is clear and thickened, 3 to 5 minutes. Remove from the heat, add the butter, lemon juice and zest, and just enough food coloring (if using) to tint the sauce pale yellow and stir until the butter melts.

SERVE warm, or set aside to cool to room temperature, then cover and refrigerate for up to 3 days. Slowly reheat, stirring frequently, over low heat or in a microwave oven.

Makes about 1½ cups for 6 servings.

1 cup sugar

Pinch of salt

1½ tablespoons cornstarch

3 tablespoons unsalted butter

¼ cup freshly squeezed lemon juice

1 tablespoon grated or minced fresh lemon zest

Yellow food coloring (optional)

FRESH BERRY SAUCE

Choose blackberries, blueberries, raspberries, strawberries, or other similar berries to make this simple sauce served with Panna Cotta (page 450). It is also delicious heated and served with pancakes.

IN a food processor or blender, puree the berries. Pour through a fine-mesh strainer into a bowl to remove seeds, if desired. Add the sugar and lemon juice or liqueur to taste and mix well.

SERVE immediately, or cover and refrigerate for up to 3 days.

Makes about 2 cups for 8 servings.

4 cups seasonal berries

2 to 3 tablespoons sugar, or to taste

1 tablespoon freshly squeezed lemon juice or berry-flavored liqueur, or to taste

WHIPPED CREAM

1 cup heavy (whipping) cream,
    preferably not ultrapasteurized,
    well chilled
About 2 tablespoons granulated
    sugar or powdered sugar
½ teaspoon pure vanilla extract

Cream labeled heavy whipping cream contains 36 to 40 percent butterfat, while that labeled whipping cream contains between 30 and 36 percent butterfat. Both can be whipped, but heavy cream whips quicker, easier, and lighter and offers more of that old-fashioned flavor. Ultrapasteurized, or sterilized, cream tastes blander than cream not subjected to the treatment.

For serving on the side with desserts, create crème chantilly by whipping the cream just until it holds its shape. For folding into a mousse or cake frosting or for topping a pie, whip the cream a little stiffer, but avoid overbeating. The cornstarch present in powdered sugar helps stabilize whipped cream.

PLACE a metal bowl and a wire whisk or the beaters of a hand mixer in a freezer until well chilled.

POUR the cream into the chilled bowl. Beat with the chilled whisk or hand mixer just until the cream begins to thicken. Add the sugar and vanilla and continue to beat to the desired stage (please see recipe introduction); be very careful not to overbeat if using a hand mixer (you may wish to finish the whipping by hand with a whisk). Use immediately.

Makes about 2 cups for 8 servings.

CRÈME FRAÎCHE

During storage, unpasteurized fresh cream develops a distinct flavor that is slightly sour yet sweet, mellow, and a bit nutty. Many markets now sell a cultured version, which is known as crème fraîche. If you can't locate it in the dairy sections of your local stores, it is easy to make at home.

2 cups heavy (whipping) cream,
    preferably not ultrapasteurized
¼ cup buttermilk

IN a saucepan, combine the heavy cream and buttermilk. Place over low heat and heat just until the mixture is no longer cool, 85° to 95° F.

POUR the mixture into a jar or other container, cover partially, and set aside at room temperature until it is thickened to a spoonable consistency and tastes slightly nutty; it may take several hours on a hot day or up to 2 days during cool weather.

STIR the thickened cream to smooth it, cover, and refrigerate for at least 24 hours or for up to 2 weeks. The cream will continue to thicken during refrigeration. Spoon off or stir in any watery liquid that separates during storage.

Makes about 2 cups for 8 servings.

MERINGUE TOPPING

⅔ cup egg whites (from about 5 eggs)

½ teaspoon cream of tartar

Pinch of salt

½ cup sugar

1 teaspoon pure vanilla extract

For maximum volume when beating egg whites, use a metal bowl and beaters that are immaculately clean and free of all traces of fat. (It is virtually impossible to wash away all traces of fat from plastic bowls.) If there is any doubt about oily residue, wipe out a well-washed bowl with vinegar and rub completely dry with paper toweling.

If you use a traditional unlined copper mixing bowl for beating egg whites, omit the stabilizing cream of tartar or the chemical reaction will turn the whites greenish. An aluminum bowl will turn the mixture gray.

Double or triple the recipe for cloudlike "mile-high" pie presentations.

PREHEAT an oven to 325° F.

PLACE the egg whites in a metal bowl (see recipe introduction) and beat with an electric mixer at low speed until frothy bubbles cover the surface. Add the cream of tartar and salt, increase the speed to medium, and continue beating until the whites form soft peaks when the beater is slowly raised. With the mixer running, gradually add the sugar, about 1 tablespoon at a time, then add the vanilla and continue to beat until the whites form peaks that are stiff and shiny but still moist when the beater is raised.

SPREAD the meringue over a warm cooked pudding or pie, making sure the meringue touches the inner edge of the pudding or pie dish to minimize weeping and shrinkage. Using a spatula or knife blade, swirl the top of the egg whites decoratively. Bake until lightly browned, about 20 minutes.

TO help prevent shrinkage of the baked meringue, transfer the dessert to a draft-free place that is not too cold and let stand until serving time. Do not refrigerate.

Makes enough to cover one 9-inch pie or pudding or 6 individual desserts.

LEMON OR LIME CURD

This tangy British classic is a natural partner with scones (see page 21), but it also makes a decadent filling for layer cakes. For a lighter curd texture, substitute 2 whole eggs for an equal number of yolks. If using Meyer lemons, reduce the sugar to 1 cup.

I prefer curd without flecks of zest, so I strain the zest out after it contributes the zing.

6 egg yolks

1¼ cups sugar

Pinch of salt

¾ cup freshly squeezed lemon or lime juice

1½ tablespoons grated or minced fresh lemon or lime zest

½ cup (1 stick) unsalted butter, cut into small pieces

IN a heavy nonreactive pan, combine the egg yolks, sugar, and salt and beat until light and well blended. Stir in the lemon or lime juice and zest. Add the butter, place over medium-low heat, and cook, stirring and scraping the bottom of the pan constantly, until the mixture is thick enough to coat the back of a spoon (your finger should leave a trail when you run it across the spoon) but remains pourable, 5 to 10 minutes. To prevent the eggs from curdling, do not allow the mixture to approach a boil.

POUR the curd through a fine-mesh strainer into a bowl. Immediately place a piece of plastic wrap directly onto the surface of the curd to prevent a skin from forming. Set aside to cool completely, then discard the plastic wrap, cover tightly, and refrigerate for up to 3 weeks.

Makes about 2½ cups.

VARIATIONS

Orange or Tangerine Curd. In a saucepan, place 1 cup freshly squeezed orange or tangerine juice over medium heat and cook until the juice is reduced to ¼ cup, then set aside to cool to room temperature. Make the curd as directed, reducing the sugar to ½ cup and substituting the reduced orange or tangerine juice for the lemon or lime juice and 2 tablespoons orange zest for the lemon or lime zest. Makes about 1½ cups.

Passion Fruit Curd. Reduce the sugar to 1 cup. Substitute fresh or thawed frozen passion fruit juice for the lemon or lime juice. Omit the zest.

CHOCOLATE CONTAINERS
AND DECORATIONS

½ pound finest-quality bittersweet
(not unsweetened), semisweet,
milk, or white chocolate containing
cocoa butter, coarsely chopped

Pesticide-free nontoxic leaves such as
camellia, citrus, mint, or rose (if
making chocolate leaves)

*Serve mousses, creamy custards, or ice cream in edible chocolate containers
made from fine chocolate that tastes great on its own. Choose small paper
bags, paper muffin-tin liners, or small paper boxes to use as the molds, or
create your own shapes by taping pieces of heavy paper together.*

*Chocolate leaves and other interesting shapes add a dramatic
or whimsical garnish that also tastes great.*

LINE a baking sheet or pan with kitchen parchment or waxed
paper and set aside.

MELT the chocolate as directed in the adjacent recipe.

TO make chocolate containers, dip a pastry brush or soft paint
brush into the chocolate and paint the inside of a paper mold
(see recipe introduction) to cover completely. Transfer to the
prepared baking sheet and refrigerate or freeze until firm.

CAREFULLY peel the paper mold off the chocolate, then refrigerate
or freeze again until very firm. Use immediately or transfer
chilled chocolate containers to an airtight container lined with
kitchen parchment or waxed paper and refrigerate for up to
1 week.

TO make chocolate leaves, dip a pastry brush or soft paint brush
into the melted chocolate and paint the underside of leaves;
avoid painting over the edges of the leaves. Place on the prepared
baking sheet or pan and refrigerate or freeze until firm.

CAREFULLY peel the chocolate off the leaves, then place on a
baking sheet lined with kitchen parchment or waxed paper and
refrigerate or freeze again until very firm. Use immediately or
transfer chilled chocolate leaves to an airtight container lined
with kitchen parchment or waxed paper and refrigerate for up
to 1 week.

TO make chocolate designs, cool the melted chocolate for a few
minutes, then spoon into a small pastry bag fitted with a small
plain tip or a small plastic bag and snip off one corner of the
plastic bag. Pipe designs directly onto a sheet of kitchen

parchment or waxed paper (placed over a pattern drawn onto a piece of paper if desired), then refrigerate or freeze until firm.

CAREFULLY peel the chocolate designs off the paper, then place on a baking sheet lined with kitchen parchment or waxed paper and refrigerate or freeze again until very firm. Use immediately or transfer chilled chocolate designs to an airtight container lined with kitchen parchment or waxed paper and refrigerate for up to 1 week.

Makes about 6 individual containers, about 18 leaves, or up to 24 designs.

MELTED CHOCOLATE

Use the type of chocolate called for in recipes and always use low heat to prevent scorching.

Finest-quality bittersweet, semisweet, unsweetened, milk, or white chocolate containing cocoa butter, coarsely chopped

IN a skillet or shallow saucepan, pour in water to a depth of 1 inch, place over medium heat, bring just to a simmer, and adjust the heat to maintain barely simmering water. Place the chocolate in a heatproof bowl, set the bowl in the simmering water, and stir the chocolate constantly just until melted and smooth; do not allow to burn.

ALTERNATIVELY, place the chocolate in a microwave-safe measuring cup or bowl and microwave at 50 percent power for bittersweet, semisweet, or unsweetened chocolate or 30 percent power for milk or white chocolate, stirring every 15 seconds, just until melted and smooth; do not allow to burn.

USE as directed in recipes.

CANDIED ORANGE ZEST

4 to 6 oranges

1 cup sugar

⅓ cup freshly squeezed orange juice

Freshly candied citrus zest is far superior to commercial preparations. Select the best unblemished fruit you can find. Use the same technique for glazing the zest of citron (a thick-skinned Italian citrus fruit), grapefruit, lemon, lime, or tangerine.

To candy zest that will be chopped up and added to dishes, start with strips of zest about the same size as those used as twists in drinks or about the width of a match. A citrus stripper that removes the zest in strips wider than those possible with a common zester is a handy tool that makes quick work of the task. I use a zester with a built-in stripper on its side. A vegetable peeler also does the job well, but you'll need to cut the wide pieces into narrower strips with a sharp knife.

Zest that will be candied for use as a garnish can be quickly removed with a common zester. Or cut off pieces with a vegetable peeler, then slice into fine slivers with a sharp knife.

In addition to its use in Sienese Spice Cake (page 526), the zest is delicious on ice cream, as a sweet snack, or as a garnish for cakes, puddings, and other desserts.

USING a citrus zester, stripper, or vegetable peeler, remove the zest (the colored part of the peel with none of the bitter white pith) from the oranges. (Save the peeled oranges for another use.) If using a vegetable peeler, slice enough of the zest into long, narrow strips (see recipe introduction for appropriate sizes) to measure 1 cup.

IN a saucepan, bring 3 cups water to a boil over medium-high heat. Add the orange zest, reduce the heat to achieve a simmer, and simmer, uncovered, for about 2 minutes if using thin strips or up to 10 minutes if using wider strips. Drain the orange zest, then spread on paper toweling. Use additional paper toweling to pat the zest dry.

PLACE a wire rack on a baking sheet and position alongside the stove top.

IN a small saucepan, combine the sugar and orange juice and stir well. Place over medium heat and cook, without stirring, until the sugar melts. Add the orange zest, adjust the heat to maintain

a simmer, and simmer uncovered, stirring frequently, until
the zest is well glazed, about 2 minutes for thin strips or up to
15 minutes for wide strips. Using a slotted utensil, transfer the
zest to the rack. Set aside to cool completely.

USE immediately as directed in recipes, or transfer to an airtight
storage container and refrigerate for up to several weeks.

Makes about 1 cup.

CRISP COOKIE CUPS

*While still warm from the oven, bend the soft cookies into edible bowls
for ice cream, mousses, custards, or fruits.*

PREHEAT an oven to 400° F. Using a pastry brush, grease a baking
sheet with butter or shortening. Set aside several soup bowls
that measure about 4 inches in diameter.

IN a bowl, lightly beat the eggs. Add the sugar, nuts, and flour and
stir just until blended but not smooth. Spoon the batter onto the
prepared baking sheets to form dollops that are about 3 inches in
diameter; make only as many cookies at a time as you have bowls
ready. Using the back of a spoon, spread the batter out so that
each cookie is about 5 inches in diameter and less than 1/4 inch
thick. Bake until browned around the edges, 8 to 10 minutes.

USING a spatula, carefully lift the warm cookies off the baking
sheet. Transfer each cookie to a reserved bowl and mold the
cookie to the bowl to form a cup, overlapping the edges slightly.
Cool completely, then remove from the bowl.

Makes about 8 cookie cups.

Unsalted butter or solid vegetable
    shortening, at room temperature,
    for greasing
4 eggs
1 cup sugar
1 cup finely chopped almonds, pine
    nuts, or other nuts
1/4 cup all-purpose flour

GINGER SYRUP

1 pound fresh ginger, coarsely
chopped
4 cups sugar

This throat-tingling syrup can be used to flavor a bowl of summer berries, as a topping for ice cream, to soak dry cakes, or to sweeten lemonade, limeade, or iced tea. My favorite use is fresh ginger ale made by combining the syrup to taste with sparkling water; serve over ice with a squeeze of fresh lime.

IN a large, heavy saucepan, combine 2 quarts water and the ginger. Place over high heat and bring to a boil, then reduce the heat to achieve a simmer and simmer, uncovered, until the liquid is reduced by one-half, about 1 hour. Remove from the heat and set aside to cool slightly.

POUR the liquid through a fine-mesh strainer set over a bowl; discard the strained solids. Measure the ginger-flavored liquid and add hot water if needed to equal 4 cups. Transfer the liquid to a clean heavy saucepan and stir in the sugar. Place over medium-high heat and bring the liquid to a boil, stirring to dissolve the sugar. Cook, uncovered, until the liquid is syrupy, about 15 minutes. Remove from the heat and set aside to cool to room temperature.

USE immediately, or pour into a clean, dry bottle or jar, cover tightly, and refrigerate indefinitely.

Makes about 4 cups.

SIMPLE SUGAR SYRUP

I usually keep a bottle of this versatile syrup in the refrigerator for making a spur-of-the-moment granita (page 462), moistening cake layers before frosting, offering to guests for sweetening iced tea, and a host of other possibilities.

2 cups sugar

IN a saucepan, combine the sugar and 2 cups water. Place over medium-high heat and bring to a boil, stirring occasionally until the sugar is dissolved. Continue cooking, without stirring, until the mixture is clear and the consistency of a light syrup, about 5 minutes longer. Remove from the heat and set aside to cool to room temperature.

USE immediately, or pour into a clean, dry bottle or jar, cover tightly, and refrigerate indefinitely.

Makes about 2½ cups.

INGREDIENTS

Here are some of the ingredients essential for today's more international kitchen. Other ingredients that may be unfamiliar are discussed in the recipe introductions.

With the growing interest in global cooking, supermarkets now stock many of the items called for in my recipes or can order them for you. Alternatively, seek out nearby ethnic markets. If you haven't noticed such stores in your area, ask owners of local restaurants that feature the type of cuisine you wish to cook where they buy ingredients, or look in the yellow pages. Stock up on hard-to-locate staples whenever you encounter them.

Although the flavor will only approximate the intended original taste, I've listed acceptable substitutions whenever possible.

ASIAN BASIL. The most readily available variety of this herb is the familiar sweet basil (*Ocinum basilicum*) identified with Italian cooking. Several other members of the basil family are preferred by Southeast Asians. Most popular and easiest to find in the produce section of Asian markets is a cultivar of *O. basilicum*, often sold as Thai basil and known as *bai horapah* in Thai and *rau huyng* in Vietnamese, with small leaves, purple stems, and a subtle licorice taste. Also look for peppery, fragrant, and purple-tinged holy basil (*O. sanctum*), or *bai graprao* in Thai, as well as the small-leaved lemon basil (*O. carnum*), or *bai maengluk* in Thai, sometimes referred to as bush or Greek basil. All basil varieties are easily grown from seeds or nursery seedlings in a sunny garden or in pots in full sun. Please, never use the flavorless dried form. *Substitute:* any fresh basil.

ASIAN CHILE SAUCE. Sometimes labeled chile paste, this fiery mixture is made from ground fresh red hot chiles packed in vinegar or tamarind liquid and salt. Choose from Sichuan and Hunan Chinese versions, Indonesian and Malaysian *sambal ulek*, or Vietnamese *tuong ot*. Indonesian and Malaysian *sambal bajak* is prepared from cooked red hot chiles seasoned with shallot and spices. Quality varies greatly, so you may need to sample a few to discover brands you prefer. **No substitute.**

ASIAN CHILE-GARLIC SAUCE. Similar to Asian chile sauce (see the preceding entry), with the addition of garlic, this mixture is a quick-and-easy way to add these flavors to many dishes. Look for products from China or Vietnamese *tuong ot toi*. **Substitute:** Asian chile sauce mixed with minced fresh garlic.

ASIAN SESAME OIL. This rich, amber-hued oil pressed from toasted sesame seed is usually added at the end of cooking for its unique flavor, which is easily destroyed when heated. This is not the clear sesame oil made from raw seed. Quality varies from brand to brand. **No substitute.**

CHILES AND SWEET PEPPERS. All chiles and sweet peppers (*Capsicum* varieties) are native to South America. Although they are all botanically chiles and not related to peppers, the European explorers thought they were the plants that produced peppercorns, thus the moniker chile pepper has stuck. I use the term *sweet pepper* to refer to the bells and other sweet types of chiles, but prefer the word *chile* for those with bite and *chili* to refer to dishes prepared from chiles. *Chili powder* is a commercial blend of ground dried chiles and spices.

The degree of heat varies greatly with the type of chile, ranging from mild to fiery. My recipes usually designate the preferred type, although most can be used interchangeably according to preference. Most popular in Southeast Asian cooking is the tiny bird or bird's eye variety

(*C. frutenscens*), often sold as Thai chile or *prik kii noo*. In the Caribbean, the searing Scotch bonnet and similar habanero are the chiles of preference.

All fresh chiles are sold either in their green state or ripened to various shades of yellow, orange, or red. Red chiles are also available dried and are often soaked in hot water to soften before using. *Chipotle* chiles (smoked jalapeños) are available dried, pickled, or canned in *adobo* sauce and add wonderful flavor and extreme heat to many dishes. **Substitute:** bottled chile sauce, ground dried chili (not seasoned chili powder), or dried chile flakes.

COCONUT MILK. Although the recipe on page 562 will teach you how to make coconut milk, the process is time-consuming, so I often use canned or thawed frozen coconut milk, imported from Southeast Asia. This is not the sweetened canned cream of coconut used in tropical drinks and sold in most supermarkets alongside cocktail mixes. Look for coconut milk in markets that specialize in Asian foods and in some well-stocked supermarkets. The quality varies with the brand, so try several to determine your favorite. I prefer frozen Mendonca's "Hawaiian-Style" from the Philippines or Hawaiian Sun from Honolulu and canned Chaokoh from Thailand.

When coconut milk is cooled, a thick, oily layer of "cream" rises to the top. It may be used in place of oil in cooking or stirred into dishes to add richness, or it may be mixed into the coconut milk much like cream is homogenized into whole cow's milk. When using canned or thawed coconut milk, always read the recipe prior to opening to know whether it should be shaken first, or whether to scoop the cream from the top. **No substitute.**

FISH SAUCE (Thai *nahm pla* or Vietnamese *nuoc man*). Basic to all cuisines of Southeast Asia, this thin, brown, extremely nutritious sauce, made from brined anchovies that are fermented under the blazing sun, is used to add saltiness and flavor. Fortunately, the flavor is far better than the strong aroma, and you'll quickly become accustomed or even addicted. Clear amber liquid, generally sold at a higher price, indicates that the sauce was taken from the top of the barrel and is valued as a table condiment or dipping sauce component; darker versions result from later siphoning and are usually reserved for cooking. Although produced throughout Southeast Asia and China, Vietnamese and Thai products are considered the finest. I use Three Crabs Brand from Vietnam. **Substitute:** light soy sauce combined with salt.

GALANGA. This rhizome of a *Zingiber* species, popular in Southeast Asian dishes, is also spelled galangal and galingale, and is sometimes called Java root or Siamese ginger. The skin is lighter than ginger and marked with stripes, and there are often pink shoots. Its texture is tougher and its flavor is more citruslike but less flavorful than its familiar ginger cousin. Although fresh is preferable, frozen is adequate. Avoid flavorless dried or powdered forms. Galanga is always used in cooked dishes and is never eaten raw. **Substitute:** fresh ginger.

HOISIN SAUCE. This soybean-based sauce contains five-spice powder, chile, garlic, red-dyed rice, and sugar. **No substitute.**

HOT SAUCE. Also called pepper sauce or hot-pepper sauce, this fiery liquid is made from ground chiles blended with vinegar or other acidic liquids or water; sometimes other seasonings are added. Hot sauces range from merely hot to searing. Louisiana hot sauces always contain vinegar and Caribbean-style hot sauces often have fruits or sweet vegetables added. **No substitute.**

INSTANT ESPRESSO. The freeze-dried granules of this convenience product are extracted from espresso, a very strong, dark coffee. Since it dissolves instantly in a small amount of hot liquid, it is the easiest and most effective way to add concentrated coffee flavor to desserts and sauces. No matter how finely ground, do not use coffee beans; they will add gritty residue to the dish because they will not dissolve. I prefer Medaglia d'Oro brand sold in jars in many supermarkets. *Substitute:* about twice as much freeze-dried dark-roast instant coffee, or very strong brewed coffee (use no more than the liquid called for in a recipe).

KAFFIR LIME LEAVES. Leaves of the wild lime tree (*Citrus hystrix*) are extremely fragrant, almost perfumelike, and grow in attached pairs. They are most often available frozen but occasionally fresh. Dried leaves bear little resemblance to the fresh and are not recommended. Plants are easily grown in warm climates. *Substitute:* fresh pesticide-free domestic lime or lemon leaves or freshly grated lime zest moistened with a little lime juice.

LARD. Freshly rendered pork fat has long been maligned as unhealthy, when in fact it contains about half the cholesterol of butter. It is indispensible in Mexican cooking and makes wonderful pie crusts. Hispanic and Asian markets and some meat markets often stock fresh lard, and pure leaf lard rendered from the fat near the kidney is considered the best. To make your own, chop pork fat and place in a saucepan with water to cover. Place over medium heat and cook until the water is evaporated, then reduce the heat to low and cook until the fat is rendered and the sputtering noise stops. Strain the fat into a container and set aside to cool, then cover and refrigerate for up to a week. *Substitute:* unsalted butter or solid vegetable shortening.

LEMONGRASS. Indispensable to the cooking of Thailand and Vietnam, this clumpy grass (*Cymbopogon citratus*), with its distinctive lemony aroma and flavor, is also known as citronella. Fresh stalks are now becoming more readily available in supermarkets, and the plants are easy to grow in warm, sunny gardens or pots. To prepare for cooking, cut off and discard the tough root end and green grass top, then peel off the tough outer layer from the remaining bulb and use only the tender, inner white portion. Dried or powdered forms have little flavor and should be left on the grocer's rack. *Substitute:* grated or minced fresh lemon zest moistened with a little fresh lemon juice.

MEXICAN CORN DOUGH (*masa*). Fresh dough is made from dried hominy that has been treated with slaked lime to soften and remove hulls, then stone-ground to a coarse meal and mixed with water to form a stiff dough. If you have the time and inclination to make your own, see my *Corn Cookbook*. Ready-to-use masa can often be purchased from a tortilla factory (tortillería) or Latin American market. *Substitute:* Mexican corn flour (*masa harina*; see next entry) mixed with water.

MEXICAN CORN FLOUR (*masa harina*). Dehydrated corn dough (*masa*; see preceding entry) is sold in many supermarkets. *No substitute.*

OYSTER SAUCE. This deep brown sauce, made from oysters, water, caramel, cornstarch, and salt, is used to flavor Chinese and other Asian dishes. *No substitute.*

PALM SUGAR. This ages-old sweetener from India and Southeast Asia is extracted from the sap of several species of palm trees. Sugar color varies from pale tan to dark brown and the texture ranges from rock-hard grainy blocks to a spoonable gooey paste of palm sugar and water in jars or cans. Also may be labeled coconut sugar, coconut candy, Java sugar, or *jaggery*. This is not date sugar made from date palms and sold in natural-foods stores. *Substitute:* maple sugar or brown sugar blended with a little maple syrup to moisten.

RICE NOODLES. Made from rice flour, these chewy noodles are available fresh in markets that cater to an Asian community. Dried rice noodles are more readily available in varying sizes and are often labeled rice sticks. If you wish to make your own fresh rice noodles, see the recipe in my *Pasta Cookbook*. *No substitute.*

RICE PAPER WRAPPERS (Vietnamese *bahn trang*). These tissue thin, very brittle disks or wedges made from rice flour are sold dried in various sizes and must be soaked in water to soften before using. *Substitute:* freshly made thin crepes or pancakes.

SHRIMP PASTE (Indonesian *trasi*, Malaysian *blachan* or *belaccan*, or Thai *ga-pi*). Look for this potently aromatic paste made from ground fermented shrimp in two types: bottled moist paste from Thailand, or less potent versions from China, and firm dried bricks from Indonesia and Malaysia. Don't be turned off by the strong aroma; the unique flavor that the paste adds to finished dishes is far better than the initial smell. *Substitute:* anchovy paste, ground presoaked dried shrimp, or thin Vietnamese shrimp sauce (*mam tom* or *mam ruoc*).

SOY SAUCE (Chinese *jyang-yo* or *jyoong-yao* and Japanese *shoyu*). The liquid extracted from cooked, fermented, and salted soybeans adds flavor and color. Chinese-style soy sauce is produced both in light and dark styles. Light soy sauce is thin and used in dishes where a delicate flavor is preferred. Dark soy sauce is aged longer, then mixed with molasses for a hint of sweetness and a deep, rich hue, although not as sweet as Javanese sweet soy sauce (see later entry). Japanese soy sauce is a light soy sauce that contains some wheat and is generally less salty and a bit sweeter than its Chinese counterparts. American-made Japanese-style soy sauce, which falls somewhere between light Chinese and Japanese soy sauces, was used in developing my recipes, unless otherwise specified.

Look for real soy sauces, not synthetic types quickly made from hydrolyzed vegetable protein. Also, be aware that Japanese-style soy sauces that are of varying quality and usually overpriced may be labeled *tamari*; real *tamari*, made without wheat, is difficult to find and comparable to Chinese-style light soy sauces. *No substitute.*

SWEET SOY SAUCE (Indonesian *kecap manis*). This syrupy mixture of dark soy sauce and palm sugar from Java adds richness, thickness, sweetness, and color to cooked dishes. The sauce may also contain galanga, garlic, aromatic *salam* leaves, and star anise and is the common table condiment of Indonesia. *Substitute:* Combine ½ cup soy sauce and 1 cup palm sugar (see previous entry) in a saucepan and cook over medium heat until syrupy.

THAI CURRY PASTE (*krueng gaeng*). Various mixtures of herbs and spices are ground into a paste and cooked briefly before adding to curries and many other dishes. Although freshly made pastes (pages 557–560) have much better flavor, canned pastes from Thailand are convenient. *No substitute.*

TOMATILLO. This small, round, light green fruit (*Physalis ixocarpa*) covered with a papery husk has a unique tart taste. Although not related to the tomato, it is sometimes erroneously called husk tomato or Mexican green tomato. It is, however, related to the husk-covered ground cherry. Fresh and canned tomatillos are available in Latin American markets and many supermarkets. *No substitute.*

RECIPE INDEX

TABLE OF EQUIVALENTS

The exact equivalents in the following tables have been rounded for convenience.

Liquid and Dry Measures

U.S.	Metric
¼ teaspoon	1.25 milliliters
½ teaspoon	2.5 milliliters
1 teaspoon	5 milliliters
1 tablespoon (3 teaspoons)	15 milliliters
1 fluid ounce (2 tablespoons)	30 milliliters
¼ cup	60 milliliters
⅓ cup	80 milliliters
1 cup	120 milliliters
1 pint (2 cups)	480 milliliters
1 quart (4 cups, 32 ounces)	960 milliliters
1 gallon (4 quarts)	3.84 liters
1 ounce (by weight)	28 grams
1 pound	454 grams
2.2 pounds	1 kilogram

Length Measures

U.S.	Metric
⅛ inch	3 millimeters
¼ inch	6 millimeters
½ inch	12 millimeters
1 inch	2.5 centimeters

Oven Temperatures

Fahrenheit	Celsius	Gas
250	120	½
275	140	1
300	150	2
325	160	3
350	180	4
375	190	5
400	200	6
425	220	7
450	230	8
475	240	9
500	260	10

ACKNOWLEDGMENTS

To everyone at Chronicle Books for all of their varied efforts on this and all of our previous work together. Very special appreciation is due to my editor, Bill LeBlond, and publisher, Jack Jensen, who have always believed in my abilities and have been patient and genteel throughout our 29 books together. And to my publicist, Mary Ann Gilderbloom, and Drew Montgomery, who along with Jack and Bill have been at Chronicle since I began producing books for the company. And to assistant editors Sarah Putman and Stephanie Rosenbaum for keeping this book on track through the long editorial process.

To Sharon Silva, who has copyedited most of my cookbooks, for helping me communicate my ideas clearly.

To three photographers with whom I worked before stepping behind the lens and to whom I owe a big debt of gratitude for much of my success: Tom Tracy, who photographed my first three Chronicle books; Patricia Brabant, who beautifully photographed 14 single-subject books that followed; and Jim Hildreth, who taught me to use a large-format camera and worked with me to photograph *Salads*. And to their assistants, including Seth Affoumado, Bruce Bennett, Lois Block, Nelson Brabant, Glen Carroll, Shari Cohen, Carrie Loyd, M. J. Murphy, Edy Owen, Chris Saul, Sheryl Scott, and Barbara Tracy.

To photographer Russ Fischella for many of my author portraits.

To Bill Reuter for his elegant design of this book.

To the designers and typographers with whom I've worked over the years: Cleve Gallat, who was the typographer for most of my single-subject books, and his associates who worked on various books, David Kingins, Don Kruse, Peter Linato, Samantha Schwemler, Charles Sublett; Rick Dinihanian and John Lyle, who designed my Italian and Southeast Asian cookbooks; the staff of Terrific Graphics for putting together my first two titles; Brenda Eno for designing *Cakes*; and Alan May, who offered design ideas through the years and created the original art used in *Squash*.

To my valued assistants who worked with me in the kitchen, photography studio, and office to make all of these tasks easier: Gail High, Mary Val McCoy, Diane Quan, and especially Ellen Berger-Quan, who worked on several books and joined me in learning photography.

To all of the businesses who've loaned me props for photography in my various books. Special appreciation to Steve Fletcher, Carl Croft, and Del Rimbey of Dandelion; Burt Tessler and James Wentworth of Dishes Delmar; Iris Fuller of Fillamento; William Goulet and Pam Franklin formerly of Gumps; Sue Fisher King; MacKenzie-Childs and Neiman-Marcus; Sally Tantau of Tantau; Michael Barcun of Tiffany and Company; Charles Gautreaux and John Nyquist of Vanderbilt and Company; and Susan Gravely of Vietri. And to Toshiko Chang at Britex Fabrics for assisting me with table linens.

To Brian Maynard of KitchenAid for providing equipment used in testing recipes and preparing food for the camera.

To friends, extended family, and others who have offered encouragement and support through the years, shared and tested recipes, loaned props, served me wonderful home-cooked meals, and provided other services for my books:

Sandra and Mike Albright; Antonia Allegra and

Donn Black; Margie and Greg Allen; Walter Allen and Greg Taylor; Ruby and Bobby Jack Bagwell; Wanda, Dick, Brooke, Meredith, and Kyle Bagwell; Nan and Ed Bang-Knudsen; Roz and Andy Bartlett; J. Peter Baumgartner; Shirley Beumer; Flo and Dave Braker; Almut and Rolf Busch; John Carr and Richard Ridgeway; Krista and Mark Carter; Martha Casselman and Jim Spaulding; Cynthia Clawson and Ragan Courtney; Mary Nell Coco; Amy Coleman; Christine Conn; Chris and Bob Cook; Rebecca Cordes; Margaret Cotton; Marion Cunningham; Ruth Dosher; Jan Ellis and Meri McEneny; Karla Filler; Nathan Fong; Maile, Mark, Malia, and Mochi Forbert; Ruth and Bill Ford; Carol Gallagher; Harold Gallagher; Naila Gallagher; Lew Gallo; Vi and John Gianaras; Cary Griffin and Keith Dozier; Larry Heller; Christine High; Gail and Tad High; Kim and Ken High III; Tanya High; Stan Hock; Steven Holden; Deborah and Royce Johnson; Hank Julian; Doris Keith; Barbie Knecht; Dorothy Knecht; Connie Landry; The Honorable Mark Leno; Jane Lidz and Bill Johnson; Marilyn Babs Lonon; Mimi Luebbermann; Marian May and Louis Hicks; Alan May and Blodwen Tartar; Mary Val McCoy; Elvin McDonald; Nancie McDermott; Scottie McKinney; Armistead Maupin; Lenny Meyer; Bill Moore; Sandy, Jim, Daniel, and Timothy Moore; Shellie, Richard, Erin, Elizabeth, and Emma Moore and Loren Lopez; John Nyquist and Rod Jensen; Terrance O'Flaherty and Lynn Hickerson; Peter Olsen; Robert Perez; Marjorie Poore and Alec Fatalevich; Jack Porter; Christa and Mike Preaseau; Nancy and Tom Riess; Erika Rosenthal; Teri Sandison and Hugh Carpenter; Ann and Efren Santos-Cucalon; Julie Schaper; Susannah Scher; Debbie and Dave Schneider; Alice and Billy Russell-Shapiro; Kim, Jeff, Hailey, Max, and Cassidy Shapiro; Diana Sheehan and Ethan Halm; Grant Showley; A. Cort Sinnes; Richard Snyder; Michele Sordi; Alex Spence; Jody Spence; Kristi and Bob Spence; Charles Stinson and Gary Weiss; Stephen Suzman; Chuck Swanson; Nena and Jim Talcott; Juanita Talley; Ed Thirkell and David Bashore; William Tikunoff; Sara, Brad, Masi, Kaeo, and Lyle Timpson; Felecia Vernon Chancey; Felix Wiench; Pauline Wiggington; Paul Vincent Wiseman; Barry Wolpa and Andy Tabot; Sharon Woo; and Brooksley, James, and Cameron Wylie.

To my family and friends who have departed during the work on my book series, but who contributed to or influenced my work and whose guiding presence I still feel: Ed Broussard, Eula Cain, Uncle Louis Coco, Jack Conybear, Aylett Cotton, Gene Davis, Bill Gallagher, Jon Gould, Kenneth High, Aunt Katie and Uncle Victor Holstead, Al Horton, Douglas Jackson, Grandmother Olivia Belle Keith, Uncle Sanford Keith, Gregg King, Lula Alice Little, Stephen Marcus, Alex Morgan, Phillip Quattrociocchi, Socoro Sandavol, Sharon Showley, Larry Smith, Chuck Thayer, and Uncle Albert Wiggington.

To my parents, James and Lucille McNair, who started me on the road to ethical living and good cooking. And to my sister, Martha McNair, her husband, John Richardson, and the world's greatest nephews, Devereux McNair and Ryan Richardson, who have always been there through the ups and downs of my life.

To a very special group of furred and feathered companions who've shared my homes and occasionally my meals over the years of writing and photographing cookbooks:

Addie Prey, who was listed as my "secretary" in my first single-subject book, *Cold Pasta*, was a long-haired red tabby who was named after the title of one of my favorite books and the main character in the movie version, *Paper Moon*. She sat on my desk through the writing of my first 22 books for Chronicle. She sat in my lap while I typed the final words of *Burgers* early in 1992, then died in my arms only two days later.

Buster Booroo, a three-legged companion who lost a front leg when hit by a truck, was a faithful German shepherd who loved cheese, butter, and beef. I allowed him to be put mercifully to sleep to accompany my partner Lin on their "big trip" on the same August afternoon in 1991.

Michael T. Wigglebutt and Joshua J. Chew are Golden Retriever litter mates who were named for my friends San Francisco Symphony conductor Michael Tilson Thomas and his manager, Joshua Robison. They loyally sit nearby in my little office at The Rockpile at Lake Tahoe while I write, and insist that I take much-needed breaks to accompany them to the lake and throw countless tennis balls into the chilly water for them to retrieve. And they are sitting at my feet as I type these words in San Francisco right now. I've shared them with their legal owner and my great friend, John Carr, ever since their birth in 1985, shortly before the publication of *Cold Pasta.*

Dweasel Pickle was a noisy little gray-cheeked parakeet who perched in his cage alongside my desk or on my shoulder throughout the writing of 17 cookbooks. His sweet spirit flew away during the work on *James McNair Cooks Southeast Asian* in 1994.

Beauregard Ezekiel Valentine was my last gift from Lin on Valentine's Day in 1991. He is arguably the most handsome German shepherd ever and my constant shadow, except for the two-and-a-half months that he was lost in the vineyards of Napa Valley. Searching for him led me to purchase Villa Sunshine in St. Helena. He came back to me on the same day that escrow closed on my new home, and we enjoyed a five-year sylvan sojourn in that beautiful valley of the vines before returning home to San Francisco. His favorite foods are Parmigiano-Reggiano and Milk Bones.

Miss Vivien "Bunny" Fleigh and Miss Olivia de Puss Puss are gray vineyard-cat sisters, named for the lead actresses in my favorite movie, who came to live with us in 1992. Dear girls and Andrew's "heart's delight," they constantly entertain us and add much pleasure to our home, even when their swishing tails are obliterating the office computer screens.

And finally, I simply could not have produced the vast amount of work that I have since the beginning of my Chronicle Books projects in 1985 without my two partners to whom this book is dedicated:

Lin Cotton thought that I could accomplish anything and made me believe it, too. At his insistence, after the closing of our gourmet grocery store and catering company, I searched both coasts for a publisher until Chronicle Books was willing to try their hand at cookbooks. He pushed me to grind out as many as four books a year at my peak, then would not take my no for an answer when he decided that I should become my own photographer. Lin died much too early in 1991 at the age of 44. I still miss his constant encouragement and dazzling smile.

Andrew Moore brought music and sunshine into my life and began working with me on *Burgers*. Without his devoted partnership and valued assistance, I could not have written and photographed the last nine books, much less this volume. He is a creative cook in his own right and the best recipe editor I've ever encountered. And even though he detests the tedious time in the photo studio, he has worked beside me to create hundreds of shots. Thank you, Andrew, from the depths of my heart!